Library of
Davidson College

VERÖFFENTLICHUNGEN DER
HISTORISCHEN KOMMISSION ZU BERLIN

BAND 57

BEITRÄGE ZU
INFLATION UND WIEDERAUFBAU
IN DEUTSCHLAND UND EUROPA
1914—1924

Herausgeber

GERALD D. FELDMAN
CARL-LUDWIG HOLTFRERICH
GERHARD A. RITTER
PETER-CHRISTIAN WITT

BAND 2

Walter de Gruyter · Berlin · New York

1984

THE EXPERIENCE OF INFLATION
INTERNATIONAL AND COMPARATIVE STUDIES

Edited by

GERALD D. FELDMAN
CARL-LUDWIG HOLTFRERICH
GERHARD A. RITTER
PETER-CHRISTIAN WITT

With Contributions by

WILLIAM J. BOUWSMA · ELIZABETH A. BOROSS · JONATHAN BLOOMFIELD
ZBIGNIEW LANDAU · HANS KERNBAUER · CHARLES P. KINDLEBERGER
CHARLES MAIER · CRAIG PATTON · THOMAS SARGENT
IRMGARD STEINISCH · JERZY TOMASZEWSKI · FRITZ WEBER
BERND-JÜRGEN WENDT

Walter de Gruyter · Berlin · New York

1984

DIE ERFAHRUNG DER INFLATION

IM INTERNATIONALEN ZUSAMMENHANG

UND VERGLEICH

Herausgegeben von

GERALD D. FELDMAN
CARL-LUDWIG HOLTFRERICH
GERHARD A. RITTER
PETER-CHRISTIAN WITT

Mit Beiträgen von

WILLIAM J. BOUWSMA · ELIZABETH A. BOROSS · JONATHAN BLOOMFIELD
ZBIGNIEW LANDAU · HANS KERNBAUER · CHARLES P. KINDLEBERGER
CHARLES MAIER · CRAIG PATTON · THOMAS SARGENT
IRMGARD STEINISCH · JERZY TOMASZEWSKI · FRITZ WEBER
BERND-JÜRGEN WENDT

Walter de Gruyter · Berlin · New York

1984

Die Herausgabe des vorliegenden Bandes erfolgt mit einer Druckbeihilfe
der Stiftung Volkswagenwerk, Hannover,
und der Deutschen Bundesbank, Frankfurt am Main
Die Schriftenreihe der Historischen Kommission zu Berlin erscheint
mit Unterstützung des Senators für Wissenschaft und Forschung, Berlin

Lektorat der Schriftenreihe
Christian Schädlich

Library of Congress Cataloging in Publication Data

The Experience of inflation.

(Beiträge zu Inflation und Wiederaufbau in Deutschland und Europa 1914—
1924; Bd. 2) (Veröffentlichungen der Historischen Kommission zu Berlin; Bd. 57)
Title on added t. p.: Die Erfahrung der Inflation im internationalen Zusammenhang und Vergleich.
  1. Inflation (Finance) -- Addresses, essays, lectures. I. Feldman, Gerald D.
II. Bouwsma, William J.
HG229.E9   1984   332.4'1   84-1743
ISBN 3-11-009679-X

CIP-Kurztitelaufnahme der Deutschen Bibliothek

Die Erfahrung der Inflation im internationalen Zusammenhang und Vergleich / hrsg. von Gerald D. Feldman... Mit Beitr. von William J. Bouwsma... —
Berlin; New York: de Gruyter, 1984.
  (Veröffentlichungen der Historischen Kommission zu Berlin; Bd. 57: Beitr. zu Inflation u. Wiederaufbau in Deutschland u. Europa 1914—1924; Bd. 2)
  Parallelt.: The experience of inflation, international and comparative studies
  ISBN 3-11-009679-X
NE: Feldman, Gerald D. [Hrsg.]; Bouwsma, William J. [Mitverf.]; Historische Kommission ‹ Berlin, West ›: Veröffentlichungen der Historischen Kommission zu Berlin / Beiträge zu Inflation und Wiederaufbau in Deutschland und Europa 1914—1924; PT

©

Copyright 1984 by Walter de Gruyter & Co., Berlin 30
Printed in Germany
Alle Rechte des Nachdrucks, der photomechanischen Wiedergabe,
der Herstellung von Mikrofilmen — auch auszugsweise — vorbehalten
Satz: Historische Kommission zu Berlin, Berlin 38
Druck: Werner Hildebrand, Berlin 65
Einband: Lüderitz & Bauer, Berlin 61

INTRODUCTION

This is the second volume in the series of essays and monographs produced as part of the international project on „Inflation and Reconstruction in Germany and Europe, 1914—1924." The background of this project as well as a comprehensive statement of its aims and goals may be found in the preface and introduction to the first volume of this series.[1] As noted in the preface to that volume by Otto Büsch of the Historische Kommission zu Berlin, the project included a plan to hold a two week workshop at the University of California at Berkeley in the summer of 1982 in place of its traditional three day working conferences at the Historische Kommission zu Berlin. A substantial part of this volume as well as portions of the next two volumes of collected essays now in preparation, are papers presented to the Workshop held in Berkeley from July 26 to August 6, 1982 under the auspices of the Institute of International Studies of the University of California at Berkeley and generously sponsored, as have all the project activities, by the Volkswagenwerk Foundation.[2]

The Berkeley Workshop was conceived as the high point in the fulfillment of the collaborative, interdisciplinary and international goals of the project. Its timing was determined by the expectation that, after three years of operation, our enterprise would have reached a stage where the projects of the individual participants would have become sufficiently advanced to make possible the presentation of large portions of their work for serious discussion. It would thus become possi-

---

[1] Gerald D. Feldman et al. (Hrsg.), *The German Inflation Reconsidered. A Preliminary Balance/Die Deutsche Inflation. Eine Zwischenbilanz* (= Beiträge zu Inflation und Wiederaufbau in Deutschland und Europa 1914—1924. Veröffentlichungen der Historischen Kommission zu Berlin, Bd. 54), Berlin-New York 1982, S. V ff., 1 ff.

[2] We wish to take the opportunity to express our gratitude, as always, to Dr. Werner Boder of the Stiftung Volkswagenwerk, to Professor Carl Rosberg, Dirctor of the Institute of International Studies of the University of California at Berkeley, and to his staff, especially, Mrs. Karen Beros and Mrs. Peggy Nelson, and our particular appreciation for the outstanding work of the Coordinator of the Workshop, Mrs. Karin MacHardy, and her assistant, Mrs. Madeline Hurd.

ble to collect both our findings and our thoughts, to exchange information and ideas in a sustained and considered manner, and to deal in an informed way with some of the problems that have concerned us ever since we embarked upon this large and complicated endeavor. Not all the materials presented to the Workshop, therefore, took the form of publishable papers. Many of them were summaries of completed or nearly completed individual projects as well as actual chapters or full length manuscripts, and some of the latter will soon appear in print as monographs in this series.[3]

It is our hope that the essays and monographs published here will express in their quality and in their spirit the very special advantages provided by our collaboration and the discussions of the Workshop itself. These discussions took place in five sections: (1) Macro- und Microeconomic Problems of Inflation and Reconstruction; (2) Economic and Sociopolitical Decision-Making and the Impact of Inflation and Reconstruction on the Political System; (3) Inflation and Reconstruction from an International and Comparative Perspective; (4) The Effects of Inflation and Reconstruction upon Social Groups, Occupations and Territorial Entities; (5) The Cultural and Psychological Reception of Inflation and its Consequences. Each of the sections met for at least two four hour meetings to discuss the written presentations that had been made available well in advance of the Workshop, and the main findings and points of debate and controversy were then presented to plenary sessions of the Workshop for further consideration. It thus became possible to take up such central issues as the validity of various models of inflation, the political consequences of inflation, the role of reparations and international economic conditions, standards of living and real wages in inflation, and problems of cultural and psychological anxiety, both in discussions among those doing specific research in these areas and among those with somewhat different concerns but whose work was nevertheless affected by these issues.[4]

---

[3] At the present time, the following studies are scheduled for publication in the immediate future: Merith Niehuss, *Arbeiterschaft in Krieg und Inflation. Soziale Schichtung und Lage der Arbeiter in Augsburg und Linz 1910—1925*, and Dieter Lindenlaub, *Maschinenbauunternehmen in der deutschen Inflation 1919—1923. Unternehmenshistorische Untersuchungen zu einigen Inflationstheorien*.

[4] Summaries of the discussions and a full report on the Workshop are to be found in the *NEWSLETTER: Inflation and Reconstruction in Germany and Europe 1914—1924*, No. 4/5 (April 1983), pp. 1—25, which is published for the project by the Historische Kommission zu Berlin (ed. by G. D. Feldman and I. Natz).

In planning the Workshop, great importance was attached to holding it in the United States and at the University of California at Berkeley. The latter's Institute of International Studies has been the center of the work of one of the largest groups in the project and constituted, in many respects, the twin pole of the Historische Kommission zu Berlin, and it provided an opportunity for the project to realize further its commitment to international and interdisciplinary collaboration. By meeting there, we were able to tap the resources of the United States and to include persons from a variety of fields of great value to our program whose participation might not otherwise have been possible, e. g., the economists and economic historians Charles Kindelberger, Thomas Sargent, Albert Fishlow and Marcello de Cecco; the historians Charles Maier, Jon Jacobson, Frank Costigliola, David Barclay, William Matthews and William McNeil; the Germanists Anton Kaes, Frank Trommler and Jost Hermand. Some of their presentations already appear in this volume, while others will appear in the volumes to follow. We believe, however, that their contributions demonstrate how much a project like this can attract and integrate a widening circle of scholars and specialists and thereby multiply its impact upon the field under investigation.

Finally, the Workshop attempted to meet an unavoidable if sometimes exaggerated expectation of the project, namely, to address explicitly the problem of the relevance of historical experience for contemporary problems of inflation. That it is possible for statesmen and political leaders to learn from the past is amply demonstrated by a comparison of the reconstructions after the two world wars, the subject of one of the Workshop's public plenary meetings at which Charles Maier presented the paper published in this volume. That there are parallels between contemporary and past debates over inflation was demonstrated by a paper of Marcello de Cecco comparing the debate between Costantino Bresciani-Turroni and Karl Helfferich with present day interpretations and debates in the economic literature. Whether it is true that the most successful way of ending an inflation is a rapid „regime change" of the kind described by Thomas Sargent in his paper formed one topic of lively debate in another very well attended public session of the Workshop at which he, Charles Kindleberger, Charles Maier, Albert Fishlow and Wolfram Fischer discussed „Contemporary Problems of Inflation and Historical Experience." There was a consensus that inflation cannot be truly ended so long as there are growing public deficits, a very unhappy and critical conclusion in the context of the Anglo-American situations at the present time. This, however, is a conclusion that one can also draw without the help of historical experience even if the latter adds strength and weight to such an argument. The object in any case is not to fight past wars — a practice often undertaken by generals to the great cost of their troops — but to illuminate the political and socioeconomic processes that explain developments in the past and in the present and thereby to deepen our understanding and make more intelligent and informed action possible. That is the purpose of the project, the Workshop and these volumes.

Historisches Kolleg, München
August 1983

Gerald D. Feldman

EINLEITUNG

Dies ist der zweite Band einer Reihe von Aufsatzsammlungen und Monographien, die als Teil des internationalen Forschungsprojekts über „Inflation und Wiederaufbau in Deutschland und Europa, 1914—1924" vorgelegt werden. Eine zusammenfassende Darstellung des Hintergrunds, der Ziele und Absichten dieses Projekts finden sich in dem Vorwort und in der Einleitung zu dem ersten Band dieser Reihe.[1] Wie Otto Büsch von der Historischen Kommission zu Berlin dort in seinem Vorwort angemerkt hat, bestand die Absicht, im Sommer 1982 anstelle der üblichen dreitägigen Arbeitstagungen im Hause der Historischen Kommission zu Berlin einen zweiwöchigen Workshop des Projekts an der Universität von Kalifornien in Berkeley abzuhalten. Ein wesentlicher Teil dieses sowie der in Vorbereitung befindlichen weiteren beiden Bände mit Aufsätzen gehen auf Beiträge zurück, die auf dem Workshop vorgelegt worden sind, der vom 26. Juli bis 6. August 1982 unter der Schirmherrschaft des Institute of International Studies der Universität von Kalifornien in Berkeley stattfand und der wie alle übrigen Aktivitäten des Projekts in großzügiger Weise durch die Stiftung Volkswagenwerk gefördert worden ist.[2]

Der Workshop in Berkeley war als Höhepunkt der interdisziplinären und internationalen Zusammenarbeit geplant, die zur Erreichung der Zielsetzungen des Projekts notwendig war. Sein Zeitpunkt ergab sich

---

[1] Gerald D. Feldman u. a. (Hrsg.), *Die Deutsche Inflation. Eine Zwischenbilanz. The German Inflation Reconsidered. A Preliminary Balance* (= Veröffentlichungen der Historischen Kommission zu Berlin, Bd. 54. Beiträge zu Inflation und Wiederaufbau in Deutschland und Europa 1914—1924, Bd. 1), Berlin-New York 1982, S. V ff., 1 ff.

[2] Wir möchten die Gelegenheit wahrnehmen, um unseren Dank auszusprechen an Dr. Werner Boder von der Stiftung Volkswagenwerk, an Professor Carl Rosberg, Direktor des Institute of International Studies an der Universität von Kalifornien in Berkeley, und an seine Mitarbeiter, insbesondere Mrs. Karen Beros und Mrs. Peggy Nelson; unser ganzer besonderer Dank und Anerkennung für die hervorragende Arbeit gelten aber der Koordinatorin des Workshops, Mrs. Karin McHardy, und ihrer Assistentin, Mrs. Madeline Hurd.

aus der Erwartung, daß nach einer mehr als dreijährigen Laufzeit des Projekts unser Vorhaben einen solchen Zustand erreicht haben würde, daß die individuellen Teilnehmer mit ihren jeweiligen Einzelprojekten genügend weit fortgeschritten sein würden, um größere Teilergebnisse ihrer Arbeiten einer seriösen Diskussion unterbreiten zu können. Dadurch würde es möglich sein, unsere Ergebnisse und Überlegungen zusammenzufassen, Ideen und Informationen in einer wirklich durchdachten Weise auszutauschen und einige der Probleme, die uns seit dem Beginn dieses großen und komplizierten Unternehmens beschäftigt hatten, auf einem höheren Informationsniveau zu behandeln. Nicht alle Materialien, die auf dem Workshop vorgelegt wurden, haben aufgrund dieser Voraussetzungen die Form von publizierbaren Aufsätzen angenommen. Vielmehr handelte es sich teils auch um Zusammenfassungen von abgeschlossenen oder kurz vor dem Abschluß stehenden Projekten, teils um Kapitel, teils um abgeschlossene Manuskripte, von denen einige bald als Monographien in dieser Reihe erscheinen werden.[3]

Es ist unsere Hoffnung, daß die Aufsätze und Monographien, die in dieser Reihe veröffentlicht werden, durch ihre wissenschaftliche Bedeutung und Qualität einiges von den wirklich besonderen Vorzügen unserer Zusammenarbeit in dem Projekt und der Diskussionen auf dem Workshop selber widerspiegeln werden. Letztere fanden in fünf Sektionen statt: (1) Volks- und betriebswirtschaftliche Probleme der Inflation und des Wiederaufbaus; (2) Wirtschafts- und sozialpolitische Entscheidungsprozesse und der Einfluß von Inflation und Rekonstruktion auf das politische System; (3) Inflation und Rekonstruktion in international vergleichender Perspektive; (4) Die Auswirkungen von Inflation und Rekonstruktion auf soziale Gruppen, Gewerbezweige und Gebietskörperschaften; (5) Die kulturelle und psychologische Verarbeitung der Inflation und deren Folgen. Jede der Sektionen traf sich zu mindestens zwei vierstündigen Sitzungen, auf denen die im voraus verteilten Arbeitsmaterialien diskutiert wurden; sodann wurden die wichtigsten Ergebnisse und die kontroversen Punkte der Debatten auf Plenarsitzungen des Workshops zur weiteren Diskussion gestellt. Dieses Verfahren machte es möglich, daß einige der zentralen Fragen wie die nach der Gültigkeit von unterschiedlichen Inflationserklärungsmo-

---

[3] Zur Zeit sind die folgenden Studien zur Publikation in nächster Zukunft vorgesehen: Merith Niehuss, *Arbeiterschaft in Krieg und Inflation. Soziale Schichtung und Lage der Arbeiter in Augsburg und Linz 1910—1925*, und Dieter Lindenlaub, *Maschinenbauunternehmen in der deutschen Inflation 1919—1923. Unternehmenshistorische Untersuchungen zu einigen Inflationstheorien*.

dellen, der politischen Folgen der Inflation, der Rolle der Reparationen und der weltwirtschaftlichen Rahmenbedingungen, des Lebensstandards und der Reallöhne unter inflationären Bedingungen sowie der kulturellen und sozialpsychologischen Folgen der Inflation zunächst unter den Spezialisten vorgeklärt werden konnten, dann aber mit allen jenen, deren Arbeiten trotz abweichender Fragestellungen auch jeweils von diesen Sachverhalten beeinflußt werden, weiter zu diskutieren.[4]

Bei der Planung des Workshops wurde großer Wert darauf gelegt, es in den USA, und zwar an der Universität von Kalifornien in Berkeley abzuhalten. Das dortige Institute of International Studies war das Zentrum einer der größten Arbeitsgruppen des gesamten Projekts und in mancher Hinsicht das amerikanische Gegenstück zur Historischen Kommission zu Berlin. Dieser Tagungsort gab darüber hinaus die Chance, die stets beabsichtigte internationale und interdisziplinäre Zusammenarbeit zu verwirklichen, indem auf die Ressourcen in den Vereinigten Staaten zurückgegriffen und eine Reihe von Gelehrten aus den verschiedensten Wissenschaftsgebieten hinzugezogen werden konnten, deren Teilnahme bei einem anderen Tagungsort nicht ohne weiteres möglich gewesen wäre, so unter anderem die Wirtschaftswissenschaftler und Wirtschaftshistoriker Charles Kindleberger, Thomas Sargent, Albert Fishlow und Marcello de Cecco, die Historiker Charles Maier, Jon Jacobson, Frank Costigliola, David Barclay, William Mathews und William McNeil sowie die Germanisten Anton Kaes, Frank Trommler und Jost Hermand. Einige von ihren Beiträgen werden in diesem, andere in späteren Bänden dieser Reihe erscheinen. Wir sind der Überzeugung, daß ihre Beiträge unter Beweis stellen werden, daß ein Forschungsprojekt wie dieses einen sich stets erweiternden Kreis von Spezialisten anziehen und integrieren kann und dadurch seinen forschungsstrategischen Einfluß auf dem Untersuchungsgebiet noch verstärkt.

Endlich suchte der Workshop auch die zwar unvermeidlichen, wenn auch bisweilen übertriebenen Erwartungen an ein solches Forschungsprojekt zu befriedigen, nämlich explizit auf das Problem der Relevanz historischer Erfahrungen für gegenwärtige inflationäre Prozesse einzugehen. Daß es für Staatsmänner und Politiker möglich ist, aus der

---

[4] Zusammenfassungen der Diskussionen und ein ausführlicher Bericht über den Workshop finden sich in dem NEWSLETTER: *Inflation and Reconstruction in Germany and Europe, 1914—1924*, Nr. 4/5 (April 1983), S. 1—25, der von der Historischen Kommission zu Berlin für das Projekt veröffentlicht wird (hrsg. von G. D. Feldman und I. Natz).

Vergangenheit zu lernen, ist bei einem Vergleich der Rekonstruktionsperioden nach den beiden Weltkriegen hinreichend belegt. Dies war der Gegenstand einer der beiden öffentlichen Tagungen des Workshops, auf der Charles Maier seinen in diesem Band veröffentlichten Beitrag vorstellte. Daß es Parallelen zwischen heutigen und früheren Debatten über die Inflation gibt, zeigte Marcello de Cecco in seinem Beitrag, in dem er die Debatte zwischen Costantino Bresciani-Turroni und Karl Helfferich mit heutigen Interpretationen und Kontroversen in der wirtschaftswissenschaftlichen Literatur verglich. Ob es richtig ist, daß der erfolgreichste Weg zur Beendigung von Inflationen ein schneller „Regimewechsel" von der Art ist, wie ihn Thomas Sargent in seinem Beitrag beschreibt, war Gegenstand einer lebhaften Debatte in einer zweiten, gut besuchten öffentlichen Tagung, auf der er, Charles Kindleberger, Charles Maier, Albert Fishlow und Wolfram Fischer „Gegenwärtige Probleme der Inflation und historische Erfahrung" diskutierten. Es bestand dabei Konsensus, daß Inflationen nicht wirklich erfolgreich beendet werden können, solange wachsende öffentliche Defizite bestehen, eine höchst unerfreuliche und kritische Schlußfolgerung im Kontext der gegenwärtigen anglo-amerikanischen Situation. Dies ist jedoch eine Schlußfolgerung, die man auch ohne die Hilfe historischer Erfahrungen ziehen kann, selbst wenn letztere einer solchen Argumentation zusätzliches Gewicht verleiht und sie bestärkt. In jedem Fall ist es ohnehin nicht die Aufgabe, vergangene Schlachten neu zu schlagen — eine Praxis, die allzu oft unter großen Kosten für die eigenen Trupen von Generälen eingeschlagen wird —, sondern die politischen und sozio-ökonomischen Prozesse zu erhellen und dadurch Entwicklungen in der Vergangenheit und in unserer Gegenwart zu erklären, um so unser Verständnis für solche Prozesse zu vertiefen und eine vernünftigere und kenntnisreichere Handlungsweise zu ermöglichen. Das ist der Zweck des Forschungsprojekts, des Workshops und dieser Veröffentlichungsreihe.

Historisches Kolleg, München, *Gerald D. Feldman*
im August 1983

INHALT
CONTENTS

Einleitung/Introduction von GERALD D. FELDMAN V

ERSTER TEIL
PART ONE

Inflation und Stabilisierung — Erkenntnisse
aus historischer Erfahrung

Inflation and Stabilization — Interpretations
of Historical Experience

CARL-LUDWIG HOLTFRERICH
Einleitung/Introduction 3

WILLIAM J. BOUWSMA
Inflation and Reconstruction — An Introduction 7
(Inflation und Wiederaufbau — Eine Einführung)

CHARLES P. KINDLEBERGER
A Structural View of the German Inflation 10
(Strukturelle Perspektiven der deutschen Inflation)

THOMAS J. SARGENT
Die Beendigung vier großer Inflationen 34
(The End of Four Big Inflations)

CHARLES S. MAIER

Inflation and Stabilization in the Wake of the Two World Wars: Comparative Strategies and Sacrifices 106
(Inflation und Stabilisierung nach zwei Weltkriegen: Vergleichbare Strategien und Opfer)

ZWEITER TEIL

PART TWO

Inflation in Mittel- und Osteuropa

Inflation in Central and Eastern Europe

PETER-CHRISTIAN WITT

Einleitung/Introduction 133

HANS KERNBAUER/FRITZ WEBER

Die Wiener Großbanken in der Zeit der Kriegs- und Nachkriegsinflation 142
(The Great Vienna Banks in the Period of the Wartime and Postwar Inflation)

ELIZABETH A. BOROSS

The Role of the State Issuing Bank in the Course of Inflation in Hungary between 1918 and 1924 188
(Die Rolle der staatlichen Notenbank in der ungarischen Inflation zwischen 1918 und 1924)

JONATHAN BLOOMFIELD

Surviving in a Harsh World: Trade and Inflation in the Czechoslovak and Austrian Republics 1918—1926 228
(Überleben in einer rauhen Welt: Handel und Inflation in der Tschechoslowakei und Österreich 1918—1926)

ZBIGNIEW LANDAU/JERZY TOMASZEWSKI

Poland between Inflation and Stabilization 1924—1927 270
(Polen zwischen Inflation und Stabilisierung 1924—1927)

DRITTER TEIL
PART THREE

Inflation und sozialer Konflikt in internationaler Perspektive
Inflation and Social Conflict in International Perspective

GERHARD A. RITTER
Einleitung/Introduction 297

CRAIG PATTON
Strikes in the German and British Chemical Industries 1914—1924: The Influence of Inflation and Deflation on Industrial Unrest in Post-War Europe 303
(Streiks in der deutschen und britischen chemischen Industrie 1914—1924: Der Einfluß von Inflation und Deflation auf industrielle Unruhen im Nachkriegs-Europa)

BERND-JÜRGEN WENDT
Die sozialen Folgen der englischen Wirtschaftskrise 1921/22 am Beispiel des „Engineering Lock-out" im Frühjahr 1922 339
(The Social Consequences of the English Economic Crisis 1921/22 as Illustrated by the „Engineering Lock-out" in the Spring of 1922)

IRMGARD STEINISCH
Die Auswirkungen inflationärer Wirtschaftsentwicklung auf das Arbeitszeitproblem in der deutschen und amerikanischen eisen- und stahlerzeugenden Industrie 394
(The Impact of Inflationary Economic Development on the Hours of Work Question in the German and American Iron and Steel Industries)

VERZEICHNIS DER MITARBEITER DES 1. UND 2. BANDES 425

ERSTER TEIL
PART ONE

Inflation und Stabilisierung — Erkenntnisse aus historischer Erfahrung

Inflation and Stabilization — Interpretations of Historical Experience

INTRODUCTION

Carl-Ludwig Holtfrerich

The papers in this section try to evaluate the historical experience of inflations in theoretical and comparative terms. W. J. Bouwsma perfectly grasped the approach underlying all our research efforts in his welcoming remarks to the 1982 Berkeley conference of our project. He presented his overview of the sixteenth century *Great Price Rise* and of its changing theoretical interpretations over time as a comparative reference to our research in the period of the twentieth century. His remarks testify to the validity of C. P. Kindleberger's contention that we have to beware of the „strong priors" that might be involved in theoretical interpretations of empirical developments. As Kindleberger notes, „the analyst with strong priors requires his findings to be consistent with his theory." This might well explain why Bouwsma, after reporting the divergent research findings on the causes and consequences of the *Great Price Rise*, concludes „that although we *know* a great deal more about what happened in the sixteenth century, we seem to *understand* a great deal less."

But, it seems to me, we have to live with the fact that the last word of scholarly truth is never written. In research on economic history we not only learn from the past how to interpret and, maybe, to influence current economic developments, but we also learn from current debates on economic theories how to approach historical experiences with new or different interpretive frameworks than those used before. T. Sargent's contribution is an outstanding example of analyzing four successful post-World War I stabilization processes in terms of the recently developed rational-expectations theory. Sargent shows that in each of the four post-WW I hyperinflations, namely in Germany, Austria, Hungary and Poland, it was not simply a change in the growth of money supply, which kept growing rapidly after each of the four stabilizations, but a drastic shift in the „policy regime" that changed the expectations of private economic agents and thus their economic behavior. Even these extreme inflations were stopped abruptly without excessive costs in terms of economic growth and employment when governments changed the basic rules for shaping their fiscal and monetary strategies. Sargent attributes the successful stabilization operations, first, to the creation of independent central banks that were legally committed to refuse their government's demands for credit and were required to back their money issues with gold, foreign exchange and commercial paper instead of treasury bills; second, to the return of governments to balanced budget practices with cuts in expenditures, increases in taxes and the obligation of governments to place their debt with private parties and foreign governments which would value those debts according to whether they were backed by sufficiently large prospective taxes relative to public expenditures. The economic policy implications of this analysis for recent problems of inflation or stagnation are clear enough and require no special mention.

C. P. Kindleberger in his erudite treatment of the German inflation alone takes issue with Sargent's mono-causal interpretation in offering a structural instead of a monetary view of the hyperinflation. His interpretation also contrasts with the balance-of-payments theory of the inflation, to which many contemporaries of the period adhered, including an array of German politicians. The „technical economic" theories, he maintains, fail „to specify the socio-economic matrix in which the economic events take place." Drawing on theories by M. Olson, which were also applied to Latin American cases by A. O. Hirschman and D. Felix, Kindleberger views the German inflation as the result of conflicts over income distribution between agriculture, industry and labor as well as between subgroups within each aggregate, and also between the government and private actors. The post-WW I process, he argues, „rested at basis on the incapacity of organized and powerful groups to agree on how to share among them the burdens of reconstruction and reparations (and of France and Germany to agree on how much reparation should be paid to make good the destruction of the great war)." The theory allows for incorporating monetary and fiscal as well as balance-of-payments factors in the causal chain. But these are not seen as independent variables over which governments and central banks have a free range of choice like acting in a political vacuum. „The structural-inflation school claims rather that politicians are endogenous and behave in predictable ways, responding to the explicit situation, and virtually certain to be dismissed from office if they try to behave like strict monetarists... In the structural-inflation model a good deal depends upon the nature of the underlying society." This view asks for the incorporation of a wide range of national and international historical issues into the inflation analysis and rejects an approach that concentrates on the study of economic policy „mistakes" only. Kindleberger addresses the political and social issues involved in an admirable fashion and draws on a number of historical parallels and contrasts, especially to Germany's post-WW II experience.

C. S. Maier in his discussion of inflation and stabilization experiences after the two World Wars fits well into the interpretive framework of the structural-inflation model. He demonstrates how our judgment of developments is improved by a comparative approach, both across time and national boundaries (not only within Europe, but also including the U.S. and Japan). He sees inflation closely linked to the Wars, as a means „to conscript monetary resources when the will to taxation failed." He analyzes the different phases, the economic functions (distribution of war costs, reconstruction etc.), the social and political roles of inflation, and, last but not least, the origins and terms of stabilization, the point at which countries finally abandoned the view that stabilization was too costly. He also addresses the differences in the international environment in which the monetary developments after the two World Wars took place. He points out that each of the two Wars shifted the share of public expenditures in national income to higher plateaus and that increases in taxation levels followed much more slowly. Thereby inflation was produced, which proved to be an expedient device to transfer funds into the hands of governments and at the same time to spur the economy against the background of widespread money illusion. As to the social setting, Maier argues that post-WW I inflations and stabilizations served producers' interests at the expense of middle-class savers or financial wealth holders mainly in Germany, Austria and France (but not without causing major political opposition and/or bitterness) and vice versa in Great Britain and Italy. After WW II, in contrast, when the problem was more suppressed than open inflation, the fear of unemployment and economic stagnation dominated over the fear of loss of financial wealth. As opposed to the earlier period, socialists and labor unions were now well entrenched on the political power front. Therefore, it proved politically easier after WW II to sacrifice the paper assets of the bourgeois rentiers and savers and to implement pro-employment „Keynesian" monetary reforms.

As to the international setting in which the monetary reforms took place, Maier points out the stabilizing role the U.S. was willing to shoulder for the smooth functioning of the world economy after WW II in contrast to the post-WW I period. As a „hegemonic power" it promoted a multilateral system of trade and payments and eased the deflationary consequences of stabilizations by accomodating Europe's current account deficits well into the 1960s and by accepting the role of a lender of last resort in a fixed-exchange-rate system with the dollar as the key currency. „If inflation originated in war finance, it was overcome by the United States' financing of the remaining war costs. Writing the peace required paying for the peace." Until 1967 the U.S. had been the stabilizer of last resort; however, in connection with the inflationary financing of the Vietnam War, the U.S. resorted to an inflationary „tax" on the world economy by flooding the world with dollars. Like Germany after WW I on a smaller scale, the hegemon did not want to pay the price of keeping its stabilizing role, namely to pursue sound fiscal and monetary policies with the possible deflationary consequences for the domestic economy. Instead it exerted „the inflationary thrust of the waning hegemon" that had been challenged in its privileged key-currency role by „the dog in the manger," namely by France and its policy of hoarding gold instead of dollars since 1965. Do recent anti-inflationary policies in major industrial countries, including the U.S., indicate that now a group of successors has appeared to take up the role of the „stabilizer of last resort" with cohesion and responsibility?

Inflation and Reconstruction — An Introduction

WILLIAM J. BOUWSMA

It is a privilege for me, as Chairman of the Berkeley History Department, to welcome you to our campus. We are honored by your presence, which also serves as a reminder of the important place of German history at Berkeley during the last two or three decades. Its importance is suggested not only by the presence of Gerald Feldman but also by the names of Wolfgang Sauer, Raymond Sontag, Carl Schorske, and of course — Hans Rosenberg.

But this welcome, however warm and sincere, is by itself somewhat routine and perfunctory; and I find myself yearning, as a *historian*, to have some real function in your proceedings — within, of course, the few minutes of your time to which I am entitled.

The obvious point of entry into your proceedings for a scholar who has devoted most of his career to the sixteenth century is, of course, the first extended period of inflation that attracted the attention of historians, the phenomenon known as *the Great Price Rise*. And it occurred to me that a reminder of the historiography of this earlier phenomenon might be instructive here.

The inflation of the sixteenth century stimulated discussion in its own time. A certain Monsieur Malestroit had attributed the rise in prices to the widespread debasement of coinage by governments.[1] But then — as now — scholarly assertion stimulated counter-assertion, and Jean Bodin responded. Bodin admitted that debasement had been a factor in the price rise but pointed also to other factors: monopolies, conspicuous consumption on the part of the ruling classes, the destruction of goods in war. But he gave particular emphasis to the massive importations of gold and silver from the New World, thereby providing the first primitive version of the Quantity Theory of Money.[2]

---

[1] Johan de Malestroit, *Les Paradoxes sur le faict des monnoyes*, Paris 1566.
[2] Jean Bodin, *La response a M. de Malestroit*, Paris 1568.

Historians, their attention fixed on other matters, paid little attention to the Great Price Rise, for some centuries. About 50 years ago, however, there appeared E. J. Hamilton's *American Treasure and the Price Revolution in Spain*.[3] Hamilton mostly developed Bodin's thesis, but went on to argue that, because prices rose faster than rents and wages, capital accumulated that provided much of the basis of earlier capitalism.

But it is the *sequel* to Hamilton's work that merits reflection. This was the period, unlike our own, of the individual scholarly small entrepreneur, and the accumulation of scholarly capital that is possible under the conditions of such small-scale enterprise was protracted and tedious.

For a long time after Hamilton's book, nothing much seems to have happened, except that, for a while, after they had read it, historians seemed to think they understood all about inflation in the sixteenth century — its causes and its consequences. But then, gradually, the domination of the scholarly market by one small enterprise was challenged by competitors.[4]

(1) Counter propositions of various kinds were circulated: Local studies of prices revealed great local variations that were often puzzling.

(2) It was also noticed that some areas that were least affected by the price rise had the largest accumulations of capital.

(3) Further, it could be argued — and was — that there is often little connection between price inflation and profit inflation.

(4) Finally, Malestroit's argument was re-examined and now found to have much merit — so that for a while it was possible to doubt that there was, in real terms, a price rise at all.

The result is that although we *know* a great deal more about what happened in the sixteenth century, we seem to *understand* a great deal less than we did 50 years ago about either the *causes* or the *consequences* of the Great Price Rise.

One economic historian of my own period writing about *its inflation* suggested the somewhat doleful mood in which scholars now find themselves. He wrote of the Great Price Rise, „Its causes were not

---

[3] Cambridge/Mass. 1934.

[4] All this is from Harry A. Miskimin, *The Economy of Later Renaissance Europe, 1460—1600*, Cambridge 1977, pp. 35—46.

clearly comprehended by the men of the time. Some might add that the causes of inflation are not yet fully understood."[5] So much for fifty years of scholarship carried out under conditions of small-scale competition.

The conditions of your own enterprise are, however, very different. Here cooperation and collaboration will take the place of competition, and the meeting of so many minds should serve as a guarantee that few complexities will be overlooked.

One of the most interesting dimensions of *this* meeting, then, is the new *shape* of the scholarly enterprise that it embodies.

This, as well as the importance of your subject, makes the *Workshop of Inflation and Reconstruction* a particularly interesting and significant event. We look forward to its results.

---

[5] *Op. cit.*, p. 36.

A Structural View of the German Inflation

CHARLES P. KINDLEBERGER

German inflation after World War I is rapidly becoming, like the French Revolution, a classic historical conundrum, useful because it allows ample scope for teaching undergraduates and training scholars in the complexity of social events, and furnishes a virtually infinite range for further monographic research and magisterial syntheses. Like British long-term lending to Canada from 1896 to 1913, the historical analysis is rewritten with each succeeding generation. If the German inflation achieves equal status in history, economic history, and economic analysis, it will be largely attributable to the entrepreneurial dynamism of Professors Feldman, Holtfrerich, Ritter, and Witt who have created a new industry around the problem, with workshops and meetings, an outpouring of articles, monographs, and books. On the economic side, the National Bureau of Economic Research and the University of Chicago economics department and *Jounal of Political Economy* contribute to the deluge as theories of monetarism, rational expectations, bubbles, efficient markets, rigorous purchasing-power parity and the like are measured against the somewhat spotty data of the episode.

If one were to read the entire literature on the French Revolution, that convulsive event would seem to be overdetermined. There are more independent variables than are necessary to explain the dependent variables, more equations than there are unknowns. Different schools of thought have developed encompassing theories: Marxists on the sans-culottes, historians, and economic historians on peasant-noble relationships in agriculture, on bourgeois energy which found it imperative to burst the restraints of the *Ancien Régime*, the resistance to change of the *financiers* in tax farming and handling government expenditure. The significance of the socio-political matrix to historic outcomes is illustrated in this last connection by the fact that a „financial revolution" was accomplished peacefully in England after the Glorious Revolution of 1688,[1] but required the guillotining of 28 *financiers* and *officiers* in France before the handling of governmental finances could be transformed from private enterprise into a bureaucratic governmental function.[2] Like German inflation, moreover, it is likely that the forces responsible for the convulsion were not necessarily its beneficiaries. In one usual view, the peasants led the way, and the middle class reaped the major gains. What is significant for our purposes, however, is the energy and verve that go into the study of this historical event now almost 200 years old. My historian-daughter tells me that the eighteenth century is the century of choice within French historiography and the French Revolution the central topic in that century.

Another analogy: true believers come to the French Revolution with a strong *a priori* position, seeking support in the uprising for a theory of social forces developed primarily by deduction. I refer of course to the Marxists who ascribe *causa causans* to the lumpen proletariat of the city, the *sans-culottes*, in the face of profound scepticism over the importance of this role on the part of the vast majority of mainstream scholars. So, too, the monetarist school of the University of Chicago, which has now spilled well beyond the confines of that city, comes to German inflation with what Melvin Reder calls „strong priors,"[3] — a belief in the centrality of the quantity theory of money, the efficiency of markets, rational expectations, purchasing-power parity etc. Reder notes that the analyst with strong priors requires his findings to be consistent with his theory. When an apparent inconsistency is encountered, it is treated as anomalous and as requiring either 1) re-examination of the data to produce new material that will reverse the finding; 2) redefinition or augmentation of the variables of the model; or 3) placing the finding on the research agenda as a researchable anomaly. Only *in extremis* and as a last resort, will the researcher with strong priors consider an alteration of the theory.

The problem of German inflation from 1914 to 1923 has developed at least three more-or-less distinct schools with many combinations and

---

[1] P.G.M. Dickson, *The Financial Revolution in England: A Study in the Development of Public Credit, 1688-1766*, New York, 1967.
[2] J.F. Bosher, *French Finances, 1770-1795. From Business to Bureaucracy*, Cambridge, 1970, and Guy Chaussinand-Nogaret, *Les financiers de Languédoc au XVIIIe siècle*, Paris, 1970, p. 315.
[3] Melvin W. Reder, *Chicago Economists: Permanence and Change*, in: *The Journal of Economic Literature*, 20, 1 (March 1982), pp. 1—38, esp. p. 11.

compromises among them. Economists, both at the time and today, generally fall into either the monetarist or the balance-of-payment camp, the former sometimes called the purchasing-power-parity school. Monetarists take money creation and destruction as central to inflation and deflation, and tend to believe in a fairly short-run adherence of economies to the quantity theory of money that says that prices vary positively with the current and expected money supply, and to the purchasing-power-parity doctrine that holds that with flexible exchange rates, the value of a country's currency will measure with a high degree of accuracy the relative extent of its current and expected internal inflation. The balance-of-payments school, on the other hand, maintains that exchange rates may be determined by independent movements affecting the balance of payments, and changes in rates feed back on the price level and on the money supply. On occasion, the rise in prices will lead to increases in wages which require the issue of more money to avoid unemployment. Monetarists find this anathema. With efficient markets, industrialists cannot raise prices and labor unions cannot raise wages. All inflation rests on excessive expansion of the money supply.

It is of some interest that the controversy between the monetarist and balance-of-payments schools which has been underway over the German episode since immediately after World War I is the exact replica of the argument between the Currency School and the Banking School in England almost a century earlier.[4] Monetarism was represented by the Currency School, led initially by David Ricardo, afterwards by Lord Overstone, that held that the agio on gold during the period of suspension of the gold standard — virtually the same as exchange depreciation of sterling — was the consequence of the excessive issue of banknotes by the Bank of England. The Banking School which emerged under the intellectual leadership of Thomas Tooke, a „Russian merchant" and insurance leader, ascribed the depreciation to a series of independent events adversely affecting the British balance of payments, viz. bad harvests requiring inordinately large imports of food, the Continental blockade of Napoleon which cut off British export markets, and the necessity to provide military subsidies to such Allies as Prussia, Austria, Russia, Portugal and Spain. The expansion of

---

[4] Frank Whitson Fetter, *Development of British Monetary Orthodoxy, 1797—1875*, Cambridge, MA, 1965.

banknotes took place in response to the requirements of trade — the so-called „real-bills" doctrine to which the Banking School subscribed — and was thought (erroneously) therefore to have had no effect on prices. In this view the agio (depreciation) was autonomous and led to price increases that increased the value of goods moving in trade and thus justified expansion of the money supply.

In the German case, the monetarist school — notably Bresciani-Turroni,[5] and in contemporary time, Phillip Cagan[6] blame the inflation principally on the budget deficit and its financing by short-term debt sold to banks that enlarged the money supply, whereas the balance-of-payments school — Karl Helfferich,[7] Moritz Bonn,[8] Frank D. Graham,[9] and John H. Williams[10] — placed the emphasis on exchange depreciation of the mark set in motion by the short-term need to restock the German economy with raw materials on the one hand and the long-term necessity to pay reparations on the other. Third and fourth independent sources of early exchange depreciation after the release of exchange control and a fixed rate in September 1919 were the insistence of German iron and steel industry in paying off its debts to Sweden for wartime purchases of iron ore in order to be able to buy more — a factor which could be subsumed under restocking — and an outflow of German capital.[11]

There is an important difference between the British inflation at the end of the Napoleonic Wars and the German inflation after World War I. The latter exploded; the former did not. In 1819 and in 1925, Britain

---

[5] Costantino Bresciani-Turroni, *The Economics of Inflation. A Study of Currency Depreciation in Post-War Germany, 1914-1923*, London, 1937.

[6] Philip Cagan, *The Monetary Dynamics of Hyperinflation*, in: Milton Friedman (ed.), *Studies in the Quantity Theory of Money*, Chicago, 1956, pp. 25—117.

[7] John G. Williamson, *Karl Helfferich, 1872-1924, Economist, Financier, Politician*, Princeton, 1971, pp. 383—384.

[8] Moritz J. Bonn, *Stabilization of the Mark*, Chicago, First National Bank of Chicago, April 1922.

[9] Frank D. Graham, *Exchange, Prices and Production in Hyperinflation, Germany, 1920-1923*, Princeton, 1930.

[10] Bernard Malamud, *John H. Williams on the German Inflation: The International Amplification of Monetary Disturbances*, in: Nathan Schmukler/Edward Marcus (eds.), *Inflation through the Ages. Economic, Social, Psychological and Historical Aspects*, New York, 1983.

[11] Gerald D. Feldman, *Iron and Steel in the German Inflation 1916-1923*, Princeton, 1977, pp. 93 ff., 140 ff.; and C. Bresciani-Turroni, *The Economics*...[see note 5], p. 56.

returned to the prewar gold price, at some cost.[12] German inflation has to be divided into two phases: the initial substantial inflation to about June 1922 and a hyperinflation which followed. Even confirmed monetarists recognize the necessity for this distinction. In his initial study, Cagan stopped his statistical investigation at July 1923 when the hyperinflation began to climax.[13] In a recent article, however, Flood and Garber of the monetarist persuasion seek to demonstrate that the later period was not a „bubble" in the sense that increases in the price level led to further increases in the price level.[14] I shall return to the question of dividing up the period into segments later. At the moment, I assert that despite Flood and Garber's inability to reject the hypothesis that the peak of hyperinflation was not the result of money issues, it is not self-evident that a single theory can cover the entire process of inflation.

There is a third possible school not discussed in the classic economic literature, although there are hints of it in Laursen and Pedersen (and Helfferich) who blame labor for raising real wages when depreciation of the mark started to lower them.[15] Elements of a sort that may be called „structural" can be incorporated into the balance-of-payments theory as a step between depreciation and the rise in international prices on the one hand, and the increase in the money supply on the other. But the theory may be viewed as more general. Mancur Olson, Jr. has extended his *Logic of Collective Action*[16] in a new work entitled *The Rise and Decline of Nations: Economic Growth, Stagflation and Social Rigidities*[17] which, while it does not discuss the case of the German inflation of 1923, can be applied to it. The thesis is that in a society where various interests — called „distributional coalitions" — fight for a greater share of national income in order to gain the lion's share on any increase in income, or more usually in order to avoid bearing a significant portion of a loss, inflation is a likely outcome. Olson's new book applies the

---

[12] C.P. Kindleberger, *British Financial Reconstruction, 1815—22 and 1918—25*, in: C.P. Kindleberger/G. di Tella (eds.), *Economics in the Long View*, London, 1982, vol. 3, pp. 105—120.

[13] Ph. Cagan, *The Monetary Dynamics...* [see note 6].

[14] Robert P. Flood/Peter M. Garber, *Market Fundamentals versus Price Bubbles: The First Tests*, in: *Journal of Political Economy*, vol. 88, no. 4 (August 1980), pp. 745—770.

[15] Karsten Laursen/Jørgen Pedersen, *The German Inflation, 1918-1923*, Amsterdam, 1964.

[16] Mancur Olson, Jr., *The Logic of Collective Action*, Cambridge, MA, 1965.

[17] Mancur Olson, Jr., *The Rise and Decline of Nations: Economic Growth, Stagflation and Social Rigidities*, New Haven, 1982.

theory largely to growth and lack of growth, but does spend a considerable amount of time on stagflation in the United States, where his theory produces a model with a strong family resemblance to the sociological theory of Fred Hirsch and John Goldthorpe in *The Political Economy of Inflation* and the „core inflation" theory of Otto Eckstein.[18] In the German post-World War I setting, agriculture, industry and labor — and especially subgroups within these broad aggregates — clashed over which group or groups were to bear the burdens of destruction, with its immediate loss of income, and of reparations.

The theory of structural inflation is of course not new with Olson. An early analyst with a model along these lines was Henri Aujac who ascribed inflation after World War II in France to the fact that agriculture, industry and labor all had market power and all were determined to resist having the burden of reconstruction imposed on them.[19] Agriculture resists by raising prices which increases the cost of living. This leads to a demand for higher wages, perhaps supported by strikes, which induces industrialists to raise the price of manufactured goods. If government is included in the model it is obliged to raise taxes in order to keep real spending unchanged. The rise in taxes and in industrial prices sets off new increases in farm prices and a new round. In an open economy, higher prices lead to import surpluses which typically induce exchange depreciation, raising traded-goods prices (the prices of exports and imports), and stimulating agriculture, labor, and non-traded-goods producers to push up their prices and wages. The model has been developed especially for Latin America by Albert Hirschman[20] and David Felix.[21]

The structural model is connected with monetarism and with budget deficits in a number of ways. If the government fails to raise taxes but rather runs a deficit, this is inflationary unless it is financed by real

---

[18] Fred Hirsch/John Goldthorpe (eds.), *The Political Economy of Inflation*, Cambridge, MA, 1978; and Otto Eckstein, *Core Inflation*, Englewood Cliffs, NJ, 1981.

[19] Henri Aujac, *Inflation as a Monetary Consequence of the Behavior of Social Groups: A Working Hypothesis*, in: *International Economic Papers*, No. 4 (reprinted from *Economie Appliquée*, vol. 3, no. 2 [April-June 1950], pp. 280—300).

[20] Albert Hirschman, *Inflation in Chile*, Chap. 3 in: *Journeys Toward Progress: Studies of Economic Policymaking in Latin America*, New York, 1963, esp. pp. 208 ff.

[21] See essays by David Felix in: Albert O. Hirschman (ed.), *Latin American Issues*, New York, 1961, pp. 81—94 and 95—124 resp.

savings. If it is financed by short-term debt placed with the banking system, it can be argued that the inflation is monetary. But this assumes that the government or central bank has a free range of choice, and finances the deficit through the banking system only because it made a mistake in economic policy, based perhaps on erroneous theories. The structural school would deny this. Raising taxes calls for an explicit political set of decisions on how to allocate the burden, and each group on which a significant tax may fall may either defeat the tax by the exercise of political power or render its effects nugatory economically by raising prices or wages to make up for it. Or in the case of industry, monetarists would claim that manufacturers would be unable to pay higher wages and raise prices unless the banking system provided them with additional credit, so that here again a rise of prices and wages can occur only if the banking system, including the central bank, makes the mistake of not holding down the supply of high-powered money and letting the increased demand raise interest rates until savings rise or other spending is reduced, or some combination of the two. Again it is assumed that the banking system has free will, in contrast to structural assumption that central bankers are endogenous and are forced to respond in particular ways by the pressures of the system.

Mistakes are possible, to be sure. Karl Helfferich, as Secretary of the Reich Treasury during the war, clung to a theory of war finance widely held as far back as Jacques Necker, but now recognized as untenable, that if the budget is balanced it is not inflationary, and that it is sufficient to balance ordinary receipts, including in the former, service on the debt incurred to finance the extraordinary budget including military expenditure.[22] Monetarists are right in regarding acceptance of such a theory as a serious mistake. But to the extent that Helfferich refused to balance the overall budget because he did not want to tax company profits or to levy income taxes on the rich as the Socialists desired, the resultant inflation can more properly be regarded as structural, arising from the inability of society to agree on how to bear the burden of the war.[23] After the hostilities, the tax reforms of Erzberger were sabotaged by the propertied classes. There were mistakes, to be sure, in the long lags allowed between levying and payment, but com-

---

[22] J.G. Williamson, *Karl Helfferich...* [see note 7], pp. 123—125. See also Robert D. Harris, *Necker, Reform Statesman of the Ancient Regime*, Berkeley, 1979, pp. 123—124.
[23] J.G. Williamson, *Karl Helfferich...* [see note 7], pp. 129—141.

pliance was minimal and capital flight to escape taxation took place on an important scale. After the London ultimatum of May 1921 there was a „violent" debate on taxation.[24] This was complicated to be sure by the reluctance of many groups to pay reparations to France (in sharp contrast to the attitude of the French in 1871 and 1872 when national pride united all groups in paying off the Franco-Prussian indemnity well ahead of schedule). But it would be a mistake to call the inflation of the period monetary if this implied that there was a monetary choice to be taken — by experts in a vacuum — that would have avoided the inflation.

Among the other mistakes of the Social Democratic/Center Party Coalition if one focuses narrowly on inflation was the initial reluctance to raise interest rates for fear of unemployment, though historians today are beginning to regard that as a virtue as they contemplate the deflationary troubles of the United States and the United Kingdom in 1920—21,[25] and the real-bills doctrine of the Reichsbank in June 1922 when it was discounting commercial bills at a sharply increasing rate during the credit squeeze, although recent work by Holtfrerich on Reichsbank sources suggests that the directors knew what they were doing and made their choice deliberately.[26] One can add the disregard of the quantity theory of money which is valid in the long run, even though it may not be helpful in shaping short-run policy. Wirth, the Center Party prime minister, on the other hand, is regarded as stupid.[27]

With mistakes, it is necessary for the accusor to specify the counterfactual, i.e. what would have happened if a different course had been followed. Was an optimal or even better policy possible or were there forces blocking that route so that the choice basically lay between the 5th, 6th, or 7th-best policies, or perhaps between the 4th best and the 7th best. Note that contemporaries are recorded frequently as having highly been critical of the policies followed, but on many occasions with

---

[24] C. Bresciani-Turroni, *The Economics*... [see note 5], p. 57; Klaus Epstein, *Matthias Erzberger and the Dilemma of German Democracy*, Princeton, 1959, chap. 9.

[25] See Gerald D. Feldman, *The Historian and the German Inflation*, in: N. Schmukler/E. Marcus (eds.), *Inflation*... [see note 10].

[26] Carl-Ludwig Holtfrerich, *Die deutsche Inflation, 1914-1923. Ursachen und Folgen in internationaler Perspektive*, Berlin, 1980, pp. 71—72, 307—308.

[27] J.G. Williamson, *Karl Helfferich*...[see note 7], p. 347.

nothing positive to offer as an alternative.[28] Or the Reichsbank and the government would each call on the other to take the appropriate action, as in the case today in the United States between the Treasury and the Federal Reserve System.

If one moves out from Germany alone to Germany and France together, the balance-of-payments theory can also be brought under the structural umbrella. If one aggregates Germany and France, it is clear that no peaceful compromise was possible to the reparations problem. Occupation of the Ruhr in January 1923 by France and Belgium was the violent unsuccessful method to resolve the impasse. The problem was where — in France or in Germany — to assign the burden of reconstructing northwest France. Rathenau and Loucheur had agreed on a form of reparations in kind with German workers building in France, but this was rejected by the French building unions.[29] Loucheur said „If I told the French the truth, they would kill me."[30]

Monetarists scorn the idea of structural inflation. Firstly they deny that any group has market power. In Reder's list of tight priors is included „No capacity to affect prices." Moreover, monetarists insist that if such an increase in prices were to take place, it could be stopped by central-bank refusal to expand the money supply in the amounts necessary to validate a price increase. Since the velocity of money moves only narrowly, this would mean that an attempt to raise prices or wages would induce unemployment which would halt inflation. Industrialists or labor or agriculture or government cannot raise prices or wages if the money supply is held steady. Money is a handle on the economy. It is exogenous. Mistakes occur but are errors of analysis or of judgement, or result from weaknesses of will or character. The structural-inflation school claims rather that politicians are endogen-

---

[28] See David Felix, *Walther Rathenau and the Weimar Republic: The Politics of Reparations*, Baltimore, 1971, p. 172; Robert G. Moeller, *Peasants, Politics, and Pressure Groups in War and Inflation: A Study of the Rhineland and Westphalia, 1914-1924*, in: *Journal of Economic History*, vol. 42, no. 1 (March 1982), p. 226; J.G. Williamson, *Karl Helfferich...* [see note 7], p. 362; and G. D. Feldman, *The Historian and the German Inflation...* [see note 25], à propos of the Hirsch plan, rejected by all sides without offers of an alternative.

[29] Alfred Sauvy, *Histoire économique de la France entre les deux guerres*, Tôm. 1, *1918-1931*, Paris, 1965, p. 140.

[30] *Op. cit.*, p. 148.

ous and behave in predictable ways, responding to the explicit situation, and virtually certain to be dismissed from office if they try to behave like strict monetarists. There is, on this score, limited scope for monetary choice.

In the structural-inflation model a good deal depends upon the nature of the underlying society, something on which historians dilate, but economists, political scientists and even macro-sociologists, apart from few like Dahrendorf and Crozier, do not. In this view the fact that the British achieved the financial revolution peacefully and the French shed blood a century later to accomplish the same transformation is not a random accident but an outcome shaped by national character — a weak concept and one virtually impossible to incorporate in a mathematical model, but nevertheless one which on occasion is critical.[30a]

German democracy was notoriously weak, that country having failed to overcome autocracy in the abortive revolution of 1848. Moreover the economy was strongly prone to cartel formation from at least 1880. Different groups did not trust one another. Worse, there was often hatred, both for individuals such as Erzberger, Helfferich, Rathenau, etc., and for large groups such as the Jews, accused of responsibility for German defeat through the stab in the back. David Felix's (the historian not the economist) book on Rathenau has a chapter on „The Tendency to Acts of Violence."[31] The end of one period in the inflation was marked by the Kapp Putsch, followed at the end of the hyperinflation in November 1923 by Hitler's Beer Hall Putsch. The extreme right wing of the Nationalist party was said not to be *koalitionsfähig*, lacking the ability to make the compromises necessary to work with other parties.[32] One aspect of the violence in addition to the Putsches was the series of assassinations — of Rosa Luxemburg, Liebknecht, Eisner, Erzberger, and Rathenau, the last two perhaps partly stimulated by the extravagance of the political attacks on them by Helfferich. The assassination of Rathenau marked a turning point in the rate of inflation as it changed expectations about the exchange rate, the capital flow, and hence changed the rate of exchange depreciation. There seems to be a

---

[30a] Cf. „If we wish to understand why one country yielded to inflation and another stood by its old standard, we must take into account many elements which are not primarily of an economic character." Robert S. Lopez, *The Dollar of the Middle Ages*, in: *Journal of Economic History*, 21, p. 222.

[31] D. Felix, *Walther Rathenau*... [see note 28], chap. 9.

[32] J.G. Williamson, *Karl Helfferich*... [see note 7], p. 368.

distinct ideological difference between the American assassinations and attempted assassinations of 1963 to 1981 from those of post-World-War-I Germany — though the writer's competence in the area is minimal. In the American case the attempts seemed to stem from psychological disorders — although there remains a possibility that that of John F. Kennedy had an international political element. Those of Germany in 1919—22 were strongly rooted in national politics and based on group hatred, „hatred" being a word that permeates the historiography of the period but has little place in econometric models.[33]

The monetarist school, as already discussed, emphasizes economic mistakes. The balance-of-payments school emphasizes „*forces des choses*" as opposed to „*forces des hommes*". With reparations, war debts, the need to restock and to pay off debts, inflation was inevitable regardless of the policies chosen. But this view must contend with the fact that the French paid the indemnity in 1871—72, well ahead of schedule, by means of an united effort. The Germans were united only in opposing any payment to France. Apposite is Sir Edward Peacock's remark of May 1922: „The French have been technical and unyielding... unhelpful, almost destructive, but in the main they have been technically correct. The Germans on the other hand are not only technically but to a large extent morally wrong. The French ask impossible things, but the Germans have not yet begun to do the possible."[34]

The structural school starts from a burden imposed on society — restocking, reconstruction, reparations, in today's world a sharp increase in the price of oil — which burden must be allocated. The problem is how to allocate it in an acceptable way, that is, a way acceptable to those with political and economic clout. As already

---

[33] On the hatred of Helfferich by the left see J.G. Williamson, *Karl Helfferich*... [see note 7], p. 342; that Erzberger was the object of „monumental and vicious hatred," and „His enemies could enjoy hating Rathenau," see D. Felix, *Walther Rathenau*... [see note 28], p. 126 ; and K. Epstein, *Matthias Erzberger*... [see note 24], p. 397. The prevalence of hatred and violence indicate how far postwar Germany was from the condition in which Adam Smith's „obvious and simple system of natural liberty" could establish itself. This system required the sovereign to discharge but three duties: one) to protect society from the violence and invasion of other independent societies; 2) to protect, as far as possible, every member from the injustice and oppression of every other member; 3) public works, (*The Wealth of Nations*, Cannan edition, New York, 1937, p. 651.)

[34] Richard S. Sayers, *The Bank of England, 1891-1944*, Cambridge, 1976, 1, p. 174.

noted, this was particularly difficult to do in German society which possessed strong groupings such as cartels, weak democracy, weak capacity to compromise, a tendency to hatred and violence. The Communist revolution of 1919 was violently suppressed, Karl Liebknecht and Rosa Luxemburg assassinated, the Kapp Putsch attempted and failed. The right wing was unwilling to pay taxes on profits or submit to a capital levy, the Social Democratic/Center Party Governments chose expansion over deflation as a means to ensure social peace. The Junkers according to Gerschenkron were a group with dominance that managed to land on its feet after victory, defeat, inflation, deflation.[35] Recent research has rejected Gerschenkron's view that the peasants followed the leadership of the Junkers blindly, but makes clear that the peasants were sharply opposed to labor and the Socialists over *Zwangswirtschaft* (compulsory planting of particular crops) and price controls.[36] Within industry, there were different interests of protectionist, labor-intensive, cartelized heavy industry — iron and steel, and coal — and the export-oriented capital-intensive dynamic industrial sectors — machine-building, electro-technical, and chemical.[37] Both were anxious to break the eight-hour day, increase productivity, return to piece work. Civil servants whose salaries lagged behind wages and profits were the worst hit, along with the rentier who had faithfully accumulated war loan. While these interests occasionally cooperated with one or another against the rest, for the most part they dug in. After a time it became impossible for the Social Democratic/Center Party coalition to govern. Cuno with connections to the Allies and to all business groups presumably had a better chance to reconcile the groups. One can debate how much his personal qualities handicapped him in trying to effect compromise.[38] The structural inflationist would maintain that only an unusually charismatic leader — which Cuno was not — would have had a chance to pull it off. Inflation — of the vigorous sort short of

---

[35] Alexander Gerschenkron, *Bread and Democracy in Germany*, Berkeley, 1943.

[36] Gerald D. Feldman, *The Political Economy of Germany's Relative Stabilization during the 1920-21 World Depression*, preliminary paper presented to a Lehrman Institute Study Group, December 2, 1981, pp. 30—32; R.G. Moeller, *Peasants, Politics...* [see note 28], p. 225.

[37] David Abraham, *The Collapse of the Weimar Republic: Political Economy and Crisis*, Princeton, 1981.

[38] Hermann J. Rupieper, *The Cuno Government and Reparations, 1922-23: Politics and Economics*, The Hague, 1979.

hyper-inflation — was a means of turning the task of distributing income over to outside depersonalized forces.

There is one strong argument for this view of structural inflation, based on incapacity to resolve the clashes among distributional coalitions, and one or two against. Favoring the structural explanation is the contrast between the means adopted for burden-sharing after World Wars I and II. After World War I, all groups survived intact and even strengthened by the „organizational mania" of 1918—19.[39] During the Nazi period, trade unions and a number of farm organizations were weakened. After World War II all groups were effectively dissolved. The Junkers lost their economic base in Eastern Germany. Heavy industry was handicapped both by destruction and by its record of having helped the Nazis. There were in fact no interests to stand in the way of a sensible socially-engineered solution. The Colm-Dodge-Goldsmith report of 1946, based on suggestions drawn from more than thirty memoranda by German economists, could be devised in an atmosphere that was politically free of pressures.

There are several misunderstandings about the German monetary reform of 1948. Gordon Craig has suggested that the measure was delayed for a long time because the American occupation forces were content to tolerate the black market and the cigarette economy.[40] If this meant to imply that Morgenthauism of the sort implicit in J.C.S. 1067 lasted until 1948 it is misleading. Already by the end of 1945, the U.S. Department of State had turned its back on the Morgenthau plan.[41] The Colm-Dodge-Goldsmith committee, for example, was appointed in March 1946 after some months of preparation. Charles Maier writes that both the West Germans and the occupation forces hesitated to write off the losses of the war years and avoided imposing deflationary reforms.[42] This is not my recollection and ignores the difficulties faced by the Allied Control Council in printing a new

---

[39] Gerald D. Feldman, *Iron and Steel*... [see note 11], p. 102.

[40] Gordon A. Craig, *The German People*, chap. 5, p. 33 of ms.

[41] See „Restatement of U.S. Policy on Germany: Adress by Secretary James E. Byrnes, Stuttgart, September 6, 1946" in Department of State, *Germany, 1947-1949: The Story in Documents*, Washington, 1950, pp. 3—8; and Department of State, *United States Economic Policy Towards Germany*, Washington, U.S. Government Printing Office Publication 2630, n. d. (fall 1946).

[42] Charles S. Maier, *The Two Postwar Eras and Conditions for Stability in Twentieth-Century Western Europe*, in: *American Historical Review*, vol. 86, no. 2 (April 1981) p. 343 and *Reply, op. cit.*, p. 364.

currency for a four-party monetary reform, given the suspicion in a number of quarters, especially Congressional, that the United States had been in error during the war in furnishing the Russians with plates for printing the occupation currency. The issues involved in the currency-printing question are replete with misunderstandings and errors, but that this was the cause of delay, and not any hesitation in proceeding with monetary reform, is clear to the participants, if not to the scholars of later decades.

A second error of historical understanding has to do with the Friedman view that the occupation forces had muddled monetary reform and were saved from ruining it by the wisdom and force of Ludwig Erhard. This is a thoroughly misguided view, based on strong priors, although it is part of legend.[43]

German monetary reform in 1948 was a model of social engineering. In addition to writing down monetary claims — currency, deposits, debts of all kinds, including bonds, insurance policies and the like — it imposed a mortgage of 50 percent on real property with the interest paid into a *Lastenausgleich Fonds* (Fund for the Equalization of War Losses), the proceeds of which were disbursed to sufferers in the war on the basis of need. It should be noted that labor unions demonstrated against the monetary reform in the ground that it unduly favored the propertied classes, but this demonstration appears to have been passionless and largely pro forma.[44]

This comparison between the financial aftermaths of World Wars I and II in Germany neglects the roles of GARIOA and the Marshall Plan. Holtfrerich has made the point, however, that Germany after World War I received a capital inflow from abroad which was larger than the Marshall Plan aid.[45] The comparison is of course far from

---

[43] See J. Kipp Tenenbaum, *Free to Choose*, a letter to the *New York Review of Books*, November 20 (1980); and Heinz Sauermann, *On the Economic and Financial Rehabilitation of Western Germany (1945-1949)*, in: Rudolph Richter (ed.), *Currency and Economic Reform: West Germany after World War II*, in: *Zeitschrift für die gesamte Staatswissenschaft*, Bd. 135, Heft 35 (September 1979), p. 316.

[44] Jürgen Domes/Michael Wolffsohn, *Setting the Course for the Federal Republic of Germany: Major Policy Decisions in the Bizonal Economic Council and Party Images, 1947—1949*, in: R. Richter, *Currency...* [see note 43], p. 341.

[45] C-.L. Holtfrerich *Die deutsche Inflation...* [see note 26], p. 293. Cf. also Carl-Ludwig Holtfrerich, *Amerikanischer Kapitalexport und Wiederaufbau der deutschen Wirtschaft 1919—1923 im Vergleich zu 1924—1929*, in: *Vierteljahresschrift für Sozial-und*

exact, since the Marshall Plan funds were invested positively whereas the capital inflow, apart from some portion which went into buying businesses, was largely held in short-term debt and land. A similar contrast is made for Austria between the League Loans of 1923 which served purely financial ends and Marshall Plan assistance which produced real investment.[46] It is of course possible for the recipients of financial assistance to transmute it into real investment — stocks of materials and components, machines, bricks, and mortar. As a matter of some historical interest, Helfferich worried in the early 1920s about *Überfremdung* — the over-foreignization (to coin an unattractive word) of the German economy.[47]

A second difference lies in reparations. But monetary payments from the acceptance of the London ultimatum in May 1921 until cash payments were stopped in July 1922 were 1.7 billion marks out of the 8.1 billion paid by Germany up to August 31, 1924 when the Dawes plan took over, roughly a quarter of the 7-8 billion gold marks received by Germany from the capital inflow.[48]

It should be emphasized further that Germany went well beyond Belgium, Italy and especially France in reforming the monetary system and imposing a capital levy to equalize war losses — a move discussed in Britain after the Napoleonic wars, and by the major countries in Europe after World Wars I and II, but undertaken in a significant scale only in West Germany where vested interests which might have opposed it did not exist. The French holding back from monetary reform is something of a puzzle. Certainly the view of the Resistance economic leader, René Courtin, that amputating part of the stock of currency and reducing bank deposits would have been „unpopular, unfair, arbitrary, and ineffective"[49] is difficult to comprehend unless perhaps, as seems unlikely, it refers to a monetary reform without a capital levy to equalize the burden between creditors and owners of real property.

Wirtschaftsgeschichte, vol. 64 (1977), pp. 497—529, reprinted in Michael Stürmer (ed.), *Die Weimarer Republik. Belagerte Civitas*, Königstein/Ts., 1980, pp. 131—157.

[46] See E. März, *Comment*, D.E. Moggridge, *Policy in the Crises of 1920 and 1929*, in: C.P. Kindleberger/J.P. Laffargue (eds.), *Financial Crises: Theory, History and Policy*, Cambridge, 1982, p. 190.

[47] J.G. Williamson, *Karl Helfferich*... [see note 7], p. 358.

[48] C.-L. Holtfrerich, *Die deutsche Inflation*... [see note 26], p. 145.

[49] Richard F. Kuisel, *Capitalism and the State in Modern France: Renovation and Economic Management in the Twentieth Century*, Cambridge, 1981, p. 183.

Another interesting contrast of the aftermath of war is with the position in Prussia in 1806 after the defeat at Jena and the treaty of Tilsit. New energy surged in the economy and the state, together with reforms. Moellendorff was mindful of them more than a century later.[50] But in the absence of any semblance of democracy, the reforms were imposed from above by von Stein and Hardenberg. The agricultural reforms moreover were later undermined.

The arguments against an explanation of the difference between the inflation of World War I and the monetary reform after World War II based on the survival of vested interests in the first and their dissolution on the second occasion include first that the difference may be due simply to learning. The United States learned over the quarter-century and was careful not to repeat the errors of war debts and reparations, substituting in their place lend-lease settlements and various forms of aid for reconstruction. The external burden on Germany, and some part of the internal were drastically reduced. That learning affects the operation of economic models is strikingly shown in a comparison of the speed of hyperinflation in Hungary after World War I and World War II.[51] Hyperinflation was reached in $4^1/_2$ years after the former, in thirteen months after the latter, because of a distinct difference in the anticipations of economic actors at home and abroad.

A second and more compelling argument against the structuralist view of the inflation is that while the Olson analysis applies strikingly to Germany of 1921—23 (and the opposite case to 1945—48), it is far from self-evident that it fits the other countries that experienced hyperinflation after World War I: Poland, Hungary, Austria, and Russia. Feldman has provided a useful categorization of three grades of inflation in the period: hypersubstantial, and reversible.[52] If the structural view is both necessary and sufficient, it should fit the entire class. In the hyperinflation category, however, the problems of the separate countries seem to be somewhat different, Russia with a revolution, Austria, a capital severed from its hinterland, Poland fashioned from a collection of remnants of countries — Germany, Russia, and the Austrian-Hungarian empire from which an attempt was made to forge a unit. I

---

[50] G.D. Feldman, *Iron and Steel*... [see note 11], p. 101.
[51] Bertrand Nogaro, *Hungary's Recent Monetary Crisis and its Theoretical Meaning*, in: *American Economic Review*, vol. 38 (1938), no. 4, pp 526—542.
[52] G.D. Feldman, *The Historians and the German Inflation*... [see note 25], pp. 4—5.

am not sufficiently versed in the histories of Eastern Europe to know whether there are any similarities with the German case — antithetical groups finding it difficult to agree on burden-sharing, and postponing resolution of distributional conflicts by a consensus for inflation in the early stages, followed by hyperinflation at a later stage when matters get out of hand.

There are then three schools. But there is no need for mono-causality except perhaps the academic predilection for parsimony in theorizing. It is possible that all three schools have a part of the truth, and especially that one school may be right at one time, another at another. The first suggestion along these lines was an attempt to reconcile the balance-of-payments and the monetary schools, made by Nurkse.[53] In the first stage the monetarist explanation was valid, with domestic expenditure financed by government deficits and central-bank expansion leading to rising prices followed by exchange depreciation. Foreign speculators, plus German, believed that the currency would ultimately be restored to par and supported the currency. The inflow of capital enabled the exchange rate to be overvalued. This meant that despite depreciation of the exchange rate the internal deflation was greater than the external. Germany developed an import surplus — at least relatively to other periods — though the data are poor as the *Statistisches Reichsamt* didn't publish trade statistics from the beginning of World War I until May 1921 and there was substantial smuggling in the Rhineland („the Hole in the West"). Exports from May to December 1921 covered only 60 percent of exports, according to the League of Nations, and 64 percent in 1922, as contrasted with 70 percent in 1921 and 99 percent in 1923.[54] When the inelastic expectations of a return of the exchange rate to its old level were reversed and followed by elastic expectations of continued depreciation, the monetarist model was superseded by the balance-of-payments model — a large outflow of capital, sharp depreciation of the exchange rate, external inflation leading internal inflation as the exchange rate became undervalued and pushed up prices. Exports rose and led to an export surplus. Inflation accelerated from June 1922, the time when expectations changed according to Holtfrerich. In the final stages, capital exports bypassed the

---

[53] League of Nations (Ragnar Nurkse), *The Course and Control of Inflation. A Review of Monetary Experience in Europe after World War I*, Princeton, 1946.

[54] *Op. cit.*, p. 50 n.

foreign-exchange market altogether as foreigners and Germans bought goods in Germany and shipped them for sale abroad, retaining the proceeds in foreign exchange.

In contrast to this pattern of monetarism, overvaluation and import surpluses which dampened the domestic inflation, followed by the balance-of-payments explanation of outflows, depreciation, rising prices, and money supplies trying to catch up, Bernholz has undertaken to establish an opposite sequence, of undervaluation followed by overvaluation, that is, the balance-of-payments school right in the first period, and the monetarists in the second.[55] There is great difficulty with the data because he uses the short-period tables of Bresciani-Turroni with their different base periods, no one of which bases can be said to be an equilibrium position. Thus his first period of undervaluation is measured on the basis of October 1918 (Table II in Bresciani-Turroni, p. 28 at a time when the exchange rate was pegged and controlled, and the wholesale price level was held down by price and wages controls. Holtfrerich's Table 1 (p. 15) gives October 1918 as 1.57 for the exchange rate taking 1913 as 1 and 2.34 for wholesale prices. For the second period when the exchange rate was overvalued and the monetarist theory valid, Bernholz uses Bresciani-Turroni's Table VII (pp. 35—36) with July 31, 1923 as a base. According to the previous table (VI, p. 35) however, the previous year had seen the exchange rate falling at three times the rate of the note circulation and almost twice that of the inflation in food prices. Bernholz' paper was focussed not solely on German inflation, but on the dynamic behavior of flexible exchange rates generally. He was trying to show that with the adoption of flexible exchange rates an initial period of undervaluation — because of the J-curve in imports and capital outflows — is generally followed by subsequent overvaluation when the balance of payments has had time to adjust. In this case it is not persuasive.

Other periodization includes the detailed breakdowns in diagrams of Bresciani-Turroni as follows, with an indication whether the lead is taken by the money supply (floating debt) or the exchange rate:[56]

---

[55] Peter Bernholz, *Flexible Exchange Rates and Exchange Rate Theory in Historical Perspective*, Stanford University, Center for Research in Economic Growth, Memorandum 247, March 1981, pp. 26—29.

[56] C. Bresciani-Turroni, *The Economics...* [see note 5], pp. 25—38.

1913-1918   money in circulation
October 1918 to February 1920   dollar exchange rate
February 1920 to May 1921   floating debt
May 1921 to July 1922   dollar exchange
July 1922 to June 1923   dollar exchange
July 31, 1923 to November 20, 1923   all together

Feldman's analysis provides a similar breakdown with emphasis on the difference in the rate of inflation between May 1921 — June 1922, and June 1922 to November 1923, even though both were led by the exchange rate.[57]

In addition to these differences in periodicity, there is considerable (mild) disagreement on the turning point from inflation to hyperinflation. Knut Borchardt maintains that this occurred in May 1921 at the time of the London Ultimatum.[58] Raymond Goldsmith informally pinned the inflection on the Franco-Belgian occupation of the Ruhr in January 1923.[59] Holtfrerich's candidate is June 1922 with the piling up of the French rejection of any change in the reparation agreement, the J.P. Morgan committee insistance that reparations had to be changed to make possible an American loan, and finally, and most critical, the assassination of Walther Rathenau.[60] The mark went from 272 to the dollar on June 1 to 318 on the 12th when the Morgan report came out, and from 332 to 355 on the day of the assassination (June 24). On June 30 it hit 374, and the next day 401. By July 31 it was 670 and by the end of August 1,725. Speculation in favour of the mark by foreigners (and some Germans) had been completely reversed.

This analysis suggests that the path of German inflation after World War I involved changing balance-of-payments and domestic monetary and fiscal forces, against the background of a struggle of vested interests that can be regarded as the fundamental pattern of structural inflation that can be succinctly summarized as follows:

1. Versailles to the Kapp Putsch of March 1920, marked by revolution, counter-revolution, assassinations of Liebknecht and Luxemburg. Exchange control was abandoned in September 1919, and the exchange rate depreciated under the influence of payments for raw materials,

---

[57] G.D. Feldman, *The Historian and German Inflation*... [see note 25], pp. 7-8.
[58] In a private discussion.
[59] *Idem*.
[60] C.-L. Holtfrerich, *Die deutsche Inflation*... [see note 26], pp. 287—291.

repayment of Swedish debts by iron and steel manufacturers, and some capital outflow. At the same time, there were internal causes of inflation from the center-left programs of work creation, support for unemployment, a relaxed attitude toward price and wage increases, the eight-hour day. The first attempt at fiscal reform was unsuccessful. It is possible to make a case of either the balance-of-payments or the monetarist school, against the background of structural inflation. Any monetarist explanation, however, has a strong admixture of the Laursen and Pedersen view, with inflation emanating from cost-push on the side of labor struggling to cut hours and raise wages.

2. From March 1920 to May 1921, relative stability, brought about by the inflow of capital. The exchange rate had plunged from $2^1/_2$ in March 1919, on the basis of 1913 as 1, to 23,6 in February 1920 before recovering to a range of 9 to 18. In May 1921 it was 14.8. This stability was based entirely on the inflow of capital from abroad. Wholesale prices were held down by the fall in import prices and the import of goods. Because of the limitations in Erzberger's financial reforms, domestic debt almost doubled from 92 to 162 billion marks, and the volume of high powered (Reichsbank) money rose from 67 billion marks at the end of February 1920 to 102 billion marks at the end of April 1921.[60a] Allowing for the world depression abroad, German exports were relatively strong because of the depreciation of the mark of the previous period and despite the relative import surplus. Feldman makes the point that booming exports and somewhat expansionary policy based on the capital inflow spared Germany the deflation and unemployment of other countries.[61] The period fits into none of the three inflationary models being characterized by overvaluation of the currency, expansion of the money supply, and a fall in prices from 17 (1913 = 1) in March 1920 to 13 in May 1921.

3. The third period runs from the acceptance of the London Ultimatum in May 1921 — characterized in Germany as the second stab in the back — to the traumatic events of June 1922. The dollar exchange rate and the prices of imported goods rose together, closely followed by the prices of domestic commodities and the cost of food. Expansion of the floating debt and the volume of circulation lagged behind. There was a „violent" struggle over new taxes to pay the agreed reparations, the

---

[60a] *Op. cit.*, pp. 51—52.
[61] G.D. Feldman, *The Historian and the German Inflation*... [see note 25], p. 5.

assassination of Erzberger in August 1921, and inability of the Wirth government to find a satisfactory basis for meeting the obligations it had accepted. Labor pushed hard to keep pace with rising prices, to furnish support to the Laursen-Pedersen model. In general it may be characterized as a period of „distress" — to use a word borrowed from financial crises[62] — with rising tension but before an absolute break. Foreign capital stopped coming in, and perhaps began slowly to ebb away. But the panic rush to withdraw was yet to occur.

4. The break came, as already noted, in June 1922, with the French rejection of a change in reparations, the J.P. Morgan refusal to lend in these circumstances, and the Rathenau assassination. Foreign capital which had been favouring the mark from March 1920 to May 1921, and wavering and uncertain to June, now took the bit in its teeth and headed out of Germany, closely followed by German speculation. The exchange rate led the expansion of money in circulation and the floating debt, to conform to the balance-of-payments model, but the Reichsbank undertook to expand its portfolio of commercial bills, at low or negative real rates of interest. In part, however, it was a deliberate decision to try to maintain the liquidity of the banking system in the face of pell-mell foreign (and domestic) dumping of German money for foreign exchange. To this extent the Reichsbank was acting as a lender of last resort to prevent a breakdown in the banking system.

This fourth period could be further disaggregated to mark a shift in the fall of 1922 to direct valuations in foreign prices instead of calculating through to foreign prices from domestic prices and the exchange rate; and again, with the occupation of the Ruhr in January 1923, when the Reichsbank turned on the presses full speed to assist the government in subsidizing the strikers. At the end, as already noted, internal and external inflation exploded together.

The explosion and the possibility of disintegration of the country as the Rhineland contemplated separation, including a separate currency and Bank of the Rhineland, substituted the stabilization consensus for the inflation consensus.[63] How the Rentenmark and the Reichsmark, plus the German acceptance of the Dawes loan fit into the structural model is a topic worth pursuit, but not in an already overlong paper.

---

[62] See my *Manias, Panics and Crashes*, New York, 1978, pp. 100 ff.

[63] See Karl Erich Born, *The German Inflation after the First World War*, in: *Journal of European Economic History*, vol. 6, no. 1 (Spring 1977), p. 116; and R.S. Sayers, *The Bank...* [see note 34], I, p. 177.

In normal historiography and economic history, and especially in a discussion of the structural model of inflation, it is useful to sort out which groups won and which groups lost. Again, I have little time or space to review this extensive literature, but I should like to record my objection to the implicit conclusion of a number of historian revisionists that the inflation after World War I in Germany was on the whole relatively inconsequential, with no group losing particularly, in fact, not much worse than a bad cold. It is true that the inflation may have been superior to violent revolution and internecine warfare, on the model of the Spanish revolution. The consensus for inflation was a comparative one, not absolute. I admire the work of Gerschenkron, Moeller, Webb, Feldman, Holtfrerich et al. in sorting out the winners and groups that held their own, but it seems to me clear that the inflation was fateful for the German middle class, including large parts of the peasantry, and that its memory shaped and distorted policy choices of the country for the next half century or more.[64] It may be that the emergence of the Nazis in government in the 1930s is overdetermined, like the French Revolution and the German inflation, finding its origins in German national character, the depth of the depression in Germany after foreign borrowing stopped, the deflationary policies of Bruening, etc. It would be hard, however, to deny a significant role to the trauma of the German middle class in the years from 1914 to 1924.

A corollary of the point of view presented in this paper — that the German inflation rested at basis on the incapacity of organized and powerful groups to agree on how to share among them the burdens of reconstruction and reparations (and of France and Germany to agree on how much reparation should be paid to make good the destruction of the great war) overlain by policy decisions, including mistakes, in which monetary, fiscal and exchange policy in Germany and speculation for and against the mark abroad and at home form a confusing pattern — is that much of the technical economic literature on the German inflation is beside the point because it fails to specify the socio-political matrix in which the economic events take place. Especially is this true of testing of theories involving tight priors, such as:

1) Inflation is purely monetary, or purely the result of depreciation of

---

[64] See my *Collective Memory vs. Rational Expectations: Some Historical Puzzles in Macro-economic Behavior*, in: *Economic Essays in Honour of Jørgen H. Geltung, Tillae snummer til Nationaløkonomisk Tidsskrift*, Copenhagen, 1982, pp.118—128.

the exchange rate based on balance-of-payments events of an automous sort.

2) The rate of exchange is always at the purchasing-power-parity level,[65] or is almost never there.

3) The forward exchange rate is an unbiassed estimator of the future exchange rate.[65]

4) Speculation is always stabilizing.[66]

5) Demand functions for money can be written as if domestic holders and foreign holders respond in the same way to the same economic events and stimuli.[67]

6) Because of rational expectations and efficient markets, there cannot be price bubbles.[68]

Economists seem frequently to take up the German inflation to prove some point in monetary or foreign-exchange theory and study little more than statistical series with no flesh and blood, no political parties, interest groups, politics, revolutions, violence, assassinations, etc. When they bring out their conclusions that the German inflation supports the theory they brought to its study, I am led to react with the Duke of Wellington when someone approached him and said „Mr. Johnson, I believe;" „If you believe that you can believe anything."

---

[65] J.A. Frenkel, *A Monetary Approach to the Exchange Rate: Doctrinal Aspects and Empirical Evidence*, in: Scandinavian Journal of Economics, vol. 78, no. 2 (1976), pp. 200—224.

[66] J.A. Frenkel, *The Forward Exchange Rate, Expectations and the Demand for Money: The German Hyperinflation*, in: American Economic Review, vol. 67, no 4 (September 1967), pp. 653—670; M.K. Salemi's *Comment*, in: American Economic Review, vol. 70, no.4 (September 1980), pp. 663—670; and J.A. Frenkel's *Reply, op. cit.*, pp. 671—775.

[67] See the *Comments* by Jean-Claude Debeir and by Jacob A. Frenkel, to Carl-L. Holtfrerich's *Domestic and Foreign Expectations and the Demand for Money during the German Inflation, 1920-1923*, in: C.P. Kindleberger/J.P.Laffargue (eds.), *Financial Crises...* [see note 46], pp. 132—136 and pp. 136—143, resp.

[68] A.P. Flood/P.M. Garber, *Market Fundamentals...* [see note 14].

Summary

The impressive literature on the German inflation of 1914 to 1923 is for the most part divided in economic, as distinct from political history, into the monetarist and balance-of-payment schools. The monetarists blame the issue of money to finance government deficits: the balance-of-payments school tends to regard the causation coming from international payments, largely for reparations, which lead to depreciation of the mark, higher import prices and only finally to an expansion of money. One variant of the balance-of-payments version attaches importance to the role of labor insisting on higher wages as the cost of living is raised by import and export prices. The clash between monetary and balance-of-payments explanations is by no means confined to the German inflation, but is present in the Banking vs the Currency School debate in England after the Napoleonic war, and in other debates.

This paper makes two main points: 1) that there is a third „structural" explanation at a more profound level which emphasizes the burden that German society had to bear and the difficulty of distributing it in a society where various competing interests were antagonistic and unwilling to compromise. Emphasis on labor's drive for higher wages touches only one aspect of this. Other interest groups — large-scale business in iron and steel, chemicals, electricity and the like, the Junkers in agriculture, the peasants of western Germany, civil servants, etc. all resisted. Temporizing solution was found by giving various groups the nominal income they sought, with real burden being allocated by rising prices. Economic policy is thus powerless.

In the second place, there is no need to subscribe to any one explanation, good for the entire period. At one time and another, monetary expansion, the balance of payments, and interest demands take the lead. Such a theory is less parsimonious, but far richer.

Die Beendigung vier großer Inflationen*

THOMAS J. SARGENT

Einleitung

In den letzten fünfzehn Jahren haben viele westliche Volkswirtschaften anhaltende Inflationen mit wachsenden Preissteigerungsraten durchgemacht. Einige prominente Ökonomen und Politiker sind inzwischen davon überzeugt, daß solche Inflationen eine hartnäckige, sich selbst tragende Eigendynamik entfalten und daß die konventionellen Gegenmaßnahmen einer restriktiven Geld- und Fiskalpolitik entweder nicht greifen oder aber sich wegen der weitverbreiteten und anhaltenden Arbeitslosigkeit, welche solche Maßnahmen nach sich ziehen, als viel zu kostspielig erweisen. Oftmals wird von einer „unterschwelligen Inflationsrate" gesprochen, die nur langsam, wenn überhaupt, auf restriktive geld- und fiskalpolitische Maßnahmen anspreche.[1] Nun ist diese unterschwellige Inflationsrate offenbar eben jene Rate, die Unternehmer und Arbeitnehmer für die Zukunft erwarten. In beiden Gruppen dürften sich die Erwartungen so bilden, daß frühere

---

* Mit den oben dargelegten Ansichten kann der Autor nur für sich selbst sprechen und nicht notwendigerweise auch für die Federal Reserve Bank of Minneapolis oder für das Federal Reserve System. Der Aufsatz war ursprünglich ein Beitrag zu einer Konferenz über Inflation, die vom National Bureau of Economic Research gefördert wurde. Preston Miller, John Kennan, Peter Garber und Gail Makinen lieferten hilfreiche Kommentare zu früheren Versionen dieses Aufsatzes, und die allgemeine Erörterung des Themas mit Michael K. Salemi und Neil Wallace war sehr förderlich. Gail Makinen machte mich auf die Arbeitslosenzahlen für Polen aufmerksam.

Aus dem amerikanischen Original übersetzt von Barbara Fremdling und Carl-Ludwig Holtfrerich.

[1] „Die meisten Ökonomen glauben, daß die unterschwellige Inflationsrate — grob definiert als Lohnkostensteigerungen minus Produktivitätsgewinne — gegenwärtig 9 bis 10 Prozent betrage und daß sie nur in einem langfristigen Prozeß von Beschränkungen bedeutend zu senken sei." *Newsweek*, 19. Mai 1980, S. 59.

Inflationsraten in die Zukunft extrapoliert werden, wodurch der Prozeß der Inflation seine Eigendynamik gewinnt. Wenn das zutrifft, dann müßte die Inflationserfahrung der letzten fünfzehn Jahre bei Unternehmern und Arbeitnehmern eine Erwartungshaltung von hohen Inflationsraten aufgebaut haben, die sich allenfalls langsam, wenn überhaupt, mit restriktiven geld- und fiskalpolitischen Maßnahmen bekämpfen lassen. Nach dieser Ansicht führen derartige restriktive Maßnahmen zunächst zu einer erheblichen Verminderung des Output und der Beschäftigung, kaum aber zu einer Reduzierung der Inflationsrate. Für die US-amerikanische Wirtschaft wird häufig die Schätzung zitiert, nach der das Land für jeden Prozentpunkt, um den man die jährliche Inflationsrate mit Mitteln der restriktiven Geld- und Fiskalpolitik senkt, 220 Milliarden Dollar des jährlichen Bruttosozialprodukts (GNP) einbüßt. Bei dem amerikanischen Bruttosozialprodukt von ca. 2,5 Billionen Dollar (1980) wären nach dieser Schätzung die Kosten allerdings in der Tat äußerst hoch, wenn man die Inflationsrate auf Null herabsenken wollte.

Autoren mit alternativer Sehweise, die von der Annahme rationaler Erwartungsbildung ausgehen, bestreiten, daß der gegenwärtige Inflationsprozeß eine Eigendynamik besitze.[2] Sie räumen zwar ein, daß Unternehmer und Arbeitnehmer zur Zeit hohe Inflationsraten für die Zukunft erwarten und sich ökonomisch entsprechend verhalten;[3] doch

---

[2] Paul Samuelson hat diesen Ansatz, der von einer rationalen Erwartungsbildung ausgeht, treffend so beschrieben: „Es gibt eine neue Schule, die sogenannten ‚rational expectationists'. Sie sind zuversichtlich, daß Inflationen mit geringen gesellschaftlichen Kosten beendet werden können, wenn nur die Regierung ihre Entschlossenheit zu diesem Unterfangen *glaubhaft* macht. Aber weder die Geschichte noch die Vernunft läßt es zu, diese Zuversicht zu teilen." *Newsweek*, 28. April 1980. Der zweite Satz dieses Zitats enthält vermutlich die scharfsinnigste Kennzeichnung dieser Ansicht, die von einem einzelnen Satz geleistet werden kann. Es fällt jedoch schwer, dem dritten Satz zuzustimmen: Was die Vernunft angeht, so wird man schon zugeben müssen, daß ein logisch stimmiges und gutbegründetes Modell den Behauptungen der „rational expectationists" zugrunde liegt. Und was die Geschichte angeht, so können die Geschehnisse, von denen dieser Aufsatz handelt, sicherlich herangezogen werden, um die Vorstellungen von einer rationalen Erwartungsbildung zu stützen.

[3] Tatsächlich gibt es keine „rational expectations school" in dem Sinne, daß eine Gruppe von Ökonomen sich auf ein Wirtschaftsmodell und eine Meinung zur optimalen Geld- und Fiskalpolitik geeinigt hätte, sondern es bestehen höchst unterschiedliche Auffassungen über die geeignete Politik auch in diesem Kreis. Übereinstimmend wollen die Vertreter der rationalen Erwartungshypothese jedoch Wirtschaftsmodelle schaffen, die davon ausgehen, daß Privatpersonen die dynamischen Prozesse, an denen sie teilha-

unterstellt dieser alternative Ansatz, daß die Wirtschaftssubjekte eben deshalb hohe Inflationsraten in der Zukunft erwarten, weil die gegenwärtige und absehbare Geld- und Fiskalpolitik der Regierung eine solche Erwartungshaltung stärkt. Nach dieser Ansicht sprechen weder die augenblickliche noch die für die Zukunft erwartete Inflationsrate schnell auf *Einzelmaßnahmen* einer restriktiven Geld- und Fiskalpolitik an, denn diese werden lediglich als vorübergehende Abweichungen von einer langfristigen *Regierungspolitik* angesehen, die ansonsten durchschnittlich hohe Haushaltsdefizite und Geldmengensteigerungen in der Zukunft auslöst. Deshalb *scheint* es nur so, als ob die Inflation eine Eigendynamik entwickle, während sie in Wirklichkeit aber durch die langfristige Regierungspolitik mit den hohen Haushaltsdefiziten und den hohen Geldschöpfungsraten weiter angeregt werde. Aus dieser Sehweise ergibt sich, daß die Inflation viel rascher gedrosselt werden kann, als jene Vertreter glauben, die ihr eine Eigendynamik zuschreiben. Deren Schätzungen über die benötigte Zeit und die Kosten, die entstünden, wenn man die Inflation aufzuhalten versucht (eine Einbuße von 220 Milliarden Dollar vom amerikanischen Bruttosozialprodukt für eine Senkung der Inflationsrate um einen Prozentpunkt), stellen sich nach dieser Ansicht als falsch dar. Auch hier erscheint die Inflationsbekämpfung als äußerst schwierig, erfordert sie doch weit mehr als einige vorübergehende geld- und fiskalpolitische Maßnahmen. Vielmehr muß die *Wirtschaftspolitik grundlegend* geändert werden („a change in the policy *regime*"): Die ständig eingesetzte *Strategie* der Defizitpolitik ist sofort aufzugeben, und zwar muß das glaubhaft auch für die Zukunft zugesichert werden. Bisher verfügen die Ökonomen noch nicht über verläßliche, empirisch überprüfte wirklichkeitsnahe Modelle, mit denen sie genau vorhersagen könnten, wie schnell sich ein solcher grundlegender Wandel in der Wirtschaftspolitik, eine Änderung des „Regimes" auswirkt und welche Einbußen an Output und

---

ben, annähernd so gut wie die politischen Entscheidungsträger der Regierungen verstehen. Diese Grundüberzeugung läßt große Unterschiede in den einzelnen Merkmalen bei der Bildung eines Modells zu. Beispiele für Modelle, die zwar alle von der rationalen Erwartungsbildung ausgehen, dennoch aber verschiedene Implikationen haben, finden sich bei Lucas (21), Barro (2), Wallace (35), Townsend (34) sowie bei Sargent und Wallace (31). Bei all ihrer Unterschiedlichkeit bringen uns diese Modelle zu wesentlich anderen Vorstellungen über die optimale Regierungspolitik, als sie in der Makroökonomie üblich waren, bevor in den frühen 1970er Jahren die Doktrin der „rational expectations" aufkam.

Die Beendigung vier großer Inflationen

Beschäftigung er verursacht. Zweifellos hinge es aber von dem Grad der Entschlossenheit und erkennbaren Zielstrebigkeit des Einsatzes der Regierung ab, welche Kosten an Produktionseinbuße ein solches Vorgehen verursachen und wie schnell die beabsichtigte Stabilisierung eintreten würde.

In diesem Aufsatz werden einige dramatische historische Erfahrungen beschrieben, die meines Erachtens mit der Hypothese rationaler Erwartungsbildung verträglich sind, aber nur schwer mit der alternativen These von der Eigendynamik der Inflation in Einklang gebracht werden können. Es geht darum, von der gegenwärtigen inflationären Lage abzusehen und statt dessen die Maßnahmen zu untersuchen, mit denen galoppierende Inflationen in mehreren europäischen Ländern während der 1920er Jahre unter Kontrolle gebracht wurden. Ich werde die Vorgänge in Österreich, Ungarn, Deutschland und Polen beschreiben und interpretieren. Jedes dieser Länder machte damals eine dramatische Hyperinflation durch, bei der die Preisindizes in nur wenigen Monaten auf astronomische Höhen stiegen. Als Basisdaten der Analyse gelten die Preisindizes der ABBILDUNGEN 1—4. Sie sind auf einer logarithmischen Skala abgebildet, damit sie auf eine Seite passen. In allen vier Ländern, besonders aber in Deutschland, stieg das Preisniveau gewaltig an. Weiterhin zeigen die Abbildungen, daß die Inflationen in allen Fällen jäh beendet wurden und nicht schrittweise. Auf die Ereignisse in der Tschechoslowakei werde ich kurz eingehen. Sie war von Nachbarländern umgeben, die Hyperinflationen durchmachten, schaffte es aber, die eigene Währung stabil zu halten. An all diesen Fällen läßt sich der grundlegende Wandel in der Wirtschaftspolitik, die Änderung des „Regimes", wie in einem Laboratorium untersuchen. In Österreich, Ungarn, Polen und Deutschland änderte man die Fiskalpolitik tiefgreifend, und in jedem dieser Länder ging damit das Ende der Hyperinflation einher. Und die Tschechoslowakei, die doch etliche Probleme mit ihren vier Nachbarn teilte, hatte bewußt eine vergleichsweise restriktive Fiskalpolitik mit dem erklärten Ziel betrieben, den Wert ihrer Währung zu erhalten.

Wenngleich die österreichische, ungarische, polnische und die deutsche Hyperinflation sich in vielen Merkmalen voneinander unterschieden, so gab es doch wesentliche Züge, die allen gemeinsam waren, und zwar:

1. Die Art der Fiskalpolitik, die während der Hyperinflation verfolgt wurde: Jedes der vier Länder ließ gewaltige Haushaltsdefizite in laufender Rechnung zu.

2. Die Art der drastischen fiskal- und geldpolitischen Maßnahmen, mit denen das Ende der Hyperinflationen gezielt herbeigeführt werden sollte.
3. Die jäh einsetzende Stabilisierung des Preisniveaus und der Wechselkurse.[4]
4. Das schnelle Anwachsen von Zentralbankgeld *(high powered money)* in den Monaten und Jahren, nachdem die Hyperinflation beendet war.

Bei der Zusammenstellung und Interpretation der Fakten werde ich von einer bestimmten Ansicht ausgehen über die ökonomischen Kräfte, die dem Geld Wert verleihen, und über die Art, in der das internationale Währungssystem in den 1920er Jahren funktionierte. Zunächst soll diese Ansicht kurz dargelegt werden.

Der Goldstandard

Nach dem Ersten Weltkrieg befand sich die US-amerikanische Währung auf dem Goldstandard. Die Regierung der Vereinigten Staaten hatte sich verpflichtet, jeden Dollar auf Verlangen gegen eine bestimmte Menge Gold einzutauschen. Die Währungen in Ungarn, Österreich, Polen und Deutschland basierten nach dem Ersten Weltkrieg nicht auf dem Goldstandard, sondern sie waren als Papiergeld weitgehend ungedeckt. Um die Haushaltsdefizite zu finanzieren, griffen die Regierungen dieser Länder zu dem Mittel, weiteres ungedecktes Geld zu drucken.[5] Sie taten das in einem derartigen Ausmaß,

---

[4] Bresciani-Turroni schrieb 1937: „Wer sich mit der jüngeren Wirtschaftsgeschichte Europas befaßt, der stößt auf ein erstaunliches Phänomen, nämlich auf die schnelle Wiederherstellung der Geldwertstabilität in einigen Ländern, in denen zuvor das Papiergeld jahrelang unaufhörlich an Wert verloren hatte. In einigen Fällen wurde die Stabilisierung der Wechselkurse nicht in einem jahrelang andauernden Verfahren erreicht. Langwierige Bemühungen dieser Art hätten sich nur langsam in einer schrittweisen ökonomischen und finanziellen Wiederherstellung des Landes niedergeschlagen, wie es vor dem Krieg mit Währungsreformen in einigen bekannten Fällen geschah. Demgegenüber vollzog sich in der Nachkriegszeit die Wende von einer heftigen Entwertung der Währung zu einer fast vollständigen Stabilität der Wechselkurse sehr plötzlich." *The Economics of Inflation*, London 1937, S. 334. Vgl. diese Bemerkungen mit Samuelsons Äußerungen in Anm. 2.

[5] Der Banknotenumlauf war hauptsächlich durch Schatzwechsel „gedeckt", von denen man damals nicht erwarten konnte, daß sie aus dem Steueraufkommen getilgt würden, sondern nur durch das Drucken weiterer Banknoten oder Schatzwechsel.

daß ihre Währungen beispiellos an Wert verloren. Am Ende waren 1 000 000 000 000 Mark in Papiergeld in Deutschland so viel wert wie eine Goldmark vor dem Krieg, 1 800 000 polnische Mark entsprachen einem Goldzloty, 14 400 Kronen in österreichischem Papiergeld und 14 500 ungarische Kronen in Papiergeld einer österreichisch-ungarischen Krone aus der Zeit vor dem Krieg.[6]

Dieser Aufsatz behandelt vor allem die zielgerichtete Änderung der Wirtschaftspolitik, die in Ungarn, Österreich, Polen und Deutschland zur Beendigung der Hyperinflation führte, und beschreibt zugleich den wirtschaftspolitischen Weg, den die Tschechoslowakei einschlug, um eine Inflation von vornherein abzuwehren. Jede der Hyperinflationen wurde dadurch beendet, daß man die Konvertibilität der eigenen Währung zum Dollar und damit zugleich zum Gold ganz oder doch annähernd wiederherstellte. Nun setzte die Bindung an den Goldstandard dem staatlichen Sektor der Wirtschaft bestimmte Grenzen. Die staatlichen Organe emittierten Noten beziehungsweise Kassenscheine als Sichtverbindlichkeiten und längerfristige Staatspapiere mit der Zusicherung, diese unter bestimmten Bedingungen, nämlich unter Vorlage der Noten, in Gold einzulösen. Wahrscheinlich waren Wirtschaftssubjekte nur dann bereit, solche Forderungen zum vollen Nennwert zu halten, wenn sie erwarten konnten, daß der Staat seinem Einlösungsversprechen nachkommen würde. Das Zahlungsversprechen des Staates war aber nur teilweise durch Goldreserven gedeckt. In der Praxis erwies es sich als wichtiger, daß die Staatsverschuldung durch die Verpflichtung des Staates zur Erhebung von Steuern gedeckt war, deren Aufkommen hoch genug sein mußte, um über die Staatsausgaben hinaus die Schulden zu decken. So hing der Ausgleich letztlich von einer angemessenen Haushaltspolitik ab. In den 1920er Jahren betonte John Maynard Keynes, daß die Sicherung des Goldeinlösungsversprechens eines Staates weniger von dem Umfang seiner Goldreserven abhinge, sondern maßgeblich von der Fiskalpolitik der Regierung.[7]

---

[6] *The Course and Control of Inflation*, League of Nations, Genf 1946, S. 101.

[7] Keynes schrieb: „Es liegt nicht am Goldmangel, daß die führenden Länder Europas nicht zum Goldstandard der Vorkriegszeit zurückkehren, vielmehr sind andere interne Regelmechanismen außer Kraft gesetzt. Die meisten dieser Länder verfügen über reichliche Goldvorräte für diesen Zweck, wenn die anderen Bedingungen für die Wiedereinführung des Goldstandards erfüllt sind." Keynes (11), S. 132. Und über Deutschland schrieb Keynes 1923: „Die Regierung kann kein gesundes Geld einführen, weil der Druck ungesunden Geldes mangels anderer Einkünfte das einzige Mittel ist, von dem sie leben kann." Keynes (10), Dt. Übersetzung, S. 62.

Demnach war nicht das Ausmaß der gegenwärtigen Haushaltsdefizite ausschlaggebend, sondern der Gegenwartswert der laufenden sowie der zukünftigen Haushaltsdefizite. Die Regierung wurde hier wie eine Firma angesehen, deren voraussichtliche Einnahmen sich aus den zukünftigen Steuererhebungen ergeben würden. Der Wert der Staatsschulden entsprach dabei annähernd dem Gegenwartswert der laufenden und zukünftigen Überschüsse des Staates. Bei der Bindung an den Goldstandard verpflichtete sich die Regierung somit, ihre Schulden zu begleichen, und konnte nicht zu einer inflationären Haushaltspolitik Zuflucht nehmen. Um die Staatsschulden zu bewerten, mußte man wissen, nach welchen Grundsätzen („Regime") jeweils die Fiskalpolitik geführt wurde, das heißt, welche Regeln das Haushaltsdefizit als Funktion des gegenwärtigen wie zukünftigen Zustands der Volkswirtschaft bestimmten. Wie die Öffentlichkeit die fiskalpolitischen Grundsätze einschätzte, beeinflußte insofern den Wert der Staatsschulden, als die privaten Wirtschaftssubjekte daraus ihre Erwartungen über den Gegenwartswert der Einnahmeströme ableiteten, die diese Staatsschulden deckten.[8] Es ist nützlich, diese Überlegungen zum Goldstandard in Betracht zu ziehen, wenn wir im folgenden die wirtschaftspolitischen Entwicklungen am Ende der vier Hyperinflationen Revue passieren lassen.[9]

---

[8] Diese Argumentation kann genauer in der Fachliteratur zum optimalen Wirtschaftswachstum verfolgt werden. Als geeignetes Modell für die Goldwährung oder ein anderes Warengeld böte sich zunächst ein gleichgewichtiges Wachstumsmodell in realen Größen an, bei dem die Regierung Schulden macht, Ausgaben tätigt und Steuern erhebt. Arrow und Kurz (1) haben derartige Modelle untersucht. Darin bemessen sich die Staatsschulden nach denselben ökonomischen Erwägungen wie private Schulden, nämlich nach den künftigen Nettoeinnahmen des Schuldners. Ein solches gleichgewichtiges Wachstumsmodell in realen Größen kann auch die formale Begründung für meine weiter unten aufgestellte Behauptung liefern, daß Offen-Markt-Geschäfte mit privaten Wertpapieren, Devisen und Gold das Preisniveau, d. h. den Wert der Sichtverbindlichkeiten des staatlichen Sektors, wahrscheinlich nicht beeinflussen.

[9] Entsprechend der Argumentation in Anm. 8 lassen sich recht leicht mehrere praktikable theoretische Modelle über Warengeld oder die Goldwährung erstellen. Es ist dagegen erheblich schwieriger, ein Modell über ungedeckte Zahlungsmittel zu entwerfen, die nahezu kostenlos zu produzieren und inkonvertibel sind und keinen Nutzen außer ihrem Tauschwert haben. Kareken und Wallace (9), Wallace (35) und Townsend (34) beschreiben diesen Sachverhalt eingehender. Die praktikablen Modelle über ungedeckte Zahlungsmittel, die existieren, z. B. die von Townsend (34) und Wallace (35), lassen sofort die Frage aufkommen, ob den freiwillig im Besitz gehaltenen ungedeckten Zahlungsmitteln bei so erheblichen Haushaltsdefiziten, wie sie hier beschrieben werden,

Zuvor sollte aber noch auf den Unterschied eingegangen werden zwischen den Wirkungen isolierter *Einzelmaßnahmen* innerhalb einer vorgegebenen Gesamtstrategie und den Wirkungen alternativer Gesamtstrategien oder Regeln, in deren Rahmen bestimmte Einzelmaßnahmen wiederholt getroffen werden. Das zweite bezieht sich auf das, was ich die Änderung des „Regimes" nenne. So wären die Entscheidungen über die Höhe der Staatsausgaben und Steuersätze für ein bestimmtes Vierteljahr *Einzelmaßnahmen*, während die impliziten oder expliziten Regeln, nach denen über die Höhe der Staatsausgaben und Steuersätze wiederholt in Abhängigkeit vom Zustand der Volkswirtschaft entschieden wird, Beispiele für strategische Grundsätze sind. Die neuere Forschung mit dynamisierten makroökonomischen Modellen hat ein allgemeines Prinzip herausgefunden, nach dem eine grundlegende Änderung der *wirtschaftspolitischen Strategie* (des „Regimes") private Wirtschaftssubjekte dazu bringt, *ihre eigene* Strategie zu ändern, nach der sie Konsumquoten, Investitionsquoten, Portfolioinvestitionen und ähnliches bestimmen.[10] Da diese egoistisch oder doch zumindest zweckgerichtet handeln, liegt es in ihrem Interesse, dann ihre Strategie zu ändern, wenn dies die Regierung tut. Unter anderem besagt dieses Prinzip, daß sich die meisten empirischen Beziehungen, wie sie in den üblichen ökonometrischen Modellen dargestellt sind, bei zu erwartenden Änderungen des wirtschaftspolitischen „Regimes" ebenfalls ändern. Somit werden Prognosen unglaubwürdig, die solche Beziehungen auch dann als konstant unterstellen, wenn ein wirtschaftspolitischer „Regime"-Wechsel stattfindet. Die Schätzung, daß die amerikanische Wirtschaft 220 Milliarden Dollar ihres jährlichen Bruttosozialprodukts einbüßt, wenn die Inflationsrate um einen Prozentpunkt gesenkt wird, ist ein Beispiel für solch eine unglaubwürdige Voraussage. Ein dynamisches makro-ökonomisches Modell würde hingegen auf der Annahme basieren, daß sich das Gesamtmuster von

---

überhaupt noch ein Wert beizumessen ist. Solche Modelle legen es nahe, staatlichen Restriktionen, besonders bei Devisengeschäften, eine entscheidende Rolle bei der Aufrechterhaltung des Wertes der dann unfreiwillig gehaltenen ungedeckten Zahlungsmittel zuzuschreiben. Auch Keynes (10) und Nichols (24) betonten die Bedeutung solcher Restriktionen.

[10] Die weitreichenden Implikationen dieses Grundsatzes für die übliche Art, ökonometrische Modelle zu erstellen und zu verwenden, hat als erster Lucas (19) beschrieben. Das Prinzip selbst wurde in einer Vielzahl von Zusammenhängen, die auf der Basis dynamischer Wirtschaftsmodelle untersucht wurden, sichtbar gemacht. Einige Beispiele dafür finden sich bei Lucas (20) sowie bei Sargent und Wallace (31).

Beziehungen zwischen den einzelnen Variablen quantitativ erheblich umstrukturieren würde, wenn eine bedeutende Änderung der wirtschaftspolitischen Strategie erfolgt.

Wenn sich prinzipiell auch klar zwischen Einzelmaßnahmen und Gesamtstrategien unterscheiden läßt, so ist bei bestimmten historischen Ereignissen doch schwer zu entscheiden, ob sie Einzelmaßnahmen im Rahmen einer bereits bestehenden Gesamtstrategie oder eine grundlegend neue Gesamtstrategie staatlichen Handeln widerspiegeln.[11] Wir können uns dabei nur nach den überlieferten tatsächlich getroffenen Maßnahmen richten sowie nach den Erklärungen von Vertretern der staatlichen Bürokratie, nach Gesetzen und parlamentarischen Abstimmungen und manchmal auch nach den Bestimmungen der Verfassung. Aus all diesen Informationen ist die tatsächlich verfolgte Regierungsstrategie aufzuspüren. Schon der gesunde Menschenverstand und erst recht spezifische ökonometrische Erwägungen besagen, daß solche Interpretationen generell schwierig sind. Unter diesem Vorbehalt bin ich der Meinung, daß die folgenden Beispiele das beste sind, was das Laboratorium der Geschichte für das Studium von wirtschaftspolitischen „Regime"-Änderungen bereithält.

Österreich

Am Ende des Ersten Weltkrieges zerfiel die österreichisch-ungarische Monarchie in mehrere Nachfolgestaaten. Nachdem es das Zentrum eines Reiches gebildet hatte, das 625 000 Quadratkilometer mit 50 Millionen Einwohnern umfaßte, blieb Österreich nach der Auflösung der Doppelmonarchie als kleines Land mit 80 000 Quadratkilometern und 6,5 Millionen Einwohnern zurück. Schon während des Krieges hatte eine Wirtschaftsblockade der Alliierten eine Lebensmittelknappheit verursacht, und bei Kriegsende sah sich Österreich von neuen Staats- und Handelsgrenzen umschlossen, die das Land von den Gebieten der alten Monarchie abtrennten, welche es zuvor mit Lebensmitteln versorgt hatten. Zudem nahm die österreichische Regierung viele Beamte aus der ehemaligen Monarchie auf, die in den anderen Nachfolgestaaten nicht mehr gern gesehen waren. Die Anpassung an die neuen

---

[11] Sargent und Wallace (32) beschreiben eine Wahrnehmungssituation, in der eine Änderung des wirtschaftspolitischen „Regimes" schwer vorstellbar ist. Wie sie bemerken, führt das Nachdenken über einen solchen Wandel im Rahmen eines Modells, das rationale Erwartungsbildung unterstellt, zur Frage des freien Willens.

Staatsgrenzen und die Umstellung der Wirtschaft auf Friedenszeiten verursachten große Arbeitslosigkeit. Als Verlierer des Ersten Weltkrieges hatte Österreich zu all den Schwierigkeiten noch Reparationszahlungen zu leisten, die in ihrer Höhe lange Zeit nicht festgelegt waren, von denen man aber annahm, daß sie erheblich sein würden. Tatsächlich hielt die Reparationskommission eine Gesamthypothek auf das Vermögen und die Einnahmen des österreichischen Staates.

Die österreichische Regierung suchte diese drückenden Probleme zu lindern, indem sie großzügige Lebensmittelhilfen und Zahlungen an die Arbeitslosen leistete. Da die Regierung die Steuern und Preise ziemlich niedrig hielt, wirtschafteten staatliche Unternehmen, wie Eisenbahngesellschaften und Monopolgesellschaften, defizitär. Das Steueraufkommen deckte die Ausgaben nicht, so daß der Staat von 1919 bis 1922 erhebliche Defizite machte (vgl. TABELLE Ö 1). Sie überstiegen damals zumeist 50 Prozent der gesamten Staatsausgaben. Die Regierung finanzierte diese Defizite, indem sie Schatzwechsel an den österreichischen Zweig der Österreichisch-Ungarischen Bank verkaufte. Damit blähte sich das Volumen des Zentralbankgeldes *(high powered money)* sehr schnell auf. Darunter versteht man den Notenumlauf und die Sichtdepositen bei der Zentralbank. Nach TABELLE Ö 2 steigerte sich die gesamte Notenzirkulation der Österreichisch-Ungarischen Bank für Österreich[12] zwischen März 1919 und August 1922 um das 288fache. Diese Expansion der Zentralbanknoten resultierte hauptsächlich aus der Politik der Zentralbank, Schatzwechsel zu diskontieren. Zum Teil ist sie aber auch darauf zurückzuführen, daß die Zentralbank an Privatpersonen Darlehen und Wechselkredite zu einem nominellen Zinssatz von 6 bis 9 Prozent jährlich vergab. Angesichts der Inflationsrate, die über das Jahr ca. 1000 % und von Januar bis August 1922 wiederum ca. 1000 % betrug, war der Zinssatz bei weitem zu niedrig (vgl. TABELLE Ö 3).[13]

Als Folge dieser Wirtschaftspolitik, die auf lange Dauer angelegt zu

---

[12] Der Vertrag von St. Germain, der im September 1919 unterzeichnet wurde, erlegte den Nachfolgestaaten der österreichisch-ungarischen Doppelmonarchie auf, ihren Anteil an den Noten der österreichisch-ungarischen Bank abzustempeln. Der Stempel machte die Banknoten zur Währung des neuen Staates, zu seinen Schulden. Der österreichische Zweig der ehemals österreichisch-ungarischen Bank fungierte jahrelang nach dem Krieg als österreichische Zentralbank.

[13] Bei einem solchen Zinssatz traf die Zentralbank natürlich auf eine große Nachfrage nach Krediten und mußte diese rationieren.

sein schien, wurde die österreichische Krone international abgewertet, und die Inlandspreise stiegen rasch (vgl. TABELLE Ö 3 und Ö 4). Vom Januar 1921 bis zum August 1922 wuchs der Notenumlauf der Zentralbank um das 39fache an, während sich der Preisindex im Einzelhandel um das 110fache erhöhte (vgl. TABELLE Ö 2 und Ö 3), so daß der Realwert des Notenumlaufs in dieser Zeit der Währungsentwertung abnahm.[14] Da die Wirtschaftssubjekte immer weniger bereit waren, ihr Vermögen in Form der sich schnell entwertenden Krone zu halten, sondern es statt dessen in Devisen oder in Sachwerten anzulegen versuchten, trat eine „Flucht aus der Krone" ein.[15] Hinsichtlich der Finanzierung des Haushaltsdefizits lag es im Interesse der österreichischen Regierung, diese Flucht aus der eigenen Währung einzudämmen, denn sie verengte die finanziellen Ressourcen, die die Regierung durch das Drucken von Geld an sich ziehen konnte. Deshalb ließ die Regierung über eine eigens gegründete Behörde, die „Devisenzentrale", Devisenbewirtschaftung durchführen. Die Devisenzentrale sollte vor allem dafür sorgen, daß die österreichischen Bürger einen größeren Teil ihres Geldvermögens in ihrer eigenen Währung hielten. Diese Behörde ergriff dazu Maßnahmen, nach denen es illegal war oder zumindest schwierig wurde, als Österreicher Devisen oder anderen Ersatz für österreichische Kronen zu besitzen.[16] Doch viele Bürger verstießen offensichtlich gegen diese Regelungen und hielten in den Jahren 1921 bis 1922 große Geldmengen in fremder Währung.

[14] Einige Zeitgenossen führten aus, daß die wachsende Notenemission der Zentralbank nicht der Hauptgrund für die Inflation sei, weil der reale Wert des Geldumlaufs abgenommen habe und Geld deshalb in diesem Sinne knapp sei. Zuweilen wurde sogar behauptet, die Zentralbank führe einen tapferen Kampf gegen diese Knappheit, wenn sie mehr Geld drucke. Unter Makroökonomen wird die Behauptung nun zumeist als irrig angesehen; um so mehr verwundert es, eben dieses Argument auch in der gegenwärtigen Diskussion in den Vereinigten Staaten zu hören.

[15] „In Wien wurden während der Epoche des Zusammenbruchs Winkelwechselbanken an jeder Straßenecke aufgetan, wo man neue Kronen wenige Minuten, nachdem man sie erhalten, in Schweizerfranken umwandeln konnte, um so das Risiko des Verlustes während der Zeit zu vermeiden, die für den Weg zur ständigen Bank gebraucht worden wäre. Es wurde ein Saisonwitz, daß ein vorsichtiger Mann bei der Bestellung von einem Glas Bier in einem Café zugleich ein zweites bestellen sollte, trotz des Nachteils, es dann abgestanden trinken zu müssen, um Preissteigerungen in der Zwischenzeit zu vermeiden." Keynes (10), Dt. Übersetzung, S. 47.

[16] Vgl. Young (36), Bd. 2, S. 16. Daß eine Regierung, die eine inflatorische Finanzpolitik betreibt, bewußt solche Maßnahmen ergreifen könnte, hat Donald Nichols (24) herausgestellt.

TABELLE Ö 4 zeigt, daß sich die österreichische Krone im August 1922 jäh stabilisierte, und TABELLE Ö 3 weist auf eine ebenso plötzliche Festigung der Preise einen Monat später hin. Beides geschah, obwohl der Notenumlauf der Zentralbank nach wie vor rasch zunahm, wie TABELLE Ö 2 zeigt. Auch wurden weder die Währungseinheiten geändert, noch eine Währungsreform durchgeführt, jedenfalls nicht in den folgenden anderthalb Jahren. Vielmehr war es die Intervention des Völkerbundsrates, die die weitere Abwertung der österreichischen Krone so plötzlich zum Stillstand brachte. Denn in Verbindung damit wurde die Regierung Österreichs verpflichtet, ihre Fiskal- und Geldpolitik grundlegend neu zu ordnen. Nachdem die Alliierten die inständigen Bitten der Österreicher um internationale Hilfe wiederholt zurückgewiesen oder doch nur teilweise erfüllt hatten, nahm der Völkerbundsrat im späten August 1922 Verhandlungen auf, um das österreichische Finanzwesen von Grund auf zu sanieren. Die Verhandlungen wurden am 2. Oktober 1922 mit der Unterzeichnung von drei Protokollen besiegelt, die als Leitlinien des finanziellen Wiederaufbaus Österreichs dienten. Allein schon die Tatsache, daß der Völkerbund sich mit den österreichischen Schwierigkeiten ernsthaft befaßte brachte Erleichterung, noch bevor die einzelnen Bestimmungen der Protokolle öffentlich bekannt waren. Die TABELLEN Ö 3 und Ö 4 weisen darauf hin, und Pasvolsky beschreibt den Umschwung folgendermaßen: „Sobald der Völkerbundsrat beschlossen hatte, sich ernsthaft mit dem österreichischen Wiederaufbau zu befassen, war man überall davon überzeugt, daß eine Lösung der Probleme greifbar war. Diese Überzeugung verbreitete sich zunächst auf den internationalen Devisenmärkten mit ihren sensiblen Mechanismen. Fast zwei Wochen bevor Kanzler Seipel am 25. August dem Völkerbund die österreichische Frage offiziell unterbreitet hatte, schnellte der Preis ausländischer Währungen nicht weiter hoch, sondern begann sogar zu sinken, und das inländische Preisniveau senkte sich entsprechend drei Wochen später. Die österreichische Notenpresse druckte nach wie vor neues Geld, das die verschiedenen Ministerien auch weiterhin unters Volk brachten, indem sie auch jetzt ihre Haushaltsdefizite fortführten. Und doch begann der Preis ausländischer Währungen allmählich zu sinken. Die Krise war gebannt."[17]

Das erste Protokoll bestand aus einer von Großbritannien, Frank-

---

[17] Pasvolsky (25), S. 116.

reich, Italien, der Tschechoslowakei und Österreich unterzeichneten Erklärung, welche die politische Unabhängigkeit und Souveränität Österreichs erneut bestätigte.[18] Das zweite Protokoll führte die Bedingungen auf, unter denen Österreich ein internationales Darlehen von 650 000 000 Goldkronen gewährt wurde. Das dritte Protokoll, von Österreich allein unterzeichnet, legte den Plan zur Neuordnung des fiskal- und geldpolitischen Gefüges vor. Die österreichische Regierung sicherte zu, eine neue unabhängige Zentralbank zu errichten, nicht wieder so große Haushaltsdefizite zuzulassen und diese nicht über Vorschüsse von Zentralbankgeld zu finanzieren. Weiterhin stimmte die Regierung Österreichs zu, daß ein Generalbeauftragter des Völkerbundsrates die Einhaltung der österreichischen Verpflichtungen überwachen sollte. Die Regierung stellte Sicherheiten für das Wiederaufbaudarlehn aus dem Ausland bereit. Zugleich kam man darin überein, daß die Reparationskommission ihren Anspruch auf das Vermögen und die Einnahmen des österreichischen Staates aufgeben oder doch abändern sollte.

Die Regierung Österreichs und der Völkerbund machten sich schnell daran, den Plan, wie ihn die Protokolle vorsahen, auszuführen. Am 14. November 1922 wurde die österreichische Nationalbank gesetzlich gegründet. Sie trat an die Stelle des früheren österreichischen Zweiges der Österreichisch-Ungarischen Bank und übernahm auch die Aktiva und die Funktionen der Devisenzentrale. Die neue Bank nahm ihre Arbeit am 1. Januar 1923 auf. Es war ihr ausdrücklich verboten, der Regierung ohne die Absicherung durch eine gleichwertige Menge an Gold oder Auslandsforderungen Darlehen zu gewähren. Die Bank war gehalten, ihre Notenemission zu bestimmten Mindestsätzen in Gold, zinstragenden Auslandsforderungen oder Handelswechseln zu decken.

---

[18] Ein solches Protokoll zu verfassen, war sehr sinnvoll, wenn man bedenkt, daß sich der Wert der staatlichen Währung und anderer Staatsschulden zumindest unter dem Goldstandard durch die Fähigkeit des Staates bestimmt, diese Schulden mit einer angemessenen Fiskalpolitik zu „decken". In dieser Hinsicht unterscheidet sich der Staat nicht von einer Firma. 1922 war man aber in Österreich und im Ausland allenthalben besorgt, die Souveränität des Staates sei in Gefahr. (Vgl. die verzweifelte Note, die ein österreichischer Minister dem obersten Rat der alliierten Regierungen übermittelte. Der Text findet sich bei Pasvolsky [25], S. 115). Mit dem ersten Protokoll sollte klargestellt werden, daß und inwieweit Österreich als politische und ökonomische Einheit erhalten blieb und fähig war, seine Staatsschulden zu decken. Ein ähnliches Protokoll wurde unterzeichnet, als das Finanzwesen in Ungarn wiederhergestellt werden sollte.

Sobald die Staatsschulden gegenüber der Zentralbank bis auf 30 000 000 Goldkronen getilgt wären, war die Bank verpflichtet, die Goldkonvertibilität wiedereinzuführen.

Die Regierung unternahm Schritte in mehrere Richtungen, um den Staatshaushalt auszugleichen. So kürzte sie die Ausgaben, indem sie Tausende von Beschäftigten der Regierung entließ. Der Wiederaufbauplan sah vor, insgesamt 100 000 Staatsbedienstete zu entlassen. Die Defizite in den Staatsbetrieben wurden dadurch abgebaut, daß man die Preise für ihre Güter und Dienstleistungen heraufsetzte. Neue Steuern wurden geschaffen und effizientere Verfahren zur Erhebung von Steuern und Zöllen eingeführt. Welche Ergebnisse all diese Maßnahmen erbrachten, ist aus der Gegenüberstellung von TABELLE Ö 6 mit Ö 1 zu ersehen: Innerhalb von zwei Jahren vermochte die Regierung den Staatshaushalt auszugleichen.

Die Stabilisierung der österreichischen Krone wurde nicht über eine Währungsreform erreicht. Am Ende des Jahres 1924 führte man lediglich als neue Währungseinheit den Schilling ein, der 10 000 Kronen in Papiergeld entsprach. Diese Maßnahme wurde aber erst lange Zeit nach der Stabilisierung des Wechselkurses getroffen und war sicherlich von untergeordneter Bedeutung.[19]

TABELLE Ö 2 zeigt, daß von August 1922, als sich der Wechselkurs plötzlich stabilisierte, bis zum Dezember 1924 der Notenumlauf der österreichischen Zentralbank um das Sechsfache anwuchs. Zeitgenossen werteten das Zusammentreffen von errungener Preisstabilität mit einer sechsfachen Vermehrung des Zentralbankgeldes *(high powered money)* zumeist als Verstoß gegen die Quantitätstheorie des Geldes, und darum scheint es sich zunächst auch zu handeln. Doch ist das Zusammentreffen gar nicht mehr paradox, wenn man bei der Interpretation beider Phänomene scharf zwischen ungedecktem Geld einerseits *(unbacked or outside money)* und gedecktem Geld andererseits *(backed or inside money)* unterscheidet. Insbesondere hatten sich nämlich die Bilanz der Zentralbank sowie ihre Offen-Markt-Politik grundlegend geändert, seit sie die Bestimmungen der Völkerbundsprotokolle ausführte. So sind die Zahlen über die gesamte Banknotenausgabe der Zentralbank nach diesem Wandel wesentlich anders zu interpretieren.

---

[19] Die neue Bank übte zwei Jahre lang eine strenge Kontrolle über Devisengeschäfte aus. Erst nach dem März des Jahres 1925 hob man die Einschränkungen für Devisengeschäfte auf.

Zuvor waren die Verbindlichkeiten der Zentralbank hauptsächlich durch Schatzwechsel gedeckt gewesen, was aber hieß, daß sie im Grunde gar nicht gedeckt waren; denn solche Schatzwechsel bedeuteten keineswegs die Verpflichtung des Staates, Einnahmen durch zukünftige Steuererhebungen zu erzielen. Nachdem aber die Protokollbestimmungen ausgeführt worden waren, waren die Verbindlichkeiten der Zentralbank durch Gold, Auslandsforderungen, Handelswechsel und letztlich durch die Macht des Staates, Steuern zu erheben, gedeckt. Im variablen Bereich waren die Verbindlichkeiten der Zentralbank zu 100 Prozent durch Gold, Auslandsforderungen und Handelswechsel gedeckt, indem die Noten und Einlagen der Zentralbank durch Offen-Markt-Operationen mit solchen Aktiva geschaffen wurden (vgl. TABELLE Ö 5). Der Wert der österreichischen Krone wurde durch die Verpflichtung der Regierung gestützt, eine Fiskalpolitik zu betreiben, bei der die Dollarkonvertibilität der Verbindlichkeiten gewährleistet blieb. Bei einem derartigen fiskalpolitischen Grundsatz („Regime") beeinträchtigten die Aktivitäten der Zentralbank, die gleichsam als Vermittler zwischen Regierung und Kreditmark tätig war, den Wert der Krone nicht, wenn nur die Aktiva, welche die Bank erwarb, Wert genug besaßen. Demnach sind die im Anschluß an die Völkerbundsvereinbarung um das Sechsfache gestiegenen Verbindlichkeiten der Zentralbank nicht mehr als inflatorisch zu betrachten. Die Bereitschaft der Österreicher, Devisenvorräte in Kronen umzuwandeln (vgl. TABELLE Ö 5), ist nicht erstaunlich, denn mit ihrer Stabilisierung war die Krone für eine Geldanlage weitaus attraktiver als Devisen geworden.[20]

---

[20] Diese Erklärung paßt zu der Argumentation Famas (6). Ein anderer Erklärungsansatz dazu läßt die Unterscheidung zwischen gedecktem und ungedecktem Geld außer acht und erklärt die Beobachtungen mit einer Nachfragekurve für die Gesamtmenge an „Geld". So schrieb Phillip Cagan (4) die Nachfragefunktion für Geld in folgender Form:

(1) $\quad M_t - P_t = a (E_t P_{t+1} - P_t) \quad a < 0$

P_t ist der Logarithmus des Preisniveaus, M_t ist der Logarithmus des Geldangebots und $E_t P_{t+1}$ ist die Erwartung über den Logarithmus des Preisniveaus in der nächsten Periode. Es ist immer schwierig, M_t empirisch zu bestimmen, doch oft nimmt man die Noten- und Sichtverbindlichkeiten der Zentralbank, m. a. W. Zentralbankgeld *(high powered money)*. Diese Funktion der Geldnachfrage oder der Portfoliozusammensetzung geht von der Vorstellung aus, daß Wirtschaftssubjekte um so weniger ihres Vermögens in Form von Geld (real gerechnet) halten, je höher die erwarteten Preissteigerungen sind. Gleichung (1) kann umgeformt werden, um das Preisniveaugleichgewicht darzustellen:

(2) $\quad P_t = \dfrac{1}{1-a} \sum\limits_{i=0}^{\infty} \left(\dfrac{a}{a-1}\right)^i E_t M_{t+i}$

$E_t M_{t+i}$ ist, was für den Zeitpunkt t an Geldangebot für den Zeitpunkt t+i erwartet wird.

Die verfügbaren Daten über die Beschäftigung besagen, daß die Stabilisierung der Krone mit einer erheblich gesteigerten Arbeitslosigkeit einherging, wenngleich die Steigerung schon zuvor eingesetzt hatte (vgl. TABELLE Ö 7). Die Anzahl der Personen, die staatliche Arbeitslosenunterstützung empfingen, vermehrte sich von 8700 im De-

Im folgenden werden zwei Gedankenexperimente angestellt: Im ersten geht man davon aus, daß die Regierung eine im voraus *allgemein bekannte* Wirtschaftspolitik verfolgt, nach der das Geldangebot mit der konstant hohen Rate von $\mu > 0$ in der Zeit von 0 bis T-1 anwächst und vom Zeitpunkt T an mit der Rate Null. In diesem Fall würde sich ein Inflationsverlauf abzeichnen, wie er in ABBILDUNG 1 skizziert ist.

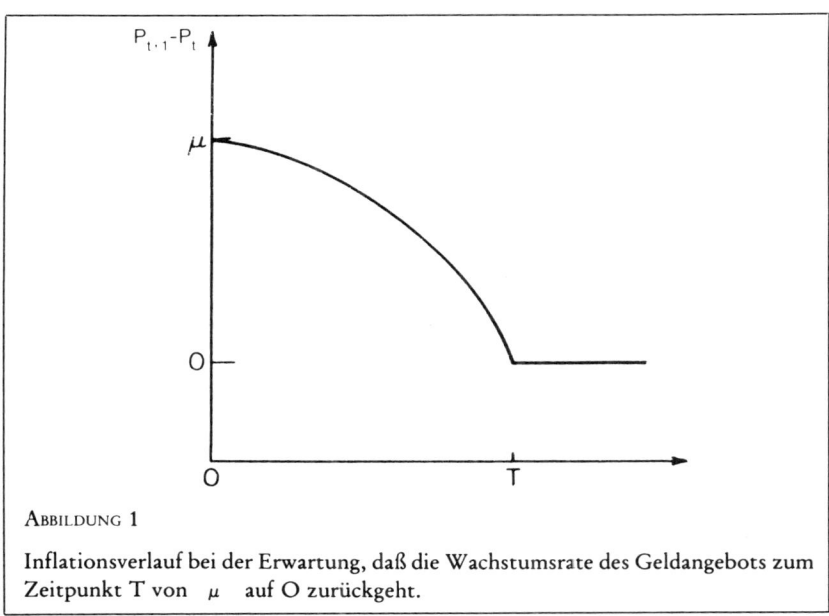

ABBILDUNG 1

Inflationsverlauf bei der Erwartung, daß die Wachstumsrate des Geldangebots zum Zeitpunkt T von μ auf 0 zurückgeht.

Das zweite Experiment geht von folgendem aus: Ursprünglich wird allgemein ein Geldangebot angenommen, das fortwährend mit der konstanten Rate μ ansteigt; jedoch stellt sich zum Zeitpunkt T heraus, daß es von nun an auf Dauer mit der Rate 0 wächst, also konstant bleibt. In diesem Fall fällt die Inflationsrate zum Zeitpunkt T jäh ab, wie in ABBILDUNG 2 dargestellt. Da nun in diesem Fall sowohl die Inflation als auch die erwartete Inflationsrate zum Zeitpunkt T plötzlich absinken, ergibt sich aus Gleichung (1), daß der Realwert der Geldmenge zum Zeitpunkt T anwachsen muß. Das setzt einen einmaligen abrupten *Rückgang* des Preisniveaus zum Zeitpunkt T voraus.

Das zweite Beispiel von einem zuvor nicht erwarteten Absinken der Inflationsrate bietet einen Erklärungsansatz für das steigende Geldangebot nach der Stabilisierung der

zember 1921, dem Tiefstand, auf 83 000 im Dezember 1922. Bis März 1923 stieg sie noch auf 167 000, um dann bis zum November 1923 auf

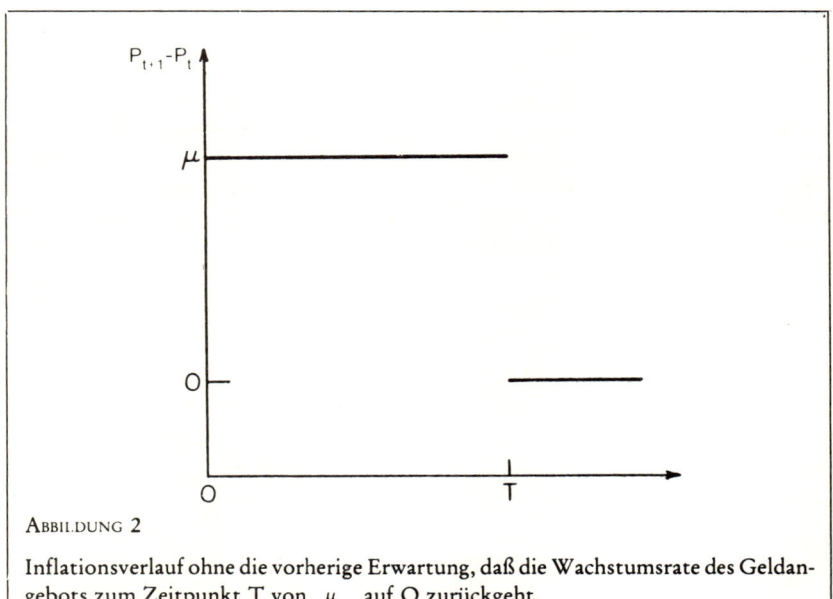

ABBILDUNG 2

Inflationsverlauf ohne die vorherige Erwartung, daß die Wachstumsrate des Geldangebots zum Zeitpunkt T von μ auf O zurückgeht.

Währung. Bei einem zuvor unerwarteten einmaligen und dauerhaften Rückgang der Wachstumsrate des Geldangebots könnte man nur dadurch ein plötzliches Absinken des Preisniveaus vermeiden, daß man die Wirkung des *Rückgangs* des Geldmengenwachstums durch eine einmalige *Vergrößerung* des Geldangebots kompensiert. Um das Preisniveau bei einer verminderten Wachstumsrate der Geldmenge zu *stabilisieren*, muß das Niveau des Geldangebots einmalig erhöht werden.

In den vier hier untersuchten Ländern vergrößerte sich das Geldangebot nicht plötzlich und einmalig, sondern nahm über mehrere Monate allmählich zu. Das könnte mit den Beobachtungen im Rahmen des ersten Modells in Einklang gebracht werden, wenn man unterstellte, daß die Wirtschaftssubjekte sich der Stabilisierung erst nach und nach bewußt wurden und ihre Inflationserwartung folglich nur langsam abnahm, als die Währungsstabilisierung anhielt. Ich kann diese Erklärung nur schwer akzeptieren, eine Möglichkeit ist sie aber immerhin.

Ein anderer Ansatz, die Ergebnisse des ersten Modells damit in Einklang zu bringen, daß das Zentralbankgeld nach der Stabilisierung allmählich anstieg, bietet sich, wenn man Anpassungsverzögerungen in die Funktion der Portfoliozusammensetzung einbaut (1). So könnte die Gleichung (1) durch (1') ersetzt werden:

$$(1') \quad (M_t - P_t) = a\,(E_t P_{t+1} - P_t) + \lambda\,(M_{t-1} - P_{t-1})$$
$$a < 0,\; 0 < \lambda < 1$$

76 000 abzusinken.²¹ Wieviel von dieser Arbeitslosigkeit auf die Währungsstabilisierung zurückzuführen ist und wieviel auf die Zerrüttung der österreichischen Wirtschaft, die nun wirksam wurde, ist nicht auszumachen. Festzuhalten bleibt jedenfalls, daß die Währungsstabilisierung in Österreich ausgesprochen schnell erreicht wurde und dies zu Kosten (gesteigerte Arbeitslosigkeit und Einbuße an Output), die weitaus geringer waren als der Verlust von 220 Milliarden Dollar am US-Bruttosozialprodukt für die Minderung der Inflationsrate um einen Prozentpunkt, die Zahl, die in den jüngsten Diskussionen in den Vereinigten Staaten genannt wurde.

Ungarn

Wie sein früherer Partner in der Habsburger Doppelmonarchie ging Ungarn aus dem Ersten Weltkrieg als ein Land hervor, das viel an Fläche, Bevölkerung und Macht eingebüßt hatte. Ihm blieben nur etwas über ein Viertel seines einstigen Territoriums (von 325 000 Quadratkilometern 92 000) und 37 Prozent seiner ehemaligen Einwohnerschaft (von 21 Millionen 8 Millionen). Das Wirtschafts- und Finanzleben war durch die neu errichteten Staatsgrenzen gestört, denn sie trennten Ungarn von Völkern und wirtschaftlichen Institutionen ab, die zuvor in die Habsburger Doppelmonarchie einbezogen waren.

Bei Kriegsende kam es zu politischem Aufruhr, als die Regierung des Prinzen Karolyi den Habsburger König Karl ablöste. Im März 1919 wurde die Karolyi-Regierung von den Bolschewisten unter Bela Kun gestürzt. Dessen Regime hielt sich nur vier Monate lang, bis Rumänien in Ungarn einmarschierte, das Land einige Wochen lang besetzt hielt und sich dann wieder zurückzog. Dann übernahm ein repressives, rechtsorientiertes Regime unter Admiral Horthy die Macht. Der „Weiße Terror", den Anhänger Horthys gegen Linke ausübten, forderte mehr Todesopfer als der „Rote Terror" unter Bela Kun.

Bei Kriegsende bestand die ungarische Währung aus Noten der Österreichisch-Ungarischen Bank. Die Friedensverträge von Trianon

---

In diesem Fall führt eine abrupte Stabilisierung der Inflationserwartung zu einer nur allmählichen Anpassung des Realwerts der Geldmenge mit einer Steigerungsrate von $1 - \lambda$ pro Periode.

Ich würde aber einer Erklärung den Vorzug geben, die einen deutlichen Unterschied zwischen gedecktem und ungedecktem Geld macht.

[21] Vgl. Pasvolsky (25), S. 161.

und St. Germain sahen vor, daß die Nachfolgestaaten der Doppelmonarchie die Noten der Österreichisch-Ungarischen Bank, die im Besitz ihrer Einwohner waren, stempelten. Dadurch wurden diese Noten im Grunde als Schulden des jeweiligen neuen Staates anerkannt. Doch bevor Ungarn diese Bestimmungen aus dem Vertrag von Trianon ausführen konnte, spitzten sich die Währungsschwierigkeiten zu, denn das bolschewistische Regime hatte Zugang zu den Druckplatten für Ein- und Zwei-Kronen-Noten der Österreichisch-Ungarischen Bank erhalten und machte Gebrauch davon. Auch brachte die bolschewistische Regierung erstmals sogenannte „Weiße Banknoten" in Umlauf. Die nachfolgenden Regierungen erkannten jede der von den Bolschewisten herausgegebenen Währungseinheiten an.

Die Österreichisch-Ungarische Bank wurde am Ende des Jahres 1919 aufgelöst und durch einen österreichischen sowie durch einen ungarischen Zweig ersetzt, und im August 1921 übernahm ein staatliches Noteninstitut unter der Kontrolle des Finanzministers die Funktionen des ungarischen Zweiges der ehemals Österreichisch-Ungarischen Bank. Im August 1921 emittierte dieses Noteninstitut eigene Noten, die ungarische Krone, im Austausch gegen von Ungarn gestempelte Noten der Österreichisch-Ungarischen Bank sowie verschiedene andere Noten, einschließlich derjenigen, die von dem bolschewistischen Regime in Umlauf gesetzt worden waren.

Der Vertrag von Trianon sah für Ungarn als Verlierer des Ersten Weltkrieges Reparationszahlungen vor. Die Reparationskommission hatte ein Pfandrecht auf die Einnahmen und Vermögenswerte des ungarischen Staates, doch standen noch Jahre nach Beendigung des Krieges weder die gesamte Schuldensumme noch ein Zeitplan zu ihrer Begleichung fest. Allein wegen dieser Unsicherheit vermochte Ungarn den Wert seiner Währung und anderer Schulden kaum zu stabilisieren, denn die in ihrer Höhe offene Reparationsschuld machte es fraglich, welche Einnahmen und Vermögenswerte die Staatsschulden deckten.

Von 1919 bis 1924 wies der ungarische Staatshaushalt erhebliche Defizite auf. TABELLE U 1 führt die Angaben der Regierung zu den Staatshaushalten auf. Pasvolsky weist darauf hin, daß sie das Defizit erheblich unterschätzen.[22] Finanziert wurden diese Defizite mit Krediten des staatlichen Noteninstituts und waren so hauptverantwortlich dafür, daß deren Noten- und Sichtverbindlichkeiten rasch anwuchsen.

---

[22] Vgl. a.a.O., S. 298.

Die Beendigung vier großer Inflationen 53

Aber auch die Darlehen und Wechselkredite, die Privaten in wachsendem Umfang gewährt wurden, ließen die Verbindlichkeiten der Notenbank ansteigen (vgl. TABELLE U 2). Das Noteninstitut vergab die Kredite zu äußerst niedrigen Zinsen, wenn man den schnellen Preisauftrieb berücksichtigt, so daß sie weitgehend Geschenke an die begünstigten Kreditnehmer darstellten. Der Anteil, mit dem die Kreditgewährung an die Privatwirtschaft zum Anwachsen der Zentralbankgeldmenge *(high powered money)* beitrug, war in Ungarn viel höher als in den anderen drei Hyperinflationen, die hier untersucht werden.

TABELLE U 3 zeigt, daß die ungarische Krone auf den ausländischen Devisenmärkten rasch an Wert verlor und die Inlandspreise stark anzogen. Zwischen Januar 1922 und April 1924 stieg der Preisindex um das 263fache. Da sich zugleich die gesamten Verbindlichkeiten des Noteninstituts (Noten und Depositen) um das 85fache vermehrten, verminderte sich deren realer Wert erheblich. Wie in Österreich so zeigte dies auch hier die „Flucht aus der Krone" an, da die Bürger möglichst wenige ungarische Kronen in ihrem Besitz haben wollten und Anlagen in stabileren Währungen bevorzugten. Die ungarische Regierung trat dieser Entwicklung wie die österreichische entgegen, indem sie im August 1922 eine ungarische Devisenzentrale innerhalb des staatlichen Noteninstituts einrichtete.

Aus TABELLE U 3 geht hervor, daß der Preisanstieg sowie die internationale Abwertung der Krone im März 1924 jäh zum Stillstand kamen. In beiden Bereichen trat die Stabilisierung ein, obwohl die Verbindlichkeiten der Zentralbank zwischen März 1924 und Januar 1925 mit einem Faktor von 3,5 weiterhin anwuchsen (vgl. TABELLE U 2). Der Prozeß vollzog sich ähnlich und aus ähnlichen Gründen wie in Österreich.

Auch in Ungarn gelang der Wiederaufbau des Finanzgefüges mit Hilfe des Völkerbundes. Zusammen mit der Reparationskommission und der ungarischen Regierung arbeitete der Völkerbund einen Plan aus, der die nunmehr verminderten Reparationsverpflichtungen Ungarns festlegte, eine internationale Anleihe zur Mitfinanzierung der Staatsausgaben bereitstellte und Ungarn verpflichtete, einen ausgeglichenen Staatshaushalt aufzustellen und eine Zentralbank einzurichten, der es gesetzlich untersagt blieb, dem Staat ungedeckte Kredite einzuräumen. Am 21. Februar 1924 erklärte sich die Reparationskommission bereit, auf ihr Pfandrecht an den Einnahmen und dem Vermögen des ungarischen Staates zu verzichten, so daß diese nun zur Absicherung der Wiederaufbauanleihe herangezogen werden konnten. Mehrere westliche Länder gaben ihre Pfandrechte gegenüber dem ungarischen

Staat ebenfalls auf, damit Ungarns internationale Anleihe erfolgreich lanciert werden konnte.

Der Völkerbund formulierte seinen Wiederaufbauplan in zwei Protokollen. Das erste, von Großbritannien, Frankreich, Italien, der Tschechoslowakei, Rumänien und Ungarn unterzeichnet, garantierte die „politische Unabhängigkeit, territoriale Integrität und Souveränität Ungarns". Das zweite Protokoll führte die Bedingungen für den Wiederaufbauplan auf und verpflichtete Ungarn, einen ausgeglichenen Etat aufzustellen und eine vom Finanzministerium unabhängige Zentralbank einzurichten. Zudem hatte die ungarische Regierung einen Generalbeauftragten zu akzeptieren, der dem Völkerbund gegenüber verantwortlich war und darüber wachen sollte, daß die Regierung ihrer Verpflichtung nachkam, das Fiskal- und Geldgefüge zu reformieren.

Im Juli 1924 war die internationale Wiederaufbauanleihe von 250 000 000 Goldkronen im Ausland erfolgreich untergebracht. Sie war durch Zolleinnahmen, Zuckersteuern und Einnahmen der Salz- und Tabakmonopole abgesichert. Die Anleihe sollte der ungarischen Regierung Mittel an die Hand geben, schon jetzt über zukünftige Steuereinnahmen zu verfügen, ohne mit diesen Schulden das eigene Land zu belasten.

Am 26. April 1924 wurde die Ungarische Notenbank gesetzlich gegründet und nahm ihre Geschäfte am 24. Juni auf. Sie übernahm die Aktiva und Passiva des früheren Noteninstituts und übte auch die Devisenkontrolle, die Funktionen der früheren Devisenzentrale, aus. Es war der Nationalbank verboten, der Regierung irgendwelche zusätzlichen Kredite oder Vorschüsse zu gewähren, die nicht ganz durch Gold oder Devisen abgesichert waren. Ihre Verbindlichkeiten mußte die Bank zu einem festgelegten Prozentsatz in Goldreserven gedeckt halten.

Mit Ausgabenkürzungen und Steueranhebungen gelang es der ungarischen Regierung schnell, ihren Staatshaushalt auszugleichen (vgl. TABELLE U 4). Tatsächlich wurde sogar das Aufkommen aus der Wiederaufbauanleihe weitaus langsamer eingesetzt, als der Plan des Völkerbundes vorgesehen hatte.

TABELLE U 2 bestätigt, daß die Stabilisierung der Krone mit einem erheblichen *Zuwachs* aller Verbindlichkeiten der Zentralbank einherging. Doch wie es am österreichischen Beispiel erläutert wurde, macht die grundlegende Wende in der Fiskalpolitik, die „Regime"-Änderung, die ja zur Stabilisierung geführt hatte, eine andere Interpretation solcher Zahlen als vorher erforderlich. Nach den Bestimmungen aus dem

Protokoll des Völkerbundes war die Zentralbank gehalten, ihre Verbindlichkeiten (Noten und Depositen)' im variablen Bereich zu 100 Prozent durch Gold, Devisen und Handelswechsel zu decken. TABELLE U 2 belegt, daß sie sich daran hielt. Hatten die Verbindlichkeiten zuvor ungedecktes Geld dargestellt, so waren sie seit der Völkerbundintervention weitgehend durch Devisenforderungen in britischen Pfund Sterling gedeckt.[23] Großbritannien hatte sich nur unter der Bedingung bereiterklärt, zur Wiederaufbauanleihe beizutragen, wenn Ungarn seine Währung gegenüber dem britischen Pfund stabilisierte.

TABELLE U 5 enthält Zahlen über die Arbeitslosigkeit in Ungarn, jedoch setzt die Reihe leider erst ein, nachdem die Preise sich gerade stabilisiert hatten. So ist aus diesen Zahlen nichts weiter abzulesen, als daß die Arbeitslosigkeit unmittelbar nach der Preisstabilisierung nicht höher als ein oder zwei Jahre später war. Diese Beobachtung ist mit zwei unterschiedlichen Hypothesen erklärbar: Zum einen könnte die Preisstabilisierung auf den Anstieg der Arbeitslosigkeit so langfristig gewirkt haben, daß sich in der kurzen Zeitspanne, welche die Zahlen abdecken, eine Linderung der Arbeitslosigkeit nicht zeigen konnte; zum andern, und das halte ich für wahrscheinlicher, könnte die Preisstabilisierung die Beschäftigungslage kaum beeinträchtigt haben.

Polen

Am Ende des Ersten Weltkrieges bildete sich der neue polnische Staat aus Gebieten, die zuvor zu Deutschland, Österreich-Ungarn und Rußland gehört hatten. Als Polen gegründet wurde, bestand der dortige Geldumlauf aus verschiedenen Elementen, aus russischen Rubeln, Kronen der Österreichisch-Ungarischen Bank, deutscher und polnischer Mark. Letztere waren von der Staatlichen Darlehensbank Polens emittiert worden, die Deutschland in dem von ihm während des Krieges besetzten Teil Polens gegründet hatte, um die Währung dort zu kontrollieren. Der Waffenstillstand von 1918 brachte Polen keinen Frieden, vielmehr führte es noch von März bis Oktober 1920 einen verlustreichen Krieg gegen Sowjetrußland. So blieb Polen am Ende von den Kämpfen und von den Demontagen der Deutschen während des Krieges verwüstet zurück.[24]

---

[23] Nach anderthalb Jahren wurde dies zu einer Forderung auf Gold, da Großbritannien zum Goldstandard zurückkehrte.

[24] Im Gegensatz zu Österreich, Ungarn und Deutschland hatte Polen keine Reparationszahlungen zu leisten.

Die neue Regierung Polens machte bis 1924 große Haushaltsdefizite (vgl. TABELLE P 1). Finanziert wurden sie durch Kreditaufnahmen bei der Staatlichen Darlehensbank Polens, welche die neue Regierung von den Deutschen übernahm. Von Januar 1922 bis zum Dezember 1923 vermehrten sich die ausstehenden Noten der Staatlichen Darlehensbank in Polen um das 523fache (vgl. TABELLE P 2). Zur selben Zeit stieg der Großhandelspreisindex um das 2402fache und der Preis eines US-Dollars um das 1397fache (vgl. TABELLE P 3 und P 4). Wie bei den Inflationen in den anderen Ländern, die hier untersucht werden, verminderte sich der Realwert des Notenumlaufs durch die einsetzende „Flucht aus der polnischen Mark". Umfassende staatliche Devisenkontrollen wurden eingerichtet, um diese Entwicklung aufzuhalten.

Die TABELLEN P 3 und P 4 zeigen an, daß die galoppierende Inflation und die Abwertung des Wechselkurses plötzlich im Januar 1924 zum Stillstand kamen. Während aber Österreich und Ungarn ihre Stabilisierungen mit Eingriffen und Anleihen aus dem Ausland einleiteten, stützte sich Polen erst dann auf ein erhebliches Darlehen aus dem Ausland, als 1927 eine erneute Währungsabwertung drohte.[25] Die Inflation wurde aber in Polen ansonsten mit ähnlichen grundlegenden Änderungen in der Fiskal- und Geldpolitik (im „Regime") beendet wie in Österreich und Ungarn. Gemeint ist die Wende hin zu einem ausgeglichenen Staatshaushalt und damit verbunden die Einrichtung einer unabhängigen Zentralbank, die der Regierung nur gegen Sicherheiten zusätzliche Kredite gewähren durfte. Im Januar 1924 erhielt der Finanzminister weitgehende Machtbefugnisse, das Geld- und Fiskalgefüge zu reformieren. Sofort ließ er die Bank von Polen einrichten, welche die Funktionen der Staatlichen Darlehnsbank Polens übernahm. Die neue Bank sollte letztlich die Goldkonvertibilität der polnischen Währung wiederherstellen und mußte ihre Banknoten zu 30 Prozent mit Reserven in Gold, Devisen und Geldforderungen in stabilen Auslandswährungen decken. Neben dieser Reserve sollten die Banknoten durch private Handelswechsel und Silber abgesichert sein. Der Regierung wurde ein Höchstkredit von 50 000 000 Zloty zugestanden. TABELLE P 1 zeigt, daß auch die Regierung schnell zu einem ausgeglichenen Staatshaushalt kam.

Im Januar 1924 wurde der Goldzloty als neue Währungseinheit eingeführt. Er entsprach 1 800 000 Papiermark und hatte einen Gold-

---

[25] The Course and Control of Inflation... (13), S. 111.

wert von 19,29 amerikanischen Cents. Aus TABELLE P 2 ist zu ersehen, daß der Notenumlauf der Zentralbank (in Goldzloty umgerechnet über den Dollarwechselkurs) sich von Januar 1924 bis Dezember 1924 um das 2,9fache steigerte, während das Preisniveau und der Wechselkurs relativ stabil blieben (vgl. TABELLE P 3 und P 4). Die Entwicklung vollzog sich in Österreich und Ungarn ähnlich und hatte dieselben Ursachen. Wie aus TABELLE P 2 zu ersehen ist, war der zusätzliche Notenumlauf damals praktisch zu 100 Prozent durch Gold, Devisen und private Wechsel gedeckt.

In TABELLE P 5 sind die verfügbaren Daten zur Arbeitslosigkeit zusammengetragen. Die Stabilisierung des Preisniveaus im Januar 1924 ging mit einer abrupten Steigerung der Arbeitslosenzahlen einher, und im Juli 1924 erhöhten sie sich erneut. Wenngleich die Zahlen eine erhebliche Arbeitslosigkeit gegen Ende des Jahres 1924 belegen, so sprengte sie doch nicht den Rahmen dessen, was vor der Preisstabilisierung üblich gewesen war. Und ohne Zweifel war die Arbeitslosigkeit tatsächlich nirgends annähernd so groß, wie sie sich darstellt, wenn man sie nach dem Verfahren berechnet, das gegenwärtig zur Vorhersage in den USA verwendet wird. (Demnach bedingt ja die Herabsetzung der Inflationsrate um einen Prozentpunkt eine Einbuße von 220 Milliarden Dollar am jährlichen Bruttosozialprodukt.)

Der polnische Zloty verlor international seit dem Ende des Jahres 1925 an Wert und stabilisierte sich im Herbst 1926 dann bei ungefähr 72 Prozent seines Wertes vom Januar 1924. Zur gleichen Zeit festigte sich das inländische Preisniveau auf einem Niveau, das ungefähr 50 Prozent höher lag als im Januar 1924. Daß die Inflation erneut aufzuflammen drohte, wird der vorzeitigen Lockerung der staatlichen Devisenkontrollen zugeschrieben und der Neigung der Zentralbank, Kredite an die Privatwirtschaft zu unzureichendem Zinssatz zu vergeben.[26]

Deutschland

Nach dem Ersten Weltkrieg schuldete Deutschland den Alliierten phantastische Reparationszahlungen. Diese Last beherrschte das öffentliche Finanzwesen in Deutschland von 1919 bis 1923 und war einer der bedeutendsten Einflußfaktoren für die Hyperinflation.

Bei Kriegsende machte Deutschland eine politische Revolution

---

[26] A.a.O., S. 108.

durch und führte die republikanische Staatsform ein. Die ersten Nachkriegsregierungen wurden mehrheitlich von gemäßigten Sozialisten gebildet, die sich aus vielerlei Gründen mit den militärischen und industriellen Machtzentren aus der Vorkriegszeit arrangierten.[27] Diese Gruppen setzten der Bereitschaft und Fähigkeit der Regierung Grenzen, die notwendigen Staatseinnahmen, die in der Tat gewaltig sein mußten, durch Steuern zu bekommen.

Deutschland machte die schlimmste Inflation von den vier Ländern durch, die hier untersucht werden. Die in TABELLE D 1 und D 2 angegebenen Großhandelspreise und Wechselkurse bestätigen das. Nachdem Frankreich das Ruhrgebiet im Januar 1923 militärisch besetzt hatte, verschärfte sich die Inflation aufs äußerste. Die deutsche Regierung entschloß sich, der französischen Besetzung passiven Widerstand entgegenzusetzen, indem sie streikende Arbeiter direkt mit Mitteln bezahlte, die sie durch Diskontierung von Schatzwechseln bei der Reichsbank aufbrachte.

TABELLE D 3 gibt Schätzungen über den deutschen Staatshaushalt in laufender Rechnung von 1920 bis 1923 wieder.[28] Daraus ist abzulesen, daß der Haushalt (bis auf das Jahr 1923) gar nicht so unausgeglichen gewesen wäre, wenn Deutschland nicht die massiven Reparationszahlungen hätte leisten müssen. Wie tief die Reparationen das Finanzwesen erschütterten, wird noch gewiß unterschätzt, wenn man nur die Zahlen über die tatsächlich geleisteten Reparationen untersucht. Zum einen hatte man ursprünglich erheblich höhere Summen erwartet, als Deutschland dann tatsächlich bezahlen konnte; zum andern lagen weder das Ausmaß der gesamten Verpflichtungen noch der Zeitplan, nach dem sie zu erfüllen waren, fest. Darüber wurde noch laufend verhandelt. Wenn aber der Wert der Währung und der sonstigen Schulden eines Staates weitgehend von der beabsichtigten Fiskalpolitik bestimmt wird, dann mußte die Ungewißheit über die Reparationsschulden des Deutschen Reiches die Aussichten, zu einer stabilen Währung zu kommen, von vornherein untergraben.

TABELLE D 4 zeigt auf, daß der Notenumlauf der Reichsbank zwischen 1921 und 1923 gewaltig anstieg, insbesondere in den Monaten vor dem November des Jahres 1923. Wie Young [36] herausgearbeitet hat, waren Ende Oktober 1923 mehr als 99 Prozent aller ausstehenden

---

[27] Vgl. den Bericht bei Paxton (26), S. 146—150.
[28] Vgl. auch Graham (7), S. 40—41.

Die Beendigung vier großer Inflationen 59

Reichsbanknoten innerhalb der vergangenen 30 Tage in Umlauf gekommen.[29] TABELLE D 4 macht auch das Ausmaß deutlich, in dem der Notenumlauf der Reichsbank durch diskontierte Schatzwechsel „gedeckt" war. Im zweiten Halbjahr 1922 begann die Reichsbank auch Handelswechsel in großem Umfang zu diskontieren. Da diese Kredite zu Zinssätzen vergeben wurden, die nominell weit unter der Inflationsrate lagen, stellten sie im Grunde staatliche Transferzahlungen an die Kreditnehmer dar.

Vor allem während der großen Inflation von 1923 kam ein Umstand zum Zuge, der sich auch auf die anderen Hyperinflationen, die hier untersucht werden, ausgewirkt hatte. Auf Grund der Tatsache, daß die Steuern nominell festgesetzt wurden, schmälerte sich in der Zeitspanne, die zwischen der Steuerfestsetzung und der Einziehung verstrich, der Realwert der Einnahmen des Staates. Denn die Regierung unterschätzte fortwährend die zukünftige Inflationsrate, und die Bürger ließen sich ihrerseits von der galoppierenden Inflation motivieren, ihre Steuerzahlungen hinauszuzögern. Damit wäre das geringere Steueraufkommen in den ersten neun Monaten des Jahres 1923 teilweise zu erklären. Auch die französische Besetzung des Ruhrgebietes führte zur Senkung der Steuereinnahmen des deutschen Staates.

Obwohl die Regierung Devisenkontrollen verhängte, löste das inflatorische öffentliche Finanzwesen eine Flucht aus der deutschen Mark aus, durch die sich der reale Wert der Reichsbanknoten drastisch minderte. Die TABELLEN D 1 und D 4 führen Zahlen auf, nach denen sich zwischen Januar 1922 und Juli 1923 die Großhandelspreise um das 2038fache und der Reichsbanknotenumlauf um das 378fache steigerten. Zwischen Januar 1922 und August 1923 stiegen die Großhandelspreise mit einem Multiplikator von 25 723, und der Umlauf der Reichsbanknoten steigerte sich um das 5748fache. Die Tatsache, daß die Preissteigerung die Erhöhung des Umlaufs von Reichsbanknoten mehrfach überstieg, spiegelt das Bestreben der Deutschen wider, möglichst wenig von der sich schnell entwertenden deutschen Mark im Besitz zu halten. Gegen Ende der Hyperinflation war man bestrebt, überhaupt keine Mark mehr zu besitzen, sondern statt dessen große Mengen von Devisen, mit denen nun auch die alltäglichen Transaktionen ausgeführt

---

[29] Keynes schrieb: „Eine Regierung, selbst die deutsche oder die russische, kann sich lange durch den Druck von Papiergeld am Leben erhalten... sie kann durch dieses Mittel leben, wenn sie durch kein anderes mehr leben kann." Keynes (10), Dt. Übersetzung, S. 42.

wurden. Es gibt eine grobe Schätzung, nach der gegen Ende Oktober 1923 der Realwert fremder Währungen, die in Deutschland im Umlauf waren, dem der umlaufenden Reichsbanknoten zumindest gleichkam, wenn er ihn nicht sogar um ein Mehrfaches überstieg.[30]

Die Zahlen in TABELLE D 1 und D 2 zeigen an, daß der Preisanstieg sowie die Wechselkursentwertung im späten November des Jahres 1923 jäh zum Stillstand kamen. Im Rahmen einer Geldreform war am 15. Oktober 1923 die Schaffung der Rentenmark als neue Währungseinheit beschlossen worden. Sie entsprach 1 000 000 000 000 Papiermark. Diesem Wechsel in der Währungseinheit ist zwar zuweilen eine große psychologische Bedeutung zugeschrieben worden, jedoch ist sie an sich eher eine kosmetische Maßnahme, aus der sich wohl kaum wesentliche Wirkungen herleiten lassen.[31] Die eigentliche Bedeutung der Verordnung vom 15. Oktober lag in der Errichtung einer Rentenbank, welche das Notenemissionsrecht der Reichsbank übernahm. Die Verordnung schränkte das Gesamtvolumen an Rentenmark, das emittiert werden durfte, verbindlich auf 3 200 000 000 Mark ein und setzte die Höchstsumme, die der Regierung überlassen werden konnte, mit 1 200 000 000 Mark fest. Diese Kreditgrenzen wurden der Regierung zu einer Zeit gezogen, als sie die Staatsausgaben praktisch zu 100 Prozent über die Notenemission finanzierte.[32] Im Dezember 1923 wehrte die Rentenbank Vorstöße der Regierung ab, die Kreditgrenzen zu erweitern.

So wurde sofort dreierlei gleichzeitig erreicht: Die zusätzliche Kreditaufnahme des Staates bei der Zentralbank hörte auf, der Staatshaushalt kam ins Gleichgewicht, die Inflation wurde zum Stillstand gebracht. TABELLE D 5 zeigt, wie schnell man in den Monaten nach der Rentenbankverordnung den Staatshaushalt auglich. Die Regierung schaffte das über eine Reihe von auf Dauer angelegten Maßnahmen zur Steueranhebung und Ausgabenkürzung. Young führt dazu folgendes

---

[30] Vgl. Young (36), Bd. 1, S. 402 und Bresciani-Turroni (3), S. 345.

[31] Nachdem er eine frühere Fassung dieses Aufsatzes gelesen hatte, machte mich John Kennan auf den folgenden Abschnitt aus Constance Reids Biographie des Mathematikers Hilbert aufmerksam: „Im Jahre 1923 hörte die Inflation plötzlich wegen der Schaffung einer neuen Währungseinheit, der Rentenmark, auf. Obgleich Hilbert skeptisch dazu bemerkte: ‚Man kann kein Problem lösen, indem man den Namen der abhängigen Variablen ändert', stabilisierten sich die Umstände allmählich." Reid (27), S. 162—163.

[32] Young (36), Bd. 1, S. 421.

aus: „Die Personalverordnung vom 27. Oktober 1923 sah vor, die Anzahl der Beschäftigten im öffentlichen Dienst um 25 Prozent zu vermindern, wobei alle befristeten Angestellten entlassen und alle, die älter als 65 Jahre waren, pensioniert werden sollten. Bis zum Januar 1924 war weiteren 10 Prozent der Staatsbediensteten zu kündigen. Die Reichsbahn, die wegen der Demobilisierungsmaßnahmen seit Kriegsende ohnehin übersetzt war, entließ 1923 120 000 Beschäftigte und 1924 weitere 60 000. Die Reichspost kürzte ihr Personal um 65 000. Und die Reichsbank, die ihr Personal von 13 316 am Ende des Jahres 1922 auf 22 909 ein Jahr später vermehrt hatte, begann schon im Dezember, sobald die Stabilisierung fühlbar wurde, überschüssige Arbeitskräfte zu entlassen."[33]

Die Haushaltssituation festigte sich auch durch die Entlastung bei den deutschen Reparationsverpflichtungen. Die Reparationszahlungen wurden zeitweise eingestellt, und der Dawesplan sah einen weitaus eher zu bewältigenden Zeitplan für die Zahlungen vor.

TABELLE D 4 belegt, daß die deutsche Stabilisierung sich nach dem gleichen Muster vollzog wie die drei anderen Hyperinflationen: In den Monaten *nach* der Währungsstabilisierung stieg das Volumen der Banknoten und Sichtverbindlichkeiten der Zentralbank erheblich an. Wie in den drei anderen Ländern ist dieser Anstieg nach dem Ende der Inflation am besten damit zu erklären, daß die zusätzliche Banknotenausgabe nach der Inflation nun nicht mehr durch die Staatsverschuldung „gedeckt" war, sondern in Deutschland weitgehend durch diskontierte Handelswechsel. Das Wesen der Forderungen und Zahlungsversprechen, die hinter den Verbindlichkeiten der Zentralbank standen, änderte sich, sobald die Reichsbank nach der Rentenbankverordnung vom 15. Oktober 1923 dem Staat keine weiteren Kredite gewähren durfte. Folglich sind auch hier die Zeitreihen über Notenumlauf und Depositen der Zentralbank seit diesem Zeitpunkt anders zu interpretieren.

Nach jedem verfügbaren Maßstab ging die Festigung der deutschen Mark mit steigendem Output und erhöhter Beschäftigung einher, und die Arbeitslosigkeit sank.[34] Wenngleich 1924 auch keineswegs als gutes Geschäftsjahr für die deutsche Wirtschaft zu bezeichnen ist, so war es doch weit besser als 1923. TABELLE D 6 gibt die von Graham zusammen-

---

[33] A. a. O., Bd. 1, S. 422.
[34] Vgl. Graham (7), Kapitel XII.

gestellten Daten wieder, die zeigen, daß 1924 gegenüber 1922 ein schwaches Jahr war, sich aber schon 1925 als günstig erwies. Aus diesen Daten läßt sich für 1923 kaum ein positiver Zusammenhang zwischen Inflation und Produktionstätigkeit herstellen, war doch das Jahr mit der spektakulärsten Inflationsentwicklung zugleich eine Zeit großer Arbeitslosigkeit und geringer Produktion. Natürlich sind die schlechten Ergebnisse dieses Jahres großenteils auch mit der französischen Besetzung des Ruhrgebietes und dem passiven Widerstand dagegen zu erklären.

Obwohl sich aus den Zahlen in Tabelle D 6 und D 1 für 1923 offensichtlich kein Zusammenhang zwischen Inflation und realem Output herstellen läßt, wie ihn die Phillipskurve unterstellt, gibt es zahlreiche Anhaltspunkte dafür, daß die deutsche Inflation zuvor keineswegs „neutral" war, sondern daß wichtige „reale Effekte" wirksam waren. Graham [7] legt Material vor, nach dem die Inflation und die damit in Verbindung stehende Minderung des Realzinssatzes für Zentralbankgeld und andere Staatsschulden mit realer Überinvestition in verschiedenartige Kapitalgüter einherging.[35] Die „irrationale" Struktur des Kapitalstocks nach der Stabilisierung in Deutschland beschwor ohne Zweifel einige Anpassungsprobleme auf dem Arbeitsmarkt sowie auf anderen Märkten herauf.

Tschechoslowakei

Der neue Staat Tschechoslowakei wurde nach dem Ersten Weltkrieg aus Gebieten gebildet, die zuvor zu Österreich und Ungarn gehört hatten. Unter der Führung des sehr fähigen Finanzministers Dr. Alois Rasin entschied sich die tschechoslowakische Regierung unmittelbar nach dem Krieg für eine konservative Fiskal- und Geldpolitik, zu der ihre Nachbarn erst dann gelangten, als ihre Währungen schon gewaltig an Wert verloren hatten. Mit der frühzeitigen Entscheidung vermied die Tschechoslowakei von vornherein eine Hyperinflation, wie die Nachbarn sie alle durchmachten. Rasin stellte klar, daß die tschechoslowakische Regierung ernsthaft entschlossen war, die Währung stabil zu halten. Bevor die Friedensverträge dies vorschrieben, stempelte sie

---

[35] Geldtheoretische Auffassungen, die mit Vorstellungen Samuelsons (29) übereinstimmen, besagen, daß zu viel Kapital akkumuliert wird, wenn eine verschwenderische Fiskalpolitik das Geld wertlos macht. Vgl. Samuelson (29) und Wallace (35).

schon die Noten der Österreichisch-Ungarischen Bank, die in der Tschechoslowakei zirkulierten, mit ihrem Zeichen und erkannte sie somit als eigene Schulden an. Dieser Vorgang vollzog sich unter dramatischen Umständen: Die Nationalversammlung hatte die Stempelaktion in geheimen Sitzungen am 25. Februar 1919 beschlossen. Vom 26. Februar bis zum 9. März wurden die Staatsgrenzen überraschend geschlossen und der Postverkehr mit dem Ausland unterbrochen. Dadurch konnten nur Banknoten, die sich im Inland befanden, zur Stemplung vorgelegt werden. Im Verlauf der Stempelaktion behielt die Regierung einige Banknoten als Zwangsanleihe ein.[36] Ungefähr 8 000 000 000 Kronen wurden gestempelt.

Eine Bankenabteilung im Finanzministerium übernahm die Geschäfte der ehemaligen Österreichisch-Ungarischen Bank. Die Tschechoslowakei schränkte per Statut den gesamten Notenumlauf des Staates schnell ein und verhinderte eine inflatorische Entwicklung des staatlichen Finanzwesens. Am 10. April 1919 engte ein Gesetz den Umlauf ungedeckter Banknoten der Bankenabteilung auf ca. 7 000 000 000 Kronen ein. Dieses Gesetz wurde befolgt und zwang die Regierung, die Staatsausgaben über Steuereinnahmen oder Staatsschulden zu finanzieren. Wegen der per Statut eingeschränkten staatlichen Notenemission wurden diese Staatsschulden als Zusage zur künftigen Steuererhebung aufgefaßt.

Von 1920 an wiesen die laufenden Haushalte in der Tschechoslowakei nur mäßige Defizite auf (vgl. TABELLE T 1). Neben anderen Steuern erhob die Tschechoslowakei eine progressive Vermögensabgabe, die bis 1925 einen kumulierten Betrag von 11 000 000 000 Kronen aufbrachte. Zudem mußten die Tschechoslowaken den Wertzuwachs, den sie während des Krieges erworben hatten, versteuern.

TABELLE T 2 führt die Verbindlichkeiten der Bankenabteilung an Noten und Depositen auf. Darin spiegelt sich der Verzicht der Regierung auf eine inflatorische Haushaltspolitik wider. TABELLE T 3 zeichnet die Entwicklung der Wechselkurse nach. Bis November 1921 sank der Wechselkurs, doch dann stieg die tschechoslowakische Krone schnell auf einen Wert von ca. 3 amerikanischen Cents. TABELLE T 4 zeigt die Preisentwicklung. Von 1922 bis 1923 machte die Tschecho-

---

[36] Die Grenzen wurden geschlossen, um das Eindringen von Banknoten aus Österreich und Ungarn in das Land zu verhindern. Der Vertrag von St. Germain, der am 10. September 1919 unterzeichnet wurde, sah vor, daß die Nachfolgestaaten die Noten der Österreichisch-Ungarischen Bank stempelten, womit sie deren Schulden übernahmen.

slowakei sogar eine Deflation durch. Finanzminister Rasins ursprünglicher Plan hatte tatsächlich darin bestanden, für die tschechoslowakische Krone die Goldparität der ehemaligen österreichisch-ungarischen Krone wiederherzustellen. Nach Rasins Ermordung gab man diesen Plan auf und stabilisierte den Wert der Krone bei ungefähr 2,96 Cents.

Schlußfolgerung

Die wesentlichen Maßnahmen, mit denen man in Deutschland, Ungarn, Österreich und Polen die Hyperinflation beendete, waren erstens die Gründung einer unabhängigen Zentralbank, der es gesetzlich untersagt war, der Regierung zusätzlich ungedeckte Kredite zu gewähren, und zweitens eine gleichzeitig durchgeführte grundlegende Änderung in der Fiskalpolitik („Regime"-Änderung).[37] Die Einzelmaßnahmen standen miteinander in einer Wechselbeziehung und wurden koordiniert. Sie zielten darauf ab, die Regierung zu verpflichten, Staatsschulden bei Privaten oder bei ausländischen Regierungen zu machen, die diese Schulden danach bemessen würden, ob sie unter Berücksichtigung der öffentlichen Ausgaben noch ausreichend durch künftige Steuereinnahmen gedeckt wären. In all den Ländern, die hier untersucht wurden, endete die Inflation und stabilisierten sich die Wechselkurse, sobald sich die Überzeugung festgesetzt hatte, daß die Regierung zur Finanzierung des Staatshaushaltes nicht auf die Zentralbank zurückgreifen würde. Die vier Fälle haben weiterhin belegt, daß die Hyperinflation nicht einfach von der wachsenden Menge der Zentralbanknoten verursacht wurde, stieg doch in allen Fällen der Notenumlauf weiterhin schnell an, nachdem der Wechselkurs und das Preisniveau sich stabilisiert hatten. Die Ursache ist vielmehr in der Zunahme von ungedeck-

---

[37] Über ein inflatorisches Finanzwesen schrieb Keynes: „Man tut gewöhnlich so, als ob das Volk von Steuern verschont bliebe, wenn eine Regierung durch Inflation sich finanziert. Wir haben gesehen, daß dies nicht zutrifft. Was durch Notendruck aufgebracht wird, wird der Bevölkerung genau so weggenommen, wie eine Bierabgabe oder eine Einkommensteuer. Was eine Regierung ausgibt, muß die Bevölkerung bezahlen. So was wie ein ungedecktes Defizit gibt es nicht. Aber in einigen Ländern kann man, wenigstens eine Zeitlang, offenbar Beifall und Befriedigung in der Bevölkerung erregen, indem man ihr für die Steuern, die sie bezahlt, fein gravierte Quittungen auf Papier mit Wassermarken gibt. Die Einkommensteuerquittungen, die wir in England vom Finanzamt bekommen, werfen wir in den Papierkorb; in Deutschland nennt man sie Banknoten und tut sie in die Brieftasche; in Frankreich werden sie als ‚Renten' bezeichnet und in den Familiengeldschrank eingeschlossen." Keynes (10), Dt. Übersetzung, S. 64.

tem Geld zu sehen oder von Geld, das nur durch Schatzwechsel gedeckt war, bei denen aber kaum die Aussicht bestand, daß sie je über Steuereinnahmen eingelöst würden.

Die Maßnahmen, mit denen man die Hyperinflationen beendete, bestanden nicht in isolierten Einzelschritten, die in dem vorgegebenen wirtschaftspolitischen Rahmen vollzogen wurden. Frühere Versuche, die Wechselkurse zu festigen (verschiedentlich in Deutschland sowie in Ungarn unter Hegedus)[38] scheiterten eben daran, daß sie nicht die Grundregeln (das „Regime") änderten, nach denen die Fiskalpolitik zu führen war.[39]

In Diskussionen über dieses Thema wurde mir zuweilen entgegengehalten, die hier beschriebenen Umstände seien zu extrem und überspitzt, als daß man sie auf die gegenwärtige Inflation in den Vereinigten Staaten übertragen könnte. Doch sind sie im Gegenteil gerade deshalb relevant, weil sie extrem waren. In der Extremlage aller vier Beispiele wirkten nämlich die elementaren Kräfte, welche Inflationen auslösen und deren man sich bedienen kann, um sie zu beenden, so ausgeprägt, daß sie wie in einem Laborexperiment leichter erkennbar werden. So glaube ich, daß aus den beschriebenen Inflationen sehr viel für unsere heutigen, weniger drastischen inflatorischen Entwicklungen zu lernen ist, wenn wir sie nur richtig interpretieren.

---

[38] Vgl. Pasvolsky (25), S. 304—307.

[39] Ein wichtiger Einwand gegen die Interpretation in diesem Abschnitt kann aus der Argumentation von Sargent und Wallace (31) abgeleitet werden, die darlegen, daß für eine einzelne Volkswirtschaft kein rationales Erwartungsmodell vorstellbar ist, in dem sich ein grundlegender Wechsel der Fiskal- und Geldpolitik, eine Änderung des „Regimes", vollziehen könnte. Insbesondere die grundlegenden Änderungen in diesen Bereichen der Politik, die mit dem Ende der Inflationen in den vier Ländern einhergingen, können ihrerseits als Folge von vorausgegangenen ökonomischen Ereignissen angesehen werden. Aus dieser Sicht wären strategische Änderungen der Wirtschaftspolitik, die ich als „Regime"-Änderungen interpretiert habe, lediglich die Wahrnehmung von Ereignissen und die Reaktionen der Menschen darauf innerhalb eines einzigen komplexen „Regimes" oder Systems. Ein solches System („Regime") müßte in einem weitaus umfassenderen Zusammenhang und mehr auf den Staat bezogen dargestellt werden, als es hier bei dem einfachen wirtschaftspolitischen „Regime" und seiner Änderung geschah, die ich beschrieben habe. Ich vermute, daß man die Daten dieses Aufsatzes mit jenem breiteren Ansatz interpretieren könnte, doch erforderte das umfangreiche Modifikationen und eine erheblich kompliziertere Terminologie, ohne daß die wichtigsten praktischen Schlußfolgerungen sich dadurch änderten.

Literaturverzeichnis

1. Kenneth J. Arrow/Mordecai Kurz, *Public Investment, the Rate of Return, and Optimal Fiscal Policy*, Baltimore-London 1970.
2. Robert J. Barro, *Are Government Bonds Net Wealth?*, in: *Journal of Political Economy*, 82 (1974), No. 6, pp. 1095—1118.
3. Costantino Bresciani-Turroni, *The Economics of Inflation*, London 1937.
4. Philipp Cagan, *The Monetary Dynamics of Hyperinflation*, in: *Studies in the Quantity Theory of Money*, ed. Milton Friedman, Chicago 1956, pp. 25—117.
5. J. van Walre de Bordes, *The Austrian Crown*, London 1924.
6. Eugene F. Fama, *Banking in the Theory of Finance*, in: *Journal of Monetary Economics*, 6 (1980), No. 1, pp. 39—58.
7. Frank D. Graham, *Exchange, Prices, and Production in Hyperinflation: Germany, 1920—23*, New York 1930.
8. John H. Kareken/Neil Wallace (Hrsg.), *Models of Monetary Economics*, Minneapolis 1980.
9. John H. Kareken/Neil Wallace, *Introduction* zu *Models of Monetary Economics*, Minneapolis 1980. (8)
10. John Maynard Keynes, *A Tract on Monetary Reform*, New York 1924. Deutsch: *Ein Traktat über Währungsreform*, München-Leipzig 1924.
11. John Maynard Keynes, *The United States and Gold*, in: *European Currency and Finance*, Bd. 1, ed. John Parke Young, Washington D. C. 1925, pp. 131—133.
12. W. T. Layton/Charles Rist, *The Economic Situation of Austria*, Report presented to the Council of the League of Nations, August 19, 1925, Genf 1925.
13. League of Nations, *The Course and Control of Inflation*, Genf 1946.
14. League of Nations, *The Financial Reconstruction of Austria: General Survey and Principal Documents*, Genf 1926.
15. League of Nations, *The Financial Reconstruction of Hungary: General Survey and Principal Documents*, Genf 1926.
16. League of Nations, *Memorandum on Currency and Central Banks, 1913—1925*, Bd. 1, Genf 1926.
17. League of Nations, *Memorandum on Public Finance (1922—1926)*, Genf 1927.
18. League of Nations, *Memorandum on Currency and Central Banks, 1913—1924*, Bd. 1, Genf 1925.
19. Robert E. Lucas Jr., *Econometric Policy Evaluation: A Critique*, in: *The Phillips Curve and Labor Markets* (= Carnegie-Rochester Conference Series on Public Policy, ed. K. Brunner/A. H. Meltzer), Bd. 1, Amsterdam 1976, pp. 19—46.
20. Robert E. Lucas Jr., *Econometric Testing of the Natural Rate Hypothesis*, in: *The Econometrics of Price Determination Conference*, ed. Otto Eckstein, Washington D.C. 1972.
21. Robert E. Lucas Jr., *Equilibrium in a Pure Currency Economy*, in: *Models of Monetary Economics*, Minneapolis 1980. (8)
22. Robert E. Lucas Jr./Thomas J. Sargent, *After Keynesian Economics*, in: *Quarterly Review*, Federal Reserve Bank of Minneapolis (1979), spring issue.
23. Robert E. Lucas Jr./Thomas J. Sargent, *Rational Expectations and Econometric Practice*, einleitender Essay zu *Rational Expectations and Econometric Practice*, ed. R. E. Lucas Jr., T. J. Sargent, Minneapolis 1982.

24. Donald Nichols, *Some Principles of Inflationary Finance*, in: *Journal of Political Economy*, 82 (1974), No. 2, Teil 1, pp. 423—430.
25. Leo Pasvolsky, *Economic Nationalism of the Danubian States*, New York 1928.
26. Robert O. Paxton, *Europe in the Twentieth Century*, New York 1975.
27. Constance Reid, *Hilbert*, New York 1979.
28. Michael K. Salemi, *Hyperinflation, Exchange Depreciation, and the Demand for Money in Post World War I Germany*, unveröffentlichte Ph. D.-Dissertation, University of Minnesota 1976.
29. Paul A. Samuelson, *An Exact Consumption-Loan Model of Interest with or without the Social Contrivance of Money*, in: *Journal of Political Economy*, 66 (1958), pp. 467—482.
30. Thomas J. Sargent, *Rational Expectations and the Reconstruction of Macroeconomics*, in: *Quarterly Review*, Federal Reserve Bank of Minneapolis (1980), summer issue.
31. Thomas J. Sargent/Neil Wallace, *Rational Expectations, the Optimal Monetary Instrument, and the Optimal Money Supply Rule*, in: *Journal of Political Economy*, 83 (1975), No. 2.
32. Thomas J. Sargent/Neil Wallace, *Rational Expectations and the Theory of Economic Policy*, in: *Journal of Monetary Economics*, 2 (1976), No. 2, pp. 169—183.
33. *Statistisches Jahrbuch für das Deutsche Reich*, 1924/25.
34. Robert M. Townsend, *Models of Money with Spatially Separated Agents*, in: *Models of Monetary Economics*, Minneapolis 1980. (8)
35. Neil Wallace, *The Overlapping Generations Model of Fiat Money*, in: *Models of Monetary Economics*, Minneapolis 1980. (8)
36. John Parke Young, *European Currency and Finance* (= Commission of Gold and Silver Inquiry, U. S. Senate, Serial 9), Washington, D. C. 1925, Bd. 1 u. 2.

ANHANG

TABELLE Ö 1

Staatshaushalt Österreichs 1919 bis 1922
(in Mio. Kronen)

Haushaltsjahr	Einnahmen	Ausgaben	Defizit	Ausgabenanteil, der durch zusätzliche Papiergeldemission finanziert wurde, in %
1. Januar—30. Juni 1919	1.339	4.043	2.704	67
1. Juli 1919—30. Juni 1920	6.295	16.873	10.578	63
1. Juli 1920—30. Juni 1921	29.483	70.601	41.118	58
1. Januar—31. Dez. 1922	209.763	347.533	137.770	40

Quelle: Pasvolsky (25, S. 102).

TABELLE Ö 2

Gesamter Notenumlauf österreichischer Kronen
(in Tsd. Kronen)

Jahr	Monat	Wert	Jahr	Monat	Wert
1919	Januar	—		März	304.063.642
	Februar	—		April	346.697.776
	März	4.687.056		Mai	397.829.313
	April	5.577.851		Juni	549.915.678
	Mai	5.960.003		Juli	786.225.601
	Juni	7.397.692		August	1.353.403.632
	Juli	8.391.405		September	2.277.677.738
	August	9.241.135		Oktober	2.970.916.607
	September	9.781.112		November	3.417.786.498
	Oktober	10.819.310		Dezember	4.080.177.238
	November	11.193.670	1923	Januar	4.110.551.163
	Dezember	12.134.474		Februar	4.207.991.722
1920	Januar	13.266.878		März	4.459.117.216
	Februar	14.292.809		April	4.577.382.333
	März	15.457.749		Mai	4.837.042.081
	April	15.523.832		Juni	5.432.619.312
	Mai	15.793.805		Juli	5.684.133.721
	Juni	16.971.344		August	5.894.786.367
	Juli	18.721.495		September	6.225.109.352
	August	20.050.281		Oktober	6.607.839.105
	September	22.271.686		November	6.577.616.341
	Oktober	25.120.385		Dezember	7.125.755.190
	November	28.072.331	1924	Januar	6.735.109.000
	Dezember	30.645.658		Februar	7.364.441.000
1921	Januar	34.525.634		März	7.144.901.000
	Februar	38.352.648		April	7.135.471.000
	März	41.067.299		Mai	7.552.620.000
	April	45.036.723		Juni	7.774.958.000
	Mai	45.583.194		Juli	7.995.647.000
	Juni	49.685.140		August	5.894.786.367
	Juli	54.107.281		September	7.998.509.000
	August	58.533.766		Oktober	8.213.003.000
	September	70.170.798		November	8.072.021.000
	Oktober	—		Dezember	8.387.767.000
	November	—	1925	Januar	7.902.217.000
	Dezember	—		Februar	7.957.242.000
1922	Januar	227.015.925		März	7.897.792.000
	Februar	259.931.138		April	7.976.420.000

Quelle: Young (36, Bd. 2, S. 292).

TABELLE Ö 3

Einzelhandelspreise in Österreich 1921 bis 1924
(Januar 1921 = 100)

Jahr	Monat	Index der Einzelhandelspreise auf der Basis von 52 Waren	Jahr	Monat	Index der Einzelhandelspreise auf der Basis von 52 Waren
1921	Januar	100		Oktober	18.567
	Februar	114		November	17.681
	März	122		Dezember	17.409
	April	116	1923	Januar	17.526
	Mai	121		Februar	17.851
	Juni	150		März	18.205
	Juli	143		April	19.428
	August	167		Mai	20.450
	September	215		Juni	20.482
	Oktober	333		Juli	19.368
	November	566		August	18.511
	Dezember	942		September	20.955
1922	Januar	1.142		Oktober	21.166
	Februar	1.428		November	21.479
	März	1.457		Dezember	21.849
	April	1.619	1924	Januar	22.941
	Mai	2.028		Februar	23.336
	Juni	3.431		März	23.336
	Juli	4.830		April	23.361
	August	11.046		Mai	23.797
	September	20.090		Juni	24.267

Quelle: Young (36, Bd. 2, S. 293).

TABELLE Ö 4

Wechselkurse, Österreichische Kronen pro US-Dollar in New York

Monat	1919	1920	1921	1922	1923	1924
Januar	17,09	271,43	654,00	7.375,00	71.500,00	70.760,00
Februar	20,72	250,00	722,50	6.350,00	71.150,00	70.760,00
März	25,85	206,66	676,00	7.487,50	71.000,00	70.760,00
April	26,03	200,00	661,00	7.937,50	70.850,00	70.760,00
Mai	24,75	155,83	604,00	11.100,00	70.800,00	70.760,00
Juni	29,63	145,00	720,00	18.900,00	70.800,00	70.760,00
Juli	37,24	165,00	957,00	42.350,00	70.760,00	70.760,00
August	42,50	237,14	1.081,50	77.300,00	70.760,00	70.760,00
September	68,50	255,00	2.520,00	74.210,00	70.760,00	70.760,00
Oktober	99,50	358,33	4.355,00	73.550,00	70.760,00	70.760,00
November	130,00	493,66	8.520,00	71.400,00	70.760,00	70.760,00
Dezember	155,00	659,40	5.275,00	70.925,00	70.760,00	70.760,00

Quelle: Young (36, Bd. 2, S. 294).

Tabelle Ö 5

Monatsausweise der österreichischen Nationalbank 1923 bis 1925
(in Mio. Kronen)

Monats-ende	Gold	Devisen und Sorten	Kredite und diskontierte Handelswechsel	Schatzwechsel	Notenumlauf	Einlagen
1923						
Januar	49.304	1.058.244	731.046	2.556.848	4.110.551	279.092
Februar	83.438	1.029.134	728.884	2.552.682	4.207.992	178.752
März	86.097	1.336.385	821.397	2.550.159	4.459.117	329.109
April	73.270	1.439.999	741.858	2.550.159	4.577.382	226.273
Mai	73.391	1.682.209	875.942	2.550.159	4.837.042	343.339
Juni	73.391	2.532.316	730.848	2.547.212	5.432.619	362.237
Juli	73.391	2.947.216	658.966	2.539.777	5.684.134	535.121
August	73.391	3.050.085	647.936	2.538.719	5.894.786	413.383
September	73.391	3.126.599	863.317	2.537.661	6.225.109	373.673
Oktober	62.117	3.356.232	1.069.340	2.536.604	6.607.839	414.882
November	62.117	3.504.652	1.094.620	2.535.547	6.577.616	617.321
Dezember	83.177	3.832.132	1.325.380	2.534.490	7.125.755	649.424
1924						
Januar	91.274	3.811.148	1.253.110	2.533.434	6.735.109	536.982
Februar	105.536	3.921.594	1.737.334	2.532.379	7.364.441	558.800
März	106.663	3.953.872	1.733.400	2.295.428	7.144.901	752.814
April	107.059	3.669.333	2.131.984	2.294.471	7.315.471	696.141
Mai	107.443	3.344.337	2.660.449	2.259.839	7.554.620	641.001
Juni	107.762	3.178.339	3.092.470	2.237.794	7.774.958	741.400
Juli	108.342	3.254.477	3.304.876	2.231.173	7.995.647	896.032
August	108.256	3.453.177	3.226.962	2.219.459	8.002.142	997.677
September	108.950	3.724.916	2.852.688	2.210.527	7.998.509	890.537
Oktober	109.327	4.032.485	2.379.700	2.202.106	8.213.003	502.579
November	110.643	4.312.355	1.945.627	2.196.181	8.072.021	484.750
Dezember	110.890	4.770.548	1.881.593	2.178.185	8.387.767	533.450
1925						
Januar	111.314	3.337.911	1.545.295	2.172.491	7.902.217	438.390
Februar	111.474	3.310.032	1.285.158	2.150.151	7.957.242	315.771
März	111.649	3.202.802	1.047.719	2.107.949	7.897.792	295.498
April	112.168	3.474.672	1.059.069	2.088.777	7.976.420	236.957

Quelle: Young (36, Bd. 2, S. 291).

TABELLE Ö 6

Staatshaushalt Österreichs 1923 bis 1925
(Ist-Rechnung, in Mio. Schilling)*

	1923	1924	1925
Gesamte Einnahmen	697,4	900,6	908,5
Laufende Ausgaben	779,6	810,0	741,4
Defizit (-) oder Überschuß (+)	- 82,2	+ 90,6	+167,1
Investitionsausgaben	76,0	103,6	90,6
Gesamtbilanz	-158,2	- 13,0	+ 76,5

* 1 Schilling = 10 000 Papierkronen

Quelle: Pasvolsky (25, S. 127).

TABELLE Ö 7

Empfänger von Arbeitslosenunterstützung in Österreich
1922 bis 1926 (in Tsd.)

Monatsanfang	1922	1923	1924	1925	1926
Januar	17	117	98	154	208
April	42	153	107	176	202
Juli	33	93	64	118	151
Oktober	38	79	78	119	148

Quelle: The Financial Reconstruction of Austria (14, S. 87).

TABELLE U 1

Staatshaushalt Ungarns 1920 bis 1924
(Voranschläge in Mio. Papierkronen)

Haushaltsjahr	Einnahmen	Ausgaben	Defizite	Ausgabenanteil, der durch zusätzliche Papiergeldemission finanziert wurde, in %
1920—21	10.520	20.210	9.690	47,9
1921—22	20.296	26.764	6.468	24,1
1922—23	152.802	193.455	40.653	21,0
1923—24	2.168.140	3.307.099	1.138.959	34,4

Quelle: Pasvolsky (25, S. 299).

TABELLE U 2

Monatsausweise der Nationalbank bzw. des staatlichen Noteninstituts Ungarns 1921 bis 1925
(in Mio. Kronen)*

Monat	Goldmünzen und -barren	Silbermünzen	Devisen und Sorten	Diskontierte Wechsel	Lombardkredite	Vorschüsse an die Regierung	Notenumlauf	Einlagen
1921								
Januar	—	—	—	10.924	195	—	15.206	3.851
Februar	—	—	—	13.202	162	—	15.571	5.531
März	—	—	—	12.862	160	—	15.650	5.246
April	—	—	—	12.178	110	—	13.114	6.802
Mai	—	—	—	11.847	111	—	13.686	5.760
Juni	—	—	—	11.693	108	—	18.096	1.162
Juli	—	—	—	11.787	107	—	15.799	3.532
August	4	1	—	17.799	1.199	—	17.326	2.975
September	5	1	—	20.994	1.194	—	20.845	2.407
Oktober	12	1	—	22.403	1.185	900	23.643	2.154
November	12	1	—	23.650	1.176	1.000	24.742	2.353
Dezember	12	1	—	23.859	1.158	900	25.175	2.240
1922								
Januar	13	1	—	24.195	1.147	1.300	25.680	2.488
Februar	13	1	—	23.952	1.504	1.900	26.758	2.354
März	13	1	—	24.574	1.565	3.000	29.327	2.224
April	13	1	—	25.120	1.565	4.100	30.580	2.901
Mai	13	1	—	25.326	1.560	5.500	31.930	3.289

Tabelle U 2 *(Fortsetzung)*

Monatsausweise der Nationalbank bzw. des staatlichen Noteninstituts Ungarns 1921 bis 1925
*(in Mio. Kronen)**

Monat	Goldmünzen und -barren	Silbermünzen	Devisen und Sorten	Diskontierte Wechsel	Lombardkredite	Vorschüsse an die Regierung	Notenumlauf	Einlagen
Juni	13	1	—	25.445	1.556	6.900	33.600	3.741
Juli	13	1	—	28.783	1.546	7.200	38.357	3.929
August	13	1	—	37.617	1.773	7.600	46.242	5.417
September	14	1	—	46.963	1.848	8.900	58.458	5.929
Oktober	14	1	—	51.631	1.728	12.000	70.005	5.189
November	15	1	—	49.246	1.861	12.500	72.016	6.408
Dezember	16	1	—	50.702	2.016	16.500	75.887	4.761
1923								
Januar	14	1	—	54.516	2.007	20.000	73.717	5.888
Februar	23	1	—	58.358	2.013	24.000	75.135	6.600
März	23	1	—	71.284	2.584	29.000	82.205	11.152
April	23	1	—	83.800	2.817	37.000	100.101	9.793
Mai	23	1	—	93.396	1.763	47.200	119.285	10.609
Juni	23	1	—	120.608	2.490	59.700	154.996	12.742
Juli	22	1	—	165.927	1.762	79.700	226.285	21.977
August	22	1	—	273.605	1.789	143.000	399.487	23.629
September	22	1	—	380.454	1.776	243.000	588.810	60.246
Oktober	23	1	—	494.501	1.663	269.000	744.926	60.176
November	23	1	—	531.403	1.047	306.000	853.989	74.970
Dezember	23	1	—	582.117	935	401.000	931.337	84.791

TABELLE U 2 *(Fortsetzung)*

Monatsausweise der Nationalbank bzw. des staatlichen Noteninstituts Ungarns 1921 bis 1925 (in Mio. Kronen)*

Monat	Goldmünzen und -barren	Silber-münzen	Devisen und Sorten	Diskontierte Wechsel	Lombard-kredite	Vorschüsse an die Regierung	Noten-umlauf	Einlagen
1924								
Januar	24	1	—	654.294	9.346	526.000	1.084.677	105.481
Februar	23	1	—	746.471	34.023	699.000	1.278.437	164.838
März	24	1	—	802.756	4.598	824.000	1.606.875	253.935
April	24	1	—	1.125.898	12.456	944.000	2.098.091	308.121
Mai	24	1		1.420.385	13.437	1.054.000	2.486.257	527.137
Juni[1]	246.947	9.823	681.268	1.192.517	17.566	1.980.000	2.893.719	1.135.710
Juli	441.832	13.545	1.110.926	1.257.597		1.980.000	3.277.943	1.424.578
August	449.945	13.558	1.382.885	1.438.454		1.978.130	3.659.757	1.473.231
September	540.425	13.560	1.385.880	1.756.636		1.977.306	4.115.925	1.416.400
Oktober	503.377	13.301	1.658.674	1.872.385		1.976.455	4.635.090	1.465.356
November	508.411	13.301	1.816.102	1.984.540	—	1.975.631	4.442.644	1.929.754
Dezember	532.842	13.299	1.933.356	1.976.888	—	1.974.781	4.513.990	2.069.468
1925								
Januar	509.848	12.373	1.967.314	1.848.620	—	1.973.930	4.449.650	2.138.629
Februar	596.334	12.374	1.989.096	1.676.594	—	1.973.163	4.237.985	2.542.262
März	669.107	12.374	1.984.006	1.514.532	—	1.969.809	4.270.096	2.552.762
April	653.534	12.136	2.081.998	1.485.898	—	1.968.987	4.526.216	2.470.507

* Vor Juni 1924 handelt es sich um die Ausweise des staatlichen Noteninstituts. Die ungarische Nationalbank nahm ihre Tätigkeit am 24. Juni 1924 auf und übernahm zu diesem Zeitpunkt die Geschäfte des Noteninstituts.
[1] Von diesem Monat an werden die Gold- und Silberbestände nicht mehr in Gold, sondern in Papierkronen bewertet. Die neue ungarische Nationalbank nahm im Juni 1924 auch andere Änderungen in der Darstellung ihrer Konten vor.

Quelle: Young (36, Bd. 2, S. 321).

TABELLE U 3

Ungarn — Preis- und Wechselkursentwicklung
1921 bis 1925

Monat	Ungarischer Preisindex*	Cents pro Krone in New York	Monat	Ungarischer Preisindex*	Cents pro Krone in New York
1921			Mai	94.000	0.0191
Juli	4.200	0.3323	Juni	144.500	0.0140
August	5.400	0.2629	Juli	286.000	0.0097
September	6.250	0.1944	August	462.500	0.0056
Oktober	6.750	0.1432	September	554.000	0.0055
November	8.300	0.1078	Oktober	587.000	0.0054
Dezember	8.250	0.1512	November	635.000	0.0054
			Dezember	714.000	0.0052
1922					
Januar	8.100	0.1525	1924		
Februar	8.500	0.1497	Januar	1.026.000	0.0039
März	9.900	0.1256	Februar	1.839.100	0.0033
April	10.750	0.1258	März	2.076.700	0.0015
Mai	11.000	0.1261	April	2.134.600	0.0014
Juni	12.900	0.1079	Mai	2.269.600	0.0012
Juli	17.400	0.0760	Juni	2.207.800	0.0011
August	21.400	0.0595	Juli	2.294.500	0.0012
September	26.600	0.0423	August	2.242.000	0.0013
Oktober	32.900	0.0402	September	2.236.600	0.0013
November	32.600	0.0413	Oktober	2.285.200	0.0013
Dezember	33.400	0.0430	November	2.309.500	0.0013
			Dezember	2.346.600	0.0013
1923					
Januar	38.500	0.0392	1925		
Februar	41.800	0.0395	Januar	2.307.500	0.0014
März	66.000	0.0289	Februar	2.218.700	0.0014
April	83.500	0.0217	März	2.117.800	0.0014

* Von Juli 1921 bis einschließlich November 1923 handelt es sich um einen Einzelhandelspreisindex (1914 = 100), der auf der Grundlage eines Warenkorbs von 60 Gütern erstellt wurde. Die Angaben für Dezember 1923 bis einschließlich März 1925 sind der Großhandelspreisindex (1913 = 100), der vom ungarischen Zentralen Statistischen Amt errechnet wurde. Die Erhebungen wurden jeweils am letzten Tag des Monats vorgenommen und beziehen sich auf einen Warenkorb von 52 Gütern.

Quelle: Young (36, Bd. 2, S. 323).

TABELLE U 4

Staatshaushalt Ungarns 1924 bis 1925
(in Mio. Kronen)

Periode	Vorläufige Haushaltsanschläge des Finanzministeriums			Wiederaufbauplan		
	Einnahmen	Ausgaben	Überschuß (+) oder Defizit (-)	Einnahmen	Ausgaben	Überschuß (+) oder Defizit (-)
Juli-Dez. 1924	208,0	205,9	+ 2,1	143,8	186,3	- 42,5
Jan.-Juni 1925	245,1	216,9	+ 28,2	150,0	207,6	- 57,6
Haushaltsjahr 1924—25	453,1	422,8	+ 30,3	293,8	393,8	- 100,1

Quelle: Pasvolsky (25, S. 322).

TABELLE U 5

Arbeitslose in Ungarn 1924 bis 1926 (in Tsd.)*

Monatsende	1924	1925	1926
Januar		37	28
Februar		37	29
März		37	29
April	22	36	26
Mai	23	30	28
Juni	25	34	26
Juli	31	32	
August	30	27	
September	20	25	
Oktober	30	23	
November	31	26	
Dezember	33	27	

* Die Angaben beziehen sich nur auf die Mitglieder der Sozialistischen Arbeitergewerkschaft.

Quelle: Financial Reconstruction of Hungary... (15, S. 50).

Tabelle P 1

Staatshaushalt Polens 1921 bis 1925 (in Tsd. Zloty)*

	1921	1922	1923	1924	1925
Einnahmen					
Verwaltung	261.676	467.979	—	—	1.491.743
Staatsbetriebe	11.413	14.556	—	—	133.530
Monopole	72.222	47.893	—	—	356.611
Insgesamt	345.311	530.428	426.000	1.703.000	1.981.884
Ausgaben					
Verwaltung	765.263	734.310	—	—	1.830.231
Staatsbetriebe	115.589	145.003	—	—	106.343
Monopole	—	—	—	—	45.019
Insgesamt	880.852	879.313	1.119.800	1.629.000	1.981.593
Defizit	535.541	348.885	692.000	—	—
Überschuß	—	—	—	74.000	251

* Umrechnung von polnischer Mark in Zloty auf folgender Basis: 1921, 1 Zloty = 303,75 Mark. 1922, 1 Zloty = erstes Quartal 513,52 Mark; zweites Quartal 691,49 Mark; drittes Quartal 1.024,97 Mark; viertes Quartal 1.933,87 Mark.

Quelle: Young (36, Bd. 2, S. 183).

TABELLE P 2

Monatsausweise der Bank von Polen 1918 bis 1925*

Monatsende	Gold[1]	Silber[1] einschl. Scheidemünzen	Devisen	Wechsel- kredite	Vorschüsse an Geschäftswelt	Vorschüsse an Regierung	Noten- umlauf
				in Mio. Mark			
1918							
Oktober	—	—	—	7,0	180,8	—	880,2
November	—	—	—	7,0	184,0	13,9	930,5
Dezember	—	—	—	6,4	183,7	117,8	1.023,8
1919							
Januar	—	—	—	5,0	194,7	209,9	1.098,1
Februar	—	—	—	4,2	196,4	315,0	1.160,0
März	3,7	4,2	3,9	3,5	189,7	400,0	1.223,2
April	3,7	4,4	9,4	2,5	192,8	575,0	1.346,0
Mai	3,7	8,9	5,8	1,8	193,2	925,0	1.548,3
Juni	4,9	14,8	14,6	1,3	185,9	1.125,0	1.784,6
Juli	5,7	20,1	13,3	1,1	193,0	1.925,0	2.087,9
August	6,1	20,5	20,3	0,7	107,4	2.525,0	2.466,6
September	6,3	21,6	69,8	0,1	218,9	3.225,0	2.964,7
Oktober	6,5	24,3	91,0	0,3	242,4	4.375,0	3.723,6
November	6,6	24,6	151,6	3,4	270,2	5.375,0	4.236,2
Dezember	6,6	25,5	344,6	3,9	243,8	6.825,0	5.316,3
1920							
Januar	6,6	25,5	244,1	3,7	278,5	8.275,0	6.719,9
Februar	6,8	25,9	565,7	6,4	303,0	10.775,0	8.300,3
März	6,8	25,9	685,4	8,2	319,1	14.775,0	10.690,6
April	6,8	25,9	685,5	14,8	316,7	19.375,0	16.027,9

TABELLE P 2 (Fortsetzung)

Monatsausweise der Bank von Polen 1918 bis 1925*

Monatsende	Gold[1]	Silber[1] einschl. Scheidemünzen	Devisen	Wechsel-kredite	Vorschüsse an Geschäftswelt	Vorschüsse an Regierung	Noten-umlauf
				in Mio. Mark			
Mai	6,8	25,9	565,7	47,2	320,9	22.375,0	17.934,7
Juni	6,8	25,9	894,7	161,4	488,2	27.625,0	21.730,1
Juli	6,8	25,9	1.130,9	325,9	847,3	33.375,0	26.311,4
August	9,0	33,8	1.273,4	465,8	1.466,1	39.625,0	31.085,8
September	9,1	34,1	174,9	333,9	1.862,9	40.625,0	33.203,5
Oktober	9,5	34,4	236,7	259,1	2.577,0	46.925,0	38.456,8
November	10,1	35,4	203,8	396,0	3.278,4	49.625,0	43.236,2
Dezember	12,4	37,6	80,7	611,6	3.999,2	59.625,0	43.236,2
Dezember	12,4	37,6	80,7	611,6	3.999,2	59.625,0	49.361,5
1921							
Januar	12,7	39,2	205,8	1.040,2	4.100,2	65.625,0	55.079,5
Februar	12,8	39,2	476,0	955,1	4.143,5	77.125,0	62.560,4
März	13,1	39,8	908,5	781,0	4.745,7	93.625,0	74.087,4
April	13,4	40,3	870,7	927,0	4.994,4	106.625,0	86.755,3
Mai	13,5	40,1	536,5	1.395,2	4.979,0	117.625,0	94.575,8
Juni	14,3	41,1	493,6	1.557,3	5.306,5	130.625,0	102.697,3
Juli	19,1	41,5	601,3	2.504,2	6.291,5	140.625,0	115.242,3
August	19,2	42,0	368,7	3.885,4	7.776,9	158.000,0	133.734,2
September	19,4	42,5	1.217,5	6.237,3	9.878,6	178.000,0	152.792,1
Oktober	20,2	42,9	2.341,3	9.529,5	12.022,3	198.500,0	182.777,3
November	22,6	43,5	7.040,1	14.347,2	15.144,3	214.000,0	207.029,0
Dezember	24,9	43,9	12.707,9	15.324,4	19.300,0	221.000,0	229.537,6

Die Beendigung vier großer Inflationen

TABELLE 12 (Fortsetzung)

Monatsausweise der Bank von Polen 1918 bis 1925*

Monatsende	Gold[1]	Silber[1] einschl. Scheidemünzen	Devisen	Wechselkredite	Vorschüsse an Geschäftswelt	Vorschüsse an Regierung	Notenumlauf
				in Mio. Mark			
1922							
Januar	26,3	44,2	13.614,2	15.951,6	21.776,9	227.350,0	239.615,3
Februar	28,3	44,4	14.207,7	19.555,0	22.327,7	230.600,0	247.209,5
März	29,0	44,7	1.156,4	25.451,1	25.473,3	232.100,0	250.665,5
April	29,5	45,2	7.388,0	28.688,8	29.063,7	220.000,0	260.553,8
Mai	30,1	45,3	23.073,4	34.555,0	26.067,0	217.000,0	276.001,1
Juni	30,9	45,3	20.521,4	46.629,8	24.499,5	235.000,0	300.101,1
Juli	31,5	45,4	21.741,0	47.661,2	24.054,4	260.000,0	335.426,6
August	31,6	45,4	51.747,2	56.366,6	21.079,9	285.000,0	385.787,5
September	32,4	45,4	67.384,1	64.093,0	22.239,4	342.000,0	463.706,0
Oktober	33,5	45,4	64.060,9	81.781,9	26.576,5	453.500,0	579.972,7
November	33,8	45,4	78.959,0	107.320,1	41.278,1	519.500,0	661.092,4
Dezember	41,0	45,4	48.580,4	133.400,8	47.901,1	675.600,0	793.437,5
1923							
Januar	41,1	44,1	34.721,8	174.950,1	51.899,9	799.500,0	909.160,3
Februar	41,4	44,1	71.883,7	219.610,7	61.037,1	1.085.000,0	1.177.300,8
März	41,7	44,2	29.868,7	274.657,8	85.323,2	1.752.000,0	1.841.205,6
April	41,9	44,2	50.851,9	304.725,4	156.815,4	2.161.500,0	2.332.396,8
Mai	41,9	44,3	43.900,7	449.440,7	217.162,3	2.377.000,0	2.733.794,1
Juni	43,9	39,8	276.506,3	627.339,5	310.862,7	2.996.500,0	3.566.649,1
Juli	46,9	34,8	384.375,1	758.112,8	390.850,9	4.190.500,0	4.478.709,0
August	48,0	32,9	340.354,4	1.372.150,9	637.268,2	6.473.000,0	6.871.776,5
September	53,2	20,7	857.084,5	2.077.128,6	670.019,6	10.265.500,0	11.197.737,8
Oktober	54,2	19,1	1.510.794,3	3.540.434,4	1.836.712,7	19.080.500,0	23.080.402,2

TABELLE P 2 (Fortsetzung)
Monatsausweise der Bank von Polen 1918 bis 1925*

Monatsende	Gold[1]	Silber[1] einschl. Scheidemünzen	Devisen	Wechsel-kredite	Vorschüsse an Geschäftswelt	Vorschüsse an Regierung	Noten-umlauf
			in Mio. Mark				
November	54,3	19,5	6.499.791,5	8.467.033,7	3.951.781,9	42.854.000,0	53.217.494,6
Dezember	54,9	19,6	57.499.741,7	20.588.037,9	28.065.396,8	111.332.000,0	125.371.955,3
1924							
Januar	66,2	19,8	91.533.085,2	43.916.802,8	54.181.445,2	238.200.000,0	313.659.830,0
Februar	66,7	19,8	172.626.128,8	67.216.289,7	83.829.440,5	291.700.000,0	528.913.418,7
März	68,0	20,3	220.658.210,7	138.649.934,8	81.231.988,5	291.700.000,0	596.244.205,6
April	55,7	21,1	277.340.925,7	199.248.956,4	60.589.081,0	291.700.000,0	570.697.550,5
	Nach der Umwandlung der staatlichen Darlehnsbank in die Bank von Polen in Goldzloty (1 Zloty = 19,3 cents)						
Mai	11.684.963[2]		214.191.336	126.522.906	1.801.936	—	244.977.010
Juni	83.392.914[2]		256.972.386	138.862.243	5.826.971	—	334.405.730
Juli	93.683.430[2]		272.137.898	166.713.469	8.236.693	—	394.262.550
August	98.288.324[2]		266.390.583	199.710.736	8.224.610	—	430.263.045
September	99.900.015[2]		233.646.562	233.788.177	9.230.850	—	460.383.770
Oktober	100.686.634	16.521.223	241.894.738	245.054.984	12.374.342	—	503.701.830
November	102.809.285	21.951.828	247.034.974	249.560.999	12.371.166	—	497.600.470
Dezember	103.362.870	27.543.698	269.045.551	256.954.853	23.897.766	—	550.873.960

TABELLE P 2 (Fortsetzung)

Nach der Umwandlung der staatlichen Darlehnsbank in die Bank von Polen*

Monatsende	Gold[1]	Silber[1] einschl. Scheidemünzen	Devisen	Wechsel-kredite	Vorschüsse an Geschäftswelt	Vorschüsse an Regierung	Noten-umlauf
1925							
Januar	104.249.258	27.658.749	242.115.258	270.423.615	23.468.829	—	553.174.980
Februar	107.032.735	27.481.871	206.317.320	286.229.180	28.467.930	18.222.212	549.637.420
März	116.619.825	28.158.597	259.392.902	306.562.690	25.477.638	403.354	563.171.945
April	117.428.697	28.358.000	216.114.621	294.632.508	27.319.944	35.977.630	567.178.830

* Staatliche Darlehnsbank Polens bis Mai 1924.
[1] Gold bewertet mit der offiziellen Parität; Silbermünzen mit ihrem Nennwert.
[2] Gold und Silber.
Quelle: Young (36, Bd. 2, S. 343).

TABELLE P 3

Großhandelspreisindex in Polen 1921 bis 1925

(1914 = 100)

Jahr	Monat	Großhandels-preisindex	Jahr	Monat	Großhandels-preisindex
1921	Januar	25.139		September	152.365
	Februar	31.827		Oktober	201.326
	März	32.882		November	275.647
	April	31.710		Dezember	346.353
	Mai	32.639	1923	Januar	544.690
	Juni	35.392		Februar	859.110
	Juli	45.654		März	988.500
	August	53.100		April	1.058.920
	September	60.203		Mai	1.125.350
	Oktober	65.539		Juni	1.881.410
	November	58.583		Juli	3.069.970
	Dezember	57.046		August	5.294.680
1922	Januar	59.231		September	7.302.200
	Februar	63.445		Oktober	27.380.680
	März	73.465		November	67.943.700
	April	75.106		Dezember	142.300.700
	Mai	78.634	1924	Januar	242.167.700
	Juni	87.694		Februar	248.429.600
	Juli	101.587		März	245.277.900
	August	135.786		April	242.321.800

Quelle: Young (36, Bd. 2, S. 349).

TABELLE P 4

Polen — Wechselkursentwicklung 1919 bis 1925

Jahr	Monat	Cents pro polnische Mark	Jahr	Monat	Cents pro polnische Mark
1919	Juli	6,88	1922	August	0,0135
	August	5,63		September	0,0127
	September	3,88		Oktober	0,0095
	Oktober	3,08		November	0,0065
	November	1,88		Dezember	0,0057
	Dezember	1,29	1923	Januar	0,0043
1920	Januar	0,70		Februar	0,0025
	Februar	0,68		März	0,0024
	März	0,67		April	0,0023
	April	0,60		Mai	0,0021
	Mai	0,51		Juni	0,0013
	Juni	0,59		Juli	0,0007
	Juli	0,61		August	0,0004
	August	0,47		September	0,00035
	September	0,45		Oktober	0,0001113
	Oktober	0,37		November	0,0000502
	November	0,26		Dezember	0,0000234
	Dezember	0,16	1924	Januar	0,0000116
1921	Januar	0,145		Februar	0,0000109
	Februar	0,130		März	0,0000113
	März	0,132		April	0,0000114
	April	0,130		Mai	—
	Mai	0,124			Cents pro Zloty
	Juni	0,082			
	Juli	0,0516		Juni	10,29
	August	0,0489		Juli	19,25
	September	0,0256		August	19,23
	Oktober	0,0212		September	19,22
	November	0,0290		Oktober	19,22
	Dezember	0,0313		November	19,21
1922	Januar	0,0327		Dezember	19,20
	Februar	0,0286	1925	Januar	19,18
	März	0,0236		Februar	19,18
	April	0,0262		März	19,18
	Mai	0,0249		April	19,18
	Juni	0,0237		Mai	19,18
	Juli	0,0185		Juni	19,18

Quelle: Young (36, Bd. 2, S. 350).

Tabelle P 5

Arbeitslose in Polen 1921 bis 1924

1921		1923	
Januar	74.000	Januar	81.184
Februar	90.000	Februar	106.729
März	80.000	März	114.576
April	88.000	April	112.755
Mai	130.000	Mai	93.731
Juni	115.000	Juni	76.397
Juli	95.000	Juli	64.563
August	65.000	August	56.515
September	70.000	September	—
Oktober	78.000	Oktober	—
November	120.000	November	—
Dezember	173.000	Dezember	67.581
1922		1924	
Januar	221.444	Januar	100.580
Februar	206.442	Februar	110.737
März	170.125	März	112.583
April	148.625	April	109.000
Mai	128.916	Mai	84.000
Juni	98.581	Juni	97.870
Juli	85.240	Juli	149.097
August	69.692	August	159.820
September	68.000	September	155.245
Oktober	61.000	Oktober	147.065
November	62.000	November	150.180
Dezember	75.000	Dezember	159.060

Quelle: *Statistisches Jahrbuch für das Deutsche Reich*, 1924/25 (33).

TABELLE D 1

Großhandelspreise in Deutschland 1914 bis 1924
(1913 = 100)

Jahr	Monat	Großhandelspreisindex	Jahr	Monat	Großhandelspreisindex
1914	Januar	96		Februar	158
	Februar	96		März	159
	März	96		April	163
	April	95		Mai	163
	Mai	97		Juni	165
	Juni	99		Juli	172
	Juli	99		August	203
	August	109		September	199
	September	111		Oktober	201
	Oktober	118		November	203
	November	123		Dezember	203
	Dezember	125	1918	Januar	204
1915	Januar	126		Februar	198
	Februar	133		März	198
	März	139		April	204
	April	142		Mai	203
	Mai	139		Juni	209
	Juni	139		Juli	208
	Juli	150		August	235
	August	146		September	230
	September	145		Oktober	234
	Oktober	147		November	234
	November	147		Dezember	245
	Dezember	148	1919	Januar	262
1916	Januar	150		Februar	270
	Februar	151		März	274
	März	148		April	286
	April	149		Mai	297
	Mai	151		Juni	308
	Juni	152		Juli	339
	Juli	161		August	422
	August	159		September	493
	September	154		Oktober	562
	Oktober	153		November	678
	November	151		Dezember	803
	Dezember	151	1920	Januar	1.260
1917	Januar	156		Februar	1.690

TABELLE D 1 *(Fortsetzung)*

Großhandelspreise in Deutschland 1914—1924
(1913 = 100)

Jahr	Monat	Großhandels-preisindex	Jahr	Monat	Großhandels-preisindex
	März	1.710		August	19.200
	April	1.570		September	28.700
	Mai	1.510		Oktober	56.600
	Juni	1.380		November	115.100
	Juli	1.370		Dezember	147.480
	August	1.450	1923	Januar	278.500
	September	1.500		Februar	588.500
	Oktober	1.470		März	488.800
	November	1.510		April	521.200
	Dezember	1.440		Mai	817.000
1921	Januar	1.440		Juni	1.938.500
	Februar	1.380		Juli	7.478.700
	März	1.340		August	94.404.100
	April	1.330		September	2.394.889.300
	Mai	1.310		Oktober	709.480.000.000
	Juni	1.370		November	72.570.000.000.000
	Juli	1.430		Dezember	126.160.000.000.000
	August	1.920	1924	Januar	117.320.000.000.000
	September	2.070		Februar	116.170.000.000.000
	Oktober	2.460		März	120.670.000.000.000
	November	3.420		April	124.050.000.000.000
	Dezember	3.490		Mai	122.460.000.000.000
1922	Januar	3.670		Juni	115.900.000.000.000
	Februar	4.100		Juli	115[1]
	März	5.430		August	120[1]
	April	6.360		September	127[1]
	Mai	6.460		Oktober	131[1]
	Juni	7.030		November	129[1]
	Juli	10.160		Dezember	131[1]

[1] Reichsmarkpreise (1 Reichsmark = 1 Bio. Papiermark).
Quelle: Young (36, Bd. 1, S. 530).

TABELLE D 2

*Deutschland — Wechselkursentwicklung
1920 bis 1925*

Jahr	Monat	Cents pro Mark	Jahr	Monat	Cents pro Mark
1920	Januar	1,69		Juli	0,20
	Februar	1,05		August	0,10
	März	1,26		September	0,07
	April	1,67		Oktober	0,03
	Mai	2,19		November	0,01
	Juni	2,56		Dezember	0,01
	Juli	2,53	1923	Januar	0,007
	August	2,10		Februar	0,004
	September	1,72		März	0,005
	Oktober	1,48		April	0,004
	November	1,32		Mai	0,002
	Dezember	1,37		Juni	0,001
1921	Januar	1,60		Juli	0,0003
	Februar	1,64		August	0,0000339
	März	1,60		September	0,00000188
	April	1,57		Oktober	0,000000068
	Mai	1,63		November	0,00000000043
	Juni	1,44		Dezember	0,0000000000227
	Juli	1,30	1924[1]	Januar	22,8
	August	1,19		Februar	21,8
	September	0,96		März	22,0
	Oktober	0,68		April	22,0
	November	0,39		Mai	22,3
	Dezember	0,53		Juni	23,4
1922	Januar	0,52		Juli	23,9
	Februar	0,48		August	23,8
	März	0,36		September	23,8
	April	0,35		Oktober	23,8
	Mai	0,34		November	23,8
	Juni	0,32		Dezember	23,8
			1925[1]	Januar	23,8

[1] Cents pro Rentenmark und nach Oktober 1924 pro Reichsmark. 1 Rentenmark = 1 Reichsmark = 1 Bio. Papiermark. Die Reichsmark entspricht einer Goldmark = 23,82 cents.

Quelle: Young (36, Bd. 1, S. 532).

TABELLE D 3

Staatshaushalt des Deutschen Reiches, in reale Größen umgerechnet über den Lebenshaltungskostenindex
(in Mio. Goldmark)

April—März	Einnahmen				Ausgaben					
	Steuern	Sonstige Einnahmen	Kreditfinanziertes Defizit	Gesamt	Tilgung schwebender Schulden	Zinsen für schwebende Schulden	Subventionen an die Eisenbahnen	Ausführung des Versailler Vertrages	Sonstige Ausgaben	Gesamt
1920—21	4.090,8	132,9	7.041,9	11.265,6	821,7	—	—	—	—	11.265,6
1921—22	5.235,7	100,5	6.627,4	11.963,6	1.039,5	811,6	1.114,4	5.110,6	5.738,4	11.963,4
1922—23	3.529,1	51,4	6.384,5	9.965,0	81,0	344,4	1.685,5	3.600,0	4.254,1	9.965,0
1923—24[1]	1.496,1	180,6	11.836,5	13.513,2	—	931,0	3.725,0	—	—	13.513,2

[1] Nur die ersten neun Monate.
Quelle: Young (36, Bd. 2, S. 393).

Die Beendigung vier großer Inflationen 93

Monatsausweise der Reichsbank, 1921 bis 1924
(in Tsd. Papiermark, seit Januar 1924 in Tsd. Rentenmark[1] oder Reichsmark[2])

	Diskontierte Wechsel			Vorschüsse an die Regierung	Wertpapiere	Notenumlauf	Kurzfristige Einlagen			Forderungen der Rentenbank
	Schatzwechsel	Handelswechsel	Diskontierte Wechsel ingesamt				Öffentliche Einlagen	Andere Einlagen	kurzfristige Einlagen ingesamt	
1921:										
Januar	50.594.540	2.742.406	53.336.946	8.881	147.126	66.620.804	4.055.904	11.778.060	15.833.964	
Februar	53.690.412	2.760.927	56.451.339	11.522	185.877	67.426.959	7.291.052	10.066.036	17.357.088	
März	64.533.894	2.268.745	66.802.639	2.805	217.044	69.417.228	15.206.381	12.836.292	28.042.673	
April	58.841.630	2.052.099	60.803.729	9.238	225.777	70.839.725	11.595.618	9.260.271	20.855.889	
Mai	62.953.604	1.809.936	64.763.540	16.624	258.664	71.838.866	3.548.492	10.545.201	14.093.693	
Juni	79.607.790	1.565.406	81.172.196	6.079	282.716	75.321.095	5.647.805	14.744.903	20.392.708	
Juli	79.981.967	1.135.529	81.117.496	10.686	282.831	77.390.853	4.810.026	11.014.130	15.824.156	
August	84.043.891	1.002.497	85.046.388	7.704	258.319	80.072.721	4.850.843	8.798.756	13.649.599	
September	98.422.137	1.142.218	99.564.355	3.289	277.977	86.384.286	4.618.087	15.362.208	19.980.295	
Oktober	98.704.768	881.474	99.586.242	47.775	282.179	91.527.679	5.239.628	13.063.035	18.302.663	
November	114.023.417	1.445.667	115.469.084	90.370	247.699	100.943.632	5.144.615	20.168.499	25.313.114	
Dezember	132.380.906	1.061.754	133.392.660	8.476	195.912	113.639.464	7.591.343	25.314.330	32.905.673	
1922:										
Januar	126.160.402	1.592.416	127.752.818	20.548	198.725	115.375.766	5.286.950	18.125.502	23.421.452	
Februar	134.251.808	1.856.936	136.108.744	62.305	215.362	120.026.387	5.806.922	20.719.150	26.576.072	
März	146.531.247	2.151.677	148.682.924	20.688	205.936	130.671.352	7.743.735	25.614.597	33.358.332	
April	155.617.524	2.403.044	158.020.568	134.314	229.242	140.420.057	7.577.862	24.038.306	31.616.168	
Mai	167.793.922	3.376.599	171.170.521	54.361	199.314	151.949.179	7.711.279	25.416.711	33.127.990	
Juni	186.125.747	4.751.748	190.877.495	58.994	307.564	169.211.792	10.125.837	27.047.908	37.173.745	
Juli	207.858.232	8.122.066	215.980.298	141.276	313.488	189.794.722	9.197.727	30.778.489	39.976.216	
August	249.765.773	21.704.341	271.470.114	172.966	241.162	238.147.160	13.708.213	42.416.241	56.124.454	
September	349.169.650	50.234.414	400.004.064	61.516	416.193	316.869.799	30.034.309	79.978.068	110.012.377	
Oktober	477.201.494	101.155.267	578.356.761	624.368	502.348	469.456.818	34.270.926	106.508.333	140.779.259	
November	672.222.197	246.948.596	919.170.793	51.425.030[3]	381.068	754.086.109	50.353.945	190.615.514	240.969.459	
Dezember	1.184.464.359	422.235.296	1.606.699.655	773.974	469.972	1.280.094.831	153.190.991	377.335.296	530.526.287	

[1] Eine Rentenmark = 1 Reichsmark = 1 Bio. Papiermark.
[2] Die Reichsmark entspricht einem Goldmarkwert von 23,82 Cents.
[3] Der starke Anstieg der Vorschüsse an die Regierung im November 1922 war darauf zurückzuführen, daß die Reichsbank von den Darlehnskassen vorübergehend die Finanzierung der Nahrungsmittelversorgung übernahm, da letztere die benötigten Kredite nicht mehr gewähren konnte, weil die emittierten Darlehnskassenscheine den gesetzlichen Höchstbetrag erreicht hatten.

TABELLE D 4 *(Fortsetzung)*

	Diskontierte Wechsel			Vorschüsse an die Regierung	Wert-papiere	Noten-umlauf	Kurzfristige Einlagen			Forderungen der Rentenbank
	Schatz-wechsel	Handels-wechsel	Diskontierte Wechsel insgesamt				Öffentliche Einlagen	Andere Einlagen	kurzfristige Einlagen insgesamt	
1923:										
Januar	1.609.081.121	697.216.424	2.306.297.545	95.316.552	483.318	1.984.496.369	157.058.537	605.205.692	763.264.229	
Februar	2.947.363.994	1.829.341.080	4.776.705.074	27.422.282	1.209.935	3.512.787.777	253.915.266	1.329.065.770	1.582.981.036	
März	4.552.011.661	2.372.101.757	6.924.113.418	2.132.906	1.690.011	5.517.919.651	368.550.293	1.903.533.291	2.272.083.584	
April	6.224.899.348	2.986.116.724	9.211.016.072	20.466.948	1.207.105	6.545.984.355	454.403.079	3.399.871.714	3.854.274.793	
Mai	8.021.904.840	4.014.693.720	12.036.598.560	61.030.322	697.611	8.563.749.470	652.575.366	4.410.494.865	5.063.070.231	
Juni	18.338⁴	6.914.198.630	25.252.198.630	188.548.574	344.819	1.648.114.327	8.304.602.339	9.952.716.666		
Juli	53.752⁴	18.314⁴	72.006⁴	2.553.177.597	1.422.291	43.595⁴	3.779.235.298	24.078⁴	27.857⁴	
August	987.219⁴	164.644⁴	1.151.863⁴	25.261⁴	15.539.853	663.200⁴	206.168⁴	384.912⁴	591.080⁴	
September	45.216.224⁴	3.660.094⁴	48.876.318⁴	98.522⁴	1.801.579.570	28.228.815⁴	8.186.467⁴	8.781.150⁴	16.966.617⁴	
Oktober	6.578.650.939⁴	1.058.129.855⁴	7.636.780.794⁴	41.787.532⁴	9.536.953⁴	2.496.822.909⁴	606.660.673⁴	3.261.424.030⁴	3.868.085.703⁴	
15. Nov.	189.801.468.187⁴	39.529.577.254⁴	229.331.045.441⁴	535.714.637⁴	8.901.495⁴	92.844.720.742⁴	72.457.230.513⁴	57.095.366.904⁴	129.552.597.417⁴	
30. Nov.	96.874.330.250⁴	347.301.037.776⁴	444.175.368.026⁴	7.742.665.263⁴	336.495.629⁴	400.267.640.302⁴	120.478.936.906⁴	253.497.803.653⁴	373.976.740.559⁴	
Dezember⁵	⁴ 322.724.948.986⁴	322.724.948.986⁴	268.325.819.530⁴	65.791.385⁴	496.507.424.772⁴	303.114.560.004⁴	244.906.637.001⁴	548.024.197.005⁴		
1924:⁵										
Januar	—	—	755.866	336.520	12	483.675	492.985	281.320	281.305	200.000
Februar	—	—	1.165.649	306.618	25	587.875	367.551	282.958	650.509	400.000
März	—	—	1.767.443	143.102	533	689.864	352.360	352.334	704.694	800.000
April	—	—	1.916.969	156.362	91.984	776.949	474.411	330.561	804.972	800.000
Mai	—	—	1.954.930	128.597	80.011	926.874	545.252	259.203	804.455	800.000
Juni	—	—	1.897.959	108.789	76.378	1.097.309	493.043	280.884	773.927	800.000
Juli	—	—	1.798.097	62.489	76.509	1.211.038	452.597	290.390	742.987	800.000
August	—	—	1.860.843	59.983	76.331	1.391.895	264.064	297.791	561.855	800.000
September	—	—	2.169.684	54.424	78.305	1.520.511	307.515	362.581	670.096	800.000
15. Oktober⁶	—	—	2.153.943	15.947	77.517	1.396.748	—	—	828.511	800.000
31. Oktober	—	—	2.339.616	33.443	77.699	1.780.930	—	—	708.728	800.000
November	—	—	2.290.166	18.628	77.808	1.863.200	—	—	703.938	684.664
Dezember	—	—	2.064.094	16.960	77.999	1.941.440	—	—	820.865	456.508

⁴ In Milliarden.
⁵ Entsprechend der Verordnung vom 15. November 1923 stellte die strukturierten Reichsbank.
⁶ Für den 15. Oktober 1924 erschien der erste Ausweis der neu-

Die Beendigung vier großer Inflationen

TABELLE D 5

Ordentliche Einnahmen und Ausgaben der Regierung des Deutschen Reiches in den Monaten November 1923 bis Oktober 1924
(in Mio. Goldmark)

	Ordentliche Einnahmen		Ordentliche Ausgaben	Überschuß der Einnahmen (+) oder Ausgaben (-)
	Gesamt	Steuereinnahmen		
1923				
November	68,1	63,2	—	—
Dezember	333,9	312,3	668,7	-334,8
1924				
Januar	520,6	503,5	396,5	+ 124,1
Februar	445,0	418,0	462,8	- 17,8
März	632,4	595,3	498,6	+ 133,8
April	579,5	523,8	523,5	+ 56,0
Mai	566,7	518,7	459,1	+ 107,6
Juni	529,7	472,3	504,5	+ 25,2
Juli	622,2	583,1	535,1	+ 86,9
August	618,2	592,0	597,6	+ 20,6
September	665,6	609,2	581,6	+ 84,0
Oktober	714,3	686,7	693,0	+ 21,3

Quelle: Young (36, Bd. 1, S. 422).

TABELLE D 6

Index der Güterproduktion pro Kopf der Bevölkerung in Deutschland 1920 bis 1927
(1913 = 100)

Jahr	Index der Güterproduktion
1920	61
1921	77
1922	86
1923	54
1924	77
1925	90
1926	86
1927	111

Quelle: Graham (7, S. 287).

Tabelle T1

Staatshaushalt der Tschechoslowakei 1919 bis 1925
(ausschließlich kreditfinanzierter Investitionsausgaben)
(in Mio. tschechischen Kronen)

	1919		1920		1922		1922	
	Soll	Ist	Soll	Ist	Soll	Ist	Soll	Ist
Einnahmen:								
Ordentliche	2.614	—	7.950	—	15.923	—	17.291	—
Außerordentliche	1.096	—	2.477	—	1.376	—	1.593	—
Gesamt	3.710		10.427		13.455	17.299	21.894	18.884 17.733
Ausgaben								
Ordentliche	2.610	—	7.175	—	10.672	—	13.289	—
Außerordentliche	6.005	—	8.103	—	7.354	—	6.524	—
Gesamt	8.615	7.450	15.278	13.931	18.026	18.558	19.813	18.663
Defizit	4.905	—	4.851	476	727	—	929	930
Überschuß	—	—	—	—	—	3.336	—	—

	1923		1924		1925	
	Soll	Ist	Soll	Ist	Soll	Ist
Einnahmen:						
Ordentliche	17.961	—	15.987	—	—	—
Außerordentliche	851	—	404	—	—	—
Gesamt	18.812	15.664	16.391	—	15.702	—
Ausgaben						
Ordentliche	13.605	—	12.200	—	—	—
Außerordentliche	5.773	—	4.703	—	—	—
Gesamt	19.378	16.540	16.993	—	15.974	—
Defizit	565	876	603	—	272	—
Überschuß	—	—	—	—	—	—

Quelle: Young (36, Bd. 2, S. 71).

TABELLE T 2

Notenausgabe der Bankenabteilung des tschechoslowakischen
Finanzministeriums
1919 bis 1924
(in Tsd. tschechischen Kronen)

Monat		Notenumlauf	Monat		Notenumlauf
1919	April	—		Mai	9.717.750
	Mai	—		Juni	9.838.205
	Juni	—		Juli	9.916.077
	Juli	161.106		August	10.171.383
	August	664.997		September	10.196.880
	September	1.443.570		Oktober	10.139.366
	Oktober	2.512.199		November	9.996.550
	November	3.513.405		Dezember	10.064.049
	Dezember	4.723.303	1923	Januar	9.222.434
1920	Januar	5.574.688		Februar	8.947.988
	Februar	6.462.825		März	9.157.407
	März	7.216.438		April	9.567.369
	April	7.216.438		Mai	9.327.676
	Mai	8.268.695		Juni	9.375.991
	Juni	9.729.233		Juli	9.448.086
	Juli	9.267.874		August	9.218.475
	August	9.814.920		September	9.311.378
	September	10.310.228		Oktober	9.278.999
	Oktober	10.920.514		November	9.250.688
	November	10.946.653		Dezember	9.598.903
	Dezember	11.288.512	1924	Januar	8.820.093
1921	Januar	10.888.319		Februar	8.506.467
	Februar	10.914.786		März	8.280.390
	März	10.921.956		April	8.198.653
	April	10.928.560		Mai	9.078.418
	Mai	10.851.403		Juni	8.081.106
	Juni	11.167.515		Juli	8.090.034
	Juli	11.134.327		August	9.139.792
	August	11.455.175		September	8.222.658
	September	11.570.881		Oktober	8.585.847
	Oktober	12.327.159		November	8.500.942
	November	11.871.647		Dezember	8.810.357
	Dezember	12.129.573	1925	Januar	7.916.540
1922	Januar	11.230.065		Februar	7.727.880
	Februar	10.743.958		März	7.680.867
	März	10.323.069		April	7.525.934
	April	10.075.757			

Quelle: Young (36, Bd. 2, S. 305—306).

TABELLE T 3

*Tschechoslowakei — Wechselkursentwicklung
1919 bis 1924*

	Monat	Cents pro Krone		Monat	Cents pro Krone
1919	Januar	—	1922	April	1,960
	Februar	—		Mai	1,921
	März	—		Juni	1,924
	April	6,135		Juli	2,185
	Mai	—		August	2,902
	Juni	—		September	3,231
	Juli	5,625		Oktober	3,285
	August	4,575		November	3,176
	September	4,575		Dezember	3,097
	Oktober	3,100	1923	Januar	2,856
	November	1,950		Februar	2,958
	Dezember	1,900		März	2,969
1920	Januar	1,425		April	2,978
	Februar	0,975		Mai	2,979
	März	1,275		Juni	2,993
	April	1,530		Juli	2,997
	Mai	2,195		August	2,934
	Juni	2,335		September	2,995
	Juli	2,195		Oktober	2,971
	August	1,810		November	2,906
	September	1,535		Dezember	2,925
	Oktober	1,245	1924	Januar	2,898
	November	1,165		Februar	2,902
	Dezember	1,190		März	2,902
1921	Januar	1,300		April	2,957
	Februar	1,290		Mai	2,939
	März	1,307		Juni	2,936
	April	1,365		Juli	2,953
	Mai	1,460		August	2,979
	Juni	1,420		September	2,993
	Juli	1,312		Oktober	2,981
	August	1,225		November	2,989
	September	1,160		Dezember	3,018
	Oktober	1,049	1925	Januar	3,00
	November	1,038		Februar	2,96
	Dezember	1,249		März	2,97
1922	Januar	1,732		April	2,96
	Februar	1,855		Mai	2,96
	März	1,733		Juni	2,96

Quelle: Young (36, Bd. 2, S. 307).

TABELLE T 4

Tschechoslowakei — Großhandelspreisindex
1922 bis 1924
(Juli 1914 = 100)

Monat		Großhandels-preisindex	Monat		Großhandels-preisindex
1922	Januar	1.675		September	957
	Februar	1.520		Oktober	973
	März	1.552		November	965
	April	1.491		Dezember	984
	Mai	1.471	1924	Januar	974
	Juni	1.471		Februar	999
	Juli	1.464		März	1.021
	August	1.386		April	1.008
	September	1.155		Mai	1.015
	Oktober	1.059		Juni	981
	November	1.017		Juli	953
	Dezember	999		August	986
1923	Januar	1.003		September	982
	Februar	1.019		Oktober	999
	März	1.028		November	1.013
	April	1.031		Dezember	1.024
	Mai	1.030	1925	Januar	1.045
	Juni	1.001		Februar	1.048
	Juli	968		März	1.034
	August	958		April	1.019
				Mai	1.006

Quelle: Young (36, Bd. 2, S. 307).

Abbildung 1
Großhandelspreise in Österreich

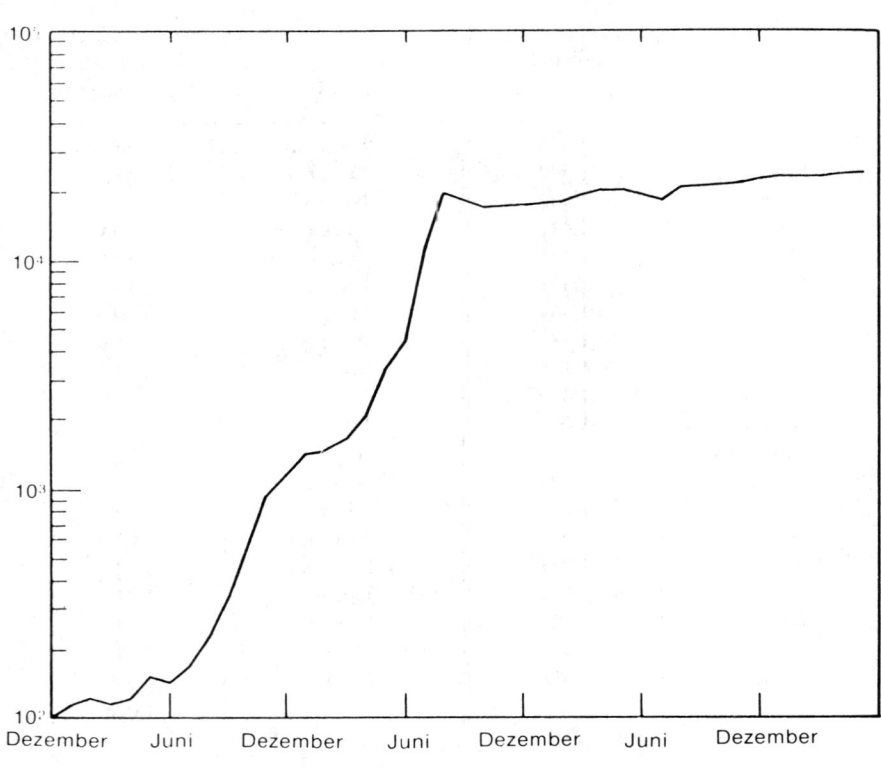

1921—1924

Abbildung 2
Großhandelspreise in Ungarn

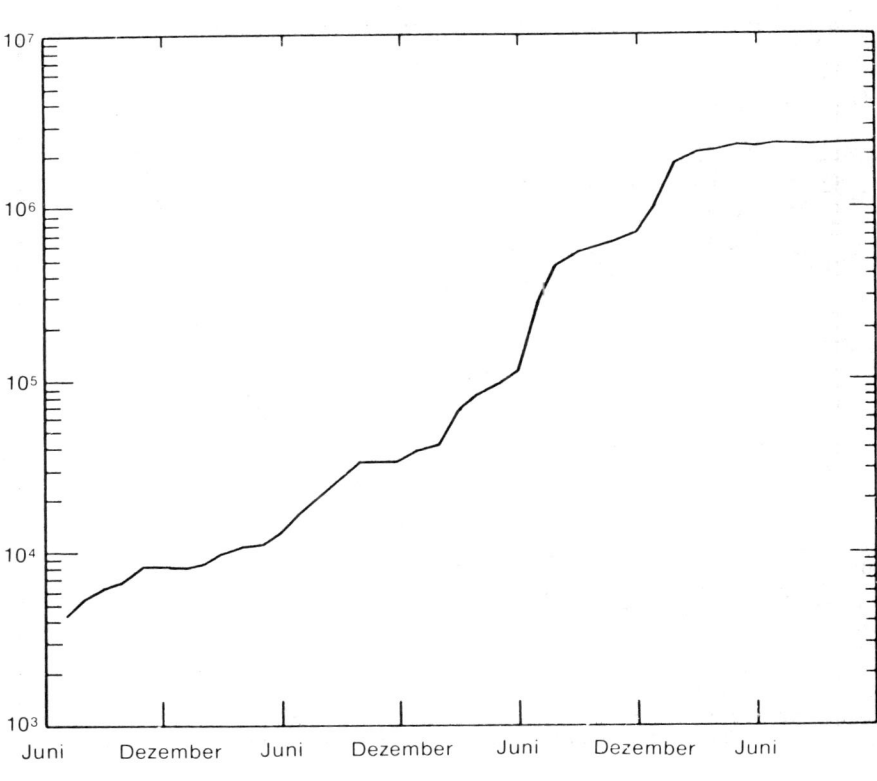

1921—1924

Abbildung 3
Großhandelspreise in Polen

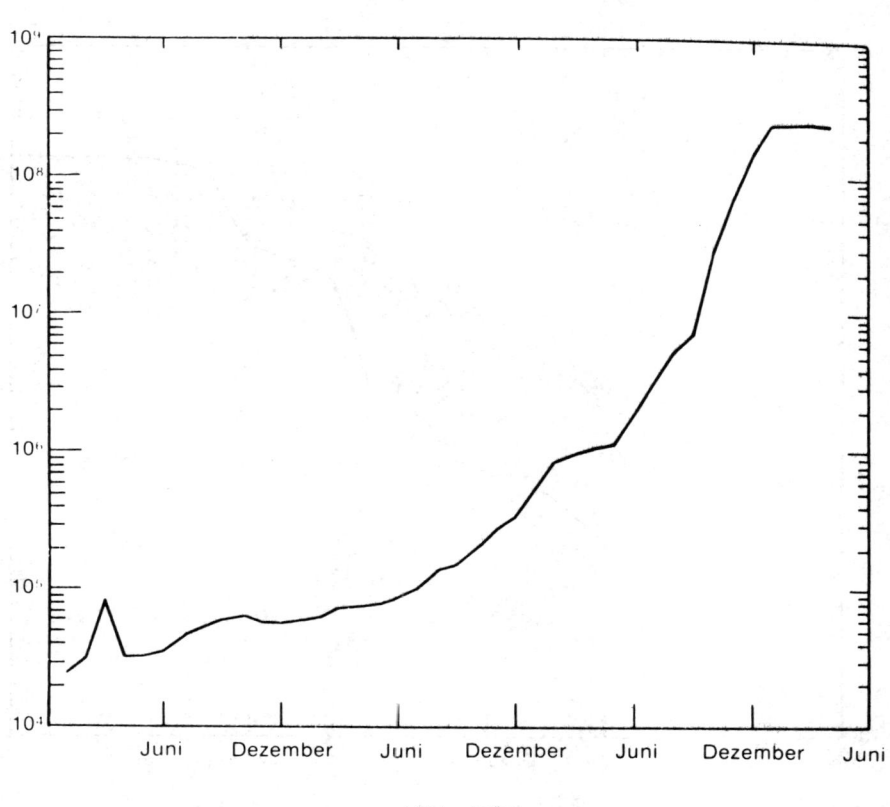

1921—1924

Die Beendigung vier großer Inflationen 103

ABBILDUNG 4

Großhandelspreise in Deutschland

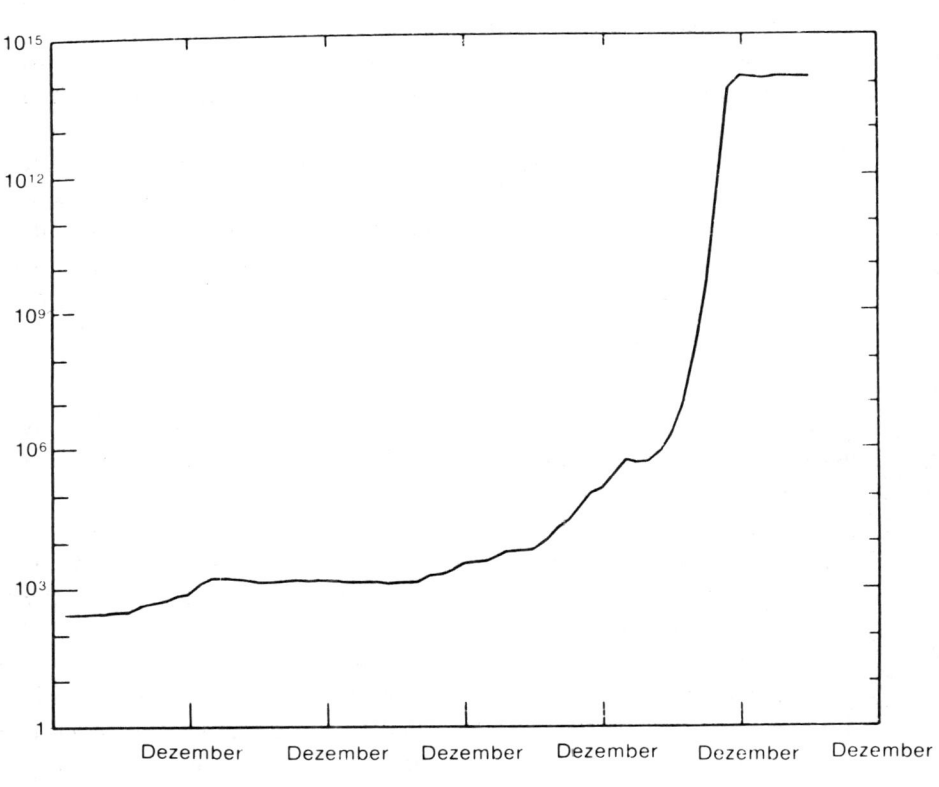

1919—1924

Summary

In his paper Sargent states that there are two views which explain persistent inflation in recent years:
1. (a) Inflation has a self-sustaining momentum the cost of eradicating which is prohibitively high, or
   (b) there is an underlying rate of inflation which responds slowly to monetary and fiscal measures, and which would cause substantial reductions in output and employment.
2. An alternative rational expectations view states that people expect high rates of inflation precisely because governments' monetary and fiscal policies warrant that expectation, i.e. the apparent self-sustaining momentum is actually due to the government's persistent large deficits. The implication of this is that inflation can be stopped more quickly than is currently thought. This is not easy, and requires an abrupt change in the government's policy *regime* as to the budget deficits.

The paper describes four historical experiences, believed consistent with the rational expectations view, in Austria, Hungary, Germany and Poland, where in each case hyperinflation was stopped abruptly. They had many features in common — persistent budget deficits, a deliberate fiscal and monetary policy to end hyperinflation, the immediate stabilization of the price level and the rate of exchange, a rapid rise in the supply of high-powered money after the end of the inflation.

Hyperinflation was in each case ended by restoring convertibility with the dollar, equivalent to a return to the gold standard. This implied, Sargent emphasizes, that thenceforth the governments concerned issued notes and other debts backed by the commitment to levy taxes sufficient to back such debts, i.e. by means of an appropriate budget policy. In this connection, Sargent notes that recent work in economics has established the principle that a change in a government regime will stimulate private economic agents to change their rules for choosing economic targets.

Sargent then describes the events in the four countries. All the countries
1. faced new national borders and trade barriers which cut them off from food sources;
2. faced a large unemployment problem;
3. had to make large expenditures on food relief;
4. except for Poland, faced large reparations claims.

In consequence they all ran large deficits, financed to a great extent by selling Treasury Bills to the Central Bank in return for money creation. As a result there were rapid price increases and falls in the exchange rate, leading to a flight from the national currency into stable foreign currencies, and further increases in prices and falls in the exchange rate.

In all four cases the currency was abruptly stabilized, even though the note issues of the central bank continued to grow rapidly. In the case of Austria and Hungary, the stabilization was achieved by the intervention of the League of Nations, which provided conditions for an international loan, and laid down a plan for fiscal and monetary reconstruction by establishing a new central bank, by the government agreeing to cease running large budget deficits, and by the government binding itself not to finance deficits by means of advances from the central bank. The two governments proceeded to carry out all the conditions required by the League, and, instead of being backed mainly by Treasury Bills, the liablilities of the Central Banks became backed by gold, foreign currency assets and commercial paper. The League of Nations also reduced and clarified their reparations commitments.

Poland achieved her stabilization in 1924 without foreign loans or intervention, but as in Austria and Hungary the government committed itself to a balanced budget and to a new central bank which ceased to make loans to the government. Although the note circulation continued to rise, it rapidly became effectively backed by gold, foreign exchange and private commercial paper.

In Germany the stabilisation was also achieved by her own efforts. It was accompanied by a „currency reform" which had only an important psychological effect. More important was the creation of a new central bank, with limits on the total issuable note circulation; government borrowing from the central bank was stopped, and the budget was balanced by a series of deliberate efforts to raise taxes and eliminate expenditures.

Thus the essential measures to end hyperinflation in all four countries were:
1. The creation of an independent central bank committed to refuse the government's demands for credit;
2. A simultaneous alteration in the fiscal policy regime.

Inflation and Stabilization in the Wake of the Two World Wars: Comparative Strategies and Sacrifices

CHARLES S. MAIER

The two world wars devastated monetary systems as thoroughly as they ravaged landscapes, cities and populations. Nations hardly welcomed wartime inflation, but they could still exploit inflation as a strategy for mobilizing national resources. Inflation had its uses in allocating productive energies first for wartime exertion, then for postwar reconstruction. The Bolshevik revolutionaries would liken inflation to the machine gun of the proletariat; let us carry the metaphor further. Inflation could serve to conscript monetary resources when the will to taxation failed: the continental countries drafted men and assets, while British society relied longer on voluntary social pressure and accepted heavier taxation than other countries to generate men and material for her war effort. Inflation could provide a scorched-earth retreat or guerrilla-like resistance even after formal hostilities had ended; nationalist circles and policy-makers in Germany understood this function well in the years after World War I. And inflation would also remain after the armies were disbanded, to corrode civic cohesion at home, as did the „psychologically undemobilized" veterans after World War I or the recriminations about collaboration after World War II. Monetary regimes in short underwent the trials and assaults of political ones in the era of world wars.

The problem originally set for this paper was one aspect of this monetary struggle: the comparative uses of inflation in the process of reconstruction after the two world wars. But the onset of inflation and the uses of inflation turn out to be only half the story of significance: Sarajevo or Verdun without Versailles. The problem of ending inflation is as historically significant and challenging as the course of inflation itself. As in the case of war, most countries tend to stumble into inflation, and we can speak of their „choice" of inflation largely as a preference revealed by their avoiding stringent efforts at stabilization. To undergo inflation certainly represents a result of national policies and testifies to implicit priorities that announced programs do not reveal. Still inflation is often a passive result. Ending inflation with its requirement of finally counting up the economic casualties and notifying the survivors entails the positive effort. Ending inflation requires confirming, or compensating for the social dislocations accumulated during the period of rising prices and recourse to the printing press. To write a meaningful evaluation of the role of monetary dislocation in the wartime and postwar periods thus requires considering inflation and monetary stabilization together.

This paper thus focuses on the related issues of inflation and stabilization in postwar societies. It addresses several key issues in turn. First, but most briefly, it asks what was the inflationary process? How did inflation develop and gather momentum? Can we mark its course like the widening interventions in the world wars from 1914 to 1917 or 1939 to 1941? Second, did inflation play different political and social roles after the First and Second World Wars? Similarly, did stabilization of currencies require different political and social exertions after the two conflicts? If monetary stabilization proved easier after World War II, why did it? Third, what role did inflation play within the international political economies that were reconstructed after the two wars? How must calculations about inflation change when, as is always the case, nations operate within the context of other countries' policies or transnational economic arrangements. Was there an inflation for victors and an inflation for the defeated, or more generally a monetary policy for world powers and another for the weak?[1]

---

[1] Earlier versions of this paper were presented at the conference on the German inflation held at the University of California at Berkeley in July and August 1982, then to the Seminar on Political Economy and to the Economic History Workshop at Harvard University. I am grateful to discussants at these presentations for valuable questions and suggestions. This paper seeks to refine and apply for a particular historical period the typologies of inflationary political coalitions that I outlined in *The Politics of Inflation in the Twentieth Century*, in: Fred Hirsch/John Goldthorpe (eds.), *The Political Economy of Inflation*, London-Cambridge, Mass. 1978, pp. 37—92. It draws upon contributions to the Berkeley conference that were then available in manuscript.

I

The Mobilization of Resources:
the Process of Inflation during and after Wartime

It is a useful starting point to distinguish three steps to the inflationary process in the wake of world war. The process of inflation refers not to its underlying causation but to the ways in which inflation gathers momentum and accelerates. The first stage derived from the massive resort to money creation to finance an extraordinary increase in public spending. The First World War, after all, required states which in 1913 had claimed, perhaps, only about 10 to 15 percent of national income for public expenditure, now to muster upward of 30 to 40 percent. Once the war ended, European governments were probably spending close to one quarter of their respective national incomes, as they still had debts to service and pensions to meet. That shift in plateau was accompanied by a decade of inflation. Unemployment relief, rearmament, and the demands of World War II moved public spending of Western societies probably to about a level of one third of national income. Although price rises in the immediate recovery from the Depression can probably be construed merely as the „reflation" of the earlier decline that had testified to hard times, after 1936 inflationary pressures grew beyond just what recovery alone might account for. The shift upward in public spending from the late 1930's to the early 1950's brought another major surge of prices and/or money supply — one that a British author who reviewed the phenomenon in 1951 termed „the great inflation."[2]

During these upward shifts in public-sector claims, taxation simply did not keep up with expenditure. During wartime, above all, expenditure was financed by money creation, largely by requiring central bank to accept government debt in return for legal-tender bank notes. To

---

[2] A. J. Brown, *The Great Inflation, 1939—1951*, London 1955. The range of public expenditure ratios to GNP must remain estimates in the absence of precise national income statistics for many countries. Perhaps the most reliable are in Alan J. Peacock/Jack Wiseman, *The Growth of Public Expenditure in the United Kingdom*, Princeton 1961. They arrive at ratios of 12,8 % in 1910, 26,1 % in 1920, 24,2 % in 1928, 30,1 % in 1938, 39,3 % in 1950 (p. 42). German ratios may have been higher before the two world wars: 14,8 % (1913), 25 % (1925), 42,4 % (1938), 40,8 % (1950). See Suphan Andic/Jendřich Veverka, *The Growth of Government Expenditure in Germany since the Unification*, in: *Finanzarchiv*, 23 (1964). For a compendium of statistics since the 1950's see G. Warren/Nutter, *Growth of Government in the West*, Washington, D.C. 1978.

take the case of Germany in World War I — whose behavior did not represent so deviant a case as has sometimes been stressed — the German floating debt increased from 0.3 to 55 billion marks. Half was taken up by financial intermediary institutions and represented, in effect, forced savings. But the other half was held by the Reichsbank and thus served as the counterpart for direct money creation. Paper money in circulation could rise, therefore, from about 2.7 to 33 billions (10^9) marks. The process of floating-debt expansion was to prove in general less devastating before and during World War II. After 1933 private industrial firms, as well as financial intermediaries, were required to accept government paper in Germany — a sort of compulsory „crowding out" that set limits on private investment initiative — and price control may have been more effective. The characteristic result in Germany and elsewhere was so-called suppressed inflation with a large monetary „overhang". How to cope with this potential avalanche of purchasing power was to become the most preoccupying financial policy issue of the Liberation period. And the debate over measures designed to „sterilize" this purchasing power recapitulated the conflicts after World War I that had accompanied the policies aimed at stabilizing already rampant inflations.[3]

Historians have often suggested that the reliance upon money creation to finance war costs should have been greatly diminished. But many factors militated against a less inflationary policy, especially in Germany and France. Antiquated tax systems, sharp class divisions, propaganda about the future fruits of victory limited the capacity for fiscal sacrifice. Moreover, tax burdens probably did increase to a degree that contemporaries perceived as a major claim. Order-of-magnitude estimates suggest that if taxes covered about two thirds of Britain's 12 to 15 percent of GNP as public expenditure in 1914 and then were raised to cover, say, one quarter to one third of the 40—45 percent of

---

[3] Carl Ludwig Holtfrerich, *Die deutsche Inflation 1914—1923*, Berlin-New York 1980, table 20, p. 64, for the monetary statistics. Gerald Merkin's essay in this volume *German Finance of the First World War and its Consequences*, suggests that money supply (not notes) rose by a multiple of 4,36, which gives less drastic an impression of inflationary potential. On the problem of post-World War II „overhang" see John G. Gurley, *Excess Liquidity and European Monetary Reform, 1944—1952*, in: *American Economic Review*, 58 (1953), pp. 76—100; and Fritz Grotius, *Die europäischen Geldreformen nach dem Zweiten Weltkrieg*, in: *Weltwirtschaftliches Archiv*, 63 (1949: II), pp. 106—152, 276—325.

GNP collected to fight the war, real tax burdens would thus have risen from 8—10 percent of national income to about 15 percent. This represented an increase in the tax burden of 50 to 100 percent or more, alongside of which the public was asked to subscribe to long-term war loans. Increasing a country's tax bill by a half meant, moreover, levying direct taxes on the lower middle classes largely spared earlier, or imposing what was felt to be virtually confiscatory treatment of middle and upper-class elements.[4] Even in financially feckless Italy the progressivity of „supertaxes" by 1919 approached a 100 percent marginal rate and income from interest and dividends was threatened by the registration of bearer securities. This measure, threatened later in France as well, would have identified bondholders and facilitated taxation hitherto evaded. To be sure implementation would be repeatedly postponed then finally cancelled by the Mussolini government. Still bourgeois circles felt a new degree of threatened burdens after as well as during the war.[5] Obviously the French slogan that the task of the Treasury was to pluck the chicken without making it squawk was an inadequate fiscal maxim in an age of world war. Still, even though more feathers were ruffled than plucked, the chickens did have reason for clamor.

The problem of war finance, moreover, was a two-sided one. One challenge was to place purchasing power in the hands of the state, but the other essential task was to preclude private consumption. Some degree of inflation efficiently solved both problems. In reflecting on the lessons of World War I, Keynes conceded its inevitability: „we also know that the political argument in favor of inflation is almost over-

---

[4] Sir Josiah Stamp, *Taxation during the War*, London-New Haven 1932, estimates that the taxes on an earned income of £ 200 rose from 4 % to 11 % and from 5 % to 14 % on an income of £ 1,000, while the overall burden increased from about £ 3,5 to £ 22 per capita, which would have been about 3,5 times in real terms. Excess profits taxes on firms bore much of the load (p. 219). French tax burdens are estimated (actually over-estimated because of the low national income figures used) by Jean Dessirier, *La progression des impôts en France et en divers pays*, in: *Bulletin de la Statistique Générale de la France*, 14, 4 (1925); also Edgard Allix/Marcel Lecercle, *L'impôt général sur le revenu*, 2 vols., Paris 1926. France lagged in direct taxes: only 92,000 were hit by surtax, farmers were largely spared, and the 7,2 % flat tax on wages and salaries hit a maximum of 2,8 million employees by 1923 and was then made more selective.

[5] Luigi Einaudi, *La guerra e il sistema tributario italiano*, Bari-New Haven 1927, pp. 130—131, 160—161. Perhaps more revealing than the actual tax burden, which struck businesses more than individuals and kept getting modified in any case, was Einaudi's use of terms such as „confiscation" and „decimation."

whelming. No one has to take the responsibility for inflation, not even the Chancellor of the Exchequer ... It will just happen. It is nature's remedy, ebbing up like the tides, silently and imperceptibly and irresistibly... It greatly benefits some important interests. It oils the wheels everywhere, and a regime of rising wages and profits spreads an illusion of prosperity. So if one is to bet on the field, inflation must always be the favorite."[6] As Keynes formulated the process, money creation and inflation allowed the state to coax extra work from labor through higher nominal wages, which could then be recouped by firms through higher prices, and finally could be captured by the government through greater taxes. As was the case with other Keynesian prescriptions, war finance relied on an initial degree of money illusion. Keynes understood, however, that illusion would soon dissipate, and he also felt that reliance on the inflationary mechanism alone was unjust: „It is no use to say that we got through the last war on a voluntary basis. No doubt we can get through this war in the same way if we are prepared to allow the same degree of inflation. But we do not thereby avoid compulsion. Compulsory savings or compulsory inflation? It is compulsory either way."[7] Keynes's own suggestion was a progressive withholding levy on income, to be divided, again on a progressive basis, between outright taxes and a loan, in the form of a blocked postal-savings account, that would be released when postwar deflation threatened. The forced loan would serve not merely to postpone inflation but could thus avert depression as well. For without a purposely accumulated monetary overhang, Keynes anticipated postwar depression, as did many forecasters in Britain and the United States.[8] In fact, rationing and shortages led to forced savings during wartime even without the Keynesian compulsory loan. Governments substituted non-market allocation of goods for the indirect rationing of inflation. They avoided

---

[6] Letter to *The Times*, November 28, 1939, now in Donald Moggridge (ed.), *The Collected Writings of John Maynard Keynes*, 22, London 1978, p. 77. See also J. Stamp, *Taxation during the War*... [see note 4], p. 213: „It is idle to state ... that ... inflation is unnecessary. This is a counsel of perfection."

[7] J. M. Keynes, *The Collected Writings*... [see note 6], p. 81.

[8] There were some exceptions to the concern about a relapse into depression. See Wladimir Woytinski, a Russian emigré then German trade-union economist and a drafter of the ADGB public-works programme in the Depression, who then ended up in Washington: „Economic Perspectives, 1943—1948," Social Security Board, „Memo No. 52," Now in National Archives, Washington, Pasvolsky Papers, Box 6.

varying degrees of wartime inflation at the cost of incurring varying doses of postwar inflation. They did not, could not, and probably should not have worked to eliminate all inflation.

The second phase of the inflationary process that we can discern in the wake of world war did not involve money creation during the conflict, but usually set in afterward. It entailed government and private-banking money creation to sustain private credit, keep industry afloat, and avoid recession, unemployment, and social unrest. Salient episodes include the period of German inflation, after June 1922 when the Reichsbank had to substitute for foreign capital imports by discounting commercial paper; during this period the private bills it accepted exceeded even governmental advances. Similarly in Italy during 1946 and 1947, and in Japan during the same postwar period business credits proliferated. These private-sector loans added further impetus to already rampant inflations that had originated with state deficits. The resulting inflations had to be ended by tourniquetting credit to firms with a forcefulness that angered businessmen along with spokesmen for labor. In Italy, Luigi Einaudi carried through this policy with the backing of Prime Minister De Gasperi and the implicit support of the United States; in occupied Japan, the Detroit banker Joseph Dodge arrived to dictate a restrictive policy to the Yoshida-Ikeda government.[9]

The third and final process of major inflation involved the everyday turn to foreign currencies for the denomination of domestic prices. Different indicators suggest that this process set in in Germany between late 1921 and mid-1922, as when an exasperated Carl Siemens, director of one of the Germany's major electrical concerns, burst out: „If a carpenter used an elastic yardstick one would call him crazy, but we are being asked to use rubber money!"[10] By this point, the society

---

[9] There is now a massive literature on the Italian reforms. For opposing evaluations: Marcello De Cecco, *Sulla politica di stabilizzazione del 1947*, in: *Saggi di politica monetaria*, Milan 1968; George H. Hildebrand, *Growth and Structure in the Economy of Modern Italy*, Cambridge, Mass. 1965.

[10] Cited from the Wirtschaftspolitischer Ausschuß of the Vorläufiger Reichswirtschaftsrat, August 29, 1922, Zentrales Staatsarchiv, Potsdam, Bd. 393, p. 246. See also C. L. Holtfrerich, *Deutsche Inflation*... [see note 3], pp. 66—67, and on reliance on the exchange rate for pricing: Gerald Merkin, *Towards a Theory of the German Inflation: Some Preliminary Observations*, in: Gerald D. Feldman/Carl Ludwig Holtfrerich/Gerhard A. Ritter/Peter Christian Witt (eds.), *Die deutsche Inflation*, Berlin-New York 1982, esp. pp. 44—45.

enters a period of self-fulfilling expectations of accelerating depreciation. It is with this third stage that hyperinflation can be said to begin. Even gallopping inflations need never really degenerate into hyperinflation; Keynes proposed in the 1923 *Tract on Monetary Reform* that money supply had to double every three months, or grow sixteen fold per year, for citizens to abandon pricing in the domestic currency. However, once this third stage of psychological flight from a currency does intervene, it is hard to stabilize without what Thomas Sargent terms a „regime change" (that is, without convincing institutional strictures on new note issues).[11] By and large this third stage did *not* occur in Western Europe after World War II. Although the German Reichsmark became increasingly unacceptable as a currency during the period of occupation, its loss of value occured in part because for two years a drastic currency reform on the part of the allies appeared imminently forthcoming.

To summarize, the inflations spanning the world wars and postwar years unfolded in three different processes: the inflationary financing of a sudden, major rise in public spending by creating government and central-bank liabilities; the financing of private industry by ready rediscounting; and in some cases, abandonment of the currency as a measure (and not merely a store) of value. The third process aggravated the first two, but it did not inevitably follow from them. Each stage of inflation corresponded to new policy choices, but choices usually resolved by passivity. As in a war that is easily or unforesightfully entered, but terminated only with difficulty, acceptance of a monetary settlement seemed repeatedly too costly. To understand the logic of the inflation thus requires thinking about the sacrifices of stabilization, long deferred and too often divisively imposed.

II

A Stabilization for Savers or Producers?

Faced unavoidably with some degree of inflation, how would different societies react? Granted that disorderly war finance left inflation-

---

[11] Thomas Sargent, *The Ends of Four Big Inflations* (= NBER Paper, August 1980; revised for this volume). Cf. Martin Spechler, *Ending Big Inflations: Lessons from Comparative Economic History* (= Working Paper), pp. 23—81, Foerder Institute For Economic Research, University of Tel Aviv 1982.

ary legacies, significant policy choises still remained at the outset of the two postwar eras. Finance officials could attempt rigorous and rapid monetary stabilization or they could defer it. In different countries they chose differently, more or less resolutely and with more or less conflict among the social groups that had an influence on decisions. Can the historian discern any pattern or logic to the differing approaches? How did the choices of stabilization respond to the structures of power and class at home, and the distributions of power internationally? We will address the first issue in this section, the international question, in the following part.

Consider first the German and Austrian hyperinflations.[12] While they raged, the two episodes reflected a latent inflation consensus in which industrial leaders and labor spokesmen found it originally more advantageous to acquiesce in inflation than to risk the unemployment and renewed social unrest involved in ending it. The early postwar consensus derived from the class stalemate left by the Central European revolutions, and it was reinforced in Germany by the broad national resentment against reparations: Why stabilize the currency ultimately for the benefit of the recent enemy? By the summer of 1921, the Social Democrats in the renewed Weimar Coalition saw the urgency of ending inflation, but found their demands for the needed tax reforms frustrated by key industrial groups. The Austrian and German inflations in short began with a shared acceptance that inflation was an acceptable second-best economic policy, less preferable than inflation-free high employment but less risky than recession. Labor groups repented of the inflationary stance first, but could not impose their preferred path to stabilization. Only when conservative forces and business spokesmen finally perceived their own interest also to lie in stabilization, could a political decision to halt inflation be imposed. Social Democrats ended

---

[12] For the Austrian inflation, J. van Walré de Bordes, *The Austrian Crown: Its Depreciation and Stabilization*, London 1924; for the French inflation, among other sources: Georges Lachapelle, *Le crédit public*, 2 vols., Paris 1932; James Harvey Rogers, *The Process of Inflation in France, 1914—1927*, New York 1929; Stephen A. Schuker, *The End of French Predominance in Europe*, Chapel Hill 1976, esp. chaps. 2, 4, 5, and Charles S. Maier, *Recasting Bourgeois Europe*, Princeton 1975, pp. 458—480. For the German inflation, the diverse titles of this series and still: Costantino Bresciani-Turroni, *The Economics of Inflation*, Millicent Sayres, trans., London 1937, and Frank D. Graham, *Exchange, Prices and Production in Hyper-Inflation: Germany, 1920—1923*, Princeton 1930.

up accepting stabilization on the conservatives' terms even though this entailed major political setbacks. In Austria the terms of Chancellor Seipel's foreign loan agreements in 1922 excluded parliament from altering the budget, while the SPD had to sacrifice the eight-hour day a year later.

Stabilization in Germany, however, presented a dual political aspect. Certainly it signalled a decisive loss of influence on the part of social democracy for the benefit of industrialists. On the other hand, it remained a victory for producer groups as a whole vis-à-vis rentiers and savers. Legal efforts to reestablish the value of private debts (insurance policies, industrial bonds) were successful only to a very limited degree, and the state debt remained annulled. Working-class spokesmen and industrialists shared the belief that revaluation requirements would burden German firms with crippling debts and taxes.

It is instructive to compare the German inflationary settlement with the French inflation. After continuing incrementally from 1918, franc depreciation accelerated briefly in 1923 and then more rapidly under left governments from 1924 to 1926. The French inflation, which for a few months in 1926 climbed toward an annual rate of 100 percent, was far less wrenching a social upheaval than the German one. Yet in a society that set great value upon savings, it also evoked a deep malaise.

Ironically the French underwent what might be termed a rentier's inflation, but a producer's stabilization. Inflation resulted from a general bourgeois reluctance to accept the costs of postwar reconstruction. Rebuilding was pursued energetically but in the hope that the financing of the capital expenditure would be charged to the German taxpayer. In Germany an effective tax and financial policy foundered on institutional impediments (delayed collection of taxes during a period of rapid depreciation) and fundamental social conflicts: the Socialist desire to tax industrial capital collided with business's insistence on immunizing corporate assets as a citadel of stable values. In France critical differences on fiscal policies divided even members of the victorious Cartel des Gauches of 1924. If German Social Democrats clashed with spokesmen for industry, in France the Socialists clashed with the representatives of middle-class and bourgeois bond holders; patrimony not production was at stake. When Poincaré stabilized the franc in 1926, he sought originally to redeem savings and to elevate the franc to its prewar level. But after two years of waiting, during which growth began to surge, the reluctant prime minister finally confirmed the level of the franc at one fifth of the gold equivalent it had held from 1803 to 1914. French conservatives had to accept the depreciation of their franc-denominated assets in part because they had resisted a fiscal program for stabilization earlier. France in short courted inflation because of the strength of rentier conservatism, but she ended up with a stabilization favorable to producer interests. Her earlier tax holiday precluded the currency revaluation that her bourgeois interests had yearned for.

In contrast to Germany and France, Great Britain furnishes the clearest example of a stabilization undertaken to satisfy financial interests at the cost of producer concerns. Earlier than in other countries British financial authorities determined to suppress the wartime pressures for inflation, which had continued to intensify during the ebullient markets of 1919. Despite taxation that was heavier in Britain than elsewhere, so the Chancellor of the Exchequer reported in April 1919, only 28.5 percent of wartime expenses had been covered by tax revenues.[13] The national debt at that date stood at £ 7.5 billion of which £ 1.35 billion was owed abroad and 1.4 billion represented floating debt. But at the moment Bank-of-England and Treasury authorities worked together in early 1920 to end the inflation they saw building, they leaned procyclically against the brief boom at the very moment it was abating in any case, thus producing the sharp recession of 1920—21. Similar restrictive policies had to be applied as Britain returned to the gold standard in 1925. It is noting the obvious to observe that the Labour Party was too feeble to forestall a policy that took high and lasting unemployment in stride. The collapse of trade-union unity on „black Friday" in March 1921 and the failure of the General strike five years later only revealed this weakness for all to see. The more intriguing question remains why the industrial interests in the Conservative party accepted so deflationary a policy. In part they were persuaded that any difficulties would be transitional. Exchequer officials also argued that a policy of paying off bondholders would allow saving to be directed into industrial undertakings.[14]

---

[13] F. W. Hurst/S. E. Allen, *British War Budgets*, London-New Haven 1926, pp. 242—247.

[14] Susan Howson, *Domestic Monetary Management in Britain, 1919—1938*, Cambridge 1975, pp. 12—13. French partisans paying off the state debt also differentiated between unproductive loans to the state and the productive ones to industry (those with a *contrepartie productive*). Excessive revaluation also marked the creation of the Czech crown after an initial expansionary start. See Zora P. Pryor, *Czech Economic Development in the Interwar Period*, in: V. S. Mamatey/R. Luza (eds.), *A History of the Czechoslovak Republic, 1918—1948*, Princeton 1973, pp. 192—197.

In 1926 Mussolini likewise opted for an over-valued exchange rate — the so-called *quota novanta* (90 lire per £) but without being able to claim the need to preserve credibility as an international banking center, that the City and British Treasury could offer. Rather, Mussolini chose a damaging exchange in part to trump the „Anglo-Saxons," in part to demonstrate his independence vis-a-vis the Italian Industrialists he wished to dominate, and in part because the fascist regime sought the support of the conservative middle classes and landowners who desired stable financial assets. While in the immediate postwar period British policymakers in effect adopted a course opposite to that of Germany, Mussolini chose the opposite post-inflationary policy from France. Poincaré came to accept the fact that property should not over-burden current production; Mussolini rebuffed his industrialists' pleadings, but largely to assure his political supremacy.[15]

Halting inflation meant that the period of disguising the costs of war and reconstruction must come to an end. What remained to pay could be thrown upon the shoulders of current producers — owners of industrial shares, managers, and labor — in order to preserve the value of bonds and savings, or upon the shoulders of savers to spare the implicit coalition of producers. To be sure, producers and savers were social roles often united among the same groups, and this contributed to ambivalent and confused political-party attitudes. By and large producer roles prevailed in Germany and came reluctantly to be recognized in France once monetary depreciation ended. Asset holders were rewarded in Britain and belatedly protected in Italy. (Industrialists could hardly complain in view of the labor discipline the regime provided!)

In each case stabilization did entail what amounted to an economic „regime change" in that new restrictive ground rules for money creation were instituted with sufficient credibility. But these were formal procedures and each economic regime change really rested on a major political change, namely the exclusion of European socialists from influence over national economic policy. In Austria Chancellor Seipel accepted the condition as part of the Geneva loan package; in Germany the SPD felt compelled to withdraw during the crisis of 1923; in Italy

---

[15] For Italy, Gian Giacomo Migone, *Gli Stati Uniti e il Fascismo*, Milan 1980, pp. 179—199; and Ch. S. Maier, *Recasting*... [see note 12], pp. 573—578, both with further titles.

decimation of the Socialists was a premise of fascism; and in France the Radical Socialists finally quarantined the S.F.I.O. Ultimately rescuing currency stability after World War I meant keeping the Socialists from power.

Let us move forward two decades to review the choices that were required in the wake of World War II. Almost every country had to face the problem of suppressed inflation even if, as in the case of Italy and France, open inflation had not already become critical. At the official rates of exchange the paper claims piled up in bank accounts had the potential to unleash a wild inflation, or might not be accepted in transactions whatsoever. The liberation governments had reflected on the problem of monetary overhang but arrived at different answers. The Belgian authorities returning to their newly liberated country in late 1944 quickly blocked bank accounts and converted them at rates that represented a sharp write-off of assets. Throughout the years that followed Belgians maintained a policy of hard money, convertibility of the Belgian franc and of strong central-bank influence that made them European paragons of stable exchange rates. It was entirely fitting that the architect of the Belgian currency reform, Camille Gutt, should go on to chair the new International Monetary Fund, which reflected the same priorities. Likewise the Banque Nationale de Belge (itself headed by the former Chairman of the 1921 Committee of Guarantees, Maurice Frère) along with the IMF and the division of the American Treasury for international affairs (IASIA) became postwar champions of currency convertibility and stable exchange rates. Brussels in effect became the anchor of American Treasury policy in Europe (not of overall American policy however, which often represented the more Keynesian precriptions of Marshall-Plan authorities) as it ran a balance of payments surplus with its soft-money neighbors. This rigorous monetary policy required a social consensus that emerged from the long-term triangular party coalitions in Belgium among Liberals, Catholics, and Socialists, and from a new pact of social pacification between unions and employers that amounted to a welfare-state charter at the outset of liberation.[16]

Blocking of accounts, conversion of currency, and the drastic writing-down of money assets proved a common pattern after World War II. It

---

[16] Leon H. Dupriez, *Monetary Reconstruction in Belgium*, New York 1947, and the titles in note 3, above.

ensued in Czechoslovakia, Austria and eventually Germany. There, of course, the Allies imposed reform in June 1948, although German memoranda and plans envisaged similar sorts of schemes. In each case of currency reform, naturally, policy makers and advisers gave thought to the sacrifices imposed upon the holders of bank deposits and paper assets. In each case the help finally provided, or compensation offered, was relatively low. To be sure in the German case a subsequent *Lastenausgleich* or equalization of burdens imposed a mortgage upon real property to benefit those who had lost property in the war or in subsequent flight from the East. But the original idea — embodied for instance in the 1946 Colm-Dodge-Goldsmith plan — of also compensating those who would sacrifice their savings by virtue of the currency amputation itself had to be dropped. Likewise the Belgian scheme provided only minimal redressal and redistribution of burdens.[17] In effect, the occupation authorities and the Belgians in the second postwar era resolutely took the decision that Poincaré had only reluctantly accepted in 1928, *i.e.* not to burden current production with the obligation of restoring money assets.

Not all governments accepted this choice. In liberated France, the young Mendès-France, de Gaulle's minister of economics, also proposed a currency reform along the lines pursued in Belgium. His measures incurred opposition across the political spectrum. French communists argued against monetary expropriation to demonstrate their respectability for postwar political coalitions. They sought to combine wage increases for their constituency and to woo peasant voters as well. Mendès also ran afoul of his colleague, Rene Pleven, at the traditionally strong Ministry of Finance when he brashly demanded a superministerial power that could only have aroused resentment and jealousy. Pleven claimed that in a society whose current national income was about half of that of 1939 (probably excessively pessimistic an assessment), rationing the losses by inflation would produce less demoralization and conflict than Mendès' levy on bank deposits. Stabilization had enjoyed a broad constituency in 1926 when the alternative seemed further erosion of paper assets. But stabilization had only a few suppor-

---

[17] For Germany: Hans Möller, *Die Westdeutsche Währungsreform von 1948*, in: Deutsche Bundesbank (ed.), *Währung und Wirtschaft in Deutschland 1876—1975*, Frankfurt/M. 1976, pp. 433—483. Also: Gerhard Weisser, *Die Gesetzgebung über den Lastenausgleich*, in: *Finanzarchiv*, N. F., 16 (1955/56), pp. 62—80.

ters in 1944—45, when it itself apparently required the clearest confiscation of the paper in the vaults. The Communists and many Socialists, spokesmen for the patronat, and de Gaulle, who himself acquiesced in the false prospect that economic revival would reduce inflationary pressures and that ministerial decrees might control prices and wages — all formed an inflation consensus against a handful of reformers.[18]

We may briefly consider the case of Italian finances. Between 1938 and 1944 Italy had already undergone a fourteen-fold increase in money supply and a sixteen-fold price increase. After a half year of relative stability, price levels more than doubled in late 1946 and 1947. Part of the difficulty derived from continued state deficits, as budget shortfalls lira depreciation, and price rises all raced each other in familiar sequence. Yet a major impulse also stemmed from firms seeking to produce and acquire material at all costs. While the Bank of Italy lent 109 billion lire to the public sector between July 1946 and September 1947, private banks lent 420 billion to firms in the same period. Stabilization came, not in the form of a monetary reform, but a stringent rationing of credit as effective fractional reserve requirements were finally imposed and banks were constrained to accept government paper instead of lending to firms. Advances to the state were also pared as Luigi Einaudi at the Budget Ministry and Donato Menichella at the Bank of Italy imposed what amounted to a new „regime." That it was also a change of political regime was indicated by the exclusion of the Communists from the cabinet before the reform and the subsequent defeats of the labor unions. A similar scenario was played in Japan, where even the conservatives followed a policy of easy money for industry until American authorities imposed an anti-inflationary credit squeeze.[19]

What generalizations can the historian derive from these diverse experiences? Political decisions centered not on the issue whether to accept inflation (it could hardly be avoided), but when and how to end

---

[18] Richard F. Kuisel, *Capitalism and the State in Modern France*, Cambridge 1981, pp. 191—202. Jean Bouvier, *Sur la politique économique en 1944—1946*, in: *La libération de la France* (= Comité d'histoire de la deuxième guerre mondiale, *Actes du Colloque... octobre 1974*), Paris 1976, pp. 835—856.

[19] For Italy, see note 9 above. For Japan see John Dower, *Aftermath of Empire: Yoshida Shigeru and the Japanese Experience, 1878—1954*, Cambridge, Mass, 1979, chaps 9—10; and the Joseph Dodge Papers in the Detroit Public Library: Japan Assignment, Box 1, F.: „Budget: Ikeda Interviews."

it. This meant resolving how finally to distribute the costs which inflation had imposed only in a disguised manner. By and large the societies that stabilized in the wake of World War II found it less acceptable to incur unemployment than those stabilizing after World War I. After World War I, Britain, Austria and Germany, and Italy accepted major unemployment and remained exceptionally vulnerable to it throughout the 1920's. Only France escaped more than a minimal stabilization crisis. But if unemployment could be taken in stride by policymakers, acceptance of the fact that savings had been lost irretrievably proved far more politically explosive. In Germany the revaluation crisis helped provoke major fragmentation of the political center. In France, Poincaré required two years to accept the fact that the patrimony of the good *père de famille* could no longer be reconstituted. In Italy, Mussolini insisted on revaluing as much of the state debt and other claims as possible. In contrast, after the Second World War Belgium led the way in blocking accounts and cancelling claims. Austria, Czechoslovakia, and finally Germany followed suit. The struggle over the value of paper claims, which had caused so much bitterness in the 1920's, could be accomplished with far less controversy. In addition, after World War II, although artificially high exchange rates were often clung to for longer than advisable, no society undertook the deflationary heroics of Britain or Italy in the mid-1920's. In return, unemployment effects were minimized except where, as in the case of German refugees from the East or Italians in the South, political or structural reasons kept many out of work.

Stabilization after World War I thus reflected the preponderance of financial and savers' interests; after the second war it responded to concerns of employment and recovery. After 1944 it proved easier to sacrifice paper assets. The first reason for the change was just the lesson that had been derived from the inflations in the wake of the first war. Then, economists and politicians and the public had to learn firsthand the sad truth that Keynes formulated so wittily in his 1923 *Tract on Monetary Reform*, namely that inflation represented a tax. The experiences in France and Germany revealed that rejecting taxation or capital levies did not really spare savings; inflation silently eroded their value to the same degree or more that tax avoidance sought to spare them. There was general understanding after 1944 that it would be better to face up to the losses at the outset and not burden the polity with the social and psychological tolls of acute inflation. (This insight did not always mean that the political will was present: obviously it could not be mustered at first in Italy and in France.) Prompt monetary reform, moreover, could also appeal to conservatives, for it might limit state intervention to a quick surgical coup, whereas lingering inflation might militate for a continuing demand for government planning and controls.

Political alignments also changed critically from one postwar era to the next. Stabilization after the first war had been achieved in effect by excluding social democrats from national office. This partisan operation was no longer feasible after 1945. The cooperation of socialists did not mean there could not be stabilization, but stabilization had to follow upon different terms, that is, without long, recessionary crises. Labor movements enjoyed a new and enhanced legitimacy after their sacrifices under fascism or in the Resistance.

Italy and France proved to be exceptions for different reasons. In France the working class parties opposed early stabilization along with key middle class interests. Stabilization was seriously attempted only a year after the removal of the Communists from the coalition (under René Mayer in 1948) and proved successful only when a renewed right-center party, the Independents and Peasants under Antoine Pinay, became the major force during 1952—53. In Italy, De Gasperi's 1947 government ousted the Communists and encouraged the approach of the traditionalist *liberisti* who returned to influence after a twenty-year absence. They indeed imposed deflation but without currency reform and at the cost of an expansionary policy. In France and Italy a pro-employment „Keynesian" monetary reform did not have support to prevail. Policy veered from an original acquiescence in inflation to a stabilization that avoided currency amputation. In effect, since stabilization ensued relatively late, both countries could dispense with Communist approval. They relied instead on American assistance to replace labor cooperation.

Although France and Italy hesitated to tackle inflation until American support was at hand, there was generally greater European willingness to write down assets or to block bank accounts and immobilize savings after the Second World War. Sacrificing bondholders and savers had seemed a graver injustice after World War I when a stronger bourgeoisie exerted greater influence. After the second war, too, aerial bombing, heavy civilian casualties (50 percent of those killed in World War II as compared with only 5 percent in World War I), and the uprooting of populations made the sacrifice of savings appear a small cost in perspective. After World War I the memory of gold money, of 3 percent consols and *rentes*, of money as the emblem of stability and the ligament of bourgeois society and families still remained fresh. By 1945 such an awareness was almost beyond recall.

III
Inflation and Stabilization in their International Context

To this point, analysis has been restricted to developments within each country. But a major reason stabilization proved less costly after the Second World War derives from the structure of international relations. The United States intervened to ease the constraints of international payments and their deflationary pressures.

The United States pursued a two-fold role as a „hegemonic power" after World War II. On the one hand, interested in benefiting from a multilateral system of trade and payments, American policy makers sought price stability and the convertibility of a key-currency system. On the other hand, until the 1960's Americans proved willing to subsidize the operation of the international economic system they preferred by helping to finance Europe's balance-of-payments deficits. Given the urgent needs of the postwar economies, this dual policy provided the incentive abroad for ending inflation. For not all inflation must be ended. Hyperinflations must indeed end, for they destroy the value of money balances and circulating money in general. But the chronic galloping inflation characteristic, say, of Latin America can be accommodated far longer. In the latter case inflation often persists for years and decades. This is the story of French inflation for a long period: a history of partial stabilizations in 1944, 1947—48, 1953 (the most effective), 1958, 1976, and perhaps 1982; of Brazilian and Argentine inflation, and of Israeli inflation. (Italy, often taken as a model of chronic inflation, in fact enjoyed enviable price stability after 1949.)[20]

Why end inflation? Why not resort to general indexation as a permanent regime? In general, I would argue, Western countries needed price stability to allow successful capital accumulation once the international economy was dominated by a leading economy that sought to impose

---

[20] See Ch. S. Maier, *The Politics of Inflation* ... [see note 1], for Latin inflation; and on failed stabilizations, see Thomas Skidmore, *The Politics of Economic Stabilization in Postwar Latin America*, in: James Malloy (ed.), *Authoritarianism and Corporatism in Latin America*, Pittsburgh 1976.

currency convertibility and multilateral trade. This does not mean inflation is incompatible with accumulation in all circumstances. Certainly it was not incompatible in the case of Brazil; the evidence is unclear during the case of the German inflation, but inflation seems to have abetted accumulation until mid or late 1922; and in interwar Hungary inflation seems to have facilitated capital-formation strategies. Nevertheless, it entails increased isolation or impoverishment to persist in inflation once the system-wide rules become those imposed by a leading country with a key currency and in search of multilateral exchange.

It was no accident that stabilization was sought in Italy, Germany, and in France after decisive United States intervention in Europe after 1947. Washington could then impose the rules of the international regime because it accepted the role of banker of last resort, the funder of Europe's current-account deficits. This acceptance meant that the concepts of stability enshrined in the IMF and the U.S. Treasury Department became the only viable path to growth and accumulation for countries that wished to benefit from American capital and not persist in autarkic development. Europeans brought stabilization on producer terms after the Second World War because Americans helped them pay for it.[21]

Yet let us look ahead. The very prerogatives inherent in the economic role of the key-currency country also suggested that the interests of the hegemon might themselves turn inflationary. This development was to characterize the third major era of twentieth-century inflation (1967—82), when the guarantor of stability, what might be termed the stabilizer of last resort, refused to pay for the public good of price stability as it had in the 1940's. (This was one reason why the inflation of the 1967—82 period, although not rooted in so profound an upheaval as either world war, still proved so persistent.) U.S. policy after 1960, in fact, followed similar British devices after 1944. Any country that enjoyed an international reserve currency, as the United Kingdom still did in part, might exploit its privileges of not having its own currency cashed in for gold or for another reserve in order to avoid the bruising

---

[21] On U.S. policies and their evolution: Fred Block, *The Creation of International Economic Disorder*, Berkeley-Los Angeles 1977; Charles S. Maier, *The Politics of Productivity: Foundations of American International Economic Policy after World War II*, in: Peter Katzenstein (ed.), *Between Power and Plenty*, Madison, Wisc. 1978, pp. 23—49; David Calleo, *The Imperious Economy*, Cambridge, Mass. 1982.

social conflicts of a stabilization program. It could have jam today and jam tomorrow — although in fact Britain renounced jam for a lingering financial imperialism. Between 1944 and 1947 Britain sought to delay the necessity of deflation by maintaining direct import controls with rationing and by reliance on her reserve position within the sterling block. In this respect she sought to exploit her key-currency legacy, much as the United States was to attempt when financing the Vietnamese War or pumping dollars abroad after 1966. I have labelled this strategy the inflationary thrust of the waning hegemon: a sort of international buck passing or perhaps pound passing to avoid deflation. In effect London outlined the approach as early as 1922 with the Genoa gold-exchange-standard proposals, then pursued it later in the 1920's when the Bank of England sought to keep interest rates low in New York or to limit the French Treasury from cashing in its sterling holdings for gold after 1927. In each episode Britain sought to avoid the deflation that would otherwise be required to sustain the high value of the pound. More systematically, Keynes' wartime proposals for the IMF-to-be, including the suggestion that a country in persistent surplus be subject to interest payments while nations in deficit should have extensive overdraft privileges — also reflected British interests in avoiding deflationary stabilization. During 1947—1948, London suggested further that Britain be allowed to pass along Marshall Aid to the so-called Suez-to-Singapore countries so that they might purchase British goods rather than have to cash in their accumulated sterling claims for dollars. (Washington did not approve the imperial international leverage that Britain was seeking to perpetuate and argued that scarce Marshall Plan dollars could only go to alleviate the European dollar gap, not of the world at large.) Later during intra-European payments negotiations in 1948 and during the negotiations for the European Payments Union in 1950, London consistently sought to insulate her economy against foreigners drawing out reserves with accumulated pounds.[22]

---

[22] For the events of the 1920s see Stephen V. O. Clarke, *Central Bank Cooperation 1924—1931*, New York 1967. John Maynard Keynes, *Plans for an International Currency (or Clearing) Union*, 1942, in: D. Moggridge (ed.), *Collected Writings...* [see note 6], 25, London 1980, pp. 177 ff.; also pp 46—47 and *passim*. For the 1948 suggested expedients, see United States Department of State, *Foreign Relations of the United States*, 1948, 3, pp. 442—443, 450—452, 486—489. For a general treatment, William Diebold, Jr., *Trade and Payments in Western Europe*, New York 1952.

From the viewpoint of the Americans, who, in fact, usually ended up granting London much of what she sought, these policies represented efforts to pass along the costs of an earlier hegemonic position that could no longer be supported: the economics of nostalgia. For the Labour Party then in power, and the civil servants framing policy, these approaches comprised a way to avoid a relapse into deflation and unemployment without the sacrifice of remaining imperial assets. Had not Britain incurred, in proportional terms, they argued to Washington policymakers, the major sacrifices of men and material in the common wartime cause? And of course, Americans who cold-bloodedly saw through the self-interest of the British after World War II sought to play a similar game in the years after 1967, first by inflationary war finance with a key currency; then by breaking the Bretton Woods requirements Washington had largely drafted and forcing a renegotiation of parities; then with efforts to force revaluation upward on other countries rather than allowing the dollar to sink downward; and finally, when allowing the dollar to sink, by exhorting strong-currency countries to take the lead in a pro-inflationary reflation (the „locomotive" policy of 1978).

These inflationary efforts of the waning hegemon sometimes provoked the resistance of strong-currency countries. To the faltering economic power, whether Britain in the 1940's or the United States in the late 1960's, such resistance appeared churlish, obstreperous, and deflationary for the system as a whole: a short-sighted failure to see the need for sufficient international liquidity. In the 1970's Americans argued that the German Federal Republic and Japan kept their currencies persistently undervalued, and that Japan especially would not play according to the rules of multilateral trade. But over the longer term it has been France that has been cast in the role of „spoiler" or dog in the manger: the hoarder of scarce currency and gold who refuses to see the international function of the privileged Anglo-American moneys. France appeared in this invidious role during the mini-crisis of the international bankers during 1927 and again during the more fateful events of 1931. In 1948 Paris angered Britain by instituting a two-tiered currency market that strained the over-valued pound sterling (at $ 4.10), while in 1965 de Gaulle took on not merely London, but the United States. Obviously the „waning hegemon" and the „dog in the manger" are reciprocal perceptions: one economy's over-valued currency must imply an undervalued one, and vice-versa.

It is only fitting that to complete the picture of inflation in an international context we return to the German experience of 1921—1923. For if the buck-passing of the waning empire is one international configuration, the other — applicable to secondary powers — is the implicit extortion-from-weakness of the second-tier economies: the exploitation of inflation to threaten sabotage of the international economic system as a whole. The German inflation served both to pressure London to resist French reparation demands, and to pressure Washington to pay for them insofar as they could not be resisted. In a sense Germany behaved as the proverbial maniac with nitroglycerin in a crowded room; putting her own society and economy through the wretchedness of the hyperinflation only made the threat plausible. There is, of course, nothing unique in weaker partners coercing stronger ones by appealing to the shared interest in system stability. The threat now operates across economic blocs: witness the case of Poland. And if monetary stability and multilateral exchange are indeed the shared value and the major goal of the guaranteeing power, it is rational to subsidize them when necessary.

What unites the two periods after the world wars, or perhaps the punctuated single epoch, was that the United States learned fitfully that is wished to enjoy the benefits of being a leading power in order to support a host of values it cherished — some political, such as liberalism, others economic, such as trade opportunities, high employment, and prosperity. In such an international political economy, inflation was viewed as counterproductive and harmful: harmful in the social ills it generated, and harmful in that it represented efforts (except when practiced by the United States itself) to isolate individual societies from the international economy. Inflation was thus a form of resistance to U.S.-sponsored integration and — no coincidence — largely overcome with the two major efforts at integration: the fragmentary and partial one of 1924—31, and the more coherent and purposeful one of 1947—71. During these periods United States bankers or tax payers at least paid for currency stability and for limited economic coordination. This required funding Europe's deficits and in particular funding Germany's international obligations arising from the two world wars. If inflation originated in war finance, it was overcome by the United States's financing of the remaining war costs. Writing the peace required paying for the peace.

In these respects the two periods of wartime and postwar inflation — 1914—24, 1938—49 (then Korea, 1951—53) — can be understood both in terms of domestic and international coordinates. In both periods the

United States could end inflationary expedients by underwriting the system of international exchange. This separates both periods, or perhaps the whole considered as one period, from the most recent major period of inflation since the late 1960's, when the guarantor of stability itself created monetary instability — perhaps because economic power was now escaping its grasp and no ready successor or group of successors appeared to take it up with cohesion and responsibility.

Summary

This essay seeks to compare the patterns of inflation and monetary stabilization during and after the two world wars. It decomposes the process of inflation into three phases: the initial recourse to treasury advances and floating debt to finance the sharp rise in public expenditure associated with the war; then a postwar continuation of easy credit to finance business activity and prevent depression; finally, in cases of hyperinflation, the public's abandonment of the domestic currency as a standard of value.

Following this exposition, the essay suggests that the two postwar periods followed different paths to bring wartime inflation to a halt. By and large — with the major exception of Germany — monetary stabilization after World War I aimed at protecting rentiers more than after World War II. Policy makers sought to prevent the writing down of money denominated assets or to reconstitute the prior value of currencies. By over-valuing their currencies in international terms Britain and Italy both sacrificed employment to savings. France initially courted inflation rather than accept stringent taxation: its bourgeois circles feared a tax on capital but ended up having to accept the levy imposed by inflation. But French policy makers did finally accept stabilization at a low rate that in turn encouraged business activity. After World War II more countries (first among them Belgium) froze bank accounts or reduced paper-money claims to quell inflation. In general statesmen were more willing to write down money assets instead of seeking to reconstitute savings at the cost of current employment, although Italy and France resisted the course of currency reform. There were several reasons: the accumulated experience of the Depression and the more powerful political position of organized labor after the defeat of fascism.

This paper finally asks about the international politics of inflation, including the British reliance on the sterling bloc to postbone deflationary choices. The paper argues that the final motive for monetary stabilization occurred when the United States encouraged stabilization as a condition for its investments (1924—29) or foreign aid (1948—53). To have persisted in inflation then would have meant renouncing American assistance. Until the late 1960's U.S. policies rewarded stabilization; thereafter the United States itself became a generator of international inflation.

ZWEITER TEIL
PART TWO

Inflation in Mittel- und Osteuropa

Inflation in Central and Eastern Europe

EINLEITUNG

von Peter-Christian Witt

Die Aufsätze dieser Sektion werden, so unterschiedlich ihre konkreten Fragestellungen auch sind, zusammengehalten durch ein gemeinsames Problem: Die Nachfolgestaaten der Doppelmonarchie Österreich-Ungarn, die Tschechoslowakei, Österreich und Ungarn, ebenso wie Polen sahen sich nach dem Ersten Weltkrieg vor die Aufgabe gestellt, erst einmal zu einer nationalen Identität zu finden. Österreich und Ungarn mußten sich mit dem Verlust des größeren Teiles ihres alten Staatsgebiets, der politischen und wirtschaftlichen Hegemonie in ihrer jeweiligen Reichshälfte abfinden und sahen sich zurückgeworfen auf den Status von Kleinstaaten, belastet mit den Kosten eines verlorenen Krieges, aber auch belastet mit einer administrativen und ökonomischen Infrastruktur, die unter dem Gesichtspunkt der Herrschaftsausübung über einen sehr viel größeren Raum aufgebaut worden war. Was vielleicht ein Gewinn hätte sein können, nämlich die Tatsache, daß weder Österreich noch Ungarn weiterhin mit starken nationalen Minoritäten innerhalb ihres Staatsverbandes belastet waren, wirkte sich so nicht aus, sondern entscheidender für die innere wie äußere Entwicklung wurde die Tatsache, daß ein Teil der deutschen beziehungsweise magyarischen Bevölkerung nicht in Österreich oder Ungarn, sondern in die übrigen Nachfolgestaaten, Polen, Rumänien und Jugoslawien inkorporiert worden war. Diese deutschen und ungarischen Minoritäten außerhalb der Grenzen des neuen Österreich und des neuen Ungarn belasteten einmal die Beziehungen aller südosteuropäischen Staaten sowie Polens untereinander, förderten die Abgrenzungspolitik der neu- oder wiederentstandenen beziehungsweise vergrößerten Staaten gegenüber Österreich und Ungarn und hatten wiederum für deren Innenpolitik die fatale Folge einer Stärkung der auf eine Revision der Friedensverträge drängenden Kräfte. Die Tschechoslowakei und Polen gehörten äußerlich zu den Siegerstaaten, besaßen Reparationsansprüche gegenüber den Mittelmächten, waren eingebunden in ein ihren Besitzstand scheinbar garantierendes Bündnissystem mit den Westmächten — und dennoch unterschied sich ihre Ausgangsposition nicht so grundlegend von der Österreichs und Ungarns. Nationale Identität zu gewinnen, war weder für die Tschechoslowakei mit ihrem aus den beiden Reichshälften der alten Doppelmonarchie stammenden Territorium und einer starken deutschen Minorität noch für Polen, dessen Reichsgebiet aus ehemals deutschen, österreichischen, ungarischen und russischen Territorien bestand und das sich zugleich deutschen und russischen Revisionsansprüchen ausgesetzt sah, die sich jeweils auf nicht unerhebliche nationale Minoritäten innerhalb des polnischen Staatsverbandes stützen konnten, eine leichte Aufgabe. Wenn äußerlich auch die wiedergewonnene Unabhängigkeit eine starke nationale Identifikationsmöglichkeit bot, so waren damit die praktischen Probleme der Staatsbildung nicht gelöst: Sowohl in Polen wie in der Tschechoslowakei mußten Gebiete mit ganz unterschiedlicher administrativer Struktur, unterschiedlicher politisch-kultureller Tradition und nicht zuletzt mit unterschiedlicher ökonomischer Entwicklung und Infrastruktur zu einem neuen Staatsgebilde zusammengefügt werden.

Politische Konsolidierung war auf jeden Fall für Österreich, für Ungarn, für die Tschechoslowakei und für Polen nach dem Ende des Ersten Weltkrieges die wichtigste Aufgabe, und sie wurde allen Staaten dadurch nicht erleichtert, daß sie, gleich ob formal zu den Siegern oder den Verlierern des Krieges gehörend, schwer an der Erbschaft des Krieges zu tragen hatten: Zerrüttete Staatsfinanzen, Inflation und das Auseinanderbrechen gewachsener ökonomischer Binnenstrukturen waren für alle diese Staaten eine gemeinsame Erfahrung. Hinzu kam, daß auch die wirtschaftlichen Außenbeziehungen neu zu regeln waren und daß hierfür nicht nur, vielleicht nicht einmal vornehmlich, ökonomische Rationalität der wichtigste Bestimmungsfaktor war, sondern wiederum politische Fragen, sei es die Sicherung der nationalen Unabhängigkeit gegenüber den alten Hegemonialmächten der Doppelmonarchie, so vor allem im Falle der Tschechoslowakei, sei es die Anlehnung an die Westmächte oder aber an Deutschland wie im Falle Österreichs und Ungarns jeweils unter dem Gesichtspunkt einer Revisionspolitik, eine gewichtige Rolle spielten. Auf diesem komplexen innen- wie außenpolitischen Problemhintergrund sind die vier hier zum Abdruck gelangenden Aufsätze zur Inflation in den österreichisch-ungarischen Nachfolgestaaten und Polen zu sehen.

Hans *Kernbauer* und Fritz *Weber* untersuchen die Geschäftspolitik der Wiener Großbanken in den Jahren 1914 bis 1925 und gehen dabei insbesondere zwei Fragen nach: Welche Bedeutung hatte die Kriegskonjunktur für die traditionell engen Beziehungen zwischen den Wiener Großbanken und der Großindustrie Österreich-Ungarns und wie reagierten die Wiener Banken auf das Auseinanderbrechen der Doppelmonarchie am Ende des Krieges und den dann beginnenden Prozeß der „Nationalisierung" in den Nachfolgestaaten. Beide Fragenkomplexe sind offensichtlich eng miteinander verbunden; denn die Wiener Großbanken beherrschten am Vorabend des Ersten Weltkriegs die Wirtschaft Österreich-Ungarns, jedenfalls soweit es sich um den industriellen Sektor handelte, durch ihre enge Verflechtung mit der Industrie als Kapitalgeber und Anteilseigner. Während der ersten Jahre des Krieges, als zumindest jede kriegswichtige industrielle Betätigung durch eine bedenkenlose öffentliche Auftragspolitik gewinnbringend war, lockerten sich diese traditionellen Bindungen. Die hohe Liquidität der industriellen Unternehmungen gab ihnen einen größeren Handlungsspielraum gegenüber den Großbanken, während diese zunehmend mit der Finanzierung des Krieges beschäftigt waren. Allerdings, und dies ist ein bemerkenswertes Ergebnis, gelang es den Wiener Großbanken offensichtlich während des letzten Kriegsjahres, einen großen Teil der von ihnen gehaltenen Kriegsanleihen wieder abzustoßen oder bei der Notenbank zu beleihen, so daß sie insgesamt am Ende des Krieges in der nicht ungünstigen Position eines Nettoschuldners gegenüber der öffentlichen Hand waren. Mochte dies auch ein Vorteil sein, schwerer wog die Tatsache, daß die Auflösung der Habsburger Doppelmonarchie auch die Auflösung der bestehenden Filialnetze der Wiener Großbanken und ihrer industriellen Besitzungen außerhalb des neuen österreichischen Staates mit sich brachte. Wie der österreichische Staat so hatten auch die österreichischen Banken die Wahl, sich mit dieser Entwicklung abzufinden und ihre Geschäftätigkeit auf den neuen österreichischen Staat zu beschränken oder aber eine Gegenstrategie zu entwickeln, mit der sich trotz der Unabhängigkeitsbestrebungen der Nachfolgestaaten auch auf wirtschaftlichem Gebiet dennoch die gewachsenen Geschäftsbeziehungen aufrechterhalten ließen. Die Wiener Banken entschieden sich für den letzteren Weg; er bewahrte sie zwar nicht vor Verlusten im Bank- und Industriegeschäft in den Nachfolgestaaten, war auch nur erzielbar um den Preis einer verhältnismäßig starken ausländischen Beteiligung an ihrem Kapital (wobei mit der Länderbank und der Anglobank zwei Institute sogar mehrheitlich in französischen beziehungsweise britischen Besitz übergingen), aber er eröffnete immerhin die Möglichkeit, etwas von dem alten wirtschaftlichen Einfluß in dem gesamten Donauraum aufrechtzuerhalten. Auch in ihrem Verhältnis zur Industrie standen die Wiener Großbanken nach Kriegsende vor einer ähnlich schwierigen Wahl: Der Krieg hatte die alten engen Beziehungen gelockert, nach dem Kriege bot sich die Chance, sich entweder auf die Position normaler Geschäftsbanken zurückzuziehen, das heißt, sich aus der allzu engen Bindung an die industriellen Unternehmungen zu lösen, oder aber durch ein verstärktes industrielles Engagement Wachstum und Rückgewinnung ökonomischen Einflusses sicherzustellen. Die österreichischen Großbanken wählten den letzteren Weg, wobei letzten Endes nicht völlig klar ist, ob sie wirklich eine Wahl hatten: Denn ihre Option für die Aufrechterhaltung einer über die Grenzen des neuen Österreich hinausreichenden Geschäftspolitik war nur mit ausländischer Hilfe durchführbar und diese scheint nur gewinnbar gewesen zu sein, weil sich die ausländischen Kapitalgeber gerade von der engen Verflechtung zwischen Wiener Großbanken und österreichischer Industrie einen ökonomisch lukrativen Einfluß auf den gesamten Donauraum versprachen, eine Tatsache, die unterstrichen wird durch die gleichzeitige Beteiligung dieser ausländischen Kapitalgeber an den Konzernbanken der Wiener Institute in den Nachfolgestaaten. Insgesamt freilich, so das überzeugende Ergebnis von Kernbauer und Weber, brachte das Festhalten der Wiener Großbanken an ihrem traditionellen Geschäftsgebaren diesen nur Nachteile, da die Industrie in Österreich während der Zwischenkriegszeit stagnierte, das Engagement in der Industrie der Nachfolgestaaten zu viele Risiken enthielt und in der Weltwirtschaftskrise hierdurch schwere Verluste für die Wiener Großbanken bis hin zum eigenen Zusammenbruch entstanden.

Während die privaten Geschäftsbanken in Österreich immerhin noch eine verhältnismäßig große Wahlfreiheit bei der Neuformulierung ihrer Geschäftspolitik nach Kriegsende hatten, standen der ungarischen Notenbank beziehungsweise ihren Vorläufern nach 1918 offensichtlich, wie Elizabeth *Boross* in ihrem Aufsatz darlegt, kaum Optionen offen. Zwei Revolutionen, Besetzung durch fremde Truppen, Konterrevolution und royalistische Putsche machten die Wiedergewinnung politischer Stabilität zu dem vorrangigen Ziel, dem alle anderen Überlegungen untergeordnet wurden. Wie schon während des Krieges wurden daher auch in den beiden ersten Nachkriegsjahren die Masse der — aus mannigfachen Gründen anschwellenden — öffentlichen Ausgaben durch Kredite — und das hieß in der Praxis durch Vergrößerung der Geldmenge — gedeckt. In dieser Phase der ungari-

Einleitung

schen Inflation lassen sich zahlreiche Parallelen hinsichtlich der Ursachen des Haushaltsdefizits wie der Methoden zur Finanzierung zur Inflation in Deutschland feststellen: Einer kaum wirksamen Besteuerung standen aus innen- wie außenpolitischen Gründen steigende Staatsausgaben gegenüber, und jeder Versuch, Einnahmen und Ausgaben der öffentlichen Hände wieder ins Gleichgewicht zu bringen, stieß auf den vereinten Widerstand von Arbeiterschaft und wirtschaftlichen Interessenten, da sie — wenn auch aus unterschiedlichen Überlegungen heraus — die politischen und sozialen Kosten einer Stabilisierung der Währung durch Beendigung der Defizitwirtschaft des Staates für weniger tragbar hielten als die Inflation. Auch nach der relativen politischen Konsolidierung und der Errichtung der neuen ungarischen Notenbank, derer sich die Regierung nicht mehr wie zuvor in unbegrenztem Maße zur Finanzierung ihres Haushaltsdefizits bedienen konnte, im Jahre 1921 ließ sich die Inflation nicht stoppen, sondern die Vermehrung der Geldmenge, der Verfall des Außenwerts der ungarischen Währung und die Preissteigerungen beschleunigten sich noch. Ursache hierfür war nun nicht mehr überwiegend das Haushaltsdefizit, sondern die überaus großzügige Kreditgewährung der neuen Notenbank an die Privatwirtschaft. Obwohl die Verbände von Industrie und Handel, die fast ausschließlich von dieser Kreditpolitik der Notenbank profitierten, ähnlich wie die Interessenorganisationen von Industrie und Handel in Deutschland damit argumentierten, daß in realen Werten diese Kreditgewährung eher unzureichend war und bei weitem nicht die Vorkriegswerte erreichte und daher auch nicht inflationär wirken konnte, sondern schon deswegen notwendig war, um die ökonomische Gesundung als die entscheidende Vorbedingung für den Ausgleich des Staatshaushalts und einen dann auch erfolgreichen Versuch zur Beendigung der Inflation voranzutreiben, läßt sich die inflationäre Wirkung dieser Kredite der Notenbank, die zunächst ausschließlich über die privaten Geschäftsbanken, seit 1923 aber für die größten industriellen Unternehmungen auch direkt gewährt wurden, nicht wegdiskutieren. Auch die Notenbank scheint sich nicht im unklaren über diese Folgen ihrer Politik gewesen zu sein; aber auch hier stand die Notenbank, wie Elizabeth Boross zeigt, vor einer Situation, die ihr kaum Handlungsfreiheit ließ: Ohne kräftige Kapitalspritzen ließ sich die Masse der industriellen Unternehmungen des neuen Ungarn nicht aufrechterhalten. Ausländisches Kapital, das vor 1914 zu einem wesentlichen Teil die industrielle Entwicklung Ungarns finanziert hatte, stand nicht beziehungsweise nur in unzureichendem Maße zur Verfügung; sollte die ungarische Industrie nicht völlig zusammenbrechen, blieb der Notenbank gar keine andere Wahl, als den Kapitalbedarf von Industrie und Handel zu befriedigen und damit die Inflation anzuheizen.

Das Auseinanderbrechen der österreichisch-ungarischen Doppelmonarchie nach dem Ersten Weltkrieg bedeutete auch für den Außenhandel der Nachfolgestaaten einen tiefen Einschnitt. Österreich-Ungarn war, auch wenn sein Außenhandel in den letzten beiden Jahrzehnten vor dem Ersten Weltkrieg verhältnismäßig hohe Zuwachsraten zu verzeichnen hatte, doch noch ein relativ autarkes Reich geblieben. Gebiete mit hoher landwirtschaftlicher Überschußproduktion und relativ entwickelte Industrieregionen, vor allem in Böhmen und Mähren sowie den deutsch-österreichischen Landen, ergänzten sich und sorgten für eine verhältnismäßig geringe außenwirtschaftliche Abhängigkeit. Sicherlich spiegelte sich darin auch die verhältnismäßig rückständige Wirtschaftsstruktur der Doppelmonarchie insgesamt, aber sich gegenseitig ergänzende Absatzmärkte für landwirtschaftliche und industrielle Produkte innerhalb der Grenzen eines Großreichs bedeuteten gerade wegen der relativen ökonomischen Rückständigkeit nicht nur Nachteile. Die Auflösung der Doppelmonarchie veränderte diese Situation schlagartig: Gewachsene ökonomische Beziehungen und Austauschverhältnisse wurden abrupt abgeschnitten und häufig aus dem Bestreben, gegenüber den alten Hegemonialmächten Österreich und Ungarn die neue politische Unabhängigkeit auch wirtschaftlich zu untermauern, eine wirtschaftliche Umorientierung eingeleitet, die für sich wohl das politische Kalkül, nicht in jedem Fall aber die ökonomische Rationalität hatte. Jonathan *Bloomfield* untersucht diesen Prozeß für die beiden am meisten industriell entwickelten Nachfolgestaaten, Österreich und die Tschechoslowakei. Obwohl beide neue Staaten am Ende des Krieges vor allem im Bereich der Nahrungsmittelproduktion vor ähnlichen Problemen standen und für das unmittelbare Überleben auf ausländische Hilfe angewiesen waren, unterschied sich ihre ökonomische Ausgangslage doch signifikant: Die Tschechoslowakei war das industriell am meisten entwickelte Gebiet der alten Doppelmonarchie (selbst unter Einschluß der überwiegend agrarischen Slowakei), seine Industrie war auch verhältnismäßig diversifiziert, vor allem die wichtige Nahrungsmittelindustrie verarbeitete im Lande produzierte Rohstoffe und war damit nicht von Rohstoffzufuhren abhängig, und darüber hinaus besaß die Tschechoslowakei eine beachtliche eigene Steinkohlenproduktion, was gerade in den ersten Nachkriegsjahren, als ganz Europa unter Kohlenknappheit litt, besonders vorteilhaft war. Österreich dagegen war in einer sehr viel ungünstigeren Position; zwar besaß es eine beachtliche Textilindustrie (doch handelte es sich überwiegend um Spinnereien, während Webereien kaum vorhanden waren, so daß Garn in großem Umfang exportiert und Stoffe dafür importiert werden mußten) und auch die elektrotechnische wie die Maschinenbauindustrie waren verhältnismäßig hoch entwickelt, aber dafür gab es mit Ausnahme einiger Braunkohlenvorkommen keinerlei eigene Kohleproduktion. Die Energieknappheit in den ersten Nachkriegsjahren traf Österreich daher viel härter als die Tschechoslowakei. Wichtiger aber noch als die ungünstigere wirtschaftliche Ausgangslage waren politische Faktoren: Österreich gehörte zu den Verlierern des Krieges, ausländische Hilfe, wie sie der Tschechoslowakei zuteil wurde, konnte nicht erlangt werden und, während die Tschechoslowakei als Siegerstaat volle Handlungsfreiheit in der Außenhandelspolitik besaß, seine Industrie also durch Hochschutzzölle gegen ausländische Konkurrenz abschirmen konnte, war Österreich dieser Weg versperrt. Hinzu kam ein psychologischer Faktor: Während in Österreich Pessimismus vorherrschte, vor allem nach dem Verbot des Anschlusses an Deutschland kaum jemand an die Lebensfähigkeit der österreichischen Republik glauben wollte, herrschte in der Tschechoslowakei eine große Zuversicht, daß sich der neue Staat würde politisch und ökonomisch behaupten können. Auf diesem Hintergrund analysiert Bloomfield die Entwicklung des Außenhandels beider Staaten und fragt dabei auch nach den spezifischen Wirkungen, die die Inflation, im österreichischen Fall, und die Deflation, im tschechoslowakischen Fall, für die Handelsbilanz, die Zusammensetzung von Exporten, die regionale Verteilung des Handels und für die *terms of trade* hatten. Schließlich fragt er nach den Rückwirkungen dieser Entwicklungen im Außenhandel für die Industriestruktur beider Staaten. Das statistisch sorgfältig abgesicherte Ergebnis zeigt, daß die bewußt deflationäre Politik in der Tschechoslowakei weder seine industrielle Entwicklung noch die schnell fortschreitende regionale Diversifizierung seines Außenhandels oder die Zusammensetzung seiner Exporte dauerhaft beeinflußte, während die Vorteile, die die Inflation zunächst für die österreichischen Exporte mit sich brachte, nur ganz vorübergehender Natur waren, langfristig sich dagegen eine deutliche Verringerung der Fertigwaren- und eine ebenso deutliche Erhöhung der Halbwaren- und Rohstoffexporte Österreichs ergaben.

Der letzte Beitrag in dieser Sektion von Zbigniew *Landau* und Jerzy *Tomaszewski* untersucht die politischen Voraussetzungen der Stabilisierung der polnischen Währung in den Jahren zwischen Ende 1923 und Ende 1927 und nimmt damit aspektweise den hier ebenfalls abgedruckten Aufsatz von Thomas *Sargent* wieder auf, in welchem die polnische Stabilisierung bereits als eines der Fallbeispiele für die Beendigung von Inflationen durch einen schnellen, grundlegenden Wandel der Geld- und Fiskalpolitik der Regierung diskutiert worden ist. Bemerkenswert an dem polnischen Fall ist zunächst, daß trotz der vielleicht besonders ungünstigen Voraussetzungen in Polen, dessen Staatsgebiet erst 1921 seine endgültige Gestalt erhalten hatte und das — betrachtet man seine Finanzpolitik — schon deswegen mit besonderen Problemen konfrontiert war, da es aus Gebieten mit vier höchst unterschiedlichen Steuer- und Abgabensystemen entstanden war, die Stabilisierung der Währung aus eigenen Kräften versucht wurde. Diese, im wesentlichen von dem Ministerpräsidenten und Finanzminister Grabski (Dezember 1923— November 1925) verantwortete Entscheidung hatte zunächst außenpolitische Gründe: Stabilisierung mit ausländischer Hilfe, die wohl sowohl von Frankreich wie von Großbritannien erhältlich gewesen wäre, hätte einen außenpolitischen Preis verlangt und hierzu war Grabski nicht bereit. Er setzte daher auf eine aus eigener Kraft erfolgende Stabilisierung und erreichte zunächst durch einschneidende steuerliche Maßnahmen und Ausgabensenkungen auch sein Ziel. Erst der Handelskrieg mit Deutschland im Jahre 1925 und die durch die Stabilisierungskrise geschwächte Wirtschaft führten zu einem neuerlichen Ansteigen des Preisniveaus und einem Verfall des Außenwertes der polnischen Währung während des Jahres 1925, so daß eine erneute Stabilisierung notwendig wurde. Landau und Tomaszewski argumentieren, daß auch diese zweite Stabilisierung aus eigener Kraft erreichbar gewesen wäre, da sich gegen Ende des Jahres 1925 die wirtschaftliche Lage verbesserte und infolge wachsender Exportüberschüsse die polnische Notenbank zugunsten des Zloty auf dem Devisenmarkt intervenieren konnte, wenn nicht durch den Sturz der Regierung im April 1926 und den Staatsstreich Pilsudskis im Mai des Jahres ein Moment politischer Unsicherheit zu einem erneuten Sturz des Zloty an den Devisenmärkten geführt hätte. Die binnenwirtschaftliche, insgesamt sehr positive Entwicklung wurde offensichtlich durch diese politischen Wirren nicht negativ beeinflußt; vor allen Dingen gelang es aufgrund steigender Steuereinnahmen und höherem Verkehrsaufkommen der Eisenbahnen das erneut entstandene Haushaltsdefizit von der Einnahmen- und Ausgabenseite her abzubauen. Allein schon durch diese Tatsachen verbesserte sich der Kurs des Zloty an den Devisenmärkten; eine volle Stabilisierung der Währung bedeutete dies allerdings nicht, da diese nur in einem festen Austauschverhältnis zum Gold und in der Einführung einer Gold-Devisen-Deckung gesehen wurde. Letztere erfolgte im Oktober 1927, nun allerdings mit Hilfe einer ausländischen Anleihe, deren Wert Landau und Tomaszewski allerdings zwiespältig beurteilen. Sie leugnen zwar nicht einen positiven psychologischen Effekt, der schon vor der Gewährung der Anleihe einsetzte, verweisen aber auf die hohen Kosten dieser Operation für den Staatshaushalt.

Die Wiener Großbanken in der Zeit der Kriegs- und Nachkriegsinflation (1914—1922)*

HANS KERNBAUER/FRITZ WEBER

I
Einleitung

Die Wiener Großbanken befanden sich im letzten Jahrzehnt vor dem Ersten Weltkrieg auf dem Höhepunkt ihrer Entwicklung. Das rasche Wachstum der Industrieproduktion, die im Jahre 1912 um fast 53 % über dem Niveau von 1900 lag,[1] hatte seinen Niederschlag auch in den Bilanzen der Wiener Aktienbanken gefunden. Deren enge Verbindung zur Industrie machte ihre Ertragsentwicklung in besonderem Maße

---

* Die vorliegende Studie verdankt ihre Entstehung Überlegungen, die die Verfasser als Mitarbeiter an einem von Professor Eduard März geleiteten größeren Projekt über österreichische Bankengeschichte gewonnen haben. Wir möchten an dieser Stelle Professor März für Anregungen, Diskussion und Kritik danken. Zu Dank sind wir auch der Direktion der Creditanstalt-Bankverein in Wien verpflichtet, die uns die Möglichkeit gegeben hat, Materialien aus dem Archiv der Bank für die Abfassung dieser Arbeit zu verwenden.

[1] Anton Kausel, *Österreichs Volkseinkommen 1830 bis 1913. Versuch einer Rückrechnung des realen Brutto-Inlandsproduktes für die österreichische Reichshälfte und das Gebiet der Republik Österreich*, in: Geschichte und Ergebnisse der zentralen amtlichen Statistik in Österreich 1829—1979, in: Beiträge zur österreichischen Statistik, H. 550 (1979), S. 706. E. März hat das letzte Jahrzehnt der Habsburgermonarchie wegen seines beachtlichen wirtschaftlichen Aufschwungs nicht zu Unrecht als „Zweite Gründerzeit" bezeichnet. Vgl. Eduard März, *Zur Genesis der Schumpeterschen Theorie der wirtschaftlichen Entwicklung*, in: On Political Economy and Econometrics. Essays in Honour of Oskar Lange, Warschau 1964, S. 371.

vom Gang der Konjunktur abhängig.² Die Wiener Banken hatten sich in den Jahren von 1890 an in besonderem Maß der Industriefinanzierung zugewandt, während von ihrer Gründung im dritten Viertel des 19. Jahrhunderts bis zu diesem Zeitpunkt das Eisenbahngeschäft und Kredit- und Anleiheoperation für den Staat im Mittelpunkt ihrer Aktivitäten gestanden hatten.³ Die Intensivierung der Beziehungen der Banken zur Industrie kann am Beispiel der Creditanstalt in Wien illustriert werden:

Die „Rothschildbank" erhöhte die Anzahl ihrer Beteiligungen an Wirtschaftsunternehmungen von zwei im Jahre 1890 auf 103 im Jahre 1913.⁴ Die „Symbiose" zwischen Banken und Industrie, die ihren sichtbaren Ausdruck in der Übernahme zahlreicher Verwaltungsratsstellen durch Bankdirektoren fand,⁵ entwickelte sich aus dem Bedürfnis der Banken nach der Erschließung neuer Tätigkeitsbereiche neben und an Stelle der traditionellen Geschäftszweige (Eisenbahnbau und Staatskredit). Aber auch die Unternehmungen selbst suchten die Verbindung zu den Aktienbanken zu vertiefen, da ihnen nach dem Börsenkrach von 1873 der Weg der Neuemission von Aktien weitgehend versperrt war und auch ein Markt für Industrieobligationen im notwendigen Umfang nicht existierte.⁶ Sofern Aktienemissionen durchgeführt wurden, erfolgten sie unter Mitwirkung der Banken, die nach einer Untersuchung von Reik⁷ in den Jahren 1907 bis 1913 rund zwei Drittel des Aktienkapitals von neugegründeten Industrieunternehmen in ihr Portefeuille nahmen. Nicht immer beteiligten sich die Banken freiwillig an

---

² Walter Reik, *Die Beziehungen der österreichischen Großbanken zur Industrie*, Wien 1932, S. 14.

³ Eduard März, *Österreichische Industrie- und Bankpolitik in der Zeit Franz Josephs I. Am Beispiel der k. k. priv. Österreichischen Credit-Anstalt für Handel und Gewerbe*, Wien 1968; Egon Scheffer, *Das Bankwesen in Österreich*, Wien 1924; David F. Good, *Financial Institutions and Economic Growth. The Evidence of pre-1914 Austria*, Phil. Diss., Pennsilvania 1972.

⁴ Eduard März, *Österreichische Bankpolitik in der Zeit der großen Wende 1913—1923. Am Beispiel der Creditanstalt für Handel und Gewerbe*, Wien 1981, S. 54.

⁵ Ludwig Neurath, Direktor der Creditanstalt, hatte im Jahre 1913 29 Verwaltungsratsstellen inne. Gleichzeitig war er Direktoriumsmitglied in fünf weiteren Konzernbetrieben. Vgl. *Compass* 1914, Bd. 3, S. 322.

⁶ Die „Abneigung gegen Spekulationspapiere", die sich als Folge der ungeheuren Verluste wegen des Kurssturzes von 1873 gebildet hatte, konnte in Österreich bis heute nicht überwunden werden: Der Aktienmarkt hat nach wie vor eine untergeordnete Bedeutung für die Mobilisierung von Investitionskapital für die Unternehmungen.

⁷ W. Reik, *Die Beziehungen...* [wie Anm. 2], S. 25.

Gründungen von Aktiengesellschaften, wie zum Beispiel bei der Umwandlung der „Carl Spaeters Veitschen Magnesitwerke" in die „Veitscher Magnesitwerke A.G."[8] In vielen Fällen wandelten sie „eingefrorene" Kredite in Beteiligungen um und plazierten die Aktien an der Börse erst zu einem Zeitpunkt, als die Öffentlichkeit bereits Vertrauen in die Lebensfähigkeit und Rentabilität der neuen Gesellschaft gewonnen hatte.[9]

Die beherrschende Stellung der Banken[10] im Wirtschaftsleben Österreich-Ungarns hatte Folgen sowohl für die Struktur der Wirtschaft als auch für die Entwicklung der Banken selbst. Von den strukturellen Auswirkungen soll hier nur die große Anzahl an Kartellen in Österreich erwähnt werden, die vor allem auf Bestrebungen der Banken, geordnete Marktverhältnisse an die Stelle der Unsicherheiten der Konkurrenzwirtschaft zu setzen, zurückzuführen war.[11] Die Rückwirkungen der Patronisierung der Industrie durch die Banken auf diese selbst zeigen sich insbesondere im Bereich der Liquidität und der Rentabilität. Die Wiener Aktienbanken hatten einen vergleichsweise hohen Prozentsatz der eigenen Mittel in „illiquiden"[12] Effekten- und Konsortialbeständen gebunden: Im Jahre 1913 betrug das Verhältnis von Effekten- und Konsortialbeständen zu den eigenen Mitteln bei den

---

[8] Friedrich Walter, *Veitscher Magnesitwerke Actien-Gesellschaft 1881—1951*, o. O., o. J. (Wien 1951), S. 49 ff. Carl Spaeter, dem Gründer der Veitscher Magnesitwerke, gelang sein Vorhaben nicht, durch die Umwandlung des Unternehmens in eine Kapitalgesellschaft die Mittel für die Finanzierung von Erweiterungsinvestitionen zu erschließen und gleichzeitig seine beherrschende Stellung in der Gesellschaft zu verteidigen. Wenige Jahre schon nach der Gründung der AG im Jahre 1899 wurde der Einfluß Spaeters auf die Leitung des Unternehmens stark beschnitten.

[9] E. März, *Österreichische Industrie- und Bankpolitik...* [wie Anm. 3], S. 297.

[10] Die enge Verbindung zwischen Banken und Industrieunternehmungen bezeichnete Gerschenkron als typisch für relativ rückständige Länder, die in den Industrialisierungsprozeß eingetreten sind. Vgl. Alexander Gerschenkron, *Wirtschaftliche Rückständigkeit in Historischer Perspektive*, in: Hans-Ulrich Wehler (Hrsg.), *Geschichte und Ökonomie*, Köln 1973, S. 127.

[11] Herbert Matis/Karl Bachinger, Österreichs industrielle Entwicklung, in: *Die Habsburgermonarchie*, Bd. 1: *Die wirtschaftliche Entwicklung*, hrsg. von Alois Brusatti, Wien 1973, S. 134 ff.

[12] Größere Effektenbestände waren auf der Wiener Börse wegen der Enge des Marktes nur zu einem beträchtlichen Kursabschlag zu realisieren. Der Hinweis auf hohe stille Reserven in den Bankbilanzen muß im Hinblick auf die geringe Aufnahmefähigkeit des Marktes beurteilt werden, die die Banken zwang, große Effektenbestände dauernd im Portefeuille zu halten.

Wiener Großbanken zwischen 38 und 57 % gegenüber 41,5 % bei den Berliner Großbanken und knapp 23 % bei den „Privaten Kreditbanken" Deutschlands.[13]

Die Rentabilität von Banken, die sich einen Industriekonzern angegliedert haben, ist größeren konjunkturellen Schwankungen ausgesetzt, als die Ertragsentwicklung von Handelsbanken englischen Typs. Die Gewinne aus Effekten- und Konsortialgeschäften sind besonders konjunkturabhängig und verstärken damit die sich prozyklisch verändernden Zinseinnahmen. Die Verzinsung der Wertpapierbestände inklusive der Beteiligung variierte bei der Creditanstalt in den Jahren 1906 bis 1913 zwischen 1,1 und 4,8 %, bei anderen Wiener Großbanken waren ähnliche Schwankungen zu registrieren.[14] Die starke Konjunkturempfindlichkeit der Ertragsrechnung von Konzernbanken begünstigt eine Dividendenpolitik, die bei längerdauernden Krisenperioden für die Banken existenzgefährdend sein kann: Um aus Gründen der Kreditwürdigkeit eine gewisse Konstanz der Börsennotierung der eigenen Aktien zu gewährleisten, werden die Ausschüttungen bei Gewinnrückgängen nicht reduziert. Auch das Überschußangebot an Aktien wird ins Portefeuille genommen, was einer Rückzahlung von Eigenkapital gleichkommt. Die Konzernbetriebe können zu einer ähnlichen „Kurspflegepolitik" angehalten werden, die, wie Ausch gezeigt hat,[15] einen wesentlichen Anteil an den Erschütterungen des österreichischen Banksystems in der Zwischenkriegszeit hatte.

Am Vorabend des Ersten Weltkriegs waren im Wiener Bankwesen keine Anzeichen einer Krise zu erkennen. Der Aufschwung der österreichischen Wirtschaft seit der Jahrhundertwende,[16] der durch das

---

[13] *Compass* 1915, Bd. 1, und Untersuchungsausschuß für das Bankwesen 1933, *Untersuchung des Bankwesens 1933*, T. 2, *Statistiken*, Berlin 1934, S. 100 ff. Die Vergleichbarkeit der Bilanzen ist wegen des Fehlens strikter Bewertungsvorschriften natürlich eingeschränkt.

[14] *Compass* 1915, Bd. 1, S. 431 f. und W. Reik, *Die Beziehungen...* [wie Anm. 2], S. 77 f.

[15] Karl Ausch, *Als die Banken fielen. Zur Soziologie der politischen Korruption*, Wien 1968, S. 343 ff.

[16] In der Periode von 1900 bis 1910 war das Wirtschaftswachstum in Österreich (Cisleithanien) sogar höher als in Deutschland, dessen Industrialisierung seit den 1850er Jahren eine größere Dynamik aufgewiesen hatte. Vgl. Hans Kernbauer/Eduard März, *Das Wirtschaftswachstum in Deutschland und Österreich von der Mitte des 19. Jahrhunderts bis zum Ersten Weltkrieg — eine vergleichende Darstellung*, in: Wilhelm H. Schröder/Reinhard Spree (Hrsg.), *Historische Konjunkturforschung*, Stuttgart 1980, S. 50.

Einströmen ausländischen Kapitals gefördert wurde,[17] hatte auch die Position der Banken gefestigt. Doch Krieg und Inflation sollten binnen einem Jahrzehnt den österreichischen Kreditinstituten derart schwere Schläge versetzen, daß sie sich davon in den wenigen Jahren der Hochkonjunktur in den 1920er Jahren nicht mehr erholen konnten.

II
Die Wiener Banken am Ende des Ersten Weltkrieges

Der Ausbruch des Ersten Weltkrieges verbreitete große Unsicherheit über die weitere Entwicklung der österreichischen Wirtschaft, die im ersten Halbjahr 1914 begonnen hatte, sich langsam von dem Konjunktureinbruch des Vorjahres zu erholen. Doch die Umstellung der Produktion auf die Bedürfnisse der Kriegsführung wurde zügig in Angriff genommen und erfolgte ohne die von vielen Beobachtern erwarteten Krisensymptome. Die Neuorientierung der österreichischen Wirtschaft wurde durch eine Vielzahl von direkten und indirekten staatlichen Maßnahmen erleichtert, die mit Fortdauer des Krieges zu einem immer umfassenderen Lenkungssystem ausgebaut wurden.[18] Für die Geschäftstätigkeit der Banken war, als erste in einer langen Reihe von staatlichen Reglementierungen, der Erlaß eines Moratoriums am 31. Juli 1914 von besonderer Wichtigkeit, das die Zahlungsfähigkeit der Banken angesichts befürchteter Angstabhebungen sichern sollte. Obwohl die Banknotenpressen mit voller Kapazität arbeiteten, war es der Oesterreich-ungarischen Bank in den ersten Wochen nach der Mobilisierung nicht möglich, den gewaltig angeschwollenen Bargeldbedarf der Heeresverwaltung und der Kreditinstitute zu decken.[19]

Die Inanspruchnahme eines großen Teils des Produktionspotentials der Wirtschaft für die Erzeugung kriegswichtiger Güter hatte bedeutende Rückwirkungen auf die finanziellen Beziehungen zwischen den Banken und ihren Konzernunternehmungen. Da die Heeresverwaltung die bestellten Güter prompt bezahlte — um den Krieg populär zu machen, schreibt Rašin, pumpte das Kriegsministerium in den ersten 14 Kriegstagen über 2 Milliarden Kronen in die Wirtschaft für Lieferun-

---

[17] Fritz Weber/Karl Haas, *Deutsches Kapital in Österreich. Zur Frage der deutschen Direktinvestitionen in der Zeit vom Ende des Ersten Weltkrieges bis zur Weltwirtschaftskrise,* in: *Jahrbuch für Zeitgeschichte 1979,* Wien 1980, S. 173.
[18] E. März, *Österreichische Bankpolitik...* [wie Anm. 4], S. 121 ff.
[19] Alexander Popovics, *Das Geldwesen im Kriege,* Wien 1925, S. 47 f.

gen zu weit überhöhten Preisen[20] —, erhöhte sich der Liquiditätsgrad der Unternehmungen sprunghaft, was ein Sinken des Zinsfußes und einen Rückgang des Wechselumlaufes zur Folge hatte.[21] Die Kreditnachfrage der Unternehmungen verringerte sich, während die Einlagen bei Banken und Sparkassen eine nie zuvor erreichte Höhe erreichten. In dieser Phase des Krieges waren Anzeichen dafür erkennbar, daß sich Teile der Industrie — vor allem die Unternehmungen, die für die Heeresverwaltung produzierten — von der Bevormundung durch die Banken emanzipierten.[22] Einen Hinweis darauf gibt auch ein Vergleich der Entwicklung von Debitoren und Kreditoren bei vier Wiener Großbanken vor und während des Krieges: Beginnend mit dem Jahr 1914, wachsen die Kreditoren stärker als die Debitoren und übersteigen diese im Jahre 1918 um mehr als 28 %. (Vgl. Anhang, TABELLE 1.)

Der reichliche Zustrom von fremden Mitteln verschlechterte das Verhältnis der eigenen zu den fremden Geldern bei den Banken kontinuierlich. Trotz einer Reihe von Kapitalerhöhungen während der Kriegsjahre war der Anteil des Eigenkapitals an der Bilanzsumme bei den zehn größten Wiener Aktienbanken im Jahre 1918 auf die Hälfte des entsprechenden Wertes von 1913 gesunken.[23] Die Bilanzsumme der zehn Kreditinstitute war im Jahr 1918 um ca. 180 % höher als 1913, das Eigenkapital wies nur eine Steigerung von etwa 51 % auf.

Das wichtigste Betätigungsfeld der Banken während des Krieges war die Placierung der Kriegsanleihen beziehungsweise die Erteilung von Vorschüssen auf die diversen Emissionen. An den acht österreichischen Kriegsanleihen im Nominalbetrag von über 34 Mrd. K. beteiligten sich die Banken (und Wechselstuben) mit eigenen Zeichnungen in der Höhe von 5,4 Mrd. K., das heißt mit einem Anteil von 15,4 %. Für die Unterbringung des Großteils dieser Titel im Publikum entfalteten die Kreditinstitute einen ungeheuren Propagandaaufwand, der den Apparat der Banken aufs äußerste beanspruchte und sie mit Agenden belastete, die ihnen bisher fern gelegen hatten.[24]

---

[20] Alois Rasin, *Die Finanz- und Wirtschaftspolitik der Tschechoslowakei*, München-Leipzig 1923, S. 14. Zwei Milliarden Kronen entsprachen im Jahre 1913 ca. 1 % des nominellen Bruttoinlandsprodukts Cisleithaniens. Vgl. Anton Kausel, Österreichs Volkseinkommen..., in: *Geschichte und Ergebnisse*... [wie Anm. 1], S. 718.

[21] Max Sokal, *Die Tätigkeit der Banken*, Wien 1920, S. 4 und S. 37ff.

[22] Stefan Müller, *Die finanzielle Mobilmachung Österreichs und ihr Ausbau bis 1918*, Berlin 1918, S. 58.

[23] *Compass* 1915 und 1920, jeweils Bd. 1.

[24] M. Sokal, *Die Tätigkeit der Banken*... [wie Anm. 21], S. 5.

Gegen Ende des Krieges versuchten die Banken ihre Portefeuillebestände an Kriegsanleihen zu veräußern oder bei der Oesterreichischungarischen Bank belehnen zu lassen. So stieg die Höhe der Lombarddarlehen der Notenbank allein im Oktober 1918 um 1,2 Mrd. K.,[25] in den beiden letzten Monaten des Jahres 1918 zusammen sogar um 3,6 Mrd. K. auf insgesamt 8,3 Mrd. K.[26] Ende 1917 hatten die Darlehen gegen Handpfand nur einen Stand von 3,4 Mrd. K. aufgewiesen.[27]

Die Veränderungen, die sich während der Kriegsjahre in der Geschäftspolitik der Banken vollzogen, schlagen sich nur zum Teil in den veröffentlichten Bilanzen nieder, die wegen des den Unternehmensorganen eingeräumten großen Gestaltungsspielraums nur ein ungenaues Bild der tatsächlichen Lage vermitteln. (Vgl. Anhang, TABELLE 2.)

Bei einem Vergleich der Bilanzen für die beiden letzten Kriegsjahre fällt in erster Linie das starke Anwachsen der liquiden Mittel im Jahre 1918 auf, das sich bei allen Instituten feststellen läßt. Darin kommt einerseits die Stockung im Wirtschaftsleben nach dem Zusammenbruch der Monarchie zum Ausdruck, vielleicht in stärkerem Maße aber das Bestreben der Banken, ihre Effektenbestände zu liquidieren oder zumindest bei der Notenbank belehnen zu lassen. In eine ähnliche Richtung weist der anteilsmäßige Rückgang der Debitoren inklusive der Effektenvorschüsse — manche Institute verbuchten die Vorschüsse auf Kriegsanleihe unter „Debitoren" —, die durchgängig im Jahre 1918 einen geringeren Wert aufwiesen als ein Jahr zuvor.

Durch die Abstoßung von staatlichen Wertpapieren beziehungsweise durch deren Lombardierung gelang es den zehn größten Aktienbanken zum Jahresende 1918 gegenüber dem öffentlichen Sektor eine Nettoschuldnerposition einzunehmen. Zu diesem Zeitpunkt besaßen sie Forderungen an den österreichischen beziehungsweise österreichisch-ungarischen Staat aus laufenden Krediten in der Höhe von insgesamt 1,5 Mrd. K.,[28] was 15,2 % der Debitoren oder 8,7 % aller Aktiva entsprach. Der Kriegsanleihebesitz betrug Ende 1918 ca. 600 Mio. K.;[29]

[25] A. Popovics, Das Geldwesen... [wie Anm. 19], Anhang.

[26] Siegfried Pressburger, Das österreichische Noteninstitut 1816—1966, T. 2, Bd. 4, Wien 1976, S. 1979.

[27] A.a.O., S. 1876f.

[28] Archiv des österreichischen Finanzministeriums, Wien (im folgenden FA zitiert), Zl. 89 309/1919, Stand der Banken Österreichs am 31. Dezember 1918.

[29] Ebda. Die Creditanstalt wies Ende 1918 einen Kriegsanleihebesitz von 44,9 Mio. K. aus: 88 % aller Nostrozeichnungen hatte die Bank zu diesem Zeitpunkt bereits veräußert. Zum Jahresende 1918 waren nur mehr 1,4 % aller Aktiva in Kriegsanleihen veranlagt.

Die Wiener Großbanken in der Kriegs- und Nachkriegsinflation 149

etwa 90 % der Nostrozeichnungen von zusammen 5,4 Mrd. K. hatten die Banken bereits abgestoßen. Diesen Forderungen standen Lombardverbindlichkeiten gegenüber der Oesterreichisch-ungarischen Bank entgegen, die zum Bilanzstichtag 1918 5,6 Mrd. K. erreichten:[30] Somit ergibt sich eine Nettoschuldnerposition der Wiener Aktienbanken von etwa 3,5 Mrd. K.

Bei der Berechnung der Nettoschuldnerposition der Banken wurden bisher nur die direkten Forderungen und Verbindlichkeiten berücksichtigt, nicht aber die Forderungen der Konzernbetriebe aus Kriegslieferungen an den Staat. Diese waren im letzten Kriegsjahr stark gestiegen, da das Militär bei der Begleichung der Fakturen in einen immer größeren Rückstand geriet. Die Höhe der Lieferforderungen der österreichischen Industrie an den Staat ist einem Bericht des Militärliquidierungsamtes an das Finanzministerium aus dem Jahr 1920 zu entnehmen: Danach betrug die Höhe der „liquiden, nicht beglichenen Forderungen der Gesamtindustrie Österreichs" im November 1918 mindestens 2 Mrd. K., wovon etwa zwei Drittel auf Unternehmungen entfielen, die ihren Sitz in der Republik Österreich hatten.[31] Welcher Teil dieser Forderungen auf Konzernbetriebe der Banken entfiel, vermutlich der Großteil, läßt sich heute nicht mehr eruieren. Doch auch dann, wenn man vom ungünstigsten Falle ausgeht, bleibt die erstaunliche Tatsache, daß die Großbanken inklusive ihrer Konzernbetriebe Ende 1918 höhere Verbindlichkeiten als Forderungen gegenüber dem öffentlichen Sektor (Staat und Notenbank) besaßen. Wenn man außerdem noch berücksichtigt, daß Rüstungsunternehmen mit hohen Außenständen im Jahre 1919 veräußert werden mußten,[32] wird die Tatsache erhärtet, daß die Wiener Banken aus den durch den Krieg veranlaßten finanziellen Transaktionen mit dem Staat nur unbedeutende Verluste erlitten.

Auch wenn aus den direkten Geschäften der Banken mit dem Staat nur geringe Verluste in der Höhe des im Portefeuille verbliebenen

---

[30] S. Pressburger, *Das österreichische Noteninstitut...* [wie Anm. 26], S. 2004 f. Der angeführte Betrag stellte die Forderung der Notenbank aus Lombarddarlehen an alle in Wien ansässigen Banken dar. Man kann davon ausgehen, daß der überwiegende Teil der 5,6 Mrd. K. Lombardverpflichtungen der Wiener Aktienbanken repräsentierte.

[31] FA, Zl. 55.021/1920.

[32] Das bekannteste Beispiel dafür sind die Skodawerke. Vgl. Alice Teichova, *An Economic Background to Munich. International Business and Czechoslovakia 1918—1938*, Cambridge 1974, S. 92 ff.

Kriegsanleihebesitzes resultierten, so kann daraus nicht der Schluß gezogen werden, daß die Banken den Krieg ohne Vermögenseinbußen überstanden. Im Gegenteil, der mit der Auflösung der Monarchie verbundene Zerfall des einheitlichen Wirtschaftsgebietes und die bald nach Kriegsbeginn einsetzende Geldentwertung[33] fügten den Wiener Banken schwere Verluste zu.

Der Index der Lebenshaltungskosten stieg vom Juli 1914 bis Oktober 1918 auf das 16,4fache, das Eigenkapital der Wiener Aktienbanken war nur um 51 %, die Bilanzsumme nur um ca. 180 % höher als 1913. Ein Vergleich dieser Zahlen mit dem Index der Geldentwertung soll aber nicht den Schluß nahelegen, daß das Vermögen der Banken Ende 1918 nur mehr einen Bruchteil des Vorkriegswertes ausmachte. Durch eine einfache Deflationierung der Bankbilanzen — was wäre ein angemessener Deflator? — können die inflationsbedingten Vermögensverluste nicht bestimmt werden. Folgende Methode der Ausschaltung inflationärer Einflüsse ist für Bankbilanzen adäquater: Die fremden Gelder sind mit den Ausleihungen entsprechender Fristigkeit zu kompensieren (Gläubiger-Schuldner-Hypothese). Dabei ist zu berücksichtigen, daß Kreditoren und Debitoren sich in der Zusammensetzung nach Währungen unterscheiden können, ein Umstand, der erst in der Nachkriegsinflation eine große Rolle spielen sollte, als ein größerer Teil der Kreditoren als der Debitoren auf „harte" Währungen lautete.

Die eigenen Mittel der Banken sind zum überwiegenden Teil langfristig gebunden: in Grundstücken und Gebäuden, in Wertpapieren und in langfristigen Ausleihungen. Die Entwicklung des Eigenvermögens der Banken während einer Inflation ist im wesentlichen davon abhängig, wie sich die Bewertung der „illiquiden" Vermögensteile in Relation zur Preissteigerungsrate entwickelt.

Wie hoch der Rückgang des Reinvermögens der Banken im Zeitraum 1913 bis 1918 war, weil die Obligationenkurse in dieser Zeit weitgehend konstant blieben und die Steigerung der Aktienkurse geringer war als die Inflationsrate,[34] läßt sich aus den Bilanzen aus zwei Gründen nicht bestimmen: Zum einen war die Bewertung der Aktien zum Jahresende 1918 angesichts der weitgehenden Unsicherheit über die allgemeine politische und wirtschaftliche Zukunft im allgemeinen, das Schicksal einzelner Unternehmungen (in den Sukzessionsstaaten) im beson-

---

[33] Über die Entwicklung des Binnen- und des Außenwertes der Krone in den Jahren 1914—1922 gibt das Diagramm 1 im Anhang Auskunft.
[34] M. Sokal, Die Tätigkeit der Banken... [wie Anm. 21], S. 44f.

ren, vollkommen willkürlich, zum anderen ist aus den veröffentlichten Zahlen kein Aufschluß über die Struktur der Debitoren und Kreditoren hinsichtlich der Fristigkeit und Währungszusammensetzung zu gewinnen. In den darauffolgenden Jahren wurden die Bilanzen noch unübersichtlicher. Die Bilanzierungsmethoden divergierten nicht bloß von Bank zu Bank, sie änderten sich auch bei den einzelnen Instituten manchmal von Jahr zu Jahr.[35]

In den Bilanzen der Jahre 1919 bis 1923 erscheinen die Einflüsse der Inflation vermengt mit den Auswirkungen des Zerfalls der Monarchie. Die Konturen des daraus zu gewinnenden Bildes sind aber zu unscharf, als daß sie eine quantitative Analyse ermöglichten. Eine Bilanz der Substanzverluste der Wiener Banken kann somit erst mit der Neubewertung aller Vermögenspositionen in den Goldbilanzen (zum 1. Januar 1925) gezogen werden. Die Veränderungen gegenüber der Vorkriegszeit sind dabei teils auf die Geldentwertung, teils auf den Verlust wichtiger Beteiligungen, die von den Nachfolgestaaten „nationalisiert" wurden, zurückzuführen.

III

Die Reaktion der Wiener Großbanken auf den Zerfall der Donaumonarchie

Der militärische und politische Zusammenbruch Österreich-Ungarns war begleitet von einer Welle des Nationalismus auch auf ökonomischem Gebiet. Die neuen Regierungen in Prag, Belgrad usw. propagierten die politische *und* wirtschaftliche Selbständigkeit ihrer Staatsgebilde, die „Nationalisierung" der Industrie und des Kreditwesens. Die Einflußsphäre der Wiener Banken in den Nachfolgestaaten (Filialen

---

[35] Siehe: *Compass* 1921—1925, jeweils Bd. 1. So ist es z. B. unmöglich, den Bilanzen der Jahre 1919—1923 Informationen über die tatsächliche Höhe der Kreditoren und Debitoren zu entnehmen: Im Fall der Niederösterreichischen Escomptegesellschaft wurden die beiden Posten, soweit sie auf fremde Währungen lauteten, zum Vorkriegskurs eingestellt; ab 1920 wurden auf gleiche Währung lautende Konti, soweit sie sich kompensierten, in Friedenskronen eingesetzt und nur die Saldi zum Kurs des Bilanztages verbucht. Bei der Creditanstalt wurden seit 1921 Debitoren und Kreditoren in fremder Währung weitgehend kompensiert und nur die Saldi in Kronen umgerechnet. Dem Vorgehen der Creditanstalt schlossen sich auch der Wiener Bankverein und die Bodencreditanstalt an. Andere Banken nahmen keine Kompensationen vor oder rechneten Konti, die auf Nachfolgestaatenwährungen lauteten, im Verhältnis 1:1 in österreichische Kronen um.

und Industriebeteiligungen) schien aufs schwerste gefährdet. Auf diese Herausforderung waren zwei alternative Antworten möglich:
— Ein genereller Rückzug der Banken aus dem Donauraum (bei gleichzeitiger Reduzierung des Bankapparats) und Konzentration auf die Bedürfnisse der österreichischen Volkswirtschaft.
— Der Versuch einer Verteidigung der traditionellen Interessengebiete (womöglich mit Unterstützung ausländischer Bündnispartner).

Der Weg der „Austrifizierung" des Wiener Banksektors, der vor allem vom ehemaligen Generaldirektor der Creditanstalt und nunmehrigem Gouverneur der Österreichisch-ungarischen Bank, Alexander Spitzmüller, befürwortet wurde, stieß bei den Vertretern der Großbanken auf ungeteilte Ablehnung.[36] Die Entscheidung für die „Multinationalisierung" fiel daher sehr rasch; sie wurde vom damaligen Finanzminister Joseph Schumpeter unterstützt[37] und entsprach auch den Anschauungen eines Großteils der österreichischen Industrie.[38] Konzediert wurde allenfalls ein gewisser „taktischer" Rückzug aus Positionen im „Neuausland" — auf Grund politischen oder administrativen Drucks oder vorübergehender Schwierigkeiten bei der Finanzierung der außerhalb Österreichs gelegenen Konzernunternehmen.

Einen charakteristischen Niederschlag fand diese Haltung in einem Memorandum mit dem Titel „Gegenwärtiger Stand und Zukunft der Banken Österreichs", das Paul Hammerschlag, ein Mitglied der Direktion der Creditanstalt, im Herbst 1919 verfaßte. Hammerschlag schloß zwar die Möglichkeit einer gewissen Einschränkung des zukünftigen Wirkungskreises der Berliner Banken „infolge der Bildung der Sukzessionsstaaten und der Zerspaltung der ehemaligen österreichisch-ungarischen Währung" nicht aus; er hielt es sogar für möglich, „daß aus diesem Grunde Umwandlungen (Fusionierungen) stattfinden werden". Seine optimistische Prognose gipfelte jedoch in der Feststellung: „Aber zunächst wird die große Geschäftserfahrung und die internationale Stellung der Wiener Banken und insbesondere das Vertrauen, das sie im

---

[36] Alexander Spitzmüller, „... und hat auch Ursach' es zu lieben", Wien 1955, S. 332. Ähnliche Ansichten finden sich auch im sogenannten Steirischen Wirtschaftsprogramm der Christlich-sozialen aus dem Jahr 1925. Siehe dazu: Jacob Ahrer, *Erlebte Zeitgeschichte*, Wien-Leipzig 1930, S. 213 ff.

[37] Siehe: E. März, *Österreichische Bankpolitik*... [wie Anm. 4], S. 333 ff.

[38] Siehe: *Berichte und Anträge der wirtschaftlichen Korporationen Deutschösterreichs zu den Bedingungen des Friedens mit Österreich*, Wien 1919.

Die Wiener Großbanken in der Kriegs- und Nachkriegsinflation 153

internationalen Verkehr genießen, wohl auch für die Zukunft ihre Bedeutung behalten, und es werden sich aus den wirtschaftlichen Beziehungen, die zwischen den Sukzessionsstaaten und Deutschösterreich naturnotwendig eintreten müssen, zweifellos neue Impulse für die Tätigkeit der Wiener Institute ergeben."[39]

In den ersten Jahren nach 1918 waren die Wiener Banken daher in ein zähes Ringen um die Aufrechterhaltung ihres Besitzes im „Neuausland" verwickelt, wobei sich bald herausstellte, daß eine Weiterführung des alten Filialnetzes unmöglich war. Die in den Nachfolgestaaten gelegenen Zweigstellen mußten entweder in selbständige Banken umgewandelt oder bereits bestehenden Kreditinstituten angegliedert werden. Von den 144 ausländischen Filialen der zehn größten Wiener Banken waren im Jahr 1924 nur mehr neun vorhanden, davon als einzig bedeutende die Budapester Niederlassung des Bankvereins.[40] In der folgenden Zusammenstellung sind die neuen Kreditinstitute, an denen die vier österreichischen Großbanken (Creditanstalt, Bodencreditanstalt, Bankverein und Escomptegesellschaft) mit zum Teil beträchtlichen Quoten beteiligt blieben, angeführt.[41]

Beteiligungen der Wiener Großbanken an Kreditinstituten in den Nachfolgestaaten (Stand Ende 1923)

Tschechoslowakei

Böhmische Escomptebank und
Kreditanstalt* (1919)** . . . . Creditanstalt (22,5 %), Escomptegesellschaft (22,5 %)
Allgemeiner Böhmischer Bankverein* (1921) . . . . Bankverein (35 %)
Slowakische Allgemeine Kreditbank (1921) . . . . Creditanstalt

Polen

Warschauer Discontobank* (1919) . . . . Creditanstalt (30 %)
Galizische Aktien-Hypothekenbank* (1919) . . . . Creditanstalt (30 %)
Bank Malopolski (1920) . . . . Bodencreditanstalt
Schlesische Kredit-Anstalt (1921) . . . . Creditanstalt
Allgemeiner Bankverein in Polen* (1923) . . . . Bankverein (40 %)

---

[39] FA, Zl. 83.623/1919.
[40] Quelle: *Compass* 1919 und 1925, jeweils Bd. 1. Siehe auch: Anhang, TABELLE 4.
[41] Auch die Wiener Mittelbanken (Depositenbank, Mercurbank, Unionbank und Verkehrsbank) trafen bezüglich ihrer neuausländischen Filialen ähnliche Arrangements.

Jugoslawien***

Kreditanstalt für Handel und
Industrie, Laibach* (1919) .... Creditanstalt (vermutlich Majorität)
Kroatische Allgemeine Kreditbank (1921) .... Creditanstalt, Bodencreditanstalt
Kroatisch-Slawonische Landes-Hypothekenbank (1921)......... Bodencreditanstalt
Agrar- und Industriebank, Belgrad (1923) .... Creditanstalt

    * Durch Umwandlung oder Einbringung von Filialen entstanden. Bei den übrigen angeführten Banken handelt es sich entweder um Neugründungen oder um den Erwerb größerer Aktienposten durch Wiener Institute.
    ** Gründungsjahr bzw. Jahr der Beteiligung
    *** Der Wiener Bankverein wandelte seine jugoslawischen Filialen erst Anfang 1929 in den *Allgemeinen Jugoslawischen Bankverein* um. Das Institut war 1922 kurzfristig auch an der *Laibacher Kreditbank* beteiligt.

Quellen: *Compass* 1925, Bd. 1; 1930, Bd. 1. Verwaltungsrats-Protokolle der Creditanstalt. Administrationsrats-Protokolle des Bankvereins.

Neben den eben angeführten Banken gab es in den Nachfolgestaaten noch andere Institute, die Beteiligungen von Wiener Großbanken aus der Zeit vor 1918 aufwiesen: die *Landesbank für Bosnien und Hercegovina* (Bankverein), die *Rumänische Kommerzialbank*, die *Rumänische Kreditbank* (seit 1923 Creditanstalt, vorher Anglobank), die *Banque Balkanique* in Sofia sowie die *Banque Générale de Bulgarie* (Bodencreditanstalt).

Die weitgehende Aufrechterhaltung der Geschäftsbeziehungen zu den Nachfolgestaaten hatte eine Ausweitung des Betriebs der Wiener Banken zur Folge: Früher in einheitlicher Währung getätigte Transaktionen mußten nun in sechs verschiedenen Währungen abgewickelt werden, die in der ersten Hälfte der zwanziger Jahre einem unterschiedlichen Rhythmus der Entwertung unterlagen. In dieselbe Richtung wirkten auch die Inflation in Österreich selbst (wegen des Fehlens von Rechenmaschinen), die Börsenspekulation und verschiedene staatliche Eingriffe in das Wirtschaftsleben (Vermögensabgabe etc.). In einem Schreiben des „Verbandes österreichischer Banken und Bankiers" an den Völkerbundkommissär vom 26. August 1925 heißt es dazu rückblickend, „daß die Banken genötigt waren, nach dem Krieg ihren Personalstand in ganz außerordentlichem Maße zu erhöhen. Die vom Staate auferlegte Notwendigkeit, eine Reihe von Steuern ... für ihn einzuheben und zu verrechnen, ferner die durch den Friedensvertrag bedingten Arbeiten ... verursachten ein großes Maß an unfruchtbarer Arbeit, zu dessen Bewältigung neues Personal eingestellt werden mußte. Weiter

Die Wiener Großbanken in der Kriegs- und Nachkriegsinflation 155

führte die Einführung selbständiger Währungen in den Sukzessionsstaaten, sowie der Umstand, daß während der Währungskrise die Klientel selbst die kleinsten Eingänge in ausländischen Währungen in diesen Währungen erhalten wollte, zu der Notwendigkeit, für jeden einzelnen Klienten zahlreiche Konti statt eines einzigen zu führen. Endlich wurde die Summe der Arbeit durch die vielstelligen Zahlen, welche infolge der Entwertung der Währung sich ergaben, wesentlich gesteigert."[42]

Die Zahl der Bankangestellten in Österreich stieg von etwa 8000 im Jahr 1913 und 12 600 (1919) auf 24 000 zu Anfang des Jahres 1924.[43] Von diesen waren ungefähr 20 000 bei Instituten beschäftigt, die dem exklusiven „Verband österreichischer Banken und Bankiers" angehörten. Es kann also angenommen werden, daß sich die Zahl der Mitarbeiter der „alten" Banken — auf die allgemeine Expansion des österreichischen Bankwesens in der Inflationsperiode werden wir weiter unten eingehen — um 150 % vermehrte. Wie das Beispiel der Creditanstalt zeigt, verlief die Entwicklung bei den Großbanken in denselben Bahnen: 1913 hatte die größte österreichische Bank auf dem Gebiet der späteren Republik 956 Mitarbeiter beschäftigt; der höchste Stand in der Nachkriegszeit wurde im März 1922 mit 2432 erreicht, was einer Steigerung um das Eineinhalbfache entspricht.[44]

Von den 20 000 Angestellten wurden zwar bis Mitte 1925 6100 wieder entlassen, aber für das — im Vergleich zur Vorkriegszeit — real stark geschrumpfte Geschäftsvolumen der Wiener Banken bildete der hohe Angestelltenstand eine empfindliche Belastung, zumal die Kreditinstitute Arbeitskräfte horteten: „Im übrigen darf nicht übersehen werden", wurde dazu im erwähnten Schreiben des Bankenverbandes vom August 1925 festgestellt, „daß die Wiener Banken großen Wert darauf legen, zur Erhaltung ihres internationalen standing und ihrer Leistungsfähigkeit ihren alten und für den Verkehr mit den mittel-, süd- und osteuropäischen Wirtschaftsgebieten eingerichteten Apparat *nicht allzu stark zu reduzieren*, weil sie die *Hoffnung* hegen, *daß die internationale finanzielle Stellung Wiens sich behauptet*, Wiens alte internationale Beziehungen aufrecht bleiben und wiederhergestellt wer-

---

[42] FA. Zl. 76.843/1926.
[43] Walther Federn, *Die österreichischen Banken*, in: *10 Jahre Nachfolgestaaten*, Wien 1928, S. 56.
[44] *Der österreichische Volkswirt* (im folgenden ÖVW zitiert), 22. Jg. (17. Mai 1930), *Die Bilanzen*, S. 375.

den, und somit auch die Umsätze der Wiener Banken wachsen werden".[45] Erst mit der Rationalisierung des Bankbetriebes durch Einführung von Rechenmaschinen im weiteren Verlauf der zwanziger Jahre sowie durch Bankfusionen und Straffung des Filialnetzes wurde die Zahl der Bankangestellten weiter reduziert. Sie betrug Mitte 1928 rund 9100.[46]

Die Bestrebungen der Regierungen in den Nachfolgestaaten, zu einer „Nationalisierung" der Wirtschaft zu gelangen, richteten sich sowohl gegen die Filialen der Wiener Kommerzbanken als auch gegen die mit diesen verbundenen Industriegesellschaften. Im allgemeinen hatten die Industrieunternehmen, auch wenn ihre Betriebsstätten über die ganze Monarchie verteilt waren und die Hauptbetriebe in anderen Landesteilen lagen, ihre Zentralverwaltung in Wien. Nach 1918 wurden die Industrie-Aktiengesellschaften dazu angehalten, ihren Hauptsitz in den jeweiligen neuen Staat zu verlegen oder das Unternehmen zu teilen und eigene nationale Firmen ins Leben zu rufen. Allein bis Mitte August 1919 hatten bereits 44 AGs mit einem Gesamtaktienkapital von etwa 400 Mio. Kronen ihre Sitzverlegung in die Tschechoslowakei entweder beschlossen oder durchgeführt.[47] Die österreichischen Banken versuchten der völligen Aufsplitterung von Konzernunternehmen mit Hilfe einer geschickten Gegenstrategie zu begegnen: Zugleich mit der Errichtung nationaler Aktiengesellschaften gründeten die Banken im westlichen Ausland *Holdinggesellschaften*, welche die im Portefeuille der Wiener Institute befindlichen Aktienpakete der Konzernfirmen übernahmen. Beispiele dafür sind:

Textilindustrie

Transalpina Industrie- und Handels AG, Zürich . . . . S.M.v. Rothschild
Tarbouches Trust S.A., Zürich . . . . Creditanstalt
Färbereien und Druckereien Trust AG, Chur . . . . Creditanstalt

Erdölindustrie

Vereinigte Fanto Petroleum AG, Genf . . . . Bodencreditanstalt
N.V. Nederlandsche Petroleum
Maatschappij Photogen . . . . Creditanstalt, S.M.v. Rothschild

---

[45] FA, Zl. 76.843/1926. Hervorhebung des Verfassers.
[46] W. Federn, *Die österreichischen Banken*, in: *10 Jahre*... [wie Anm. 43], S. 56.
[47] ÖVW, 11. Jg. (23. August 1919), S. 893. Ein Akt des Finanzministeriums aus dem Jahr 1922, der eine Zusammenstellung über alle bis zu diesem Jahr erfolgten Sitzverlegungen enthielt, ist leider einer Skartierungsaktion zum Opfer gefallen.

Holzindustrie

Mundus, Allgemeine Handels- und Industrie AG, Zürich . . . . Creditanstalt
Timber Holding-Gesellschaft für Werte der Holzindustrie, Zürich . . . . . . Unionbank

Neben den Nationalisierungsbestrebungen der Nachfolgestaaten gefährdete der Friedensvertrag von Saint Germain die Stellung der Wiener Banken im Donauraum. Der ursprüngliche Entwurf enthielt einen Passus, wonach das österreichische Vermögen im Ausland, also auch in den Sukzessionsstaaten, ohne Entschädigung enteignet werden konnte. Die Anwendung dieser Bestimmung wurde im endgültigen Vertrag auf jene Länder eingeschränkt, die außerhalb der ehemaligen österreichisch-ungarischen Monarchie lagen. Die tatsächliche Regelung war noch günstiger: Der Wiener Bankverein mußte zwar seine Filialen in Konstantinopel und Smyrna aufgeben, er erhielt dafür jedoch eine angemessene Entschädigung, die er zur Finanzierung seiner Beteiligung an der Banque Francaise des Pays d'Orient verwendete. Die Bank war zur Übernahme der Geschäfte der genannten Filialen gegründet worden.[48] Für den Verkauf der Aktien der Bank für Orientalische Eisenbahnen erlöste der Bankverein im Jahr 1920 55,6 Mio. Kronen. Auch der Besitz der Wiener Banken an Orientbahn-Aktien — im Jahr 1913 hatte ein österreichisch-ungarisches Bankenkonsortium 51 % des Aktienkapitals übernommen — konnte zu relativ günstigen Bedingungen an eine französische Bankengruppe veräußert werden.[49] Bezüglich einiger Kreditinstitute am Balkan trafen die beteiligten Wiener Banken vorteilhafte Arrangements mit westeuropäischen Finanzkreisen; in keinem Fall kam es zu Enteignungen.

Gefahr drohte den österreichischen Banken auch von Artikel 248 des Friedensvertrages. Dieser besagte, daß die privaten Vorkriegsschulden in der Originalwährung zurückzuzahlen seien oder, wenn sie in Kronen eingegangen worden waren, in der Währung des Gläubigerlandes zum Vorkriegswechselkurs. Aber auch die *Valorisierung der Kronenschulden* erwies sich letzten Endes als keine allzu große Belastung, denn die ausländischen Gläubiger waren zu großen Konzessionen hinsichtlich der Rückzahlungsbedingungen bereit: „Bis Ende 1924 wurden zwischen den englischen Gläubigern und den österreichischen Vorkriegs-

---

[48] *Jahresbericht der Direktion des Wiener Bankvereins an den Administrationsrat für das Jahr 1920.* Archiv der Creditanstalt-Bankverein, Wien (im folgenden *CA-Archiv* zitiert).
[49] *Ebda.* Sowie: FA, Dept. 17, Sammelakt 16 — *Orientbahn-Aktien.*

schuldnern Vergleiche in der Höhe von 4 Mio. Pfund geschlossen. Hiervon wurden mindestens drei Viertel durch Aufnahme neuer Kredite konvertiert. Etwa 10 % wurden mit sequestrierten österreichischen Forderungen an englische Schuldner kompensiert. Kaum eine halbe Million Pfund wurden in bar bezahlt. Mit Frankreich, Belgien und Italien konnte Österreich ähnliche Vergleiche abschließen."[50] Mit dem Vorkriegsschuldengesetz vom 16. Juli 1921 übernahm der Bundesschatz die Tilgung eines Teils der Verbindlichkeiten. Zu diesem Zweck wurden sogenannte Abrechnungsschuldverschreibungen ausgegeben.[51]

In zwei Fällen strebten die Auslandsgläubiger *und* die Wiener Bankdirektoren eine gänzlich andere Lösung an: Die Anglobank und die Länderbank hatten vor dem Krieg Filialen in London beziehungsweise London und Paris unterhalten und waren daher in besonderem Maß an das westliche Ausland verschuldet. Da eine Rückzahlung dieser Kredite zu den im Friedensvertrag festgelegten Bedingungen nach Ansicht der Bankleitungen die Existenz der Institute aufs schwerste gefährden mußte, schlugen sie eine Sitzverlegung ins Ausland vor, wobei eine Umwandlung der französischen und englischen Forderungen in Aktien ins Auge gefaßt wurde. Die Anglobank wies, laut Generalbilanz vom 31. Dezember 1920, valorisierte Kronenschulden im Gesamtbetrag von 5,5 Mrd. — bei einem Eigenkapital von 402 Mio. Kronen — aus. Die Verpflichtungen der Länderbank aus demselben Titel beliefen sich, bei einem Eigenkapital von 817 Mio. — auf 7,7 Mrd. Kronen. Vom österreichischen Parlament eingesetzte Gutachter kamen jedoch, unter Hinweis auf die Auslandsschuldenverträge und bestehende Forderungen der Banken, zu dem Schluß, daß weder vom staatlichen noch vom Gesichtspunkt der Banken aus eine zwingende Notwendigkeit der Umwandlung in ein englisches beziehungsweise französisches Institut gegeben sei. Trotzdem traten sie für eine „Verausländerung" der beiden Institute unter gewissen Kautelen — so sollte die Verwendung eines bestimmten Teils der Aktiva für den Geschäftsbetrieb in Österreich zwingend vorgeschrieben sein — ein und verwiesen auf die Vorteile einer solchen Regelung: Sie könne wesentlich zur Aufrechterhal-

---

[50] Friedrich Hertz, *Zahlungsbilanz und Lebensfähigkeit Österreichs*, München 1925, S. 35.

[51] W. Federn, *Das österreichische Bankwesen*, in: *10 Jahre...* [wie Anm. 43], S. 55; Max Sokal, *Die Banken*, in: *Geldentwertung und Stabilisierung in ihren Einflüssen auf die soziale Entwicklung in Österreich* (= Schriften des Vereins für Sozialpolitik, Bd. 169), München-Leipzig 1925, S. 36.

tung der finanziellen Stellung Wiens im Donauraum beitragen.[52] Im Oktober 1921 gab der österreichische Nationalrat seine Zustimmung zur Überführung der beiden alten Finanzinstitute in englischen beziehungsweise französischen Besitz. Der neue Name der Anglobank lautete Anglo-Austrian Bank Ltd.; der Anteil des Aktienkapitals, der in den Besitz eines englischen Konsortiums unter der Führung der Bank of England überging, betrug 55,6 %. Die österreichische Länderbank, deren Aktienkapital nach der Expatriierung zu etwa 70 % in französischen Händen lag, wurde in Banque des Pays de l'Europe-Centrale umbenannt.[53]

Die „Nationalisierung" des neuausländischen Filialnetzes der Wiener Banken bedeutete in den meisten Fällen das Ende der intensiven Beziehungen zur Großindustrie der Monarchie und damit einen realen Rückgang des laufenden Bankgeschäftes: Nachdem die Creditanstalt im Jahr 1919 die Umstrukturierung ihrer ausländischen Zweigstellen abgeschlossen hatte, stiegen die Debitoren und Kreditoren gegenüber 1918 um 52,9 % beziehungsweise 19,5 %; beim Bankverein hingegen, dessen Filialnetz 1919 noch intakt war, lauteten die entsprechenden Werte 94,5 % beziehungsweise 99,1 %. Disaggregiert man die Daten für die Creditanstalt, so zeigt sich, daß das laufende Geschäft — bei einer Inflationsrate von etwa 100 % — bloß um 6,2 % zunahm, während die Guthaben bei Kreditinstituten um 124 % anstiegen.[54] Das Beispiel der Creditanstalt kann als typisch angesehen werden: An die Stelle der Kreditgewährung an die Industrie in den Nachfolgestaaten traten Einlagen bei den nationalen Bankinstituten, in welche die Filialen der Wiener Banken eingebracht worden waren. Dies gilt in besonderem Maß für die Tschechoslowakei und Oberitalien. In Jugoslawien und Polen vermochten die österreichischen Banken in einem weit größeren

---

[52] Allgemeines Verwaltungs-Archiv Wien, Sozialdemokratischer Parlamentsklub, Karton 45, *71-Angelegenheit Länderbank.*

[53] *Records of Department of State Relating to Internal Affairs of Austria-Hungary and Austria 1910—1927*, National Archives, Washington. Microfilm Publications No. 695, Roll 51, C. 692 und 734. Siehe zur Verausländerung der beiden Banken auch: Marie-Luise Recker, *England und der Donauraum 1919—1929*, Stuttgart 1976, S. 60 ff., sowie Alice Teichova, *Versailles and the Expansion of the Bank of England into Central Europe*, in: *Recht und Entwicklung der Großunternehmen im 19. und frühen 20. Jahrhundert*, hrsg. von Norbert Horn und Jürgen Kocka, Göttingen 1979, S. 368 ff.

[54] Quelle: *Compass 1921*, Bd. 1. Ab 1920 entfiel die detaillierte Gliederung der Debitoren in den Bilanzen der Creditanstalt.

Ausmaß auch nach 1918 ihre Rolle als Kreditgeber der Industrie aufrechtzuerhalten.[55]

In der Tschechoslowakei und in Oberitalien — die ungarischen Banken hatten immer eine relativ eigenständige Rolle gespielt — standen finanzielle Institutionen bereit, die tendenziell die Rolle der Wiener Banken übernehmen konnten. Die engen Verbindungen zur oberitalienischen Industrie und zu den großen Schiffahrtsunternehmen (Stabilimento Tecnico Triestino, Österreichischer Lloyd, Austro-Americana) gingen bereits 1919/20 verloren; die unter Beteiligung von Wiener Banken gegründete Banca Commerciale Triestina, die sich schon vor dem Krieg weitgehend von Wien emanzipiert hatte, löste im Jahr 1919 vorzeitig ihre vertraglichen Bindungen mit dem Wiener Bankverein und gliederte sich die Triester Filiale der Creditanstalt an. Zu ihren neuen Konzernunternehmen zählten im Jahr 1923 fast alle oberitalienischen Großunternehmen, die mit den Wiener Banken zusammengearbeitet hatten.[56]

In der Tschechoslowakei blieben zwar Creditanstalt und Niederösterreichische Escomptegesellschaft über die Böhmische Escomptebank und Kreditanstalt (Bebka) weiter mit ihren alten Konzernunternehmen in Fühlung, aber nur als Unterbeteiligte an einem Finanzierungssyndikat, das von der Živnostenská banka geleitet wurde. Die im Besitz der tschechoslowakischen Filialen der Creditanstalt befindlichen Industriebeteiligungen und Konsortialbestände wurden von der Bebka erworben. Das Zuckergeschäft der Creditanstalt ging verloren.[57] Die Bodencreditanstalt, die über kein Filialnetz verfügte, übertrug den größten Teil ihres laufenden Geschäfts in der Tschechoslowakei noch im Jahr 1919 an die Živnostenská banka.[58] Nur dem Wiener Bankverein scheint es, in enger Kooperation mit befreundeten belgischen Banken, gelungen zu sein, den Einfluß auf den Allgemeinen Böhmischen Bankverein und dessen Geschäftsführung weitgehend zu wahren. Für die

---

[55] Diesen Eindruck vermitteln nicht nur die Verwaltungs- bzw. Administrationsrats-Protokolle der Creditanstalt und des Bankvereins, sondern auch die Angaben über die regionale Streuung der Konzernbetriebe der Großbanken.

[56] Siehe: *Triests Wiederaufbau*, in: ÖVW, 16. Jg. (10. Mai 1924), S. 987.

[57] Abschrift des Vertrages zwischen der Creditanstalt und der Böhmischen Escomptebank und Kreditanstalt, FA, Zl. 57.606/1919. Über die Details der Abmachungen zwischen der Bebka und der Niederösterr. Escomptegesellschaft ist nichts bekannt. Die Böhmische Escomptebank, die unter Eingliederung der Creditanstalt-Filialen in die Bebka umgewandelt wurde, war bis 1919 zu 100 % im Besitz der Escomptegesellschaft.

[58] ÖVW, 15. Jg. (23. Dezember 1922), *Die Bilanzen*, S. 89.

Die Wiener Großbanken in der Kriegs- und Nachkriegsinflation 161

Tschechoslowakei trifft am ehesten zu, was der bekannte österreichische Wirtschaftspublizist Walther Federn rückblickend über die Auslandsbeziehungen der Wiener Banken in den zwanziger Jahren konstatierte: „Sie hatten zunächst nach der Auflösung der Monarchie mit der Bildung eigener Währungen als Kreditgeber überhaupt ausgespielt. In der Inflationszeit waren die Wiener Banken nicht in der Lage, ausländische Unternehmungen mit Kredit zu versorgen. Wohl waren und blieben sie noch Großaktionäre von Banken und Industrieunternehmungen in den Nachfolgestaaten und sie behielten auch Einfluß auf diese, aber dieser war überwiegend ein persönlicher der Wiener Bankleiter... Erst nach der Stabilisierung der österreichischen Währung wurden die Kreditbeziehungen in größerem Umfang wieder aufgenommen. Aber sie hatten ihren Charakter geändert. Für den normalen laufenden Kredit waren weder Banken noch Industrie der Nachfolgestaaten auf die Wiener Banken angewiesen, am wenigsten in der Tschechoslowakei, wo die Kreditbedürfnisse zum größten Teil im Lande selbst gedeckt werden konnten... Den Wiener Banken überließ man... die Dauerkredite an Unternehmungen, die nicht prosperierten."[59]

Über das Ausmaß des Aktienbesitzes der Wiener Banken an neuausländischen Unternehmen gibt es keine zuverlässigen Angaben. Mitte 1919 schätzte man den Wert aller österreichischen Besitzansprüche an Industrieunternehmen in den Nachfolgestaaten auf 20 bis 30 Mrd. Kronen.[60] Am zuverlässigsten dürften die Daten sein, die der Bankierverband dem österreichischen Finanzministerium im Juni 1919 zur Verfügung stellte: Danach betrug der Wertpapierbesitz (Nostro- und Kommittentenbesitz) von 24 österreichischen Banken (6 Groß- und 3 Mittelbanken, 9 kleinere Aktienbanken und 6 Privatbankfirmen) an Industrieunternehmen in den Sukzessionsstaaten zu diesem Zeitpunkt etwa 3,8 Mrd. Kronen.[61] Dies entsprach einem Wert von ungefähr 12,6 Mio. Dollar.[62] In der Folgezeit mußten die Wiener Banken auch auf

---

[59] Walther Federn, *Der Zusammenbruch der Österreichischen Kreditanstalt*, in: *Archiv für Sozialwissenschaft und Sozialpolitik*, Bd. 67 (1932), S. 411f.

[60] *Berichte und Anträge der wirtschaftlichen Korporationen...*, Beilage: *Deutschösterreichs Interessen an Industrieunternehmungen der Sukzessionsstaaten*, S. 1.

[61] FA, Zl. 39.014/1919.

[62] Eine ähnliche Kompilation des Bankenverbandes nach dem Stand vom Oktober 1919, die sich auf den alt- *und* neuausländischen Aktienbesitz der Wiener Banken bezieht, weist den Wert der Industriebeteiligungen mit 2,2, den Gesamtwert des ausländischen Aktienbesitzes (inklusive Banken, Versicherungen und Transportunternehmen) mit 5,6 Mrd. Kronen aus. FA, Zl. 89.813/1919.

dem Feld der neuausländischen Industriebeteiligungen größere Einbußen hinnehmen; sie verloren gerade ihre wertvollsten Aktienbestände — neben denen der bereits erwähnten oberitalienischen Firmen auch in der Tschechoslowakei und in Rumänien. Die Bodencreditanstalt veräußerte den größten Teil ihres Besitzes an Aktien der Berg- und Hüttenwerke (Tschechoslowakei) an Schneider-Creuzot. Die schwerindustriellen Besitzungen der von der Bank kontrollierten Staatseisenbahn-Gesellschaft (STEG) gingen an die Acieres et Domaines de Resita in Rumänien über, von deren Aktienkapital die englische Firma Vickers & Co 1922 einen beträchtlichen Anteil erwarb.[63] Die Niederösterreichische Escomptegesellschaft verkaufte ihren Besitz an Aktien der Skodawerke und der Prager Eisenindustrie-Gesellschaft.[64] Die Creditanstalt verlor bereits 1919 ihre Beteiligungen an den Skodawerken, der Prager Maschinenbau AG und an der Firma Breitfeld, Danek & Co, größtenteils an Schneider-Creuzot.[65] In den ersten Jahren nach 1918 vollzog sich allgemein ein Prozeß der Abwanderung von in Wien placierten Wertpapieren nach Prag.[66]

IV

Die Beteiligung ausländischer Kreditinstitute an den Wiener Großbanken 1918 bis 1923

Die Umwandlung des neuausländischen Filialnetzes und der Versuch, die Verbindungen zur Industrie der Nachfolgestaaten im größtmöglichen Ausmaß aufrechtzuerhalten, bildeten einen Aspekt der Strategie der Wiener Banken, ihre Geschäftspolitik auf eine neue *transnationale* Grundlage zu stellen. Die andere Seite dieses Prozesses war die Beteiligung westlicher Finanzgruppen an den österreichischen Großbanken selbst. An einer solchen Kooperation waren beide Seiten interessiert: Sollte Wien weiter das wichtigste Finanzzentrum des Donauraums bleiben, so war es unabdingbar, die Eigenkapitalbasis der Großbanken zu stärken und die Kreditbeziehungen zum westlichen Ausland zu intensivieren. Zur Fortführung des Aktivgeschäftes auf

---

[63] ÖVW, 13. Jg. (16. Oktober 1920), *Die Bilanzen*, S. 11; *Compass* 1925, Bd. 1, S. 555 und 764 f.
[64] ÖVW, 13. Jg. (22. Jänner 1921), *Die Bilanzen*, S. 60.
[65] *Compass* 1920, Bd. 1, S. 1348 ff. Siehe dazu auch: A. Teichova, *An Economic Background...* [wie Anm. 32], S. 195 ff.
[66] Walther Federn, *Die Börse*, in: *10 Jahre...* [wie Anm. 43], S. 64.

multinationaler Basis hätten die österreichischen Ersparnisse auch unter „normalen" Umständen nicht ausgereicht, um so weniger konnten sie dies unter den Bedingungen der Inflation und des Währungsverfalls. Der Versuch der Wahrung der wirtschaftlichen Einflußsphären in den Nationalstaaten hatte die Ersetzung der verlorengegangenen Kreditoren durch Einlagen aus dem westlichen Ausland zur Bedingung. Über das Ausmaß, das dieser Substitutionsprozeß in den Jahren der Nachkriegsinflation erreichte, geben die Bankbilanzen keinen Aufschluß. Es existieren lediglich Schätzungen einiger kompetenter Zeitgenossen: „Obwohl darüber keine näheren Daten vorliegen", heißt es in einer Analyse der Creditanstalt-Bilanz für das Jahr 1920, „steht es außer Zweifel, daß die Einlagen in fremder Währung und die Kronenguthaben von ausländischen Firmen einen großen Teil der sprunghaft angeschwollenen Kreditoren der Bank bilden."[57] Nach den Angaben Walther Federns sollen die ausländischen Kreditoren „zeitweilig bei einzelnen Banken bis zur Hälfte der Gesamtsumme" betragen haben.[68] Darunter befanden sich jedoch auch die eigenen Vorkriegsverbindlichkeiten der Banken gegenüber dem westlichen Ausland beziehungsweise — aus der Zeit vor der Währungstrennung stammende — gegenüber den Nachfolgestaaten.[69] Zum geringeren Teil enthielten die Auslandskreditoren auch Guthaben österreichischer Bankkunden in fremder Währung. Verläßliche Daten über die kurzfristige Auslandsverschuldung der Wiener Großbanken stehen auch für die späteren Jahre nicht zur Verfügung. Nur für den 31. Dezember 1924 existiert eine vertrauliche Zusammenstellung des „Verbandes österreichischer Banken und Bankiers": Danach machten die Fremdwährungsguthaben ausländischer Kreditinstitute 22,1 % der gesamten Einlagen und Kreditoren von fünf Banken (Creditanstalt, Bankverein, Bodencreditanstalt, Escomptegesellschaft und Unionbank) aus. Nach Abzug der Remboursverpflichtungen und der Guthaben affiliierter Institute erreichte die kurzfristige Auslandsverschuldung 12,4 % der Gesamtkreditoren.[70]

Da von einer engen Kooperation mit westlichen Banken auch eine Stärkung der Verhandlungsposition gegenüber den Regierungen der Nachfolgestaaten erhofft wurde, setzte bald nach dem Krieg eine rege

---

[67] ÖVW, 13. Jg. (16. Juli 1921), *Die Bilanzen*, S. 167.
[68] Walther Federn, *Die Kreditpolitik der Wiener Banken*, in: *Geldentwertung und Stabilisierung...* [wie Anm. 51], S. 66.
[69] ÖVW, 14. Jg. (8. Juli 1922), *Die Bilanzen*, S. 251.
[70] FA, Zl. 76.843/1926.

„diplomatische" Reisetätigkeit der Wiener Bankdirektoren mit dem Ziel ein, beteiligungswillige Finanzgruppen zu gewinnen.[71] Um die ausländischen Banken für Wien zu interessieren, plante der Bankenverband Anfang 1920 die Publikation einer eigenen „Propagandaschrift", die, nach den Worten des Sekretärs des Verbandes, „auf die ersten Finanzkreise in den Ententeländern Eindruck zu machen geeignet wäre".[72] Im Fall der Creditanstalt entschloß sich deren Großaktionär Louis von Rothschild zu einem spektakulären Schritt, indem er im Sommer 1921 die Funktion des Verwaltungsrats-Präsidenten übernahm und so gegenüber den „ersten Finanzkreisen" des Westens dokumentierte, daß die Bank weiterhin den Rückhalt des angesehenen Privatbankhauses genoß.[73] Das Haus Rothschild hatte schon vorher bei der Anknüpfung von Auslandsbeziehungen und der Mobilisierung westlicher Kredite eine wichtige Rolle innegehabt, die es der Creditanstalt ermöglichte, selbst in der Periode des Währungsverfalls Kapital langfristig im Ausland anzulegen und ihre außerhalb Österreichs gelegenen Konzernunternehmen zu finanzieren.[74] Mit Unterstützung des Bankhauses S.M.v. Rothschild gründete die Creditanstalt 1920 in Holland die Amstelbank, die als Vermittler für ausländische Kredite sowohl an die Anstalt selbst als auch direkt an Konzernfirmen in den Nachfolgestaaten fungierte.[75] Im selben Jahre beteiligte sich die Creditanstalt an der International Acceptance Bank in New York, wobei ein Großteil der für die Zeichnung des Aktienkapitals und der als Sicherstellung für künftige Remourskredite notwendigen Summe von 2 Mio. Dollar vom Haus Rothschild aufgebracht wurde.[76]

Welches waren die Motive für ausländische Kreditinstitute, sich an den Wiener Großbanken zu beteiligen? Ihnen erschienen die öster-

---

[71] Siehe: Philip L. Cottrell, *Aspects of Western Equity Investment in the Banking Systems of East Central Europe.* Unveröffentl. Manuskript. University of East Anglia International Symposium in Economic History 1979.

[72] FA, Zl. 13.410/1920. Auch die Kennzeichnung der Broschüre als „Propagandaschrift" stammt von Max Sokal, dem Sekretär des Bankenverbandes. Es ist den Verfassern allerdings nicht bekannt, ob die Broschüre, die detaillierte Angaben über den Industriekonzern der Banken enthalten sollte, tatsächlich zur Verteilung gelangte.

[73] Verwaltungsrats-Protokoll der Creditanstalt vom 29. Juli 1921. CA-Archiv.

[74] Zwischen 1919 und 1923 konnte die Creditanstalt 35 namhafte Neugründungen oder -beteiligungen im Ausland durchführen (davon nur vier Umwandlungen von Filialen). Siehe: E. März, *Österreichische Bankpolitik*... [wie Anm. 4], S. 534.

[75] *Ebda.*, S. 449ff.

[76] FA, Zl. 80.242/1920, 105.707/1920, 35.428/1921 und 52.278/1921.

Die Wiener Großbanken in der Kriegs- und Nachkriegsinflation 165

reichischen Mobilbanken mit ihren weitverzweigten Industriekonzernen — jener der Creditanstalt umfaßte 1923 hundert Industrieaktiengesellschaften — als gleichsam riesige „*Holdinggesellschaften*".[77] Die Beteiligung an einer Wiener Bank eröffnete den Zugang zum zentraleuropäischen Industriemarkt, ohne daß man das Risiko einer Direktbeteiligung an einem Industrieunternehmen mit ungewissen Zukunftsaussichten auf sich nehmen mußte. Tatsächlich bildeten Industriebeteiligungen westlichen Kapitals in Österreich zu dieser Zeit die Ausnahme, wohingegen Kapital aus Deutschland hauptsächlich in den industriellen Sektor eindrang.[78] Als Beispiel für westliche Bankbeteiligungen in Österreich, die mit Blickrichtung auf eine Kooperation im Industriebereich erfolgten, seien die Interessennahme der Union Européenne Industrielle et Financiere (Schneider-Creuzot) an der Niederösterreichischen Escompte-Gesellschaft als Konzernbank der Alpine Montangesellschaft und die Übernahme eines Aktienpakets der Bodencreditanstalt durch die Mutuelle Mobiliere et Immobiliere (Solvay-Gruppe) genannt, die Interesse für den tschechoslowakischen Chemiekonzern des Wiener Instituts bekundete.[79]

Im Vergleich zu den Möglichkeiten, die sich den ausländischen Finanzgruppen durch eine Beteiligung an einer Wiener Großbank eröffneten, war das finanzielle Risiko — wegen des Wertverfalls der österreichischen Krone auf den Devisenmärkten — gering (siehe Anhang, TABELLE 3). Für einen Betrag von bloß 70 000 £ erwarb im Winter 1922 ein anglo-amerikanisches Bankensyndikat (Morgan und Schroeder) 500 000 Aktien (etwa 21 % des Aktienkapitals) der Bodencreditanstalt.[80] Insbesondere nach der Stabilisierung der Krone wurden die österreichischen Bankaktien im westlichen Ausland zu „Modeeffekten für große Finanzgruppen".[81]

---

[77] In diesem Sinn wurden die ausländischen Banken auch von den westlichen Botschaften in Wien informiert. So machte der englische Botschafter bereits im September 1920 darauf aufmerksam, daß „any cooperation with the Boden-Credit-Anstalt means an entrance into the most important industries and companies of Central Europe". Zit. nach M. L. Recker, *England und der Donauraum*... [wie Anm. 53], S. 72, Anm. 137.

[78] Siehe: F. Weber/K. Haas, *Deutsches Kapital*... [wie Anm. 17], in: *Jahrbuch für Zeitgeschichte*, (1979), S. 185 ff.

[79] Siehe: Benedikt Kautsky, *Volkswirtschaft*, in: *Arbeit und Wirtschaft*, Nr. 13 (1923), Sp. 494, sowie A. Teichova, *An Economic Background*... [wie Anm. 32], S. 279 ff.

[80] P. L. Cottrell, *Aspects*... [wie Anm. 71]

[81] W. Federn, *Die Kreditpolitik der Wiener Banken*, in: *Geldentwertung und Stabilisierung*... [wie Anm. 51], S. 61. Manchmal wurden alte Geschäftsverbindungen auf ein

Das Kapital, das den Wiener Großbanken durch die Plazierung von eigenen Aktien im Ausland zufloß, stammte hauptsächlich aus den Siegerstaaten des Ersten Weltkrieges sowie von neutralen Finanzplätzen (Belgien, Holland, Schweiz). An der Mercurbank beteiligte sich deutsches Kapital (Darmstädter Bank), an der Depositenbank — vorübergehend — eine italienische Bankengruppe in größerem Ausmaß.[82] Der Gesamtbetrag der den Banken durch diese Transaktionen zugeflossenen ausländischen Gelder kann wegen des Fehlens zuverlässiger Angaben über die Übernahmekonditionen und Einzahlungstermine nicht geschätzt werden. Im Fall der Creditanstalt machten sie etwa 800 000 $ aus.[83] Die Folge der wiederholten Aktienverkäufe war eine drastische Änderung der Eigentumsverhältnisse bei den Wiener Banken gegenüber 1913:

Auslandsanteil am Aktienkapital der größten Wiener Banken 1913 und Ende 1923 (in %)

	1913	1923
Creditanstalt	3,9	20,2
Bodencreditanstalt	17,8	ca. 46
Niederöst. Escomptegesellschaft	0,7	36,0
Wiener Bankverein	18,3	38,4
Länderbank	31,4	ca. 70*
Anglobank	3,0	55,6**
Unionbank	1,5	ca. 10
Mercurbank	3,4	60,0
Verkehrsbank	?	37,6
Depositenbank	?	16,3
Insgesamt (1923 ohne Anglo- und Länderbank)	10,4	30,5

* Französisches Institut.
** Englisches Institut.

Quelle: Nat. Archives, MC. No. 695, Roll 51, C. 337 ff., 692 und 734. *Compass* 1918 und 1925 jeweils Bd. 1; Bilanzbesprechungen des *Österreichischen Volkswirts*.

quasi „höheres" Niveau gehoben: So hatte die Creditanstalt bereits vor dem Krieg über das Hamburger Bankhaus M. M. Warburg & Co. Kontakte zu amerikanischen Banken geknüpft, die während des Krieges nie ganz abrissen. Diese Banken — Kuhn, Loeb & Co. und die Guaranty Trust Company of New York — partizipierten im Frühjahr 1920 an einer Kapitalerhöhung der Creditanstalt. Ihr Vertrauensmann im Verwaltungsrat des

Die neuen Großaktionäre beteiligten sich meist auch an den Konzernbanken der Wiener Institute in den Nachfolgestaaten. Dies trifft in besonderem Maß auf den Wiener Bankverein zu, der seinen belgischen und Schweizer Freunden beträchtliche Quoten am Böhmischen Bankverein (40 %) und am Allgemeinen Bankverein in Polen (25 %) überließ.[84] Im allgemeinen behielten die ausländischen Institute die Wiener Bankaktien auch nach Ablauf der ausgehandelten Sperrfristen im Portefeuille, zum Teil nahmen sie an Kapitalerhöhungen in der zweiten Hälfte der zwanziger Jahre teil; in manchen Fällen kamen auch neue Großaktionäre aus dem Ausland hinzu. Erst gegen Ende des Jahrzehnts scheinen die westlichen Banken größere Posten von Aktien abgestoßen zu haben. Ebenso dauerte der Zufluß kurzfristiger Auslandsgelder zu den österreichischen Banken bis zum Jahr 1929 fort. Dieser ermöglichte die Aufrechterhaltung bestehender beziehungsweise das Eingehen neuer Engagements in den Nachfolgestaaten.[85] Insbesondere 1928 dürfte „ein Jahr des Kapitalexports" gewesen sein.[86] Ein beträchtlicher Teil der Auslandsgelder muß aber zweifellos in Österreich selbst investiert worden sein, weil sonst unerklärlich bliebe, wie das chronische Defizit der Leistungsbilanz finanziert wurde.

Wiener Instituts war Max Warburg. Siehe: E. März, *Österreichische Bankpolitik...* [wie Anm. 4], S. 353 und 541; *Ein Jahrhundert Creditanstalt-Bankverein*, Wien 1957, S. 139.

[82] Siehe: F. Weber/K. Haas, *Deutsches Kapital...* [wie Anm. 17], in: *Jahrbuch für Zeitgeschichte*, (1979), S. 186.

[83] Nat. Archives, Mc. No. 695, Roll 51, C. 342. Auch über die Währung, in der das Aktienkapital zur Einzahlung kam, ist in den meisten Fällen nichts bekannt. Einer der wenigen Hinweise findet sich in einem Aktenstück des österreichischen Finanzministeriums, FA, Zl. 52.684/1920. Es lautet: „Laut mündlicher Mitteilung: Warburg, Kuhn, Loeb Co. etc. Einzahlung dürfte in Mark erfolgen (ca. 27 Mill.?)."

[84] *Tätigkeitsbericht der Direktion an den Administrationsrat des Wiener Bankverein für das erste Halbjahr 1921*. CA-Archiv. Auch an der Böhmischen Escomptebank und Kreditanstalt waren die ausländischen Freunde der beteiligten Wiener Banken interessiert.

[85] Siehe: W. Federn, *Der Zusammenbruch...*, in: *Archiv...* [wie Anm. 59], Bd. 67, S. 406 ff., sowie: K. Ausch, *Als die Banken fielen...* [wie Anm. 15], S. 307 ff.

[86] *Wirtschaftsstatistisches Jahrbuch*, (1928), hrsg. von der Kammer für Arbeiter und Angestellte, Wien 1929, S. 393.

V

*Die Geschäftspolitik der Großbanken
in der Zeit der Nachkriegsinflation*

Die ersten Nachkriegsjahre standen im Zeichen einer ungeheuren Expansion des österreichischen Kreditsektors. 1913 hatte es auf dem Gebiet der späteren Republik 27 Aktienbanken und 150 Privatbankfirmen gegeben; Ende 1923 war ihre Zahl auf 76 beziehungsweise 282 angewachsen. Den meisten dieser neugegründeten Institute war jedoch keine lange Lebensdauer beschieden. 1927 existierten in Österreich nur mehr 40 Aktienbanken und 152 private Kreditinstitute.[87] Das Entstehen einer so großen Anzahl neuer Banken trug zur Verschärfung der Konkurrenz im Inland, insbesondere auf dem Gebiet des Einlagengeschäftes, bei und trieb das Zinsniveau zusätzlich in die Höhe. Die Konkurrenz um die Einlagegelder erreichte ihren Höhepunkt allerdings erst nach dem Ende der Inflation: Während der großen Börsenhausse des Jahres 1923 beschafften sich die neuen Banken die Mittel zur Geschäftsführung vielfach durch Attraktion von Tag- und Wochengeld, für das in einzelnen kurzen Phasen Zinssätze in der Höhe von 200—250 % p.a. geboten wurden.[88]

Bis 1918 hatten sich die Wiener Großbanken auf die Betreuung der industriellen Großkundschaft konzentriert und daher den Alpengebieten geringeres Augenmerk zugewandt. In den Nachkriegsjahren versuchten sie verstärkt, in der österreichischen Provinz Fuß zu fassen. Die Zahl der Großbankenfilialen in den Bundesländern vermehrte sich, wie aus TABELLE 4 (siehe Anhang) hervorgeht, von 1918 bis 1922 um das Zweifache. Im Zusammenhang damit gewann auch die Pflege des Privatkundengeschäfts an Bedeutung.[89]

---

[87] W. Federn, *Das österreichische Bankwesen*, in: *10 Jahre...* [wie Anm. 43], S. 56. Besonders spektakulär verlief diese Entwicklung in den österreichischen Bundesländern: Von den 27 Aktienbanken des Jahres 1913 hatten nur drei ihren Sitz außerhalb Wiens; 1923 gab es 22 Provinzbanken, 1927 nur noch zehn. Siehe dazu: Fritz Weber, *Der finanzielle Länderpartikularismus. Aufstieg und Fall der Provinzbanken in der Ersten Republik.* Unveröffentl. Manuskript. Symposium der Kommission zur wissenschaftlichen Erforschung der österreichischen Geschichte der Jahre 1918 bis 1938, Wien 1981.

[88] W. Federn, *Die Kreditpolitik der Wiener Banken*, in: *Geldentwertung und Stabilisierung...* [wie Anm. 51], S. 64; sowie: *Die Geldknappheit*, in: ÖVW, 15. Jg. (10. Februar 1923), S. 493.

[89] So heißt es 1920 in einem Akt des Finanzministeriums, FA Zl. 39.205/1920: „Auch in der Praxis der alten großen Aktienbanken ist insoferne eine gewisse Änderung

Die Wiener Großbanken in der Kriegs- und Nachkriegsinflation

Eine quantitative Analyse der Geschäftspolitik der Wiener Großbanken in der Inflationsperiode muß notwendigerweise spekulative Züge tragen. Für die Bankbilanzen dieser Zeit gilt noch mehr als sonst, daß aus ihnen nur zu ersehen ist, was erkannt werden soll. Schon die zeitgenössischen Bilanzanalytiker haben festgestellt, „daß ... sowohl im Bilanz-, als auch im Gewinn- und Verlustkonto vielfach soweit von der Wirklichkeit abweichende Bewertungen und Ertragsziffern eingesetzt sind, daß die Rechnungsabschlüsse nur als *Entwicklungsbild* und auch das nur mit großen Vorbehalten gewertet werden können, nicht aber als ein tatsächliches Bild der finanziellen Situation der Bank(en)".[90]

Besonders starke Verzerrungen erfuhren die Rechnungsabschlüsse durch den transnationalen Charakter des Bankgeschäftes. Auf dieses Problem ging der *Österreichische Volkswirt* anläßlich der Besprechung der Bilanz der Niederösterreichischen Escomptegesellschaft für das Jahr 1922 ein: „Dabei wären die Bilanzansätze", hieß es, „noch ungleich größer gewesen, wenn die Bank nicht ... alle auf gleiche fremde Währung lautende Konti miteinander kompensiert und nur die Saldi aller in ein und derselben Auslandswährung geführten Konti unter den Kreditoren zu den Kursen des Abschlußtages, unter den Debitoren etwas niedriger in die Bilanz eingesetzt hätte. Wenn die Bank nicht so vorgegangen wäre, so hätten die Debitoren und Kreditoren nicht nahezu eine Billion, sondern mehrere Billionen erreicht ... In den Erträgnissen ist der Spielraum für eine künstliche Verminderung der ausgewiesenen Summen natürlich ungleich größer, daher läßt das Steigen des Reingewinnes von 10,6 Millionen im Jahre 1913 ... auf das 1400fache absolut nicht den Schluß zu, daß die Erträgnisse tatsächlich in Goldrechnung auf den zehnten Teil zurückgegangen sind."[91] Vielfach wurden Gewinne aus Konsortialgeschäften nicht verrechnet. So war bekannt, daß die Creditanstalt 1922 von 300 derartigen Transaktionen nur 30 verbucht hatte.[92] Wie groß die nicht ausgewiesenen Erträge waren, mag der Tatsache entnommen werden, daß die Dividenden, die der Escomptegesellschaft im Jahr 1922 aus dem Besitz an Aktien der Böhmischen

---

eingetreten, als sie durch ihre Filialen, welche seit dem Umsturze in vermehrter Zahl auch an kleineren Orten errichtet wurden, mehr als bisher das kleine Geschäft zu pflegen begannen."

[90] *ÖVW*, 15. Jg. (14. April 1923), *Die Bilanzen*, S. 213. Hervorhebung von den Verfassern.
[91] *Ebda.*
[92] *ÖVW*, 15. Jg. (19. Mai 1923), *Die Bilanzen*, S. 254.

Escomptebank und Kreditanstalt zuflossen, zum Kurs des Bilanztages „nahezu den ganzen Reingewinn, weit mehr als die ausgeschüttete Dividende", ausmachten.[93] Durch die bewußte Niedrighaltung der ausgewiesenen Erträgnisse und die Beschränkung der Dividendenausschüttung versuchten die Banken der Scheingewinnbesteuerung zu entgehen und Mittel für die Aufrechterhaltung des Bankbetriebs sowie zur Absicherung gegen die Geldentwertung zu erhalten.[94]

Wenn die in den Rechnungsabschlüssen erscheinenden Zahlen auch kein realistisches Bild von der Höhe der Gewinne vermitteln, so veranschaulicht der veränderte Stellenwert der einzelnen Gewinnquellen doch die Verschiebungen, die sich gegenüber 1913 in der Inflationsperiode ergaben (siehe Anhang, TABELLE 5). Die auffallendsten Veränderungen betreffen die Gewinne aus Devisen beziehungsweise Effekten und Konsortialgeschäften, die nach dem Krieg in wesentlich größerem Maß zum gesamten Rohertragnis beitrugen als vor 1914. Beide waren 1923 auch in Goldkronen gerechnet mehr als doppelt so hoch wie 1913. In diesen zwei Posten spiegelt sich einerseits der multinationale Charakter des Bankgeschäftes wider, andererseits drückt sich darin die gute Börsenkonjunktur dieser Jahre aus. Dagegen ging der Zinsenanteil am Gewinn nur *scheinbar* von 70,3 % (1913) auf 25,7 % (1923) zurück. Zinsen und Provisionen müssen, wie es in einem Bericht der Direktion des Wiener Bankvereins heißt, „insoferne in ihrer Gesamtheit" betrachtet werden, „als sie das Entgelt für die der Kundschaft zur Verfügung gestellten Gelder und für den großen Arbeitsaufwand, den das reguläre Bankgeschäft erfordert, bilden".[95] Zwar gelangten auf dem Provisionskonto auch Syndikatsprovisionen und — als Besonderheit bei der Creditanstalt — Gewinne der Warenabteilungen (Handel mit Zucker und Textilien) zur Verrechnung, doch muß der überwiegende Teil den Zinsenerträgnissen zugerechnet werden. Ein zeitgenössischer Kommentator bezeichnete die Zunahme der relativen Bedeutung der Provisionsgewinne seit 1921 als „charakteristisch". Sie sei Ausdruck einer geänderten Art der Zinsberechnung, „die heute komplizierter ist

---

[93] ÖVW, 15. Jg. (14. April 1923), *Die Bilanzen*, S. 214.

[94] Eine namentlich nicht genannte „Autorität" teilte der Wirtschaftsabteilung der US-Botschaft in Wien mit, daß die österreichischen Aktiengesellschaften vor dem Krieg etwa 70 % der erzielten Erträgnisse ausgewiesen hätten, nach 1918 aber nur noch ungefähr 15 %. Nat. Archives, MC. No. 695, Roll 51, C. 463.

[95] *Bericht der Direktion des Wiener Bankvereins an den Administrationsrat für das Jahr 1922*. CA-Archiv.

und bei der die Provisionen eine viel größere Rolle spielen als früher. Unter den Bankkonditionen ist der reine Zinssatz heute nicht mehr allein ausschlaggebend. In der Form von Provisionen und anderen Titeln werden dem Kreditnehmer Beträge angerechnet, die häufig über das Ausmaß der reinen Zinsen hinausgehen."[96] Noch im ersten Halbjahr 1924 war die sogenannte „Vorlageprovision" für Kontokorrentkredite an erste Industriekunden fast so hoch wie der Debetzinssatz.[97]

Die Entwicklung der auf diese Weise entstandenen „realen" Zinsspanne ist aus den veröffentlichten Bilanzdaten nur als Trend zu rekonstruieren, dessen Aussagekraft sehr stark eingeschränkt ist, weil wir über den — sowohl tatsächlichen als auch rechnungsmäßigen — Anteil des in österreichischen Kronen abgewickelten laufenden Bankgeschäfts keinerlei Anhaltspunkte besitzen.

Der für die Zeit vor dem Weltkrieg errechnete Zinsensaldo (siehe Anhang, TABELLE 6) stimmt mit den Schätzungen zeitgenössischer Experten überein.[98] Dagegen scheint für die Nachkriegsjahre der Überschuß der Zinsen *und* Provisionen ein wirklichkeitsnäheres Bild der Entwicklung zu geben (wobei die außerordentlich günstigen Ziffern für 1923 und 1924 das infolge der Börsenkonjunktur und der Deflation exorbitant hohe Debetzinsniveau reflektieren). Für die Jahre 1921 und 1922 bleibt jedoch selbst die aus den Bilanzdaten sich ergebende „reale" Zinsspanne hinter jenen Werten zurück (mindestens 4 % 1921, 6 % oder mehr 1922), die der *Österreichische Volkswirt* auf Grund genauer Kenntnis der Lage errechnet hatte.[99]

Während des Weltkrieges hatte die Liquidität der Industrieunternehmen beträchtlich zugenommen. Diese Tatsache kam in dem starken Überhang der Bankkreditoren über die Debitoren zum Ausdruck. Auf Grund der Unzuverlässigkeit der Daten, die eine Aufgliederung in Kronen- und Fremdwährungspositionen nicht erlauben, ist die Aussagekraft einer solchen Berechnung für die Nachkriegszeit sehr eingeschränkt, doch indiziert auch sie eine Umkehr des Trends (siehe Anhang, TABELLE 1).

---

[96] Benedikt Kautsky, *Die Bankbilanzen des Jahres 1925*, in: *Arbeit und Wirtschaft*, 1. September 1926, Sp. 693.
[97] W. T. Layton/Charles Rist, *Die Wirtschaftslage Österreichs*, Wien 1925, S. 92.
[98] A.a.O., S. 19, wird berichtet, daß die Zinsmarge vor 1914 „etwas weniger als 3 %" betrug.
[99] ÖVW, 14. Jg. (2. Mai 1922), *Die Bilanzen*, S. 184; 15. Jg. (14. April 1923), *Die Bilanzen*, S. 214.

Die Jahre der Nachkriegsinflation waren von einer ständig wachsenden Nachfrage der Industrie nach Kredit geprägt. Diese war zum Teil eine Folge der Zerreißung des einheitlichen Wirtschaftsgebietes der Donaumonarchie. Kohle, Rohstoffe und Halbfertigwaren mußten nun in großem Ausmaß aus dem Neuausland bezogen werden. Beim Export von Fertigwaren ergaben sich längere Umschlagsfristen der Produktion; Außenstände waren schwerer mobilisierbar, weil die auf ausländische Währung lautenden Wechsel nicht bei der Notenbank eskomptefähig waren.[100] Zum anderen benötigte die Industrie Investitionskredite zur Umstellung von der Kriegs- auf Friedensproduktion. Eine der wesentlichen Ursachen für die in diesen Jahren vielbeklagte „Kapitalnot" der Industrieunternehmen dürfte jedoch in den Folgen der Mitte 1920 einsetzenden „Ausverkaufskonjunktur" und des Valutadumpingexports zu suchen sein. Als Folge verfehlter Kalkulationsmethoden wurden Industrieprodukte unter ihrem Wert verkauft, was bedeutete, daß ein Teil des Betriebsvermögens der Unternehmen verlorenging. Die Preisberechnung zum Wiederbeschaffungswert wurde offenbar — insbesondere in den ersten beiden Nachkriegsjahren — nur von wenigen Firmen angewandt.[101] Aber selbst wenn die Gesellschaften methodisch richtig kalkulierten, war es nicht einfach, die künftige Entwertungsrate korrekt zu antizipieren. Der Wertverfall der Krone unterlag einem wechselnden Rhythmus und war immer wieder von Perioden der zeitweiligen Erholung unterbrochen.[102] Dementsprechend folgte jedem stärkeren Inflationsstoß „für eine Zeit eine Periode intensiver Geldverknappung..., trotz stetig steigenden Notenumlaufes".[103]

Im Jahr 1921 setzte die Flucht aus der Krone verstärkt ein. Devisenerlöse aus dem Warenexport wurden gehortet,[104] Kronen zu spekulati-

---

[100] W. Federn, *Die Kreditpolitik der Wiener Banken,* in: *Geldentwertung und Stabilisierung...* [wie Anm. 51], S. 62.

[101] Siehe dazu: Viktor Wutte, *Lebenslauf.* Masch.schrift. Manuskript. Wutte, ein steirischer Industrieller, berichtet, daß die Kalkulation der Verkaufspreise auf Grund der jeweiligen Einkaufspreise in den Jahren 1919 und 1920 durchaus üblich war.

[102] Siehe: Adele Wieser, *Die Verwertungsmöglichkeit der Arbeitskraft in der Industrie,* in: *Geldentwertung und Stabilisierung...* [wie Anm. 43], S. 99 ff.

[103] Max Sokal, *Die Tätigkeit der Banken in den Jahren 1919 und 1920,* Wien 1921, S. 8.

[104] Im *Bericht der Direktion des Wiener Bankvereins an den Administrationsrat für 1921* (verfaßt im Juni 1922) heißt es, „daß viele unserer Schuldner in ausländischer Valuta, die sich aus der heimischen Industrie und Kaufmannschaft rekrutieren, vorderhand auch einer nur teilweisen Erfüllung ihrer Verpflichtung aus dem Wege zu gehen trachten." CA-Archiv.

ven Zwecken ins Ausland transferiert.[105] Dadurch und auf Grund der Flucht in die Sachwerte (Umwandlung von Geldkapital in Immobilien, Aktien etc.) nahmen die Einlagen bei den Banken rascher ab, als dies dem Tempo der Geldentwertung entsprochen hätte. Je allgemeiner die Fluchtbewegung wurde, desto fühlbarer war die Knappheit und Verteuerung des Kredits, zumal die Banken selbst, um sich gegen die Folgen der Geldentwertung zu schützen, große Guthaben in ausländischer Währung unterhielten und ihr Eigenkapital in ausländischen Wertpapieren anlegten.[106]

Neue Mittel zur Befriedigung der wachsenden Kreditnachfrage beschafften sich die Banken durch wiederholte Kapitalvermehrungen. Die Erhöhung des Aktienkapitals der vier größten Wiener Kreditinstitute machte (im Zeitraum Oktober 1918 bis September 1922) zwischen 460 % (Bodencreditanstalt) und 1290 % (Bankverein), im Durchschnitt etwa 1000 % aus. Trotzdem verschlechterte sich das Verhältnis zwischen den — ausgewiesenen — eigenen und fremden Mitteln kontinuierlich. Es betrug bei der Creditanstalt im ungünstigsten Fall (1921) 1 : 45.[107]

Auf Grund des Einlagenrückgangs und der Verknappung des Kreditangebotes stiegen die Zinssätze, die während des Krieges auf einem niedrigen Niveau verblieben waren. Sie dürften im Frühjahr 1921 unter Einrechnung der verschiedenen Gebühren und Provisionen für erste Adressen mindestens 10 bis 14 % betragen haben.[108] 1922 machten sie, da die Banken auch eine Risikoprämie für die Geldentwertung in Rech-

---

[105] Nach den Schätzungen von Schweizer Banken erreichten die österreichischen Guthaben in der Schweiz Anfang 1922 die Höhe von 18 Mio. £. Walré de Bordes, *The Austrian Crown. Its Depreciation and Stabilization*, London 1924, S. 192.

[106] Eine realistische Wiedergabe dieser Tatsache in den Bilanzen hätte zu bizarren Verzerrungen geführt: 1922 wies die Creditanstalt ein Effekten- und Konsortialkonto von 54 Mrd. Kronen aus. Allein der Kurswert ihres Besitzers an Aktien der Böhmischen Escomptebank und Kreditanstalt machte 150 Mrd. aus. (ÖVW, 15. Jg. [19. Mai 1923], *Die Bilanzen*, S. 253 f.)

[107] Im Herbst 1922 wurde den Banken die Möglichkeit gegeben, durch Aufwertung von Aktienbeständen eine Aufstempelung des eigenen Aktienkapitals durchzuführen. Bei der Creditanstalt betrug der Aufstempelungssatz 1 : 10, bei den anderen Großbanken lag er etwas niedriger. Um ein höheres Eigenvermögen auszuweisen, brauchte die Creditanstalt bloß zwei in ihrem Portefeuille befindliche Aktienpakete ausländischer Unternehmen aufzuwerten. (Siehe: *Compass* 1925, Bd. 1, S. 370.)

[108] FA, Zl. 37.397/1921 (Zeitungsausschnitt, *Frankfurter Zeitung* vom 19. April 1921). Genaue Angaben über die Höhe der Debetzinsen wurden von den Banken nicht veröffentlicht.

nung stellten, 20 bis 30 % aus. Für die normale Industriekundschaft lagen sie noch weit höher.[109] Schließlich gingen die Banken sogar zu einer Kontingentierung der Kronenkredite über.[110] Kontokorrentkredite in inländischer Währung wurden im Stadium der Hyperinflation offenbar „auf das zu Lohnzahlungen benötigte Maß" beschränkt[111] und die darüber hinaus notwendige Kreditgewährung an heimische Industrieunternehmen in fremder Währung abgewickelt, um das Kursrisiko bei Außenhandelstransaktionen zu eliminieren beziehungsweise die einem Gläubiger in der Inflation allgemein drohende Gefahr des Verlustes auszuschalten.[112]

Eine Begrenzung der Kreditgewährung in Kronen[113] erschien, neben den bereits angeführten Gründen, auch wegen der Notwendigkeit einer hohen Kassenhaltung geboten. Diese wurde von den Banken auf die große Fluktuation bei den Einlagen und auf den hohen Geldbedarf an Lohnzahlungstagen zurückgeführt. Die Kassabewegung bei der Niederösterreichischen Escomptegesellschaft machte im Endstadium der Inflation an Samstagen 80 bis 90 Mrd. Kronen aus.[114] Aus demselben Grund sahen sich die Banken auch veranlaßt, ein beträchtliches Wechselportefeuille zu halten. Seit Ende 1921 nahm der Wechseleskompte, der in den Jahren vorher eine geringere Rolle gespielt hatte, wieder an Bedeutung zu.[115] Die Inanspruchnahme des Reescomptes der Notenbank durch die Banken kann TABELLE 7 (Anhang) entnommen werden.

An dieser Stelle erscheint es angebracht, auf einen grundlegenden

---

[109] W. Federn, *Die Kreditpolitik der Wiener Banken*, in: *Geldentwertung und Stabilisierung...* [wie Anm. 51], S. 64. Noch 1924 betrugen die Debetzinsen (inkl. Provisionen) über 20 %. W. T. Layton/Ch. Rist, *Die Wirtschaftslage...* [wie Anm. 97], S. 92.

[110] Max Sokal, *Die Tätigkeit der Banken in den Jahren 1921 und 1922*, Wien 1923, S. 5.

[111] ÖVW, 15. Jg. (14. April 1923), *Die Bilanzen*, S. 213.

[112] M. Sokal, *Die Tätigkeit der Banken in den Jahren 1921 und 1922...* [wie Anm. 110], S. 6.

[113] Eine interne Zusammenstellung der Creditanstalt über den ihren österreichischen Konzernunternehmen bewilligten Kronengesamtdebetsaldo weist — für Anfang Oktober 1922 — eine Summe von 52,3 Mrd. Kronen aus (*Verwaltungsrats-Protokoll der Creditanstalt vom 4. Oktober 1922*. CA-Archiv). Dies entspräche — nimmt man die Bankbilanz von 1922 als Bezugspunkt — einem Anteil von etwa 5,5 % an den gesamten Nichtbanken-Debitoren der Creditanstalt.

[114] ÖVW, 15. Jg. (14. April 1923), *Die Bilanzen*, S. 214. Auf die Notwendigkeit einer hohen Kassenhaltung wird auch in den Direktionsberichten des Wiener Bankvereins an den Administrationsrat wiederholt hingewiesen.

[115] M. Sokal, *Die Tätigkeit der Banken in den Jahren 1921 und 1922...* [wie Anm. 103], S. 13. Die Belebung des Wechseleskomptes fiel charakteristischerweise mit dem

Unterschied zu Deutschland hinzuweisen: Während die deutschen Banken in den ersten Nachkriegsjahren bereitwillig kurz- und langfristige staatliche Schatzanweisungen und Wechsel eskontierten, haben sich die Wiener Banken „nach dem Zusammenbruch dem Staat fast ganz versagt... In Österreich bestand von Anfang an kein Zutrauen zu dem neuen Staate... und seiner Währung... Bis auf eine bescheidene Losanleihe... konnte der Staat sein gewaltig anschwellendes Defizit nur mit der Banknotenpresse decken..."[116]

Im Vergleich zu Deutschland erscheint auch eine zweite Besonderheit der Geschäftstätigkeit der österreichischen Banken in der Inflationszeit von Bedeutung. Während sich im Deutschen Reich die Großindustrie während der Inflation von den Banken emanzipierte und das Emissionsgeschäft bei den Kreditinstituten eine untergeordnete Rolle spielte,[117] vermochten die österreichischen Großbanken ihren Konzern zum Teil beträchtlich zu erweitern, da die Schrumpfung des Betriebskapitals eine große Anzahl selbst renommierter und alteingesessener Privatfirmen zwang, sich an die Kreditinstitute um finanziellen Beistand zu wenden.[118]

Die Abhängigkeit vom Bankkredit bildete in den meisten Fällen die Vorstufe zur „Veraktionierung" der Unternehmen: Ein wichtiger Bestandteil der Bankenstrategie zur Sicherung des Eigenvermögens bestand in der Umwandlung von Kontokorrentforderungen in Aktienbeteiligungen. „Der erste Vizepräsident einer der führenden Banken", berichtete die amerikanische Botschaft, „wurde... von einem amerikanischen Ökonomen gefragt, ob die Banken nicht wüßten, daß Kredite, die in einer Periode der Geldentwertung vergeben würden, in Kronen von geringerem Wert zurückgezahlt werden würden... Die Antwort war, daß die Bankiers sehr wohl erkannten, welches die wahrscheinliche Entwicklung der Krone sein würde, daß es aber zwei zwingende Gründe für die Gewährung von Darlehen gab: Der eine war ihre Tradition der

Beginn der Hyperinflation (Oktober 1921) zusammen. In der Folge führte die Einstellung der staatlichen Lebensmittelunterstützung und die Erhöhung der Lebensmittelpreise zu einer außerordentlichen Geldknappheit. A. Spitzmüller, „... und hat auch Ursach'..." [wie Anm. 36], S. 334 f.

[116] W. Federn, Die Kreditpolitik der Wiener Banken, in: Geldentwertung und Stabilisierung... [wie Anm. 51], S. 59 f.

[117] Siehe: Karl Erich Born, Die Deutsche Bank in der Inflation nach dem Ersten Weltkrieg, in: Deutsche Bank. Beiträge zu Wirtschafts- und Währungsfragen und zur Bankgeschichte, Nr. 17, Frankfurt/Main 1979, S. 27 f.

[118] Nat. Archives, MC 695, Roll 51, C. 508.

Verantwortung für die Aufrechterhaltung des Geschäftslebens... Eine Weigerung, Geld zu verleihen, würde ökonomische Sabotage für das gesamte Land bedeutet und größte soziale Unruhen ausgelöst haben. Der zweite Grund war, daß die meisten dieser Darlehen der Bank zu einem größeren Anteil an den Handels- und Industrieunternehmen verhalfen. Was die Bank als Kreditgeber einbüßte, konnte sie mehr als wettmachen durch den höheren Wert ihres Anteils an kontrollierten Unternehmen."[119] Die Praxis der „Veraktionierungen" begann in größerem Stil 1920[120] und erreichte ihren Höhepunkt in den Jahren 1922 und 1923, als neue Wertpapiere an der Börse leicht unterzubringen waren. Den Banken flossen so reichliche Emissionsgewinne zu, die Industriefirmen konnten ihre Bankschuld reduzieren und erhielten neues Betriebskapital. Allein zwischen September 1922 und Oktober 1923 wurden an der Wiener Börse Aktien neuer Unternehmen mit einem Marktwert von 60 Mrd. Kronen emittiert, die Neuemissionen alter Aktiengesellschaften betrugen 180 Mrd. Kronen.[121] Angaben über die Höhe der Verluste, die den österreichischen Banken in der Inflationszeit aus dem laufenden Geschäft erwuchsen, wären nur möglich, wenn verläßliche Daten über die Fristigkeit und die Währungszusammensetzung der Kreditoren und Debitoren zur Verfügung stünden. Die Abgänge müßten um so höher sein, je weiter die Höhe der Fremdwährungskreditoren die auf Kronen lautenden Debitoren überstieg. Unter der Voraussetzung, daß Einlagen und Kredite auf gleiche Währung lauten, tragen die Gläubiger der Banken das Risiko der Geldentwertung. Der Verlust der Banken besteht in diesem Fall in der Differenz zwischen der Zinsspanne und der Inflationsrate, das heißt im niedrigeren Realwert des Zinsgewinns.

Das Verhältnis der Fremdwährungskreditoren zu den Debitoren dürfte in der Tat ungünstig gewesen sein. In einem Rückblick auf die Entwicklung des österreichischen Bankwesens vertrat der Generaldirektor der Creditanstalt-Bankverein, Josef Joham, 1937 die Auffassung, daß die Entwertung der inländischen Debitoren in der Entwertung der Kronenkreditoren „nur ein unvollkommenes Korrelat" ge-

---

[119] A.a.O., C. 504 f.
[120] M. Sokal, *Die Tätigkeit der Banken in den Jahren 1919 und 1920*... [wie Anm. 103], S. 12.
[121] Nat. Archives, MC 695, Roll 51, C. 333. Siehe auch die bei E. März, *Österreichische Bankpolitik*... [wie Anm. 4], S. 430, wiedergegebene Tabelle über die Vermehrung des Nominalkapitals der österreichischen Aktiengesellschaften 1919—1924.

funden habe, „denn den ausländischen Kreditoren gegenüber blieben die Verpflichtungen der Banken in der Höhe des vollen Goldwertes bestehen".[122] Joham spielte dabei vor allem auf die Vorkriegsschulden der Banken an. In welchem Ausmaß die Wiener Kreditinstitute neue Fremdwährungskredite in Anspruch genommen haben, ist unbekannt. In den Jahren 1919 und 1920 standen ihnen Kronenguthaben von Ausländern in nicht bekannter, aber beträchtlicher Höhe zur Verfügung, die in der Hoffnung auf ein Steigen des Kronenkurses deponiert worden waren.[123] Diese waren Mitte des Jahres 1919 noch höher als die Guthaben, die von Ausländern in fremder Währung bei den österreichischen Banken gehalten wurden.[124] Sogar 1921 sollen die Kroneneinlagen des Auslandes in Wien noch eine „ganz gewaltige Summe" erreicht haben.[125] Die großen Schwankungen des Wechselkurses der Krone in diesem Jahr dürften zum Teil auch auf die Bewegungen dieser Spekulationsgelder zurückzuführen sein.

Eine Aussage zum Verhältnis von ausländischen Kreditoren und Debitoren ist nur insofern möglich, als feststeht, daß ein großer Teil der auf fremde Währung lautenden Debitoren, nämlich die Guthaben bei den affiliierten Kreditinstituten in den Nachfolgestaaten, nicht mobilisierbar war. Deren Anteil an den Gesamtdebitoren betrug nach den Rechnungsabschlüssen für 1922 bei den einzelnen Banken zwischen 30 und 40 %.[126] Über die Höhe der Einlagen der neugewonnenen westlichen Geschäftspartner in Wien gibt es, wie bereits erwähnt, keine Angaben. Dagegen kursierten bei den Zeitgenossen Schätzungen darüber, in welchem Ausmaß es den Wiener Banken gelungen war, ihr Eigenvermögen — durch eine Politik der „Hortung" von Sachwerten — über die Zeit der Inflation hinweg zu erhalten: Auf dem Höhepunkt der Börsenhausse Ende des Jahres 1923 soll ihr Vermögen 50—60 % des Vorkriegsstandes betragen haben.[127] Aber innerhalb eines Jahres fiel

---

[122] Josef Joham, *Geld- und Kreditwesen in Österreich*, in: *Österreichische Zeitschrift für Bankwesen*, 2. Jg. (1937), Nr. 2/3, S. 4.
[123] M. Sokal, *Die Tätigkeit der Banken in den Jahren 1919 und 1920...* [wie Anm. 103], S. 8, berichtet, „daß ein Teil der verfügbaren Kronenguthaben Auslandsguthaben waren, deren dauernde Veranlagung nicht feststand".
[124] FA, Zl. 46.531/1919.
[125] ÖVW, 14. Jg. (17. Juni 1922), *Die Bilanzen*, S. 229.
[126] ÖVW, 15. Jg. (28. April 1923), *Die Bilanzen*, S. 229; (19. Mai 1923), *Die Bilanzen*, S. 254; 14. Jg. (8. Juli 1922), *Die Bilanzen*, S. 252.
[127] Walther Federn, *Goldbilanzen*, in: ÖVW, 16. Jg. (27. September 1924), S. 1569.

das Kursniveau an der Aktienbörse um über 55 %.[128] Außerdem hatte sich die Zusammensetzung des Aktienportefeuilles gegenüber dem Vorkrieg qualitativ verschlechtert,[129] und die Banken waren während des Jahres 1924 (und später) gezwungen, übergroße Bestände von Wertpapieren ihrer Konzernunternehmen zur Kursstützung aufzukaufen.

VI

Die Goldbilanzen

Da die Bilanzen der Banken in den Inflationsjahren nur ein sehr ungenaues Bild der wirklichen Lage vermittelt hatten, war es nach dem Ende der Geldentwertung notwendig geworden, eine völlige Neubewertung aller Vermögens- und Schuldenpositionen vorzunehmen. Die gesetzliche Grundlage hierfür bildete das Goldbilanzgesetz vom 4. Juni 1925.[130]

Bei einem Vergleich der Goldbilanzen (per 1. 1. 1925) mit den Jahresabschlüssen für 1913 fällt vor allem die starke Schrumpfung der Bilanzsummen und des Eigenkapitals der Banken ins Auge. Dabei ist der Rückgang der eigenen Mittel — trotz der seit 1913 vorgenommenen Kapitalerhöhungen — deutlich stärker, so daß sich das Verhältnis von Eigenkapital zu Bilanzsumme merklich verschlechterte. Eine Ausnahme bildet nur der Wiener Bankverein, der den Eigenkapitalanteil von 18,9 % im Jahre 1913 auf 20,6 % erhöhen konnte. Doch auch der Bankverein wies in den Goldbilanzen ein Eigenkapital aus, das nur 15,4 % des Wertes von 1913 (zuzüglich der seither durchgeführten Erhöhungen) entsprach. (Siehe Anhang, TABELLE 8.)

Die Entwertung des Eigenvermögens der Wiener Banken zeigt sich auch bei einer Gegenüberstellung der eigenen und der in Effekten und Konsortialbeständen dauernd gebundenen Mittel. Im Jahre 1913 waren bei den vier angeführten Instituten zwischen 20 und 57 % des Eigenkapitals in langfristigen Anlagen gebunden, in den Goldbilanzen erreichte dieser Wert zwischen 49,5 (Bankverein) und 116,6 % (Bodencreditan-

---

[128] W. T. Layton/Ch. Rist, *Die Wirtschaftslage...* [wie Anm. 97], S. 82. Der dort angeführte Aktienindex bezieht sich allerdings nur auf die Aktien von 77 österreichischen Gesellschaften, die bereits vor dem Krieg bestanden.

[129] E. März, *Österreichische Bankpolitik...* [wie Anm. 4], S. 534 ff.

[130] Siehe dazu: Franz Rust, *Das österreichische Goldbilanzgesetz*, in: *Mitteilungen des Verbandes österreichischer Banken und Bankiers*, 7. Jg. (1925), S. 97 ff.

stalt).[131] Die Relation war bei jenen Banken besonders ungünstig, die ihr Wertpapierkonto — im Vergleich zu 1923 — in starkem Maße aufwerteten.[132]

Es gibt eine Reihe von Indizien, die den Schluß nahelegen, daß die Goldbilanzen ein zu optimistisches Bild von der Lage der Großbanken zeichneten und daß ein wesentlicher Grundsatz des Gesetzes — die Rücksichtnahme auf die Ertragsfähigkeit bei der Bewertung des Vermögens — außer acht gelassen wurde. Die Erklärung für das leichtfertige Vorgehen der Banken liegt nicht bloß in allzu optimistischen Zukunftserwartungen, sondern auch in der Tatsache, daß die Goldbilanzen mit Blickrichtung auf das westliche Ausland erstellt wurden: Die Wiener Kreditinstitute sollten als im Kern gesunde und potente Partner erscheinen, in die weitere Gelder zu investieren sich lohne[133] — dies, obwohl zum Zeitpunkt der Goldbilanzlegung bekannt war, „daß man in London einen Kapitalisierungsanspruch von 8 bis 10 % an kontinentale Papiere stellen wird"[134] und daß zumindest eine Großbank die Dividende für das Jahr 1924 aus ihren Reserven hatte bestreiten müssen.[135]

Spätere Untersuchungen haben ergeben, daß auch in den folgenden Jahren Dividenden ausgezahlt wurden, die die Banken nicht verdient hatten. Darüber hinaus hatten die Banken verschiedentlich Konzernunternehmen dazu angehalten, bei der Goldbilanzerstellung ebenfalls ein überhöhtes Eigenkapital auszuweisen. Aus Gründen der „Kurspflege" mußten diese Firmen Dividenden ausschütten, die — um es überspitzt zu formulieren — mit dem Kredit der Mutterbank finanziert wurden. Auch hinsichtlich der ausländischen Industriebeteiligungen scheinen die Wiener Kreditinstitute eine wenig glückliche Ge-

---

[131] *Mitteilungen des Direktoriums der Oesterreichischen Nationalbank*, Nr. 7 (1926).

[132] Das Ausmaß der Höherbewertung betrug bei der Escomptegesellschaft 27, beim Bankverein 49, bei der Creditanstalt 117 und bei der Bodencreditanstalt 138 %. Siehe: Benedikt Kautsky, *Die Bankbilanzen des Jahres 1925*, in: *Arbeit und Wirtschaft*, 1. September 1926, Sp. 688.

[133] Bei den Verhandlungen des Goldbilanzgesetzes wiesen die Vertreter der Banken darauf hin, daß bei einer Bewertung der Effekten zum Kurs von Ende 1924 „die Goldbilanzen der Banken ein so kleines Eigenvermögen ergeben (würden), daß im Ausland der schlechteste Eindruck hervorgerufen würde". Vorstandssitzungsprotokoll der Bodencreditanstalt vom 8. Mai 1925, CA-Archiv.

[134] Direktionssitzungsprotokoll des Bankvereins vom 6. Mai 1925, CA-Archiv.

[135] Vorstandssitzungsprotokoll der Bodencreditanstalt vom 15. Mai 1925, CA-Archiv.

schäftspolitik betrieben zu haben. Hier erwiesen sich die Konzernunternehmen im Textil- und Mineralölsektor als besonders problematisch.[136] Der Schein der Prosperität des Bankwesens ließ sich daher nur für wenige Jahre und nur so lange aufrechterhalten, als der Zustrom kurzfristiger Gelder aus dem westlichen Ausland anhielt und die stillen Reserven der Institute noch nicht aufgezehrt waren.

Möglicherweise wäre es den Großbanken unter günstigeren ökonomischen Umweltbedingungen gelungen, ihre durch die Inflation und den Verlust der Filialen in den Nachfolgestaaten geschwächte Position allmählich zu konsolidieren, zumal ihnen von der internationalen Bankwelt ein beträchtlicher Vertrauens- (und Kredit)vorschuß gewährt wurde.[137] Aber die Symbiose mit der Industrie des Donauraums[138] — vor dem Krieg Quelle der Prosperität der Banken — erwies sich in den zwanziger Jahren als Achillesferse des österreichischen Crédit-Mobilier-Systems; sie potenzierte die Fehlentscheidungen, die bei der Erstellung der Goldbilanzen getroffen wurden. Es erscheint daher symptomatisch, daß mit der Bodencreditanstalt im Herbst 1929 jene Bank als erste in Schwierigkeiten geriet, die sich in der Goldbilanz am weitesten — und wissentlich[139] — von der Realität entfernt hatte.

---

[136] *Gutachten des Hofrates Georg Stern über die Creditanstalt* (verfaßt 1931/32). CA-Archiv.

[137] Auch die österreichischen Experten vertraten nach der Veröffentlichung der Goldbilanzen die Ansicht, daß die Banken — aus Gründen der vorsichtigen Geschäftsgebarung — ihr Eigenvermögen eher zu niedrig eingeschätzt hätten. Siehe: ÖVW, 18. Jg. (8. Mai 1926), *Die Bilanzen*, S. 240; (29. Mai 1926), *Die Bilanzen*, S. 265; (26. Juni 1926), *Die Bilanzen*, S. 301 ff.

[138] Obwohl beispielsweise die Creditanstalt nach 1918 die Fühlung mit einer Reihe großer Industrieunternehmen im Ausland verlor, erhöhte sich die Zahl ihrer industriellen Konzernfirmen zwischen 1913 und 1923 von 86 auf 100. Davon hatten fast zwei Drittel ihren Hauptsitz bzw. die Hauptbetriebe im Ausland. Siehe: E. März, *Österreichische Bankpolitik...* [wie Anm. 4], S. 536 ff.

[139] Dies geht aus dem Vorstandssitzungsprotokoll der Bodencreditanstalt vom 6. Juni 1925 hervor. Damals wurde die Frage besprochen, ob sich die Bank — im Wege des Aktientausches — an der Anglo-Austrian Bank beteiligen solle. Eine solche Transaktion wurde mit dem Hinweis abgelehnt, daß kein Interesse daran bestehe, der Bank of England Einsicht in die interne Bilanz der Bodencreditanstalt zu gewähren, weil „dann... das Umtauschverhältnis ein solches sein (würde), daß vielleicht eine größere Anzahl von B.C.A.-Aktien einer kleineren Anzahl von Anglobank-Aktien entsprechen würde".

ANHANG

Tabelle 1

Kreditoren und Debitoren von vier Wiener Großbanken*
(in Mio. Kronen)

Jahr	Debitoren	Kreditoren	Kreditoren in % der Debitoren
1910	1 422,6**	1 483,9	104,3
1911	1 689,6**	1 668,4	98,7
1912	1 758,2**	1 723,3	98,0
1913	1 869,2**	1 835,7	98,2
1914	2 049,1**	2 121,8	103,5
1915	2 415,9	2 782,2	115,4
1916	3 698,5	4 390,7	118,7
1917	4 595,2	5 771,8	125,6
1918	5 208,4	6 685,7	128,4
1919	10 159,0	11 858,0	116,7
1920	24 529,0	27 598,0	112,5
1921	207 741,0	214 964,0	103,5
1922	4 031 790,0	4 472 181,0	110,9***
1923	6 888 645,0	7 220 698,0	104,8

* Creditanstalt, Bodencreditanstalt, Bankverein, Escomptegesellschaft.

** Die Bodencreditanstalt verbucht auch die Konsortialbeteiligungen unter Debitoren. Eine Bereinigung um diesen nicht genau feststellbaren Betrag würde den Überschuß der Kreditoren um 2—3 % erhöhen.

*** Die Kassenbestände der Gemeinde Wien wurden bis 1921 bei der Länderbank gehalten, nach dem Übergang dieses Instituts in französischen Besitz aber bei der Escomptegesellschaft. Die Höhe der liquiden Mittel der Wiener Kommunalverwaltung sank mit dem Anlaufen des Wohnbauprogramms im Jahr 1923.

Quelle: Compass, diverse Jahrgänge, jeweils Bd. 1.

TABELLE 2
Bilanzstruktur der Wiener Großbanken

		Eigenkapital	Kassa	Portefeuille	Effekten	Vorschüsse auf Effekten	Konsortialbeteiligungen	Debitoren
		(in Prozent der Bilanzsumme)				(in Prozent der Bilanzsumme)	(in Prozent der Bilanzsumme)	
Creditanstalt	1913	20,6	2,6	17,1	3,9	4,3	7,2	62,2
	1917	10,0	1,0	6,7	7,7	1,9	2,3	66,0
	1918	11,1	5,2	5,0	5,7	1,0	2,9	52,5[2]
	1925*	14,8	1,4	5,3	7,6	—	5,6	78,4
Bodencreditanstalt	1913	19,0	0,9	11,8	3,6	2,9	—[1]	35,5
	1917	11,9	1,3	5,3	4,0	21,2	2,0	39,6
	1918	14,2	11,7	4,6	4,9	10,4	2,3	40,2
	1925*	14,8	1,4	5,7	10,5	—	6,8	73,9
Bankverein	1913	18,9	2,1	23,8	3,1	5,1	6,2	56,6
	1917	7,6	3,1	3,8	7,5	1,0	1,4	81,7[2]
	1918	7,2	3,8	1,0	6,3	0,7	1,6	52,5[2]
	1925*	20,6	3,0	12,1	1,4	0,0	8,9	71,2
Länderbank	1913	18,8	2,5	21,1	6,7	9,1	5,3	54,3
	1917	10,5	2,4	3,3	9,4	1,0	2,4	80,0[2]
	1918	10,7	3,6	2,8	5,4	0,6	2,5	64,2[2]
	1925[3]							
Anglobank	1913	16,9	1,9	21,3	2,8	3,1	3,6	66,5
	1917	9,1	2,4	1,7	6,3	2,5	1,9	85,3[2]
	1918	10,6	4,0	1,7	4,0	3,2	2,2	56,0[2]
	1925[3]							
Escomptegesellschaft	1913	23,2	1,8	15,4	8,7	2,5	4,6	66,6
	1917	12,1	1,1	4,6	1,2	34,8	2,1	56,2
	1918	13,5	3,1	5,8	0,5	—	2,9	84,3[2]
	1925*	17,5	4,0	5,8	1,5	—	11,1	77,5

ANMERKUNGEN zu TABELLE 2:
* Golderöffnungsbilanz vom 1. 1. 1925.
[1] In Debitoren enthalten.
[2] Inklusive Vorschüsse auf Kriegsanleihen.
[3] Diese Banken verlegten 1921 ihren Sitz ins Ausland.

Quelle: Compass, diverse Jahrgänge, Bd. 1.

TABELLE 3

Kurswert des Aktienkapitals der Creditanstalt
1913—1924 (in Mio. Dollar)

Jahr		Aktienkapital (in Mio. Kronen)	Kurswert (in Mio.)
Ende	1913	150,0	60,6
	1918	200,0	24,1
	1919	200,0	5,3
	1920	320,0	2,4
	1921	600,0	5,1
30. Juni	1922	1 000,0	1,5
Ende	1922	15 000,0	3,0
	1923	20 000,0	31,0
	1924	20 000,0	14,6

Quelle: Compass 1915, 1925, 1930, jeweils Bd. 1.

TABELLE 4

Zahl der Filialen der 10 größten Wiener Banken
außerhalb Wiens 1913—1929

Jahr	Insgesamt	Außerhalb des Gebiets der Republik Österreich	In den Bundesländern
1913	149	114	35
1918	187	144	43
1922	121	9	112
1924	104	9	95
1929*	36	3	33

* Vor der Fusion Creditanstalt-Bodencreditanstalt (7 Banken).

Quelle: Compass 1915, 1919, 1925, 1930, jeweils Bd. 1.

TABELLE 5

Zusammensetzung des Rohgewinns der Creditanstalt (ohne Gewinnvortrag) 1913—1923 (in %)

	1913	1918	1919	1920	1921	1922	1923
Zinsen	70,3	74,9	44,2	41,2	35,8	35,2	25,7
Gewinn aus Effekten- und Konsortialgeschäften	6,6	—	24,6	19,6	13,8	13,4	28,8
Provisionen und Warengewinne	20,7	22,5	18,7	17,7	38,7	43,6	37,5
Gewinne aus Devisen	2,2	2,1	12,4	21,4	11,7	7,8	8,0

Quelle: *Compass,* versch. Jahrgänge, jeweils Bd. 1.

TABELLE 6

Zinsspanne der Creditanstalt

A: Zinsensaldo in % der Debitoren
B: Zinsensaldo und Provisionen in % der Debitoren

Durchschnitt	A	B
1905—1913	2,9	3,9
1919	1,9	2,7
1920	1,6	2,3
1921	1,7	3,5
1922	2,3	5,1
1923	4,1	10,0
1924	3,3	8,3
1925	2,5	5,6

Quelle: *Compass,* versch. Jahrgänge, jeweils Bd. 1.

TABELLE 7

Wechselportefeuille der Notenbank*

	I Wechselportefeuille (in Mio. Kronen)	II Banknotenumlauf	I in % von II
31. 12. 1913	925,0	23 493,6	37,1
31. 10. 1918	12,9**	31 483,2	0,04
30. 6. 1921	1 305,8	49 685,1	2,6
30. 9. 1921	3 500,0	70 170,8	5,0
31. 12. 1921	29 373,7	174 114,7	16,9
31. 3. 1922	70 142,8	304 063,6	23,1
30. 6. 1922	175 301,4	549 915,7	31,9
31. 8. 1922	531 103,0	1 353 403,6	39,2

* 1913—1918: Österreichisch-ungarische Bank; 1921—1922: Östereichische Geschäftsführung der österreichisch-ungarischen Bank.
** Ohne Staatswechsel in der Höhe von 2,8 Mrd. Kronen.

Quelle: S. Pressburger, *Das österreichische Noteninstitut...*, passim.

TABELLE 8

Rückgang des Eigenkapitals 1925 gegenüber 1913

	Eigenkapital 1925 in % des Wertes von 1913	Eigenkapital 1925 in % des Wertes von 1913 zu- zügl. v. Kapitalerhöhungen
Creditanstalt	20,0	15,7
Bodencreditanstalt	19,0	16,2
Bankverein	24,0	15,4
Escomptegesellschaft	34,5	22,5

Quelle: ÖVW, 18. Jg. (26. Juni 1926), S. 1074.

Summary

One the eve of World War I, after a decade of rapid economic growth which tightened the links between banks and industry, the Viennese Crédit-Mobilier-banks were at the height of their influence. During the war the increasing liquidity of industrial firms led to a loosening of the symbiosis with the banks, a trend which was again reversed in 1917/18 and especially in the immediate post-war period. Although the main business of the banks, from 1914 onwards, consisted in the financing of the war, the banks managed to get into a net debtor position vis-à-vis the public sector (state and central bank) at the end of 1918.

The downfall of the Habsburg Monarchy was accompanied by the process of „nationalization" in the succession states, i.e. the dissolution of the banks' industrial conglomerates and network of branches. The Viennese banks now had to choose between restricting their business to the new Austria (a small country) or trying to uphold their sphere of influence in the Danube Basin irrespective of the hostile environment. The banks decided in favour of the „multinationalization" of their activities which also meant finding support of „Western" capital groups. Indeed, Western banks took over — and, because of the depreciation of the Austrian Crown, at a cheap price — varying portions of the Viennese bank capital, and they granted credits to the Austrian banks throughout the 1920s.

The effects of the post-war inflation on the status of the banks are not deducible from the balance sheets which were published during the inflation period. Even the so-called „gold balance sheets" (Goldbilanzen) of 1 January 1925, designed to give an exact statement of the banks' assets and liabilities after the end of inflation, showed too optimistic a picture of the Austrian banking system. The banks must have undergone losses because of the forfeiture of their branches located in the succession states, because of the unfavourable ratio of deposits in foreign currency to domestic credits, and also because they continued to grant credits in Crowns at an interest rate far below the inflation rate. But the banks hoped to compensate these losses by enlarging their influence as shareholders of their client firms, a strategy which in the end proved not to be successful, since the rate of profit of the Austrian Industry as a whole was rather low during the Twenties.

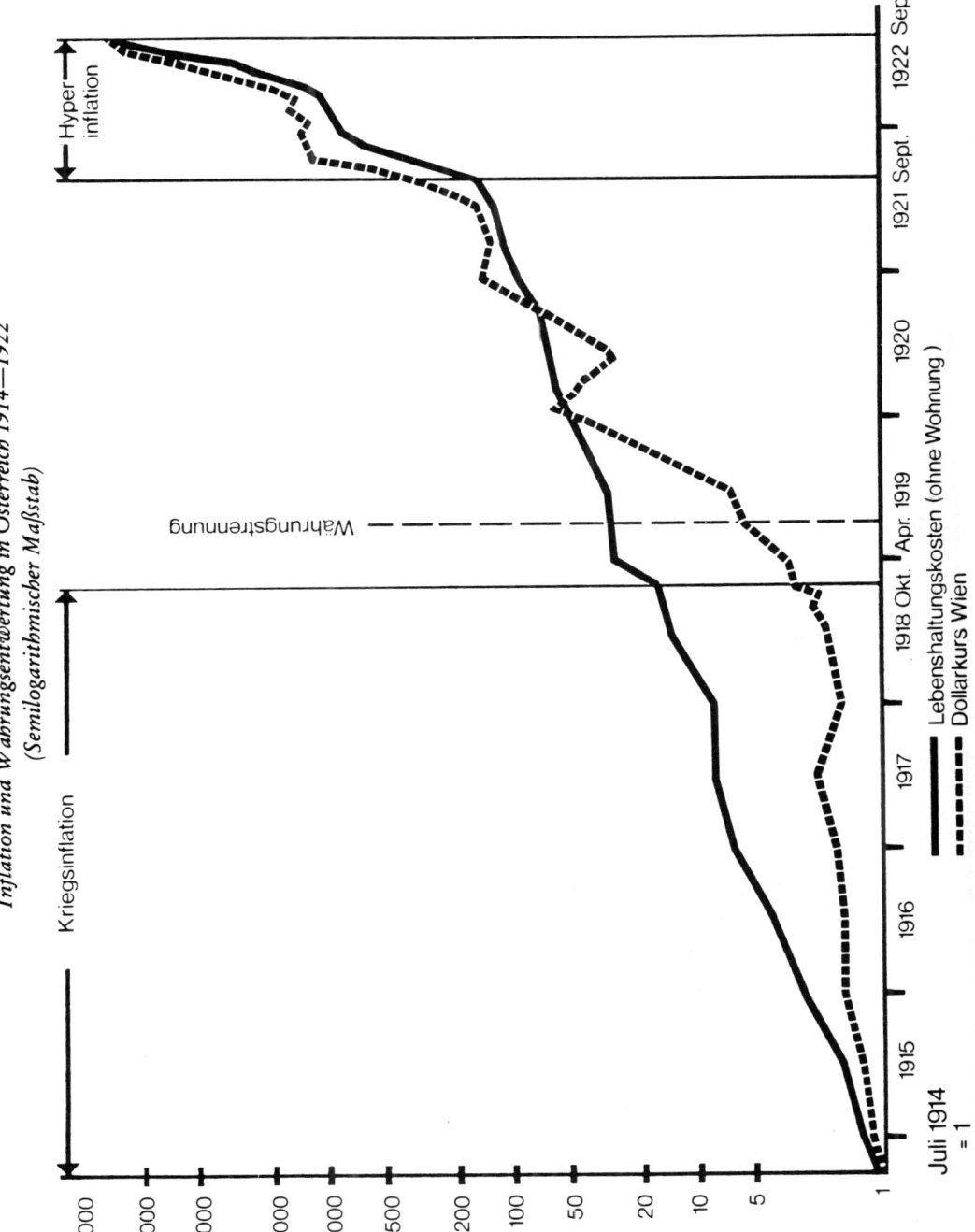

The Role of the State Issuing Bank in the Course of Inflation in Hungary between 1918 and 1924*

ELIZABETH A. BOROSS

Introduction, Periodization of Inflation

The Austro-Hungarian Crown was established by Statute XVII of 1892 during a period of stability and economic growth within the Monarchy. After two decades, however, it was destabilized by the war and its aftermath and it was drawn into an inflationary spiral. The purpose of this paper is to try and ascertain when inflation in Hungary became set on a course wich led to the collapse of the currency in 1924, following Austria (1922) and Germany (1923). More specifically the motivations and consequences of the note issuing policy of the Hungarian Government and the credit policy of the State Issuing Bank will be examined.

Nowadays theories relating to inflation — the problems of analysing the sources of inflationary pressures — constitute a complex economic science in light of the persistent nature of the phenomenon. However, inflations which occurred before World War II could be seen to reflect some particular national crisis which preceded the fall in the value of the currency. Expensive wars and their aftermath have traditionally been recognised as potent sources of inflationary pressure, being periods when governments, in an attempt to squeeze more and more out of

---

* This paper is a contribution to the research project „Inflation and Reconstruction in Germany and Europe, 1914—1924" and the author wishes gratefully to acknowledge the financial support of the Stiftung Volkswagenwerk. Thanks are due to Professor Alice Teichova and Dr. Philip L. Cottrell for their continuous assistance during the preparation of this study, and to Professor Dr. Ivan T. Berend and Dr. György Peteri for their constructive comments. For any errors and omissions the responsibility is mine.

hard-pressed wartime economies often resorted to the printing presses to provide the requisite finance for the purchase of arms, payment of soldiers, etc. It was generally assumed that once the economy returned to a more normal state of affairs, then persistent inflationary pressures would disappear. Hence theories relating to inflation in the post-World War I period were still tending to be more mono-causal, with the process being instigated by the state in abnormal circumstances, i. e. at a time of war with an economy already fully stretched in its productive capacity to wage hostilities, the issue of extra money by government simply served to bid up the prices of the limited output of that economy. The continued printing of money by the government did in such circumstances lead to a persistent tendency for prices to rise, that is, it led to inflation. The ruling contemporary inflationary theory in Hungary was broadly speaking a traditional quantity theory, that of Liefmann, Cassel and Bendixen.[1] Accordingly, inflation was seen as being caused by the exaggerated increase of the money supply (that is an increase unwarranted by the normal needs of the economic life) and the effect of this increased quantity of money caused prices to rise, the consequence of which was the deterioration of the purchasing power of a unit of the currency.[2]

As excessive issuing of notes was undertaken by Hungary during and after the war, the contemporary view of the causes of inflation generally included the disturbance of the balance of the state budget, either due to the extraordinary increase in demand, or due to the decrease in tax revenue.

It should be added, even if only in a brief and oversimplified fashion, that the view expressed by contemporary literature analysing the course of inflation in Hungary offered the following alternatives for the elimination of the budget deficit: A) to increase the state revenue within the statutory framework, i. e. taxes; B) through a loan operation, usually through mortgage bonds or debentures; C) if neither alternatives were feasible (taxes may not have been mobile enough, and a tense political or financial situation did not lend itself to a successful loan

[1] Rudolf Liefmann, *Die Goldvermehrung im Weltkriege und die Beseitigung ihrer Folgen*, Berlin 1918; Gustav Cassel, *Money and Foreign Exchange after 1914*, London 1922; F. Bendixen, *Das Inflationsproblem*, Stuttgart 1917.
[2] F. Bendixen is also quoted by Anna Löw, *A pengőérték bevezetése és értékállandósága fenntartásának feltételei* (The introduction of the Pengö value and conditions relating to the stability of the currency), Diss., Budapest 1932.

operation) the state might be forced to embark upon an increase in the money supply in order to create sufficient means to meet the demand of state expenditure. Therefore in Hungary, the First World War was seen as the initial cause of the post-war inflationary process.

It was not emphasized sufficiently in the economic literature of the period that: a) the budget deficit could also be controlled by means of reduction in expenditure. At first sight this might seem a contradiction in terms as we are talking about the war demand increasing expenditure continually, but in fact most of the state interventions in the economy during the war were aiming — at least theoretically — to reduce the deficit. To this end material distribution centres were set up, and as from 1917 the Government Price Control Centre was operating. The fact that price controls were ineffective to control inflation was the result of goods being in diminishing supply and production through various disruptions (call up system reducing employment levels, dislocation of raw material supplies etc.) was not able to keep up with demand. b) It also needs to be acknowledged that the loan operation and the inflationary note issues were not really alternatives to one another, since note issues — technically — were also state obligations between the Issuing Bank and government through Treasury bonds.

The inflationary process will be examined through the four discernible stages which can be found between the outbreak of the war and stabilization:

1) During the war the issuing of uncovered notes took place almost exclusively for the state's purposes, i.e. war requirements.

2) From the end of 1918 to September 1921 notes had to be issued for personnel expenses of the state, — one need only to mention the hugely increased volume of pensions, the influx of mostly unproductive civil servants from areas detached from Hungary, the cost of maintaining demobilized soldiers, reparation payments in kind to be reimbursed.

3) From September 1921 to late 1923, the needs of the private sector of the economy were honoured far too generously. The newly established central bank, the Hungarian State Issuing Office set up in August 1921, extended loans to aid post-war recovery, which swelled the money supply.

4) January to May 1924, during the last few months before stabilization note issuing to cover state expenses came into prominence again.

War Economy, 1914—1918

The war effected the growth in the circulating currency from two directions. First, the expansion of production necessitated an increase in the means of payment. Second, the state's financing of warfare —because the extraordinary expenses could not be met from ordinary revenue, and the proceeds of a succession of war bond issues were quickly consumed — was only possible by the repeated issue of paper notes. As opposed to the first, economically justifiable increase in the circulation money supply, the second state instigated course of action contained the dangers which led to the watering down of the value of the Crown.

Indebtedness of the state to the Austro-Hungarian Bank began to increase with a 2 Milliard Crown Lombard Loan taken out by the two Treasuries on 14th August 1914. Thereafter the governments of the Monarchy regularly resorted to the Austro-Hungarian Bank which employed different credit operations in order to cover the increasing war expenditure. On the day of the military collapse the Bank's claim on the two governments stood as follows:[3]

TABLE 1

Indebtedness to the Austro-Hungarian Bank

	Austria K	Hungary K
Consortium Loan	510,000,000	297,500,000
Lombard Loan	1,272,000,000	728,000,000
Sola Bills	1,780,800,000	1,019,200,000
Bond Notes	19,634,000,000	6,798,000,000
Treasury Notes	1,862,997,276	1,066,243,724
Total	25,059,797,276	9,908,943,724

On account of the joint currency the two governments took up loans from the Austro-Hungarian Bank in a predetermined proportion, that is Austria 63.6%, Hungary 36.4%, which was also the war expense distribution quota.

---

[3] Sándor Popovich, *A pénz sorsa a háborúban* (The fate of money during the war), Budapest 1926, p. 79.

To the end of 1916 loans were taken up according to this set quota. As from mid-1917, however, the calling up of the Austrian Parliament (30th May 1917) and the tenser internal political situation, which manifested itself in social unrest, forced the Austrian Government to greatly increase the state subsidy to the families of soldiers, war widows and orphans. The Austrian Government being unable to find another source of income, came to rely on the Austro-Hungarian Bank to a greater extent than had been set by the parity. Accordingly, although Austria's 25 Milliard Crown loan would have entitled Hungary to a 14.3 Milliard Crown loan, in fact, the Hungarian state only took up 9.9 Milliard. Hungarian opposition members called the Hungarian Government's attention to the fact that Austria depreciated the joint currency to a greater degree, because the joint Bank was drawn on for the direct increase of the purchasing power of the Austrian population. It was thought that this was an even more dangerous precedent than the Government's war time spending.[4]

The argument, however — undoubtedly fired by the Hungarian nationalists — as to who depreciated the currency to a greater degree has no relation to a quota set up decades earlier in the Austro-Hungarian Monarchy. One could only argue about responsibility for depreciating the joint currency if there was a way of calculating that Austria's contribution to the creation of the national income of the whole Monarchy was less in proportion than her inflation of the currency, and the preset quota had nothing to do with this proportion.

The volume of banknotes in circulation as of 31st July 1914 amounted to K 3,062 Million, while the Austro-Hungarian Bank's effective gold cover came to K 1,270 Million. Subsequently the volume of banknotes and the stock of gold foreign exchange reserves moved in the following way:[5]

---

[4] János Teleszky, *A Magyar Állam Pénzügyei a Háboru Alatt* (The finances of the Hungarian State during the War), Budapest 1927, p. 252.

[5] S. Popovich, *A pénz sorsa*... [see note 3], Appendix II.

TABLE 2

The Austro-Hungarian Bank's Volume of Banknotes
and Reserves

Date	Volume of Banknotes in 1000 K	Gold foreign exchange reserves in 1000 K
31st Dec. 1914	5,136,694	1,055,069
31st Dec. 1915	7,162,355	684,886
31st Dec. 1916	10,888,619	290,024
31st Dec. 1917	18,439,695	265,137
31st Oct. 1918	31,383,231	267,712
31st Dec. 1918	35,588,600	—

Between the outbreak of the war (31st July 1914) and the ending of the hostilities (26th October 1918) the Austro-Hungarian Bank's volume of Banknotes and its gold reserves showed the following change:

TABLE 3

The Development of the Austro-Hungarian Bank's
Volume of Notes and Reserves

Date	Volume of Banknotes	Reserves
31st July 1914	K 3,062,000,000	K 1,269,900,000
26th October 1918	K 30,679,900,000	K 285,500,000

While therefore the volume of banknotes increased tenfold, the gold cover dwindled to a quarter of its original value.

What is typical for the first phase of the inflationary period is that there developed a gap between the Crown's internal purchasing power and its foreign exchange value. The foreign exchange rated the growth in the money supply as being less inflationary than the internal market, as shown below:[6]

---

[6] Bela Jankovich, *A papirpénz inflációja és értéke az utolsó évtized tapasztalatai nyomán* (The inflation of paper money and its value as experienced in the last decade), in: *Közgazdasági Szemle*, (1925), p. 33.

	1913	1918
The disagio at the Zurich Exchange	1	0.29
Volume of Banknotes	1	11.46
Price index	1	8.93

This can be explained by several factors. Between 1914-18 the Austro-Hungarian Bank did not publish its accounts either at home or abroad. Furthermore the Hungarian press was not even allowed to publicise the statements issued by either the German Issuing Bank, or the Entente Power's financial reports, although the latter were available.[7] Others (cf. footnote 6) attributed the relatively favourable foreign valuation to the following factors: the extension in the use of cash which took place in all transactions instead of the normal bank and credit business; the additional need for the means of payment in occupied territories; the mounting predominance of hoarding. All these factors ensured demand for the increasing volume of notes and so allowed the unsecured paper currency to retain more than its real value.

What needs also to be added by the way of explanation is that the possibility of the gap between internal and external valuation of currency was itself contained in the elimination of the international intermediary mechanism which created a material connection between the national price levels and the currency's international valuation. In other words during the war the free movement of goods, services and capital was suspended.

While the Crown fared relatively well on the foreign exchanges, prices on the home market — although kept in the dark over the extent of money printing — indicated all the signs of an economy disrupted by war, aggravated by a diminishing supply of goods. The ever increasing demands of the Supreme Command for goods, materials, animals and increased output required everybody's intensified efforts. As it was not possible to obtain essential supplies through imports, all necessities had to be routed out from within Hungary. This was why the Supreme Command not only overlooked rising prices, but often encouraged this trend. They did not consider how much the producer or grower asked for the goods, but engaged a whole series of procurers, agents and middlemen to buy at any cost.[8]

Nevertheless, when the war ended the Crown's value had not yet

---

[7] Arpád Dános, *A valutánk rendezése* (The regularizing of our currency), Budapest 1920, p. 11.

[8] *Op. cit.*, p. 14.

dropped to a level from which recovery would not have been possible and feasible with energetic measures on the home front and international cooperation. There were, however, three obstacles in the way: lack of international understanding, paralysis of the Issuing Bank, and extremely low production levels.

With the collapse, the unity of the joint currency ceased to exist among the states of the Monarchy and the nationalization of the currencies began with the overstamping of Austro-Hungarian banknotes by individual states. Great confusion was caused as this did not occur simultaneously. Yugoslavia carried out the stamping on the 18th January 1919, Austria ordered bank closures on the 15th February to stop the import of the Crown (order issued 25th February 1919), Czechoslovakia on the 25th February 1919, Poland on the 26th March 1919, followed by Romania, each country thereby fixing its own note liability. Hungary's overstamping of the currency was delayed not only because she was engaged in effecting major social and political changes during the ensuing revolutions, but also because initially Count Károlyi (the leader of the democratic revolution) entertained federalist ideas. While recognising the desire and necessity for political autonomy, he hoped to retain some degree of economic unity among the emerging national states, and so did not want to condone the disintegration by participating in the monetary separation. In 1920, however, the Peace Treaty of Trianon (§ 189) and the Treaty of St. Germain (§ 206) unequivocally ordered the liquidation of the Austro-Hungarian Bank. Most importantly, the liabilities of the Bank were distributed among the Successor States on the basis of the quantities of notes to be found on their territory. As by this time — apart from Hungary — the other interested states had carried out their stamping operations, Hungary was the only place to which the hitherto unstamped banknotes could escape to be validated, and this inevitably led to a further increase in the volume of banknotes in circulation in Hungary (Hungary's stamping was carried out on the 17th March 1920).

A study undertaken by a Hungarian economist (Jankovich cf. footnote 6) to prove the influx of notes quantitatively concurred with this process. A calculation was made to establish the per capita volume of note circulation in Austria and Hungary based on the 1912 volume which was 3100 Million Crown over a population of 52.5 Million. The result showed that Hungary's total note circulation worked out as K 466 Million, or K 59 per capita (Population 7.9 Million) while Austria's total volume was K 500 Million, or K 81.2 per capita. This estimate is borne out by aggregating the July 1919 note volumes, when both the Viennese and Budapest quotations still agreed, of which 15.3 % belonged to Hungary and 19.7 % to Austria. The reports of the overstamping that had taken place, however, showed a different result. In the first half of 1920, the Successor States all reported the amount of stamped and exchanged currency on their territory to the Austro-Hungarian Bank Liquidating Commission. The total was 44,927 Million Crowns, of which Austria claimed 7,428 Million, i. e. 16.8 %, while Hungary had 8,500 Million, i. e. 18.9 %.[9] What had taken place was that a proportion of the currency volume which had not been disclosed elsewhere was validated in Hungary.

Another fiscal operation adding to the inflationary pressure was the policy of the Austro-Hungarian Bank to issue Lombard Loans against War Bonds taken up by the public at 75 % of face value. From 22nd October 1918 to 7th November 1918 applications were received for Lombard Loans to the nominal value of K 332 Million, against which K 249 Million were issued.[10] As early as December 1918 the Austro-Hungarian Bank warned the Hungarian Finance Ministry that it would only continue to satisfy this increasing demand for the loans if the Treasury accepted the liability for any losses incurred on the bonds. In order to maintain public confidence in state securities the Council of Ministers agreed to guarantee the loans secured by the war bonds instead of restricting this very profitable credit operation, which at the low rate of interest of 5 % only fuelled inflation by increasing demand in the circulating money supply.

Revolutions and Economic Instability

The following period was characterised by revolutionary upheavals, over and above the war-time disorganization of the economy. It was impossible to even contemplate the introduction of a systematic economic policy. Not only did the chaotic revolutionary conditions prevent the formulation and carrying out of a policy, but during the

---

[9] B. Jankovich, *A papirpénz*... [see note 6], p. 22; quoted from the *Memorandum sur les monnais 1913-1922*, Geneve 1923, p. 88.

[10] Országos Levéltár Budapest (Hungarian National Archives — OL) Magyar Kir. Minisztertanács jegyzökönyvei, K27 NO.68, 17. December 1918. Also quoted by György Péteri, *A Magyar Tanácsköztársaság iparirányitási rendszere* (The system of industrial management in the Hungarian Soviet Republic), Budapest 1979, p. 27.

Károlyi regime, (31st October 1918 to 21st March 1919) for instance — contrary to the armistice provisions — the political and economic demarcation lines kept changing. The Government could never be certain of the extent and scope of its activities, both as far as the governing authority or boundaries were concerned. State administration, under the circumstances, was conducted first at biweekly, and from the end of November 1918 to January 1919 in a three monthly estimation of expenses, which in effect could only indicate foreseeable money requirements.[11] The shock of losing the war with the disruption caused by the breakup of the centuries old working order debilitated all established institutions. Count Károlyi came into power on the strength of being able to provide an equitable peace to the exhausted population. Only the organised labour force, particuarly the trade unions in the capital, who had gained strength during the war, had a programme which was not affected by the constitutional change. Károlyi — idealistically — embraced this programme as governing principles for the future. Initially, however, the population, exhausted by the demands of war, was seeking peace and easier living conditions, not further sacrifices and self-denial in order to build a new socialist economic order. Consequently only those aspects of the socialist programme were instigated in the short period of time, which resulted in the more even distribution of wealth and which under the circumstances amounted to state aid; particularly, as increases in production to pay for these benefits were not realisable, since the lack of raw materials and the lack of transport crippled the economy.

One needs to consider the psychological elements in order to understand why the post-war revolutionary period became the eldorado of state spending. To mention just a few examples: it is unquestionable that the high war-time prices and the depreciating currency placed the heaviest burden on those living on a fixed income. Therefore it was expected that a revolutionary democratic government would bring the level of earning up to the level of inflated prices. The new Government, partly in order to secure continued support and popularity and also in recognition that the level of pay for the fixed income sectors lagged inequitably behind prices, had to give a substantial increase in pay to civil servants and workers. Naturally, once this was granted in the

---

[11] OL., Kállay Documents, K275 7/VI/I, Memorandum to the Peace Negotiations and Reparation Commission. Extracts printed in: *Közgazdasági Szemle*, (1920).

public sector its soon filtered through to the private sector as well. To satisfy to some extent the clamouring demands, it put a yearly amount of some 1.27 Milliard Crowns as permanent excess expenditure on the budget. The Council of Ministers decided that MAV (Hungarian State Railways) employees who had been discharged from the forces were to receive a once and for all demobilizing subsidy on the 15th November costing 33.8 Million Crowns, and from the 15th December railway employees were to draw a regular familiy benefit allowance amounting to 51.3 Million Crowns.[12] Altogether an estimated 1.5 Milliard Crowns were spent by the War Ministry and Public Order Institution between October 1918 and march 1919 on demobilized soldiers who had families to support and often no jobs to sustain them. Increasing amounts had to be spent on those unemployed, since the sudden stop of war deliveries left the majority of factories without orders. Those industries which did not have to convert to peace production and were already operating, such as mines, were also faced with wage demands. For instance, the coal mining interests notified the Government of the extraordinary pay rises demanded by the miners retrospectively from 1st October 1918, amounting to a monthly increase in the wage bills of 12.52 Million Crowns, which they could not absorb and would be passed on to consumers. The Council of Ministers felt compelled — in order to ensure intensified coal production vital to the whole economy and in order to keep the price of coal down — to undertake to foot the wage bill. An amount of 25.04 Million Crowns was issued for October-November and the Government also announced that in these extraordinary circumstances this procedure was to be a maintained until further notice.[13] This was modified in January 1919 to the extent that 25 % of the so-called coal aid (wage increases) were to be borne by the employers and 75 % by the Treasury.[14] The following estimate of expenditure and income for the 5 months period is quoted in the Kallay Documents[15] as reconstructed in 1920 for the peace negotiations:

---

[12] OL, K27 No. 42, 8 November 1918.
[13] *Op. cit.*, No. 56, 25 November 1918.
[14] *Op. cit.*, No. 3, 5 January 1919.
[15] OL, K275 VII/6/1.

TABLE 4

*Expenditure of the Károlyi Government
31st October bis 21st March 1919*

	Million Crowns
State debt service incurred	476.9
Public employees and works' aid in State Industries	632.4
Aid to Servicemen's families to February 1919	428.0
War widows, orphans, disabled aid	56.4
Unemployment aid, extraordinary wage allowances	312.7
Aid to Transylvanian Hungarian population	148.3
War Ministry and Public Order expenses:	
National Guard & Military Council organization	95.5
Demobilizing Allowance	600.0
Other expenses of the War Ministry	825.9
Ministry of Food, ensuring essential food supply	205.9
Expenses re liquidating the Monarchy's affairs	434.6
Expenses re French occupational forces	77.5
The cost of administration	545.7
Total	4,800.0

This amount of 4,800 Million Crowns is equivalent to a monthly average of 1,000 Million, whereas even in the last stages of the war the monthly State expenditure did not amount to more than 700—800 Million Crowns. Under the circumstances — with production almost at a standstill — tax income became drastically reduced, hence less than 10 % of expenditure was covered by ordinary revenue, and State indebtedness to the Austro-Hungarian Bank rose accordingly. Estimated State revenue during this period amounted to only 400 Million Crowns.

On the 21st March 1919 a transfer of power took place to the Hungarian Soviet Republic, led by Béla Kun. Its stated policy was to establish the dictatorship of the proletariate in order to bring about a socialist system of government. Under the continuing disrupted conditions it proved to be too ambitious in its radical goals, especially in an economy of shortages. As far as providing revenue for the administration of government, these had to be improvised, as the Austro-Hungarian Bank refused to provide the requirements. Appoximately 253.7 Million Crowns were issued through the Postatakarék Pénztár (Post Office Saving Banks) and about 5.6 Milliard Crowns worth of banknotes were put into circulation through the „nationalized" Budapest branch of the Austro-Hungarian Bank.

State expenditure during the March—July 1919 period was estimated at about 4,889 Million Crowns and ordinary revenue at 473 Million Crowns.[16] The dictatorship of the proletariate tried to transform the production relations in a fast and radical manner as was reflected by its expropriation policy from the very first day of its existence. The thus acquired State property necessarily facilitated the development of an absolute centralization in the given period and created a state-owned sector too large to be controlled by the central organs. The precipitate policy during a war economy of shortages was doomed to failure. Tension was enhanced by the positive mechanism of interplay between the expropriation policy and the practice of nationalization under the conditions of economic shortages, i.e. the more radical aims the former set, the more numerous the spontaneous capital expropriation became owing to competition forced by the scarcity of resources bursting even the framework determined by this very policy.[17] Contemporary leaders called this process the „tantrums of nationalization". The attempts —lasting over four months — at radical reorganization of the economic system not only set back production futher, but created tensions between the urban proletariate, where the strength of the leadership lay, and the rural population. These tensions crippled the exchange of goods between town and country, necessitated forced requisitions and also led to the decline in the volume of agricultural output, as the rural population resorted to a subsistence economy.

Finally, the Romanian occupation, which put an end to the Soviet experiment, was seen by contemporaries as having been more damaging to the economy than war itself. Requisitioning was not only employed to sustain the occupying forces. Apart from exhausting the limited stock of resources the Romanian army dismantled a large proportion of industrial and agricultural machinery, livestock and rolling stock on withdrawal from Hungary.

Even after nine months of revolutionary upheavals economic consolidation and financial stabilization had to be delayed, because the Government constantly had to grapple with internal and external political threats. Although all financial discussions centred upon more effective taxation measures in order to attempt to reduce the budget deficit,

---

[16] Public Record Office (PRO), Foreign Office Documents (FO) 371*6140/C12707 Annual Report on Hungary, 16 January 1921.

[17] Gy. Péteri, *A Magyar Tanácsköztársaság*... [see note 10], p. 280.

while at the same time trying to leave enough incentives in the economy to aid recovery, effective measures could not be implemented.

An attempt was made to introduce a deflationary policy in Hungary in 1920 when the stamping of notes took place in June. 50 % of the stamped value was withheld as a forced loan, and only 7 Milliard opposed to 14 Milliard Crowns was immediately returned to circulation. This deflationary attempt floundered, for at the same time the rapidly growing state expenditure forced the Government to release the notes back into circulation.

The financial measures of the immediate post-war years show a pattern of coping with issues on a day to day basis, and the inability to carry out medium term policies even if some were formulated in theory. Haphazard daily measures they might have been, but the government itself was in a state of transition. Poor harvests followed, the reparation debt cast a cloud of uncertainty over finances, the final evacuation of the Romanian occupation army was not completed until April 1920, all preventing anything like the proper functioning on the state revenue collecting apparatus. The Peace Treaty was not ratified and did not come into force until the end of July 1921, Karlist putches disrupted the political consolidation twice in 1921, while industry lacked raw materials and exports were being inhibited by market restrictions.

Between the years 1918 and 1920, the continuous depreciation of the Crown may not have been halted due to a lack of decisive measures — for instance by efforts to balance the state budget — yet, it cannot be claimed that Government embarked upon a specifically inflationary policy.[18] Note issuing was not resorted to on a scale which would have created an inflationary boom. Even well informed outside opinion voiced: „It is difficult to give a proper appreciation of the financial position of Hungary during 1920, because there had been no budget passed, and questions of reparation and currency have prevented anything in the nature of an approximate understanding of Hungary's indebtedness."[19] Or: „crisis of every description, financial, commercial and political — even meteorological — have each had their turn collectively and singly to try the temper of the nation."[20]

Another more decisive attempt to deflate was undertaken by Loránt

---

[18] Ivan T. Berend/György Ránki, *Magyarország gazdasága az elsö világháború után 1919-1929* (The Hungarian Economy after World War I), Budapest 1966, p. 70.
[19] PRO, FO 371/7632/C3299, Annual Report on Hungary, 1921.
[20] PRO, FO 371/6140/C12707, Johnson to Lord Curzon, 16 June 1921.

Hegedüs, the ex-President of the Commercial Bank, Finance Minister from December 1920. His concept closely followed the conservative school of thought, recognising a close parallel between the volume of notes in circulation, the Crown's foreign valuation, and rising price levels. He considered that the newly issued notes watered down the value of the existing currency, so rising prices were the direct result of the State's note issuing. The *sine qua non* of a healthy economy was the re-establishment of the balance of public finances and the stabilization of the currency. His programme was based on achieving two main tasks: to bring about a substantial rise in the value of the Crown and to balance the budget by introducing strict financial measures, and reducing the rate of interest on outstanding State debts from 5.5 % to 4 %. To achieve the former Hegedüs wanted to discontinue the use of the printing presses and turn the balance of payments in a positive direction. The raising of the value of the Crown was to be carried out as a *precondition* to gain the confidence of the foreign money market which — Hegdüs believed — once convinced of an effective Hungarian financial policy and will in self-help would come in to help *keep* the stability of the currency. Although the Hegedüs attempt has always been judged to have failed because he tried to stabilize the Crown by Hungary's own efforts, evidence shows that he always kept in mind the need for foreign loans at a later stage, to help sustain the precarious value of the Crown stable. In his announcement to the Council of Ministers on the 17th December 1920, he stated in his plan that in January or February (1921) he would put forward a loan proposal in which parliament was to empower him to undertake negotiations with interested powers — in accordance with instructions of the Reparation Commission — regarding foreign credit being extended to Hungary.[21]

Meantime, to set the Crown — which he believed to be valued unwarrantedly low — on the road to recovery he set about to find the means to enable him to do without the printing presses. His plan involved a whole series of deflationary measures. First of all he blocked the bank accounts and levied a 20 % capital levy on deposits over 1000 K.[22] This was followed by the Limited Companies having to surrender 15 % of their share capital, (Statute XV 1921). Other measures followed regarding houseowners, foreign securities held, as well as cur-

---

[21] OL, K27 Box 129, 17 December 1920.
[22] *Ibid.*, 23 December 1920, Decree 10589/1920.

rency, covering both mobile and immobile assets in order to withdraw a proportion of bank and treasury notes. As direct personal taxation was not elastic enough, his taxation programme was based on turnover and consumption taxes, which were to ensure a constantly increasing state revenue once the economy recovered.

However, as the capital levy both on land and shares could be paid in kind, the actual surrendering took time to materialize, publicly accountable companies had to authorise special share issues, and the post-war disorganised financial and tax collection apparatus was too cumbersome to carry out such a huge undertaking efficiently. Nevertheless, he was successful in creating a positive frame of mind in the public at home and abroad, and his deflationary policy resulted in a marked improvement in the valuation of the Crown. The Zurich exchange which was just over 1 cent at the beginning of the year went up to 2.85 cents by May 1921, which was accompanied by a reduction in prices.[23] Although the Zurich quotation of the Crown improved, inflation was not brought under control permanently. The capital levy, apart from lacking mobility, could not substitute as permanent cover for ordinary state revenue and finding the means to create permanent ordinary revenue broke on the resistance of the agrarian sector of the economy. Not only did they object to the levy on the land, in which they saw far reaching consequences of precedent, they also sought exemption from the application of turnover tax on growers, which was being planned as a permanent financial fixture and source of revenue. Therefore, from the beginning the balancing of the state budget encountered very serious obstacles. With a budget deficit of 10 Milliard Crowns and important factors such as reparation liability not being known, economic life was kept jittery, some fearing that signs of economic recovery would lead to even greater reparation burdens and this fear was constantly fuelled by political rumours. The Hegedüs policy could not be maintained in the face of sustained resistance, he could not carry out the internal measures however appropriate and, so some saw, heroic they were; therefore the external aid which he was counting upon did not come about either. Hegedüs left the ministerial chair a broken man both in spirit and health in September 1921, and the deterioration in the value of the Crown accelerated at a speed previously unknown in Hungarian finan-

---

[23] See B. Jankovich, *A papirpénz*... [see note 6], Table 10 and 11 appended, pp.00000.

cial history. To provide an indication of the movement of the exchange rate the table below gives the Zurich quotation in monthly averages:[24]

TABLE 5

Monthly Rates of Exchange of the Hungarian Crown at Zurich

	1921	1922	1923
January	1.16	0.78	0.2059
February	1.16	0.77	0.1956
March	1.62	0.63	0.1530
April	2.11	0.63	0.1160
May	2.62	0.66	0.1038
June	2.34	0.56	0.0800
July	1.97	0.39	0.0554
August	1.53	0.31	0.03187
September	1.14	0.22	0.03020
October	0.77	0.22	0.0300
November	0.57	0.22	0.0300
December	0.76	0.23	0.0300

The Role of the State Issuing Bank 1921—1923

The third period from September 1921 to late 1923 was characterized by the private sector of the economy utilizing the newly established State Issuing Bank's credit facilities. The 1921 Statute XIV, created the central bank which began operations on the 1st August 1921. It was intended as a temporary institution, a necessity resulting from the liquidation of the Austro-Hungarian Bank according to the Peace Treaty of Trianon. The Law only authorized the issuing of notes in the following circumstances: to exchange the Austro-Hungarian Bank's notes as well as to exchange the Postsparcasse notes issued during the Hungarian Soviet Republic, and against such cover as was prescribed in the Statutes. The Law delimited the amount of the State note contingency to two Milliard Crowns. Despite these limitations one can go as far as stating that the issuing Bank *in effect* became the source of

[24] *Magyar Statisztikai Évkönyv* (Hungarian Statistical Yearbook), (1919—1922), p. 123; *Op. cit.*, (1923-1925), p. 174.

unbound inflation, although the reasons why the Bank became the source of inflation, particularly in its credit policy towards the private sector of the economy needs to be highlighted.

The State Issuing Bank took over only a small quantity of bills from the Austro-Hungarian Bank. While the Crown was appreciating or remained stable during the Hegdüs administration, there was a pause in the extension of commodity credit, which was the most natural basis for the growth of money supply. Only after the depreciation began again in the Autumn of 1921, coupled with prices rises and an upturn in industrial production, did an increase in credit demand develop. Temporary credits were granted for the successful marketing of agricultural produce, for grain purchases to secure the flour and bread requirements of the destitute, and seasonal credits for some industrial concerns in the public sector for operational costs. Soon after the Issuing Bank started its operation the Government took advantage of its authority to increase its note contingency in excess of the 2 Milliard Crowns and continued to issue notes through uncovered Treasury Bills. By the 6th April 1922 the Council of Ministers increased the state note contingency to 6 Milliard Crowns.[25] By May 31st it was increased again to 8 Milliard Crowns.[26]

One can take the view, if one seeks a single issue over which the financial policy of the inflationary period was most far reachingly at fault, that it must be the credit policy of the Issuing Bank. This can be supported by the fact that the growth of the credit demand was greater than the depreciation of the Crown's purchasing power would have warranted, yet these demands were met. Yet a word of explanation is needed from the Hungarian Government's point of view, as to why for instance the Bank was not encouraged to pursue a strict deflationary course.

In a period of unprecedented European economic dislocation the only example of a deflationary policy pursued among the Successor States was that of A. Rašín, the Finance Minister of Czechoslovakia. This was a topic discussed and analysed nationally and internationally as an example of what effect a ruthless policy of deflation had on the Czechoslovak economy, foreign trade, unemployment levels, etc. Even

---

[25] OL, Állami Jegyintézet (Hungarian State Issuing Bank) Z2 Bundle 1, Board Meeting, 6 April 1922.
[26] *Ibid.*, 31 May 1922.

Keynes quoted the Czecholovak example as a deterrent to engaging in a similar deflationary policy in Britain. However, a combination of contemporary circumstances, not least Rašin's open market operations, softened the effect of the deflationary policy.[27] In the long term the policy was effective so far as the Czech population was spared the ravages of the worst inflation.

This is how the Directors Meeting at the Hungarian Issuing Bank reflected upon the Czechoslovak monetary policy on 22nd February 1922:[28] „The artificially improved and maintained currency allowed Czechoslovakia to purchase a large quantity of American grain cheaply, but not enough to satisfy demand until the next harvest. *We shall only be able to judge the cost of this currency-hausse to the Czech economy, when the balance sheets of those industrial works will be published, which had to cease operating.*" (My emphasis — EAB.) Or more appropriately of the period 24th August — 23rd September 1922: „Due to the improvement in the foreign valuation of the sokol (the new Czech currency) the crisis in the Czech industry deepens. Particularly deteriorating was the position of the textiles, steel, glass and leather (shoe) industries. The number of unemployed is estimated at 600 000. The Czechoslovak Government, which is being attacked by the industrialist circles on account of the artificial improvement in the sokol's foreign valuation, is now trying to bring the prices and wages to similiar levels."

So one must keep remembering that in a country such as Hungary, where during the past three years two revolutions and a counter-revolution had taken place, and where the ruling regime's consolidation was far from accomplished, where instead of solving old social tensions even more were created (see the plight of 300 000 refugees from territories lost to Hungary) those responsible for the financial policy of the country — especially with the Czecholovak example highlighting the difficulties — were reluctant, even unwilling to pursue a deflationary policy. The very potent ‚real-political' consideration having been that the price of deflation in terms of unemployment, social unrest, political instability was far greater to the country than that of inflation. These considerations did not mean that the Issuing Bank embarked upon a conciously inflationary policy, only that it had good reasons for not following a deflationary policy.

---

[27] Alice Teichova, *A Comparative View of Inflation of the 1920s in Austria and Czechoslovakia*, (forthcoming).

[28] OL, Z2 Bundle 1, 22 February 1922.

Another, and very important factor in determining the Issuing Bank's credit policy had to be the undisputed shortage of investment capital in Hungary. Even before 1914, in the decades leading up to the war, economic growth was achieved with the aid of substantial injections of foreign capital. On the other hand, particularly in the immediate post-war years, when foreign capital could not be attracted on account of the uncertain reparation liability hanging over the economic future of Hungary, the lack of investment capital was a crippling bottleneck in the attempts of economic reorganization and adjustment to the post-Trianon framework, which had reduced Hungary to one-third of its original size.

The central Bank therefore discounted 3 monthly bills of exchange for the use of the private economy, rather almost exclusively for commerce and industry. These credits — due to the loss in the value of the Crown — were repaid at very much reduced sums to the Bank, with the low interest rates prevailing (6—8 % in 1922; 8—18 % in 1923) while the value of the Crown would drop by as much within a few weeks, and at a later stage in days. The low interest rates were again an attempt not to fuel inflation, while the ever-increasing extension of credits was to serve to keep the productive enterprises alive and to enable them to increase their output. In the policy of the Issuing Bank, the rationale was that, if injection of credits produced increased output it need not necessarily be inflationary.

Needless to say that the Hungarian Government (as in Germany and other countries suffering from inflation)[29] was pressured by advocates of an inflationary policy. They were trying to prove that the national economy, far from enjoying excessive credit facilities, when calculated in gold (Swiss francs), the value of credits showed a declining tendency. This way they were able to claim that the credit contingency made available for Trianon Hungary was even lower than that of the pre-war Hungary.

The main spokesman of the inflationary policy, the Confederation of Hungarian Industry (GYOSZ) and the Hungarian National Union of Commerce (EMKE) in other words, those economic interest groups who benefited most from these credit operations — saw the depreciation of the currency as a result of the war-time devastation of capital,

---

[29] Costatino Bresciani-Turroni, *The Economics of Inflation: A Study of Currency Depreciation in Post-War Germany*, London 1937, pp. 183-223.

the threat of excessive reparation liability, unfavourable conditions in foreign relations causing marketing restrictions and in the balance of payment deficit resulting from these and international speculations. Even the moderates, those who did not believe in an inflationary policy, claimed that the economy's recovery could only be ensured if the infusion of those credits, which were to serve productive purposes, were allowed to be obtained. According to them, only after the private sector of the economy was functioning properly could the restoration of public finances be undertaken. Their proposal for restricting credit applications was that applicants need not only prove their creditworthiness but that they have to meet productivity requirements as well.

The deflationists, on the other hand, demanded control over commercial credits through a Draconian interest rate policy, even if this would temporarily affect production critically.[30]

Thus a communitiy of interest arose between the Government and industrialists, the latter being able to threaten with dire economical and political consequences if working capital was not found for productive enterprises. According to the Statutes, the Issuing Bank could not get involved in direct credit extension, but was able to discount bills of the leading commercial banks of the country. These bills discounted at the Issuing Bank came to constitute the major business activity of the large banks. Through them the banks were able to extend credits to industrial and commercial companies in their sphere of interest. On the 1st August 1921, the Issuing Bank's holding of bills receivable amounted to 93.1 Million Crowns, while the volume of notes circulating came to 17.325 Million Crowns. In other words, the holding only amounted to 0.53 % of the volume of the notes. By the end of 1921, bills receivable amounted to 3,900 Million, and reached a peak on 31st October 1922 at 29.5 Millard Crowns.[31] The following development took place during 1923:[32]

---

[30] Béla Imreh, *Az inflációs évek hitelpolitikája* (The credit policies of the inflationary years), Budapest 1926, pp. 10-11.

[31] Elemér Hantos, *A pénz problémája középeurópában* (The problem of money in Central Europe), Budapest 1925, p. 36.

[32] A Magyar Kir. Állami Jegyintézet 1923 évi jelentése (The 1923 report of the Hungarian State Issuing Bank), Appendix II and IV.

TABLE 6

Hungarian State Issuing Bank Report — 1923

1923	Discounted Bills	Treasury Notes	Volume of notes in circulation
	in Million Crowns		
January	34,847	20,000	73,716
February	38,635	24,000	75,135
March	51,552	29,000	82,205
April	64,051	37,000	100,101
May	73,643	47,000	119,285
June	100,843	59,700	154,996
July	146,156	73,700	226,284
August	253,831	143,000	399,486
September	360,680	243,000	588,809
October	474,727	269,000	744,925
November	511,627	306,000	853,988
December	562,340	401,000	931,337

The Table shows that the private sector utilization throughout the year was more important than the Treasury advances. This was consistently so through 1922 and in the first half of 1923, when in the first seven months discounted bills increased by 319 % and the Treasury bills by 269 %. In the last five months of 1923 the State utilization of the Issuing Bank intensified, nevertheless the total increase in the discounted bills over the year 1923 amounted to 1511 %. Finally, when comparing the value of discounted bills in proportion to the volume of notes in circulation, the proportion which in August 1921 had been 0.53 %, by June 1923 had increased to a staggering 65 %.

On the first anniversary of the Issuing Bank's existence, the Board evaluated its role in the reconstruction of the economy. They admitted to having been criticised in their credit policy of being both parsimonious and overgenerous, especially where the discounting of bank and commercial bills was concerned. They claimed not have responded to either extreme, but had aimed at satisfying legitimate business as long as it rested on a healthy and sound basis. They prided themselves on the fact that „the major part of note circulation was no longer buttressed by the State, but by the strength of the whole economy."[33] An indication

---

[33] OL, Z2 Bundle 1, Board Meeting, 20 December 1922.

of this policy is shown in a confidential list dated 30th November 1921 which itemized the Council of the Issuing Bank's approvals of discounting bills to a large number of enterprises as „singular credits". Singular credits — in the case of banks meant — amounts over and above those already granted, or in the case of individual companies, over and above existing overdraft and other loan arrangements.[34] (See TABLE 7).

To show the extent of the increasing credit demand one can quote that a year later, in 1923, Ganz Danubius and Ganz Electric (claiming K 50 Million credit in 1922) approached the Issuing Bank directly to request a 300—400 Million Crown credit with the justification that they have to keep 9000 men at work and want to be able to increase their outpout. They were claiming this special privilege as the country's foremost machine engineering concern, because their bankers, the Credit Bank and the Discounting Bank had refused to grant credit facilities in *excess of their 1000 Million Crown* credit limit.[35] The Board of the Issuing Bank had been aware that business development was suffering from a company „floatation fever", yet did not restrict their credit policy. „Besides our capital shortage, that forced pace is beginning to tell, through which our enterprises try to maintain the position they held in the pre-war league, often not only maintaining their status but by setting up new companies they even improve on them."[36]

TABLE 7

Hungarian State Issuing Bank — Approved credits registered as Singular Credits — 30 November 1921

	Million Crowns
Anglo-Hungarian Bank	300
Hazai Bank Ltd (Domestic Bank)	150
Hungarian Credit Bank (MAH)	500
Hungarian Land Credit Institute	40
Hungarian Discounting Bank	150
Hungarian-Italian Bank	300
Commercial Bank of Pest (PMKB)	500
Anglo-Austrian Bank — Budapest branch	100
Wiener Bankverein — Budapest branch	100

[34] OL, Z5 Bundle 1, Credit Department.
[35] *Ibid.*, Bundle 2, Ref: 805/1922.
[36] OL, Z2 Bundle 1, 20 December 1922.

	Million Crowns
Central Credit Institute (PK)	500
Lloyds Bank Ltd	50
Ganz Electric Ltd	20
Ganz Danubius Co Ltd	30
Rimamuranyi Salgotarjan Iron Works Ltd	60
Salgotarjan Coal Mines Ltd	80
Hofherr-Schrantz-Clayton Machine Mfg Ltd	10
Manfred Weiss Conserve & Tin Factory Ltd	60
Manfred Weiss Steel & Metal Ltd	25
Sam. Goldberger & Sons Ltd — Textile Co	5
L. Lang Machine Works Ltd	10
Hungarian Textile Industry Ltd	8
Hungarian General Coal Mine Ltd (MAK)	50
Dr. Liptak & Co Building and Iron Ind. Ltd	50
and about a dozen power mills...	

They also felt alarmed by the newspaper reports giving lists of new companies floated in 1922, which indicated that 722 new limited companies had been founded with a share capital of 5 Milliard Crowns. „Considering that the Issuing Bank is unable to satisfy even the old established companies' capital and credit requirements in present day Hungary, and that there are first rate idustrial concerns we are unable to accomodate, without doubt we are facing a company floatation fever, which can only do damage to the economy."[37]

The policy of the Bank as regards controlling the money supply by the variation in the bankrate was certainly not restrictive enough. The rates charged were:[38]

1st August 1921	6 %
19th October 1921	7 %
20th December 1922	8 %
25th April 1923	12 %
4th July 1923	18 %

While they closely watched the attempts of the Austrian, German, Czecholovak Issuing Banks as they varied their rates, the Hungarian Issuing Bank feared that raising the bankrate would result in further price explosions — considering the interest rate as a cost factor — and

---

[37] *Ibid.*, 31 January 1923.
[38] *Ibid.*, From Minutes of Board Meetings on those dates.

so followed a policy of moderation in line with other Issuing Banks.[39] This policy, of course, encouraged banks and companies to take advantage of the relatively easy and cheap credits, as the losses in the value of the currency always nullified the effect of the bankrate changes. By 1923, the 18 % interest charged on the discounted bills did not even impose the 6—8 % liability of 1922.[40] The combination of unvalorized credits and the gathering pace of inflation manifested itself increasingly in a flight from holding cash reserves or deposits, which in turn resulted in speculative Stock Exchange activity. This is clearly shown in the proliferation of the so called „cost money". These were very short term, usually weekly loans, at exorbitant rates of interest. On 28th February 1923 the Board of the Issuing Bank stated that „cost money swallows up enormous sums to the detriment of other credit in the economy. Parallel with the rise in Stock market quotations such vast amounts were channelled into cost money placements and such high rates of interest, the likes of which is not to be found in the history of the Budapest Stock Exchange."[41]

At the beginning of February the weekly rates were $2—2^5/_8$ %, at the end of February 6—6½, by the end of March 1923 exceeded 13 % weekly, equalling 676 % per annum. The buying and selling of stocks and shares in January alone amounted to 27 Milliard Crowns, again unprecedented and increased throughout February.[42]

As the large banks had access to fast depreciating State credits through the Issuing Bank and passed them on — admittedly at a higher rate — to companies operating in their orbits this resulted in creating an investment boom. The falling value of the currency which rendered these loans to worthless paper, not only allowed but encouraged industry to purchase machinery, put up new buildings and accumulate raw materials which all promoted large inflationary profits. The amounts involved can be seen from the Minutes of the Board Meeting at the Issuing Bank on the 30th January 1924, which reported on bank discounting for the five largest banks in Budapest.[43]

---

[39] *Ibid.*, 31 January 1923.
[40] I.T. Berend/Gy. Ránki, *Magyarország gazdasága*... [see note 18], p. 81.
[41] OL, Z2 Bundle 1, Board Meeting, 28 February 1923.
[42] *Ibid.*, 28 February 1923.
[43] *Ibid.*, 30 January 1924.

Hungarian General Credit Bank (MAH)   113.9 Milliard Crowns
Hungarian Discounting Bank   85.5 Milliard Crowns
Anglo-Hungarian Bank   63.2 Milliard Crowns
Central Finance Institute (PK)   54.7 Milliard Crowns
Commercial Bank of Pest (PMBK)   42.5 Milliard Crowns
The Total was   359.8 Milliard Crowns

when the total amount of discounted bills held by the Issuing Bank (31st December 1923) amounted to some 562,3 Milliard Crowns. The profit to be gained from these credit transactions can also be gauged, not from various company balance sheets — where they where not disclosed publicly — but from reports to the Issuing Bank, when credit requests had to be justified and therefore undervalued investments, or undeclared profits had to be disclosed. TABLE 8 indicates the growth of latent company reserves, which often amounted to tenfolds of the combined share capital and ordinary reserves.

TABLE 8

Schedule from the Györ District sent in for Credit Approval: 24th April 1923[44]

Name	Share Capital	Ordinary Reserves	Total	*Latent Reserves*	Credit Approved
	In Million Crowns				
Black Hermann Cylinder Mill	8.5	1.0	9.5	400	100
Györ Oilworks Ltd.	25.0	40.0	65.0	200	50
Györ Distillery	10.0	44.0	54.0	600	100
Hungarian Waggon & Machinery	40.0	52.8	92.8	1000	200
Oil Refinery Ltd.	60.0	514.0	574.0	1000	300

One can also tell the importance and the volume of undisclosed or undervalued investments by the policy adopted by the Issuing Bank after 1922. When it determined the credit extension limit of applying banks and companies, in addition to share and reserve capital it took into consideration at least a quarter (usually more, since they were

---

[44] OL, Z5 Bundle 5, Credit Documents, Ref: 349/1923.

always the larger) of the latent reserves.⁴⁵ To some extent, especially in the later stages of inflation, this investment potential was limited by inflation itself, because speculative material hoarding and the ensuing scarcity made it difficult to obtain even capital goods. Despite these limitations the unvalorized credits became the mainstays of the inflationary boom.

Hyperinflation January-June 1924

As was indicated in the preceding pages, the source of inflation was initially the State itself. Those barriers which had existed between the State and the Issuing Bank were set aside during the war. The statutes regulating the Issuing Bank's activities sidestepped as a matter of expediency and governments authorised themselves to acquire Treasury advances which set off inflation. During the war and for three years afterwards the volume of the Treasury notes in relation to the total volume of note circulation was always higher than the discounted bills. The setting up of the Issuing Bank in August 1921 reversed this trend; the accommodation of credit requirements took precedence over State needs and although by 31st December 1921 State advances amounted to 900 Million Crowns, it was only one sixth of the private sector's demands.⁴⁶

But from then the share of the Treasury advances grew gradually to May 1923 to about 40 % of the total circulation, still behind the private sector's proportion. In early 1924, however, at the height of the raging inflation the printing presses started rolling again for State requirements. In April-May 1924 notes were issued at a weekly rate of 30 Milliard Crowns, and in the last week before stabilization it jumped to 696 Milliard Crowns. While in the first half of 1924 the volume of discounted bills doubled, the State share increased four-fold.⁴⁷

In January-February 1924 the introduction of the Savings-Crown, a valorization attempt which only applied to newly taken out loans, slowed down the clamouring for credits. From January-February 1924 the State's major role in depreciating the value of the currency came about through the more intensive settlement if its own debts from the

---

⁴⁵ OL, Z2 Bundle 1, Board Meeting, 27 March 1923.
⁴⁶ E. Hantos, *A pénz problémája*... [see note 31], pp. 37—38.
⁴⁷ *Op. cit.*, p. 38.

proceeds of the printing presses, all in preparation for creating a favourable climate for a forthcoming internal loan, which was planned as a preamble to the setting up of the National Bank. This was only established, however, with the help of a substantial international loan operation in June 1924.[48]

Price Behaviour and the Depreciation of the Crown

When causes of the currency depreciation are examined, the analysis of purely fiscal measures are insufficient. Obviously the effects of internal and external political issues, trade and consequent balance of payment deficit, speculation at home and abroad, lack of proper strategy in economic policy also aggravate the fate of the currency. As was aptly put, this was a period when „peace was none other than the continuation of war by other means".[49]

In this preliminary outline viewing the course of inflation, however, there is not sufficient scope to develop the role of all these factors, but at least one other important factor needs to be examined, that is the behaviour of prices in relation to the falling value of the Crown. A study of inflation was published by the Hungarian economist Béla Jankovich in 1925 (cf. footnote 6) and observations relating to prices are based on the statistical tables presented in his study. In these tables he established the statistical symptoms of inflation as reflected in the changes in the money supply, the external value of the Crown as shown in the Zurich quotation, and the internal value of the Crown as indicated in the wholesale price movement. (See TABLE 10 and 11, below pp.)

In this table he calculated the percentage increase in the money supply, the currency agio percentage based on the pre-war quotation of 105 Swiss centimes = K 1.00, and the wholesale price index (1913 = 100 %) as was reconstructed by the Hungarian Central Statistical Office. The latter index is based on the average monthly Budapest wholesale prices of 45 items, which follows the British Sauerbeck system. As from January 1924 the Hungarian Statistical Office issued an official monthly average wholesale price index based on 52 items. *The overall theory is that in the initial stages of inflation it is the shortage of commodities, while in the latter stages it is the increasing money supply which is the objective cause — the main factor in the increase of prices.*

---

[48] B. Imreh, *Az inflációś évek*... [see note 30], p. 19.
[49] E. Hantos, *A pénz problémája*... [see note 31], p. 38.

The compiled indices indicate that inflation (of money supply), agio of exchange, and price index moved together and continuously from the beginning of the war. Initially inflation led, followed by the price index, which in turn was followed by the agio increase. At the end of 1918, the note volume had increased by 1148 %, the price index 893 %, and the agio by 344 % as shown by the detailed Table.

During the war years of economic segregation of the Central Powers it was not difficult to keep the prices and exchange agio down. This was aided by the maximized prices and the setting up of the Devisenzentrale in 1916.

When the war ended the agio went up suddenly to 3280 %, the price index to 3954 % and by the end of 1919 both had surpassed the money supply increase of 1985 %. This sudden and substantial change. was connected naturally with concurrent political changes. The dissolution of the Monarchy into Successor States not only upset faith in existing institutions, but also shook the financial position of the Austrian and Hungarian States. In 1919, after the separation of the currencies, the percentage increases of the indicators continued their more or less parallel rising tracks. The increase was higher in Austria, but it levelled off in 1922 due to stabilization. In Hungary the rising levels continued to the end of 1923, drawing ever nearer to the Austrian level. Apart from these general observations the noticeable fact ist that the proportion between the percentage indicators changes over time. Since in the beginning both the agio and price indices were lower than the money supply index, we can see that the effect of inflation was not fully reflected either in internal prices or in the external rate of exchange. Paper note issuing, however, began to assume increasingly larger proportions after the conclusion of peace, partly to replace the shortage of state revenue and partly to satisfy credit demands. Such a vast-scale and continously increasing volume of notes was diminishing the value of the currency, so much so, that it caused a loss of the confidence in the currency, so that the price and agio index exceeded the rate of inflation. Beyond this cross-over point both price and agio indices remained above the inflation level. In other words, as people got rid of liquid reserves, velocity increased.

Why should it happen, that after these indices had crossed one another, i. e. after the money supply reached a certain proportion, the level of increases in both prices and exchange ratio remained higher than inflation? In the first stage of inflation, when the loss of money value was relatively slight and price increases followed this slowly, the public hardly noticed the change. Being used to considering money as a stable value, the public's realization that the price increases are caused by the growth in the money supply is slow and in the given circumstances it was taken as the effect of the war. The excess paper money does initially increase the circulating capital in production and commerce and the price increases seemingly indicate an economic boom and prosperity. The excess notes, however, circulate in the economy to the detriment of the consumer, as he is able to buy less goods for the same money than he would have done without the price increases or without the excess circulating capital. Hence, while initially inflation benefits the producer and trade, it damages the consumer, especially those on a fixed income. This is then followed by inflation-induced movements for higher wages, which even if satisfied to a large extent, always lag behind the price increases, in other words the *effect of inflation is not yet noticeable because it is financed by the consumer, by this indirect method of unfair taxation.*

We might consider the war-induced price increases to be the result of a stronger demand on the economy, which in the short term was financed by the extra issuing of notes by the State. Towards the end of the war and certainly afterwards in the second stage of the inflation, there was a scarcity of goods, while waves of the circulation medium kept flooding the economy. So although a stronger demand for goods remained a feature, this demand was based on artificial purchasing power, not in the growing wealth of the nation. The continually diluting money value was further reduced — over and above the proportion of the volume of new note issues — by an inflationary phenomenon known as „die Flucht vor dem Gelde". In order to escape the losses in money depreciation, everyone tried to get rid of cash holdings and sought to place them in stocks, capital goods, shares or foreign currency, which they hoped would maintain their value better than paper money.

Jankovich with his *consumer oriented* argument drew the attention of the Hungarian Government to that „odious policy" which was being followed especially in 1922, after the setting up of the Issuing Bank, when the instrument of inflation was not only used to cover the State deficit, but through the discounting of bills the private sector's credit demands were also satisfied in this way. At that time respectable leaders of public opinion took opposite views, stating that inflation was the consequence, not the cause of rising prices, and that only through satisfying credit claims could production be maintained, which in any case could not be harmful if credits were used for productive purposes. Jankovich's argument was that the issuing of paper money depreciated the currency regardless for what purposes it was issued. While it increased the circulating capital, it increased the capital for production and commerce, but at the same time the countervalue was drawn from the consumers on fixed incomes, who were indirectly taxed by the fact that their pay always lagged behind prices.

If the State was forced to do this in the short term — say during a war — in its own interest, it might be justified on the grounds of common public interest. But if the Government used this method of indirect taxation for the satisfaction of the private sector's credit demands through the Issuing Bank, it placed both its own and the consumers' interests at the mercy of those demands. With this concession Government not only made consumer subsistence more difficult, but became the destroyer of its own financial resources, because the amount of money excess reduced the value of all its income: „as long as we use the opiate of inflation for propping up production, commerce and the Stock Exchange, not only can we not improve our economic situation, but we shall sink to the same depths as other nations whence we can only escape through a much greater sacrifice — through foreign tutelage".[50]

The Jankovich line of thought is seductive from the consumer point of view, nevertheless some points need to be qualified in the given circumstances. His conclusion is not all self-evident that on the one hand the excess notes do initially increase the circulating capital of production and commerce, and the price increases indicate an economic boom, (see p. 21) nor that on the other hand, the excess notes circulate in the economy to the detriment of the consumer, as he is able to buy less goods for the same money than he would have done without the price increases, i. e. without the excess capital. Simply because the excess notes could have increased for instance the salaries of state officials. But even if the excess capital is employed in production, it is by no means certain which prices will be affected. If it pushes up consumer prices, it can only happen if this excess circulating capital was spent on salaries and wages, as opposed to raw materials or generally for production's operating expenses. But if that is the case, then the excess circulating capital is serving the very function of adjusting wages to

---

[50] B. Jankovich, *A papirpénz...* [see note 6], in: *Közgazdasági Szemle*, (1925), p. 92.

prices (provided that it is used for wage increases only and not for drawing in additional workforce), therefore the opposite of his argument stands, i. e. the excess circulating capital is *not* to the detriment of the consumer. Further, assuming that the excess capital was spent on purchasing raw materials, etc., it is again questionable whether it will be to the detriment of the consumer, namely, the price of production-goods will increase first (provided there is no substantial over-supply — which there was not — and the additional purchasing power is not used to offset this) and only the related consumer goods will suffer the spin-off price effect. But if all this results in a substantial growth in output, possibly increasing the supply of goods, it need not necessarily fuel inflation.

As the whole purpose of the credit policy of the Hungarian Issuing Bank was directed towards supplying the necessary credits to improve the output of a disrupted economy, one can and should examine perhaps the prudence exercised in the *allocation* of such credits, but it is difficult to state categorically that it was deliberately inflationary in principle.

As other factors, such as internal and external political pressures, the effect of adverse balance of trade due to autarchial aspirations of the complementary economies and traditional markets of Hungary, state budget and balance of payment deficits were also a determining influence on the fate of the Crown — but are outside the scope of this study — we have to limit ourselves to stating that the discount policy of the Issuing Bank was also a major contributing factor to the downfall of the currency.

It is fairly evident from the information published in the *Economist*[51] that depreciation of currency was infinitely greater in countries where discounting by Issuing Banks for private credit requirements was high.

---

[51] *The Economist*, December 1923.

Table 9

State and Private Credit Balances of various Issuing Banks

	Volume of Notes	Treasury Loans (1)	Internal Loans (2)	Percentage of total volume of notes (1)	(2)
December 1923 French francs	37,905 Million	23,000 Million	6060.6 Million	60.7 %	16.0 %
December 1923 Italian lira	12,628 Million	5,838 Million	3301.8 Million	46.3 %	26.2 %
November 1923 German mark	184 Trillion	82.8 Trillion	137.7 Trillion	45.0 %	73.0 %
November 1923 Czech Kč	9,898.9 Million	—	1997.5 Trillion	—	20.6 %
November 1923 Austrian Crown (stabilized in 1922)	7.1 Billion	2.5 Billion	1.3 Billion	35.2 %	18.3 %
December 1923	931 Milliard	401 Milliard	563.2 Milliard	44.1 %	60.5 %

Discounting was lowest in France and Czechoslovakia whose inflationary experience was less damaging, highest in Germany and Hungary where inflation assumed a hyper-inflationary character. With this over generous credit accommodation the Issuing Bank and through it the government speeded up the deterioration of its own financial affairs, not only to the extent that it allowed credits to the private sector, but to a multiple of that amount, because the value of the currency also fell many times exceeding that of the note issue proportions. For this reason the State also had to resort to the instrument of inflation for its own purposes to a much greater extent in the final months of the inflationary period.

The fact that the state budget deficit was not possible to eliminate in Hungary — which necessarily meant financing it by increasing the amount of money in circulation — had its roots in social and political causes. Both in Hungary and in other defeated countries, after the war and revolutionary transformations, the power of the State was not sufficiently consolidated to implement a resolute and equitable taxation policy through which it could obtain the means to cover state requirements. At that stage it did not even have the strength to refuse or even wanted to restrict the ever increasing credit demands of various economic pressure groups. Thus resorting to the printing presses seemed the only, i.e. the most convenient, way of financing the stage budget.

In conclusion, one can state that the State Issuing Bank played a decisive role in the course of the Hungarian inflation by its unrestricted, unvalorized credit discounting policy, which from late 1922 and throughout 1923 increased the tempo of inflation. The extent of its damaging policy is indicated by the fact that by mid-1923 some 60 % of the total volume of notes in circulation were represented by the commercial bills discounted by the Bank.

The point at which inflation in Hungary can be seen to have been set on a definite inflationary course was after the establishment of the Issuing Bank (August 1921) and its sustained credit policy can be deemed to have led to the hyper-inflationary period.

TABLE 10

Monthly Statistics Hungary

Date	Volume of Notes in circulation	Postsparcasse Notes	Total Volume	Percentage Increase
		In Million Crowns		
1918				
July	25,365.6	—	25,366	817 %
August	26,990.5	—	26,990	871 %
September	28,646.0	—	28,646	924 %
October	31,483.2	—	31,483	1015 %
November	33,825.3	—	33,825	1901 %
December	35,588.6	—	35,589	1148 %
1919				
January	36,507.4	—	36,507	1177 %
February	37,569.6	—	37,570	1212 %
March	37,965.3	—	37,965	1224 %
April	39,438.8	—	39,439	1273 %
May	39,949.9	(19.0)	39,950	1290 %
June	41,761.4	(95.5)	41,761	1347 %
July	6,513	240.9	6,754	1450 %
August	6,669	549.7	7,219	1545 %
September	7,020	964.8	7,985	1715 %
October	7,520	974.8	8,495	1823 %
November	7,830	1002.8	8,833	1900 %
December	8,240	1002.8	9,243	1985 %

Date	Volume of Notes in circulation	Postsparcasse Notes	Total Volume	Percentage Increase
		In million Crowns		
1920				
January	8,482	1002.8	9,485	2036 %
February	8,658	1027.8	9,686	2078 %
March	8,872	1127.8	10,000	2146 %
April	9,034	1168.8	10,202	2189 %
May	8,996	1217.8	10,214	2190 %
June	8,840	1237.8	10,078	2164 %
July	8,860	1397.8	10,258	2200 %
August	11,580	1397.8	12,978	2786 %
September	11,550	1397.8	12,948	2778 %
October	11,889	1397.8	13,287	2850 %
November	12,975	1401.8	14,377	3084 %
December	14,308	1403.7	15,712	3372 %
1921				
January	15,206	1411.2	16,617	3566 %
February	15,571	1414.3	16,985	3644 %
March	15,650	1414.3	17,064	3662 %
April	13,114	1421.8	14,536	3120 %
May	13,686	1421.8	15,308	3284 %
June	18,096	1423.8	19,520	4190 %
July	15,799	1423.8	16,223	3482 %
August	17,326	582	17,808	3824 %
September	20,845	342	21,187	4540 %
October	23,643	337	23,980	5140 %
November	24,742	277	25,019	5370 %
December	25,175	249	25,424	5453 %
1922				
January	25,680	228	25,908	5560 %
February	26,758	215	26,973	5730 %
March	29,327	142	29,469	6210 %
April	30,580	113	30,693	6570 %
May	31,930	75	32,005	6870 %
June	33,600	69	33,669	7220 %
July	38,357	65	38,422	8245 %
August	46,242	62	46,305	9930 %
September	58,458	59	58,517	12560 %
October	70,005	58	70,063	15020 %
November	77,016	57	77,073	16540 %
December	75,887	56	75,943	16300 %

Date	Volume of Notes in circulation	Postsparcasse Notes	Total Volume	Percentage Increase
			In million Crowns	
1923				
January	73,717	45	73,762	15820 %
February	75,135	42	75,177	16130 %
March	82,205	40	82,245	17650 %
April	100,101	—	100,101	21500 %
May	119,285	—	119,285	25600 %
June	154,996	—	154,996	33270 %
July	226,285	—	226,285	48550 %
August	399,487	—	399,487	85620 %
September	588,810	—	588,810	126300 %
October	744,926	—	744,926	160000 %
November	853,989	—	853,989	183400 %
December	931,337	—	931,337	200000 %
1924				
January	1,084,677	—	1,084,677	232700 %
February	1,278,437	—	1,278,437	274600 %
March	1,606,875	—	1,606,875	344800 %
April	2,098,091	—	2,098,091	450200 %
May	2,486,257	—	2,486,257	533500 %
June	2,893,719	—	2,893,719	621000 %
July	3,277,943	—	3,277,943	704700 %
August	3,659,757	—	3,659,757	785900 %
September	4,115,925	—	4,115,925	883200 %
October	4,635,090	—	4,635,090	994100 %
November	4,442,635	—	4,442,635	953400 %
December	4,515,990	—	4,515,990	920000 %

Source: Bela Jankovich, *The Inflation of Paper Money and its Value, as Experienced in the Last Decade*, in: *Hungarian Economic Review*, (1925). Total volume to 1/7/1919 is based on the joint data. Separate Hungarian volume total as from only 1919, the percentage indicator is based on K 466 Mill.

TABLE 11

Monthly Statistics Hungary

Date	1 Zurich Exch. Monthly Av.	2 Agio Percentage 1 K = 105 Swiss Cents.	3 Price Index 1913 = 100 (wholesale)
1918			
July	40.54	259	—
August	32.28	267	—
September	37.93	277	—
October	43.05	244	—
November	36.35	289	—
December	30.59	344	Yearly av. 893
1919			
January	29.93	350	1035
February	25.46	412	1056
March	22.46	468	1129
April	18.58	566	1169
May	21.23	493	1256
June	17.90	586	1447
July	16.08	652	1983
August	11.63	905	2287
September	8.24	1275	2651
October	5.95	1765	2876
November	4.35	2415	3496
December	3.20	3280	3954
1920			
January	2.33	4510	5014
February	2.30	4565	5823
March	2.39	4390	6223
April	2.57	4086	6212
May	2.73	3845	6086
June	3.19	3290	6024
July	3.47	3026	6045
August	2.86	3673	6407
September	2.21	4753	8265
October	1.68	6250	10327
November	1.31	8015	10805
December	1.24	8100	11405

	1 Zurich Exch. Monthly Av.	2 Agio Percentage 1 K = 105 Swiss Cents	3 Price Index 1913 = 100 (wholesale)
1921			
January	1.16	9050	10314
February	1.16	9050	9878
March	1.62	6485	8975
April	2.11	4980	7647
May	2.62	4010	6736
June	2.34	4490	6623
July	1.97	5330	7325
August	1.53	6865	8271
September	1.14	9210	9574
October	0.77	13640	11254
November	0.57	18420	13873
December	0.76	13810	12509
1922			
January	0.78	13460	11962
February	0.77	13690	12923
March	0.63	16670	14769
April	0.63	16670	16465
May	0.66	15900	17203
June	0.56	18750	20259
July	0.39	26920	27257
August	0.31	33860	34468
September	0.22	47730	44293
October	0.217	48390	53182
November	0.223	47130	52875
December	0.227	46250	53742
1923			
January	0.2059	48800	58448
February	0.1956	53700	63926
March	0.1530	65690	85346
April	0.1160	90520	128235
May	0.1038	101150	145527
June	0.0800	131250	191378
July	0.0554	189530	323370
August	0.03187	330400	589101
September	0.03020	347600	662334
October	0.0300	344480	685497
November	0.0300	350000	755777
December	0.0300	350000	831786

	1 Zurich Exch. Monthly Av.	2 Agio Percentage 1 K = 105 Swiss Cents	3 Price Index 1913 = 100 (wholesale)
1924			
January	0.0229	458500	1026600
February	0.01795	585000	1839100
March	0.00904	1163000	2076700
April	0.00768	1367900	2134600
May	0.00650	1618000	2229600
June	0.00650	1618000	2207800
July	0.00674	1558000	2294500
August	0.00683	1515000	2242000
September	0.00690	1522000	2236600
October	0.00679	1546000	2285200
November	0.00691	1519000	2309500
December	0.00701	1500000	2346690

Source: Bela Jankovich, *The Inflation of Paper Money and its Value, as Experienced in the Last Decade,* in: *Hungarian Economic Review,* (1925).

Summary

This study analyses and describes the course of the Hungarian inflation through its various phases from the outbreak of World War I to the collapse of the currency before stabilization in June 1924. It examines the turbulent years following defeat which resulted in the dissolution of the old political and economic order. The limited range of choices the Hungarian government had in economic policy formulation and application in the transitional (i. e. inflation) period are highlighted. The study focuses on the credit policy of the Hungarian State Issuing Bank: it is argued that this may have been the source of growing inflation during the period August 1921 to December 1923. The discounting of short term commercial bills at relatively low rates of interest (6—8 % in 1921; 8—18 % in 1923) the magnitude of which grew (in relation to the total volume of notes in circulation) from 0,53 % in August 1921 to 65 % in June 1923 was evidence of this policy. The factors which determined the Government's and the Bank's credit policy were: 1) the chronic shortage of investment capital in Hungary: Before 1914 economic growth achieved only took place with the aid of substantial injections of foreign capital. In the immediate post-war years foreign capital could not be attracted because of the problem of uncertain reparation liabilities which overshadowed the economic future of the country. The lack of investment capital was a crippling bottleneck in the necessary economic reorganization to the post-Trianon framework. 2) The ruling regime was far from established. Externally it experienced political and economic hostility from the Successor States. Two revolutions, counter-revolution and royalist putsches delayed political consolidation internally. Accordingly very potent „real-political" considerations ruled the day: the cost of deflation (the only example, that of Czechoslovakia, was seen as a deterrent) in terms of unemployment, social unrest, political instability was seen as being far more damaging to the country's future than that of inflation. Under these circumstances the State Issuing Bank embarked upon supplying the credit needs of the economy, thus playing a decisive role in the course of the Hungarian inflation through its unrestricted, unvalorized credit discounting policy which increased the tempo of inflation.

Surviving in a Harsh World: Trade and Inflation in the Czechoslovak and Austrian Republics 1918—1926*

JONATHAN BLOOMFIELD

Introduction

The outcome of the First World War was dramatic. Political upheaval, social conflict, economic distress, and national sentiment fused in an explosive mixture. The Habsburg, Ottoman and Tsarist empires collapsed. From the Baltic to the Mediterranean new nation states emerged as in the chaos and confusion the map of Eastern and Central Europe was completely redrawn. Ravaged by the war and frequently riven by sharp social divisions, these states, having achieved national independence, still had to secure their economic future. This paper assesses how the economies of two of these states, Austria and Czechoslovakia, adapted to the initial realities of independence, particularly in regard to foreign trade.

Both countries suffered from inflation after the war. This was much more severe in Austria, which experienced a dramatic hyperinflation. Whereas the Czechoslovak crown fell from 35 Swiss centimes in May 1919 to 5.1 centimes in November 1921 and then rose, following government deflation policies to 19.2 centimes by October 1922, the

---

* This paper is a contribution to the research project „Inflation, Foreign Trade and Investment; a comparative study of Austria and Czechoslovakia, 1918—1926" under the direction of Professor Alice Teichova. The author wishes to acknowledge gratefully the financial assistance of the Stiftung Volkswagenwerk. My thanks are due to Professor Alice Teichova and Dr. Philip Cottrell for their considerable assistance, diligence and advice and to the staff in libraries and archives in Birmingham, London and Vienna for their help and guidance. Responsibility for the content of the paper rests with the author.

Austrian krone never gained more than temporary respite from the inflationary pressures which had been exerted upon it in the war. The descent into uncontrollable hyperinflation culminated in September 1922 when the Austrian krone was worth a mere 1/15,000th of its pre-war value. Only with the guarantee of a League of Nations loan accompanied by strict monetary controls was the currency stabilized.

It is not the purpose of this paper to study the mechanism and process of inflation in detail. Most orthodox contemporary analyses sought monocausal explanations in the high levels of government expenditure resulting in heavy budgetary deficits covered by an excessive — and inflationary — printing of paper currency. Such views have recently come back into favour. However, they remain partial and limited, investigating symptoms rather than causes. In this paper some of the international, economic, political and social factors affecting these new states and their recovery and reconstruction will be indicated. It is from this wide gamut of political and economic factors that the origins and explanation of inflation can be sought and the reasons for the differing capacity of Czechoslovakia and Austria to cope with it can be found.[1]

The main focus of this paper is the foreign trade of the two countries between 1918 and 1926, comparing and contrasting how they faced the harsh realities of economic independence and how they coped with the differential impact of inflation. To this end, the legacy bequeathed to the two new states at the end of the war is considered; then the general trends in their balance of trade, imports and exports are analysed; and the influence of inflation and deflation on the trade and economic patterns of the two countries considered, as are further aspects of foreign trade of the two countries. The relatively advantageous position the Czechoslovak Republic enjoyed vis à vis the Austrian one found expression in most comparisons of trade and economic indices. Although not a central theme of this paper, this obviously had important consequences for the course and mechanism of inflation in both countries. Thus the Austrian economy's substantial and persistent trade deficit indicated a severe structural imbalance. This not only made the country economically and politically dependent on the West-

---

[1] Alice Teichova, *A Comparative View of the Inflation of the 1920s in Austria and Czechoslovakia*, N. Schmukler (ed.), *Inflation Through the Ages*, New York 1983, pp. 531—567.

ern powers, forfeiting full control of its economy, but also undermined efforts to stabilize the currency. In contrast, the Czechoslovak economy achieved a surplus trade balance from 1920. This undoubtedly aided confidence in the economy and helped the government to check any uncontrolled inflation. These factors require more detailed examination; here primary attention is focused on the impact which inflation itself had on the foreign trade of the two countries.

This is of particular interest to students and historians of the period for two main reasons. Firstly, it is important to gauge the effect of inflation on a crucial area of economic activity. The very existence of both republics meant that foreign trade became a central focus of economic life, since the previous semi-autarkic Imperial system had collapsed. Secondly, through a careful study of foreign trade indices it is possible to analyse the impact of inflation and hyperinflation on the industrial structure. In this instance, the effect of the inflationary period on the industrial composition of Austrian and Czechoslovak exports is analysed to consider whether the process aided or hindered their respective industrial development.

I

The Legacy of the new States

Industrial and Economic Capacity

In Autumn 1918, as the war came to an end, the Habsburg Empire collapsed. As Eduard März has commented, „The very swiftness with which the Monarchy departed from the historic scene indicates that it was no living political organism when the final act of surgery was performed."[2] Severe economic turmoil inevitably resulted from the rapid demise and disintegration of the Empire, combined with the cumulative depredations of the war. Prior to 1914 the Monarchy had largely been self-sustaining in its economic activity. The different component parts of the Empire were able to supply the bulk of the food, raw materials and manufactured goods that were required. There had been a rising trend in foreign trade in the two decades before the war and after 1908 a growing import surplus.[3] However, in 1913 Austria-Hungary of

---

[2] Eduard März, *The Austrian Economy in Transition: Heritage and Formative Years of the Austrian Republic*, unpublished thesis, Harvard 1948, p. 212.

[3] *Österreichisches Statistisches Handbuch*, 1913, p. 213.

all the major European countries aside from Tsarist Russia, had the lowest level of trade per capita.[4] This relative self-sufficiency disguised the general economic backwardness of the region. While pockets of advanced industrial development were to be found, especially in the Western parts of the Empire, overall the region was economically underdeveloped. The war and its aftermath were to confirm this painful fact.

Thus a difficult legacy was bequeathed to those new nation states established in 1918 on the territory of the old Empire. All suffered from the chaos and devastation of the war. Food production had fallen sharply during the hostilities and showed few signs of imminent recovery. The self-sufficient pattern of the Monarchy had disintegrated and inevitably there was disruption as the successor states, often uncertain of their new boundaries even, sought to achieve a new economic pattern with direct access to far fewer resources than the old Empire. The inevitable consequence was that foreign trade assumed a much more significant role within economic life. This was particularly the case with regard to Austria and Czechoslovakia. Neither were large-scale producers of staple foods, which had been supplied from other parts of the Empire. These previously internal transactions weighed heavily in the import balance of the new states. To compensate, Austria and Czechoslovakia had to rely on their industries. Their territory included the most advanced industrialised areas of the Habsburg Empire. In this respect they were reasonably placed to survive in the post-war world.

Czechoslovakia was the more populated nation with 13.6 million people to Austria's 6.5 million. It was also the more industrialised, at least in Bohemia and Moravia. While the Czechoslovak state acquired around 60 % of the industrial capacity of Cisleithania, Austria gained probably 30 %.[5] In contrast to the Czech Lands, Austria had a preponderance of small and medium sized enterprises and lacked large-scale undertakings. Both countries had significant textile industries; along with metallurgical, electrical and machine industries. Heavy industry was more developed than elsewhere in the old Empire with Austria retaining one-third of iron and steel capacity and Czechoslovakia approaching three-fifths. In the sphere of consumer goods, aside

---

[4] Walter Thomas Layton & Charles Rist, *The Economic Situation of Austria*, League of Nations report, 1925, p. 76.

[5] These figures are approximate estimates and are sometimes exaggerated.

from textiles, Czechoslovakia had a very substantial glassware industry while both made leather goods. Agriculture contributed distinctively to the Czechoslovak economy with beet, barley and hops being cultivated and utilised in the sugar, malt and brewing industries which constituted a powerful export sector. Czechoslovakia also benefitted from the possession of considerable supplies of good quality coal, producing 31 million tons in 1920. This was in marked contrast to the new Austrian Republic which possessed significant reserves of lignite but negligible supplies of indigenous coal. Austria's main raw material assets were its forests, with timber being both a major export product and a resource for the paper, hardware and furniture industries; high quality iron ore located in the Erzberg in Styria; and an enormous potential for hydro-electric power.[6]

Political Outlook

From the point of view of overall balance and technical level, the Czechoslovak Republic was definitely in a stronger position to face the economic realities of the post-war world. This position was buttressed and reinforced by the buoyancy of the successful nationalist movement which had gained the country's independence. There existed a confidence in the country's political and economic future, sustained by the favourable treatment which the new republic received at the hands of the Entente powers.

The despair and pessimism expressed in contemporary Vienna stood in stark contrast. The overwhelming weight of political and economic opinion believed that the German-Austrian remains of the old Empire did not constitute a viable state. The dire food and fuel shortages gave apparent substance to this belief. The alternative proposition canvassed was for a union with Germany. To prepare the way for „the great idea of uniting the German people" the Foreign Minister, Bauer, commenced negotiations with the German government. „The policy of ‚Anschluss' was approved by all parties in the National Assembly"[7]

---

[6] For Austria see Gustav Stolper's articles in *Der Österreichische Volkswirt*, (1918), No. 8, No. 9; (1920), No. 16: Gustav Slavik, *Der Außenhandel und die Handelspolitik Österreich 1918 bis 1926*, Klagenfurt 1928, pp. 9—10. For Czechoslovakia see Rudolf Ol'šovský, *Přehled hospodářského vývoje Československa v letech 1918—1945* (A Survey of the Economic Development of Czechoslovakia from 1918—1945), Prague 1963.

[7] *Ein Jahr Republik: Österreich 1918/1919*, Wien 1919, p. 21.

although there were differing reasons, some pan-Germanic others pragmatic, motivating this policy from varying parts of the political spectrum. The case continued to be presented even after the Entente had effectively vetoed it in the Treaties of Versailles and St. Germain. Certainly it was a recurrent theme in the influential, economic journal *Der Österreichische Volkswirt*.[8] The effect was to magnify the difficulties facing the new state and to minimise its assets. Unbalanced assessments of Austria's economic prospects undoubtedly hindered the country's adaptation to the new situation. This was combined with a general inability or unwillingness, stretching across the political spectrum, to outline a national perspective for the new state.[9] The idea of ‚Anschluss' acted as a psychological parachute, which avoided confronting awkward realities. Such political escapism was not to help the Austrian people face the traumas of post-war reconstruction.

The New Boundaries

The territory of the new states of East Central Europe was decided by a combination of factors. National identity; historic boundaries; military defensibility; economic cohesion: all influenced the outcome. The precise mixture varied in each case, as political factors came into play. In this respect the Czechoslovak government, as an associate of the victorious Entente powers, had powerful levers at its disposal which ensured a favourable allocation of territory. In contrast the Austrian government's bargaining position was slight. They found the negotiations at St. Germain objectionable,[10] but their claims were always going to be refuted by the Entente. The ascendant nationalist movements held the upper hand and the twin oppressors of the old Empire suffered accordingly.

The new boundaries inevitably reflected this uneven mixture of principles. Significant national minorities remained in most of the new states. Some boundaries were more ‚historic' than others. Economic cohesion and compactness was not common. Often there was scant

---

[8] See for example 1918, No. 8: *Unsere wirtschaftliche Zukunft:* 1919, No. 4: *Ententes hilfe;* 1920 No. 42: *Um den Anschluß*.

[9] For an interesting view of the outcome of the Social Democrats' nationality policy, see Raimund Loew, *The Politics of Austro-Marxism*, in: *New Left Review*, (1979), No. 118.

[10] *Ein Jahr Republik...* [see note 7], p. 22.

convergence between the new national boundaries and the disposition of raw materials. Thus Austria was bequeathed an extremely acute problem as regards fuel. Pre-war the area had used an average of 15 ½ million tons of coal annually. In the new state, aside from the lignite reserves in Upper Austria and Styria there was almost no coal, which meant all supplies had to be imported.

Previous industrial patterns were dislocated. Prior to the war a division of labour had operated in the textile industry. Spinning and finishing had been concentrated in Austria, with weaving being the speciality of the Czech Lands. The break-up of the Empire disrupted this pattern. Austria received 25 % of the cotton spindles of the old Monarchy but only 9 % of the weaving machines. Consequently two-thirds of its yarn had to be sent abroad and then a similar share of fabric imported again for finishing. The position as regards wool was even more serious since the new republic did not possess a single major weaving mill.[11] This imbalance affected Czechoslovakia as well, but less dramatically. Its cotton industry was concentrated in Northern Bohemia and possessed 86 spinning mills along with 617 weaving mills.[12]

Czechoslovakia was more affected by the impact of the new boundaries on its transport system. Previously the area had enjoyed direct access to the ports of Rjeka and Trieste. These direct connections with the sea were severed with the break up of the Monarchy and only its access to the Danube at Bratislava remained. For a state dependent in large measure on foreign trade, this was a serious handicap. The Austrian economy did not escape from this difficulty either, although the Danube gave her valuable access to the sea. Czechoslovakia's internal railway network was moulded by the logistical and political priorities of the old Empire. It was oriented southwards and towards Vienna, while connections between the Czech Lands and Slovakia, which had been previously attached to Hungary, were inadequate.

Yet the most significant aspects of the new boundaries concerned the trade and commercial policies of the states that had arisen on the ruins of the old Monarchy. National sentiment had been one of the most powerful components in the movement which broke the Monarchy. In the post-war world this assumed a protectionist economic character, a

---

[11] *Der Österreichische Volkswirt*, (January 1920), No. 16, p. 298.
[12] Robert H. B. Lockhart, *Report on the Industrial and Economic Situation in Czechoslovakia to June 1921*, Department of Overseas Trade, (London), p. 23.

development fuelled by the famine and disruption of transport and coal supplies in the immediate post-war period. The relative economic backwardness of the region was ascribed primarily to a lack of national sovereignty, with other factors being underestimated.[13] Throughout East Central Europe the translation of nationalist principles into economic practice meant protective tariffs, with import duties being raised to very high levels. Despite gestural references — and even agreements — at several international conferences,[14] the creation of a free trade area within the Successor states was a dead letter. This had severe implications for Austria and Czechoslovakia as both were heavily reliant on trade with the Danubian states. Again Austria was the more affected. While Czechoslovakia imposed its own tariffs with high duties protecting the export sector of its economy,[15] Austria, as a defeated power, was hampered from doing so by the Peace Treaties. These stipulated that the Austrian government had to grant the allied and associated powers unconditional, unilateral, most-favoured nation treatment for five years.

The Effects of the War

The dislocation arising from the dissolution of the Empire was exacerbated by the effects of the war. The return to civilian production was a disjointed, precarious process for both states, although the Czechoslovak economy was better placed to resolve these difficulties.

Both countries' railway system suffered from wartime neglect, with lack of investment and repair. In January 1920 over one-third of the locomotives in each country were unfit for service. Czechoslovakia was better placed in respect of trucks and wagons with 88 % in operation, as against only 67 % in Austria.[16] This situation was clearly unsatisfactory but in Austria's case this problem was secondary. Its transport system was threatened above all by the lack of coal. The Communications

---

[13] Iván Tibor Berend, *The Problems of Eastern European Economic Integration in a Historical Perspective*, in: Imṛe Vajda/Mihály Simai (eds.), *Foreign Trade in a Planned Economy*, London 1971, pp. 1—6.

[14] Brussels 1920; Portorose, Yugoslavia 1921; Genoa 1922.

[15] Vaclav Průcha (ed.), *Hospodářské dějiny Československa v 19. a 20. století* (An Economic History of Czechoslovakia in the 19th and 20th Centuries), Prague 1974, p. 144.

[16] *The European Transport Situation*, Paper No. 9 for International Financial Conference, London 1920, pp. 3—5.

Section of the Supreme Economic Council considered the shortage of coal so serious as to threaten „a total collapse of transportation".[17] Indeed the lack of coal supplies undermined every sphere of Austrian economic life immediately after the war. In the general disruption each Successor state sought to renew coal output for domestic consumption first. Coal exports were a relatively low priority. This had calamitous consequences for Austria with no hard coal of its own. Even the rather dilatory Allied powers felt obliged to guarantee Austria some coal supplies from neighbouring states. However, as TABLE 1* indicates,[18] the post-war recovery in coal and the coke consumption was very slow. This bottleneck had a stranglehold effect on the country's industrial revival with many industries working at only 25 % of capacity in 1919, and the iron industry much less. This shortage of coal, combined with a shortage of foreign currency to purchase other raw materials, crippled Austria's economic restoration. Austria's industrial production index, taking 1928 as 100, was 34 for 1919 and 41 for 1920. While Czechoslovakia experienced some raw material supply difficulties, for example with cotton, its position „was notably better than that of the surrounding countries."[19] Economic reconstruction was correspondingly swifter with the country's index of industrial production (1928 = 100) being 58 in 1919 and 53 in 1920.

The war severely weakened both countries' agriculture, although again Austria appears to have suffered more. Between 1913 and 1918 the area under cultivation dropped by 22 % while the drop in yield per hectare ranged from 35 % for barley, to 41 % for wheat, to 46 % for potatoes and 47 % for oats.[20] The factors contributing to this alarming decline — shortage of labour and equipment; lack of fertilizers and

---

* This and all subsequent tables are to be found in the Appendix.

[17] *Op. cit.*, p. 3.

[18] Dept. of Overseas Trade. *Report on the Economic and Commercial Situation of Austria to July 1922*, O. S. Phillpotts, p. 17. These figures represent the consumption of the post-war Austrian Republic. Hence the pre-war figure is an estimate for those lands. The severe shortages of coal had dramatic effects on all aspects of ordinary life with power cuts, cessation of tram and train services and absence of fuel for domestic heating. Some indication of the desperate situation of the Austrian republic and especially Vienna in the immediate post-war period is given by the material in the Haus-, Hof- and Staatsarchiv, Trade Policy section. HP14. K705. 1919 and 1920.

[19] *Europe's Overseas Needs and How They Were Met*, League of Nations, Geneva 1943, p. 39 & figs. p. 40.

[20] Figures calculated from *Statistische Monatsschrift*, (1920), p. 21.

manure; poor seedcorn; slaughter of animals during the war — were not easily overcome. When a broader time period is compared, the decline remains considerable. Thus comparing 1919/1922 with 1910/1914 the drop in yield per hectare for barley was 23 %, for wheat 23 %, potatoes 21 %, oats 24 % and rye 29 %. Steady improvements were made in subsequent years but most agricultural indicators were still below pre-war levels in 1925.[21] Consequently, food imports were a prominent feature of Austria's trade in this period, with emergency relief supplies being vital in the immediate post-war years. This also was the case with Czechoslovakia although its plight was less desperate. The war had also affected its agricultural production with yields per hectare in 1919 for wheat down 17 %, barley 18 % and rye 31 % as compared with 1909/1913.[22] While this created considerable difficulties they were not of the same scope as those of Austria.

The International Setting

In considering the international balance of power Austria's legacy was extremely burdensome. At the end of the war the victorious Entente powers required a new bulwark in Central Europe to block any renewed German expansionism and urgently wanted to give concrete expression to their victory over Germany. A further central consideration was the containment of the Bolshevik revolution. Viewed in this way Czechoslovakia seemed the most appropriate bulwark among the Successor states while reparations were to ensure that Germany undertook no swift recovery. Furthermore, any wish by the new Austria for a union with Germany was firmly ruled out. ‚Anschluss‘ would seriously undermine the victory which had just been won.[23]

[21] W. T. Layton & C. Rist, *The Economic Situation*... [see note 4], pp. 61—75, Roman Sandgruber, *Österreichische Agrarstatistik 1750—1918*, Wien 1978, pp. 134—136.
[22] R. H. B. Lockhart, *Report*... [see note 12], p. 25.
[23] Ernest Llewellyn Woodward/Rohan Butler, (eds.), *Documents on British Foreign Policy*, Vol. 6 (1919), see two memoranda of Sir Francis Oppenheimer enclosed in a note from Curzon to Balfour on 9 July 1919. There is a growing body of literature on this topic, see Marie Luise Recker, *England und der Donauraum*, Stuttgart 1976, Robert Hoffman, *Die wirtschaftlichen Grundlagen der britischen Österreichpolitik, 1919*, in: *Mitteilungen des Österreichischen Staatsarchivs*, vol. 30 (1970). Anne Orde, *Großbritannien und die Selbständigkeit Österreichs, 1918—1938*, in: *Vierteljahrshefte für Zeitgeschichte*, (1980), pp. 224—247. Philip Cottrell, *Austria between Bankers and Diplomats 1918—1938* (forthcoming).

Consequently Czechoslovakia gained favourable treatment from the Peace Treaties agreed at the Paris peace conference. As an associate of the victorious power the government was also able to secure financial credits. In contrast Austria was left with the rump of an empire — what remained once all other national claims had been settled. With such chaotic origins, the new state required not only far-sighted domestic, political leadership. Its future was also intimately connected to the political wishes of its international creators.

The Entente victory had only been secured with American help. The United Kingdom no longer dominated the world as in its Victorian heyday, yet the Americans were still reluctant to assume this mantle.

Thus a crisis of hegemony existed in Europe. At its heart lay Austria. No country had the power or the will to revive the dismembered torso of the old Empire. The Foreign Office was keen to help Austria's recovery with food and fuel credits and generous financial aid. This would „bar German designs in the Balkans" and would create for Britain „a paramount position, commercially and politically in Central Europe." The Treasury, recognising the country's financial limitations, cold shouldered all such ideas.[24] When Foreign Office pressure led to discussions in Washington the British Ambassador, Viscount Grey, reported that the American government was not willing to sanction any direct credits to Austria.[25]

Given this attitude by the world's two leading nations it was not surprising that the Austrian situation deteriorated. In all of war-torn Europe — Russia excepted — the plight of the Austrian people was the most severe, with the most desperate situation affecting the citizens of Vienna. Goode, the British Director of Relief, was moved to comment that as well as negligible food and fuel he had found on his trip in October 1919 „for the first time in my life... a whole nation or what was left of it in utter, hopeless despair".[26] As well as drastic shortages of cereals the city's milk supply had been decimated. In 1918 deaths in Vienna from tuberculosis were double the 1914 figure, while only 8 % of the city's schoolchildren were in a satisfactory state of health.[27]

---

[24] *Ibid.* for the correspondence which forcefully expresses the differences of opinions in none-too diplomatic language, see especially FO Memorandum on 15 August and Treasury note on 20 August.

[25] *Ibid.*, 3. December 1919.

[26] Sir William Goode, *Economic Conditions in Central Europe (I) Parliamentary Paper 521*, 1920, p. 9.

[27] Data taken from report in *Haus-, Hof- und Staatsarchiv, Handelspolitik section*, HP228, File 170, No. 3054.

The disruption of economic life meant that the whole of Central and Eastern Europe required immediate relief supplies and credits to help restore their battered economic condition. This was mostly carried out by the American Relief Administration (A.R.A.) created by the U.S. government but operating for a period as an executive body of the Allied Supreme Council. Reflecting the changed world balance arising from the war, it was the U.S. „which alone had large supplies and adequate finances at her disposal."[28] The priority for aid was afforded to the Allied and Associate Powers. By the end of 1919 the Czechoslovak government had received $ 76,610,000 in credits from the A.R.A. plus some limited aid from Britain, France and Italy.[29] This amounted to 456,128 metric tons of supplies, mainly of food.[30] This aid helped smooth the transition to civilian industrial and agricultural production, as did the ability of the new government to raise loans to finance necessary reconstruction. However, for the Austrian government the position was much more desperate. As an ex-enemy country Austria was not entitled to American credit. Yet its plight was so serious and the contingent political prospects so alarming for the Allied politicians that an adroit proposal for aid presented by J. M. Keynes was agreed. To avert famine and consequent social upheaval the British, French and Italian government each borrowed $ 16 million from the U.S. Treasury, which was spent on buying food supplies of American origin for Austrian relief. Combined with credits from other countries this enabled 452,169 metric tons of relief supplies to be delivered to Austria during 1919, mainly cereals.[31] Yet even this „had been insufficient to provide more than a bare subsistence."[32] Despite receiving approximately the same quantity of supplies as Czechoslovakia and having only half its population, the Austrian position at the end of 1919 was much more dire. Relief did little more than prevent the country's complete collapse. With its assets still held by the Reparations Commission Austria was unable to raise loans abroad. As disputes among the Allies over reparations continued, the doubts over Austria's economic viability grew. The disagreements and divisions among the Al-

---

[28] Sir W. Goode, *Economic Conditions... (I)...* [see note 26], p. 5.
[29] Sir W. Goode, *Economic Conditions in Central Europe (II). Parliamentary Paper 641*, 1920, p. 18.
[30] Sir W. Goode, *Economic Conditions... (I)...* [see note 26], p. 15.
[31] *Ibid.*
[32] Sir W. Goode, *Economic Conditions... (II)...* [see note 29], p. 6.

lied and Associate Powers over the future of Austria and the inability of the two most powerful to encourage a programme of economic recovery created a most inhospitable climate for the new republic. The calamaties which befell the Austrian Republic in its early years were due in no small measure to these inauspicious beginnings.

II
General Patterns of Trade

The diverse origins of the two states and arising from them the relative advantages accruing to Czechoslovakia found expression in economic developments in the early post-war years. In the new circumstances of both states foreign trade became a crucial indicator of economic performance.

The Balance of Trade

The figures for the balance of visible trade in TABLE 2[33] indicate the difficulties under which the Austrian economy was labouring. Throughout this period the Austrian economy had a persistent and substantial negative trade balance. Although Czechoslovakia had a significant deficit in 1919, thereafter its trade balance was always positive. Its trade figures closely followed the course of the domestic economic cycle with a post-war boom 1920—21, followed by a sharp slump in 1922—23, with a significant recovery in the next two years, but then falling off slightly in 1926. Aside from 1924 when the recovery brought a disproportionate rise in imports the balance of trade remained in comfortable surplus. The much greater strength of the Czechoslovak economy is indicated by TABLE 3, which shows the percentage of exports to imports, annually, for each economy. This table emphasises the catastrophic position of the Austrian economy, with the export boom of 1922 at the peak of hyperinflation, according only a temporary amelioration. A slight improvement occurred from 1925 but Austria's export/import ratio remained the worst in Europe. In contrast Czechoslovakia's remained one of the strongest.[34]

---

[33] See Appendix for all information concerning the sources for the statistical data from which this and subsequent tables have been compiled.

[34] See W. T. Layton & C. Rist, *The Economic Situation...* [see note 4], p. 77 for a comparative table for 1924 of 13 European countries and the U.S.A. in which Austria clearly had the worst export/import ratio.

The volume figures in TABLE 4 bear out the resilience of the Czechoslovak economy. The immediate post-war export boom is clearly evident while the crisis of 1922 was marked by a decline in both imports and exports. However, exports rose sharply in 1923 and were relatively stable thereafter and imports rose considerably from 1923 to 1925. Both data series suggest that the economy was not too severely affected by the slump. For Austria the picture is significantly different. The sharp rise in export volume at the peak of inflation is very marked as is the export revival after stabilisation, yet the gap between export and import volumes remained wide throughout.

Sectoral Breakdown of Trade

The breakdown of trade reveals the economic character and specificities of the new states. TABLE 5 classifies Austria's trade by group, TABLE 6 by individual category. (In the official publications of both countries the trade tables are divided into fifty-one separate product categories). Both illustrate the country's serious shortfall in food and meat products, which consistently accounted for over one-quarter of the country's import bill. Coal imports were another prominent feature. The tables indicate the predominance of manufactured goods among Austria's exports, with a broad spectrum of industries involved, textiles being the most conspicuous. The rising share of raw materials and partly manufactured goods — from 15.4 % to 21.8 % — suggests that the production of wood, iron, and other raw materials was increasing its share within their own individual categories. While the diversity of exports had positive advantages, the data also indicates that the new republic had no outstandingly strong sector on which it could rely.

This was one of the contrasts with the Czechoslovak economy along with certain broad similarities revealed in TABLES 7 and 8. The basic pattern of the economy was similar with a preponderance of food and raw materials among the imports, and manufacturing goods dominating the export sector. As with Austria, food imports consistently constituted between one-quarter to one-third of the import bill. In the export sector a smaller number of sectors predominated, compared with Austria, and textiles were again prominent. Czechoslovakia had several significant raw material exports, most notably coal and sugar beet. The latter was the most important of a number of agricultural exports, which were a distinctive feature of the Czechoslovak economy as compared to the Austrian.

Trade in 1919

As has already been described, both states required considerable relief supplies in the immediate aftermath of the war. This is revealed in the data compiled for Czechoslovak trade in 1919. While available only in terms of value, it indicates that almost 35 % of the country's imports in 1919 consisted of two food products, cereals and fats. The considerable extent of relief deliveries in Czechoslovak imports is confirmed by the fact that the United States was the source of 28.41 % of the nation's imports in that year, more than double the figure of the next largest supplier, Germany. These relief deliveries undoubtedly contributed to the country's negative trade balance in 1919. This deficit was not very substantial, however, and was partly alleviated by the substantial exports of sugar beet the Czechoslovaks were able to deliver to the French, whose beet fields had been devastated in the war. This was one example of how the favoured position the Czechoslovak Republic occupied in the Entente's view of post-war Central Europe had beneficial economic repercussions. Subsequent years were to show that the country's trade balance would regularly be in surplus.

In contrast the Austrian trade data for 1919 foretold the future all too accurately. For the Austrian Republic only trade data by volume is available for 1919.[35] This indicates the reliance of the new state on imports for its basic foodstuffs and fuel. The volume of coal supplies was well below the levels necessary to restore industrial production and transport while the inadequacy of the food supplies has been commented upon in an earlier section of this paper. Each month's figures showed a marked deficit of exports as against imports. Cumulatively they illustrated the huge dimensions of the economic tasks of the Austrian Republic.

III

Inflation and its Impact on Trade

As stated in the introduction, one of the main purpose of this paper is to consider the impact of inflation on the foreign trade of the two countries. A swiftly depreciating currency cheapens exports. To what

---

[35] Data for the six months, July—December 1919, was officially published. Monthly trade tables from March-October 1919 are to be found in the trade policy section of the Haus-, Hof- und Staatsarchiv, HP986, Z.63762.

extent did this stimulate exports in the two countries? To what degree was this ‚greenhouse' growth, spawned by inflation and destined to wither once the exceptional conditions disappeared? Clearly there was a range of factors influencing trade but by selecting certain data it is possible to assess the impact and effect of inflation on trade in the two countries.

The Effect on Exports

As regards exports, there seems no doubt that a depreciating currency acted as a stimulus. A sharp upturn in export volume coincided with the years of peak currency depreciation and a world slump. In Czechoslovakia the volume of exports increased by 41.15 % between 1920 and 1921, in Austria by 42.32 % between 1921 and 1922. The changing pattern of exports for the main products of both countries is outlined in TABLE 9. This table calculates the volume change per year using 1920 as the base of 100. For Czechoslovakia some of the manufacturing sectors showed considerable growth, although the index for cotton goods is exaggerated by a relatively low base. Of the main exports only glassware and machinery showed a persistently poor performance. The Austrian picture is more varied. The textile sector enjoyed above growth throughout the period. In heavy industry, iron and ironware was well below par, aside from the special cicumstances of 1923 with the French occupation of the Ruhr which also boosted the Czechoslovak iron industry. Other heavy industrial sectors held their own in the immediate post-war period but then fell away badly. This suggests that it was within this sector that export growth generated in the inflation was most transitory.

This appears to be confirmed by the data compiled in TABLE 10. This contrasts the share by value accruing to four of the main groups of exports between the inflationary boom period and the relatively tranquil conditions of the mid-1920s. (Owing to the different peaks of inflation the starting date for the Austrian figures in one year later than for the Czechoslovakian). The table indicates a sharp contrast in the export patterns of the two economies.

Czechoslovak heavy industry was able to retain and marginally increase its share of the export trade while in Austria there was a marked decline in this sector and a noticeable growth in the share of textiles and exports of timber. Although the share of textiles in Czechoslovakia's trade pattern fell appreciably, this was not indicative of a post-inflation permanent decline, as the data in TABLES 9 and 11 confirm. In contrast it is clear that Austrian heavy industry fell victim to a false boom during the inflation. This point is amplified by the contrast drawn in TABLE 11 of the export volume of key products during the inflation period as compared with the mid-1920s.

In the Czechoslovak section of TABLE 11, eight categories of manufactured goods are listed. In all but two of these — glassware and machinery — the increase in gross volume was above average. The buoyancy of the textile and iron industry was most marked. This data confirms that the bulk of the economy was able to recover from the deflation of 1922/33 and that the inflation boom did not seriously distort the economy by promoting greenhouse economic growth.

The position of Austrian manufactured goods was much less positive. Except for the silk trade, their growth in exports was much more sluggish with only two of the ten manufactured categories showing an increase in gross volume above the average. The cotton, wool and iron industries all lagged well below the average growth rate. Although they held their share of the total value of Austrian exports, their volume growth rate was very poor compared to their Czechoslovak equivalents. Light industries such as leatherware and wooden products experienced an absolute decline as did the capital goods sector of machines and electrical machinery. Even if the figures for wood exports (Category 15) are removed from the data, leaving an average volume increase of 20.15 %, half of the products in TABLE 11 remain below that level.

The substantial increase in Austrian timber exports indicated in both TABLES 10 and 11 was part of a general trend, boosting the share of raw materials in Austrian exports. In an oblique way this trend further expressed the difficulties of the country's manufacturing sector. These were even more apparent when trade product categories were subdivided. Raw materials, semi-manufactured and finished goods were often contained within the same category. TABLE 12 analyses the components of three particular categories. The table shows clearly how raw material exports rose while that of manufactured products fell steeply. The table provides further evidence of the damage wrought by hyperinflation to the export position of Austrian industry.

Imports: a less significant influence

Inflation appears to have had less impact on imports. The depreciating currency made imports more expensive. In such situations the tendency is for import levels to be reduced as their comparative cost advantage over domestic products disappears. However, where a substantial segment of a nation's imports are food and raw materials, then swift domestic substitution is not a realisable option. In this instance, the recovery and development of both Czechoslovak and Austrian agriculture was bound to be slow, while Austrian investment in hydro-electric power could not conceivably resolve the country's fuel shortage in the short-term. Yet the dramatic collapse of the brief post-war boom after summer 1920 acted as a powerful countervailing tendency. Raw material prices slumped, in many instances falling at a faster rate than the depreciation of currencies. This explains the anomaly whereby between 1920 and 1921 the volume of Austrian imports rose by 35.22 % yet their value actually decreased by 0.05 %. In the same period the same trend is evident, but less sharply, in the Czechoslovak figures with import volumes rising by 2.07 % while the value of imports fell by 4.07 %. This development had the effect of sheltering both countries but especially Austria from some of the most calamitous consequences of inflation. The figures compiled in TABLE 13 illustrate this in more detail. They take eight leading imports of both countries in the inflation period and compare the shifts in the volume and value of those imports. For the years 1920—21 when both currencies were depreciating, a priori the value should have been significantly higher than that for volume. This should still hold for Austria when comparing 1921 and 1922, but should be reversed for Czechoslovakia as there was a sharp appreciation of the Kč during 1922. Indeed this was the case with the value figures being lower than the volume figures in all eight categories in that period. Yet when comparing 1920 with 1921 it is only with the indices for coal that the predicted pattern holds. In every other instance and with all the Austrian imports of that period, the shift in volumes was higher than those in value. Sometimes the discrepancy was considerable as with textiles and food. The clear implication of the data is that inflation did not have the impact on either the value or volume of imports that could have been expected. In contrast the deflationary measures by which the Czechoslovak government sought to control the inflation had a swift impact, reducing import volumes by one-fifth in 1922. By then the fall in world prices was abating, permitting the normal pattern of trade/currency relations to assert itself. As the Czechoslovak crown appreciated during 1922, imports became cheaper and the country's import bill dropped by twice as much as the fall in volume.

Inevitably the economies of both countries were heavily influenced by fluctuations in the world economy. Thus Czechoslovakia's initially favourable terms of trade, achieved largely by the high unit price of its exports in 1920 during the general restocking of manufactures, disappeared with the world recession, while the government's deflationary domestic policy with an appreciating Kč. resulted in a sharp fall in the unit price of imports in 1922 and 1923. Austria's initially favourable position was sustained in 1921 largely by a massive fall in its unit price of imports but the terms of trade fell steeply in the peak year of hyperinflation. 1923 and 1924 saw a relative stabilisation in both countries' terms of trade, but whereas Czechoslovakia's improved with the upturn in its economy, Austria's continued to worsen. The unit price of Czechoslovak exports underwent some recovery after 1923, lending further weight to our argument that once relatively normal conditions returned, the Czechoslovak economy was in a position to adapt to them effectively. In contrast the shift in both the composition of Austria's exports towards weak areas of world trade, e. g. textiles, and towards primary and semimanufactured products of low added value (see TABLES 10 and 12) meant that the unit price of Austrian exports fell sharply from 128.01 in 1924 to 89.05 in 1926. So while the Czechoslovak economy's terms of trade improved in these years those of Austria continued to decline, as TABLE 14 shows.

The character and extent of both countries' inflation was closely related to their overall economic and political position. A close inspection of the import figures lends further weight to the argument that the Austrian economy faced a grave situation. Its severe structural imbalance was highlighted by the high import content of its major export products. This is illustrated by TABLE 15 with its breakdown of Austrian and Czechoslovak cotton and wool imports, which indicate the substantial advantage of the Czechoslovak industries. The overwhelming bulk of its imports in these categories were raw materials, while the proportion of fully manufactured goods was negligible. This was not due merely to the slump of 1922, since the same pattern held true during the boom of 1921. In contrast only one-quarter to one-third of Austrian imports in these categories were raw materials with between one-half and two-thirds being manufactured goods. This pattern was broadly reproduced throughout the period to 1926 and does not seem to have been related directly to inflation.

IV
Further trade Contrasts

Tariff Policy

The more significant factor affecting this pattern of trade was the respective tariff policies of the two governments. The Czechoslovak government, as with other Successor states, took advantage of its status as an associate of the victorious powers to introduce a series of wide-ranging controls on its trade, with an extensive system of import and export licences in the immediate post-war period. From 1918 to 1924 there were high customs duties, which in some of the economy's main export branches, such as textiles, assumed an almost prohibitive character.[36] Their effectiveness is indicated by the negligible level of manufactured imports displayed in TABLE 15. This course of action was more difficult to Austria, as a defeated power, due to its treaty obligations. Furthermore, the characteristic thinking of the international bankers, economists and politicians who became involved in Austrian affairs was firmly free trade, linked to the gold standard. They objected to restrictive tariff policies. The country's industry was given little breathing space in which to recover from the dislocation of war and the break-up of the Monarchy. A glance at the proportion of manufactured goods in the country's cotton and wool imports illustrates the problem .

This is not to suggest that a tariff policy was the panacea for Austria's trade imbalances and economic shortcomings. That belief was one of the illusions retained by several Successor and Balkan states who failed to appreciate the general technical backwardness of the region in relation to the world economy. A tariff policy was one component of the wide-ranging programme of economic measures necessary if all these states were to modernise and develop their economies. As the major element of that programme it proved severely inadequate.

Into a Wider World

In fact, the main effect of the widespread tariff policy pursued by most states in East Central Europe was to accelerate the break-up of the pre-war trade patterns. The region was integrated increasingly into the

---

[36] V. Průcha (ed.), *Hospodářské dějiny Československa*... [see note 15], p. 144.

international economy. This process was apparent in both Czechoslovakia and Austria. TABLE 16 indicates this trend, which was especially marked for Czechoslovakia. Its exports to the Danubian states fell from one-half to one-third of the total over the period 1920—1926. The main area of expansion was to markets beyond Continental Europe which took over one-quarter of the country's exports by 1926 as compared with one-tenth in 1920, while imports from these regions rose by one-third.[37] This trend to markets beyond Continental Europe is also clear in the Austrian export figures, although the decline in its exports to the Danubian states was less marked.

One particular aspect of this decline was the fall in trade between the two states. From 1920 to 1926 in Czechoslovakia's import bill, Austria's share halved in value, dropping from 13.01 % in 1920 to 6.51 % in 1926. The decline in Czechoslovak exports to Austria was even more significant, Austria's share falling from 35.10 % in 1920 to 16.26 % in 1926. TABLE 17 breaks down Czechoslovakia's export trade with the Danubian states in three major products and indicates that it was the substantial decline in trade with Austria which accounted primarily for the declining share of the Danubian states in Czechoslovakia's exports. Hungary's share also dropped sharply but Yugoslavia's showed a more varied, contradictory picture, while Romania represented a significantly expanding market. The overall trend, however, was clearly negative with a sharp fall coinciding with Czechoslovakia's deflation in 1922. In that year both Austrian and Hungarian shares of Czechoslovak exports fell by one-quarter. From then on there was no likelihood of either country recouping their former position. The impact of Austrian hyperinflation on Czechoslovakia's export needs further investigation since this may have contributed substantially to the fall in 1922. Yet in the shifting patterns of trade there were many factors at work, with the break-up of the Monarchy and subsequent nationalist economic policies being primary among them. The comparable Austrian figures (TABLE 18) are harder to evaluate, since only export volumes are available for 1920 and 1921. Yet they suggest a similar picture. The main decline came with Hungary and Czechoslovakia (although comparing with volumes makes this judgement tentative) while trade with Romania expanded slightly.

---

[37] This figure includes exports through the free ports of Hamburg and Bremen.

Transit Trade

Pre-war Vienna had been the most important banking, commercial and trading city in East Central Europe. One of the potential assets of the new Austrian Republic lay in the regeneration under the new conditions of the transit trade. There were high hopes that Vienna's standing as a financial and commercial centre would survive the downfall of the Monarchy and that its situation on the Danube would ensure its continued importance as a transit centre. Some of the hopes concerning Vienna's continuing financial prestige were swiftly dispelled but the volume of transit trade did climb steadily after the war. By 1922 the volume of transit trade was almost 38 million quintals, equivalent to 51 % of total import volume. Thereafter there was a decline till 1925 but by 1926 the volume of transit trade exceeded its 1922 peak. The main goods transported were food, especially sugar, cereals, fruit and vegetables, coal and minerals with Germany, Italy and Czechoslovakia being the main sources of transit goods and the same countries and Hungary being the primary destinations. By reason of its location, commercial experience and favourable railway and river network, Vienna was more advantageously placed than Prague to develop this trade. Yet as the size of the new republic was not great and as many goods transversed the country by the shorter North-South route, as with Czechoslovak and German coal to Italy, the actual revenues accruing to the Austrian government from this trade appear not to have been as substantial as initially hoped.[38] Nevertheless, despite the disruptive effects of hyperinflation the basically favourable conditions for transit trade were evident in its revival in the mid-1920s. This was one area where the growth of the early 1920s did not wither away with hyperinflation.

V

Conclusion

This paper has analysed the legacy bequeathed to the new Austrian and Czechoslovak republics; their overall patterns of trade from their foundation until 1926; the impact of their respective inflations on these trade patterns; and several further contrasting trade features. A number of sharp contrasts have been drawn between the two states and it has

---

[38] For an indication of this see Gustav Stolper, in: *Der Österreichische Volkswirt*, No. 37, (11 June 1921), p. 680.

been argued that the outcome of the war shaped the economic environment and prospects of both. The qualitatively more advantageous position of the Czechoslovak Republic found reflection in most economic indicators and enabled the republic to cope with some of its initial economic problems. In contrast the Austrian people gained neither systematic international aid from the Entente nor a clear-sighted national policy from their political leaders. In consequence the country was not able quickly to overcome the economic difficulties arising from its inchoate origins. The country's trade problems analysed in this paper give a clear indication as to the scale of these difficulties without suggesting that they were insurmountable. Undoubtedly the turmoil of these years reshaped and weakened Austria's industrial structure. Whether it could be refashioned and modernised remained a task for the future.

Appendix

The statistical information in this article has been drawn from the official trade data to be found in the government publications listed at the end of this appendix. An extensive range of publications have been consulted in various libraries and institutions in Vienna and London.

The various tables, time-series, sectoral breakdowns, etc., are based on the annual and monthly data for imports and exports which can be located in these publications. The trade tables of both governments were based on a common division into fifty-one categories of product, thereby permitting direct comparison between them. In 1925 the Austrian government altered its categorisation slightly but for the purposes of this article the Austrian data for 1925 and 1926, where necessary, has been recalculated into the original categories. All the tables have been calculated from this data base. The construction of these eighteen tables has often involved considerable re-working of this data, to group it into the appropriate categories prior to recalculation.

One of the minor effects of the collapse of the Austro-Hungarian Empire and the uncertainty of new state boundaries was the disruption of official data collection. This was especially true in the new republic of ‚German-Austria'. No official trade statistics were published before mid-1919, although I have located some monthly, stencilled tables in the Haus-, Hof- und Staatsarchiv in Vienna. For the second half of 1919 trade data in volume only was published. While information on trade by value by product category is available from 1920, no official data for the value of trade by country was given until 1922.

In contrast the Czechoslovak figures appear complete from 1920, with monthly breakdowns as well. Only in 1923 does it appear that the Austrian government officially began the publication of quarterly trade figures. For 1919 Czechoslovak figures (in value only) can be calculated from information available in the *Ceskoslovenský Statistický Věstník*, the Manuel Statistique (1920) as well as the Monthly Bulletin of the Supreme Economic Council. This disparity in the data base available for the two countries has meant that certain comparisons for the immediate postwar years are difficult to make.

As regards to the data by value the Czechoslovak Kč is expressed at current prices, while the Austrian figures for 1920—1924 are expressed in Schilling. This currency was introduced in 1925 and the previous Gold Kronen figures have been converted by the appropriate ratio. To ensure as great a degree of consistency as possible in the construction of my data base, each year's figures have been drawn from the full, annual set of data as it appears for that year. I have not used trade figures published subsequently which may have been corrected or adjusted. Hence there are bound to be slight inaccuracies in the data as well as those inevitably arising from the inadequacies of the contemporary, statistical returns. However, these appear unlikely to alter significantly the overall statistical trends.

TABLE 1

Austrian Coal and Coke Consumption
('000 tons)

	Pre-war circa	1919	1920	1921
Austrian	2,600	2,076	2,076	2,607
Imported	12,790	3,030	4,065	5,928
Total	15,390	5,106	6,141	8,535

TABLE 2

Balance of Trade by Value, 1919—26

Year	AUSTRIA (Schilling)			CZECHOSLOVAKIA (Kč)		
	Exports	Imports	Balance	Exports	Imports	Balance
1919	n.a.	n.a.		5,323,260	6,555,417	- 1,232,157
1920	1,341,863	2,449,670	- 1,107,807	27,569,414	23,384,411	+ 4,185,003
1921	1,311,813	2,448,454	- 1,136,641	27,311,585	22,433,293	+ 4,878,292
1922	1,518,944	2,292,859	- 773,915	18,086,348	12,695,515	+ 5,390,833
1923	1,494,307	2,665,331	- 1,171,024	12,573,315	10,222,287	+ 2,351,028
1924	1,988,099	3,473,784	- 1,485,685	15,666,721	15,261,239	+ 405,482
1925	1,954,485	2,891,424	- 936,939	18,821,117	17,618,110	+ 1,203,007
1926	1,744,930	2,844,553	- 1,099,623	17,856,559	15,276,671	+ 2,579,999

TABLE 3

Exports by Value as a percentage of Imports

Year	Austria	Czechoslovakia
1919	n.a.	81.20
1920	54.78	117.90
1921	53.58	121.75
1922	66.25	142.46
1923	56.06	123.00
1924	57.23	102.66
1925	67.60	106.83
1926	61.34	116.89

TABLE 4

Austrian and Czechoslovak Trade by Volume 1919—26
(measured by quintals, 1 q = 100 kg)

Year	AUSTRIA			
	Exports	% annual change	Imports	% annual change
1919 VI—XII	4,992,753		20,679,603	
1920	13,175,800	+ 163.90	60,610,719	+ 193.09
1921	14,868,546	+ 12.85	81,955,578	+ 35.22
1922	21,161,963	+ 42.32	74,483,008	- 9.11
1923	21,976,281	+ 3.85	76,824,755	+ 3.14
1924	25,975,222	+ 18.20	90,651,154	+ 18.00
1925	32,458,908	+ 24.96	82,403,886	- 9.10
1926	32,281,886	- 0.55	82,627,966	+ 0.27

Year	CZECHOSLOVAKIA			
	Exports	% annual change	Imports	% annual change
1919	n.a.		n.a.	
1920	69,002,209		39,101,560	
1921	97,427,354	+ 41.15	39,911,743	+ 2.07
1922	94,902,625	- 2.59	31,942,150	- 19.97
1923	113,095,983	+ 19.17	41,956,502	+ 31.35
1924	122,991,569	+ 8.75	56,057,447	+ 33.61
1925	121,541,030	- 1.18	66,524,694	+ 18.67
1926	127,965,410	+ 5.29	65,708,441	- 1.23

TABLE 5

Pattern of Austrian Trade by product group as % of total value (using Brussels Convention Classification)

	IMPORTS					EXPORTS				
	1922	1923	1924	1925	1926	1922	1923	1924	1925	1926
Live animals	5.0	6.4	6.9	9.0	9.6	0.8	1.3	0.8	1.5	1.3
Articles of food & drink	25.6	26.1	26.9	26.6	27.3	2.0	1.5	2.3	1.9	1.9
Materials, raw or part manufactured	31.0	31.5	29.5	29.6	26.8	15.4	15.5	18.1	20.1	21.8
Manufactured articles	38.3	35.9	36.0	32.2	33.5	81.1	81.8	77.8	73.3	72.6
Gold & silver	0.1	0.1	0.7	2.5	2.8	0.7	0.7	0.9	3.2	2.4

TABLE 6

Austria's Major Imports/Exports by category as a % of total value (usually over 3%)

Category	1920	1921	1922	1923	1924	1925	1926
Imports							
C6 Cereals	18.93	15.52	12.61	14.00	12.29	12.87	12.85
C7 Fruit & veg.	3.14	3.06	3.38	2.73	3.02	3.18	3.31
C8 Cattle	1.17	2.77	5.33	5.97	6.83	8.92	9.42
C14 Foodstuffs	6.49	4.37	3.02	3.07	3.61	2.87	3.34
C15 Coal & wood	8.22	8.34	11.44	10.30	8.69	8.32	7.70
C22 Cotton & goods	9.00	11.06	12.14	14.57	12.73	12.27	10.04
C24 Wool & goods	9.13	11.42	9.21	9.30	8.36	7.14	7.06
C25 Silk & goods	3.58	4.77	3.77	4.60	4.66	4.74	4.99
Exports:							
C15 Wood & Coal	4.66	4.51	5.66	6.80	7.31	9.53	9.97
C22 Cotton & goods	12.06	8.71	12.27	12.22	14.11	13.71	12.92
C24 Wool & goods	3.06	4.00	5.30	6.38	7.07	5.38	5.45
C25 Silk & goods	4.35	4.15	3.52	5.65	6.13	5.55	6.53
C26 Made-up articles	5.65	5.62	6.02	5.98	6.07	4.63	3.97
C29 Paper & goods	5.99	7.20	7.30	8.79	6.54	7.53	8.88
C32 Leather & wares	5.55	5.30	4.62	4.83	5.02	4.53	4.05
C34 Wood products	5.34	5.53	5.06	3.07	3.60	2.61	2.32
C38 Iron & ironware	13.10	11.00	9.94	11.90	7.89	10.51	9.58
C39 Base metals	3.29	4.23	4.80	6.04	6.98	5.27	5.47
C40 Machinery	5.47	6.67	5.20	3.25	3.34	3.66	3.82
C41 Elect. machines	4.07	4.64	4.94	3.78	3.28	3.01	3.37

TABLE 7

Czechoslovakia's Pattern of Foreign Trade

Imports   % of Total imports in value

	1920	1921	1922	1923	1924	1925	1926
Raw materials	44.24	53.64	57.13	63.93	45.36	59.35	54.94
Semi-manufactured goods	14.29	12.33	13.29	12.15	19.28	11.12	11.77
Manufactured goods	41.47	34.03	29.58	23.91	35.36	29.53	33.29

Exports   % of Total exports in value

	1920	1921	1922	1923	1924	1925	1926
Raw materials	10.74	14.30	19.12	23.60	16.54	16.92	17.52
Semi-manufactured goods	10.94	10.35	17.02	17.46	17.87	16.62	15.35
Manufactured goods	78.32	75.35	63.86	58.94	65.59	66.46	67.13

Ratio of Imports: Exports, according to value

	1920	1921	1922	1923	1924	1925	1926
Raw materials	1:0.29	1:0.32	1:0.47	1:0.45	1:0.39	1:0.30	1:0.37
Semi-manufactured goods	1:0.90	1:1.02	1:1.81	1:1.75	1:0.99	1:1.60	1:1.52
Manufactured goods	1:2.23	1:2.69	1:3.05	1:3.00	1:1.99	1:2.41	1:2.35

TABLE 8

Czechoslovakia's Major Imports/Exports by category as a
% of total value (usually exceeding 3% of value)

Category	1919	1920	1921	1922	1923	1924	1925	1926
Imports:								
C6 Cereals	22.03	9.84	20.20	9.93	8.51	15.40	14.38	12.24
C7 Fruit & veg.	1.25	2.91	3.18	3.53	3.27	3.14	3.18	3.83
C8 Cattle	0.45	0.58	0.32	4.05	6.32	5.42	4.36	3.94
C11 Fats	12.89	4.62	3.65	6.60	8.40	5.23	3.83	4.11
C22 Cotton & goods	14.00	21.51	15.36	15.54	17.25	17.34	18.29	13.90
C24 Wool & goods	8.45	9.46	9.47	12.65	12.40	11.39	10.08	10.30
Exports:								
C4 Sugar	29.52	12.35	13.71	7.74	14.98	15.52	12.34	12.58
C15 Coal & wood	11.54	6.31	10.27	14.10	18.58	14.19	10.40	9.81
C22 Cotton & goods	1.88	9.16	13.92	14.19	12.61	14.88	17.05	13.91
C24 Wool & goods	6.05	24.24	15.03	15.52	9.23	10.88	9.55	9.02
C35 Glassware	6.96	6.88	7.59	11.32	7.65	7.89	6.90	6.55
C38 Iron & ironware	5.91	5.48	5.01	4.24	7.70	4.85	6.54	7.02

TABLE 9
Changing Pattern of Exports by Main Products, 1920—26 by volume
(1920 = 100)

Product	CZECHOSLOVAKIA						AUSTRIA					
	1921	1922	1923	1924	1925	1926	1921	1922	1923	1924	1925	1926
C4 Sugar	184	129	209	295	363	405	—	—	—	—	—	—
C6 Cereals	42	264	452	234	307	407	—	—	—	—	—	—
C15 Wood, coal	148	140	163	176	158	165	116	214	236	356	488	480
C22 Cotton & goods	301	436	380	529	726	616	185	275	242	282	343	291
C24 Wool & goods	117	176	163	225	224	234	184	296	322	406	330	312
C25 Silk & goods	—	—	—	—	—	—	181	159	268	388	430	507
C29 Paper & goods	105	127	123	139	151	169	129	189	242	256	289	292
C32 Leather & goods	210	213	180	149	259	339	212	334	293	370	284	224
C34 Wooden products	107	99	87	138	173	158	162	172	156	182	160	149
C35 Glassware	97	87	74	115	122	121	—	—	—	—	—	—
C38 Iron, ironware	124	120	346	203	315	293	106	127	191	111	147	157
C39 Base metals	—	—	—	—	—	—	137	159	157	187	170	184
C40 Machinery	123	75	64	91	123	110	190	151	99	108	105	90
C41 Elec. Machinery	—	—	—	—	—	—	158	163	128	123	118	99
Overall	141	137	164	178	176	185	113	161	167	197	246	245

TABLE 10

The Pattern of Exports by Principal Groups (by value)

Czechoslovakia	1920—21 (Kč)	% of total	1925—26 (Kč)	% of total
C15 Wood & coal	4,546,630	8.28	3,709,827	10.11
C22—26 Textiles	20,188,885	36.79	12,104,365	33.00
C29 Paper & goods	1,349,295	2.46	696,770	1.90
C38—42 Metal and manufactured goods	5,500,516	10.02	4,178,326	11.39
Austria	(Schilling)		(Schilling)	
C15 Wood & coal	145,106	5.13	360,302	9.74
C22—26 Textiles	731,287	25.83	1,132,469	30.61
C29 Paper & goods	205,363	7.25	302,096	8.17
C38—42 Metal and manufactured goods	832,961	29.43	826,889	22.35

TABLE 11
Changing Pattern of Export Volumes of Key Products (by quintals)

Products	CZECHOSLOVAKIA						AUSTRIA				
	1920–21		1925–26		% Gross volume increase/decrease		1921–22		1925–26		% Gross volume increase/decrease
	Export volume	% of total	Export volume	% of total			Export volume	% of total	Export volume	% of total	
C4 Sugar	7,056,871	4.24	19,089,357	7.65	170.51		—	—	—	—	—
C6 Cereals	1,226,576	0.74	6,185,090	2.48	404.26		—	—	—	—	—
C15 Wood & coal	128,771,901	77.36	167,429,840	67.10	30.02		12,396,820	34.41	36,344,597	56.14	193.18
C22 Cotton & goods	432,707	0.26	1,446,643	0.58	234.32		406,147	1.13	552,810	0.85	36.11
C24 Wool & goods	228,303	0.14	481,005	0.19	110.69		100,568	0.28	134,244	0.21	33.49
C25 Silk & wares	—	—	—	—	—		18,564	0.05	51,022	0.08	174.84
C29 Paper & goods	1,572,387	0.94	2,451,444	0.98	55.91		2,821,825	7.83	5,157,203	7.97	82.76
C32 Leather & goods	87,547	0.05	169,054	0.07	93.10		152,790	0.42	142,455	0.22	- 6.76
C34 Wooden products	359,301	0.22	576,023	0.23	60.32		815,764	2.26	752,937	1.16	- 7.70
C35 Glassware	2,758,671	1.66	3,403,494	1.36	23.37		—	—	—	—	—
C38 Iron, ironware	3,674,071	2.21	9,963,301	3.99	171.18		4,290,027	11.91	5,623,164	8.69	31.08
C39 Base metals	—	—	—	—	—		391,846	1.09	469,626	0.73	19.85
C40 Machinery	901,940	0.54	942,092	0.38	4.45		963,420	2.67	550,286	0.85	- 42.88
C41 Elect. Machinery	—	—	—	—	—		227,037	0.63	153,898	0.24	- 32.21

TABLE 12

Breakdown of Three Austrian Product Categories into constituent parts (by volume) quintals

Products	1921—22	1925—26	% Gross volume change per constituent part	% Gross volume change per category
C29 Paper & goods	2,821,825	5,157,209		+82.76
— stationery	189,918	70,009	-63.09	
— paper	2,631,137	5,087,106	+93.34	
C32 Leather & goods	152,790	142,455		-6.76
— shoes	25,406	6,763	-73.38	
— leather	103,533	116,365	+12.39	
C38 Iron & ironware	4,290,027	5,623,164		+31.08
— ironware	1,398,633	1,081,784	-22.65	
— raw & pig iron	2,127,285	3,800,534	+78.66	

TABLE 13
The Shifts in Value and Volume of Eight Major Imports in the Inflation Period

Product	CZECHOSLOVAKIA				AUSTRIA			
	Shift in value (%) 1920–21	Shift in volume (%) 1920–21	Shift in value (%) 1921–22	Shift in volume (%) 1921–22	Shift in value (%) 1920–21	Shift in volume (%) 1920–21	Shift in value (%) 1921–22	Shift in volume (%) 1921–22
Cereals	+97.04	+219.11	-72.17	-44.47	-18.03	+23.85	-23.89	-13.11
Fats	-24.15	- 7.09	+ 2.24	+44.02	-52.12	-17.01	- 5.71	- 9.07
Coal	+10.62	-13.81	-48.27	-37.45	+ 1.43	+43.36	+28.44	-12.20
Foodstuffs	—	—	—	-32.39	-32.68	-25.86	-35.20	-20.62
Minerals	-16.29	-10.98	-41.76	- 6.58	—	—	—	—
Mineral oils	-47.38	-19.52	-50.61	—	—	—	—	—
Cotton	-31.48	+37.70	-42.77	-16.65	+22.77	+138.08	+ 2.81	+ 0.46
Wool	- 3.90	+53.89	-24.46	- 5.74	+25.01	+156.53	-24.41	- 3.22
Silk	—	—	—	—	+33.12	+109.76	-26.07	-23.58
Iron	-41.83	+ 7.02	-20.42	+78.97	- 2.86	+104.40	-28.68	-19.41
Total	- 4.07	+ 2.09	-43.41	-19.97	- 0.05	+35.22	- 6.35	- 9.11

TABLE 14

Estimated Terms of Trade, 1920—1926
1925 = 100

	Czechoslovakia	Austria
1920	114.22	146.22
1921	85.30	170.29
1922	82.02	128.37
1923	78.04	118.59
1924	80.03	115.71
1925	100.00	100.00
1926	102.64	91.46

TABLE 15

Percentage Breakdown of Austrian and Czechoslovak Textile Imports (by value)

	1921	1922	1923	1924	1925	1926
C22						
— Raw cotton						
Austria	26.92	25.02	26.15	27.74	38.98	30.81
Czechoslovakia	86.33	88.96	89.62	90.51	86.61	82.75
— Cotton yarn						
Austria	7.12	5.02	5.27	6.89	8.99	10.81
Czechoslovakia	8.87	7.68	6.36	3.31	8.86	11.28
— Cotton goods						
Austria	65.82	69.88	68.56	65.35	52.02	58.37
Czechoslovakia	4.80	3.36	4.01	6.18	4.53	5.97
C24						
— Wool						
Austria	17.57	22.91	26.45	29.04	34.93	33.06
Czechoslovakia	76.12	78.34	86.60	82.04	80.23	78.27
— Woollen yarn						
Austria	4.31	10.78	12.47	16.16	14.36	14.48
Czechoslovakia	18.84	16.68	10.16	15.10	13.51	13.99
— Woollen goods						
Austria	78.12	66.29	61.06	54.79	50.70	52.44
Czechoslovakia	4.63	4.19	3.24	2.86	6.26	7.74

TABLE 16

Changing Trade Patterns (%)

	Imports (value)			Exports (value)			
	1920	1922	1925	1920	1922	1925	1926
Czechoslovakia:							
Danubian States	18.58	18.66	17.49	50.79	37.95	32.42	33.21
North Central Europe	25.67	30.41	25.68	17.25	22.18	25.99	21.94
West Europe	25.43	17.47	16.72	21.57	21.34	18.10	17.46
Other	30.32	33.46	40.11	10.39	18.53	23.49*	27.39*
Austria	volume	value	value	volume	value	value	value
Danubian States	44.5	41.16	38.91	38.4	41.74	34.28	36.89
North Central Europe	42.3	27.50	24.38	20.9	24.83	23.50	15.76
West Europe	6.7	16.22	17.09	38.1**	22.48	23.16	24.90
Other	6.5	15.22	19.62	2.6	10.95	19.09	22.45

Key: Danubian States: Hungary, Yugoslavia, Romania, Austria/Czechoslovakia. North Central Europe: Germany, Poland. West Europe: Belgium, France, Holland, Italy, Switzerland, United Kingdom.

* includes free ports, notably Hamburg
** excludes Belgium.

TABLE 17

Changing Trade Patterns. Selected Products & the Danube States
Czechoslovak Exports % by value

	1920	1921	1922	1923	1924	1925	1926
C22 Cotton & goods							
Hungary	13.27	19.24	16.97	11.10	14.39	11.39	13.35
Austria	45.24	47.44	31.13	37.65	31.51	22.99	21.18
Romania	1.70	4.92	5.97	8.33	9.44	10.83	13.50
Yugoslavia	5.99	14.19	8.45	13.45	10.11	9.75	11.67
Total	66.20	85.79	62.52	70.53	65.45	54.96	58.70
C24 Wool & woollen goods							
Hungary	19.04	22.75	14.54	6.55	10.28	9.75	9.63
Austria	59.61	51.75	35.84	34.88	32.96	27.92	27.00
Romania	1.25	4.17	2.58	5.41	5.38	4.79	5.12
Yugoslavia	4.61	6.31	6.09	6.13	6.36	7.73	8.05
Total	84.51	84.98	59.05	52.97	54.98	50.19	49.80
C38 Iron & ironware							
Hungary	9.12	11.34	6.34	3.89	4.62	4.01	3.40
Austria	34.51	18.63	14.63	6.90	12.83	12.67	11.41
Romania	6.11	10.17	11.25	7.95	10.60	14.69	17.04
Yugoslavia	6.25	11.92	8.50	3.99	8.19	5.02	9.09
Total	55.99	52.06	40.72	22.73	36.24	36.39	40.94

TABLE 18

Changing Trade Patterns. Selected Products & Danube States
Austrian Exports (%)

	1920 (q)	1921 (q)	1922 (sch)	1923 (sch)	1924 (sch)	1925 (sch)	1926 (sch)
C22							
Cotton & cotton goods							
Czechoslovakia	27.73	27.74	10.72	6.35	6.41	6.89	6.71
Hungary	17.61	20.00	22.83	15.80	17.01	15.46	17.05
Romania	1.20	4.63	8.80	13.67	12.73	13.63	15.11
Yugoslavia	3.57	13.01	12.18	17.81	11.70	10.55	11.68
Total	50.11	65.38	54.53	53.63	47.85	46.53	50.55
C24							
Wool & woollen goods							
Czechoslovakia	59.26	46.53	15.92	11.33	13.06	15.68	13.68
Hungary	12.42	12.39	15.81	9.27	15.72	13.64	15.30
Romania	1.02	4.30	5.90	7.93	5.92	6.32	8.42
Yugoslavia	5.49	7.87	7.90	10.42	9.41	10.92	9.49
Total	78.19	71.09	45.53	38.95	44.11	46.52	46.89
C38							
Iron & ironware							
Czechoslovakia	43.64	30.57	8.08	5.37	8.81	9.92	11.26
Hungary	8.24	7.85	11.96	6.77	6.18	5.35	8.55
Romania	3.86	3.93	10.26	8.09	10.04	8.48	8.59
Yugoslavia	8.12	24.89	23.55	20.67	21.76	17.48	14.49
Total	63.86	67.24	53.85	40.90	46.79	41.23	42.89

Sources

Československý Statistický Věstnik 1920 (Czechoslovak Statistical Bulletin 1920), Praha 1920.
Commerce Extérieur de la Republique Tchéchoslovaque en 1921, Prague 1922.
Commerce Extérieur de la Republique Tchéchoslovaque en 1922, Prague 1923.
Commerce Extérieur de la Republique Tchéchoslovaque en 1923, Prague 1924.

Zahraniční Obchod Republicky Československé v roce 1924 (Foreign Trade of the Czechoslovak Republic in 1924), Praha 1925.
Zahraniční Obchod Republicky Československé v roce 1925 (Foreign Trade of the Czechoslovak Republic in 1925), Praha 1926.
Zahraniční Obchod Republicky Československé v roce 1926 (Foreign Trade of the Czechoslovak Republic in 1926), Praha 1927.
Manuel Statistique de la Republique Tchéchoslovaque, No. 1, Prague 1920.
Manuel Statistique de la Republique Tchéchoslovaque, No. 2, Prague 1925.
Supreme Economic Council. Monthly Bulletin 1919—20, Vol. 1, London 1920.
Statistický Přehled Zahraničního Obchodu Republicky Československé, Nos. 1—6 (Statistical Survey of the Foreign Trade of the Czechoslovak Republic) Jan—June 1921, Prague 1921.
Aperçu Statistique du Commerce Extérieur de la République Tchéchoslovaque, Jan—Dec 1922, Nos. 1—2, Prague 1922.
Zahraniční Obchod Republicky Československé 1923, Nos. 1—12 (Foreign Trade of the Czechoslovak Republic 1923), Prague 1923.
Zahraniční Obchod Republicky Československé 1924, Nos. 1—12 (Foreign Trade of the Czechoslovak Republic 1924), Prague 1924.
Měsíční Přehled Zahraničního Obchodu Republicky Československé 1925, Nos. 1—12, (Monthly Survey of the Foreign Trade of the Czechoslovak Republic 1925), Prague 1925.
Měsíční Přehled Zahraničního Obchodu Republicky Československé 1926, Nos. 1—12, (Monthly Survey of the Foreign Trade of the Czechoslovak Republic 1926), Prague 1926.
Österreichisches Statistisches Handbuch 1913, Wien 1914.
Statistisches Handbuch für die Republik Österreich, Year I, Wien 1920.
Statistisches Handbuch für die Republik Österreich, Year II, Wien 1921.
Statistisches Handbuch für die Republik Österreich, Year III, Wien 1923.
Statistisches Handbuch für die Republik Österreich, Year IV, Wien 1924.
Statistisches Handbuch für die Republik Österreich, Year V, Wien 1924.
Statistisches Handbuch für die Republik Österreich, Year VI, Wien 1925.
Statistisches Handbuch für die Republik Österreich, Year VII, Wien 1926.
Statistisches Handbuch für die Republik Österreich, Year VIII, Wien 1927.
Österreichisches Jahrbuch 1922, Wien 1923.
Statistische Monatschrift 1919, 1920, 1921, Wien 1919, 1920, 1921.
Statistische Übersichten über den auswärtigen Handel Österreichs im zweiten Halbjahre 1919, Wien 1920.
Statistische Übersichten über den auswärtigen Handel Österreichs im Jahre 1920, Wien 1921.
Statistische Übersichten über den auswärtigen Handel Österreichs im Jahre 1921, Wien 1922.
Statistische Übersichten über den auswärtigen Handel Österreichs im ersten Halbjahre 1921, Wien 1921.
Außenhandel Österreichs im Jahre 1922, Wien 1923.
Memorandum on Balance of Payments and Foreign Trade Balances 1910—1923, Volumes 1 & 2, League of Nations, Geneva 1924.

Summary

This paper assesses how the economies of the two most industrially-developed Successor States, Czechoslovakia and Austria, adapted to their new conditions of national independence. The paper concentrates on the foreign trade of the two countries between 1918 and 1926. It compares and contrasts the response of both nations to the harsh realities of economic independence and the differential impact of inflation.

It begins by a consideration of the political, economic and diplomatic legacy bequeathed to the two new states; then the general trends in their balance of trade, imports and exports, are analysed; and the influence of inflation and deflation on the trade and economic patterns of the two countries considered, as are further aspects of their foreign trade. The relatively advantageous position of the Czechoslovak Republic vis-a-vis Austria is confirmed by the comparison of these trade and economic indices.

Particular attention is focussed on the impact which inflation itself had on the foreign trade of the two countries. With the collapse of the previous semi-autarchic Imperial system, foreign trade became a central focus of economic life for both states. Inflation had important effects on this crucial area of economic activity, especially as regards exports. The evidence drawn from an extensive study of official contemporary publications — which form the core of the paper's 18 tables — indicates that while Czechoslovak heavy industry was not unduly affected by inflation, in Austria the export growth in this sector generated in the inflationary period was transitory. It withered once the exceptional conditions disappeared. Indeed, a number of the foreign trade indices illustrate the differential impact of inflation on the industrial structure of the two states. While the composition of Czechoslovak exports altered little during this period, there was a discernible shift in Austrian exports away from manufactured products with semi-manufactured goods and raw materials increasing their percentage share. This retrogression in the Austrian economy is one of the most important features to emerge from this study.

The structural imbalance in Austria's balance of trade, the high import content of its major export products, notably textiles, and its weakening terms of trade from 1922 are further examples indicated in the paper of the difficulties faced by the Austrian republic in these initial years. The qualitatively more advantageous position of the Czechoslovak Republic found reflection in these and other economic indicators, including its ability to penetrate into markets beyond Continental Europe, although this diversification was also a feature of Austrian trade. The marked disparity in the economic and foreign trade performance of the two states was related to a series of domestic and international political factors which require integration into an overall analysis. The Austrian people gained neither systematic international aid from the Entente powers nor a clear-sighted national policy from their political leaders. In consequence the country was not able to overcome quickly the economic difficulties arising from its inchoate origins.

Poland between Inflation and Stabilization 1924—1927

ZBIGNIEW LANDAU
JERZY TOMASZEWSKI

I
The Grabski Stabilization Program, December 1923—November 1925

After Poland regained independence in autumn 1918 one of her most complicated problems was to set the note circulation and public finance in order. A disorganized tax system, the collapse of production and trade due to the First World War, the need to create a new Polish army, administration, educational system etc. — all this brought serious budget expenditures while the revenues remained quite insufficient. The large budget deficit was covered by issuing notes.

At first the moderate inflation of the years 1918 to 1921 promoted economic reconstruction. Depreciation of the currency — at that time it was the Polish mark — stimulated exports and checked imports. Industrial products could easily be sold, and this induced increased production. Inflation meant a decrease of the share of wages in the costs of manufacture. Government banks granted loans for reconstruction. Since these loans were paid off in a depreciating currency, they actually were state subsidies for private firms.

The inflation, however, accelerated in 1923. At the end of January 1923 the Polish mark circulation amounted to 909,160 million, at the end of April to 6,871,077 million, and at the end of December 1923 to 125,371,955 million Polish marks. The rate of exchange to the US dollar also grew more and more rapidly, especially in the second half of 1923. While at the end of January the price of 1 US dollar was 35.7 thousand Polish marks, at the end of August it amounted to 360 thousand and the end of December to 6,375 thousand Polish marks.

The dramatic breakdown of the Polish currency brought about a total disorganization of the economy. Exporters faced growing difficulties, sales at home fell, credits practically disappeared, while entrepreneurs calculated and settled accounts in foreign currencies, above all in US dollars. The Polish mark was losing its role as means of circulation.[1]

In autumn 1923 serious political problems also appeared. In November there was a series of riots and demonstrations in Southern Poland, which, in Cracow, led to a scuffle with police and soldiers. The government faced events which could be interpreted as a direct threat of revolution. The currency stabilization could therefore determine not only the economic situation but also the political fate of the Polish Republic.

Under these circumstances the center-rightist government of Wincenty Witos, responsible for the policy which led to a financial disaster, fell. On 19 December 1923 a well-known economist, Professor Władysław Grabski, took over the office of Prime Minister and the Minister of Treasury. On 20 December he presented his program to the Sejm: „Today ... we have arrived at such a state of affairs that any progress is impossible unless we solve the financial difficulties which not only paralyze improvement of the internal situation and threaten the social peace but also are detrimental to our defensive system. And we must do it very soon."[2] He predicted that all possible efforts would be made to liquidate the budget deficit by means of increased taxation, seeking domestic and foreign loans and reduction of budget expenditures. In contrast to previous policies, this program was very concrete and was based on a plan prepared early in 1923 when Grabski was the Head of Treasury in General Władysław Sikorkski's government. The new program was different from the original plan in two respects: It was mainly focussed on the currency reform and its realization was to be accelerated.

Poland was then not the only country trying to overcome inflation and to set the budget in order. What was unique about the Grabski reform, however, was that it relied on domestic resources without

---

[1] Z. Landau/J. Tomaszewski, *Gospodarka Polski międzywojennej 1918—1939* (The Polish Interwar Economy 1918—39), Vol. 2, *Od Grabskiego do Piłsudskiego* (From Grabski to Piłsudski), Warsaw 1971, p. 279 ff.

[2] *Sprawozdanie stenograficzne z 89 posiedzenia Sejmu w dn. 20 grudnia 1923 r., łam 5* (Stenographic Report of the 89th Sitting of the Sejm, 20 December 1923, column 5).

waiting for foreign aid. In the already quoted Sejm speech Grabski said: „Improvement of the fiscal situation may be based either on foreign aid or on a common effort of the whole society. Without neglecting benefits to be gained from foreign aid, the Government will make it its business to stimulate the country's own efforts so that it can extricate itself from the present critical state of affairs." And further on „The financial difficulties of our country disheartened some people to such an extent that anxious suggestions were made to the effect that the only way out for Poland was a kind of financial wardship by foreign powers. The government will do its best to eliminate any reason for such a solution."

Caution in seeking foreign loans resulted from fears about their political implications. At that time Warsaw received a British financial expert, Hilton E. Young, who came on an invitation by the previous government. The Young recommendations threatened to weaken Poland's position vis à vis Germany, which had territorial claims against Poland. There was knowledge of cooperation of London and New York banks with the German financial circles. There was a real danger that credits granted by the two world's largest monetary markets would become politically harmful to Poland and result in the subordination of her economy to German interests.[3] Thus Grabski did his best to get rid of the Young mission in a diplomatic manner and sought credits from politically neutral banks. However he placed the main emphasis on solving the problem by means of the country's own resources.

On 11 January 1924 the Sejm passed a bill concerning reform of the budget and a monetary reform. It included a general power for the president to issue appropriate decrees in this respect for half a year. This power, though slightly limited, was afterwards prolonged.[4] This made it possible to legislate by means of immediate decisions, which

---

[3] Z. Landau, *Polityczne aspekty działalności angielskiej misji doradców finansowych E. Hiltona Younga w Polsce* (Political Aspects of the British Mission of Financial Advisors Headed by E. Hilton Young to Poland), in: *Zeszyty Naukowe Szkoły Głównej Planowania i Statystyki*, (1958), No. 9.

[4] *Dziennik Ustaw Rzeczypospolitej Polskiej* (The Law Gazette of the Polish Republic — cited hereafter on as DURP), (1924), No. 4, item 28; No. 71, item 687. Cf. also, J. Tomaszewski, *Stabilizacja waluty w Polsce. Z badań nad polityką gospodarczą rządu polskiego przed przewrotem majowym* (Currency Stabilization in Poland. A Study in the Economic Policy of the Polish Government before the May Coup d'Etat), Warsaw 1961, pp. 41—44, 91—93.

would be impossible if all questions involved were discussed and settled by the Sejm. Thus in mid-January 1924 the government disposed of both a program and the necessary powers to implement it.

In January 1924 the note circulation still grew while the value of the Polish mark fell. At the end of January the circulation amounted to 313,660,000 million Mkp. On 10 January the price of 1 US dollar reached 9,875 thousand Mkp. But then the Prime Minister recommended that the Polska Krajowa Kasa Pożyczkowa, a state-owned central bank of issue, intervene to support the Polish mark with its remaining foreign currency resources. With new hopes arising from the clear and concrete Government's program, this action checked currency depreciation and stabilized the rate of exchange at 9,350 thousand Mkp to the US dollar. Within following weeks the exchange rate even improved slightly.[5] Owners of foreign currencies thought they might lose, and some of those who had invested their capital in foreign currencies began to sell them to the Polska Krajowa Kasa Pożyczkowa. Thus the bank could not only support the Polish mark but also increase its foreign currency resources.[6]

The basic objective of the Government was to balance the budget. In order to avoid losses connected with depreciation of the Polish mark all public offices, institutions and state-run enterprises were obliged to conclude contracts with foreign partners only in US dollars and with home customers only in gold franks. On 29 January a decree was passed moving up the date of payment of the capital and rent tax. On 16 February penalties were imposed on those who were delinquent in paying their turnover and income taxes in the amount of 0.5 % of the arrears per day of delinquency.[7]

Particularly important was acceleration of the date of payment of the property tax. A draft bill concerning this extraordinary tax, which amounted to a total of 1,000 million gold Swiss franks, had been prepared by Grabski during his previous term in office at the beginning of 1923. The Sejm passed it in August 1923. According to the decree of 15 January 1924 the second advance payment of this tax — the first one

---

[5] J. Zdziechowski, *Finanse Polski w latach 1924 i 1925* (Polish Finance in the Years 1924 and 1925), Warsaw 1925, p. 15.

[6] A. Krzyżanowski, *Polityka i gospodarstwo* (Politics and Economy), Cracow 1931, p. 96.

[7] J. Tomaszewski, *Stabilizacja...* [see note 4], p. 49.

was collected in autumn 1923 — was to amount to 131 million gold Sfr. However payments were dragging, and the revenue boards started preparations for a compulsory collection in February.[8] The Government also undertook energetic steps against entrepreneurs violating the tax law, which was especially frequent in Poland's southern and central provinces. Tax evasion was also committed on a large scale by certain Upper Silesian enterprises in German hands.[9] Vigorous collection of the property tax brought quick results. By the end of April, 72 % of the second advance payment had been collected, and in the end almost 80 % of the sums due were paid.[10]

This aspect of the Government's activity deserves special attention. In contrast to previous cabinets, Grabski decided to place the monetary and budget reform burden above all on the propertied classes. Moreover, this was approved by the Central Association of Polish Mining, Industry, Trade and Finance (the so-called „Lewiatan"), an organization representing the big business circles.[11] This was the result of the alarming political situation of the country at the end of 1923 and the economic disorder directly threatening the conduct of business.

The Government also made other decisions increasing budget revenues and prepared an increase of other tax rates and charges. On 1 March 1924 it was decided to increase future earned income and land taxes, to introduce fiscal charges on school certificates, and to raise the railway and mail rates. Some industrial plants were to be sold by the state along with the government owned shares. The sale of goods and property received from the USSR under the Polish-Soviet peace treaty of March 1921 was begun. Individual ministries made attempts to obtain additional income themselves.[12] The budget revenues were also increased by internal loans. In January 1924 subscription of a dollar premium loan was started in the amount of US $ 5 million. A railway loan was announced to help liquidate the railway deficit.[13] The state-

---

[8] *Op. cit.*, p. 50.

[9] For documents cf.: Archiwum Akt Nowych (Contemporary Record Archives — cited hereafter as AAN), Kauzik 30, Ministerstwo Skarbu 542; Z. Landau/J. Tomaszewski, *Misja profesora Artura Benisa* (Professor Artur Benis' Mission), in: *Teki Archiwalne*, (1959), No. 6.

[10] J. Tomaszewski, *Stabilizacja...* [see note 4], p. 50.

[11] E. R[ose], *Program p. Grabskiego* (Mr. Grabski's Program), in: *Przegląd Gospodarczy*, (1924), No. 2.

[12] J. Tomaszewski, *Stabilizacja...* [see note 4], pp. 50—51.

[13] DURP, (1924), No. 5, item 40; No. 12, item 103.

run credit instituions limited lending while new deposits were earmarked for the purchase of government securities.[14] Although these individual sources of revenue, except for the property tax, were rather small, altogether they made it possible to reduce the budget deficit.

At the same time the Treasury Ministry started a rigid saving action. First of all it was necessary to set in order the budget of the state-owned railway company. Subsidies to this company accounted in 1923 for almost half of the budget deficit.[15] The railway rate schedule was valorized, investments were suspended and, in March, passenger ticket prices were increased.[16] Also other ministries limited expenditures. Competence of the Extraordinary Saving Commissioner was extended to include a program for „necessary saving in state administration and public enterprises, reorganization and simplification of office work".[17]

The Government thought that simultaneous efforts aimed at reduction of expenditures and increase of revenues would balance the budget and thereby eliminate the basic reason for inflation. It was expected that after employing the revenues from the extraordinary property tax, the national economy would be strong enough so that normal budget revenues would cover the expenditures. This program was however hard to carry out. It struck directly at the interest of the propertied classes which were to pay the extraordinary tax and bear other burdens of the new tax system. Grabski understood that this was the only way to obtain the means required by the Treasury. The wage earners and small farmers were too poor to bear new charges for the benefit of the state and their capacity to pay was unsatisfactory from the budgetary point of view. That was the basic novelty of his program: Grabski managed to treat the matter from a broader perspective beyond the immediate interest of social groups he represented, and to act in the national interest for the purpose of stabilization of the economy and neutralization of the revolutionary atmosphere.

This however did not mean that the Government would free other social groups from the tax burden. In the course of 1924 the earned income tax was raised along with the land-value and indirect taxes. Gradually the Government unified the direct taxes all over Poland, as

---

[14] *Protokoły Komitetu Dyrekcyjnego ze stycznia 1924 r.* (Records of the Directing Committee of the Postal Savings Bank), AAN, Pocztowa Kasa Oszczędności 7.
[15] *Wiadomości Statystyczne*, (1924), No. 4, p. 17.
[16] J. Tomaszewski, *Stabilizacja*... [see note 4], pp. 53—54.
[17] DURP, (1927), No. 11, item 93.

hitherto the tax burdens differed in various parts of the country formerly partitioned under Prussia, Russia, and Austria. Only the land-value tax continued to remain different in each of the three former partitions.

Another source of budget revenues were the state monopolies of tobacco, matches, and spirits.[18] On the other hand foreign loans played an incidental role. Although the Government negotiated with foreign financial groups and private stock companies looked for credits abroad, the only result was the Government's contract with Banca Commerciale Italiana in Milan. At the beginning of March 1924 a credit contract was signed concerning a loan of Lit 400 million (about 90 million Sfr) secured by the revenues and assets of the State Tobacco Monopoly. The financial conditions of the contract proved very difficult for Poland, and the inflow of foreign currency was of a minor importance for the improvement of the Polish financial situation.[19]

Energetic Government action made it possible to proclaim on 1 February 1924 that further issuing of Polish marks for budgetary purposes would be stopped.[20] This had above all a psychological meaning, since the Treasury far-sightedly gathered certain note reserves. Nevertheless, the rate of growth of note circulation diminished, and at the beginning of April it fell slightly — a symptom of the Government's success.

Stabilization of the price for the Polish currency and suspension of note issuing created grounds for replacement of the depreciated currency by a new one.[21] The latter was called „złoty". One złoty was divided into 100 groszy, equal to the Swiss frank and included 1/31 g of gold. In practice this rate of exchange proved too high and diminished the competitiveness of Polish exports. The złoty was covered by gold, foreign exchange, and currencies up to 30 % of the circulation. Convertibility into foreign currencies exchanged for gold corresponded with

---

[18] For details cf. W. Mateńko, *Zagadnienie monopolów skarbowych w Polsce* (The Question of State Monopolies in Poland), Warsaw 1939.

[19] Z. Landau, *Pożyczka tytoniowa* (The Tobacco Loan), in: *Zeszyty Naukowe Szkoły Głównej Planowania i Statystyki*, (1956), No. 3.

[20] F. Młynarski, *Przełomowe lata* (Decisive Years), in: *Przemysł i Handel*, (1924), pp. 133—135.

[21] Z. Karpiński, *Ustroje pieniężne w Polsce od roku 1917* (Monetary Systems in Poland after 1917), Warsaw 1968, p. 57 ff.

contemporary monetary concepts. It was thought that such a solution would prevent depreciation of the currency, as its excess could always be exchanged for other currencies. The size of circulation was also secured by the gold and exchange reserves of the issuing bank. As it soon proved, these hopes for prevention of depreciation of the złoty were in vain.

The privilege of issuing złoty banknotes was given until 1944 a newly established private stock company — Bank Polski. This solution, based on the British experience, was to limit the possible pressure from the Government to raise the circulation above the economic requirements. Floating of shares of the Bank Polski proved, however, to be a difficult task.[22] Its subscriptions did not arouse particular interest in business circles, as they feared the reform would be a failure and felt the growing tax burden. In many circles buying these shares was treated as a patriotic duty and not a profitable investment. Finally the Government had to resort to pressure, threatening that the firms which avoided buying the Bank Polski shares might be refused credit.

On 28 April Bank Polski started issuing złoty banknotes. The disposable reserves of gold, foreign exchange, and valuables covered 87.3 % of the circulation in 1924. Apart from banknotes the circulation included coins and small paper notes issued by the Treasury, initially up to 9.5 zł per inhabitant. Polish marks were exchanged in relation 1 zł for 1.8 million Mkp,[23] while for a few months payments could be executed either in złotys or in Polish marks.

The first months of the monetary and budgetary reform brought a success which influenced the social and political atmosphere all the more because there was a slight increase of real wages in the spring of 1924. At the same time, however, stabilization of currency in Poland finally liquidated benefits resulting from inflation for Polish exports. Already in autumn 1923 symptoms of depression had appeared with production falling and unemployment growing. This, of course, affected the paying capacity of the tax payers. Even more significant, however, were the effects of political stabilization. Removal of the „specter of revolution" made the business circles start a new offensive against workers. In June 1924 nominal wages began to fall. In that month also a serious conflict broke out in Upper Silesia on the question

---

[22] J. Tomaszewski, *Stabilizacja*... [see note 4], pp. 79—82.
[23] Z. Landau/J. Tomaszewski, *Gospodarka*... [see note 1], Vol. 2, pp. 191—192.

of the projected extension of the working time. A large wave of strikes ended with the workers' defeat. In metallurgy the working time was extended to 10 hours a day in exchange for a slight increase of wages. The working day in mining remained unchanged, but wages were reduced.[24]

Simultaneously tax payments brought in by the propertied classes diminished. Comparisons of subsequent tax instalments paid in the course of 1924 is very significant: while 80 % of the prepayment was paid up, the government received only 63 % of the first payment and only 30 % of the second.[25] Responsibility for the growing arrears lay mainly with the wealthiest taxpayers. A comparison of the percentages of actual receipts for specific taxes in 1924 is also instructive. 52 % of the income tax, 60 % of the property tax, 88 % of the land-value tax, 118 % of the turnover tax, 134 % of the indirect taxes, 173 % of the monopoly revenues, and 190 % of the customs duties were received in that year.[26] These data refute the contention that tax payments diminished due to the business setback. If so, the fall of tax payment would be more or less proportional in all kinds of taxes. The quoted data show that especially those taxes levied on the wage-earners were overfulfilled. In other words, contrary to the Government's program the burden of the reform was to a great extent shifted onto the working people in the second half of 1924.

From the formal point of view the year 1924 ended with a budget surplus. There even remained a reserve of 59.4 million złoty and a credit in Bank Polski in the amount of 29.3 million złoty.[27] This however did not mean that the budget was really balanced. The budget expenditures were covered in 1924 not only by regular revenues but also by receipts from liquidation of the state-owned Polska Krajowa Kasa Pożyckowa, by internal loans, credits in Bank Polski, issuing of coins, and sale of state property. If these sums are deducted, then the budget deficit would amount to more than 170 million złoty. Besides, a major item of receipt was the extraordinary property tax in the amount of about 200 million złoty; it was to cover the deficit in the interim period.[28] Thus

---

[24] J Tomaszewski, *Stabilizacja*... [se note 4], pp. 97—100.

[25] *Op. cit.*, p. 119.

[26] *Rocznik Ministerstwa Skarbu* (The Treasury Ministry Annual), Warsaw 1924; Warsaw 1925, pp. 178—179.

[27] J. Zdziechowski, *Finanse*... [see note 5], pp. 38—49.

[28] *Op. cit.*, p. 38; *Rocznik*... [see note 26], pp. 174—176.

about 370 million złoty were extraordinary revenues covering about 23 % of the budget expenditures. Despite the key role played by such exceptional revenues, the situation was a real improvement over the previous year. Moreover, resources available for the budgetary reform were not exhausted.

The monetary situation depended not only on the balancing of the budget but also on the economy and especially on foreign trade. In the latter field the year 1924 brought further aggravation, unchanged by a temporary and slight improvement in autumn. Stabilization of the Polish currency showed that average costs of production in Poland were higher than in other countries. This resulted in a growing deficit in the trade balance. A bad harvest in 1924 made it necessary to increase importation of foodstuffs, and this threatened to produce a gold and foreign exchange outflow from the Bank Polski. The deficit could be possibly covered by foreign loans. Apart from the mentioned tobacco loan, Poland also received a $ 6 million loan in return for leasing the match monopoly to the Swedish Ivar Kreuger concern.[29] Finally, the Government started negotiations with the US bank of Dillon, Read and Co.[30] They proved to be very difficult. The Polish negotiators overlooked the slyness of the American finanicers, who granted only $ 21 million in cash while retaining an option to provide a further loan and imposing an obligation on the Poles not to start negotiations with other banks. Dillon did not make use of the option, but the Polish Government was pegged down in seeking foreign credits when financial conditions were most difficult. Grabski still refused all offers of credit aid involving political or economic supervision by the creditor. For instance, he did not accept the project of the Financial Committee of the League of Nations to grant Poland a big loan in return of a League's control.[31] He feared that in view of the prevailing British influence in the Committee, such a control would lead to subordination of Poland

---

[29] Z. Landau, *Działalność koncernu Kreugera w Polsce* (The Kreuger Concern Activities in Poland), in: *Przegląd Historyczny*, (1958), No. 1.
[30] Z. Landau, *Pożyczka dillonowska. Przyczynek do działalności kapitałów amerykańskich w Polsce* (The Dillon Loan. A Contribution to American Capital Activities in Poland), in: *Kwartalnik Historyczny* (1957), No. 3.
[31] *Sprawozdanie naczelnika wydziału Ministerstwa Skarbu z podróży do Genewy z 1 marca 1925 r.* (A Report by the Head of a Department in the Ministry of the Treasury on a Trip to Geneva on 1 March 1925), AAN, Kauzik 6.

to the interests of Great Britain and consequently to the increased influence of Germany in Poland.

In 1925 the economic situation of Poland deteriorated further. Another decrease of budget revenues from taxes, duties, and monopolies was accompanied by an increase of state expenditures.[32] The Government had to support private entrepreneurs on the verge of bankruptcy, and maintain or even raise the unemployment benefits introduced to ease the political tension as well as finance public works. In order to help the private firms it proved essential to reduce some taxes.[33] At the same time the inflow of foreign currencies decreased. In January 1925 the demand of Polish importers for foreign exchange grew, while the sums paid to Bank Polski were lower than in previous months. The outflow of currency amounted to 25 million złoty and in February to another 32 million.[34] Credits granted to Polish firms diminished and loans already given were withdrawn.[35]

In summer 1925 a Polish-German economic war contributed to the aggravation of the situation.[36] The conflict was largely due to political issues. In Germany it was thought that the economic weakness of Poland along with her dependence on trade with Germany would soon make the Polish Government politically compliant in exchange for credits and economic benefits. Certain businessmen in Germany were interested in checking imports from Poland, especially those competitive with German products. This referred above all to coal and foodstuffs. Also general conditions made German economic policy makers stop imports from Poland: German international obligations were quite heavy and, apart from regular trade, Germany needed the means to cover war reparations.

In January 1925, article No. 264 of the Versailles Treaty expired which had provided Poland and other Allies with the most-favored-

---

[32] *Podatki bezpośrednie w latach 1924 i 1925* (Direct Taxes in the Years 1924 and 1925), in: *Przemysł i Handel*, (1926), pp. 230—232.

[33] K. Ostrowski, *Polityka finansowa Polski przedwrześniowej* (The Financial Policy of Poland before September 1939), Warsaw 1958, p. 284.

[34] *Protokóły posiedzeń Rady Banku Polskiego z 14 lutego i 12 marca 1925 r.* (Record of the Meetings of the Bank Polski Board on 14 February and 12 March 1925), AAN, Bank Polski 70.

[35] A. Krzyżanowski, *Pauperyzacja Polski współczesnej* (The Pauperization of Contemporary Poland), Cracow 1925, pp. 102—103.

[36] For details cf. B. Puchert, *Der Wirtschaftskrieg des deutschen Imperialismus gegen Polen 1925—1934*, Berlin 1963.

nation clause in trade with Germany. In mid-June 1925 the term of economic clauses of the 1922 Upper Silesian convention also expired. They provided for privileged trade turnover between both parts of Upper Silesia which had been divided between Poland and Germany. Under these circumstances it was inevitable to start negotiations on further economic relations between both countries. Talks faced grave problems, as the German side tended to view mutual relations in terms of utilizing the German economic predominance and links created during the years of partition. The Polish side wanted to resist German expansion and to strengthen Poland's independence. Therefore it refused to talk about political conditions. Negotiations broke down, and on 15 June 1925 Germany stopped coal imports from Poland. Following this decision both sides imposed import prohibitions, and this meant the outbreak of an economic war. The German embargo affected 57 % of Polish exports to Germany, which was equal to 27 % of the total Polish exports. The Polish prohibitions affected 47 % of the German exports to Poland, but this was only about 3 % of the total exports of the Reich.[37] The conflict brought a dramatic fall of Polish exports, while imports could be reduced much less. Replacement of the lost market proved difficult and required time.

Since the beginning of 1925 the Government covered the growing deficit of the budget by issuing coins and small paper notes without regard to real circulation requirements. At the same time, the banknote circulation diminished, which was connected with the outflow of gold and foreign currencies of the Bank Polski. From 31 December 1924 to 30 June 1925 banknote circulation fell from 551 to 503 million złoty, while the circulation of coins and small paper notes issued by the Treasury grew from 123 to 244 million złoty. At the end of 1925 circulation in Poland included 382 million złoty of banknotes and 434 million złoty of money issued by the Treasury.[38] The overissue of coins in spring 1925 caused anxiety. In order to avoid buying foreign currencies for the money issued by the Treasury, Bank Polski introduced double accounts and sold foreign currencies only for złoty banknotes. This meant a double monetary system. One hundred złoty banknotes

---

[37] Z. Landau: J. Tomaszewski, *Gospodarka...* [see note 1], 2, p. 280.
[38] *Rocznik Statystyki R. P.* (Statistical Yearbook of the Polish Republic), (1927), p. 269.

were sometimes sold for coins at a few złotys' higher price.[39] Even more serious were the effects of the growing discrepancy between the domestic production and currency circulation. Since the end of 1923 production had been falling while circulation had been growing. In spring 1924 the latter fell slightly. It was then estimated that the optimum circulation for Poland should be about 600 million złoty but since the end of 1924 this level was considerably exceeded. Prices began to increase again.

At first the inflationary trend was only very small and did not cause economic trouble. Remembering the disastrous problems and hyperinflation of 1923, however, the society felt uneasy, especially the more that salaries were paid with coins in small sacks. People began to sell złotys and buy gold and foreign currencies. This made the situation of Bank Polski even more difficult, as it lost coverage for the złoty banknotes. In June 1925 a $ 6 million credit from the American Irving Bank temporarily eased the tension.[40] However the economic war with Germany brought another stroke in July 1925. At the end of this month restrictions were introduced on foreign currency sales that forced the Polish importers to pay in złotys. An increase of supply of Polish złotys on foreign money exchanges brought about a collapse of the rate of exchange of the złoty. On 29 July 1925, one US dollar was paid 5.8 to 6.0 złoty, while the gold parity rate of exchange was 1 : 5.18.[41]

In order to counteract the collapse of the złoty, Bank Polski started a monetary intervention. It consisted of selling foreign currencies at their gold parity rate and buying them at a current rate. Costs of this operation proved very high: about 1.5 million złoty were spent daily for this purpose.[42] Moreover, it required a constant replenishing of foreign exchange and currencies. Both the Government and Bank Polski sought new credits in foreign banks. Of major importance in July were 123 million złoty of the Dillon loan and an intervention credit received by Bank Polski from the Federal Reserve Bank of New York in the amount

---

[39] W. Grabski, *Dwa lata pracy u podstaw państwowości naszej 1924—1925* (Two Years of Work of Founding the Polish Statehood 1924—25), Warsaw 1927, p. 161.

[40] *Protokół posiedzenia Rady Banku Polskiego z 9 czerwca 1925 r* (Record of the Meeting of the Bank Polski Board on 9 June 1925), AAN, Bank Polski 70.

[41] *Protokół... 17 lipca i 18 sierpnia 1925* (Record... on 17 July and 18. August 1925) [see note 40], AAN, Bank Polski 70.

[42] *Protokół... 18 sierpnia 1925 r.* (Record... on 18 August 1925) [see note 40], AAN, Bank Polski 70.

of $ 10 million.[43] Apart from these credits, Poland received a short-term aid: 20 million SFr from the Banque de Suisse, £ 250 thousand from the British Overseas Bank and $ 600 thousand from the Bank Francusko-Polski in Paris.[44] These sums were immediately utilized for current intervention. Bank Polski planned to start selling foreign currencies at increased prices from 3 August, but on the Prime Minister's request this decision, which would practically mean devaluation of the Polish złoty, was postponed.[45] Intervention brought temporary improvement of the złoty price, especially after 21 August.[46]

The Government faced the problem of saving the złoty. Despite a temporary stabilization, a further decrease of the złoty price could be expected, and this would mean the return of inflation. On 30 September 1925, Grabski presented the Council of Ministers with a new program for złoty stabilization.[47] It provided for maintaining a standard money, independent of the Government. The circulation of coins and small change was not to exceed 12 złoty per capita, which seems too high a standard under the existing circumstances. The note circulation was to increase only if there was an improvement of the trade balance or inflow of new foreign credits. Grabski decided to run the probable risk of foreign control inviting a British financial expert, William Goode, to Poland.[48]

But the foreign aid did not come, and the domestic economic disturbances grew. The fall of the złoty caused a run on banks in autumn. Deposits were withdrawn and exchanged into stable currencies.[49] The Government was forced to assign large sums to save private banks from bankruptcy. On 12 November 1925, the President of Bank Polski, Stanisław Karpiński, refused to continue intervention aimed at maintaining the price of the złoty, which fell on the same day from 6.2 to 6.9 złoty per US dollar.[50] Under these circumstances, in view of the failure of his policies, Prime Minister Grabski resigned.

[43] Z. Karpiński, *Bank Polski 1924—1939*, Warsaw 1958, pp. 27—28.
[44] *Op. cit.*, p. 28.
[45] *Op. cit.*, pp. 26—28.
[46] *Bieżąca sytuacja walutowa* (Current Monetary Situation), in: *Przemysł i Handel*, (1925), p. 1194.
[47] *Protokół posiedzenia Rady Ministrów z 30 werześnia 1925* (Record of the Meeting of the Council of Ministers on 30 September 1925), AAN, Protokóły Rady Ministrów 30.
[48] For correspondence cf. AAN, Kauzik 18 and AAN, Sokołow 3,15.
[49] A. Krzyżanowski, *Polityka...* [see note 6], p. 326.
[50] A. Krzyżanowski, *Dwa programy finansowe/jesień 1925 i wiosna 1926* (Two Financial Programs — Autumn 1925 and Spring 1926), Cracow 1927.

II

The Second Stabilization, 1925—1927

In a new coalition cabinet of Aleksander Skrzyński the portfolio of Treasury was given to Jerzy Zdziechowski. He inherited a very difficult economic situation and a budget deficit but also one positive element: since September 1925 the trade balance was showing a surplus.[51] At first it allowed only for paying off the most urgent foreign obligations, but new hopes arose for inflow of foreign exchange to Poland and, therefore, for stabilization of the złoty. The trade surplus was mainly due to depreciation of the złoty which stimulated exports and checked imports. Grabski had concentrated his efforts on the monetary and budgetary reform. Zdziechowski from the beginning connected the monetary question with the general economic situation. He thought that a permanent stabilization of the złoty should be based on a firm market. In his opinion a certain decrease of the rate of exchange of the złoty might have positive effects by stimulating exports and, as a consequence, production. He warned, however, that the currency depreciation should not be too high.[52]

The new Treasury Minister opposed issuing money to cover the budget deficit, but in practice he still increased the coin circulation. On the other hand, he downright refused plans to introduce auxiliary money, for instance secured by motgages.[53] The basic problem of the Treasury was how to balance the budget. The rightist parties, represented by Zdziechowski, thought the best solution would be to reduce salaries of the state officials and to decrease the property tax burden. The Left, represented in the Government by the Polish Socialist Party, suggested reduction of the number of police, shortening of the military service, and energetic collection of the overdue taxes.[54] In practice, a

[51] S. Pszczolkowski, *Stabilizacja kursu złotego* (Stabilization of the Złoty Rate), Warsaw 1926, pp. 3—4.

[52] J. Zdziechowski, *Sytuacja gospodarezo — skarbowa Polski i drogi naprawy* (Economic and Budgetary Situation of Poland and Methods for its Improvement), Warsaw 1926, p. 8.

[53] J. Zdziechowski, *O pieniądzu i budżecie* (On Currency and Budget), Warsaw 1926, pp. 7—8; E. Taylor, *Druga inflacja polska* (Second Polish Inflation), Poznań 1927, p. 78; B. Hausner, *Sanacja polskiego pieniądza bez pomocy zagranicy* (Improvement of the Polish Currency Without Foreign Aid), Warsaw 1926, pp. 12—20.

[54] A. Próchnik, *Pierwsze piętnastolecie Polski niepodległej* (The First Fifteen Years of Independent Poland), Warsaw 1957, p. 213.

compromise was adopted. The salaries of state officials were reduced for three months and the military service was shortened. These decisions however were temporary, and more permanent methods of balancing the budget had to be found. This was the source of a conflict within the cabinet coalition. The Zdziechowski plan to raise all taxes except for the property tax, to introduce new indirect taxes, to dismiss a large number of the civil servants and to reduce salaries of the remaining ones, faced firm resistance from the socialists, who left the coalition and brought about a cabinet crisis.[55]

Meanwhile the Government was helped by a factor even more important than the projects of the Treasury Minister. Improvement of the balance of trade was accompanied by a recovery of the market after February 1926. Tax revenues began to increase and the budget deficit diminished. In April, it was a mere 2 million złoty. These circumstances strengthened the position of the złoty. The free foreign exchange convertibility was temporarily limited, and the increasing foreign trade receipts made it possible again for Bank Polski to intervene on the monetary exchanges. As a result the price of the US dollar began to fall. In mid-December 1925, it reached the maximum of 10.5 zł for one dollar (unofficially it was exchanged for up to a maximum of 14 zł), and at the end of December it fell to 8.35 zł. On 10 January 1926 it was exchanged for 7.3 zł.[56]

In February and March 1926 the rate of exchange of the złoty remained at a similar level. A sudden collapse came in April when one US dollar was sold for 9 zł.[57] This time the reasons were of a political nature. The fall of the Skrzyński government brought back the fears that the increasing struggle for power might have far-reaching economic and political consequences. These fears proved correct. In mid-May 1926 a coup d'état brought Józef Piłsudksi to power, and at the end of May, one US dollar cost more than 11 zł.[58]

---

[55] *Op. cit.*, pp. 218—219; *Protokół posiedzenia Rady Ministrów z 17 kwietnia 1926 r.* (Record of the Meeting of the Council of Ministers on 17 April 1926), AAN, Protokóły Rady Ministrów 33.

[56] J. Zdziechowski, *O pieniądzu*... [see note 53], p. 9, 11; *Sytuacja walutowa* (Monetary Situation), in: *Przemysł i Handel*, (1925), p. 1606; *Zmiany w reglamentacji obrotu dewizami i walutami* (Changes in Foreign Exchange and Currency Control), in: *Przemysł i Handel*, (1926), pp. 1011—1012.

[57] *Annuaire statistique du Ministére des Finances*, Varsovie 1931, p. 388.

[58] *Przegląd Gospodarczy*, (1926), pp. 477, 527, 577 and 623.

The May coup d'état was staged under circumstances favorable for its initiators: the market was recovering. In summer 1926 an external random factor contributed to the rise in exports — a long-lasting strike of British coal-miners made it possible for Polish hard coal to enter the Scandinavian markets. At the same time, the post-May government inherited all positive effects of the previous monetary and budgetary reforms. The Grabski government had managed to create an orderly budget, to stop hyperinflation, and all this had been achieved almost entirely from Poland's own resources with only slight aid from abroad. Failure of the Government's economic policy had resulted above all from the unfavorable economic conditions and circumstances independent of the Government: the economic war with Germany and evasion of taxes by entrepreneurs. When some of these conditions disappeared or were replaced by other factors, the subsequent cabinets could finally set the budget and the currency in order.

Piłsudski as a rule underestimated the importance of economic problems, but he attached importance to maintaining a stable currency. This was probably due to the influence a stable money could have on the international situation of Poland and to the political effects of late 1923 hyperinflation. Immediately after his coup d'état he ordered that the złoty was to be a stable currency. This task was hardly feasible as there were no reserves of gold and foreign exchange for stock intervention.[59]

The first Treasury Minister after the coup was Gabriel Czechowicz. Then, between 8 June and 30 September 1926, this post was held by Czesław Klarner, after whom Czechowicz returned. Both ministers continued the policy of Zdziechowski in the field of monetary and budgetary questions introducing projects for which the previous government did not have time.[60] They acted under much happier circumstances as business conditions were rapidly recovering and, even before the direct tax rate increases could bring results, the budget was balanced virtually automatically. The increasing production and turnover brought higher tax receipts, and the growing employment had the same effect. The railway traffic expanded and so did the State Railway Company income. State monopolies brought growing revenues from April to December 1926, and monthly receipts of the Treasury grew

---

[59] Cf. F. Młynarski, *Wspomnienia* (Memoirs), Warsaw 1971, p. 280.
[60] Z. Landau/J. Tomaszewski, *Gospodarka*... [see note 1], Vol. 2, p. 218.

from 136.6 million złoty to 234.6 million złoty. Effects of the increasing taxation played only a secondary role.⁶¹

By July 1926 the budget was balanced. Therefore it was not hard for Klarner to fulfil his pronouncement of 22 June 1926: „It is ... my duty to state solemnly from this place that the Government will not balance the budget by means of printing notes."⁶² Particularly opportune for him was the fact that after a brief period of hesitation reflecting concern about the nature of the Polish coup d'état, the monetary exchanges showed appeasement and the price of the US dollar began to fall to an average of 9.18 złoty in July and to 9 złoty in August.⁶³ Holders of foreign currencies, uneasy about probable losses, started selling out their reserves, and this increased the foreign exchange supplies of the Bank Polski.

In September 1926 Klarner could declare in a speech: „Concern about the currency is gone. The situation of the Bank Polski is favorable.... The rate of the złoty which reached 11 złoty for one US dollar in May was brought down to 9 zł. in July and maintained at this level. The monetary speculation has lost all foundation and has been liquidated."⁶⁴ In the second half of 1926 the circulation was stabilized at the level of about 1,000 million złoty, including some 57 % of the Bank Polski notes. The gold reserves grew only slightly, from 133.8 million złoty in January to 138.8 million złoty in December 1926, but reserves of foreign exchange and currencies increased considerably. In January the Bank Polski obligations were higher than reserves by 2.8 million zł, while in December, reserves were higher than obligations by 125.2 million zł.⁶⁵ It may be therefore stated that the Polish currency was actually stabilized in the second half of 1926. It was accompanied by a budget surplus and a favorable trade balance. The budget surplus was maintained for a few years, while the trade balance deficit returned in

---

⁶¹ *Rocznik Statystyki R. P.* (Statistical Yearbook of the Polish Republic), (1927), pp. 511, 513; Z. Landau, *Plan stabilizacyjny 1927—1930. Geneza, założenia, wyniki* (The Stabilization Plan 1927—1930. Origin, Assumptions, and Results), Warsaw 1963, p. 70.

⁶² C. Klarner, *Drogi sanacji gospodarczej* (Ways of Economic Improvement), Warsaw 1926, p. 6.

⁶³ *Sprawozdanie Banku Polskiego za rok 1926* (Report of the Bank Polski for 1926), Appendix No. 10.

⁶⁴ Cz. Klarner, *Dorobek czeterech miesięcy/dwi mowy programowe* (Achievements of the Four Months. Two Program Speeches), Warsaw 1926, p. 12.

⁶⁵ Z. Landau/J. Tomaszewski, *Gospodarka...* [see note 1], Vol. 2, p. 203.

the following year. At that time, however, the foreign trade deficit played a lesser role as Poland received — though in not really considerable amounts — foreign credits.

Stabilization of the złoty was only the beginning of a new stage of the currency improvement. In order to restore a full trust it was necessary to stabilize the currency in legal terms. The Government however feared to act hurriedly as it wanted to connect the legal stabilization of the złoty with the inflow of foreign capital to Poland. After the May coup d'état, negotiations started by previous cabinets were continued, and the previously prepared agreements — e.g., with William Averell Harriman granting privileges in the zinc industry in which his US firm wanted to invest, with an American group of Ullen and Co. for loans to municipalities, and with a French group which was to finance construction of the railway line Upper Silesia-Gdynia, — were concluded, although some of these transactions were decidedly unfavorable for Poland.

The Government representatives explicitly stated that gaining of foreign capital was a primary task. Klarner said: „We badly need capital ... therefore securing foreign investments in Poland is a top priority".[66] Czechowicz stated: „We must clearly say that without an inflow of considerable foreign capital ... our economic life will not be able to develop at a rate which is required".[67] Similar opinions were also formulated by the Prime Minister Kazimierz Bartel and the Minister for Industry and Trade Eugeniusz Kwiatkowski.[68] Such views were quite popular in contemporary Poland and were also expressed by such well-known economists as Adam Krzyżanowski, Feliks Młynarski, Ferdynand Zweig, Henryk Tennenbaum, Wacław Konderski or Roman Rybarski.[69] It may be therefore said without exaggeration that

[66] Cz. Klarner, *Dorobek*... [see note 64], p. 21, 36.

[67] *Sprawozdanie stenograficzne z 306 posiedzenia Sejmu w dn. 13 listopada 1926, łam 15* (Stenographischer Report of the 306th Meeting of the Sejm on 13 November 1926, column 15).

[68] K. Bartel, *Mowy parlamentarne* (Parliamentary Speeches), Warsaw 1928, p. 91; E. Kwiatkowski, *Przemówienie w Komisji Budżetowej Sejmu w dn. 6 grudnia 1926* (A Speech in the Budgetary Commission of the Sejm on 6 December 1926), Warsaw 1926, p. 13.

[69] A. Krzyżanowski, *Dwa programy*... [see note 50]; A. Krzyżanowski, *Rządy Marszałka Piłsudskiego* (Marshal Piłsudski's Rule), Cracow 1926; F. Mlynarski, *Wspomnienia*... [see note 59]; F. Zweig, *O programie gospodarczym Polski* (On the Economic Program for Poland), Warsaw 1926; H. T[ennenbaum], *Przegląd sytuacji* (Review of the

almost everybody in Poland wanted contraction of foreign loans.[70] A turn towards foreign loans resulted among others from a partial failure of the reform based on the country's own resources. It was however forgotten that Grabski's failure was mainly due to recession, which affected not only Poland, and that, given economic recovery, the złoty stabilization based on the country's own efforts was truly realized.

The Government thought that legal stabilization of the złoty coordinated with exports abroad would be an initial step towards encouragement of foreign capital investment in Poland. Such an opinion was also expressed by Professor Edwin Walter Kemmerer, an American financial expert invited by Zdziechowski and then again by the post-May governments.[71] Kemmerer told the President of the Polish Sejm: „Improve your economy and the loans will come."[72] In this connection stabilization had to be carried out so that foreign creditors could be satisfied. Its fulfilment had to be controlled by foreign experts whose opinions were authoritative for banks abroad.[73] Representatives of the latter suggested the złoty stabilization be based on an international loan despite the firm position of the Polish currency. Meanwhile, at the end of 1926, the economic situation of Poland made it possible to settle the currency problem and waiting for the loan was only due to the Government's hopes that such a credit would raise foreign interest in investing in Poland.

A project of granting Poland an international loan for the złoty stabilization was formulated by governors of the Bank of England and the Federal Reserve Bank of New York in September 1925. One of the

---

Situation), in: *Przegląd Gospodarczy*, (1926), p. 1178; W. Konderski, *Koniunktura światowa a nasza polityka gospodarcza* (The World Market Trends and Our Economic Policy), Cracow 1927; R. Rybarski, *Polityka i gospodarstwo* (Politics and Economy), Warsaw 1927.

[70] Z. Landau, *Plan*... [see note 61], pp. 63—88.

[71] For details cf. Z. Landau, *Misja Kemmerera* (The Kemmerer Mission), in: *Przegląd Historyczny*, (1957), No. 2; Z. Vidi, *Na marginesie pożyczki stabilizacyjnej* (Side-Note on the Stabilization Loan), in: *Sprawy Międzynarodowe*, (1957), No. 2; As to Kemmerer's view cf. E. W. Kemmerer, *Sprawozdanie oraz zalecenia Komisji Doradców Finansowych pod przewodnictwem*... (Report and Recommendations of the Financial Experts' Commission Headed by...), Vol. 1—3, Cracow 1926.

[72] M. Rataj, *Pamiętniki 1918—1927* (Memoirs 1918—1927), Warsaw 1965, p. 348.

[73] *Przedmówienie ministra skarbu Gabriela Czechowicza na posiedzeniu Rady Banku Polskiego w dn. 24 czerwca 1926 r.* (A Speech Made by the Minister for Treasury on the Meeting of the Bank Polski Board on 24 June 1926), AAN, Bank Polski 70.

conditions was establishment of a supervision of the Polish public finance by the creditors, and that was precisely what Grabski had feared.[74] Similar suggestions were repeated in the West in autumn 1926.[75] Initiators of the plan, mainly the governor of the Bank of England cooperating quite closely with the governor of the Reichsbank, hoped that the loan and foreign supervision of Polish finance would make it possible to draw Poland into the sphere of German economic influence. At that time, Germany reconstructed its economy on the basis of the Dawes plan and was given substantial credits from the USA and Great Britain. In 1927, however, similar expectations were hardly feasible. Firstly, improvement of the economic situation in Poland resulted in an actual stabilization of the currency without foreign aid; secondly, the projects of the Bank of England and the Reichsbank began to be torpedoed by the leadership of the Bank of France and the Federal Reserve Bank of New York whose governor, Benjamin Strong, changed his views and no longer supported the policy of the governor of the Bank of England, Montagu Norman.[76]

In spite of unfavorable conditions put forward by foreign creditors, the post-May government did their best to obtain a stabilization loan. It was still thought that it would involve, just as in other countries, the inflow of large capital investments from abroad. This was why a direct investment credit was given up for the time being. Such a policy was short-sighted and risky. If the currency stabilization based on foreign credits did not attract capital from abroad, costs of the stabilization action would mean a loss from the point of view of the Polish economy. And so it was.

On 13 October 1927, the President of the Polish Republic signed a decree concerning a stabilization plan and a loan of $ 62 million and £ 2 million.[77] The plan took into account recommendations formulated by

---

[74] Z. Landau, *Polski zagraniczne pożyczki państwowe 1918—1926* (Polish Government Loans from abroad 1918—26), Warsaw 1961, pp. 143—170.

[75] For details cf. Z. Landau, *Plan*... [see note 61], chapter 4.

[76] Cf. also E. Moreau, *Souvenirs d'un Gouverneur de la Banque de France. Histoire de la stabilisation du Franc (1926—1928)*, Paris 1956, pp. 254—256; P. Einzig, *Montagu Norman. A Study in Financial Statesmanship*, London 1931, p. 88.

[77] DURP, (1927), No. 88, item 789. Cf. also J. F. Dulles, *Poland's Plan of Financial Stabilization 1927*, New York 1928; B. Blumenstreich, *Le nouveau régime monetaire en Pologne et son role dans l'économie nationale*, Nancy 1932; L. Costa de Beauregard, *L'evolution économique de la Pologne et les reformes monétaires depuis 1920*, Paris 1928.

experts headed by Kemmerer and particularly modified as a result of negotiations with bankers financing the whole operation. Nevertheless, the plan pinned down the Government and the Bank Polski considerably with regard to their financial policy. The stabilization plan served as the basis for decrees concerning stabilization of the złoty, a change of the monetary system and of the Bank Polski statute.[78] They provided for devaluation of the złoty. It was settled that 1 kg of gold would serve as coverage for 5,924.44 zł while formerly it was 3,100 zł. This meant a decrease of the parity by 42 %. The US dollar was settled at the level of 8.91 zł.[79] The złoty was convertible into gold and foreign currencies without limitations, the only restriction being the exchange into gold of sums above 20 thousand zł. The minimum coverage of banknotes with gold was raised to 40 %. In order to extend the activities of the Bank Polski, its share capital was increased from 100 to 150 million zł. The plan provided for an obligation to maintain the budget in balance and to diminish the Treasury issues of coins and small change. All limitations of the free flow of currency in foreign transactions were to be removed. Many of the stabilization plan stipulations were to safeguard interests of the creditors and probable foreign investors rather than of the national economy of Poland. This was especially the intention of the free flow of currency, whose guarantee meant that both profits and principal investments could be withdrawn from the country.

Expenditures connected with fulfilment of the plan were covered by the loan. For instance, it supplied the increased capital of the Bank Polski, its take-over of half of the Treasury issue, i.e. exchange of coins and small paper notes into banknotes, conversion of a part of the Treasury issue into silver coins or remission of the Treasury debt in the Bank Polski. Altogether stabilization absorbed almost 80 % of the obtained means. The rest remained for investment.[80] Fulfilment of the stabilization plan in Poland was supervised by an American adviser of the Polish Government, Charles Dewey. For three years, he also served as a full member of the Board of the Bank Polski with extensive

---

[78] DURP, (1927), No. 88, item 790; No. 97, item 855 and 856.

[79] The problem of the level at which the złoty was to be stabilized was a matter of discussion. Cf., e. g., Z. Karpiński, *Ustroje...* [see note 51], p. 96; S. Pszczółkowski, *Stabilizacja...* [see note 51], passim.

[80] Z. Landau, *Plan...* [see note 61], p. 216.

authorities to control the effective realization of the plan.[81] It is noteworthy that this was the only case when the Polish Government made such far-reaching concessions toward the outside world. No pre-May government would accept such terms. In practice, however, the foreign control brought no harmful effects to the Polish economy and international position. One must admit that the task of the adviser was all the easier because the rapid recovery of the Polish economy gave the Government a certain amount of financial freedom, and he had no reasons to intervene. Odds were that his attitude towards the Polish state was quite positive, and his reports — published according to the stabilization plan provisions — contributed to strengthening of trust in the firm position of the Polish economy.

The new reform finally settled the monetary system in Poland. Correct proportions between circulation of coins and banknotes were restored. At the end of March 1927, the whole circulation amounted to 1,091 million zł, including 668 million zł of banknotes. At the end of March 1929, the circulation amounted to 1,572 million zł, while banknotes were valued at 1,333 million zł. Until March 1929, the gold reserves of the Bank Polski grew to 623 million zł, and the reserves of foreign exchange and currencies (obligations deducted) to 530 million zł. This meant a 62.5 % coverage of the circulation.[82] The stabilization loan accelerated processes going on before it was contracted. From this point of view it played a positive role. But it also had a negative side. The budget revenues were not additionally stimulated, while the Treasury was charged with new obligations. When hopes for a considerable inflow of foreign capital proved in vain, the loan appeared practically useless, although expensive.

In the years 1927—29 the monetary situation of Poland was quite favorable. Even a foreign trade deficit which reappeared in April 1927 was not a serious threat to the złoty. Business firms enjoyed foreign short-term credits, which to a great extent diminished the deficit of the

---

[81] Cf. among others Ch. Dewey, *Sprawozdanie zagranicznego członka Rady Banku Polskiego i doradcy finansowego rządu polskiego nr. 1—12* (Reports of the Foreign Member of the Bank Polski Board and the Financial Adviser of the Polish Government, No. 1—12), Warsaw 1928—1930. For details concerning his activities cf. Z. Landau, *Plan*... [see note 61], chapter 9.

[82] *Sprawozdanie Banku Polskiego za 1927 r.* (Report of the Bank Polski for 1927), pp. 11—12; for 1928, pp. 12—13, for 1929, p. 11, 13.

balance of payments. Prosperity all over the world, and especially in the United States, maintained the inflow of means from other sources and particularly remittances from Polish emigrants. In other words, the monetary situation depended not on the economic policy but on economic conditions. When the latter began to deteriorate at the beginning of 1929, monetary disturbances reappeared. The price of US dollars began to increase and although this trend was soon stopped,[83] it was a symptom of a new period in the economic development of Poland and the whole world. Different conditions now required new monetary policies.

Summary

This paper describes Polish efforts to stabilize her currency after she achieved independence in 1918. By the end of 1923, the Polish inflation had reached such serious proportions that a major stabilization effort had to be undertaken, and this task was assumed by Wladyslaw Grabski, who became Prime Minister and Treasury Minister in December 1923. The Grabski effort was unique in that it relied on domestic resources without waiting for foreign aid. Within the context of previous Polish efforts at stabilization, it was also unique in placing the chief burdens of monetary and budgetary reform on the propertied classes. By the end of 1924, Poland had a new currency, the zloty, and her budgetary situation was vastly improved. In 1925, however, conditions deteriorated again because of high domestic production costs and an unfavorable trade balance, and Grabski resigned in November 1925. While certain aspects of the economic conditions improved under the governments which followed, economic conflicts with Germany, entreprenurial resistance to taxation, and domestic political difficulties prevented Grabski's basic reforms from having their full effect. Improved economic conditions permitted a balancing of the budget in the summer of 1926 and a true stabilization in the second half of the year. This was followed by a persistent government effort to secure foreign

---

[83] *Przemówienie pana kierownika Ministerstwa Skarbu na Radzie Finansowej* (A Speech of the Managing Director of the Ministry of Treasury on the Financial Council), in: *Przemysł i Handel*, (1929), p. 1150.

loans, despite the unsatisfactory conditions that were being offered, and a stabilization loan finally was negotiated in October 1927. The latter did not pave the way for the anticipated inflow of foreign capital and proved quite expensive. The monetary situation between 1927 and 1929, however, was favorable, and Poland was able to participate in the brief worldwide prosperity.

DRITTER TEIL
PART THREE

Inflation und sozialer Konflikt in internationaler Perspektive

Inflation and Social Conflict in International Perspective

EINLEITUNG

von Gerhard A. Ritter

Im Mittelpunkt dieser Sektion stehen die Auswirkungen von Inflation und Deflation auf Struktur, Lage und Verhalten wichtiger gesellschaftlicher Gruppen, darunter vor allem deren Konsequenzen für die Form und die Intensität der Konflikte zwischen Arbeitgebern und Arbeitnehmern. Dabei wird entweder ausdrücklich, wie in den Studien von Craig Patton und Irmgard Steinisch, oder doch implizit wie in dem Aufsatz von Bernd-Jürgen Wendt, das methodisch anspruchsvolle Instrument des Vergleichs zwischen bestimmten Industrien verschiedener Länder angewandt, um Gemeinsamkeiten und Unterschiede der Entwicklung schärfer herauszuarbeiten, als das bei der isolierten Betrachtung der Verhältnisse in einem Lande möglich gewesen wäre. Obwohl die Analysen auf die Zeit von der Zuspitzung sozialer und politischer Auseinandersetzungen unmittelbar nach Ende des 1. Weltkrieges bis zur Stabilisierungskrise in Deutschland 1923/24 begrenzt sind, beziehen sie doch auch längerfristige, weitgehend durch den 1. Weltkrieg beschleunigte Wandlungsprozesse in den behandelten Industrien, in der Struktur der Belegschaften und der organisatorischen Vertretung von Interessen ein. Zwar wird das am deutschen Beispiel entwickelte Modell einer durch die Struktur der Gesellschaft und besonders die Intensität der Verteilungskonflikte mit bedingten Inflation von C. P. Kindleberger nicht herangezogen, aber dennoch lassen sich viele Ergebnisse der einzelnen Studien relativ gut in dieses Konzept einordnen und damit auch zur Klärung der Unterschiede in der deutschen Entwicklung einerseits und der englischen und amerikanischen Entwicklung andererseits verwenden.

Craig *Patton* geht in seiner Untersuchung über Arbeitskonflikte in der deutschen und britischen chemischen Industrie 1919—1924 von den Zahlen der amtlichen Statistik über die Häufigkeit, die Teilnehmerzahl, die Dauer und die durch verlorene Arbeitstage gemessene Intensität von Streiks aus. Er weist anhand eines Vergleichs dieser Angaben mit der genau in einzelne Phasen gegliederten unterschiedlichen Konjunkturentwicklung in Deutschland und Großbritannien nach, daß wirtschaftliche Expansion oder Schrumpfung, die ihrerseits durch die bis 1923 in Deutschland bestehende Inflation beziehungsweise die von der Regierung in Großbritannien vertretene deflationäre Politik entscheidend beeinflußt wurden, signifikante Konsequenzen für die Häufigkeit und die Form der Arbeitskonflikte hatten.

Die Inflationskonjunktur habe die Streikaktivität in Deutschland angeheizt und zu einer relativ hohen Zahl offensiver und erfolgreicher Streiks geführt, während umgekehrt die von der ökonomischen Depression 1920/21 schwer getroffene und sich auch danach nur langsam erholende britische chemische Industrie seit 1921 einen Rückgang der Streikaktivität, insbesondere der offensiven und der mit einem Sieg der Gewerkschaften endenden Streiks, zu verzeichnen hatte. Wenn auch nicht alle Indikatoren eindeutig die These von der primären Abhängigkeit der Streiks und Streikformen von der die Lage auf dem Arbeitsmarkt bestimmenden konjunkturellen Entwicklung bestätigen — auch längerfristige Traditionen wie die Struktur der Arbeiterschaft, die Stärke der Organisation der Arbeitgeber und der Gewerkschaften sowie politische Faktoren spielten eine nicht zu unterschätzende Rolle —, so wäre es doch wünschenswert, wenn mehr Untersuchungen über den Zusammenhang der ökonomischen Entwicklung und des Streikverhaltens für andere Industrien, andere Länder und andere Zeitepochen vorgenommen würden.

Allerdings wird man sich davor hüten müssen, von einem Rückgang von Streiks, der durch die eindeutige Unterlegenheit der Gewerkschaften in Zeiten der Depression verursacht sein kann, auf einen Abbau sozialer Spannungen und Interessengegensätze zwischen Arbeitnehmern und Arbeitgebern zu schließen. Der Aufsatz von Bernd-Jürgen *Wendt* über die große Aussperrung in der metallverarbeitenden Industrie Großbritanniens im Frühjahr 1922 zeigt, wie die prekäre Situation der Gewerkschaften in einer Zeit wirtschaftlicher Krise von den Arbeitgebern genutzt wurde, um die Löhne herabzusetzen und die Stellung der Gewerkschaften und der Betriebsräte in den Betrieben zu erschüttern. Der Aufsatz macht klar, daß die grundsätzlichen Konfliktlinien, weitgehend durch Wandlungen im Produktionsprozeß bedingt, auf das letzte Viertel des 19. Jahrhunderts zurückgingen und durch die Kapazitätserweiterungen, die Veränderungen in der Struktur der Arbeitgeberschaft sowie die tendenzielle Verlagerung der Auseinandersetzungen von den Spitzenverbänden auf die Einzelbetriebe im 1. Weltkrieg intensiviert wurden.

Einleitung 299

Der offene Ausbruch der Gegensätze hing aber doch damit zusammen, daß die langfristigen Modernisierungs- und Wachstumsprobleme der britischen Wirtschaft durch das Zusammentreffen der 1920/21 einsetzenden Weltwirtschaftskrise mit der unter dem Primat der Wiederherstellung der Vorkriegsparität des Pfundes stehenden Deflationspolitik der britischen Regierung entscheidend verschärft wurden. In dieser Situation sahen die britischen Metallarbeitgeber den einzigen Weg zur Behauptung ihrer Position auf den ausländischen Märkten (vor allem gegenüber der deutschen Konkurrenz, die, inflationsbedingt, durch Abwertung der deutschen Währung begünstigt wurde) in einer rigorosen Senkung der Arbeitskosten und Minderung des Einflusses der Gewerkschaften auf den Produktionsprozeß. Sie setzten sich mit dieser Auffassung gegenüber den Gewerkschaften durch. Die Gewerkschaften wollten die britische Wirtschaft und die metallverarbeitende Industrie unter anderem durch die Steigerung der Nachfrage auf dem Binnenmarkt, den Abbau der Staatsschulden mit Hilfe einer allgemeinen Kapitalsteuer und das Abstoppen der Inflation in anderen Ländern durch internationale Abmachungen und einen Wandel der Reparationspolitik sanieren.

In Deutschland wurde eine ähnliche Politik von den Arbeitgebern, mit einer Phasenverschiebung von einigen Jahren im Vergleich zu Großbritannien, erst nach der Stabilisierung der deutschen Währung verfolgt. Die unterschiedliche Entwicklung in den ersten Nachkriegsjahren wird durch die zunächst stärkere Stellung der Gewerkschaften und Arbeiterparteien in Deutschland nach der Revolution von 1918/19 und durch die mit der Inflation in Deutschland und der Deflation in Großbritannien gegebenen, ganz andersartigen ökonomischen Rahmenbedingungen erklärt. Während durch die Inflation die grundlegende Frage, wer für die Kosten des Krieges, des Wiederaufbaus und der Reparationen zu zahlen hatte, in Deutschland zunächst noch verdeckt und damit die neu geschaffene parlamentarische Demokratie in den Krisenjahren bis 1923 entlastet wurde, hat Großbritannien aufgrund der Stärke des englischen Staatswesens und des in seiner Legitimität ernsthaft nur von Randgruppen in Frage gestellten politischen Systems schon 1921/22 die durch die Politik der Deflation bewirkte offene Austragung und Zuspitzung der Verteilungskonflikte ertragen können. Allerdings haben neben der Schwäche der demokratisch-parlamentarischen Traditionen und Institutionen in Deutschland auch weitere politisch soziale Rahmenbedingungen — die Niederlage im Krieg, die Ablösung des bestehenden Systems durch eine unvollendete

Revolution und die deutsche Tradition relativ starker staatlicher Eingriffe in das wirtschaftliche und soziale Leben — das Risiko einer deflationären Wirtschaftspolitik in den turbulenten Nachkriegsjahren kaum noch kalkulierbar gemacht.

Die entscheidende Bedeutung dieser und anderer politischer und sozialer Faktoren unterstreicht die vergleichende Untersuchung von Irmgard *Steinisch* über das Problem des 8-Stundentages in der deutschen und amerikanischen eisen- und stahlerzeugenden Industrie 1918—1924. In Deutschland wurde der Übergang vom Zweischichtensystem zum Dreischichtensystem und damit von einer 12- zur 8-stündigen Arbeitszeit unter dem Druck der Revolution plötzlich und ohne Vorbereitung der Industrie unter Bedingungen vollzogen, die von der Arbeiterschaft diktiert wurden. In den Vereinigten Staaten setzte sich dagegen der 8-Stundentag unter dem Einfluß der Öffentlichkeit und der Regierung 1923/24 in einer Situation durch, in der die Stellung der Gewerkschaften in der Industrie durch eine vorangegangene Streikniederlage stark geschwächt worden war, der Staat von direkten sozialpolitischen Interventionen absehen und die Bedingungen der Arbeitszeitverkürzung von den lange auf diesen Schritt vorbereiteten amerikanischen Unternehmern weitgehend bestimmt werden konnten.

So kam es im Gegensatz zu Deutschland, wo ein voller Lohnausgleich gewährt, die Zahl der höher bezahlten Überstunden durch schematische Regelungen drastisch beschränkt sowie Lohnanreize durch Akkord- und Prämienzahlungen weitgehend abgebaut wurden, in den Vereinigten Staaten zu einer Teilung der Kosten der Arbeitszeitverkürzung zwischen Arbeitgebern und Arbeitnehmern und zur unveränderten Übernahme der vorher bestehenden Akkord- und Prämienlöhne. Auch behielten die amerikanischen Unternehmer die Möglichkeit, Überstunden zum normalen Lohnsatz von ihren Arbeitern zu verlangen. Während in den Vereinigten Staaten durch die Straffung der Betriebsorganisation und die Verringerung der Belegschaft pro Schicht eine erhebliche Steigerung der Produktivität pro Arbeitsstunde erreicht werden konnte und damit die Umstellung weitgehend kostenneutral war, trat in Deutschland, wo man an den betriebsorganisatorischen Mustern der Vorkriegszeit festhielt, ein starker Leistungsrückgang ein. Dieser war allerdings — im Gegensatz zu der seit 1920 einsetzenden massiven Kampagne der Industrie für die Abschaffung des 8-Stundentages — keineswegs allein durch die Arbeitszeitverkürzung, sondern auch durch mangelnde Rationalisierung, die schlechte Ernährungssituation der Arbeiter und politische Unruhen zu erklären.

Einleitung

Nachdem durch den Verfall der deutschen Währung die Position der deutschen Industrie auf dem Weltmarkt zunächst noch behauptet werden konnte, sahen die deutschen Unternehmer nach der Währungsstabilisierung Ende 1923 in einer Politik des sozialen Dumping die einzige Möglichkeit, die internationale Konkurrenzfähigkeit ihrer Industrie zu erhalten. Zum Symbol dieser Politik, die sich auch gegen andere soziale Errungenschaften aus Krieg und Revolution (das System bindender Tarifverträge, das staatliche Schlichtungswesen und die Betriebsräte) wendete, wurde der Ende 1923 von der deutschen eisen- und stahlerzeugenden Industrie im internationalen Alleingang erzwungene Übergang zum 12-stündigen Doppelschichtsystem in den Hochofen-, Stahl- und Walzwerken. Diese Herausforderung der Gewerkschaften, die durch die bewußte Stilisierung der Arbeitszeitfrage zu einer politischen und wirtschaftlichen Machtfrage noch verschärft wurde und sich angesichts der traditionellen, wenn auch durch ihre wirtschaftliche Bedeutung im Rahmen der Gesamtwirtschaft nicht mehr gerechtfertigten, sozialpolitischen Führungsposition der Schwerindustrie auch auf andere Industriezweige auswirkte, stellte schon vor der Weltwirtschaftskrise eine schwere Hypothek der parlamentarischen Demokratie und des unmittelbar in die Auseinandersetzungen der Kampforganisationen der Arbeitgeber und Arbeitnehmer hineingezogenen Weimarer Staates dar.

Die durch Krieg und Niederlage, die Kosten der sozialen Errungenschaften der Revolution, mangelnde Modernisierung bis zur Stabilisierung, den Aufbau von Überkapazitäten durch die Bedürfnisse der Kriegswirtschaft, fehlgeleitete Investitionen und andere Schwächen des Managements, die Polarisierung zentraler gesellschaftlicher Kräfte, die geringe Integrationskraft der die Republik tragenden Parteien und die mangelnde Legitimität des politischen Systems bedingten Probleme wurden offenbar zunächst durch die Inflation weitgehend verschleiert. Diese ermöglichte andererseits die wenigstens vorübergehende Lösung der Verteilungskonflikte zugunsten der Produzenten (Arbeitgeber und Arbeitnehmer) auf Kosten der kaum organisierten Konsumenten, erlaubte die pazifizierende Überleitung revolutionärer Unruhen in Lohnbewegungen, half bei der schnellen Überwindung der im Gefolge der Demobilmachung auftretenden Arbeitslosigkeit, erleichterte der deutschen Industrie die Wiedergewinnung der im Kriege verlorenen Exportmärkte und schirmte Deutschland weitgehend von den Auswirkungen der internationalen Depression 1921 ab. Damit hat die Inflation wahrscheinlich zunächst entscheidend zur Erhaltung der bis Ende 1923 ständig gefährdeten parlamentarischen Demokratie beigetragen. Gleichzeitig hat aber die Vertagung notwendiger struktureller Anpassungen und die Schaffung neuer inflationsbedingter Hypotheken — unter anderem das oft im Antisemitismus zum Ausdruck kommende Ressentiment der Inflationsgeschädigten und die Erschütterung der Autorität des Staates und der demokratischen Parteien durch ihren vergeblichen Kampf gegen Wucherer, Preistreiber und Inflationsgewinnler — die Erkenntnis der neuen Gegebenheiten erschwert und einen Problemstau für die Zeit nach der Stabilisierung bewirkt. In dieser Situation, die sich mit der für den deutschen Sozialstaat typischen, in den Vereinigten Staaten und Großbritannien nicht in gleicher Weise gegebenen direkten Politisierung ökonomischer und sozialer Fragen verband, war längst vor der Weltwirtschaftskrise das Überleben des politischen Systems und der durch die Revolution von 1918 geschaffenen sozialen Verhältnisse ernsthaft gefährdet.

Strikes in the German and British Chemical Industries 1914—1924:

The Influence of Inflation and Deflation on Industrial Unrest in Postwar Europe

CRAIG PATTON

I

Introduction

The years following the First World War were characterized by intense industrial unrest in many countries of Western Europe. These conflicts have been the subject of a number of monographs and articles, but serious gaps still exist in our knowledge of labor conflict in this period. In particular, despite a relatively extensive literature on individual strikes or particular strike waves in various countries, there are few if any studies which analyze general strike patterns, i. e. frequency, duration, number of participants, goals and success or failure, during these years. Those works which do discuss strike patterns in the years 1919—1924 in one way or another tend to be very general accounts of the evolution of labor conflict over an extended period of time. Their coverage of the immediate postwar period is thus usually sketchy and tends to focus either on changes in strike patterns for industry in general or in a few major industries.[1] The importance of these studies should not be minimized, but for a thorough understanding of the

---

[1] Heinrich Volkmann, *Modernisierung des Arbeitskampfes? Zum Formwandel von Streik und Aussperrung in Deutschland 1864—1975*, in: *Probleme der Modernisierung in Deutschland. Sozialhistorische Studien zum 19. und 20. Jahrhundert* (= Schriften des Zentralinstituts für sozialwissenschaftliche Forschung der Freien Universität Berlin, Bd. 27), ed. Hartmut Kaelbe, Opladen 1978, pp. 110—170; Edward Shorter/Charles Tilly, *Strikes in France 1830-1968*, Cambridge 1974; James E. Cronin, *Industrial Conflict in Modern Britain*, London 1979.

contours of industrial unrest in the crisis-plagued years 1919—1924 we need more detailed studies devoted to the pattern of conflict in different branches of industry and in different regions of individual countries and to the similarities of differences between various countries.

This paper attempts to contribute to the already existing fund of literature concerned with labor unrest after the First World War along these lines. The essay examines and compares strike patterns in the British and German chemical industries in 1919—1924 in connection with the economic development of each industry during the same period and seeks to demonstrate the influence of the latter on the former. Several considerations affected the choice of both topic and approach. The chemical industry was chosen as the focus of research because it was one of the „new" industries of the early twentieth century which by the World War had already begun to replace older, established industries such as mining, iron and steel, or textiles as the „leading sectors" of the European economy. Although much has been written about differences in the economic performance of these „old" and „new" industries during the interwar years, relatively little attention has been paid to the implications of this difference for labor relations. We are comparatively well-informed about the severe labor unrest often experienced by many of the older industries after the war, but far less has been written about such conflicts in the „new" industries.[2] This paper seeks to rectify this situation somewhat by providing a general overview of strike activity in the two largest chemical industries of Western Europe.

The essay also deliberately concentrates on the role of „economic" factors in shaping strike patterns in the British and German chemical industries in 1919—1924. This is not because „political" factors were

---

[2] With regard to the chemical industry this situation is improving. Among recent works in this area the best is undoubtedly that of Dieter Schiffmann, *Arbeit und Konflikt in der Badischen Anilin- und Sodafabrik 1918-1924. Ein Beitrag zur Geschichte der pfälzischen Arbeiterbewegung*, Phil. Diss., Mannheim 1981. Other works include Eva Cornelia Schoeck, *Arbeitslosigkeit und Rationalisierung. Die Lage der Arbeiter und die kommunistische Gewerkschaftspolitik 1920—1928*, Frankfurt/Main 1977; Uta Stolle, *Arbeiterpolitik im Betrieb. Frauen und Männer, Reformisten und Radikale, Fach- und Massenarbeiter bei Bayer, BASF, Bosch und in Solingen (1900—1930)*, Frankfurt/Main 1980; Willi Breuning, *Soziale Verhältnisse der Arbeiterschaft und sozialistische Arbeiterbewegung in Ludwigshafen am Rhein 1869—1919* (= Veröffentlichungen des Stadtarchivs Ludwigshafen a. Rh., Bd. 5), Ludwigshafen a. Rh. 1976.

unimportant, but precisely because many of the existing accounts of postwar labor unrest tend to emphasize its social-political aspects. This is understandable since one of the major features of industrial unrest after the First World War, especially in the years 1919—1920, was the emergence of demands for sweeping social and political change. However, the available evidence indicates that the majority of strikes in both England and Germany after the war were inspired or conditioned by economic developments. Moreover, as the postwar revolutionary threat ebbed and then largely vanished in 1920—1921 strikes became more purely „economic" conflicts.³

The study's concern with economic developments as a causal, or at least conditioning, factor in strike activity is also due to its focus on the relatively brief period 1919—1924 rather than a longer period of time. Other studies have shown that over short periods of time cyclical economic developments tend to exercise a greater influence on strike behavior than structural factors. These works, most of which focus on the late nineteenth and early twentieth century, have demonstrated a tendency for years of economic expansion to exhibit higher levels of strike activity than years of economic contraction.⁴ This essay will show that this pattern was true for both the English and German chemical industries in the period 1919—1924.

However, it has a broader goal as well. The years 1919—1924 were a period of pronounced inflation and deflation in both Germany and England. This essay attempts to show how inflationary and deflation-

---

³ Gerald D. Feldman, *Streiks in Deutschland 1914—1933: Probleme und Forschungsaufgaben*, in: *Streik. Zur Geschichte des Arbeitskampfes in Deutschland während der Industrialisierung*, ed. Klaus Tenfelde and Heinrich Volkmann, München 1981, pp. 272—273. The shift from „political" to „economic" strikes is dated earlier, and given a different significance, by Bernd-Jürgen Wendt, *‚Deutsche Revolution' — ‚Labour Unrest'. Systembedingungen der Streikbewegungen in Deutschland und England 1918—1921*, in: *Archiv für Sozialgeschichte*, 20 (1980), pp. 49—53.

⁴ Hartmut Kaelble/Heinrich Volkmann, *Konjunktur und Streik während des Übergangs zum Organisierten Kapitalismus in Deutschland*, in: *Zeitschrift für Wirtschafts- und Sozialwissenschaften*, 92 (1972), Nr. 5, pp. 513—544 (esp. 526—527, 539); Klaus Schoenhoven, *Arbeitskonflikte in Konjunktur und Rezession. Gewerkschaftliche Streikpolitik und Streikverhalten der Arbeiterschaft vor 1914*, in: *Streik. Zur Geschichte des Arbeitskampfes in Deutschland während der Industrialisierung*, ed. Klaus Tenfelde and Heinrich Volkmann, München 1981, pp. 177—193 (esp. 184—185, 189); H. Volkmann, *Modernisierung des Arbeitskampfes?* ... [see note 1], pp. 153—155, 157, 161—163; E. Shorter/C. Tilly, *Strikes in France* ... [see note 1], pp. 10, 83, 341.

ary developments helped condition short-run economic fluctuations during this period. In particular, it seeks to illustrate the way in which phases of economic expansion corresponded with periods of inflation while phases of economic contraction were associated with periods of deflation. Methodological problems make it impossible to assess that exact effect which inflation and deflation *per se* may have had on strike activity in the German and English chemical industries in these years, but the correspondence of periods of inflation with those of economic expansion, when strike activity tended to increase, and periods of deflation with those of economic contraction, when strike activity generally waned, suggests that inflationary and deflationary developments had a strong, if indirect, effect on labor unrest during the period under review. This effect was mediated through general economic developments, which were, of course, shaped by many other factors, both long- and short-run, than just inflation or deflation. Nonetheless, one cannot understand either the short-run cyclical economic fluctuations or short-term variations in strike activity during the years 1919—1924 without reference to the role of inflation and deflation.

For reasons of space this study deals almost exclusively with strikes rather than with labor protest in general. Consequently, many types of industrial conflict, particularly lockouts, are not discussed. These other forms of labor conflict were certainly important in both Germany and England during the period under review and deserve our attention, but they have been omitted from the present essay so as to devote as much attention as possible to strikes, which remained the dominant form of labor conflict over these years. Similar considerations also mean that many other issues connected with labor unrest during this period are either not discussed at all here or are only briefly treated in passing. For example, the extent to which changes in the nature of strikes in the British and German chemical industries in these years were a continuation or interruption of prewar trends is only occasionally discussed. Likewise, the degree to which these changes support or contradict current theories concerning the „modernization" of labor conflict in the late nineteenth and early twentieth centuries is only mentioned in passing.

II

Economic Trends in the German and British Chemical Industries

In order to appreciate the particular influence which economic developments exerted on strike activity in the German and British chemical industries, it is first necessary to know something of the quite different experience of the chemical industry in each of the two countries in 1919-1924. As will be seen, the period was not one of uniform development in either England or Germany for in both nations the industry experienced periods of good and poor business conditions. However, the German chemical industry enjoyed „boom conditions" to a much greater extent than its British counterpart. The chief determinant of the *Hochkonjunktur* enjoyed by the German industry throughout most of 1919—1924 was the depreciation of the Mark which greatly facilitated exports and also stimulated domestic sales. In contrast, the English chemical industry suffered greatly during the severe depression which gripped the British economy in 1920—1921, and its recovery over the course of 1922—1924 was painfully slow.

Turning our attention first to the German chemical industry, six different phases of development can be discerned during the half-decade 1919—1924. The first of these lasted from November 1918 to mid-1919 and was one of extremely limited sales and production. Output was severely handicapped because of a) the need to convert back to peacetime production, b) shortages of raw materials and fuel, especially coal, c) political uncertainty caused by the revolutionary unrest which followed the collapse of the imperial regime, and d) the Allied occupation of the Rhineland and other parts of Western Germany, where much of the chemical industry was located, and their blockade of trade between occupied and unoccupied Germany until the Treaty of Versailles was signed in June 1919.[5]

The second phase in the development of the German chemical industry lasted from mid-1919 to mid-1920 and was characterized by brisk

---

[5] *Verhandlungsbericht der 41. Hauptversammlung des Vereins zur Wahrung der Interessen der Chemischen Industrie Deutschlands. Berlin, 25. Oktober 1919*, Beilage in: *Die Chemische Industrie*, 42. Jg. (1919), pp. 7—8, 13; Farbenfabriken vorm. Friedrich Bayer & Co., Leverkusen, *Bericht des Vorstands und des Aufsichtsrats über das Bilanzjahr 1919*, p. 2.

business. The gradual elimination or easing of the aforementioned obstacles to production in spring and summer 1919 allowed the chemical industry to take advantage of the *Warenhunger* for its products both at home and abroad. This was particularly true for the dyestuffs industry, but was also the case for the nitrogenous fertilizer industry in which BASF was now leader thanks to its facilities at Oppau and Leuna.[6] The decline of the value of the Mark throughout most of this phase acted as a major stimulus to the sale of German chemical products abroad. This was especially important to the largest chemical firms such as Bayer, BASF, and Hoechst which were heavily export-orientated and now faced new competition from the greatly expanded chemical industries of other nations.[7]

The third stage, from roughly mid-1920 to Autumn 1921, was one of relative stagnation for the German chemical industry. There was a slowdown in domestic sales in most branches of the industry as pent-up demand was gradually satisfied and an even more dramatic fall in exports. The sharp drop in foreign sales in large part simply reflected the problem of worldwide excess capacity once the initial backlog of demand built up by four years of war had been statisfied. The chemical plants constructed by both belligerents and neutrals during the First World War in their effort to become independent in the area of vital chemical products were capable of producing much greater quantities

---

[6] *Verhandlungsbericht der 41. Hauptversammlung...* [see note 5], p. 8; Farbenfabriken vorm. Friedrich Bayer & Co., Leverkusen, *Bericht des Vorstandes und des Aufsichtsrats über das Bilanzjahr 1920*, p. 2; Badische Anilin- und Sodafabrik Ludwigshafen am Rhein, *Bericht des Vorstands und Aufsichtsrats über das Geschäftsjahr 1920*, p. 3; L.F. Haber, *The Chemical Industry 1900-1930. International Growth and Technological Change*, Oxford 1971, pp. 249-250.

[7] On the role of the value of the Mark in stimulating sales during this period, and throughout the postwar inflation, see Carl Ludwig Roedler, *Grundzüge der deutschen Konjunkturbewegung 1920-1925 unter besonderer Berücksichtigung der chemischen Industrie*, Wirt.- und Sozialwiss. Diss., Frankfurt/M. 1926, *passim*, who treats this topic at some length, if not as systematically as one might wish. Roedler's observations form the basis of many of the present author's own judgements on the chemical *Konjunktur* between 1919 and 1924, and although the work will not be cited again (so as to save space), it should be understood that Roedler's book informs much of the following discussions on the German chemical industry. Subsequent footnotes on this topic will chiefly serve to indicate other primary and secondary sources that pertain to this issue. Thus, for the period late 1919 — early 1920 see Farbenfabriken Bayer, *Bericht...* [see note 6], p. 2; Badische Anilin- und Sodafabrik, *Bericht...* [see note 6], p. 4.

of both organic and inorganic chemicals than the world required during peacetime.[8] However, the decline in German exports was also conditioned by economic depression in the U.S. and Great Britain which not only reduced sales to these countries, but also lowered the price of American and British chemical products, making them more competitive with German ones in other countries. The relative stability of the Mark during this same period further aggravated the export problems of the chemical industry.[9] An additional handicap to the industry at the end of this phase was the *Rheinzollgrenze* and other sanctions imposed by the Allies in April—October 1921 in connection with the London Ultimatum. Some measure of the impact of these different factors on the German chemical industry can be gained by looking at the production figures for the dyestuffs producers in the *Interessengemeinschaft* (IG) that had been formed in 1916 and had a virtual monopoly in this branch of the chemical industry. Whereas in the second half of 1920 they had produced approximately 69.4 million pounds of dyestuffs, during the first and second halves of 1921 these firms produced only 53.1 million and 63.1 million pounds respectively.[10] The major exception to the generally gloomy picture was in the area of synthetic nitrogen and nitrogenous fertilizers which were sold almost exclusively at home and enjoyed growing demand as German agriculture struggled to increase its production after four years of neglect.

Despite these hardships the chemical industry survived and during the fourth phase of its development, from autumn 1921 through January 1923, it experienced notable prosperity. Signs of improved business

---

[8] L.F. Haber, *The Chemical Industry 1900—1930*...[see note 6], pp. 251—152; League of Nations. Economic and Financial Section, *The Chemical Industry* (= Documentation. International Economic Conference, Geneva May 1927), Geneva 1927, pp. 21—29.

[9] On the mutually reinforcing impact of the worldwide depression of 1920—1921 and the relative stability of the Mark in the German chemical industry see Farbenfabriken Bayer, *Bericht*... [see note 6], p. 2, and *Bericht des Vorstands und Aufsichtsrats über das Bilanzjahr 1921*, p. 2; Badische Anilin- und Sodafabrik Ludwigshafen am Rhein, *Bericht des Vorstands und Aufsichtsrats über das Geschäftsjahr 1921*, p. 5; also see *Die Chemische Industrie*, 44, Nr. 10, 5 March 1921, p. 84; 44, Nr. 29, 13 July 1921, pp. 274—275; 44, Nr. 32, 8 August 1921, p. 309.

[10] These figures, based on those required of the IG firms by the Reparations Commission beginning in February 1920, are taken from Thomas W. Delahanty, *The German Dyestuffs Industry* (= U.S. Bureau of Foreign and Domestic Commerce. Miscellaneous Series, No. 126), Washington D.C. 1924, p. 18.

conditions were already evident in August—September 1921, and by the end of the year a full-scale „boom" was in progress. Following a mild dip in business in early 1922, conditions were generally good throughout spring and summer of that year, depending largely on fluctuations in the value of the Mark. As the Mark plummeted in the second half of 1922 chemical sales surged with foreign buyers seeking German products at bargain prices and domestic purchasers scrambling for safety by means of a *Flucht in die Sachwerte*.[11] Available evidence suggests that most, if not all, branches of the industry participated in this *Inflationskonjunktur*.[12] That this increase in domestic and especially foreign sales, and a corresponding increase in production, was primarily due to the accelerating depreciation of the Mark was explicitly recognized by the major German chemical firms and by their competitors abroad.[13] Figures on the production of dyestuffs within the IG for 1922 (compared with 1921) and on the total tonnage and value of all German chemical Export for 1922 clearly reveal the powerful stimulus which the Mark's fall had on the chemical industry.[14]

The occupation of the Ruhr by French and Belgian soldiers in late January 1923 and the German government's subsequent policy of passive resistance signalled the start of the fifth stage of the chemical

---

[11] D. Schiffmann, *Arbeit und Konflikt*... [see note 2], pp. 52—53, 69—70; Badische Anilin- und Sodafabrik, *Bericht*... [see note 9], pp. 4—5.

[12] Farbenfabriken vorm. Friedrich Bayer & Co., Leverkusen, *Bericht des Vorstands und Aufsichtsrats über das Bilanzjahr 1922*. p. 2; Badische Anilin- und Sodafabrik, *Bericht des Vorstands und Aufsichtsrats über das Geschäftsjahr 1922*, p. 3; *Die Chemische Industrie*, 45, Nr. 33, 12 August 1922, p. 503; 45, Nr. 38, 16 September 1922, p. 601; 45, Nr. 44, 28 October 1922, p. 271.

[13] Farbenfabriken Bayer, *Bericht*... [see note 9], p. 3 and *Bericht*... [see note 12], p. 2; Badische Anilin- und Sodafabrik, *Bericht*... [see note 9], p. 5; *Berliner Börsen-Zeitung*, No. 221, 15 May 1923 (quoting Agfa Geschäftsbericht for fiscal year 1922). On contemporary foreign observers' awareness and estimation of the German chemical industry's inflation advantage see T.W. Delahanty, *German Dyestuffs Industry*... [see note 10], p. 2; also W.J. Reader, *Imperial Chemical Industries. A History, The Forerunners 1870—1926* (= Vol. 1), London 1970, p. 444.

[14] In the first half of 1921 the IG firms produced only some 53,000,000 pounds of dyestuffs. In the first and second halves of 1922 the figures were 90,500,000 and 101,900,000 pounds respectively. Over the same period of time the weight of chemical exports rose from 616,000 dz. (*Doppelzentner*) in May 1921 to over 3,000,000 dz. in December 1922. For more details see T. W. Delahanty, *German Dyestuffs Industry*... [see note 10], pp. 18 & 19 and Statistisches Reichsamt, *Monatliche Nachweise über den auswärtigen Handel Deutschlands 1921, passim.; ibid., 1922*.

industry's immediate postwar history. This phase lasted until the introduction of the *Rentenmark* in November 1923. In general, conditions in the chemical industry were less favorable than during the preceding phase, but the degree of hardship experienced by different firms varied considerably. On the one hand, all the firms situated in the occupied regions suffered from declining sales and production as the French progressively cut the economic ties between occupied and unoccupied Germany. However, while some firms were forced to cease operations altogether (such as BASF in April—October), others only had to close down individual plants (as at Hoechst), and still others managed to maintain production largely without interruption although at lower than average levels (as at Bayer).[15] In unoccupied Germany, on the other hand, sales and production remained high through mid-1923. Only in July—August did signs of a downturn become evident when exports began to decline as German chemical prices reached or passed world prices and domestic sales fell due to declining purchasing power and credit shortages. These difficulties intensified through the autumn so that by the time the *Rentenmark* was introduced the chemical industry in unoccupied, as well as occupied, Germany was in a severe crisis.[16]

The sixth and final phase of the chemical *Konjunktur* of 1919—1924 lasted from the end of 1923 throughout 1924 and represented a rather bleak, although not disastrous, period for most German chemical producers. In the year following currency stabilization German chemical prices were generally above the world price level for chemicals. Consequently, exports tended to stagnate and only grew significantly toward the end of the year.[17] Simultaneously sales at home were low because

---

[15] T.W. Delahanty, *German Dyestuffs Industry*... [see note 10], pp. 26—30, 54—56, 61. On BASF see Walter Voigtlander-Tetzer, *Chronik der BASF*, Bd. 3 (1914-1925), unpub. Ms., no date, pp. 749, 854, as well as D. Schiffmann, *Arbeit und Konflikt*... [see note 2], pp. 70, 460—462. On the situation at Hoechst, see letter of Hoechst Betriebsabteilung to the Regierungspräsident in Wiesbaden 27 April 1923, Hauptstaatsarchiv Wiesbaden (HStAW), 425/82. For Bayer see Farbenfabriken vorm. Friedrich Bayer & Co., Leverkusen, *Bericht des Vorstandes und Aufsichtsrats über das Bilanzjahr 1923*, p. 3.

[16] *Die Chemische Industrie*, 46, Nr. 44, 27. October 1923, p. 618; 46, Nr. 50, 8 December 1923, p. 663; 47, Nr. 39, 27 September 1924, p. 529.

[17] Only in November—December 1924 was there a clear trend for the weight of chemical exports to exceed the average level of exports for July—December 1923. For more specific information see Statistisches Reichsamt, *Monatliche Nachweise*... *1923*; ibid. 1924 [see note 14].

tight capital and credit markets prevented many customers from obtaining funds for new purchases. This capital shortage also affected the chemical industry directly because lack of operating capital forced many firms to reduce production, close down various plants, and lay off large numbers of workers.[18] As in the case of the periods of relative stabilization from mid-1920 to autumn 1921 it was the synthetic nitrogen and nitrogenous fertilizer branch which was the chief exception to this overall trend, although there is some evidence that the pharmaceutical branch also weathered the crisis in relatively good shape.[19] Currency stabilization, stagnation or only slowing climbing sales, relatively stable production costs, and tight credit all worked to bring about the final end of the *Inflationskonjunktur* of the German chemical industry.

The experience of the British chemical industry in 1919—1924 was quite different from that of the German industry. Its development exhibited fewer swings between periods of good and poor business conditions and, more importantly, the period of favorable economic conditions was much shorter than in Germany. The dominant fact of life in the English chemical industry in this period was the abrupt end of a postwar boom in mid-1920 and the onset of a depression whose aftereffects pervaded the next four years. A closer examination of this process reveals three general phases.

The first phase of the English chemical industry's postwar development lasted from the end of 1918 to roughly mid-1920 and was one of generally favorable economic conditions. British firms benefited from the pent-up demand for products created by the war at an earlier date than their German counterparts because they were spared the consequences of defeat and revolution. The absence of significant German competition until late 1919 allowed the British chemical industry to do well both at home and abroad. The new English dyestuffs industry was further aided in its efforts by a government prohibition on the import of dyestuffs of 24th February 1919, which however, was later ruled invalid in December of that year.[20] Even after the Germans returned in

---

[18] Farbenfabriken vorm. Friedrich Bayer & Co. Leverkusen, *Bericht des Vorstands und Aufsichtsrates über das Bilanzjahr 1924*, p. 3; Badische Anilin- und Sodafabrik, *Bericht des Vorstands und Aufsichtsrats über das Geschäfsjahr 1924*, p. 4.

[19] On the market situation for synthetic nitrogen products see Badische Anilin- und Sodafabrik, *Bericht*... [see note 18], p. 4; for limited information in the pharmaceutical branch see Peter Waller, *Probleme der deutschen chemischen Industrie*, Halberstadt 1925, pp. 208—210.

[20] W.J. Reader, *Imperial Chemical Industries*... [see note 1], pp. 280. 430—431.

strength to international chemical markets, the English industry was in a better competitive position than before the war as a result of the expansion and improvement of production facilities during the war.[21] Producers of heavy chemicals, who were the traditional backbone of the English chemical industry, appear to have done fairly well during this postwar boom even though they faced considerably greater competition than before the war. The dyestuffs industry presents a more complex picture. Although demand for dyes was great, the largest producer, the newly-established British Dyestuffs Corporation, which controlled 40—50% of all English dye capacity, was plagued by a seemingly endless string of technical and organizational problems that reduced its ability to satisfy this demand.[22] Nonetheless, the dyestuff branch of the English chemical industry prospered during the reconversion and restocking boom of 1919—1920; a boom encouraged by the ready availability of money and generally dominated by inflationary conditions.[23]

However, this period of good business proved short-lived, and from mid-1920 to the end of 1921 the English chemical industry passed through its second stage of development after the war — one of severe depression. The depression of 1920—1921 which affected all of English industry, was brought about by a combination of many factors including consumer resistance to higher prices, growing industrial debt, a high level of bank illiquidity, and waning business confidence. The importance of the government's adoption of deflationary policies in this web of causality is disputed, but that it played a central role, even if only to aggravate the downturn, cannot be denied.[24] There is some evidence that the depression affected the chemical industry particularly hard. Figures on industrial production indicate that while output fell 18.6%

[21] *Op. cit.*, pp. 263—264, 273—280, 284—288, 291, 300—303, 310—314; L.F. Haber, *The Chemical Industry 1900-1930*... [see note 6], pp. 243—246, 250.

[22] W.J. Reader, *Imperial Chemical Industries*... [see note 13], pp. 329—332, 427—430; L.F. Haber, *The Chemical Industry 1900—1930*... [see note 6], pp. 189—193, 211—212.

[23] On the sources and impact of the abundant capital and credit which facilitated the upswing of 1919—1920 see Derek Aldcroft, *The Inter-War Economy: Britain 1919—1939*, New York 1970, pp. 35—36, 326 and Sidney Pollard, *The Development of the British Economy 1914—1967*, 2nd edition, London 1969, pp. 214-215.

[24] D. Aldcroft, *Inter-War Economy*... [see note 23], pp. 36, 327—328; S. Pollard, *The Development of the British Economy*... [see note 23], pp. 210—211, 217.

for industry as a whole during this slump, the level of production in the chemical industry fell 28.0 %.[25] The major chemical companies in all branches of the industry reported large declines in sales, widespread plant closures, and massive lay-offs of workers. Even those facilities which remained in operation worked far below capacity; some at only 20—30 % of capacity.[26]

The worst of the depression was over by the end of 1921, but the third and final phase of development, from the beginning of 1921 through 1924, remained one of only slightly improved business conditions for the British chemical industry. In fact, recovery in the chemical industry appears to have been slower than in general. Whereas all industry registered a 41.4 % increase in production over the period 1921—1925 (measured against the 1920—1921 low), output in the chemical sector rose only 32.4 %.[27] However, this conceals important intra-industry differences. The heavy, or inorganic, chemical branch did better than the dyestuffs industry. Sales and production in the former increased gradually over the course of 1922—1924, and the leading firm in the heavy metal branch — Brunner, Mond & Co. — appears to have rebounded quite quickly.[28] In the area of dyestuffs manufacture recovery was slower, in part because of fierce competition with Germany in 1922 as the latter used its inflation advantage to reconquer old markets and gain new ones.[29] The occupation of the Ruhr by French and Belgian troops in 1923 provided British dye makers with some relief, and during the first half of 1923 their exports shot up

---

[25] These figures are found in D. Aldcroft, *Inter-War Economy...* [see note 23], pp. 48—49 but are based on K.S. Lomax, *Growth and Productivity in the United Kingdom*, in: *Productivity Measurement Review*, 38 (1964), pp. 5—22. Although aspects of Lomax's indicies have been criticized by other English economic historians, notably J.A. Dowie, *Growth in the Inter-War Period: Some More Arithmetic*, in: *The Economic History Review*, 2nd series, vol. 21, no. 1 (April 1968), pp. 93—107, the critics generally accept the accuracy of his figures for the inter-war period.

[26] For a general overview of the English chemical industry's plight at this time see L.F. Haber, *The Chemical Industry 1900—1930...* [see note 6], pp. 252—253, 258; *Die Chemische Industrie*, 45, Nr. 16, 15 April 1922, pp. 252—253; 45, Nr. 23, 1 June 1922, p. 359. More detailed information on particular firms, i.e. Brunner, Mond & Co. and British Dyestuffs Corporation, can be found in W.J. Reader, *Imperial Chemical Industries...* [see note 13], pp. 332—334, 431—433, 436.

[27] D. Aldcroft, *Inter-War Economy...* [see note 23], pp. 48—49.

[28] W.J. Reader, *Imperial Chemical Industries...* [see note 13], p. 382.

[29] *Op. cit.*, p. 444.

almost 100 %.[30] Although 1924 was certainly not an exeptionally prosperous year for the dyestuffs industry, both domestic and foreign sales improved slightly.[31]

III
Strike Trends in the German and British Chemical Industries

The impact which economic developments in the British and German chemical industries in 1919—1924 had on strike patterns in the two countries is difficult to capture statistically. Only rarely did official statistics differentiate between „economic" and „political" strikes. Moreover, such distinctions are largely artificial since strikes, like all social conflicts, arise out of the complex interaction of economic, social and political phenomena, thus making it extraordinarily difficult to assign specific causal weight to particular factors. Nonetheless, some idea of the influence which prevailing economic conditions exerted on strike activity in each chemical industry can be gained through a careful examination of official strike statistics. By first tracing changes in certain crucial aspects of strike behavior such as frequency, size, duration and overall intensity, which are at least partially revealed in government statistics, and then relating these changes to simultaneous developments in the chemical industry of each country we can see the importance of cyclical economic factors in shaping strike patterns during this brief period and, at the same time, gain a general impression of the role of inflation and deflation in this process.

The two tables presented on the following pages are based on figures drawn from published and unpublished material of the *Reichsarbeitsministerium* and the Ministry of Labour. In particular, the figures for Germany in TABLE I are either taken directly from information in the „Reichsarbeitsblatt" or computed from statistics published in it. The statistics for England in TABLE II are computations derived from information contained in strike reports filed with the Ministry of Labour since prior to 1923 the Ministry (and its predecessors under the Board of Trade) did not publish strike figures for the chemical industry in its

---

[30] *Die Chemische Industrie*, 46, Nr. 37, 8 September 1923, pp. 563—564.
[31] *Op. cit.*, 47, Nr. 8, 23 February 1924, p. 74; W.J. Reader, *Imperial Chemical Industries*... [see note 13], p. 448.

„Labour Gazette." For 1923 and 1924 the figures given in the „Labour Gazette" are also listed in parantheses (); the differences in the two sets of figures highlight the caution with which we must view all the statistical material presented here. Moreover, comparisons between the figures for Germany and Britain should be judged with a very critical eye for although names of the categories in the tables are the same, important differences existed in how these categories of analysis were actually defined and how the statistical material was compiled. Despite these reservations, the figures in TABLES I and II do offer at least an image of the general contours of strike activity in the German and British chemical industries in 1919—1924.

TABLE 1

Strike Statistics — Germany

	Average 1890—1913	1919	1920	1921	1922	1923	1924
A. Number of Strikes (Frequency)	—	54	44	24	41	36	21
B. Number of Factories Affected	20	120	70	29	59	211	31
C. Greatest Number of Strikers	1465	26500	13699	13219	21642	15841	5959
D. Strikers per Strike (Size)	—	490	310	550	527	440	283
E. Total Work Days Lost	33809	330508	167627	346891	353846	107268	109901
F. Days Lost per Strike (Intensity)	—	5880	3720	14300	8432	3080	5094
G. Days Lost per Striker (Duration)	23	12	12	26	16	7	18

Source: Reichsarbeitsblatt (nichtamtlicher Teil), Neue Folge, 6. Jg. (1926), Nr. 14, S. 236—237.

TABLE 2

Strike Statistics — Great Britain

	1914	1919	1920	1921	1922	1923	1924
A. Number of Strikes (Frequency)	8	15	14	8	4	12 (14)	9 (11)
B. Number of Plants Affected	8	20	25	27	9	26 (—)	9 (—)
C. Number of Strikers	1249	1867	10745	2803	814	1517 (2000)	1448 (2000)
D. Strikers per Strike (Size)	156	125	768	350	204	112 (143)	161 (182)
E. Total Work Days Lost	31840	35997	132562	44744	27398	15500 (27000)	16721 (23000)
F. Days Lost per Strike (Intensity)	3980	2390	9440	5571	6858	1066 (1929)	1850 (2091)
G. Days Lost per Striker (Duration)	26	19	12	16	34	10 (14)	12 (12)

Source: Public Records Office, Kew Gardens, Ministry of Labour, Lab. 34/32 and Lab. 34/38—34/42.

Strike Frequency

A comparison of the figures on the number of strikes listed in TABLES I and II offers insights into the frequency of strikes in the chemical industry of each country. In every year examined the absolute number of strikes in the German chemical industry far exceeded those in the English industry. Usually the German figure was 200 % above the British one, but in 1922 it was 900 % higher while in 1924 it was only about 100 % higher. In part this difference only reflects the greater size of the German industry. Assuming all else was equal, the number of strikes in Germany could be expected to be higher simply because it employed more workers in more plants. However, this difference in size was not alone great enough to account for the dramatic difference in strike frequencies. When examined in terms of the number of strikes per 100,000 workers employed in each chemical industry, strike frequency was still consistently higher in the German than in the British chemical industry. However, when computed in this manner, the figures for strike frequency in Germany are on average 100 % higher than those for Britain (rather than 200 % when based simply on absolute number of strikes).[32] Obviously other factors must be have been at work to foster „strike fever" among the German chemical workers. The list of such possible factors is a long one and includes such diverse factors as the lower level of political legitimacy enjoyed by the Weimar Republic, the higher level of industrial concentration in Germany, and serious food shortages after the war.

Space does not permit a detailed examination of all the factors which influenced strike frequency in each country, but several features of the timing of strikes in the two industries suggest that cyclical economic developments are crucial to understanding the observed differences in strike frequency, at least over the short period of time examined here. The fact that the greatest difference in strike frequency occurred in 1922 while the smallest difference was in 1924 ist noteworthy. In 1922 the German chemical industry was in the midst of an inflation-inspired *Hochkonjunktur* while its British counterpart struggled to overcome the effects of one of the worst depressions in British history. Conversely, 1924 was a year of crisis for the chemical sector in Germany while the British chemical industry enjoyed moderately favorable, or at least satisfactory, conditions. A closer examination of the timing of strikes

---

[32] Differences in the type of industrial activity subsumed under the term ‚chemical industry' in each country or by different collectors of data within the same country preclude any exact comparison of the number of chemical workers in the two industries. However, on the basis of figures contained in the British government's *Population Census of 1921*, the 1921 edition of the German government's *Statistisches Jahrbuch für das Deutsche Reich*, and the yearly report of the German Berufsgenossenschaft der chemischen Industrie for the same year it is possible to generalize that there were roughly 200,000 chemical workers in Britain and approximately 300,000 in Germany during this period (although, of course, the numbers fluctuated yearly). In that case, the figures for strikes per 100,000 workers are

	1919	1920	1921	1922	1923	1924
Germany	18.0	14.7	8.0	13.7	12.0	7.0
Britain	7.5	7.0	4.0	2.0	6.0	4.5

in each country gives added weight to the thesis that economic factors played an essential role in determining strike frequency during this period.

In Germany the peak for strikes in the chemical industry was 1919, followed at some distance by 1920. The number of strikes fell sharply in 1921 but then rose significantly in 1922. In 1923 there were almost as many strikes as in the preceding year but 1924 saw the least number of strikes of any year of this half-decade. When this pattern of rising and falling strike frequency is compared with the *Konjunktur* of the German chemical industry during these same years one notices that years in which „boom" conditions prevailed also tended to be ones of greater strike activity while years of less favorable business conditions saw fewer strikes. This pattern conforms to the trend for strikes to increase in frequency during periods of economic expansion that has been found for the prewar decades by other researchers.[33]

However, a special aspect of the period 1919—1924 was the sharply fluctuating rate of inflation which appears to have indirectly helped shape this pattern of strike frequency through its impact on both the economic prosperity of the chemical industry and the wages of chemical workers. On one level, inflationary developments tended to stimulate sales and production in the chemical industry for both the home and, especially, the foreign market. This produced a relatively tight labor market within the industry and created a favourable situation for chemical workers to back wage and other demands with strikes. Simultaneously, inflation placed special pressure on both the worker's nominal and real wages and so inspired ever new demands on their part.

Of course such economic developments cannot completely explain all the strikes in the German chemical industry in 1919—1924. For example, the large number of strikes in 1919 and 1920 also reflect the particularly troubled political situation of these years as well as unrest caused by serious food shortages.[34] The decline of strikes in 1923 suggests that under conditions of hyper-inflation fewer German

[33] See note 4.
[34] In the largest chemical firms, which are the only ones with substantial archival material, there is no recorded instance of a strike purely over the issue of food supply or prices during this period, in large part because of the sometimes elaborate efforts of the firms to acquire and distribute food to their workers. Despite such efforts, however, the question of food, fuel and other shortages was a major contributory factor to much of the unrest of this period, and on occasion major protests over such shortages occured without necessarily creating a strike situation. For Bayer see *Wiesdorfer General-Anzeiger*, 14 March 1920, Bayer Archiv, 85/3.1. On Hoechst see *Hoechster Kreisblatt*, 25—29 June

workers were inclined to risk the loss of income or employment through strike action unless driven to do so by desperation. In general, the evidence cited here plus the nature of strike demands in these years suggest that economic developments exerted a strong influence on the timing and frequency of strikes in the German chemical industry.

The timing of strikes in the British chemical industry also tends to bear out the importance of cyclical economic changes on strike activity over the short period 1919—1924. Although 1919—1920 were the years with the greatest number of strikes in both Britain and Germany, after 1920 the patterns of strike frequency in the two countries diverge. In 1921 and especially 1922 the number of strikes in the English chemical industry fell dramatically. However, in 1923 and 1924 strikes increased significantly and approached the levels of 1919—1920. The timing of these alterations in the strike rate corresponds closely with changes in the general development of the British economy and the English chemical industry during the same period. Especially noteworthy is the decline in strikes in 1921—1922, the worst period of the chemical industry's postwar development. While the frequency of strikes in the German chemical industry increased under the impact of inflation in 1922, depressed conditions in England, which were in large part due to the government's deflationary policies, led to low strike rates in the British chemical industry.

Strike Size

TABLES I and II also contain figures on the size of strikes in the German and British chemical industries over 1919—1924. They indicate that just as the number of strikes was consistently higher in Germany than in Britain, average strike size (in terms of the number of participants per strike) also tended to be larger in the German chemical industry. Only in 1920 was average strike size larger in England than in Germany. The reasons for the particularly high level of strike size in England in this year are discussed in detail below, but they appear to have been closely linked to a combination of continued price hikes and the first signs of the coming depression. In every other year though the

1920. For an account of unrest at BASF linked to shortages and high prices during Winter 1919—1920 see D. Schiffmann, *Arbeit und Konflikt*... [see note 2], pp. 276—297, especially 276—280 and 292—297. Given the difficulties of the larger companies one might safely assume that many small and medium size firms also experienced considerable labor trouble involving food or other shortages.

average level of participation in strikes was significantly higher in the German chemical industry.

The primary reason for the observed difference in strike size between Germany and Britain over the period 1919—1924 as a whole is the structural differences in the two industries rather than short-run economic developments. The German chemical industry was characterized by a greater degree of industrial concentration than the British. Thus, when a strike did occur, it was likely to involve more workers. The English chemical industry had few if any firms with production complexes that could compare with those of BASF, Bayer, Hoechst, Agfa or the Leunawerke either in terms of physical size or number of employees.

Of course the level of strike participation is shaped by many other influences as well. One of the most important of these is the degree of trade union organization among workers. Unfortunately, no satisfactory material exists on which to base a comparision of union membership in the German and British chemical industries in 1919—1924 since the unions representing chemical workers in both countries were „general unions" with many members drawn from other industries as well as the chemical industry.[35]

If we shift our attention from average strike size in the two countries during the period 1919—1924 in general to variations in the size of strikes in each one from year to year, we once again see the importance of cyclical economic developments. Among other things changes in strike size indicate shifts in the locus of conflict from smaller to larger factories or vice versa. Such shifts in the focal point of strike activity would seem to suggest that at certain points in time different size

---

[35] There is no adequate general account of the Verband der Fabrikarbeiter, the trade union with the largest membership among the German chemical workers, during this period. Some insight into its general evolution can be gained through its own *Jubiläumsschrift 40 Jahre Kampf. Zur Erinnerung an die Gründung und den 40jährigen Kampf des Verbandes der Fabrikarbeiter Deutschlands,* Hamburg 1930. For specific developments during the period 1919—1924 one should consult the Jahrbücher which the union published annually throughout these years and the Protokolle of its Verbandstage in 1920 and 1922. In England several major unions included chemical workers in their ranks. Useful overviews include G.D.H. Cole, *Trade Unionism and Munitions* (= Economic and Social History of the Great War, British Series, no. 9), Oxford 1923; Jack Eaton/Richard Morris/Colin Gill, *The Growth of Trade Unionism in the United Kingdom Chemical Industry,* in: *Journal of Modern History,* 50, 4 (December 1978); Richard Hyman, *The Workers Union,* Oxford 1971.

chemical firms may have borne the brunt of labor conflict, possibly as a result of their peculiar economic situation under conditions of inflation or depression. A glance at shifts in strike size over time in each industry tends to support this idea, especially in the German case.

TABLE I reveals that for Germany 1921 was the year in which average strike size was largest and 1924 the year in which it was lowest. The high level of participation in 1921 implies that this was a year in which strike activity was focused in larger plants. The actual record of labor unrest confirms this deduction. There were major conflicts at Bayer in January—February, the Leunawerke in March (in connection with the KPD's Maerzaktion), and at both Hoechst and Griesheim-Elektron in September—October. Nor is it exactly surprising that strikes and other forms of labor protest centered in large plants at this particular period of time. The relative stability of the Mark from mid-1920 to mid-1921 along with a severe depression in many Western industrial countries hurt both the sales and profits of the largest German chemical firms, which were much more export-oriented than the smaller companies. This development led the large firms to adopt labor policies aimed at restoring „productivity" and „discipline"; policies at odds with their previously more flexible postwar practises.[36] The result was, predictably enough, increased labor unrest in the larger chemical plants. It should be noted that this change in employer policies was not unique to the chemical industry. Gerald Feldman has argued that during the period of relative stabilization in 1920—1921, „Both political and market conditions... conspired to restore the initiative to the employers who, under increasing economic pressure to protect their export advantages, began to put up resistance to worker demands where they had previously yielded because they could pass the costs off in higher prices."[37]

---

[36] The Arbeitgeberverband der chemischen Industrie Deutschlands has also received scant attention from historians. The policies of chemical employers during the Kapp Putsch has been discussed by Gerald D. Feldman, *Big Business and the Kapp Putsch*, in: *Central European History*, 4, 2 (June 1971), pp. 99—130. Theodor Berkel, *Die Geschichte der Reichsarbeitsgemeinschaft Chemie 1919—1924*, Phil. Diss., Marburg/Lahn 1981 contains some valuable information on the attitudes and policies of chemical employers during 1919—1920, but it suffers from a rather poor narrative style which lacks analytic clarity. For the specific policies of two of the largest firms, i. e. BASF and Bayer, see. D. Schiffman, *Arbeit und Konflikt...* [see note 2], pp. 327—328, 330 and U. Stolle, *Arbeiterpolitik im Betrieb...* [see note 2], pp. 54—56, 64—66 respectively.

[37] Gerald D. Feldman, *The Political Economy of Germany's Relative Stabilization*

The small size of strikes in 1924 reflects a completely different set of economic conditions. Among the largest chemical firms only BASF experienced a major strike or lockout during this year. There were several reasons for this lack of unrest in the large plants, including worker disillusionment and apathy following earlier defeats, but economic factors played a crucial role. Two factors were especially important. First, the crisis in which the chemical industry found itself and the high levels of unemployment which accompanied the crisis seriously reduced the willingness and ability of workers to strike. Secondly, the economic and organizational strength of the largest firms vis-à-vis their workers and the unions, which had been augmented by the inflation and hyperinflation, remained intact despite the business downturn of 1924.[38] The secure position of the largest firms made a successful strike against them virtually impossible.

In the case of the English chemical industry, 1920 was the year in which strike size was largest and 1923 the year with the smallest level of strike participation. The exeptionally large size of strikes in 1920 is primarily due to the almost simultaneous occurence of three of the largest strikes of the postwar period in May and June of that year. The fact these strikes occured when they did was almost predictable. The spring and summer of 1920 was a period of sharp price increases, leading to workers' demands for higher wages. At the same time the period brought the first signs of the coming depression, inspiring inflexibility on the part of employers.[39] As in the German chemical industry slightly later on in 1920—21 the result was an upswing in labor conflict.[40]

---

during the 1920/21 World Depression, in: *Die Deutsche Inflation. Eine Zwischenbilanz*, Gerald D. Feldman, Carl-Ludwig Holtfrerich, Gerhard A. Ritter, Peter-Christian Witt (eds.), Berlin-New York 1982, p. 204. For a specific example of this change in strategy see Gerald D. Feldman, *Arbeitskonflikte im Ruhrbergbau 1919—1922*, in: *Vierteljahreshefte für Zeitgeschichte*, 28, 2 (1980), pp. 168—223, especially pp. 199—201.

[38] Ludwig Preller, *Sozialpolitik in der Weimarer Republik*, Stuttgart 1949, p. 294.

[39] For statistics on wages and prices at this time see Arthur L. Bowley, *Prices and Wages in the United Kingdom, 1914—1920*, London 1921, pp. 70—71, 103—106. On the employers' adoption of harsher labor policies with the reversal of economic conditions see Keith Middlemas, *Politics in Industrial Society. The Experience of the British System Since 1911*, London 1979, pp. 154, 158—160.

[40] The similarity in workers' reaction in 1920/21 to the employers' adoption of less flexible labor policies, especially in the areas of wages and hours, i.e. with renewed militance, has been noted by Gerald D. Feldman, *Arbeitskonflikte im Ruhrbergbau*... [see note 37], p. 201.

The small size of strikes in the British chemical industry in 1923 is also probably related to the economic conditions prevailing at the time, but the exact nature of the mechanisms involved is unclear. On the one hand, because they tended to have less excess capacity than larger firms, the smaller British companies were likely to be more sensitive to the gradual improvement of the economy over the course of 1922 and 1923.[41] Thus, they might have been more vulnerable to strike threats and selected as targets for demands by the unions on this basis. On the other hand, it is possible that numerous smaller firms may have been so weakened by the depression of 1920—1921 that they could not afford a prolonged work stoppage which naturally would have made them particularly attractive points of action for workers fighting wage cuts or striving for pay increases. Obviously neither explanation excludes the other so both processes may have been at work. In any case, the experience of different size firms in Britain as well as in Germany at various times in the postwar economic cycle would appear to be an important factor in the observed shifts in strike size.

Strike Duration

Data on the duration of strikes in the British and German chemical industries is also contained in TABLES I and II. In neither country was there a uniform trend in this particular area of strike behavior. In each country the number of work days lost per striker fluctuated wildly over the course of 1919—1924. This naturally makes it difficult to generalize for the period as a whole, but the material does suggest that the average duration of strikes in both countries was shorter than before the war. In the case of Germany, where the statistical data is relatively straightforward, average strike duration in 1919—1924 was definitely shorter than in the prewar period — an average of 15.2 for the former period compared with 23.0 for the years 1890—1913. The situation in the British chemical industry is much less clear. Strike duration throughout 1919—1924 was shorter than in 1914, but it is questionable how repre-

---

[41] The yearly reports of the major British chemical firms from 1922 to 1924 indicate that production remained below capacity which suggests they felt little pressure from the market to accede any workers' demands. See *Die Chemische Industrie*, 46, Nr. 45, 3 October 1923, p. 629; 46, Nr. 46, 10 October 1923, p. 639; 47, Nr. 18, 3 May 1924, p. 218.

sentative the figure for 1914 is for the prewar era as a whole. The years 1910—1914 were ones of particularly intense labor conflict in England and any figures based solely on one or more of these years cannot be regarded as reliable indicators of the general prewar situation. Nonetheless, the difference in the duration of strikes in 1914 and the period 1919—1924 is noteworthy and it suggests that the shorter strike duration for this period (compared with the last prewar decades) observed in the German chemical industry may not have been an isolated development. If this is so, it would support the arguments of those who claim that there was a „modernization" of labor conflict in the late nineteenth and early twentieth centuries since these authors regard shorter duration as a crucial aspect of this process.[42] However, much more research needs to be done in this area before any definite conclusions can be drawn.

An examination of the duration of strikes in each country on a yearly basis suggests that this aspect of strike behavior was also influenced by cyclical economic factors, and thus, indirectly by inflation and deflation. Beginning with the German case, one notes that the average duration of strikes in 1919 and 1920 was relatively short, especially in comparison with the length of strikes before the war. In 1921 strike duration increased dramatically, but then in 1922 the figure fell once more. In 1923 strike duration declined even further and reached its lowest point for the period under study. During 1924 the duration of strikes increased dramatically, but even then it was still below the average for the prewar period.

The timing of these changes in strike duration in Germany suggests a connection with the inflation-conditioned *Konjunktur* of the German chemical industry. The relative brevity of strikes in 1919—1920 was no doubt influenced by the general political situation, but the generally conciliatory labor policies of the chemical employers were also due in part to the favorable business conditions which prevailed from approximately mid-1919 to mid-1920. If the chemical industrialists hoped to exploit this upswing to regain their former predominance in international markets, then labor conflicts, especially long ones, would have to be avoided. The actual record of labor relations in the chemical industry during 1919—1920 suggests that the employers strove to minimize

---

[42] H. Volkmann, *Modernisierung des Arbeitskampfes?*... [see note 1], pp. 138—13c, 166; E. Shorter/C. Tilly, *Strikes in France*... [see note 1], pp. 217—218, 343—344.

labor unrest and cultivate the goodwill of their workers and the relevant trade unions. This conciliatory policy can be seen in the speed in which the *Reichsarbeitsgemeinschaft (RAG) Chemie* was established in early 1919, the comparatively smooth course of wage negotiations at the regional and national level in late 1919 and early 1920, the relatively quick implementation of the *Betriebsrätegesetz* during the first half of 1920, and particularly in the *RAG Chemie's* unequivocal condemnation of the Kapp Putsch of March 1920.[43]

This is not to deny the very real conflicts which did occur between employers and workers or the trade unions in the chemical industry in 1919—1920. It is only to point out that during this phase of postwar developments the employers demonstrated a greater willingness to deal and co-operate with worker representatives as equal negotiating partners than had been the case before or during the war or was to be the case subsequently. Another factor which probably contributed to the short duration of strikes in 1919—1920 and should not be overlooked is that a number of them were at least partially inspired by food and other shortages. In such cases a quick solution was possible when the affected firm took steps to satisfy a minimum of the workers' most pressing needs.[44]

The longer duration of strikes in the German chemical industry in 1921 reflects the growth of a more cost-conscious, less conciliatory attitude among many employers, which has been discussed above. As business conditions worsened and the postwar revolutionary tide ebbed from mid-1920 onward, employers in all sectors of industry became less flexible in their dealings with workers.[45] This tendency appears to have

---

[43] On the history of employer organizations in the chemical industry before 1918—1919 and on the creation of the central chemical employers' association in 1919 see Dr. Jäckel, *Die Entstehung der Arbeitgeberorganisationen der chemischen Industrie*, Berlin no date (1921?), Bayer Archiv, 62/2. For a discussion of employer-trade union relations in the RAG Chemie over the course of 1919—1920 consult T. Berkel, *Geschichte der RAG Chemie*... [see note 36], pp. 37, 46, 52—54, 67, 82—83, 89—90, 101, 130—131, 139—143, 148—149. On the chemical employers' policies during and immediately after the Kapp Putsch see G. Feldman, *Big Business*... [see note 36], pp. 101—102, 111, 117, 121.

[44] In addition to the examples and sources cited in footnote 34 see the following sources for accounts of the tension generated in some of the major chemical centers by inadequate food supplies and high prices during 1919—1920. *Hoechster Kreisblatt*, 26 August 1919, 31 October 1919, 24 December 1919, 25 June 1920, 11 August 1920; *Bergische Arbeiterstimme*, 21 June 1919, 25 June 1919, 1 April 1920; *Pfälzische Post*, 30 August 1920, 5 October 1920.

[45] G.D. Feldman, *Political Economy*... [see note 37].

been particularly true of the largest chemical firms which were not only more sensitive to the changed economic conditions because of their heavy reliance on foreign markets but also tended to be in a better financial situation to weather a long strike than smaller undertakings. This was especially true of those large firms linked together in the famous *Interessengemeinschaft*. The provisions of the IG agreement of 1916 allowed a struck firm to farm out its contracts to other members of the IG and thus later recover at least some of the lost revenue through the IG's system of profit-sharing. This naturally reduced the risk of a major strike to any of the individual firms.[46]

The shorter duration of strikes in 1922 is perhaps best explained by the *Inflationskonjunktur* which the chemical industry enjoyed that year. As both domestic and foreign sales increased with the continued depreciation of the Mark most employers undoubtedly looked askance at any long work stoppage. Moreover, inflation tended to ease the actual financial burden which any wage increase placed on employers, further inclining them toward a quick settlement when only wages were at dispute. It should not be overlooked, however, that the same inflationary developments probably also reduced the willingness of the workers to engage in long strikes since an extended period of idleness meant financial disaster for them in the face of ever-rising prices. The extremely short duration of strikes in 1923 cannot be satisfactorily explained solely through specific employer policies. The chief expanation of this phenomenon was undoubtedly the inability of workers or unions to endure, much less win, a long strike under conditions of hyperinflation. Of course, the pressure on unions and employers to preserve at least a facade of national unity in the face of the French and Belgians following the occupation of the Ruhr undoubtedly also helped to bring quick settlements when strikes broke out. The increase in strike duration in 1924 was most probably due to a combination of harsher labor policies pursued by chemical employers in an attempt to deal with generally poor economic conditions and the workers' offsetting desire to resist this employer offensive wherever possible so as not

---

[46] To what extent membership in the IG affected the labor policies of the major German chemical firms is, of course, impossible to determine exactly. However, for a critical evaluation of the IG's influence in this area by an otherwise generally favorable commentator see Willi Kissel, *Die Interessen-Gemeinschaft der deutschen Teerfarben-Industrie unter besonderer Berücksichtigung der erzielten Ergebnisse*, Wirtschafts- und Sozialwiss. Diss., Köln 1925, pp. 115—116.

to sacrifice any more of the gains of the November Revolution. The strike and lockout at BASF from March to May 1924 in connection with the employers' attack on the 8-hour day is a prime example of this type of conflict.

The timing of shifts in strike duration in the British chemical industry over 1919 suggest that here economic factors also played a role, although perhaps not so obviously as in the German case. The duration of strikes in 1919 was relatively long but fell noticeably in 1920. In 1921 the average length of strikes increased slightly, but then in 1922 it rose sharply to its highest level during the period under review. Strike duration fell markedly in 1923 and was only slightly longer in 1924.

The length of strikes in 1919 is somewhat surprising given the generally favorable business conditions of that year. It seems likely that in this instance „political" factors were of overriding importance. Although there was widespread popular support for various types of social reform immediately following the First World War, there was also a distrust and fear of „excessive" and „revolutionary" demands on the part of workers; a state of affairs which the British government did its best to foster and manipulate through its campaign against „Bolsheviks" in the trade unions and the shop stewards movement.[47] This political climate may have reinforced the ingrained reluctance of many employers in the chemical industry to accede to any workers' demands that appeared to challenge their traditional powers in regulating the conditions of work, especially since the need for concessions did not appear as great as in Germany where political revolution and major social upheaval created a very different environment for industrial relations.[48] This is supported by the fact that many of the longest strikes in the British chemical industry in 1919 centered on the issue of

---

[47] The literature on this subject is relatively extensive, but here I rely primarily in the accounts of K. Middlemas, *Politics in Industrial Society*... [see note 39], pp. 130—133, 143—150 and B.-J. Wendt, *Deutsche Revolution*... [see note 3], pp. 21—22. 24—27. Other, more extensive, accounts can be found in Branko Pribicevi'c, *The Shop Stewards Movement and Workers Control, 1910—1922*, Oxford 1959, Walter Kendall, *The Revolutionary Movement in Britain 1900—1921. The Origins of British Communism*, London 1969; Rodger Charles, *The Development of Industrial Relations in Britain 1911—1939*, London 1973.

[48] For the attitudes and labor policies of English employers in general at this particular time see K. Middlemas, *Politics in Industrial Society*... [see note 39], pp. 146—147. On the traditional labor policies typical of some of the large chemical employers see W.J. Reader, *Imperial Chemical Industries*... [see note 13], pp. 233—234.

reduced hours of work, an aspect of working conditions which the employers traditionally regarded as subject to their decision alone.[49] The shorter duration of strikes in 1920 is perhaps best explained by a more flexible attitude on the part of employers in view of the good business conditions in the first half of the year, when most of the strikes occured, in conjunction with a decline in the number of strikes concerned with such particularly contentious issues as length of the working day, trade union recognition, and so forth (which had given the conflicts of 1919 a highly symbolic value to both sides and so inspired a number of long drawn-out strikes).[50]

The increase in strike duration in 1921 and especially 1922 is undoubtedly linked to the employers' reluctance to concede anything to workers in the face of the depressed conditions of these years. However, the longer duration also suggests that when workers did strike during these years, the dispute was likely to have been viewed by them as particularly intractable and consequently carried out with greater resolution on their part as well. The shorter duration of strikes in 1923 and 1924 suggests that as economic conditions slowly improved some employers were once again more interested in avoiding long work stoppages. Yet the higher failure rate of strikes in these years, which the Ministry of Labour strike data reveal, suggests that the unions found it difficult to win a strike, let alone a long financially-draining one, in the face of high levels of unemployment and declining membership and, thus, also had an interest in brief strikes.[51] In both Britain and Germany it would seem that cyclical economic developments, which were at least in part conditioned by inflationary and deflationary developments, affected the willingness and ability of both employers and workers in the chemical industry to engage in long strikes.

---

[49] The strike reports contained in the Ministry of Labour records Lab 34/38 at the PRO Kew Gardens indicate that while only one out of every three strikes in the chemical industry in 1919 involved the question of hours, four of the five longest strikes in that year raised this issue.

[50] PRO Kew Gardens, Ministry of Labour, Lab 34/39. The number of strikes involving either the question of hours or union recognition in addition to wage hikes fell from 7 in 1919 to 3 in 1920 while the number of strikes involving wage increases alone rose from 5 in 1919 to 8 in 1920.

[51] The problems plaguing the unions with members in the chemical industry are discussed by J. Eaton, et al., *Growth of Trade Unionism...* [see note 35], p. 144 and R. Hyman, *The Workers Union...* [see note 35], pp. 128—129.

Strike Intensity

Finally, TABLES I and II also contain information over the number of work days lost per strike, which can be viewed as an indicator of the general intensity of strike. The figures show that, as in the case of strike size, strike intensity (which is strike participation multiplied by duration) was significantly greater in Germany than in England for all years except 1920. However, the year to year variation in strike duration in each country discussed above worked in such a way that the difference in strike intensity was not usually as great as in strike size. A comparison of the level of strike intensity in the chemical industry of each country reveals several interesting points which once again indicate the influence of economic developments on short-run strike behavior during the period 1919—1924.

In the case of Germany, the year with the highest level of strike intensity was 1921, followed at some distance by 1922. The year with the lowest level of strike intensity was 1923 while 1920 had the second lowest level. This particular constellation suggests definite connections between the German chemical *Konjunktur* and strike intensity. 1921 was a year of particularly intense conflict because, as indicated earlier, many chemical employers sought to cope with the less favorable business conditions of mid-1920 to autumn 1921 through labor policies aimed at increasing productivity and which usually eliminated or modified concessions made to workers earlier. This led to intense strike activity especially in the larger firms. This was a dramatic change from 1920 when favorable business conditions, at least through the first half of the year, had helped keep strike intensity at a relatively low level, certainly below that of 1919. The lower level of strike intensity in 1922 was due in part to the employers' victories in 1921, which caused disillusionment and apathy among many workers, but it also reflects the effects of revitalized business activity. The improved performance of the chemical industry in 1922, which resulted from the depreciation of the Mark, enabled many employers to pay relatively high wages and thus defuse worker discontent to some extent.[52] Yet the very pace of inflation was such that it was almost impossible for wages to keep up

---

[52] Nominal and real wages in the chemical industry during this phase of the postwar inflation are exceptionally hard to determine, but for an idea of general trends see Rudolf Meerwarth, *Zur neuesten Entwicklung der Löhne*, in: Zeitschrift des Preußischen Statistischen Landesamt, 62, 3/4 (1923), pp. 327—340.

with prices, making wage disputes inevitable, which explains why 1922 still had the second highest level of strike intensity in this period.

The dramatic drop in strike intensity in 1923 was due to the unique conditions created by hyperinflation, in particular to its disastrous effect in the ability of workers to engage in protracted strikes. Thus, although discontent among workers was certainly high, their economic and organizational weakness vis-à-vis the chemical employers meant this discontent was only rarely translated into major strikes.[53] The higher level of strike intensity of the German chemical industry in 1924 was due to the particular bitterness of the few strikes that did occur. The workers resented the employers' efforts to place the main burden of the crisis on their backs while, simultaneously, the employers dogmatically pursued this goal.

The links between fluctuations in the level of strike intensity and short-run economic changes is less obvious in the British chemical industry, but several developments do stand out. The year in which strike intensity was greatest was 1920 with 1922 in second place. 1921 was also a year of relatively high strike intensity, but 1919 and especially 1923—1924 were years with a low level of strike intensity. As indicated earlier, 1920 was marked by particularly large-scale strikes. These strikes arose in large part because workers demanded wage increases to compensate for sharp price increases in the spring and summer at the same time that employers felt compelled to resist any pay hikes because of signs of the coming depression. The level of strike intensity was significantly lower in 1921 because the workers did not feel in a position to stop cuts through strike action given the miserable business condi-

---

[53] In August—September 1923, Bayer, Weiler-ter Meer, the Leunawerke, and Agfa's Treptow plant all experienced labor unrest, but only at Bayer were the number of workers involved significant. Yet this relative lack of conflict is deceptive because the available evidence suggests there was a great deal of discontent among chemical workers, but it was kept in check by the workers' fear of the potentially disastrous consequences of any strike action on their already precarious financial situation under conditions of hyperinflation. The desperate plight of the already unemployed was an obvious and persistent reminder to chemical workers of the risks they would run in any work stoppage. This point has been cogently made in the case of the BASF by D. Schiffmann, *Arbeit und Konflikt*... [see note 2], pp. 460—470. For a description of the August unrest at Bayer see U. Stolle, *Arbeiterpolitik im Betrieb*... [see note 2], pp. 89—92. On the situation at Farbwerke Hoechst see *Hoechster Kreisblatt*, 11—13 October 1923; 27 October 1923; *Freie Presse*, 1 June 1923; 7 July 1923; 7 August 1923; 19 September 1923.

tions and high level of unemployment that existed.[54] Strike intensity increased slightly in 1922. Although there were fewer strikes and strikers than the preceding year because of the poor conditions which continued to prevail in the industry, the few strikes which did occur tended to be long bitter contests. The dramatic drop in strike intensity in 1923 and 1924 was due primarily to a marked decline in the length of strikes in the chemical sector, which was in part conditioned by recent economic developments. Improving business conditions likely made some employers more willing to accede to worker demands, an idea supported by the higher percentage of successful strikes (as opposed to only partially successful strikes) in 1923—1924 than in 1921—1922.[55] Thus, fluctuations in the level of strike intensity in the German and British chemical industries also appear to have been linked to economic developments which occured at the same time.

The absence of reliable figures on the number of strikes in the German chemical industry during the prewar period and of data in general for the English industry before 1914 makes it difficult to assess how strike intensity in the two countries in 1919—1924 was different from that in the prewar years. In the case of the German chemical industry the available material suggests that the level of strike intensity in these years was greater than in the prewar period. Although strikes tended to last longer in Germany before the First World War, they involved fewer participants. In the English chemical industry the intensity of strikes was relatively high in 1914 so that while strike intensity was higher in the years 1920—1922, it was lower in 1919 and especially in 1923—1924. However, it is unclear how representative the level of strike intensity in 1914 is for the last prewar decades as a whole. Thus, it is impossible to state whether strike intensity in the British chemical industry in the period 1919—1924 as a whole was greater or lesser than in the prewar period. More research in this area is obviously required before we can ascertain to what extent long-run trends in strike intensity in the British and German chemical industry paralleled one another

---

[54] *Quarterly Report of the National Amalgamated Union of Labourers*, December 1921, p. 41.

[55] According to the records of the Ministry of Labour, Lab 34/39—34/42, in 1921 and 1922 there were no „successful" strikes in the British chemical industry while in 1923 the figure was 25 % and in 1924 it was 11 %. During the same years the proportion of „compromise" settlements was: 1921 = 71.4 %, 1922 = 100 %, 1923 = 33.3 %, and 1924 = 44.5 %).

or diverged. Until these long-run trends are known more exactly, it is impossible to judge if this aspect of strike behavior reflected the „modernization" of labor conflict that some researchers argue occurred over the later nineteenth and early twentieth centuries.

IV

The Role of Inflation and Deflation

This study of strike activity in the British and German chemical industries in 1919—1924 highlights not only the influence of cyclical economic developments in short-run fluctuations in strike behavior during these years but also the vital role of inflationary and deflationary developments in this whole process. As stated at the outset, the effect that inflation and deflation *per se* had on strike activity in the chemical industries of Germany and England is impossible to assess exactly since their impact on strike behavior was indirect. Although inflation and deflation subtly affected the entire social-political framework in which industrial relations and labor unrest took place, it was primarily through their effect on short-run business conditions that these twin phenomena exerted an influence on the extent and nature of strikes in the German and British chemical industries. It is through the mediating agency of short-term economic trends, or *Konjunktur*, that we must principally seek the linkage between inflation/deflation and strike activity. A brief review of some of the major aspects of strike activity in the British and German chemical industries during 1919—1924 can perhaps offer some idea as to the multifaceted nature of these linkages.

In the area of strike frequency, the experience of the German and British chemical industries in 1919—1924 suggests a correlation between inflation, economic expansion, and high strike frequency on the one hand, and another between deflation, economic concentration, and low strike frequency on the other hand. The German chemical industry consistently had a greater number of strikes than its English counterpart. There can be little doubt that this higher strike frequency was intimately bound up with the *Hochkonjunktur* which the German industry experienced over the greater part of this period. Likewise, it is clear that these favorable business conditions were in large part due to the depreciation of the German Mark during the same years. The smaller number of strikes which the English chemical industry experienced in these years, especially in 1921—1924, was certainly linked to the depressed conditions which generally prevailed in it, and the British economy in general, after the brief postwar boom of 1919—1920 ended. The exact role which the deflationary policies adopted and pursued by the British government after 1920 played in bringing about the severe depression of 1921 and then slowing recovery over 1922—1924 is subject to debate, but it was certainly a major contributory factor to both developments. The apparent connections between inflation and higher strike frequency and deflation and lower strike frequency discovered in this particular study would seem to be significant, but far more research is required in this area to examine and test these linkages. In particular, studies of other industries are necessary to determine if the chemical industry was representative of general tendencies in strike frequencies or if it was an exception.

The findings of this paper on changes in strike size in the German and British chemical industries suggest that inflation and deflation exert an influence over the level of strike participation as well. Year to year fluctuations in strike size in each country indicate that under conditions of inflation or deflation different size firms were the locus of strike activity. However, unlike the case of strike frequency, inflation and deflation do not appear to have worked in opposite directions, but rather to have exerted a similar downward pull on strike size in both Germany and England. The mechanisms or mediations involved in this process, however, were quite different in the two countries. For example, in the German chemical industry there was a tendency for strike size to be somewhat smaller in years of inflation. This suggests that inflation allowed the larger, export-oriented firms to reduce labor management disputes through the payment of high wages; a tactic that smaller firms could not pursue because they tended to profit less from inflation. The result was a greater proportion of strikes in small and medium-sized firms.

In Britain, however, strike size in the chemical industry declined markedly from its postwar high in 1920 with the onset of depression in 1921. However, the chief cause of lower levels of strike participation here does not appear to have been due to differences in labor policies on the part of employers, but rather the weakness of the unions which experienced drastic membership losses in 1921—1923 due to the depression. This weakness compelled the unions to focus their strike activity on smaller, weaker firms if they hoped to maximize their success. The drastic decline in strike size in the German chemical industry in 1924 is largely the result of similar developments. The different mechanisms through which inflationary and deflationary developments in the German and British economies affected strike size reveals the complexity of the processes involved. To gain further insight into the impact inflation or deflation had on levels of strike participation in different countries after the First World War we need a great deal more research into strike size in different industries in various countries and the economic, social and political framework in which changes in strike participation occured.

Developments in the German and British chemical industries during 1919—1924 also indicate a connection between inflation, economic expansion, and shorter strikes in the one hand, and another connection between deflation, economic contraction, and longer strikes on the other hand. At the risk of oversimplification, one can argue that in both Germany and England years of favorable economic conditions, which were usually associated with periods of inflationary monetary and fiscal policies, tended to be ones in which strike duration was relatively short. In contrast, strike duration tended to be longer in years of economic contraction or stagnation, such as 1921 and 1924 in Germany and 1921—1922 in England, which were also years of either relative price stability or actual deflation.

Exceptions to this general pattern of change in strike duration during these years, such as 1923 and 1924, point out the influence of other factors whose role naturally also must be considered if we are to thoroughly understand the dynamics of strike behavior in the postwar years. In the case of England in 1923—1924, short strike duration is probably attributable to the combined influence of improving economic conditions, making long work stoppages unattractive to employers, and the continued weakness of the unions due to earlier membership losses in 1921—1922, which made them less inclined to risk long strikes. In other cases though, different factors may have been at work; factors such as short-run political developments or long-run structural changes in the economy or society which it has been impossible to deal with in this essay. The overall tendency for strike duration to decline in both the British and German chemical industries over 1919—1924 suggests the influence of just such political or structural factors. Detailed research into changes in the economic, social, and political framework of labor relations of different countries is a prerequisite for understanding the particular influence which inflation or deflation may have exerted on changes in strike duration.

Variations in strike intensity in the English and German chemical industries after the First World War suggest that inflation and deflation also exercise an influence on this aspect of strike behavior. However, as in the case of strike size, which is one of the determinants of intensity along with duration, the exact nature of this influence is not always clear. It appears that no common pattern existed in the role of inflation or deflation in strike intensity in Germany and Britain at this time. Instead inflation and deflation seem to have had somewhat contradictory effects on strike intensity in the two countries. In the German chemical industry periods of greater inflationary developments, such as 1919—1920 and 1922—1923, were marked by lower levels of strike intensity while periods of either relative or absolute price stability, such as 1921 or 1924, promoted a higher level of strike intensity. In England the reverse tended to be true with strike intensity highest in 1920, which was a year marked by price increases, and then falling over the course of 1921—1924, years of deflationary government policies and economic depression.

This apparently contradictory impact of inflation and deflation in England and Germany may be somewhat illusory. It is extremely difficult to classify each separate year as totally dominated by either inflation or deflation since these had their own special phases that did not follow the calendar. Consequently, strikes in any one year do not necessarily reflect the influence of only one particular trend. For example, the high level of strike intensity in the English chemical industry in 1920 undoubtedly mirrors the discontent of workers in the face of inflationary price hikes, but there can be little doubt that it was also due in part to the growing reluctance of employers to grant concessions after early 1920 when the government began to implement its deflationary policies and signs of an economic downturn increased. Likewise, the low level of strike intensitiy in Germany in 1923 only partly reflects the ameliorating effect of inflation in labor disputes. It was also due to a growing sense that the inflation-inspired *Scheinkonjunktur* was headed for an unforeseeable but probably disastrous end, which led workers to be more cautious about risking their incomes or jobs through strike action. Political factors linked to the government's policy of passive resistance, especially the idea of national unity in the face of the French and Belgians, also probably served to hinder strike activity for a good part of 1923. Detailed analytical studies of the chronology of strikes and the phases of inflationary developments in both countries are certainly desirable, and they might reveal a common pattern in changes of strike intensity which is not obvious on the basis of the yearly statistics employed in this study.

Limitations of space have compelled this paper to focus on only a few aspects of strike behavior in the British and German chemical industries in 1919—1924. However, there is ample evidence that economic developments associated with inflation and deflation affected other areas of strike activity as well. These other effects should be noted for they indicate the multitude of ways in which cyclical economic developments inspired by inflationary or deflationary policies could shape strike behavior. Published and unpublished material of the Ministry of Labour and the *Reichsarbeitsministerium* indicate that the proportion of „offensive" strikes, e. g. those inspired by workers' demands on employers, tended to predominate in both the British and German chemical industries during the periods of economic expansion which accompanied inflationary policies in each country. Similarly, „defensive" strikes, e. g. those inspired by workers' resistance to employer initiatives (often backed by threat of a lockout), predominated during the economic downswings which tended to follow deflationary policies.[56] The long *Inflationskonjunktur* of the German chemical industry meant that there was a far larger number of „offensive" strikes in Germany than in England.

There ist also evidence that the economic conditions inspired by inflation and deflation affected the success rates of strikes in the two chemical industries. For example, in the German chemical industry years of greater inflationary price increases, such as 1920 or 1922, also tended to be the years in which the percentage of „successful" strikes (as opposed to „compromises" or „failures") was higher. A somewhat similar pattern also appears to have existed in the British chemical industry with the lowest percentage of successful strikes in the depression years of 1921—1922.[57] Thus, not only strike frequency, size, duration, and intensity were affected by the very different economic conditions inspired by inflation and deflation, but the nature of strike demands and the success/failure rate of strikes was also partly shaped by inflationary or deflationary developments. Further research into strike activity in different industries in Britain and Germany, and other countries as well, during the economically-troubled years of 1919—1924 may reveal even more ways in which inflation and deflation affected strike behavior.

[56] *Reichsarbeitsblatt* (nichtamtlicher Teil), Neue Folge, 2, 9 (1922), p. 286; 3, 4 (1923), p. 80; 3, 11 (1923), p. 240; 4, 15 (1924), p. 361; 6, 4 (1926), p. 228; Ministry of Labour, 34/38—34/42.
[57] *Ibid.*

Summary

It is virtually a truism that over short periods of time cyclical economic developments can greatly influence strike behavior. Many monographs and articles have shown that years of economic expansion tend to have higher levels of industrial unrest than years of economic contraction. This essay will demonstrate that this pattern was also true for the English and German chemical industries in the period 1919—1924. It seeks to trace certain crucial aspects of strike behavior such as frequency, size (in terms of participants) duration, and overall intensity and then relate these changes to simultaneous developments in the economic position of the chemical industry of the two countries in order to illustrate the importance of cyclical economic factors on strike patterns in the turbulent postwar years.

At the same time, the essay emphasizes the way in which inflationary and deflationary developments in the years 1919—1924 helped shape these short-run economic fluctuations and thus had a crucial if indirect effect on labor unrest during the period under review. Between 1919 and 1924 there were periods of pronounced inflation and deflation in both Germany and England. Phases of economic expansion tended to correspond with the periods of inflation while phases of economic contraction or recession were generally associated with the periods of deflation. Methodological problems make it impossible to directly assess the effect which inflation and deflation *per se* may have had on strike activity in the two chemical industries during these years, but the correspondence of periods of inflation with those of economic expansion, when strike activity tended to increase, and periods of deflation with those of economic decline, when strike activity usually waned, suggests a strong albeit indirect link between inflationary or deflationary trends and the level of strike activity. This linkage was mediated through general economic developments, which were, of course shaped by many factors in addition to inflation or deflation. Nonetheless, it is clear that one cannot understand either short-run economic fluctuations or short-run variations in strike behavior between 1919 and 1924 without reference to the role of inflation and deflation.

Die sozialen Folgen der englischen Wirtschaftskrise 1921/22 am Beispiel des „Engineering Lock-out" im Frühjahr 1922[1]

BERND-JÜRGEN WENDT

I

Zur Fragestellung

Die exemplarische Behandlung der großen Aussperrung in der englischen Metall-, Maschinen- und Schiffbauindustrie vom 11. März bis zum 13. Juni 1922 *(Engineering Lock-out)*[2] im Rahmen des Projektes bietet sich unter folgenden fünf Aspekten an:
1. Hier läßt sich beispielhaft nachweisen, wie die Kriegsentwicklung mit ihrer Aufblähung der staatlichen Nachfrage und der Produktionskapazitäten gerade im metallverarbeitenden Sektor, ihrem technologischen Modernisierungsschub (Ausbau der Massen- und Serienfabrikation), ihren dadurch bedingten nachhaltigen Strukturwandlungen auf

---

[1] Für die finanzielle Unterstützung bei den Forschungsreisen nach England sei an dieser Stelle der Stiftung Volkswagenwerk gedankt. Weiterhin danke ich für wertvolle Hilfe beim Besuch einschlägiger Archive und Bibliotheken sowie für die Vermittlung von Kontakten den Herren M. G. Thickett und E. E. Toms von der Britischen Botschaft in Bonn.

[2] Die Darstellung basiert vorwiegend auf den Archivalien im TUC-Archiv, Congress House, London: „Engineers' Dispute 1922", Box TB 19, 9/6/18, File 18, sowie auf den Periodika der A.S.E./A.E.U. *A.S.E. Monthly Journal and Report;* ab August 1920: *A.E.U. Monthly Journal and Report; A.S.E. Half-Yearly and Yearly Reports, 1918; A.S.E. Annual Report, 1919; A.E.U. Half-Yearly Reports, 1920—1922;* vgl. auch PRO: LAB 2/642. A 68/1922 I.R. 1208/1922. Vgl. weiter Günther R. Degen, *Shop Stewards. Ihre zentrale Bedeutung für die Gewerkschaftsbewegung in Großbritannien,* Frankfurt/Main-Köln 1976; J. B. Jefferys, *The Story of the Engineers,* London 1945; A. I. Marsh, *Industrial Relations in Engineering,* London 1965.

dem Arbeitsmarkt (Probleme der „*dilution*") sowie ihrer Verlagerung des Sozialkonfliktes von den Spitzenverbänden an die betriebliche Basis (Aufstieg der Shop Stewards) und die — nach einem kurzen wirtschaftlichen „Zwischenhoch" 1919/20 — dann im Herbst 1920 vehement einsetzende Nachkriegsdepression im Grunde nur Konflikte in den Sozialbeziehungen aktualisiert und dann mit sektoral unterschiedlicher Intensität dramatisch zugespitzt haben, die seit dem letzten Viertel des 19. Jahrhunderts vor allem in diesem Sektor angelegt waren. Sie hingen untrennbar mit dem technologischen Wandlungsprozeß zusammen, wie er gerade die Metallindustrie auszeichnete. Modernisierungs- und Rationalisierungsvorgänge in der Metallverarbeitung waren untrennbar verknüpft mit dem Übergang zur Fließbandarbeit, zum Akkordlohnsystem und anderen Formen des leistungsbezogenen Lohnes und zu einer stärker arbeitsteiligen Aufsplitterung der Produktion selbst; dies hatte wichtige Rückwirkungen auf einen Strukturwandel in der Zusammensetzung der Arbeiterschaft: Einer Dequalifizierung breiter Schichten stand gleichzeitig die Aufwertung eines qualifizierten Facharbeiterstammes gegenüber; der überkommene „craftism" wurde herausgefordert durch den neuen Typ des angelernten „machine man" und „handy-man"; die Tatsache, daß hochqualifizierte Wartungs-, Reparatur- und Ausbildungsarbeiten der „maintenance workers" weiterhin auf Zeit-, minderqualifizierte und repetitive Arbeiten der „production workers" jedoch zunehmend auf Akkordlohnbasis verrechnet wurden, führte zu Verzerrungen im Lohngefüge und entsprechender Mißstimmung in der Facharbeiterschaft. In Antwort auf den technologischen Wandel mußten zeitgemäße Gewerkschaftsstrategien entwickelt werden: Es galt, im Übergang vom „craft" zum „industrial unionism" nun auch stärker die An- und Ungelernten und die Frauen zu erfassen. Der gewerkschaftliche Kampf um die Beschickung und Kontrolle der neuen Maschinen *(manning)* und gegen die Einführung des Leistungslohnsystems sowie auf dem Ausbildungssektor um die Einflußnahme auf die Lehrlingsausbildung *(apprenticeship)* hatte ausgesprochen defensive Züge einer Verteidigung des traditionellen Einflusses auf den Produktionsprozeß auch unter den neuen Bedingungen des Wandels; innergewerkschaftliche Organisationsprobleme entwickelten sich im Spannungsfeld zwischen zentralistischem Spitzenverband und innerbetrieblichen Selbständigkeitsbestrebungen an der Basis um den Shop Steward als neuen Kristallisationskern; aus neuen Frontenbildungen im Arbeitskonflikt entwickelten sich neue Verfahrensregelungen zu seiner Regulierung. Auf den grundsätzlichen Charakter dieser Erscheinungen hat unter anderen Eric Hobsbawm hingewiesen: „... der Kern der neuen Industriellen Revolution lag in einem Industriezweig, der bis dahin überwiegend auf einer handwerklichen Basis von hochbezahlten, mit viel Selbstvertrauen ausgestatteten Arbeitern getragen worden war: in der Metallindustrie und im Maschinenbau. Hier mußte der Übergang zum neuen System viel bewußter zu Ende gedacht und ausgefochten werden als anderswo. Auch kann es nicht überraschen, daß als Folge davon die Metallarbeiter, die bis dahin sehr konservativ waren, in den meisten Ländern zu typischen Führern kämpferischer Arbeiterbewegungen wurden. Die Geschichte solcher Bewegungen seit der Aussperrung in Großbritannien im Jahre 1897 kann daher größtenteils als eine Geschichte der Metallarbeiter geschrieben werden..."[3]

2. Die mehr langfristigen Modernisierungs- und Wachstumsprobleme im englischen Wirtschaftsorganismus seit dem letzten Viertel des 19. Jahrhunderts mit ihren tiefgreifenden Rückwirkungen auf die Sozialbeziehungen verschärften sich kurzfristig innerhalb von wenigen Wochen mit dem vergleichsweise plötzlichen Abklingen des inflationären Nachkriegsbooms im Winter 1920/21 und dem Einsetzen der Weltwirtschaftskrise. In ihr wurde eine international-konjunkturbedingte Talfahrt für etwa zwei Jahre noch zusätzlich durch eine einseitig fiskalisch induzierte, monetär am Ziel einer Wiederherstellung der Vorkriegsparität des Pfundes (£ = $ 4.86) auf Goldbasis ausgerichtete und seit 1918 zielstrebig wesentlich vom Schatzamt und von den Rücksichten auf die USA diktierte, vielfach sogar gegen den Widerstand der Außenwirtschaftskreise durchgesetzte Deflationspolitik beschleunigt. So warnte die „Federation of British Industries", der Spitzenverband der englischen Industrie, schon 1918 das „Committee on Currency and Foreign Exchanges" (Cunliffe Committee), das Pfund mit rein monetären Mitteln wieder auf die Vorkriegsparität hinaufzudrücken und darüber das innere Preisniveau und die Absatzchancen der Ausfuhrindustrien zu mißachten. Goldstandard und starkes Pfund auf dem Vorkriegswert könnten demgegenüber nur langfristig natürliches Ergebnis eines florierenden Exports und eines kräftigen Leistungsbilanzüberschusses sein und nicht umgekehrt.[4] Lord Cunliff und sein

---

[3] Eric J. Hobsbawm, *Labouring Men*, London 1964, p. 359sq. zit. nach G. R. Degen, *Shop Stewards*... [wie Anm. 1], S. 47.

[4] Vgl. Bernd-Jürgen Wendt, *Aspekte der britischen Nachkriegsentwicklung zwischen Inflation und Deflation in Europa 1919 bis 1922*, in: Historische Prozesse der deutschen

Nachfolger als Gouverneur der Bank von England, Montague Norman, beharrten demgegenüber, unterstützt vom Schatzamt und von der Londoner City, auf dem Primat der Währungspolitik und lehnten alle Forderungen, diese im Zeichen sinkender internationaler Nachfrage den Erfordernissen einer aktiven Konjunkturpolitik unterzuordnen, strikt ab. Mit dieser deflatorischen Zielsetzung steckte der Staat wesentlich mit den Rahmen ab, in dem sich der Wirtschaftsablauf und die Sozialbeziehungen 1921/22 entwickelten: Verteuerung des Geldes durch Heraufsetzung des Diskonts am Budget Day, dem 15. April 1920, von 6 auf 7 %, zielbewußte Drosselung der öffentlichen Ausgaben und Nachfrage mit dem Ziel des Haushaltsausgleiches im Chamberlain-Budget 1920/21, Primat der Schuldenbedienung und -tilgung mit einem nationalen Schuldendienst 1920/21 von £ 350 Mill. bei einem Ausgabenvolumen von insgesamt £ 1,195 Mrd.[5] Angesichts einer staatlichen Wirtschaftspolitik, die recht einseitig an der Währungspolitik orientiert war, Warnungen insbesondere der Außenwirtschaft ignorierte und das Heil auch für den Außenhandel vor allem von der Vorkriegsparität und der Stärkung des Pfundes erwartete, mußte die zentrale Frage also lauten: Wie haben sich zum einen die Metallunternehmer in ihrer Lohn- und Unternehmenspolitik auf die konjunkturell-deflationistische Doppelkrise von 1920/21 mit einem raschen Sinken der Weltnachfrage und einem — teils von innen, teils von außen induzierten — lang anhaltenden deflationären Preisverfall (so sanken etwa die Großhandelspreise zwischen Mai 1920 und Dezember 1921 um 50 %) eingestellt, und welche Gegenstrategien haben zum anderen die Metallgewerkschaften zur Verteidigung ihres materiellen und sozialen Besitzstandes entwickelt. Hier wird das Augenmerk vor allem auf der führenden, im Sommer 1920 durch Verschmelzung von zehn kleineren Einzelgewerkschaften als Nachfolgerin der traditionsreichen und bereits siebzig Jahre alten A.S.E. gegründeten „Amalgamated Engineering Union" (A.E.U.) liegen.

3. Die strategischen Grundpositionen wie auch die mehr oder minder geschickte propagandistische Verpackung für die Öffentlichkeit lassen sich besonders dicht und geschlossen durch zwei ausführliche Propa-

---

Inflation 1914—1924. Ein Tagungsbericht, hrsg. von Otto Büsch und Gerald D. Feldman (= Einzelveröffentlichungen der Historischen Kommission zu Berlin, Bd. 21), Berlin 1978, S. 405 ff.

[5] Board of Trade, *Statistical Abstract for the United Kingdom for Each of the Fifteen Years from 1912 to 1926*, 71st Number, April, 1928, p. 111sqq.

gandaschriften der Arbeitgeber und der Gewerkschaften — *The Present Economic Position of the Engineering and Allied Industries* und in Antwort darauf *Some Comments on „The Present Economic Position of the Engineering and Allied Industries"* — nachweisen. Mit diesen Schriften läuteten der Spitzenverband der Metallarbeitgeber, „The Engineering and the National Employers' Federation", und die A.E.U. im Frühjahr 1921 unter großem Widerhall in der Öffentlichkeit ihren mehr als einjährigen Konflikt ein und begleiteten ihn dann ständig. Damit aber gewinnen die vordergründigen Konfliktpunkte der Aussperrung — Festlegung von Überstunden, Einführung von Akkord- und sonstigen Leistungslöhnen, gewerkschaftliche Vertretung und Beschäftigung von Lehrlingen, Entscheidung über die Beschickung neuer Maschinen (*manning*) — erst ihre eigentliche Tiefenschärfe im Kontext der Deflationsdepression und ihrer sozialen Kosten sowie der internationalen Wirtschaftskrise der frühen zwanziger Jahre.

4. Der „Engineering Lock-out" stellte mit all seinen zeittypischen Erscheinungen, seinem Konfliktmuster und seinem Ausgang eine letzte Aufgipfelung der sozialen Gärungen der Nachkriegszeit dar, die alle wichtigen Produktionssektoren — besonders den Bergbau, das Eisenbahnwesen, das Transportwesen sowie die Eisen- und Stahlindustrie — erfaßt hatten und die enormen Anpassungs- und Normalisierungsschwierigkeiten der Rekonstruktionsperiode im Übergang von der staatlichen Kriegs- zur reprivatisierten Friedenswirtschaft kennzeichneten.

5. Schließlich ist nicht nur in der zeitgenössischen Propaganda immer wieder zwischen dem deflationierenden und krisengeschüttelten England und dem inflationierenden Kontinent mit Deutschland an der Spitze verglichen und die deutsche Konkurrenz als *die* große Herausforderung an die britische Metallindustrie begriffen worden; hier eröffnet sich auch heute eine Möglichkeit, innerhalb des gleichen Leitsektors zweier Volkswirtschaften — der metallverarbeitenden Industrie — durch den Vergleich eines deflationierenden und von den Folgen der Weltwirtschaftskrise heimgesuchten (England) und eines in der kurzfristigen Scheinblüte eines Inflationsbooms stehenden Landes (Deutschland) nationale Besonderheiten und transnationale Gemeinsamkeiten der modernen Industriewirtschaft schärfer herauszuarbeiten und zu akzentuieren.

II

Die Hintergründe der Aussperrung in der englischen Metall-, Maschinen- und Schiffbauindustrie im Frühjahr 1922

Die strukturellen Probleme der Industriebeziehungen in der metallverarbeitenden Industrie Englands in der Zwischenkriegszeit laufen sowohl in der zeitgenössischen Argumentation als auch in der sozialgeschichtlichen Forschung im wesentlichen alle immer wieder auf einen markanten Fluchtpunkt zurück: die sogenannten „Terms of Settlement" vom Januar 1898.[6] Im Kern handelte es sich dabei um eine Neuauflage der Kapitulationsurkunde der A.S.E. nach dem ersten großen „Engineering Lock-out" 1851/52.[7] Nach einer mehrwöchigen Aussperrung der Metallarbeiter im Herbst und Winter 1897, in der es vorwiegend um die Durchsetzung der 48-Stunden-Woche, um Mindestlöhne, den Abbau von Überstunden, Abgrenzungsprobleme fachlicher Qualifikation im Arbeitsprozeß, um die Beschickung neuer Maschinen mit Un- und Angelernten oder Jugendlichen, im Kern aber ebenso wie schon 1851/52 um die Verteidigung der überkommenen „craft regulations" und „restrictive practices" gegenüber dem Vordringen vehement und extensiv beanspruchter „principles of managerial prerogatives" ging, wurde die A.S.E. am Ende zur Annahme von Bedingungen gezwungen, die den gewerkschaftlichen Einfluß am Arbeitsplatz entscheidend beschnitten: Das „General Principle of Freedom to Employers in the Management of Their Works" wurde garantiert und im Betrieb jede Einmischung seitens der Arbeitnehmer und ihrer Repräsentanten in die „managerial functions" verboten.

---

[6] Vgl. Keith Burgess, *The Origins of British Industrial Relations*, London 1975, p. 49sq.; R. O. Clarke, *The Dispute in the British Engineering Industry, 1897—1898. An Evaluation*, in: *Economica*, new Series, 24 (May 1957); H. A. Clegg/A. Fox/A. F. Thompson, *A History of British Trade Unions since 1889*, Vol. 1: *1889—1910*, Oxford 1964, p. 161sqq.; J. B. Jefferys, *The Story...* [wie Anm. 2], p. 141sqq.; B. C. M. Weekes, *The Amalgamated Society of Engineers 1880—1914: A Study of Trade Union Government, Politics and Industrial Policy*, unpublished Ph. D. Thesis, University of Warwick, 1970.

[7] K. Burgess, *Technological Change and the 1852 Lock-Out in the British Engineering Industry*, in: *International Review of Social History*, 14 (1969); ders., *Trade Union Policy and the 1852 Lock-Out in the British Engineering Industry*, in: *International Review of Social History*, 17 (1972).

Konkret hieß dies im einzelnen: Freiheit des Arbeitgebers, jeden, Gewerkschafter oder Nicht-Gewerkschafter, einzustellen, und damit Aufhebung und Verbot des „closed shop"; Recht des Betriebes auf Akkordarbeit zu individuell ausgehandelten Stücklöhnen mit einer gewissen Verhandlungsvollmacht der Gewerkschaften für ihre Mitglieder; Beschränkung der Überstunden auf maximal 40 innerhalb von vier Wochen; Freiheit der Firmenleitung, nicht gewerkschaftlich organisierte Arbeitnehmer zu gegenseitig vereinbarten Löhnen ohne Mitsprache der Gewerkschaften einzustellen, und damit die Möglichkeit, angesichts eines damals noch relativ niedrigen Organisationsgrades und heftiger Ressentiments gegenüber den alten Facharbeitergewerkschaften in der breiten Masse der Arbeiterschaft den kollektiven Tarifvertrag zu unterlaufen, zumal da seine Unabdingbarkeit und Allgemeingültigkeit (im Gegensatz zu Deutschland ab 1918) in England bis heute nicht rechtlich fixiert ist; keine Begrenzung der Lehrlinge im Verhältnis zu den Gesellen und damit Aufhebung eines der ältesten und wichtigsten zünftischen Rechte der „craft unions", durch einseitige Beschränkung und zeitliche Festlegung der Lehrlingsausbildung (oft auf sieben Jahre) das Arbeitskräfteangebot auf dem Markt für ausgebildete Fachkräfte zu regulieren und gegebenenfalls zu verknappen; Recht des Arbeitgebers, eine Maschine mit jedem passend erscheinenden „machine operator" ohne Mitsprache der Gewerkschaften zu einem gegenseitig individuell vereinbarten Lohn zu besetzen. Damit gerieten, da damals infolge des niedrigen Organisationsgrades noch ein erheblicher Teil der Metallarbeiter individuellen Verträgen unterlag, die Tarifpolitik der A.S.E. und mit ihr das gesamte „collective bargaining" unter einen permanenten Druck. Die alte Monopolstellung des Facharbeiters drohten ebenso wie die „common rules" eines ganzen Standes nachhaltig unterhöhlt zu werden. Eine außerdem zwischen den Spitzenverbänden — der A.S.E. und der 1896 gegründeten „Engineering Employers' Federation" /E.E.F. — vereinbarte Verfahrensordnung „Provisions for Avoiding Disputes" sah für den Konfliktfall in der Auslegung der „Terms of Settlement" oder bei Tariffragen eine strikte Institutionalisierung und Formalisierung der Konfliktlösung in drei Stufen — betriebliche Ebene, lokale oder Distrikt-Ebene, Zentralkonferenz zwischen den Spitzenverbänden — vor. Hier wurde der Arbeitskonflikt bereits nach der untersten Ebene der Schlichtung (Belegschaft *versus* Management/Vorarbeiter) im Falle eines Scheiterns aus dem Betrieb hinaus auf die Verbandsebene verlagert und damit den Einflüssen der unmittelbar Betroffenen am Arbeitsplatz und ihrer Vertrauensleute

(Shop Stewards) entzogen. Dies geschah mit dem Ziel, künftig im Zusammenspiel der Spitzenverbände sogenannte wilde Streiks an der Basis zu verhindern und inoffizielle Konfliktträger im Betrieb wie „unofficial shop committees" der strengen Kontrolle gewerkschaftsbürokratischer Autorität zu unterwerfen. Hinzu kam, daß alle Gewerkschaftsmitglieder bis zur Abwicklung des gesamten dreistufigen Konfliktlösungsverfahrens, das sich oft über Wochen erstrecken konnte, strikt der Friedenspflicht unterlagen und im Falle der Verweigerung damit rechnen mußten, daß ihr Streikverhalten als „verfahrenswidrig" *(unconstitutional)* oder „nicht genehmigt" *(unofficial)* eingestuft und jeder Anspruch auf gewerkschaftliche Unterstützung damit verwirkt wurde. Diese Regelung blieb im wesentlichen auch in der Zwischenkriegszeit in Kraft. Sie enthielt aber von Anfang an einen explosiven Zündstoff, der erst 1922 nach der Aussperrung verfahrensmäßig eindeutig zuungunsten der Gewerkschaften entschärft wurde: Während die Unternehmer entschieden darauf beharrten, daß einseitig diktierte innerbetriebliche Maßnahmen auch mit dem einschneidenden Charakter von „material changes" wie die Neuaufstellung von Maschinen, die Umorganisation ihrer Bedienung, die Ersetzung von Facharbeitern durch angelernte Maschinisten, die Einführung von Akkordarbeit oder die Verfügung von Überstunden und Schichtarbeit *sofort* auch gegen den Widerstand der Belegschaft und ihrer Repräsentanten innerhalb und außerhalb des Betriebes umgesetzt und damit bereits während des Abspulens der „Disputes Procedures" durchgeführt werden mußten, so daß eine präjudizierende Wirkung derartiger Maßnahmen auf die anschließenden Schlichtungsverhandlungen der verbandlichen Gremien und auf die schließlichen Lösungsregelungen keineswegs auszuschließen war, bestanden die Gewerkschaften beharrlich auf der Bewahrung des innerbetrieblichen und organisatorischen *Status quo*, bis alle Möglichkeiten einer schiedlich-friedlichen Einigung bis hinauf zur Spitze erschöpft und gegebenenfalls die Friedenspflicht damit abgelaufen war.

Seit dem ausgehenden 19. Jahrhundert lagen also die Konfliktmuster und -ursachen sowie die Frontenbildungen fest. Sie waren zugleich Ausdruck und Folge des tiefgreifenden und dynamischen technologischen Wandels von Produktion, Arbeitsplatzorganisation und Zusammensetzung der Arbeiterschaft. Dieser Wandel war in der Zwischenkriegszeit noch keineswegs abgeschlossen und nahm unter den Bedingungen der Weltkrise 1921/22 eine besonders konfliktträchtige Form an: Ging es den Gewerkschaften um Statuserhalt ihrer Facharbeiterschaft und eine Abwendung der Dequalifizierung, um Arbeitsplatzsicherung durch die Blockierung von „systematic overtime", um die Verhinderung einer erhöhten Ausbeutung durch die verschiedenen Systeme von Leistungslöhnen, um die Verteidigung des überbetrieblichen, kollektiven Tarifvertrages als Rückgrat eines hohen gewerkschaftlichen Organisationsgrades gegenüber innerbetrieblichen und individuellen Abschlüssen und Akkordfestsetzungen, um ein Mitspracherecht bei der Besetzung neuer Maschinen *(manning of machines)*, um eine Monopolstellung auf dem Arbeitsmarkt durch strenge Kontrolle der Ausbildung *(regulation of apprenticeship)*, kurz, um Mitwirkung und Kontrolle bei der Festsetzung der Arbeitsbedingungen im Betrieb und außerhalb, so setzten sich demgegenüber die Arbeitgeber entschieden zur Wehr gegen alle Versuche einer „trade union interference with management functions". Sie bestanden darauf, über die Einführung von Akkordlöhnen bei einer Standardisierung und Mechanisierung der Produktionsabläufe und beim Übergang zur Fließband- und Serienproduktion autonom entscheiden, die Besetzung neuer Werkzeugmaschinen mit an- und ungelernten Arbeitskräften *(machine men)* zu niedrigeren Lohnsätzen selbständig nach Maßgabe der Produktionserfordernisse gegenüber den alten Ansprüchen der Dreher *(turner)* und Schlosser *(fitter)* verfügen, die Senkung der Selbstkosten durch eine intensivere Ausnutzung des bestehenden Kapitalstocks und Maximierung der Produktivität ohne Einspruch durchsetzen und die Arbeitsplatzorganisation nach eigenem Gutdünken gestalten zu können. Das strikte Beharren auf den „managerial prerogatives" und der „power to manage" im Interesse erhöhter Effizienz und einer Senkung der Stückkosten stieß auf den Exklusivitätsanspruch der alten Facharbeitergewerkschaften und ihren „craft conservatism" bei der Verteidigung von tradierten „craft regulations", deren durch „Herkommen und Sitte" *(custom and practice)* verbürgte Ausweitung zu umfassenden innerbetrieblichen Mitbestimmungsrechten im Zeichen eines ungebrochenen Wirtschaftswachstums bis in die siebziger Jahre hinein kaum Kopfzerbrechen bereitet hatte, deren Durchsetzung jedoch seit dem ausgehenden 19. Jahrhundert und vor allem in der Krise der Zwischenkriegszeit unter den Bedingungen nachlassender Zuwachsraten, verschärfter internationaler Konkurrenz und schließlich einer allgemeinen wirtschaftlichen Stagnation auf immer hartnäckigeren Widerstand seitens der Unternehmer traf.

Die „Disputes Procedures" von 1898 wurden nach den ausgedehnten Streikwellen der letzten drei Vorkriegsjahre am 17. April 1914 in den

„Provisions for Avoiding Disputes" des sogenannten York Memorandums, genannt nach dem Tagungsort der regelmäßig stattfindenden Spitzengespräche der Verbände, erneut und in der Substanz unverändert verankert. Sie erfuhren nach den umfangreichen „wilden" Arbeitsniederlegungen besonders in der Rüstungsindustrie während des Krieges und der zunehmenden Verselbständigung der Belegschaften und ihrer Shop Stewards gegenüber der Kontrolle der Gewerkschaftsbürokratien, die sich seit dem „Treasury Angreement" vom März 1915 freiwillig zum sozialen Burgfrieden und zur staatlichen Zwangsschlichtung während des Krieges verpflichtet und damit selbst ihrer traditionellen sozialen Sanktionsinstrumente wie des Streikrechts praktisch zeitweilig begeben hatten, in den „Regulations Regarding the Appointment and Functions of Shop Stewards and Works Committees", die am 20. Mai 1919 zwischen den Spitzenverbänden vereinbart wurden, eine wichtige Ergänzung: Nunmehr wurden die Shop Stewards und von ihnen halbparitätisch mit Vertretern des Managements beschickte „Works Committees" zwar offiziell in die Konfliktregulierung auf der betrieblichen Ebene auf einer zweiten und dritten Stufe eingegliedert, bevor das Verfahren dann im nächsten Schritt gemäß den weiterbestehenden „Provisions for Avoiding Disputes" von 1898/1914 aus dem Betrieb hinaus auf die lokale Distriktebene in die alleinige Verantwortung der Organisationen und ihrer Vertreter verlagert wurde; gleichzeitig wurden sie aber nach ihren unkontrollierten und nicht selten auch politisch radikalisierten Emanzipationsbestrebungen im Kriege nunmehr wieder domestiziert, in einen reglementierten Verfahrensgang integriert und dadurch der strikten Aufsicht ihrer Gewerkschaften unterworfen: „Shop Stewards shall be subject to the control of the Trade Unions, and shall act in accordance with the rules and regulations of the Trade Unions and agreements with employers so far as these affect the relation between employers and work-people" ([d] General. 8.); „Employers and shop stewards and works committees shall not be entitled to enter into any agreement inconsistent with agreements between the federation or local association and the Trade Unions" ([d] General. 11.). Mit diesem „Procedure Agreement" besiegelten die beiden Spitzenverbände, „The Engineering and the National Employers' Federation" und die A.S.E., in der gleichgerichteten Absicht einer gemeinsamen Ausräumung und Entschärfung basisnaher und unkontrollierbarer Konfliktpotentiale und einer Disziplinierung und Neutralisierung ihrer möglichen Träger und Kristallisationskerne offiziell das Ende des wenige Jahre vorher noch so gefürchteten „Shop Steward

Movement". Immerhin aber beließ dieses in mehreren Stufen 1898/1914/1919 aufgebaute rechtlich-normative Rahmenwerk zur Konfliktvermeidung noch hinreichend konfliktträchtige Freiräume kontroverser Auslegung im Falle einer radikalen Verschlechterung der materiellen Situation und der „industrial relations". Hier galt der Erfahrungssatz, daß freiwillig vereinbarte und gesetzlich nicht besonders fixierte soziale Normen nur soweit trugen, wie beide Kontrahenten, im vorliegenden Falle die Tarifparteien, zum beiderseitigen Vorteil an ihrer Aufrechterhaltung interessiert waren und vor allem wie die ökonomischen und politischen Zustände es zuließen. Die Wirtschaftslage änderte sich mit dem plötzlichen Einbruch der Nachkriegskonjunktur im Herbst 1920 so nachhaltig, daß die „disputes procedures" den Belastungen zunächst nicht mehr standhielten. Der Angriff erfolgte nicht nur von der Arbeitgeberseite, die die Normen jetzt extrem restriktiv auslegte, sondern auch von den Arbeitern in den Betrieben, die unter dem Druck der allgemeinen Wirtschaftsmisere die erwähnte leidige Status-Quo-Frage, die praktisch seit zwei Jahrzehnten ungelöst im Raume gestanden hatte, zum Anlaß nahmen, um den erreichten sozialen und materiellen Besitzstand zu wahren.

Die Unternehmer trugen über ihren Spitzenverband vom Frühjahr 1921 an in auffallender Synchronisation ihren Angriff nach zwei Richtungen — gesellschafts- und lohnpolitisch — vor und trafen damit die Gewerkschaften in ihrer doppelten Funktion als Verteidiger sowohl des sozialen Facharbeiterstatus *(craft regulation)* als auch des wirtschaftlichen Lebensstandards empfindlich: Sie drängten zum einen strukturell auf eine schärfere Eingrenzung der „proper functions of the Trade Union" und der „restrictive pratices" zugunsten ihrer eigenen „managerial functions" und eines Ausbaues ihrer direktorialen Entscheidungsgewalt im Betrieb und zum anderen materiell auf einen raschen Abbau des Kriegsbonus und weiterer inflationsbedingter Zusatzzahlungen der letzten Jahre mit dem — zweifellos nicht ganz unberechtigten — Hinweis auf den seit Ende 1920 zu beobachtenden schrittweisen Rückgang der Lebenshaltungskosten:[8] Die Nahrungsmittelpreise erreichten im November 1920 mit 291 (1914 = 100) ihren Höhepunkt, um dann nach dem Jahreswechsel rasch von 278 Anfang

---

[8] Die Indexzahlen sind zusammengestellt aus *Statistical Abstract for the United Kingdom*... [wie Anm. 5], p. 93sqq., und aus den laufenden Jahrgängen von *The Labour Gazette* hrsg. vom Ministry of Labour, Vol. 26 (1918) — 30 (1922).

Januar auf 218 im Juni 1921 zu sinken. Der allgemeine Preisindex der *Labour Gazette*, der neben den Nahrungsmitteln auch Bekleidung, Miete usf. eines Arbeitenehmerhaushaltes einschloß, zeigte eine ähnlich fallende Tendenz: Dem Höhepunkt im November 1920 mit 276 (1914 = 100) folgte ein rascher Abfall auf 219 im Juni/Juli 1921.

Schon im Januar/Februar 1920 zeichnete sich bei den regelmäßigen Spitzenkonferenzen zwischen Vertretern der A.S.E. und der „Engineering and National Employers' Federation" ab,[9] daß die fortdauernde Auseinandersetzung um die 47-Stunden-Woche — für die Gewerkschaften lediglich eine vorläufige Plattform auf dem Wege zur 44-Stunden-Woche, für die Arbeitgeber das wirtschaftlich an sich nicht mehr vertretbare Maximum an Zugeständnissen — und um die Einführung von Leistungslöhnen in ihrem Kern auf die stets umstrittene Abgrenzung zwischen der Dispositionsfreiheit des Managements im Betrieb auf der einen und dem gewerkschaftlichen Mitbestimmungsrecht bei der Ausgestaltung der Arbeitsbedingungen auf der anderen Seite zielte. Überstunden und Leistungslöhne sollten bei ihrer Einführung in einem Betrieb grundsätzlich an die gewerkschaftliche Zustimmung gebunden werden.

An der Lohnfront forderten die Arbeitgeber den Abbau der Kriegs- und der inflationsbedingten Nachkriegszuschläge, die teilweise durch staatliche Lohnämter zunächst für die Rüstungsindustrien festgesetzt und dann weiter auch auf den zivilen Sektor ausgedehnt worden waren, in Höhe von 6s. plus 12 1/2 % War Bonus auf den Wochenverdienst für Zeitlöhne und 15 % plus 7 1/2 % War Bonus auf Akkordlöhne. Durch diese Zuschläge hatte sich der durchschnittliche Tarifwochenlohn eines Metallfacharbeiters bis Ende Dezember 1920 bei einer Reduktion der Wochenstundenzahl von 53/54 auf 47 Stunden gegenüber 1914 um 120—130 %, eines ungelernten Arbeiters dagegen um über 200 % erhöht. Dies führte zu einer bemerkenswerten Einebnung der ursprünglich sehr differenzierten Lohnstrukturen zwischen *skilled* und *unskilled workers*. Kam ein Schiffbauer im Zeitlohn vor dem Krieg auf 41s. 4d/Woche und ein ungelernter Arbeiter im Schiffbau auf 22s. 10d., so verminderte sich diese Differenz bis Ende 1920 auf 91s. 3d. resp. 70s. 4d.[10] Ungünstiger noch sah es für die Facharbeiter aus, wenn man ihren wöchentlichen Tariflohnanstieg bis zum 31. 12. 1920 auf 220—230

---

[9] *A.S.E. Monthly Journal and Report*, No. 2, February, 1920, p. 21 sqq.
[10] *The Labour Gazette* Vol. 29 — No. 1, January, 1921, p. 63.

(1914 = 100) korreliert mit dem etwa gleichzeitigen Höhepunkt der allgemeinen Preisentwicklung bei 291 für Nahrungsmittel und 276 für die allgemeinen Lebenshaltungskosten einer Arbeiterfamilie. Auch hier schnitten die ungelernten Arbeiter relativ mit einem Index von 300 im Vergleich zur Vorkriegszeit weitaus besser ab.

Vermehrt auftretende Verweigerungen von Überstunden seitens der Belegschaften, sofern nicht vorher die Zustimmung der örtlichen Gewerkschaften eingeholt war, die Ablehnung des Stücklohnsystems bei der Fa. Hick, Hargreaves and Co. in Bolton sowie die bei mehreren metallverarbeitenden Firmen erhobenen Forderungen lokaler Gewerkschaftsbeamter, neue Werkzeugmaschinen entweder auch weiterhin mit Facharbeitern — Drehern — oder zumindest mit Maschinisten zum Facharbeiterlohn zu besetzen, selbst wenn es sich um Serienherstellung mit relativ niedrigem erforderlichem Qualifikationsgrad bei der Bedienung handelte, führten am 7. April 1921 zur ersten Androhung einer Aussperrung seitens des Unternehmerverbandes für den Fall, daß die Arbeitsverweigerungen und die Eingriffe in die „managerial functions" nicht sofort aufhörten.[11] Damit war der Konflikt in der Metall-, Maschinen- und Schiffbauindustrie eröffnet.

Die Gewerkschaften gaben lediglich an der Lohnfront vergleichsweise schnell nach: Angesichts einer Arbeitslosenziffer von 31,9 % der gewerkschaftlichen Organisierten im Juni 1921 (25,3 % der gesamten Metallarbeiterschaft), ein Rekord, in dem sich zugleich die Folgen des großen Bergarbeiterstreiks vom Frühjahr 1921 ausdrückten, stimmten sie nach harten Verhandlungen, ohne einen Arbeitskampf zu riskieren, einer Aufhebung der Zuschläge des Jahres 1920 in zwei Etappen — Juli und August je 3s. Zeitlohnzuschlag und 7 1/2 % Akkordzuschlag — und einer solchen des War Bonus in drei Schritten — 1. November/1. Dezember/1. Januar 1922 je 1/3 von 12 1/2 % resp. 7 1/2 % zu. Dies ergab für Facharbeiter auf Zeitlohnbasis eine wöchentliche Lohnsenkung von insgesamt 16s. oder 17—18 %, für ungelernte Arbeiter von 20 %. Die generelle Lohnsenkung 1921 lag ebenfalls im Schnitt bei 20 %, der Rückgang des Nahrungsmittelindex im gleichen Zeitraum dagegen bei 33,5 %, des allgemeinen Lebenshaltungskostenindex bei 27,4 %. Bei den Metallfacharbeitern lagen Ende Februar 1922 die wöchentlichen Tariflöhne um 80 % bis 90 % über denen der Vorkriegszeit, bei den ungelernten Arbeitern immer noch 150 % höher. Der Nah-

---

[11] *A.E.U. Monthly Journal and Report*, new issue, No. 10, May, 1921, p. 12sqq.

rungsmittelindex war bis zum 28. 2. 1922 jedoch nur auf 177 (1914 = 100), der Gesamtindex auf 186 gefallen, so daß sich die Spanne zwischen dem Preisniveau und den wöchentlichen tariflichen Durchschnittslöhnen im Grunde kaum verringerte.

Während die Gewerkschaftsführungen diese Lohnvereinbarungen zweimal, im Juli und Oktober 1921, mit Erfolg einer Urabstimmung vorlegen konnten, blieben ihnen Zustimmung und Gefolgschaft der Basis in den grundsätzlichen gewerkschaftlichen Status- und Machtfragen im Winter 1921/22 versagt, so daß sich hier die Fronten am Ende entscheidend bis zum offenen mehrmonatigen Arbeitskampf verhärteten.

Der Konflikt entzündet sich allgemein an den Verhandlungen über eine praktische Umsetzung der am 19. November 1918 bei vollem Lohnausgleich erkämpften 47-Stunden-Woche (vorher 54-Stunden-Woche) vor allem im Schicht- und Akkordsystem und um die Angleichung der verschiedenen Lohnstrukturen. Sie wurden von der A.E.U.-Führung, obwohl damals mit dem Arbeitgeberverband ausdrücklich vereinbart, nur relativ unlustig geführt. Denn diese stand bereits seit Frühjahr 1919 unter dem Druck der Forderung nach Einführung der 44-Stunden-Woche seitens der Mitglieder. Konkret ging es dann ab April 1921 um eine Interpretation des am 30. September 1920 ebenfalls zwischen den Spitzenverbänden abgeschlossenen Überstunden- und Nachtschichtenabkommens. Kernpunkt des Dissens war der Absatz (j) in dem Teil „Overtime on Dayshift": „The Federation and the Trade Union agree that systematic overtime is deprecated as a method of production and that when overtime is necessary the following provisions shall apply, viz.: — No Union workman shall be required to work more than 30 hours overtime in any four weeks after full shop hours have been worked, allowance being made for time lost through sickness, absence with leave, or enforced idleness." Weitere Ausnahmen von dieser 30-Stunden-Beschränkung betrafen unter anderem Probefahrten im Schiffbau, dringende Reparaturen und einzuhaltende Lieferfristen, anstehende Ersatzleistungen oder Änderungen im Interesse des Arbeitgebers oder des Kunden.

Umstritten war und blieb die Auslegung der Begriffe „systematic overtime" und „necessary". Vor dem Hintergrund einer Massenarbeitslosigkeit von knapp 2 Millionen oder 16,2 % der Versicherten auf ihrem Höhepunkt im Winter 1921/22, davon etwa 146 000 oder 27,3 % der gewerkschaftlich organisierten Metallarbeiter[12] — allein in der

---

[12] Ende Dezember 1921 waren von 425 714 eingeschriebenen Mitgliedern der A.E.U.

A.E.U. war damit jeder Vierte bis Fünfte arbeitslos —, waren die Belegschaften geneigt, über die „Notwendigkeit" von Überstunden ein entschiedenes Mitspracherecht im Betrieb zu beanspruchen und das vereinbarte Verbot „systematischer" Überstundenregelungen im Rahmen des normalen Produktionsprozesses so extensiv auszulegen, daß es ab Frühjahr 1921 immer mehr zu „wilden" Arbeitsverweigerungen über die 47-Stunden-Woche hinaus an der betrieblichen Basis *(overtime ban)* kam. Nur so hoffte man verhindern zu können, daß durch „systematische" Überstundenarbeit den zahlreichen arbeitslosen Kollegen Arbeitsplätze vorenthalten oder wegrationalisiert wurden.

Demgegenüber sahen die Arbeitgeber angesichts der Tatsache, daß zwar die Auftragsbücher teilweise aus dem vorhergehenden Jahr *noch* relativ gefüllt beziehungsweise die Aufträge noch im Fertigungsprozeß waren, aber kaum noch Neuaufträge, vor allem aus dem Ausland, hereinkamen und deshalb in absehbarer Zeit eine empfindliche Drosselung der Produktion unabdingbar würde, nicht selten in Überstundenregelungen ein willkommenes, wenn auch infolge der 50 %igen Zuschläge nicht ganz billiges Mittel, um auf die unsichere Absatzlage relativ flexibel reagieren und die einlaufenden oder eingelaufenen Aufträge noch zügig und fristgerecht abwickeln zu können, ohne sich durch Neueinstellungen für eine recht ungewisse Zukunft noch unnötige Personalkosten aufbürden zu müssen. Ab April 1921 lag dieser Konfliktpunkt seitens der Arbeitgeber auf dem Verhandlungstisch der Spitzenverbände, und es wurden den Gewerkschaftsführern auch Sanktionen in Form von Aussperrungen angedroht, sofern sie ihre Anhängerschaft nicht soweit unter Kontrolle hätten, um sie von unbedachten Überstundenverweigerungen abzuhalten. Diese Drohungen stützten sich — formal berechtigt und nicht ungeschickt — auf das von den Gewerkschaftsführungen im Zusammenhang mit der Arbeitszeitverkürzung am 19. November 1918 eingegangene Versprechen, mit allen Mitteln dafür Sorge zu tragen, „that in the critical state through which the country has to pass the greatest possible output will be secured and maintained" (Absatz 3 des gemeinsamen Memorandums vom 19. 11. 1918 über die Verkürzung der Wochenarbeitszeit).

Freilich stieß die starre und auf dem Prinzipiellen beharrende Ver-

---

in 2013 Ortsverbänden *(branches)* 92 426 oder 26,5 % arbeitslos, Ende Januar 1922 waren es mit 92 884 Mitgliedern von 409 219, organisiert in 2008 Ortsverbänden, 27,03 %.

handlungsführung des Arbeitgeberführer Sir Allan Smith[13] auch im eigenen Lager auf Kritik und Unverständnis. Denn es wurde bezweifelt, ob es überhaupt opportun sei, die Überstundenregelung in einem Augenblick zur grundsätzlichen Frage der „managerial functions" mit dem Risiko eines Arbeitskampfes hochzuspielen, da abzusehen war, daß sie sich infolge einer rapiden Verschlechterung der Auftragslage bald von selbst erledigen würde. Auch seien mit diesem Streitpunkt, lautete der Vorwurf an Sir Allan, schwierige Probleme angesprochen, die durch einen Arbeitskampf sowieso nicht gelöst werden könnten. Ein Arbeitskampf gerade in diesem Augenblick der allgemeinen, vor allem der finanziellen Schwäche der Gewerkschaften und über diesen Punkt werde nur die negative Rückwirkung haben, die Autorität der Gewerkschaftsführungen ohne Not zu unterminieren und dadurch die Unruhestifter an der Basis zu stärken. Die Funktionäre des Spitzenverbandes, die Sir Allan überall in die Distrikte vor Beginn der Aussperrung entsandte, hatten Schwierigkeiten „to enlighten their members of the seriousness of the issues involved".[14] So gab es nach dem Bericht des staatlichen Chief Conciliation Officer aus Birmingham an das Arbeitsministerium[15] in dem Distrikt der „Coventry Engineering Employers' Federation" überhaupt keinen aktuellen Anlaß von Bedeutung, der den drastischen Schritt der Aussperrung gerechtfertigt hätte, „...and the rank and file Employers no less than the Union members need to have the issue explained and, in some cases, to be convinced that the proper time and method of forcing these issues have been taken at Headquarters". Auch gab es Anzeichen wie etwa den Protest der „Midland Engineering Employers",[16] daß die einzelnen Distrikte des Arbeitgeberverbandes sich gegen die „autocratic attitude" der Spitze wehrten und Verhandlungen mit der A.E.U. auf Distrikt- und lokaler Ebene vorzogen.

---

[13] Zu Sir Allan Smith und seiner zentralen Rolle bei der Gründung des Arbeitgeberverbandes „National Conferation of Employers' Organisations" (NCEO) 1919 vgl. Keith Middlemas, *Politics in Industrial Society. The Experience of the British System since 1911*, London 1979, pp. 113, 127sq., 146.

[14] Bericht des Chief Conciliation Officer für die Midlands aus Birmingham an das Arbeitsministerium vom 27. Februar 1922, in: PRO: LAB 2/642. A 68/1922 I.R. 1208/1922.

[15] *Ebda.*

[16] Pressebericht „Engineering Dispute" vom 3. 3. 1922, in: PRO: LAB 2/642. A 68/1922 I. R. 1208/1922.

Im Herbst 1921 verbanden die Metallarbeitgeber dann erstmalig die aktuelle Überstundenfrage ultimativ mit dem Grundproblem der „managerial functions" und des *Status quo* und setzten am 17./18. November 1921[17] bei den sehr vorsichtig und gemäßigt taktierenden A.E.U.-Führern eine verschärfte Vereinbarung durch, deren umstrittene Auslegung dann den Konflikt der folgenden sieben Monate bestimmen sollte. Im allgemeinen 1. Teil des gemeinsamen Memorandums wurde grundsätzlich festgestellt: „The Trade Union shall not interfere with the right of the Employers to exercise managerial functions in their establishment and the Federations shall not interfere with the proper functions of the Trade Union." Nach einem Hinweis auf die bekannten und nach wie vor gültigen Verfahrensregelungen im Konfliktfall vom 7. 4. 1914 (York Momorandum) und 20. 5. 1919 (Shop Stewards und Works Committee Agreement) unter Punkt 2 räumt der entscheidende Punkt 3 dann endgültig mit der *Status-Quo*-Vorstellung der Gewerkschaften und ihrer Mitglieder bei innerbetrieblichen „material changes" (dies galt auch für Überstundenregelungen) auf: „Instructions of the Management shall be observed pending any question in connection therewith being discussed in accordance with the provisions referred to" (das heißt, gemäß den unter Punkt 2 aufgeführten Verfahrensregelungen, Wdt). Der Teil II „Overtime" übertrug diesen Grundsatz noch einmal ausdrücklich auf das Überstundenabkommen vom 30. September 1920 und dekretierte: „... the Employers have the right to decide when overtime is necessary, the workpeople or their representatives being entitled to bring forward under the provision referred to (gemeint sind wiederum die Verfahrensregelungen im Konfliktfall, Wdt) any cases of overtime they desire discussed. Meantime the overtime required shall be proceeded with." In diesem Falle der Überstundenregelung erwies sich, was die Arbeitnehmer mit Recht für sich geltend machen konnten, das „disputes procedure" als ein besonders fragwürdiger Schutz, da Überstunden in der Regel sehr kurzfristig und *ad hoc* je nach besonderem Arbeitsanfall im Betrieb angesetzt wurden und infolgedessen hier ein langwieriger und bürokratischer Konfliktregelungsmechanismus überhaupt nicht rechtzeitig und mit Erfolg greifen konnte. Die Diskussionen in den folgenden Wochen und Monaten,

---

[17] The Engineering and the National Employers' Federation. The Amalgamated Engineering Union. Memorandum of Conference held on 17th and 18th November 1921. Overtime Question, in: PRO: LAB 2/642. A 68/1922 I.R. 1208/1922.

auch in den drei Monaten der Aussperrung, bewegten sich immer wieder um die drei zentralen Punkte: (a) gegenseitige konkrete Abgrenzung von „managerial functions" und „proper functions of the Trade Union", (b) Forderung nach zumindest einvernehmlicher und gemeinsamer Feststellung der „Notwendigkeit" von „nichtsystematischen Überstunden" und (c) Verlangen nach einer gewissen, freilich höchstens auf 14 Tage begrenzten Notifikationsfrist für „material changes" inklusive Überstundenregelungen durch die Betriebsführung, so daß die Belegschaften die Möglichkeit hätten, die Konfliktlösungsverfahren in diesen zwei Wochen zumindest in den ersten Stufen in Gang zu setzen, ohne daß die Anordnungen der Betriebsleitung bereits in Kraft traten (befristete *Status-Quo*-Regelung).

Die hier aufgeworfene prinzipielle Frage eines gewerkschaftlichen Mitwirkens am „management of the shops" *(shop control)*, zu der der ganze Überstundenkonflikt hochstilisiert wurde, war eine der schwierigsten in den Industriebeziehungen, und wenn sie erst einmal von einer Seite auf den Tisch gelegt wurde, in dieser generellen Form kaum lösbar.

Das mehrmonatige Tauziehen um die Auslegung des Textes des Memorandums vom 17./18. November 1921 verkomplizierte sich noch dadurch, daß die Arbeitgeber strikt darauf bestanden, unter Punkt II „Overtime" die Formulierung „the workpeople or their representatives" so eng zu interpretieren, daß unter „... their *representatives*" nur betriebsinterne Vertreter der Belegschaft verstanden wurden, nicht jedoch Gewerkschaftsvertreter von außen, so daß die „*organizer*", also Repräsentanten des örtlichen Gewerkschafts-Büros oder des Distriktes, erst relativ spät in die Stufenfolge der Verfahrensregelungen einbezogen wurden, auf jeden Fall erst nach Ablauf der Notifikationsfrist. Hier wurde schon damals von den Arbeitgebern das uns heute sehr geläufige Problem „gewerkschaftlicher Fremdbestimmung" in einem Betrieb von außen her hochgespielt und den Gewerkschaften vorgeworfen, sie wollten mit Hilfe dieser Fremdbestimmung durch ihre „organizers" (nicht „representatives"!) die Belegschaft nur aufwiegeln und einen Keil zwischen Betriebsführung und Betriebsangehörige treiben. Die alte, heftig umstrittene Frage seit dem ausgehenden 19. Jahrhundert nach der Intensität und Wirkungskraft gewerkschaftlicher Kontroll- und Mitbestimmungsrechte im Betrieb war also nach wie vor auf dem Tisch und noch keineswegs ausdiskutiert, und die Angst vor der gewerkschaftlichen Fremdbestimmung eines privaten Unternehmens ist es ganz wesentlich, die bis heute die Arbeitgeber in England vor dem Modell der wirtschaftlichen Mitbestimmung in Deutschland und der möglichen Aussicht, einmal mit Gewerkschaftsvertretern zusammen im Vorstand *(Board of Directors)* sitzen zu müssen, entschieden hat zurückschrecken lassen.

Am 27. Januar 1922 lehnten die Mitglieder der A.E.U. das November-Memorandum in einer Urabstimmung mit 50 240 gegen 35 525 Stimmen ab. Entscheidend für dieses Ergebnis waren wohl mit die Proteste der Arbeitslosen gegen Überstunden jeder Art und die grundsätzliche Weigerung, Errungenschaften, die als Ergebnis des Krieges in der Kontrolle über den Produktionsprozeß bereits gesichert schienen, wieder aufs Spiel zu setzen. Demgegenüber schien sich freilich die Mehrheit der Gewerkschaftsmitglieder, wie das Abstimmungsverhalten zeigt, entweder von der Überstundenfrage überhaupt nicht angesprochen zu fühlen, oder sie stand Überstunden sowieso positiv gegenüber, da sie eine Aufbesserung der Wochenlöhne brachten, oder sie war nach Ausweis der Quellen auch nicht bereit, Überstunden im Betrieb zu verweigern und einen Arbeitskampf zu riskieren, weil dann immerhin zu befürchten stand, daß vakante Arbeitsplätze umgehend mit einem Arbeitslosen besetzt werden würden.

So konnten es sich auch die Unternehmer in den folgenden Wochen und Monaten nicht verkneifen, zum einen auf die niedrige Abstimmungsquote überhaupt von 21 % der Mitgliedschaft hinzuweisen und zum anderen aus der Tatsache, daß sich insgesamt nur 12,3 % der Mitglieder für eine Ablehnung des Memorandums ausgesprochen hätten, den recht öffentlichkeitswirksamen Vorwurf abzuleiten, eine an sich gemäßigte und vernünftige Gewerkschaftsführung lasse sich von einer kleinen Minderheit radikaler Rebellen in den Betrieben majorisieren. Die daraufhin für den 11. März 1922 erklärte nationale Aussperrung aller A.E.U.-Mitglieder geschah durchaus in dem Bewußtsein, daß die A.E.U. mit ihren schwindenden finanziellen Mitteln nur 14 Tage werde durchhalten können. Sie wurde noch dadurch verschärft, daß die Arbeitgeber auch den anderen Metallarbeitergewerkschaften, die an sich überhaupt nicht in den Überstundenkonflikt verstrickt waren, das Novemberabkommen ultimativ zur Zustimmung vorlegten. Mehrtägige Verhandlungen[18] mit der „Federation of Engineering and Ship-

---

[18] Verhandlungsprotokolle „Special Conference between The Engineering and the National Employers' Federations and The Federation of Engineering and Shipbuilding Trades, The National Federation of General Workers, The National Union of Foundry

building Trades", der „National Federation of General Workers" und der „National Union of Foundry Workers", Zusammenschlüsse von insgesamt 47 kleineren Einzelgewerkschaften, scheiterten am 14. April endgültig an der Kernfrage, ob die Arbeitgeber allein das Recht hätten festzustellen, was ein „material change" in den Arbeitsbedingungen sei und insofern unbeschadet anschließender Schlichtungsprozeduren zunächst einmal ihrer autonomen Entscheidungsgewalt unterlag. Mit Wirkung vom 2. Mai dehnte die „Engineering and National Employers' Federation" die Aussperrung auch auf die kleineren Gewerkschaften aus, so daß am Ende mehr als 1/4 Million Metallarbeiter ausgesperrt war.

Es würde viel zu weit führen, hier den — im Arbeitgeber- wie im Arbeitnehmerlager doch sehr unpopulären und vielfach als unzeitgemäß empfundenen — Arbeitskampf in seinen einzelnen Phasen nachzuzeichnen.[19] Erwähnt sei lediglich zum einen, daß die Kontakte zwischen den Konfliktparteien unter aktiver Vermittlertätigkeit des National Joint Council, bestehend aus Vertretern des General Council des TUC, der Labour Party Executive und der Parliamentary Labour Party, während des gesamten Arbeitskampfes niemals ganz abrissen und daß es dem Unternehmerverband zeitweilig zwischen Ende März und Mitte April sogar gelang, einen Keil zwischen die bereits ausgesperrte A.E.U. und die noch verhandelnden kleineren Gewerkschaften zu treiben, bis sich auch hier die Ablehnung der Arbeitgeberforderungen in einer Urabstimmung mit 164 759 gegen 49 503 durchsetzte, und zum anderen, daß es die staatliche Exekutive, vertreten durch den Arbeitsmister Dr. Macnamara, bis Anfang Mai strikt ablehnte, offiziell aus ihrer Zurückhaltung herauszutreten und zwischen den Parteien zu vermitteln.[20] Diese Haltung offizieller Neutralität wurde den Vertre-

---

Workers" vom 10./11./12./13. April 1922, in: Box TB 19 — File 18 Engineering and Foundry Workers' Dispute 9/6/18 TUC-Archiv, Congress House, London.

[19] Zum Ablauf vgl. die Berichte in: *A.E.U. Monthly Journal*, new issue, No. 21, April, 1922, p. 11sqq., No. 22, May, 1922, p. 11sqq., No. 23, June, 1922, p. 11sqq.; *The Labour Gazette*, Vol. 30, No. 3, March, 1922, p. 106, No. 4, April, 1922, p. 156, Nr. 5, May, 1922, p. 200, No. 6, June, 1922, p. 246, No. 7, July, 1922, p. 287; PRO: CAB 23/29, 17 (22); 18 (22); 20 (22); 22 (22).

[20] Diese offiziell eingehaltene Neutralität schloß jedoch nicht aus, daß der Arbeitsminister nicht hinter den Kulissen vor Beginn der Aussperrung wie auch während des Arbeitskampfes ständig bemüht war, die Parteien an einen Tisch zu bringen. Vgl. u. a. PRO: LAB 2/642. A 68/1922 I.R. 1208/1922: Dispute in the Engineering Trades involv-

tern des National Joint Council, unter ihnen Arthur Henderson, J. R. Clynes und John Hodge, am 16. März auf einer Konferenz in 10, Downing Street durch den Gesprächsführer der Regierung, den Lordsiegelbewahrer A. Chamberlain, noch einmal mit Nachdruck deutlich gemacht:[21] „We, as a Government, of course, hold no brief for either party in this matter. The interest we desire to take is to do nothing which appears to take sides with either party. The interest which we have to consider and to protect to the utmost of our power is the interest of the community at large, and in the decision which we take we are actuated solely by our desire to do that which may best protect the country against worse misfortunes and bring the quickest possible end to the trouble in which we are already involved."[22] Mehrfach betonte Chamberlain, unterstützt vom Schatzkanzler Horne und vom Arbeitsminister Dr. Macnamara, die unparteiliche Position der Regierung und ihre strikte Abneigung gegen eine Einmischung, solange die Parteien noch untereinander verhandelten. Mit dieser Weigerung bekräftigte die Exekutive nur ihren Standpunkt, den sie seit 1919 immer wieder grundsätzlich vertreten hatte, sich schnellstmöglich aus dem Wirtschaftsbereich und hier insbesondere aus dem der Sozialbeziehungen, in den sie während des Krieges durch die staatliche Zwangsschlichtung und die Nationalisierungen als Arbeitgeber so tief verwickelt gewesen war, wieder zurückzuziehen und die traditionelle Autonomie der Sozialparteien wiederherzustellen.

Die Gewerkschaften dagegen drängten die Regierung ab Mitte März, unterstützt vom National Joint Council, pausenlos, von dem durch das Industrial Courts Act 1919 ihr gegebenen Instrument der Einsetzung eines staatlichen Untersuchungsausschusses *(Court of Inquiry)* durch den Arbeitsminister Gebrauch zu machen. Zwar hatte ein solcher Ausschuß keine Sanktionsgewalt und nur die Funktion, einen Bericht für das Parlament zu erstellen; er bot aber den Gewerkschaften die Chance, durch eine geschickte Vertretung ihrer Interessen im Zeugenstand die öffentliche Meinung wie 1919 bei der Sankey-Commission für

---

ing possibility of stoppage of work on 11. 3. 1922. Minister of Labour's Meeting, on behalf of the Prime Minister, with representatives of the Amalgamated Engineering Union, Tuesday — 7th March, 1922 at 11 a.m.

[21] National Joint Council. The Engineering Trades Dispute. Report of Interview with M. Austen Chamberlain, London 1922, in: Box TB 19 — Engineering and Foundry Workers' Dispute 1922, File 18.

[22] *A.a.O.*, p. 6.

den Bergbau für die eigene Sache zu mobilisieren und über einen moralischen Druck dieser Öffentlichkeit gegebenenfalls sogar die Unternehmer zur Aufhebung der Aussperrung und zur Wiederherstellung des *Status quo* während der anschließenden Verhandlungen zu zwingen.

Endlich am 27. April, an demselben Tage, an dem die Arbeitgeber sich bereit erklärten, individuell Arbeiter, die ihre Bedingungen akzeptierten, wiedereinzustellen, verkündete A. Chamberlain vor dem Unterhaus, da nunmehr nach dem Scheitern der Verhandlungen mit den kleineren Gewerkschaften eine Ausdehnung der Aussperrung unvermeidlich erscheine, die Einsetzung eines Court of Inquiry unter dem Vorsitz von Sir William W. Mackenzie, um der Öffentlichkeit einen unabhängigen Bericht über den Charakter des Arbeitskampfes zu vermitteln. Nach fünf Sitzungen — zwei geheimen und drei öffentlichen mit Zugang für die Presse — erging am 10. Mai 1922 der Spruch[23]: Hinsichtlich der Überstunden sei bis zur vereinbarten Höchstgrenze von 30 Stunden in vier Wochen allein das Management in der Lage, über die „Notwendigkeit" zu entscheiden. „Up to that limit there must be freedom to the Management to act in the exercise of their discretion. Beyond that limit overtime would be open to the suggestion that it is unreasonable." Auch bei dem allgemeinen Streitpunkt der „managerial functions" und der *Status-Quo*-Frage stellte sich der Ausschuß im wesentlichen auf den Unternehmerstandpunkt: Informationen über einen geplanten „workshop change" sollten normalerweise rechtzeitig vorher „to the workpeople directly concerned or their representatives in the shop", also nicht bereits in der ersten Phase Gewerkschaftsvertretern *außerhalb* des Betriebes gegeben werden, damit noch hinreichend Zeit zur Diskussion *vor* dem Inkrafttreten der betrieblichen Veränderungen sei, ohne daß diese Informationspflicht freilich zu „undue delay" führen dürfe. Sollte während dieser Diskussionsphase keine Einigung zustande kommen und die strittige Angelegenheit in den mehrstufigen Schlichtungsvorgang nach den vertraglichen Prozeduren gelangen, dürfe das Management, „if they think it necessary and in the exercise of their discretion", die Betriebsänderungen inzwischen in Kraft setzen, wobei eine spätere Übereinkunft gegebenenfalls durchaus rückwirkenden Charakter haben könne. Der Befürchtungen der Fach-

---

[23] Industrial Courts Act, 1919. Report by A Court of Inquiry concerning the Engineering Trades Dispute, 1922, London 1922, p. 19sqq.; Zusammenfassung in *The Labour Gazette*, Vol. 30, No. 5, May, 1922, p. 200.

arbeiter, sie könnten bei innerbetrieblichen Veränderungen, etwa bei der Einführung neuer, arbeitssparender Maschinen ohne ein Recht zur rechtzeitigen Mitsprache arbeitslos werden, wurde durch den doppelten Hinweis Rechnung getragen, zum einen werde ein expandierender Industriezweig wie die Metallbranche immer neue Arbeitsplätze für die freigesetzten Facharbeiter als Kompensation anbieten können und zum anderen sei es die Pflicht der Arbeitgeber und der Gewerkschaften gemeinsam, für entlassene Facharbeiter neue Arbeitsplätze mit einem entsprechenden Qualifikationsgrad bereitzustellen.

Mit diesem Spruch, mochte er auch als Empfehlung keinerlei Rechtswirksamkeit oder Zwangscharakter haben, war die Sache der Gewerkschaften in den beiden zentralen Punkten — „overtime" und „managerial functions" — im Grunde verloren, da es nicht gelang, die breite Öffentlichkeit zu mobilisieren und hinter die gewerkschaftlichen Forderungen zu scharen. Bereits Anfang Juni begann die an sich trotz der hohen Arbeitslosigkeit bewundernswerte Solidarität, durch die Wiederaufnahme der Arbeit in den kleineren Gewerkschaften und durch die verstärkte Annahme des Angebotes der Arbeitgeber zum Abschluß individueller Arbeitsverträge langsam abzubröckeln. Die A.E.U. war finanziell praktisch am Ende, nachdem durch die Erwerbslosen- und Aussperrungsunterstützung ihre Rücklagen von anfangs £ 3,25 Mill. beim Zusammenschluß im Sommer 1920 bereits vor der Aussperrung im Januar 1922 auf £ 2 382 240 und dann infolge des dreimonatigen Arbeitskampfes am Ende auf £ 32 572 zusammengeschmolzen waren, so daß die Unterhaltszahlungen für die Ausgesperrten im Mai eingestellt werden mußten. Die Arbeitslosigkeit (zusätzlich zu der Aussperrungsziffer von etwa 260 000) lag im Metall- und Schiffbaugewerbe bei den gewerkschaftlichen Organisierten im Frühjahr 1922 durchgehend um 30 % und höher, im gesamten Schiffbau allein bei knapp 40 % und in der unter der Rubrik „Engineering and Ironfounding" aufgeführten Gesamtarbeiterschaft zwischen 27 und 28 %, während allgemein die Arbeitslosenquote seit ihrem Höhepunkt im Juni 1921 mit 17,8 % kontinuierlich auf 12,7 % der Versicherten im Juni 1922 (15,6 % der gewerkschaftlich Organisierten) zurückgegangen war. Das Metallgewerbe gehörte also mit seiner zwei- bis dreifach über dem nationalen Durchschnitt liegenden Arbeitslosenquote zu den ausgesprochen krisengeschüttelten Industriezweigen, ja es war, folgen wir den seit April 1921 kontinuierlich zwischen 20 und 30 % liegenden Erwerbslosenziffern, nach dem im Winter 1920/21 endenden Kriegs- und Nachkriegsboom aus seiner Dauerkrise überhaupt nicht mehr herausgekommen.

So erfolgte am 2. Juni 1922, wie seit Wochen absehbar, eine nahezu bedingungslose Kapitulation, der sich dann elf Tage später nach erfolgreicher Urabstimmung (75 478 gegen 39 423) die Aufhebung der Aussperrung anschloß. Die von den Arbeitgebern bereits am 24. Mai formulierte und diktierte „Kapitulationsurkunde"[24] hatte praktisch alle „disputes procedures" seit 1898 bis zum Novembermemorandum von 1921 zum Inhalt, stellte aber mehrfach mit Nachdruck fest, daß (a) das Management allein über Betriebsveränderungen, selbst wenn diese personelle Umschichtungen zur Folge hätten, zu entscheiden habe und lediglich unter normalen Umständen zu einer Vorankündigung von 10 Tagen veranlaßt werden könne und (b) nach Ablauf dieser Vorankündigungsfrist die Anordnungen der Betriebsleitung ohne Rücksicht darauf, wieweit im Konfliktfall das Lösungsverfahren bereits gediehen sei, vorbehaltlos zu befolgen seien. Die Friedenspflicht der Belegschaft während der gesamten Zeit der „procedures" wurde noch einmal ausdrücklich ebenso hervorgehoben wie eine nunmehr strikte Interpretation des Punktes (J) der Überstundenregelung vom 30. September 1920, nach der die Arbeitgeber das alleinige Recht hatten, „to decide when overtime is necessary, the workpeople or their representatives being entitled to bring forward under the Provisions for Avoiding Disputes any cases of overtime they desire discussed. Meantime, the overtime required shall be proceeded with." Mit dieser eindeutigen Restabilisierung einer autoritären Führungsstruktur im Betrieb, dieser entschiedenen Beschneidung über Jahrzehnte gewachsener und einseitig ausgeübter, wenn auch nie offiziell kodifizierter „craft regulations" und zünftischer Kontrollrechte am Arbeitsplatz *(restrictive practices)* und der allgemeinen tiefen Demütigung der Metallgewerkschaften insgesamt unter dem Eindruck der schweren Wirtschaftskrise im Zeichen einer Arbeitslosigkeit von über 24 % der A.E.U.-Mitglieder verbanden sich einmal ein rapider Mitgliederschwund der A.E.U. von ursprünglich bei der Gründung im Juli 1920 über 450 000 auf 370 000 im Oktober 1922 und 252 776 dann 1924 und zum anderen ein weiterer Angriff auf die Löhne: Zwar wurde die Forderung nach Lohnsenkung um insgesamt 16s. 6d. pro Woche in drei gleichen Stufen Juli/August/September 1922 in einer Urabstimmung verworfen, aber der Executive Council der A.E.U., das Führungsorgan, gab zusammen mit den Exekutiven der

---

[24] *A.E.U. Monthly Journal,* new issue, No. 23, June, 1922, p. 14sqq., No. 24, July, 1922, p. 12sqq.

anderen Gewerkschaften die Weisung, unter Ignorierung des Abstimmungsergebnisses weiterzuarbeiten, „having regard to the recent lockout, the large number of workpeople unemployed, and the relative state of the respective organisations".

Parallel zur Aussperrung in der Metallindustrie fand von Ende März bis Anfang Mai 1922 ein Lohnkonflikt im Schiffbau, getragen von der „Federation of Engineering and Shipbuilding Trades", statt.[25] Auch in ihm ging es wie bei der A.E.U. um einen wenigstens partiellen Abbau der Kriegszuschläge in Höhe von 16s. 6d. pro Woche. Die Einigung von Anfang Mai, die zwar in der Urabstimmung vom 5. 5. 1922 zurückgewiesen wurde, dennoch aber am 8. Mai in Kraft trat, da sich nicht die vorgeschriebenen 2/3 der Abstimmenden für die Fortführung des Streiks aussprachen, sah im einzelnen folgendes vor: Die Gewerkschaft akzeptierte rückwirkend ab 29. März einen Abzug von 10s. 6d. wöchentlich; weitere Abzüge von je 3s./Woche wurden ab 17. 5 und 7. 6. vorgesehen, so daß auch hier wie bei der A.E.U. der wöchentliche Kriegszuschlag von 26s. 6d. im Sommer 1922 um 16s. 6d. auf 10s. reduziert wurde. Einen Schlußpunkt unter eine eineinhalbjährige schrittweise Lohnsenkung 1921/22 im Metallgewerbe setzte Ende 1922 die Abmachung, daß die restlichen 10s. pro Woche allen Arbeitern im Zeit- oder Stücklohn, die auf mehr als 52s. 6d. wöchentlich kamen, in vier Raten bis Januar 1923 abgezogen werden sollten. Bei geringeren Wochenverdiensten wurden die Abzüge mit sinkender Tendenz gestaffelt, so daß für alle diejenigen, die weniger als 37s. 6d. verdienten, die Abzüge überhaupt entfielen. Damit betrugen die Gesamtabzüge 1922 in der metallverarbeitenden Industrie bei Facharbeitern auf Zeitlohnbasis 24—26 %, bei ungelernten Arbeitern 32 %; im Schiffbau lagen sie zwischen 33 und 35 %. Der generelle Preisrückgang betrug im gleichen Zeitraum 15 %, die Nahrungsmittelpreise sanken um 12 %.

Eine Korrelation zwischen Löhnen und Preisen ergibt, daß die tariflichen Wochenlöhne der Facharbeiter in der Metallverarbeitung und im Schiffbau im September 1922 noch 42 %—51 %, die der ungelernten Arbeiter 75—77 % über den Vorkriegslöhnen lagen (wobei stets die Arbeitszeitsenkung von 53 auf 47 Wochenstunden zu berücksichtigen ist), während der Gesamtindex zum gleichen Zeitpunkt noch bei 178 (1914 = 100) und der Nahrungsmittelindex bei 172 lag. Die Schere zwischen Preisen und Löhnen schloß sich also 1922 weiter.

---

[25] Zur Zusammenfassung der Konfliktabläufe in der metallverarbeitenden und in der Schiffbauindustrie vgl. *The Labour Gazette*, Anm. 13.

III

Die Strategie der Unternehmer in der metallverarbeitenden Industrie in der Deflationskrise

Schon für die Phase der wissenschaftlich-technischen Revolution des ausgehenden 19. Jahrhunderts wird in der Forschung einhellig herausgestellt, daß die englischen Unternehmer, vor die Alternative gestellt, auf die neuen Wettbewerbsbedingungen auf dem Weltmarkt und hier vor allem auf die Herausforderungen aus den USA und Deutschland entweder mit kapitalintensiven Modernisierungsinvestitionen oder einer intensiven Steigerung und Maximierung der Produktion und Produktivität des bestehenden Kapitals zu reagieren, überwiegend den zweiten Weg der erhöhten Produktionsleistung und verschärften Ausbeutung pro Arbeitseinheit, verbunden mit einer Senkung der realen Kosten besonders von der Lohnsumme her, gingen. Das bedeutete schon im letzten Viertel des 19. Jahrhunderts die Einführung eines Leistungslohnsystems mit Akkord und Prämienbonus, „systematische" Überstunden bei guter Auftragslage, Disziplinierung des Arbeiters an seinem Arbeitsplatz, Angriff auf die „craft regulations", Senkung der Lohnkosten durch die Ersetzung von Facharbeitern durch an- oder ungelernte Arbeiter in mechanischen und repetitiven Fertigungsprozessen usf. und lief vor allem in wirtschaftlichen Krisenzeiten nach dem großen Konjunktureinbruch von 1873 auf eine besonders straffe und schroffe Handhabung der „management control" und „managerial functions" im Betrieb gegenüber gewerkschaftlichen Mitbestimmungsforderungen bei der Besetzung von Maschinen, Einführung von Überstunden und Akkorden, Beschäftigung von Lehrlingen, Festsetzung von bestimmten fachlichen Qualifikationsanforderungen usf. hinaus. Ein ganzer Katalog von einseitig erkämpften und in der Regel nirgendwo eindeutig kodifizierten Mitbestimmungs- und Mitwirkungsrechten, der vor allem dann im Kriege unter den Bedingungen des leergefegten Arbeitsmarktes und des Facharbeitermangels gerade in der Rüstungsindustrie, der hohen und steigenden Anforderungen des Heeres an den Rüstungs-Output und der starken Stellung der Shop Stewards in den Betrieben eine enorme Ausweitung zuungunsten der „managerial prerogatives" erfahren hatte, stand mithin wie bereits immer wieder in den vorhergehenden Jahrzehnten auch in der Rekonstruktionsperiode nach 1918 zur Disposition.

Für diesen gerade in England relativ weit verbreiteten Widerstand und dieses Mißtrauen gegen kapitalintensive Rationalisierungs- und Modernisierungsmaßnahmen und -investitionen, gegen Montageband, „Taylorism" und „scientific management" werden mehrere Gründe geltend gemacht, die hier in ihrem Gewicht nicht weiter diskutiert werden können: ein nach wie vor vergleichsweise hohes Angebot an hochqualifizierten Facharbeitern; die langdauernde Monopolstellung als „workshop of the world"; investitionshemmende Betriebsgrößen und -anlagen und eine gewisse Überkapitalisierung in den alten Leitsektoren der sogenannten ersten industriellen Revolution; eine überwiegend typisch mittelständische Unternehmermentalität im kleinen und mittleren Familienbetrieb mit einer vergleichsweise hohen Selbstfinanzierungsrate; mangelnde Kooperation von Industrie- und Bankkapital etwa im Gegensatz zu Deutschland u. a. m. Freilich wird man hier gerade für die Zwischenkriegszeit sorgfältig differenzieren müssen zwischen den älteren, mehr traditionsverhafteten und überwiegend außenwirtschaftlich orientierten Zweigen des Maschinen- (etwa Textilmaschinen) und des Schiffbaus einerseits und den jüngeren, modernen und vorwiegend auf den Binnenmarkt ausgerichteten Sektoren der Elektroindustrie, des Fahrzeug- und Motorenbaus andererseits, die in ihren Fertigungsprozessen durchaus viel stärker mechanisiert und rationalisiert und der Notwendigkeit kapitalintensiver Modernisierungsinvestitionen gegenüber recht aufgeschlossen waren. Auch war die modernere Rationalisierungs- und Investitionsstrategie des unternehmerischen Spitzenverbandes keineswegs identisch mit den Zielen all seiner Mitglieder. Das bis in die Gegenwart gerade auch aus dem Unternehmerlager immer wieder kolportierte Argument, die relativ starke Stellung der Gewerkschaften in England, an ihrer Spitze die alten Facharbeitergewerkschaften, habe aus einer Art zünftischem und versteinertem Selbsterhaltungstrieb heraus rechtzeitige Modernisierungsinvestitionen blockiert, ist stark ideologie- und apologieverdächtig und bedarf einer sorgfältigen Überprüfung an den zeitgenössischen Quellen, die im folgenden Abschnitt wenigstens ansatzweise versucht werden soll.

Die angeführten Konfliktursachen und -muster der siebziger, achtziger und neunziger Jahre des 19. Jahrhunderts waren auch nach dem Kriege nach wie vor virulent und erfuhren sogar durch den Krieg eine erhebliche Verschärfung: Die „dilution" gerade im metallverarbeitenden Gewerbe war kaum mehr umkehrbar und zwang auch die alten Facharbeitergewerkschaften zu neuen Rekrutierungsstrategien, Organisationsformen und einem neuen gewerkschaftlichen Selbstverständnis; Überkapazitäten aus der Kriegszeit erfuhren in dem kurzfristigen Nachkriegsboom 1919/20 keinen markt- und zukunftsgerechten Abbau und belasteten die Produktion dann in der weltweiten Absatzkrise für Eisen- und Stahlerzeugnisse ab Herbst 1920; gleiches galt für den Zwang, relativ starke Belastungen aus der vorangegangenen Kriegs- und Nachkriegskonjunktur — Verschuldung, hohe laufende Unkosten, ausgeweitete Kapazitäten, relativ teuer eingekaufte Rohstoffe und Verarbeitungsmaterialien — nunmehr innerhalb recht kurzer Zeit und ohne zu große Verluste irgendwie in Einklang bringen zu müssen mit den neuen Bedingungen der Depressions- und Deflationsphase: Der Großhandelspreisindex des Board of Trade[26] erreichte im Mai 1920 seinen Höchststand mit 325,5 (1914 = 100) und sank innerhalb eines Jahres bis zum Mai 1921 auf 201,7, also um 38 %. Bis zum Mai 1922 erreichte der Index 160,6, so daß sich die Großhandelspreise innerhalb von zwei Jahren praktisch halbiert hatten. Dem allgemeinen Preisverfall von 50 % stand im gleichen Zeitraum im Metallgewerbe freilich ein durchschnittlicher Rückgang der tariflichen Wochenlöhne von nur 35 % bei Facharbeitern und 42 % bei ungelernten Arbeitern gegenüber, ein Rückgang, der sich noch geringer ausnimmt, wenn man die Reduktion der Wochenarbeitszeit von 53/54 auf 47 Stunden, also um 10 % bei vollem Lohnausgleich berücksichtigt. Augenfälliger noch ist die Diskrepanz zwischen Preis- und Lohnentwicklung, wenn man die Großhandelspreise für Eisen und Stahl und die Löhne in der metallverarbeitenden Industrie — in dem Bewußtsein freilich, daß das vorliegende statistische Material hier keine volle Vergleichbarkeit sondern nur Annäherungswerte zuläßt! — Ende Februar 1922, also unmittelbar vor dem Höhepunkt des Arbeitskampfes, vergleicht: Die Eisen- und Stahlpreise erreichten ihren Höhepunkt im Juni 1920 mit 390,6 (1914 = 100) und sanken bis Februar 1922 auf 142,9, also um 63,5 %, die Großhandelspreise allgemein im gleichen Zeitraum um rund 50 %; ein Schlosser oder Dreher, der Ende 1920 auf dem Höhepunkt der Lohnexplosion auf einen wöchentlichen Tariflohn von 89s. 2d. kam, verdiente Ende Februar 1922 immer noch 73s. 6d., also etwa 18 % weniger; bei Schiff-

---

[26] *Statistical Abstract for the United Kingdom...* [wie Anm. 5], p. 190sqq. Zur Lohnentwicklung in der metallverarbeitenden Industrie vgl. *The Labour Gazette*, Vol. 27, No. 5, May, 1919, p. 173, Vol. 29, No. 2, February, 1921, p. 63, Vol. 30, No. 3, March 1922, p. 107, No. 10, October, 1922, p. 398.

bauern lagen die Größen bei 91s. 3d. resp. 75s. 1d., also mit einer Differenz von etwa 17,6 %, bei ungelernten Arbeitern im Schiffbau bei 70s. 4d. resp. 56s. 7d., das heißt mit einer Differenz von 20 %. Naturgemäß verbilligte sich für die Metallverarbeiter auch der Grundstoff Eisen und Stahl entsprechend, wenngleich anzunehmen ist, daß noch erhebliche Vorräte 1920/21 zu vergleichsweise hohen Einkaufspreisen angelegt worden waren. Immerhin dürften die Statistiken mit aller Vorsicht eine Schlußfolgerung nahelegen: Bei steigender Kaufkraft des Geldes, ausgedrückt in einem sinkenden Preisindex, schlug nicht nur eine vorher kontrahierte Schuld mit unverändertem Nominalwert immer stärker zu Buche, sondern wirkte sich auch ein relativ starres Nominallohngefüge bei rückläufiger Absatzlage, schrumpfender Produktion sowie rapidem Preisverfall in den Betriebsbilanzen zunehmend belastend und kostensteigernd aus. Nahm sich von der Arbeitnehmerseite her die Tatsache, daß sich nach der Preisexplosion im Kriege und in den ersten beiden Nachkriegsjahren besonders für den Facharbeiter die oben dargestellte Schere zwischen dem ab Winter 1920/21 sinkenden Lebenshaltungskostenindex auf der einen und dem ebenfalls durch den Abbau der Kriegszulagen und Teuerungszuschläge rückläufigen Tariflohnniveau auf der anderen Seite nur sehr zögernd und langsam wieder schloß und daß diese Entwicklung zu einer deutlichen Einebnung der differenzierten Lohnstrukturen der Vorkriegszeit geführt hatte, als besonders bedrückend und konfliktträchtig aus, so beklagten umgekehrt die Produzenten, daß sich die Löhne nicht flexibel und schnell genug der allgemeinen Preisdeflation und der kritischen Absatzlage anpaßten.

Da die metallverarbeitende Industrie Englands zu 50 % vom Weltmarkt abhängig war, machte sich der rapide Kaufkraftverfall infolge der allgemein rückläufigen Preise gerade auch für Rohstoffe und Nahrungsmittel bei den überseeischen Abnehmern englischer Fertigprodukte besonders bemerkbar. Ein kurzer Überblick über die Exportsituation Englands 1920/21 mag den Hintergrund ausleuchten, vor dem die Produzenten argumentierten.[27] Die Gesamtausfuhr der im Vereinigten Königreich produzierten Waren reduzierte sich wertmäßig in einem Jahr um 47,3 % oder, auf den Kopf der Bevölkerung gerechnet, von £ 28 14s. 4d. auf £ 15 18s. 6d., ein dramatischer Abfall, der sich nicht

---

[27] *Statistical Abstract for the United Kingdom*... [wie Anm. 5], p. 289, 298sqq., 310sq., 342sqq.

annähernd nur aus dem gleichzeitigen Preisverfall der Großhandelspreise um 36 % erklären läßt, sondern nach dem erhitzten Rekonstruktionsboom der beiden vorhergehenden Jahre eher auf eine gewisse Sättigung des Weltmarktes nach Auffüllung der kriegsbedingten Lücken und Rückstände, vor allem aber auf die totale Zerrüttung des mittel- und osteuropäischen Marktes deutet. So verminderte sich die Ausfuhr nach Deutschland (unter Berücksichtigung des neuen Reichsgebietes) um fast 20 %, während der Handel mit der USSR nahezu zum Erliegen kam, der mit Frankreich auf 1/3 zurückfiel und auch die Exporte nach Nordeuropa in der Regel um 60 % schrumpften. In der für England besonders wichtigen Klasse III der Exportartikel (Articles Wholly or Mainly Manufactured), die 1920/21 ebenfalls einen Wertrückgang um 47,4 % verzeichnete, hatten die britischen Reichsgebiete gegenüber den nichtbritischen Märkten insofern eine gewisse kompensatorische Funktion, als hier die Ausfuhren nur unterdurchschnittlich um 40,3 % gegenüber 52,2 % im nichtbritischen Bereich sanken. Dadurch steigerte sich der Anteil britischer Gebiete in der Klasse III der Ausfuhren von 40,2 auf 45,7 %, in der Gesamtausfuhr von 37,6 % auf 42,5 %. Eine exemplarische Aufschlüsselung nach zentralen Exportgütern innerhalb des Metallsektors der Klasse III unterstreicht noch einmal den außergewöhnlichen Charakter der Entwicklung zwischen 1920 und 1922: Roheisen und Eisenlegierungen gingen 1920/21 mengenmäßig um 76,6 %, wertmäßig um 83,2 % zurück, diverse Stahlsorten um 70,7 % resp. 72,3 %, Stahlröhren um 40,5 % resp. 35 %, Drähte und Drahtprodukte um 66 % resp. 67,1 %, Haushalts- und Küchengeräte aus Blech um 62,6 % resp. 60,6 %, Messing und Kupferlegierungen incl. Fertigprodukte um 61 % resp. 59,9 %. Abweichend war die Entwicklung bei Elektrogütern und Apparaten sowie bei Maschinen (incl. Elektro-, Werkzeug-, Näh-, Textilmaschinen und Verbrennungsmotoren). Im ersten Bereich war 1921 noch ein Wertzuwachs von 12,4 % zu verzeichnen, bevor dann 1922 der tiefe Einbruch mit einem Rückgang von 44 % kam; im zweiten war es ähnlich: Einem Wertzuwachs 1921 von 17,6 % stand im folgenden Jahr ein Verlust von 34,5 % gegenüber, wobei sich freilich Elektro-, Näh- und Textilmaschinen auch noch 1922 und teilweise sogar über die ganzen zwanziger Jahre hervorragend hielten. Möglicherweise lebte der englische Maschinenbau noch 1921 von einem relativ dicken langfristigen Auftragspolster aus dem Ausland und konnte auch in der Depression traditionelle Märkte, etwa für Textilmaschinen, noch vergleichsweise gut gegenüber der jüngeren Konkurrenz halten. Gleiches gilt für den Schiffbau sowie die Ausfuhr von Lokomotiven und anderem rollendem Material, zwei weiteren traditionell wichtigen Exportindustrien. Während der Verkauf von Schiffen unter fremder Flagge 1921 sogar noch wertmäßig mit 15,3 % eine gewisse Zuwachsrate aufwies und erst 1922 mit einem Rückgang von 2/3 gegenüber dem Vorjahr den dann für die zwanziger Jahre entscheidenden Einbruch verzeichnete, folgte der zweite Sektor dem Trend im Maschinenexport: Zuwachs 1921 mit wertmäßig 19 % und erhebliche Verluste 1922 mit 31 % bei weiterhin sinkender Tendenz in den folgenden Jahren. Die Produktion von Kraftfahrzeugen und -teilen sowie Motorrädern war zwar überwiegend binnenmarktorientiert, wies aber auch auf dem weniger wichtigen Ausfuhrsektor typische Merkmale einer Wachstumsindustrie in den zwanziger Jahren auf: Zwar zeigten auch hier die Jahre 1921 und 1922 gegenüber 1920 mit einem Rückgang der Ausfuhren von mehr als 50 % starke Einbrüche, dann setzte jedoch ein steiler Aufschwung der Auslandsverkäufe vor allem von Kraftfahrzeugen ein: Wurden 1920 5309, 1921 2721 und 1922 1934 Wagen verkauft, so schnellten die Ziffern zwischen 1923 und 1925 von 4232 auf 19 315 empor.

Das angedeutete Bündel von strukturellen und konjunkturellen Schwierigkeiten und der allgemein nicht nur in England zu beobachtende Trend stagnierenden oder sogar rückläufigen Wirtschaftswachstums, der der Entwicklung der traditionellen und vorwiegend ausfuhrorientierten Leitsektoren in den alten Industrieländern generell seinen Stempel aufdrückte,[28] waren naturgemäß damals in den frühen Zwanzigern wenig geeignet, ein investitionsfreundliches Klima zu schaffen. Statt teurer Kapitalaufnahme und riskanter Neuverschuldung bei ungünstiger Trendprognose lag eher der Versuch nahe, die Krise von der Angebotsseite, also von der raschen und nachhaltigen Senkung der Gestehungskosten, das hieß aber primär von den Lohnkosten mit Lohnsenkungen, Leistungslöhnen und Dequalifizierungsmaßnahmen in der Beschickung der Produktionsmittel in den Griff zu bekommen und dadurch die früher führende Stellung auf dem Weltmarkt gegen die verschärfte Konkurrenz aus dem Ausland, besonders aus den USA,

---

[28] Vgl. Wolfram Fischer, *Die Weimarer Republik unter den weltwirtschaftlichen Bedingungen der Zwischenkriegszeit*, in: *Industrielles System und politische Entwicklung in der Weimarer Republik*, hrsg. von Hans Mommsen, Dietmar Petzina, Bernd Weisbrod, Düsseldorf 1974, S. 6 ff.; ders. *Die Weltwirtschaft im 20. Jahrhundert*, Göttingen 1980; Dietmar Petzina/Werner Abelshauser, *Zum Problem der relativen Stagnation der deutschen Wirtschaft in den zwanziger Jahren*, in: *Industrielles System...*, S. 57 ff.

Deutschland und Japan, zurückzugewinnen. Diese Strategie zielte sicher primär kurzfristig auf die rasche Überwindung der Wirtschaftskrise, entbehrte aber langfristig einer strukturellen Verbesserung der Wettbewerbs- und Marktchancen durch eine energische Beseitigung des Modernisierungsdefizits und der Rückständigkeiten in weiten Bereichen der Industrie. Zugute kam ihr auch auf der Arbeitgeberseite nach dem Kriege ähnlich wie bei den Gewerkschaften (A.S.E. 1914: 170 000 — 1919: 300 000 — A.E.U. 1920: 460 000) ein recht hoher Organisationsgrad: Waren 1913 nur 714 Firmen im Spitzenverband der Metallarbeitgeber zusammengefaßt, so stieg diese Zahl 1921 auf 2600 Firmen.

Äußerungen des mit der Schiffahrt liierten Mitgliedes des Arbeitgeberverbandes Gould in der großen Unterhausdebatte zur Metallaussperrung am 20. März 1922[29] legen die Vermutung nahe, daß den Unternehmern angesichts der schlechten Auftragslage der „Engineering Lock-out" insofern gar nicht ganz ungelegen kam, als er für drei Monate die laufenden Lohnkosten drastisch reduzierte; auf jeden Fall saßen die Metallarbeitgeber in dem ganzen Konflikt angesichts der verheerenden Auftragslage in der metallverarbeitenden Industrie und im Schiffbau für die kommenden Monate gegenüber den Gewerkschaften eindeutig am längeren Hebel: „Not only the engineering industry but the shipbuilding industry is paralysed, and yet we have a dispute of this kind coming up to-day, on conditions and terms which totally ignore the economic outlook and totaly disregard the position in which the employer is placed and, as a matter of fact, the position in which the State will ultimately be placed, as regards its responsibility for maintaining these men and their dependants."

Die Argumentationslinie des Pamphletes *The Present Economic Position of the Engineering and Allied Industries*,[30] mit dem der Unternehmerverband im März 1921 die schrittweisen Lohnsenkungen und die strikte Durchsetzung der „managerial prerogatives" einleitete, kündigte sich bereits 1919 im Kampf um die 47-Stunden-Woche und um die Anpassung des Leistungslohnsystems an die reduzierte Wochenstundenzahl an. Anfang Juli stellte der Verbandsvorsitzende Sir Allan M. Smith auf einer Spitzenkonferenz mit der A.S.E. in York ernsthaft in

---

[29] *Parliamentary Debates, House of Commons*, Vol. 152, Col. 87sq.
[30] The Engineering and the National Employers' Federations: *The Present Economic Position of the Engineering and Allied Industries*, March, 1921.

Frage, ob die 47-Stunden-Woche bei vollem Lohnausgleich „wirtschaftlich gesund" sei, und begründete dies damit, daß England auf allen Weltmärkten auf dem Maschinensektor bereits unterboten werde, von Amerikanern, Indern und Deutschen teilweise um 25— 30 %.[31]

Auf der Spitzenkonferenz am 10. März 1921 wurde Sir Allan deutlicher: „Now we are faced with an extraordinary position, and I do not know that we have ever had to face it before, because not only are our costs of production in this country much greater than the sale price of articles that we make, but we find, further, that the purchasing power of the countries in the world to whom our export trade was diverted in the old days has been reduced to such an extent that until these countries come down to a proper settled state they simply do not want the stuff we were prepared to give them."[32] Um diese alten Kunden wieder zum Kauf anzureizen, komme es zuerst darauf an, „to indicate that the costs of production will be reduced". „If the costs of production are reduced then we will be able to attract those countries in a way that we could prior to the war, and in a way which we cannot to-day, on account of the cost of production and the international exchanges." Zahlreiche frühere Kunden wollten durchaus in England Bestellungen aufgeben, aber sie bekämen ihre Waren von den USA oder Deutschland „at from one-half to one-third less cost".

Im Mittelpunkt der Argumentation in dem Pamphlet *The Present Economic Position of the Engineering and Allied Industries,* das in der öffentlichen Diskussion bis in die Gewerkschaften hinein einen weiten Widerhall fand,[33] standen die schweren Beeinträchtigungen des Auslandsabsatzes durch die stetig wachsende Kluft zwischen Kaufkraftparität einerseits und offiziellem Wechselkurs andererseits gegenüber den inflationierenden Ländern mit schwacher Währung, an der Spitze Deutschland, dann folgend Frankreich, Belgien, Italien, Österreich, die Tschechoslowakei, Polen, Rußland und die Balkanstaaten.[34] Die erhebliche Überbewertung des britischen Pfundes — sie belief sich nach diesen Berechnungen der Arbeitgeber gegenüber der Papiermark im

---

[31] *A.S.E. Monthly Journal and Report,* No. 7, July, 1919, p. 19sq.
[32] *A.E.U. Monthly Journal and Report,* new issue, No. 9, April, 1921, p. 10sqq.
[33] Vgl. *A.E.U. Monthly Journal and Report,* new issue, No. 9, April, 1921, p. 12sq., No. 10, May, 1921, p. 22sqq.; *The Labour Gazette,* Vol. 29, No. 4, April, 1921, p. 179sq.
[34] *The Present Economic Position of the Engineering and Allied Industries...* [wie Anm. 30], p. 5sqq.

März 1921 auf mehr als 100 % (Kaufkraftparität zum Pfund 100 Mk, offizieller Wechselkurs 240 Mk), gegenüber dem frs. Fr auf etwa 25 % (Kaufkraftrelation £ 1 = 40 Fr, offizieller Kurs £ = 55 Fr) — im Vergleich zu den Inflationswährungen schränkte, dies war das Hauptargument für die schwierige Absatzlage, die Kaufkraft gerade bei den traditionellen Hauptkunden britischer Metallerzeugnisse auf dem Kontinent und damit die Wettbewerbsfähigkeit der Engländer um rund 50 % ein und gab dadurch gleichzeitig den Produzenten der Inflationsländer einen erheblichen Preisvorteil auf dem Weltmarkt und auch in Großbritannien selbst gegenüber britischen Angeboten. „Under these circumstances European countries are naturally turning to Germany to supply their wants, and it is manifestly becoming daily more difficult to obtain orders for British goods from the Continent."[35] „... The high exchange value of the sovereign as compared with the German mark is like an export tariff, which put us at a disadvantage of nearly 2 to 1 against German products in every other market."[36] Als illusorisch für die nächsten zwei Jahre sollte sich die Hoffnung erweisen, eine Vergrößerung des deutschen Ausfuhrvolumens werde gleichzeitig mit einem gewissen Automatismus zu einer Erholung des Außenkurses der Mark und mit einem dadurch bedingten allmählichen Schließen der Schere zwischen Kaufkraft- und Wechselkursparität zu einer allmählichen Steigerung der britischen Wettbewerbsfähigkeit führen. „... But in the meantime we are faced with a colossal handicap against which the world-wide hostile sentiment towards Germany is the only off-set, and this is of somewhat doubtful value when reckoned in terms of money. Other currencies, e. g., French, Italian, Belgian, are depreciated, and therefore they can compete against us on favourable terms just as Germany can, but their advantage is not so great as Germany's."[37] Aus der Fülle der im Anhang[38] mit genauen Preisangaben aufgeführten Konkurrenzbeispiele seien hier nur wenige herausgegriffen:

— Verkauf der auf Entschädigungskosten abgelieferten deutschen Handelsschiffe zu Lasten der britischen Werftindustrie;
— Verlust von Bau- und Reparaturaufträgen an kontinentale Werften;

---

[35] A.a.O., p. 8.
[36] A.a.O., p. 21.
[37] Ebda.
[38] A.a.O., p. 26sqq.

— Preisvorteil deutscher Landmaschinen, soweit in Pfund fakturiert, von £ 23 bis 28, bei einem gleichartigen englischen Angebot für Düngemaschinen von £ 53 10s. „On the Continent at the present time Germany is sweeping up whatever orders are going and German prices are only about half those required for British goods."[39]
— Vergabe von Lokomotivaufträgen aus Spanien und Rußland nach Deutschland. „Depreciated exchanges (Belgium and German) made successful British and American competition practically impossible."[40]

Weitere Beispiele, mit denen der Industriellenverband seine Wettbewerbsnachteile dokumentierte, betrafen Werkzeuge und Werkzeugmaschinen, Motoren und Turbinen, Ausrüstungen für chemische Fabriken und Elektromaschinen, Baustahl und Kräne sowie Fleischschneidemaschinen; überall lagen nicht nur die deutschen Preisangebote, sondern auch die Lieferfristen wesentlich unter den englischen.

In dieser zentralen Argumentationslinie des Unternehmerverbandes äußert sich noch einmal exemplarisch der Grundkonflikt zwischen Außenwirtschafts- und Finanzinteressen, der das Wirtschaftsleben Englands in der Zwischenkriegszeit bis zur Pfundabwertung 1931 kontinuierlich bestimmte: Relativ hohe Produktionskosten im Inland, nicht zuletzt auch mitverursacht durch ein insgesamt recht inflexibles Lohnniveau bei rasch fallenden Preisen, in Verbindung mit inflationären Entwicklungen bei den Hauptkunden im Ausland, hätten an sich auch für London eine behutsame und begrenzte Strategie monetärer Flexibilität im Blick auf den Außenwert des Pfundes nahegelegt. Eine derartige Politik der Anpassung des Pfundkurses an die hohen Gestehungskosten im Inland und an die allenthalben um sich greifende Inflation im Ausland stieß jedoch auf den strikten Widerstand des Schatzamtes, der Bank von England und der City mit ihren einseitig auf Aufwertung, Vorkriegsparität und Goldstandard gerichteten Prioritäten. So blieb als Alternative für die Unternehmer nur der Angriff auf die Produktionskosten.

Ein weiterer Grund für die Absatzkrise wurde in dem Verfall der Rohstoff-, Engros- und Einzelhandelspreise gesehen;[41] so stehe den vollen Lagern und den relativ hohen Einkaufspreisen der Vorjahre für

---

[39] A.a.O., p. 27.
[40] A.a.O., p. 28.
[41] A.a.O., p. 11sqq.

Rohstoffe und Verarbeitungsmaterialien eine deutliche Zurückhaltung der Käufer gerade auch in den Rohstoffländern („The Consumers' Strike") gegenüber, die angesichts der englischen Deflationspolitik bereits weitere Preisnachlässe für die Zukunft antizipierten und sich deshalb zunächst nur mit dem Nötigsten eindeckten.

Außerdem fehlte auch nicht ein kritischer Hinweis auf die „Financial Stringency"[42] und die deflationsbedingten „higher and still higher prices, which are without parallel, being offered for capital in the form of rates of interest. The high rates of interest have stimulated savings through further personal economies, but these have not been adequate, and consequently there has been a slowing down of new enterprises."[43] Das dem eigentlichen Konjunktureinbruch des Winters 1920/21 um etwa ein halbes Jahr vorausgehende Umkippen der Großhandelspreise (1914 = 100, Höhepunkt Mai 1920: 325,5 — März 1921 = 210,8), dem sich der Einzelhandel mit einer Phasenverschiebung von etwa fünf Monaten anschloß (Lebenshaltungskosten 1914 = 100, Höhepunkt 31.10.20: 276 — 28.2.21: 241), wird neben den ungünstigen Währungsrelationen zu einer Hauptursache der Krise erklärt. „Just at the time when the limit (i. e. of the strain upon the credit machine, Wdt.) was being reached, the fall of wholesale prices already referred to was beginning. Manufacturers and merchants holding of necessity great stocks of material at high prices largely paid for out of borrowed money, were unable to repay the loans from the banks, and the latter being tied up in this way were unable to provide accomodation for others who were just needing it for their enterprises, and who frequently, in consequence, did not know where to turn for the wherewithal to meet their weekly wage bill. Credit, the life blood of industry, became frozen in great stocks of materials, partly finished and fully finished goods."[44] Von dem aus dieser Misere resultierenden Zwang zu Verlustabschreibungen wird ein kurzer Bogen zu dem Allheilmittel aus der Krise geschlagen: Produktionskostensenkung. „Stocks now held will have to be reduced in value to an extent which will induce purchasers to buy, and the holders will have to cut their losses accordingly. This, however, will be possible only if the holders of stocks are able to replace them at much lower prices in future, and this, in turn, means far

---

[42] A.a.O., p. 13.
[43] A.a.O., p. 14.
[44] A.a.O., p. 15.

lower costs of production than exist at present."⁴⁵ Auch Chamberlains erstes Deflationsbudget vom April 1920, die Geld- und Kreditpolitik des Schatzamtes und deren konjunkturell prozyklisches, das heißt in diesem Fall krisenverschärfendes „timing" werden von der Kritik nicht ausgespart: Der Schatzkanzler habe bei seiner Haushaltsvorlage übersehen, daß die Ursachen, die den kommerziellen Boom bis dahin stimuliert hätten, bereits im Begriff waren zu schwinden. „Counting unjustifiably on a continuance of the boom, he naturally sought the opportunity to obtain as great a revenue as possible, for the purpose mainly of reducing our debt abroad and that form of debt at home known as the ‚Floating Debt'."⁴⁶ Die Erhebung neuer Steuern zusammen mit den bereits bestehenden, deren Ziel und Zweck die Ausbalancierung des Haushaltes von der Einnahmeseite her, die Rückzahlung der Außenschulden, die Gewährung neuer Außenanleihen und die Fundierung respektive Rückzahlung der hohen schwebenden Schuld gewesen seien und die infolgedessen schließlich zu einer Kreditdeflation im Inland geführt hätten, „imposed a heavy strain on the resources of this country". „Economically these added to our burden and aggravated the financial stringency, and therefore contributed to the present situation." „.... The supply of new capital for the maintenance and development of industry was diverted to other purposes, and the financial stringency reached such a pitch that, in combination with the other causes already described, a slump became inevitable."⁴⁷ Auftragslage und Situation auf dem Arbeitsmarkt wurden auch für die Zukunft als düster angesehen.

Ganz auf der Linie traditioneller britischer Unternehmerstrategie, Wettbewerbsnachteile und Absatzstockungen weniger durch Neuinvestitionen, für die zweifellos jetzt bei dem relativ hohen Zinsniveau auch der ungünstigste Zeitpunkt war, als durch eine stärkere Ausnutzung des bestehenden Kapitalstockes, durch Senkung der Gestehungskosten und Erhöhung der Arbeitsproduktivität aufzufangen, liegt das Argument „Productivity of Labour". Englische und übrigens auch deutsche Arbeitgeber waren sich damals einig in ihren Klagen über die niedrige allgemeine Arbeitsproduktivität nach dem Kriege, und so wird man diesem Standardargument, vor allem wenn es zur Erklärung der

---

[45] A.a.O., p. 16.
[46] Ebda.
[47] Ebda.

Wettbewerbsnachteile gegenüber Deutschland herangezogen wurde, nur mit großer Vorsicht begegnen dürfen: „The great misfortune is that at present, for a variety of reasons, the productivity of British labour is below its pre-war standard and below that of workmen in competing countries."[48] Wie weit unter dieser „Vielfalt von Gründen" nicht auch der relativ niedrige Mechanisierungs- und Rationalisierungsgrad der englischen Produktion, verglichen mit der kontinentalen, und eklatante Investitionsdefizite in den letzten 30 bis 40 Jahren eine nicht unerhebliche Rolle spielten, müßte noch genauer untersucht werden.

Angesichts der Tatsache, daß die bestehenden Nachteile wie die Überbewertung des Pfundes gegenüber den Hauptkunden auf dem Kontinent, der freilich eine sehr viel günstigere Währungsrelation gegenüber den USA, einigen südamerikanischen Ländern, Schweden, der Schweiz und Holland gegenüberstand, die Steuerlast und die Kreditverknappung respektive -verteuerung für Inlandinvestitionen zunächst einmal als kurzfristig kaum beeinflußbar hingenommen werden mußten, trat der Unternehmerverband als „Immediate Action" für eine tendenziell vorerst unbegrenzte Senkung der Lohnkosten ein, die bis zu einem gewissen Grad freilich durch eine gleichzeitige Senkung der Lebenshaltungskosten kompensiert werden sollte. Er schreckte aber auch vor einer Reallohneinbuße nicht zurück, bis die Preise für Produkte der metallverarbeitenden Industrie einen Stand erreicht hätten, an dem sich dann zusammen mit einer neuen Preisstabilität auf wesentlich niedrigerem Niveau zugleich auch wieder eine Stabilisierung der Nachfrage besonders im Ausland und ein Ausgleich von Kaufkraftparität und Wechselkurs einstellen würden. „As prices are reduced, the volume of orders will increase, but the process must continue till producers are sufficiently busy so that the consumer can no longer force reductions in prices. The fall in the cost of production and therefore of wages, profits and other expenses must inevitably go on till the point of stability is reached."[49] Getreu dem Credo der klassischen Nationalökonomie wurde eine wirtschaftliche Gesundung über die Angebotsseite und über eine drastische Senkung der Gestehungskosten, verbunden mit einer Steigerung der Produktivität, bis zum Wiedereinpendeln des Marktmechanismus von Angebot und Nachfrage auf der Talsohle

---

[48] A.a.O., p. 21.
[49] A.a.O., p. 24.

für möglich gehalten. Dabei war dieser Stabilisierungspunkt irgendwo auf dem Boden der Preisdeflation naturgemäß so vage und unbestimmt, daß von hier aus nicht nur von der wirtschaftlichen Realität, sondern auch von der Unternehmerphilosophie her in die Tarifbeziehungen während der Deflationsphase ein ständiges Moment der Labilität und Unkalkulierbarkeit vor allem für die Arbeitnehmer und Gewerkschaften gebracht war. Dies trug sicher einiges dazu bei, daß sie sich in Ermangelung irgendwelcher günstiger lohnpolitischer Perspektiven damals so vehement auf eine Verteidigung ihrer Mitwirkungs- und Kontrollrechte am Arbeitsplatz warfen. Der nahezu automatische Prozeß stellte sich für den Arbeitgeberverband so dar, daß eine Senkung der Löhne und eine Steigerung der Erzeugung pro Arbeitseinheit dann am Ende an irgendeinem Punkt des harmonischen Ausgleichs von Angebot und Nachfrage in eine Nachfrage- und Produktionssteigerung vor allem durch Auslandsaufträge umschlagen werde mit der Folge eines erneuten Lohnanstiegs „to such an extent as will greatly, if not entirely, compensate for reduction in wages rates".[50] „It is the considered opinion of the employers that a definite reduction in hourly rates and an increase in individual output are both necessary. The effect of the reduction on the standard of life will depend on the fall in the cost of living and the extent to which the workpeople maintain and increase their actual earnings by a greater intensity of output."[51] Die wichtige Frage, wieweit die englische Industrie vor allem in den älteren Sektoren, einmal unabhängig vom Preis, überhaupt noch marktgerecht produzierte und ob nicht eine Erhöhung der Produktivität wieder zu einem Überangebot auf dem Weltmarkt mit erneutem Absatzrückgang und Preisverfall führen würde, wurde hier nicht gestellt. Flankiert werden sollten die Maßnahmen zur Kostensenkung durch eine gewisse Lockerung der Deflationsbremse, nachdem der Schatzkanzler bereits eine Diskontsenkung für reichlich angebotene Schatzwechsel von 6 1/2 auf 6 % angekündigt hatte. „This will help manufacturers somewhat in their efforts to reduce the cost of production."[52] Zusammenfassend sei diese deflationistische Preis- und Lohnpolitik der Metallarbeitgeber, die sich durch eine sie begleitende Reduktion der Massenkaufkraft letztlich zugleich prozyklisch und krisenverschärfend auswirkte, noch

---

[50] Ebda.
[51] A.a.O., p. 25.
[52] Ebda.

einmal in einem Kernsatz des Memorandums dargestellt, wo es unter Bezug auf den schleppenden Absatz von Landmaschinen heißt: „High wages have produced high prices; these high prices have stifled the demand. Sellers of agricultural produce have been compelled to accept lower prices, and hence they can only afford to buy their implements at lower prices. A revival of demand can only come with lower prices, and under existing conditions these lower prices can only come with lower wages."[53]

IV

Die Gegenstrategie der Gewerkschaften in der Deflationskrise

Während der Unternehmerverband in seiner Krisenstrategie eindeutig von der *Ökonomie der Angebotsseite* und dem Zwang zur Senkung der Gestehungs- und das hieß vorwiegend der Lohnkosten her argumentierte und damit im Interesse einer Wettbewerbsverbesserung auf den Außenmärkten zugleich auf dem an sich in der Zwischenkriegszeit mächtig expandierenden und durchaus ausbaufähigen Binnenmarkt zumindest zeitweilig eine Schrumpfung der Massenkaufkraft und damit auch der Nachfrage nach Massen- und Konsumgütern (immer wieder zitiertes Beispiel war das Fahrrad als Inbegriff eines ganz neu zu erschließenden Massenmarktes im Innern) zu riskieren bereit war, was sich tendenziell zumindest im Inland im Sinne einer Verschärfung der Absatzkrise auswirken mußte, legten die Gewerkschaften in ihren *Some Comments on ‚the Present Economic Position of the Engineering and Allied Industries'*[54] unter anonymer Berufung auf nationalökonomische Autoritäten besonderen Nachdruck auf die Notwendigkeit, einmal die Krise durch eine *Stabilisierung und Hebung der Nachfrage* auf dem Binnenmarkt und das bedeutete durch eine Sicherung und Expansion der Kaufkraft vor allem für Güter des Massenbedarfs in den Griff zu bekommen, und zum anderen durch eine nachfrageinduzierte Bele-

---

[53] *A.a.O.*, p. 28.

[54] Amalgamated Engineering Union: *Some Comments on „The Present Economic Position of the Engineering and Allied Industries". Being a Reply to the Publication under that Title by the Engineering and National Employers' Federations*, April, 1921. Vgl. *The Labour Gazette*, Vol. 29, No. 5, May, 1921, p. 232.

bung des Binnenmarktes, durch Arbeitszeitverkürzung, Überstundenabbau und gleichmäßigere Verteilung der Arbeit die Arbeitslosenziffer drastisch zu senken und dadurch wiederum ebenfalls zusätzlich Massenkaufkraft zu schaffen. „It is not a ‚consumers' strike' that causes a slump in trade, but very largely the reverberation of widespread reduction of wages. Employers show an apparently invincible ignorance on this point. But it is now the assured judgement of the best economic science that, speaking generally, the only statesmanlike course, when any part of business meets with difficulties, is inflexibly to maintain the Standard Rates of Wages everywhere, at whatever temporary cost, *so as not to aggravate the evil;* and to cope with the difficulties otherwise than by wage reductions. Nothing is more calamitous to a nation than a reduction in the Standard of Life of its people."[55]

Dieses antizyklische Kaufkraftargument von der Nachfrageseite her, das auch in der deutschen Gewerkschaftsbewegung seit 1924 zunehmend Verbreitung fand und hier sicher mit auf die Unterkonsumtionstheorie von Marx zurückging, war für seine gewerkschaftlichen Verfechter durchaus nicht nur Ausdruck einer einseitig interessenpolitischen, sondern einer gesamtvolkswirtschaftlichen Orientierung. Bei ihr ging es primär darum, über Lohnerhöhung oder zumindest eine Lohnstabilisierung Massenkaufkraft zu schaffen beziehungsweise zu erhalten, um damit den Absatz zu erhöhen und gleichzeitig das Arbeitsplatzangebot zu steigern. Damit aber nahm die Kaufkrafttheorie unter den Bedingungen der Weltwirtschaftskrise 1921/22 und dann vor allem zehn Jahre später über ihren engeren lohntheoretischen Rahmen hinaus den Rang einer wirtschafts- und konjunkturpolitischen Alternativstrategie zum Argument der Produktionskostensenkung im Unternehmerlager ein.

Den Unternehmern wird in dem Gegenartikel von den Gewerkschaften der Vorwurf gemacht, ihre Verluste nicht eindeutig und überzeugend mit Bilanzen ausgewiesen, weiterhin verschwiegen zu haben, daß sie ihre seit kurzem aufgetretenen Passivsalden gegen die abgeführten Überschußgewinnsteuern *(Excess Profits Duties)* der letzten Boomjahre aufrechnen könnten, und im übrigen auch nicht darauf eingegangen zu sein, daß die metallverarbeitende Industrie für 1920 im Schnitt noch Dividenden zwischen 10 und 20 % (Metropolitan Vickers Electrical Co. 12 1/2 %, Sir W. G. Armstrong, Withworth, and Co. 10 %) ausge-

---

[55] A.a.O., p. 11 (Hervorhebung im Original).

wiesen habe und die Aktiennotierungen vom 1. April 1921, die in der Regel alle über pari lägen (Ausnahmen u. a. Sir W. G. Armstrong, Withworth, and Co. £ 0 18s. und Vickers and Co. £ 0 12s.6d.), auch nicht gerade Pessimismus in diesem Industriezweig signalisierten.[56] Freilich bleibt die A.E.U. hier in ihrer Liste ihrerseits eine genaue Differenzierung nach Betriebsgröße, Produktionsumfang, Bedeutung innerhalb der Metallbranche, nach Binnen- oder Außenmarktorientierung sowie nach Modernisierungs- und Rationalisierungsgrad schuldig, die erst näheren Aufschluß über das Ausmaß der Depression in den einzelne Produktionsrichtungen hätte geben können.

Den Währungsverfall unter den einstigen Hauptkunden Englands sieht die A.E.U.[57] als Indikator für eine total verfehlte Nachkriegspolitik der Sieger gegenüber den Besiegten, an der Spitze Deutschland, und für eine zweifelhafte Außenwirtschaftspolitik mit selektivem Produzentenschutz für den Binnenmarkt. Der Regierung Lloyd George und der sie tragenden konservativ-plutokratischen Parlamentsmehrheit wird angelastet, sie habe durch ihre Reparationspolitik, die Ausfuhrabgabe auf deutsche Waren, durch Valutaausgleichszölle gegen Valuta-Dumping und eine partielle Schutzzollgesetzgebung in wichtigen Branchen wie das 1920 erlassene „Dyestuffs (Import Regulations) Act" insbesondere gegen die Einfuhr deutscher Chemieerzeugnisse — einst vor dem Kriege Hauptexportartikel des deutschen Englandhandels! — oder das ein Jahr später eingeführte „Safeguarding of Industries Act" für feinmechanische Artikel wie optische und wissenschaftliche Präzisionsinstrumente zum einen die deutsche Exportkraft und damit den Außenkurs der Mark zusätzlich geschwächt und zum anderen die deutsche Wirtschaft geradezu unter einen Exportdruck gesetzt, um die Reparationsleistungen überhaupt aus eigener Kraft in Gold- und Devisenzahlungen zu ermöglichen. Dieser Druck mache sich jetzt allenthalben zum Schaden der britischen Ausfuhr bemerkbar. Zu denken sei hier auch an die deutschen Kohlenlieferungen auf Reparationskonto nach Belgien und Frankreich, die nachweisbar zu einer schweren Einbuße für den Absatz britischer Kohle geführt haben. „... *Who is now depreciating still further the German mark? We understand that an overwhelming majority of the British engineering employers have supported, and still support, Mr. Lloyd George's Government, with its policy of*

---

[56] A.a.O., p. 4sq.
[57] A.a.O., p. 6sqq.

‚making Germany pay', and its present proposals of high Customs duties calculated to prevent all German exports. Everything that hinders the German export trade necessarily still further depreciates the German mark; and, therefore (according to the statement of the British engineering employers), *still further strengthens the position of the German employers*. Now, the British employers contend that, because their German competitors enjoy the ‚advantage' of having a depreciated currency, the British engineering workman must accept lower wages! When the British Government, by its strangling of the German export trade, has caused a further depreciation of the German mark, presumably this extra ‚advantage' that the German employer will possess will be made the justification for still further reduction of British wages!"[58]

Ein Stück „craft"-Arroganz spricht aus der Selbsteinschätzung der Facharbeitergewerkschaften, daß zwar ein Maschinist auf dem Kontinent „on a repetition job, with foolproof machines" einen quantitativ höheren Output leisten könne. „But the fact that no employer having engineering work of first-rate quality to do ever engages a foreign workman when he can get an English or Scottish engineer, with all his faults, indicates how little ground there is for this careless slender."[59]

Die von der A.E.U. immer wieder angemahnten Auswege aus der nationalen und internationalen Krise ergeben sich nahezu zwangsläufig als Konsequenz dieser Ursachenanalyse: Hebung der nationalen und internationalen Kaufkraft für britische Erzeugnisse durch eine Liberalisierung des Welthandels und einen Abbau aller politischen und kommerziellen Hemmnisse etwa auch im Rußlandgeschäft, Wiederherstellung der Prosperität auf dem Kontinent und vor allem in Deutschland als seinem Kernland (deutlicher Hinweis auf den großen Einfluß des 1920 erschienenen und damals sofort ins Deutsche übersetzten berühmten Buches von J. M. Keynes *The Economic Consequences of the Peace*) und damit Schaffung erweiterter Nachfrage nach britischen Erzeugnissen auf der Grundlage gesundeter Austausch- und Währungsverhältnisse mit einer stabilen Angleichung von Kaufkraft- und Wechselkursparität wie vor dem Kriege. „The only way to increase our foreign trade is by adopting a policy of peace, the restoration of Europe, and free trade."[60] Dabei wandte sich die Gewerkschaft mit deutlicher

---

[58] A.a.O., p. 7sq. (Hervorhebung im Original).
[59] A.a.O., p. 19.
[60] A.a.O., p. 21.

Spitze gegen das Schatzamt und unter Berufung auf den schwedischen Nationalökonomen Gustav Cassel und sein auf der Internationalen Finanzkonferenz in Brüssel 1920 vorgelegtes Memorandum über die „World's Monetary Problems" ausdrücklich gegen eine Wiederherstellung der Vorkriegsparitäten; konstante Hinweise auf sie seien das ernsteste Hindernis für ein klares Verständnis der monetären Probleme der Welt, da diese alten Paritäten in keiner Weise mehr als normal betrachtet werden könnten.[61] Vielmehr müsse in einer internationalen Verständigung ein Ende der Inflation erreicht werden, um dann gemeinsam zu einer Stabilisierung der Währungen und ihrer gegenseitigen Relationen auf der Grundlage echter Kaufkraftparität zwischen den Ländern zu kommen und künftig Wechselkursschwankungen möglichst gering zu halten.[62] Gerade diese Passage im Anhang über das *Problem of the Exchanges*[63] liest sich aus heutiger Sicht wie eine Vorwegnahme jüngster Versuche, im Rahmen der EG und der „Euro-Schlange" zu einer möglichst störungsfreien und stabilen gegenseitigen Abstimmung der europäischen Wechselkurse als Grundlage für einen reibungslosen Warenaustausch zu gelangen: „The problem which confronts the Government is that of the stability of the exchanges. This involves two things: (1) a new equilibrium, and (2) minimising deviations from it."[64]

Breiten Raum nehmen die Vorschläge zu einer „Reduction of Workshop Costs" ein;[65] sie resultieren aus einer illusionslosen und äußerst kritischen Einschätzung der allgemeinen Überalterung und Ineffizienz des britischen Produktionsapparates im Vergleich zu Deutschland und den USA mit einem überholten Maschinenpark, schlechter Ausstattung des Arbeitsplatzes, Mißmanagement, Material- und Zeitvergeudung, unnötig hohen Erstellungskosten, mangelnder Organisation und Planung der einzelnen Arbeitsvorgänge, einem viel zu geringen Grad an Mechanisierung und Rationalisierung usf. „*The British engineering industry is, with few exceptions, badly organised from one end to the other.*"[66] Hier dürfte ein kritisches Wort zu dem bis heute bis zum Überdruß kolportierten Vorwurf der generellen Modernisie-

---

[61] A.a.O., p. 27sq.
[62] A.a.O., p. 29.
[63] A.a.O., p. 27sqq.
[64] A.a.O., p. 29.
[65] A.a.O., p. 23sqq.
[66] A.a.O., p. 23 (Hervorhebung im Original).

rungsfeindlichkeit der englischen Gewerkschaften angebracht sein. Gerade das vorliegende Memorandum zeigt,[67] daß die A.E.U. — gleiches galt übrigens nachweislich auch für die Bergarbeitergewerkschaft — damals die große Herausforderung des „scientific management" und des „Taylorism" aus den USA mit dem Zwang zur straffen Organisation und Bewertung der einzelnen Arbeitsvorgänge *(grading)* und zur leistungsgerechten Lohnbemessung *(rating)* möglicherweise viel klarer als manche Unternehmer gesehen hat. Sie sperrte sich keineswegs grundsätzlich gegen einen Wandel zur Modernität und konnte sich auch gar nicht sperren, wenn sie mit ihrem energischen Eintreten für eine Senkung der Gestehungskosten nicht über die Lohnquote, sondern über die Kapitalausstattung und die höhere Effizienz des Produktionsapparates glaubwürdig bleiben wollte. Entscheidend für die Gewerkschaften war also weniger das „Daß" als das „Wie", das heißt die intensive Beteiligung und Mitbestimmung an der Einführung neuer Maschinen, ihrer Besetzung, an der Neubewertung der Arbeitsplätze und Arbeitsabläufe und an der Festsetzung des Leistungslohnes sowie eine echte Teilhabe an den durch Produktivitätszuwachs auflaufenden zusätzlichen Gewinnen; entscheidend war aber auch die Knüpfung eines sozialen Sicherheitsnetzes mit Umschulungsmöglichkeiten, Übergangszahlungen und anderen Hilfen als Kompensation für mögliche Rationalisierungsinvestitionen und die Wegrationalisierung von Arbeitsplätzen. Damit war allerdings das heikle Prinzip der innerbetrieblichen Entscheidungsgewalt *(managerial functions)* wieder · mit Nachdruck ebenso zur Diskussion gestellt wie das Problem, wer im Betrieb der Ansprechpartner für die Leitung sein sollte, der innerbetriebliche Belegschaftsvertreter *(representative)* oder der außerbetriebliche Gewerkschaftsfunktionär *(organizer)* und welche Rückwirkungen die Einführung des Taylorismus auf das „collective bargaining" und die Lohnstrukturen haben würde. Einer Lösung ein entscheidendes Stück nähergebracht wurde dieses dornige Problem innerbetrieblicher Rationalisierung erst mit den Produktivitätsabkommen der sechziger und siebziger Jahre des 20. Jahrhunderts, an deren Anfang das richtungsweisende „productivity agreement" in der Esso-Raffinerie in Fawley stand.

Am Ende werden noch einmal komprimiert die Lösungsvorschläge der A.E.U. zusammengefaßt:[68]

---

[67] *A.a.O.*, p. 23sq.
[68] *A.a.O.*, p. 31.

— Anerkennung der Tatsache, daß gegenüber vielen Ländern eine Rückkehr zu Vorkriegsparitäten unwahrscheinlich ist;
— Schaffung von Wechselkursen, die auf der Kaufkraftparität zwischen den einzelnen Ländern basieren;
— Stabilisierung der Wechselkurse auf der Grundlage eines neuen Gleichgewichts und Verhinderung weiterer Kursschwankungen;
— Inflationsstop für die nationalen Währungen durch internationale Abmachungen und Ausbalancierung der nationalen Budgets (vor allem unter Einschränkung der Rüstungsausgaben);
— Fundierung der schwebenden auswärtigen Schulden und Liberalisierung des internationalen Handels durch internationale Abmachungen;
— Heftige Kritik an der britischen Regierung, weil ihre Politik sich noch krisenverschärfend auswirke, vor allem an ihrer Zollpolitik, die die Tendenz zu weiteren Abwertungen anderer Währungen und zu erheblichen Kursschwankungen noch fördere.

Die oben in ihrem Kern kurz skizzierte Ausarbeitung der A.E.U. hatte ihren unmittelbaren branchenspezifischen Anlaß zwar in der Denkschrift des Unternehmerverbandes, sie ist aber als Zeugnis einer wirtschaftspolitischen Krisenkonzeption der Gewerkschaften damals nur voll zu würdigen vor dem Hintergrund der gleichzeitigen umfassenden Recherchen und Expertisen eines „Joint Committee on the Cost of Living". Dieser Ausschuß setzte sich aus Vertretern des Parliamentary Committee, des Vorgängers des General Council im TUC, der Labour Party, der Genossenschaften, der Triple Alliance (Eisenbahner, Bergarbeiter, Transportarbeiter), der Federation of Engineering and Shipbuilding Trades, der National Federation of General Workers und der National Federation of Building Trades Operatives zusammen. Auf der Grundlage einer umfangreichen Expertenarbeit und Gutachtertätigkeit[69] — unter anderen von A. C. Pigou, S. Webb, J. A. Hobson — erstellte der Ausschuß zwei Zwischenberichte im September 1920 und Januar 1921 sowie dann einen eingehenden „Final Report on the Cost of Living" im Juli 1921.[70] In diesem Zusammenhang kann

---

[69] Das Untersuchungsmaterial in Box T 252 File 182. 2 TUC-Archiv, Congress House, London: *Cost of Living. T.U.C. Enquiry 1920.*

[70] Zusammenfassung in *The Labour Gazette*, Vol. 28, No. 10, October, 1920, p. 541 (1st. Interim Report), Vol. 29, No. 2, February, 1921, p. 68sq. (2nd. Interim Report), No. 8, August, 1921, p. 392 (Final Report).

auch hier nur auf die Grundgedanken verwiesen werden, soweit sie zum Verständnis der gewerkschaftlichen Strategiediskussion Anfang der zwanziger Jahre und auch später wichtig sind. Einig waren sich eigentlich alle, auch die linken Nationalökonomen in dem Ziel, daß längerfristig eine wirtschaftliche Gesundung sowohl im nationalen als auch im internationalen Maßstab nur durch eine Preisdeflation und eine behutsame Deflationierung des Pfundkurses mit einer schrittweisen Wiederangleichung des Papierpfundes an das alte Goldpfund der Vorkriegszeit zu erreichen sei, wobei freilich über die Höhe einer neuen Parität in Relation zur Kaufkraft auch im linken Lager durchaus unterschiedliche Ansichten bestanden. Herrschte also über Richtung und Ziel des monetären Weges eigentlich zwischen der Linken und der Finanzorthodoxie kaum ein grundsätzlicher Dissens, so standen sich doch in der konkreten Markierung der einzelnen Stationen dieses Deflations-Kurses die Fronten recht unversöhnlich gegenüber. Diese theoretische Frontenbildung sollte sich in der Praxis des Sozialkonfliktes und in der praktischen Formulierung der Konfliktpunkte recht genau widerspiegeln. Deutlich brachte Hugh Dalton, Nationalökonom an der London School of Economics und später einer der profiliertesten finanz- und wirtschaftspolitischen Sprecher der Labour Party, bis er unter Attlee das Schatzamt übernahm, in voller Übereinstimmung mit dem zweiten Zwischenbericht des Ausschusses in seinem Memorandum zum Ausdruck, daß die allgemeine Senkung des Preisniveaus zusammen mit einer langsamen Steigerung des Pfundkurses nur unter den Bedingungen eines hohen Beschäftigungsniveaus und zumindest einer Stabilisierung, wenn nicht eines Zuwachses der Reallöhne erfolgen dürfe. Die nationalen müßten überdies mit internationalen Anstrengungen für eine Wiederherstellung uneingeschränkter Welthandelsbeziehungen gekoppelt werden. Flankiert werden müsse die Währungs- und Preisdeflation durch eine sofortige drastische Reduktion insbesondere der nationalen schwebenden und der Außenschulden mit Hilfe einer allgemeinen Kapitalsteuer auf alle Formen des in den letzten Jahren aufgelaufenen Reichtums *(capital levy)*, da andernfalls bei steigendem Geldwert die Anleihegläubiger und Rentiers als Folge der Kriegsfinanzierung auf Kosten der Steuerzahler noch einen zusätzlichen Deflationsbonus auf ihr Kapitaleinkommen einstreichen würden. „Deflation and a capital levy are, therefore, supplementary parts of a sound financial policy."[71] Angesichts der Alternative, entweder den Steuerzahler und

---

[71] H.P.C. No. 6. Parliamentary Committee of the Trades Union Congress. Joint

den Staatshaushalt noch auf lange Zeit zu etwa 30 % (wie 1920/21) mit einer Bedienung und Tilgung der Kriegsschulden zu belasten,[72] wobei die Reallast mit steigendem Geldwert noch zunehmen werde, dadurch der öffentlichen Hand auch noch in der folgenden Generation, die mit dem Krieg überhaupt nichts mehr zu tun hatte, die notwendige Manövriermasse für kostendämpfende Maßnahmen, wie eine Herabsetzung der Steuern, insbesondere der Verbrauchssteuern auf Nahrungsmittel, und für eine Anhebung der Sozialausgaben für Erziehung, Hausbau und öffentliche Gesundheit zu nehmen, oder durch eine scharfe einmalige Besteuerung der Kriegsgewinne einen erheblichen Teil der Gesamtschuld sofort zu tilgen, was einen echten Umverteilungseffekt zugunsten der einkommensschwachen Schichten gehabt hätte, und diesen Schritt zugleich mit einer drastischen Beschneidung der Verteidigungsausgaben (1920/21 25,3 % des Gesamthaushaltes) zu verbinden, sprach sich der Ausschuß eindeutig für den zweiten Weg aus. Dieser war jedoch durch die damaligen innenpolitischen Machtverhältnisse und den finanzorthodoxen Prioritätenkatalog von Schatzamt und City völlig blockiert. Gleiches galt für die Produktionsseite. Denn nicht nur vom Haushalt und vom monetären Bereich her glaubten die linken Theoretiker, die Gewerkschaften und die Labour Party mit der rigiden Kapitalsteuer, einem schnellen Abbau der unproduktiven Lasten der öffentlichen Hand, einer Senkung der Verbrauchssteuern und der Einschränkung des Notenumlaufes wenigstens theoretisch ein erfolgreiches Rezept zur Verwirklichung eines „magischen Fünfecks" aus Vollbeschäftigung, Reallohnstabilisierung, Preisdeflation, Pfundaufwertung und wirtschaftlichem Wachstum zur Hand zu haben, sondern auch auf dem Produktionssektor. Hier lagen die Vorschläge zur Senkung der Herstellungs- und damit auch der Lebenshaltungskosten *nicht* über den Lohnfaktor, die der Schlußbericht enthielt, auf der Linie des Bekannten:[73] Effizienzsteigerung durch eine grundlegende Modernisierung und technologische Verbesserung des Produktions-

---

Committee on the Cost of Living, *Memorandum on the Cost of Living as Affected by the Government's Currency Policy,* by Hugh Dalton, p. 11.

[72] Die nationale Schuld belief sich 1914 vor Kriegsausbruch auf £ 15 pro Kopf der Bevölkerung, ihre Bedienung auf etwa einen halben Guinee (= 10s.5d.); 1920 hatte sich die Schuld mehr als verelffacht mit £ 170 pro Kopf bei einer jährlichen Bedienungslast von £ 7 pro Kopf.

[73] Parliamentary Committee, Trades Union Congress. Joint Committee on the Cost of Living, *Final Report of the Cost of Living,* July, 1921, p. 118sqq.

apparates unter Einschluß der Maschinen, der Fabrikanlagen, der sanitären Einrichtungen usf., Übergang zur echten Bedarfsdeckungswirtschaft unter besonderer Rücksichtnahme auf die Wünsche der breiten Massen und der organisierten Arbeiter, staatliches Außenhandelsmonopol, Nationalisierung des Grund und Bodens, der Eisenbahnen, der Grundstoff- und einiger ausgewählter Fertigwarenindustrien wie etwa der Wolltextilfabrikation, Einrichtung kommunaler und anderer öffentlicher Banken, Ausdehnung des Genossenschaftswesens vor allem auf dem Bausektor durch die staatliche Förderung von Building Guilds, Publizität und öffentliche Kontrolle der Gewinne, zwangsweise Einführung des Kostendeckungsprinzips, Bildung eines ständigen Verbraucherrates beim Board of Trade zur Überprüfung der Kosten und Preise, öffentliche Untersuchung verschiedener Industriezweige, Monopol- und Kartellkontrolle gegebenenfalls mit Hilfe der Wirtschaftsabteilung des Völkerbundes weltweit für die multinationalen Unternehmen. Zusammenfassend heißt es dann im Schlußbericht: „The cost of living has been reduced, but the workers are paying the price of this fall in the unemployment and lower wages. A healthy and permanent fall in prices must depend upon the adoption of the policy outlined in our Reports. It is inevitable that international trade intercourse should increase and to that extent prices should fall. But we cannot be certain that the consumer will enjoy the advantages of as large a fall in the cost of living as we believe to be possible, unless there is strong pressure on the part of the public in favour of measures for eliminating the extravagant toll levied by the capitalist and increasing the efficiency of industry."[74] Die in sich widerspruchsvolle und schwierige Harmonisierung von Effizienzsteigerung, Modernisierung, Rationalisierung und Vollbeschäftigung sollte hergestellt werden durch ein Programm, das unter dem gängigen Schlagwort „work or maintenance" auf die Funktion des Interventionsstaates als Sozialstaat verwies, bei Unterbeschäftigung oder bei der Freisetzung von Arbeitskräften durch arbeitssparende Maschinen entweder selbst eine öffentliche Arbeitsbeschaffungspolitik zu betreiben oder zumindest durch finanzielle Unterstützung einen angemessenen Lebensstandard zu garantieren.

Naturgemäß war auch dieser Forderungskatalog, der im übrigen bereits weit auf die zweite Rekonstruktionsperiode nach 1945 und auf

---

[74] A.a.O., p. 121.

den vollen Durchbruch Englands zum Wohlfahrtsstaat vorauswies, unter den damaligen politischen Machtbedingungen nicht durchsetzbar. Es erscheint auch fraglich, ob die Verwirklichung dieser Forderungen durch eine „mixed·economy" unter den damaligen Bedingungen nicht, statt, wie erhofft, die Produktivität zu steigern und damit mehr Wohlstand und Arbeitsplätze für alle zu sichern, den gegenteiligen Effekt einer Strangulierung und Blockierung der Wirtschaft gehabt und damit letzten Endes zu einer Erhöhung der Lebenshaltungskosten und der Arbeitslosenziffern sowie zu einer weiteren Herabminderung der internationalen Wettbewerbsfähigkeit Englands geführt hätte.

V

Überlegungen zu einem Vergleich zwischen England und Deutschland

Eines der zentralen gesellschaftspolitischen Probleme, mit dem sich der englische wie der deutsche Arbeiter und deren Interessenorganisationen in gleicher Weise während des Krieges und in der anschließenden Rekonstruktionsperiode konfrontiert sahen, war ihre Stellung im Produktionsprozeß, und zwar im kapitalistischen, nachdem weder hier noch dort die lange erhoffte sozialistische Wirtschaftsordnung hatte durchgesetzt werden können. Auch die Bandbreite der diskutierten und zeitweise heftig umkämpften Möglichkeiten und Wege war in beiden Ländern in etwa gleich: hier workers' control — joint or dual control, participation and consultation — one directorial authority or managerial prerogatives, dort Arbeiterkontrolle — Mitbestimmung und Sozialpartnerschaft — Betriebsabsolutismus. Während in England bereits unmittelbar nach Kriegsende, in Deutschland etwa ein Jahr später schon der Weg zur workers' control/Arbeiterkontrolle in einer vergesellschafteten Produktionsordnung endgültig verbaut war, zeigen sich in der Ausgestaltung der zweiten und in den gesellschaftspolitischen Trendverschiebungen von der zweiten zur dritten Variante zwischen beiden Ländern gewisse Unterschiede. Generell wird man sagen können, daß in Deutschland im Zeichen des Inflationsbooms mit steigenden Nominallöhnen und einer recht starken und geschlossenen Arbeiterbewegung, die über ihre Partei zumindest auf Reichsebene bis 1920 und dann auch auf verschiedenen anderen Ebenen, vor allem im preußischen Staatsministerium, bis Juli 1932 in unterschiedlicher

Weise im Gegensatz zur Labour Party an der politischen Macht teilhatte, die Bereitschaft zur partnerschaftlichen Kooperation im Zeichen der ZAG und der Branchenarbeitsgemeinschaften doch länger bis zur Stabilisierungskrise im Herbst und Winter 1923/24 anhielt. Demgegenüber war in England, wie sich auch exemplarisch an der Metallaussperrung oder ein Jahr vorher 1921 in dem großen Bergarbeiterstreik zeigt, das Maß der Gemeinsamkeit und Zusammenarbeit aus der Kriegszeit zwischen den Sozialparteien im Zeichen der Weltwirtschaftskrise seit dem Winter 1920/21 schon wesentlich früher erschöpft, und das Pendel kehrte hier schon im März/April 1921 — besonders im Bergbau und in der Metallindustrie — eindeutig wieder zum Betriebsabsolutismus der Vorkriegszeit, zum Herr-im-Haus-Standpunkt zurück, ein Vorgang, der dann von Herbst 1923 an ebenfalls vor allem in der Montanindustrie auch in Deutschland nach der Währungsstabilisierung krass zu beobachten war. Dabei erwies es sich für die englischen Gewerkschaften als besonders nachteilig, daß sie unter dem Druck sinkender Produktion und Nachfrage, hoher Arbeitslosigkeit, materieller Not und leerer Kassen ab 1921 an zwei Fronten, der gesellschaftspolitischen und der tariflichen, gleichzeitig praktisch mit dem Rücken gegen die Wand standen oder doch aus einer ausgesprochenen Position der Schwäche und der Defensive heraus operieren mußten. Es wäre in der vergleichenden Diskussion zu prüfen, ob es nur die unterschiedlichen wirtschaftspolitischen und konjunkturellen Rahmenbedingungen waren — hier Inflationsboom, dort Deflations- und Wirtschaftskrise, hier Nominallohnerhöhungen, dort Lohnabbau —, die in der Entwicklung der Industriebeziehungen/Industrial Relations in Deutschland gegenüber England zu einer Phasenverschiebung von zweieinhalb bis drei Jahren geführt haben, oder ob hier auch unterschiedliche Faktoren innerhalb der Arbeiterbewegung selbst, in ihren traditionellen Konfliktmustern und im Verhalten der Arbeitgeberseite eine Rolle gespielt haben; möglicherweise lag auch in der verschiedenen Ausgestaltung des Arbeits- und Sozialrechts in beiden Ländern nach dem Kriege ein Ansatz getrennter Entwicklung.

Wenn die unter anderen von Knut Borchardt für die deutsche Entwicklung in den zwanziger Jahren entwickelte These[75] wahr ist, daß ein

---

[75] Knut Borchardt, *Wirtschaftliche Ursachen des Scheiterns der Weimarer Republik*, in: *Weimar. Selbstpreisgabe einer Demokratie. Eine Bilanz heute*, hrsg. von Karl Dietrich Erdmann und Hagen Schulze, Düsseldorf 1980, S. 216; vgl. ders., *Zwangslagen und*

stagnierendes oder gar rückläufiges Wirtschaftswachstum die politischen und vornehmlich die Verteilungskonflikte verschärft und daß die Inflation „eine spezifische Form der Lösung von Verteilungskonflikten in politisch schwachen Staaten [ist], die es nicht wagen können, die reale Umverteilung durch eine gleichzeitige nominale Umverteilung offenbar werden zu lassen", so würde diese Aussage in doppelter Weise auch die britischen Sozialkonflikte der zwanziger Jahre erklären und zugleich auf einen grundlegenden Unterschied zwischen Deutschland und England verweisen: Während in England der plötzliche Konjunktureinbruch im Winter 1920/21 die gesellschaftlichen Konflikte vor allem im Bergbau und in der metallverarbeitenden Industrie sichtlich verschärfte, konnte es sich ein im Gegensatz zu Deutschland politisch ausgesprochen starker und stabiler Staat mit tiefverwurzelten demokratischen Traditionen noch zusätzlich primär im Interesse seiner Finanzoligarchie leisten, die Weichen zumindest kurzfristig krisenverschärfend von einer inflationären auf eine deflationäre Entwicklung zu stellen, ohne befürchten zu müssen, daß die Sprengkräfte vom sozialen auf das politisch-parlamentarische System durchschlagen würden. Eben dies war in Deutschland mit seiner noch jungen und recht instabilen demokratischen Ordnung bis 1923 offenbar nicht möglich. Erhebliche Differenzen, die in den unterschiedlichen Traditionen der englischen und deutschen Gewerkschaftsbewegung begründet lagen, ergaben sich in der formalen Ausgestaltung der mittleren Variante der Machtteilung und Mitbestimmung und damit zugleich in den Formen, Ebenen und Inhalten der Konfliktaustragung. Dies wird schon deutlich an den Prioritäten, die der Gewerkschaftsführer und profilierte Labourpolitiker Clynes in der erwähnten Unterhausdebatte vom 20. März 1922 in der konkreten Auffüllung der allgemeinen Feststellung, „Industry must be, and has been for long, restrained by at least four lines of action", setzte: „First by Legislation, of which this House has frequently approved. Secondly, by trade union action, which is commonly accepted even by employers themselves, and certainly is not resented by the employing class as a whole. Third, by joint organisation, and by such arrangements mutually entered into as are, for instance, very well symbolised in what we know as the Whitley Councils,

Handlungsspielräume in der großen Wirtschaftskrise der frühen dreißiger Jahre: Zur Revision des überlieferten Geschichtsbildes, in: *Die Weimarer Republik*, hrsg. von Michael Stürmer, Königstein/Ts. 1980, S. 318 ff.

joint organisations covering between 3 000 000 and 4 000 000 workers, and, fourth, public opinion has often exerted itself in a manner to restrain industry from tendencies which otherwise would have been shown."[76]

Während die deutsche Konzeption der „Wirtschaftsdemokratie" auf Institutionalisierung und Formalisierung in der Verfassung (Räteartikel 165 WRV), auf nationaler und Branchenebene (ZAG) und in der Betriebsstruktur (Betriebsrätegesetz) zielte, ist der Inbegriff der „industrial democracy" das „collective bargaining" (nur sehr unvollständig mit Tarifverhandlungen zu übersetzen), also die permanente Entfaltung gewerkschaftlicher Gegenmacht, die „trade union action" und hier im Konfliktfall besonders das kollektive, von den Gewerkschaften frei ausgehandelte und dementsprechend auch jederzeit aufkündbare und modifizierbare konfliktregulierende Verfahren, das „procedure agreement" respektive die „disputes procedures" oder „provisions for avoiding disputes", wie sie von der A.S.E./A.E.U. seit 1898 immer wieder — 1914/1919/1921 und 1922 — zum Gegenstand harter Auseinandersetzungen mit den Arbeitgebern, nicht selten auch erbitterter Arbeitskämpfe gemacht worden sind. Tief saß gerade in der Metallindustrie das Mißtrauen gegen alle Formen institutionalisierter Mitbestimmung, gegen „joint organisation" oder gegen den „Whitleyism", das heftig abgelehnte paritätische Mitbestimmungsgebäude der Nachkriegszeit. Nur so ist es auch verständlich, wie intensiv und penibel in der Formulierung und Auslegung der „procedure agreements" in der Metallindustrie 1921/22 um alle Punkte gerungen wurde, die — wie die Status-Quo-Regelung — auf eine Einschränkung traditioneller restriktiver Gewerkschaftspraktiken „vor Ort" am Arbeitsplatz hinausliefen. Den Faktor der „public opinion" schließlich bemühten sich Gewerkschafts- und Labour-Führung zweimal während des Arbeitskampfes, jedoch beide Male ohne sichtbare Breitenwirkung zu ihren Gunsten zu mobilisieren, zuerst in der auf Antrag der Labour-Fraktion zustande gekommenen Unterhausdebatte am 20. März und dann Anfang Mai bei der zuvor wochenlang ergebnislos angestrebten Einsetzung eines "Court of Inquiry".

Die englischen Gewerkschaften waren bereit, sich mit der Deflationsstrategie langfristig im eigenen Interesse der Wiederankurbelung

---

[76] *Parliamentary Debates, House of Commons*, Vol. 152, Col. 80.

der wirtschaftlichen Prosperität bis zu einem gewissen Punkt unter folgenden Bedingungen, wie gezeigt, zu identifizieren:
— Sicherung und gegebenenfalls sogar gewisse Hebung der Reallöhne durch die Garantie, daß die Nominallohnsenkungen nur im gleichen Rhythmus oder langsamer als die Senkung der Lebenshaltungskosten erfolgten;
— eine Senkung der Gestehungkosten und der Preise vorwiegend durch Rationalisierung und Modernisierung der Produktion, also über den kapitalintensiven Weg und nicht über die Lohnkosten und eine verschärfte Ausbeutung der Arbeitskraft;
— ein in den „procedures" geregeltes erhebliches Mitspracherecht im Betrieb bei diesem Prozeß der Modernisierung, so unter anderem bei der Ausbildung und Qualifizierung für neue Maschinen, bei ihrer Beschickung oder beim Aushandeln von Lohnstückkosten und Akkordsätzen.

Damit aber waren wiederum Grundsatzfragen ökonomischer Entscheidungsgewalt im kapitalistischen System und der Verfügungsgewalt über die Produktionsmittel auf mikro- und makroökonomischer Ebene aufgeworfen, deren Relevanz und Brisanz gerade unter den Bedingungen der Konjunktur- und Deflationskrise in England nach dem Ersten Weltkrieg am Beispiel der metallverarbeitenden Industrien besonders deutlich gemacht werden kann.

Summary

An exemplary investigation of the British engineering lock-out in the spring of 1922 in the context of a project on inflation can be justified on five grounds: First, it shows how, not only in mining, conflicts in English social relations were dramatically brought to a head whose foundation had already been laid in the last quarter of the 19th century and which were inseparable from the rapid technological and scientific transformations of that period. Second, in the metal working industry, as in mining, long term problems of modernization and growth reached a sudden high point in 1920/21, when an international economic crisis was exacerbated in England — in contrast to Germany — by the deflationary policy of the Treasury, the Bank of England and the City, all of whom were less oriented toward foreign trade than toward monetary priorities, i. e., the restoration of the prewar exchange rate of the Pound. One of the central purposes of this essay is to show how employers and workers reacted to this double crisis and to the national and international parameters of distributional conflict which it set and how the crisis exacerbated the social conflict. What was involved in the end with respect to social relations was no longer only wages but rather deep seated sociopolitical differences, which can be encompassed in slogan-like form by the terms „workers' control" versus „managerial functions." Thirdly, the basic economic positions of the employers and workers in this particular conflict are expressed especially vividly in two extensive propaganda pieces: „The Present Economic Position of the Engineering and Allied Industries" and the trade union reply, „Some Comments on ‚The Present Economic Position of the Engineering and Allied Industries.'" It is possible, therefore, to consider this labor struggle beyond its immediate causes arising out of conditions in this specific branch and to embed it in the economic discussion of the 1920's concerning cyclical management, monetary policy and potentialities for economic growth. Fourthly, the engineering lock-out was the last great outburst of the social turmoil following the reconstruction period after the First World War, a phenomenon which encompassed all sectors of production — especially mining, railroads, transportation as well as iron and steel — and which illustrated the enormous difficulties of adaptation and normalisation in the transition from the wartime to the peacetime economy. Finally — and here is the connection with Germany — there was already in the contemporary debate at the time the comparison between the deflationary crisis-racked England and the predominantly inflationary continent with Germany at its head. The German competition was recognized as *the* great challenge to the British engineering industry. This opens up the possibility for us today, within the context of the study of a leading sector of the two economies, engineering, to delineate more sharply national peculiarities and transnational comparisons of modern industrial economies through the comparison of a deflationary land which felt the full impact of the world economic crisis (England) and a land experiencing a short-term illusory inflationary boom (Germany).

These general questions are dealt with through a structuring of the investigation in four steps: a presentation of the engineering lock-out itself, its historical roots, its cause and its results, and then following an analysis of the contrasting basic positions of the employers and the unions. At the end, there is a brief sketch of the considerations involved in an comparison of England and Germany.

Die Auswirkungen inflationärer Wirtschaftsentwicklung auf das Arbeitszeitproblem in der deutschen und amerikanischen eisen- und stahlerzeugenden Industrie

IRMGARD STEINISCH

Als die deutsche eisen- und stahlerzeugende Industrie nach Beendigung der Hyperinflation Ende 1923 die Wirtschafts- und Währungskrise des Reiches dazu benutzte, um die Rückkehr zum zwölfstündigen Doppelschichtsystem in den Hochofen-, Stahl- und Walzwerken zu erzwingen, stellte dieses Vorgehen einen internationalen Alleingang dar. Reaktionen aus dem Ausland, daß das den deutschen Währungszerfall begleitende Exportdumping nun in der Form eines sozialen Dumpings fortgesetzt werden sollte, waren aus internationaler Sicht nur allzu verständlich.[1] Schließlich kämpfte die eisen- und stahlerzeugende Industrie weltweit mit Absatzschwierigkeiten und Rentabilitätsverlusten aufgrund unzureichend ausgelasteter Produktionskapazitäten, ohne sich deshalb von der Neuerung des achtstündigen Dreischichtsystems loszusagen. Darüber hinaus hatte das Deutsche Reich nach Kriegsende mit der gesetzlichen Etablierung des Achtstundentages und der 48-Stundenwoche international an der Spitze des Arbeitszeitfortschritts gestanden, um durch die gesetzliche Einschränkung des Achtstundentages während der Krise 1923/24 zum Schlußlicht dieser Entwicklung zu werden.

In keinem der wichtigen westlichen Industrieländer hatten sich, obwohl vor dem Krieg international in den durchgehend produzierenden Industriezweigen noch üblich, zwölfstündige Schichtzeiten halten können. Auf den massiven Druck der Arbeiterschaft hin sorgten zwi-

---

[1] Siehe *Die Arbeitszeit im Auslande*, in: *Stahl und Eisen*, 44. Jg., Nr. 11 (1924), S. 296.

Inflationäre Wirtschaftsentwicklung und Arbeitszeitproblem

schen 1918 und 1920 meist entsprechende Arbeitszeitgesetze dafür, daß das achtstündige Dreischichtsystem unter anderem in der eisen- und stahlerzeugenden Industrie Großbritanniens, Frankreichs, Belgiens, Österreichs und Italiens allgemeinen Einzug hielt.[2] Lediglich die amerikanische eisen- und stahlerzeugende Industrie als der mit Abstand größte Produzent auf dem Weltmarkt hatte sich dieser Arbeitszeitverkürzung nach Kriegsende zunächst widersetzen können, jedoch ohne bleibenden Erfolg. Zu dem Zeitpunkt, als die deutsche eisen- und stahlerzeugende Industrie wieder zum zwölfstündigen Doppelschichtsystem zurückkehrte, befand sich die amerkanische eisen- und stahlerzeugende Industrie gerade im Endstadium der Einführung des achtstündigen Dreischichtsystems, und letzteres wurde 1924 zur Regel.

Im Gegensatz zu den europäischen Industriestaaten stand auf amerikanischer Seite hinter dieser Einführung des achtstündigen Dreischichtsystems kein gesetzlicher Zwang, sondern allenfalls die Drohung einer möglichen gesetzlichen Arbeitszeitregelung.[3] Nach Kriegsende war nämlich noch stärker als zuvor offenkundig, daß die amerikanische eisen- und stahlerzeugende Industrie den Anschluß an die allgemeine Arbeitszeitentwicklung in den Vereinigten Staaten hoffnungslos verpaßt hatte. Durch die staatliche Unterstützung des Achtstundentags als der prinzipiellen Arbeitszeitnorm während des Krieges hatte sich der Trend zur Arbeitszeitverkürzung beträchtlich beschleunigt, so

---

[2] *Achtstundentag*, in: *Handwörterbuch der Arbeitswissenschaft*, hrsg. von Fritz Giese, Bd. 1, Halle 1930, S. 28 ff.; ferner *Der internationale Achtstundentag* (= Beilage zu den *Mitteilungen der Vereinigung der Deutschen Arbeitgeberverbände*, Nr. 20/21), Bundesarchiv Koblenz, Verein Deutscher Eisen- und Stahlindustrieller, R 13 I/368.

[3] Falls die eisen- und stahlerzeugende Industrie nicht freiwillig den Zwölfstundentag abschaffen würde, hielt man nicht nur in der sozialreformerischen Presse ein gesetzliches Vorgehen für notwendig. Ob die republikanische Regierung unter Präsident Warren G. Harding, der die staatliche Reglementierung und den Interventionismus auf ein Minimum beschränkt wissen wollte, soweit gegangen wäre, ist überaus fraglich. Darüber hinaus war ein bundesstaatliches Arbeitszeitgesetz auch verfassungsrechtlich umstritten, obwohl man auf das Beispiel des Adamson-Gesetzes von 1916, das den Achtstundentag für die Eisenbahnen gesetzlich verfügte, verweisen konnte. Vgl. dazu: Irmgard Steinisch, *Acht Stunden sind besser als zwölf: Die wirtschafts- und sozialpolitischen Probleme sowie politischen Implikationen des Kampfes um die Einführung des achtstündigen Dreischichtsystems in der deutschen und amerikanischen eisen- und stahlerzeugenden Industrie vor und nach dem Ersten Weltkrieg* [Maschinenschrift], Phil. Diss., München 1981, Kap. III,1.

daß 1919 für fast die Hälfte aller Industriearbeiter (48,6 %) eine 48stündige oder kürzere Arbeitszeit galt. Lediglich drei Prozent der Industriearbeiter arbeiteten regelmäßig länger als 60 Stunden in der Woche, wobei die eisen- und stahlerzeugende Industrie mit ihren zwölfstündigen Doppelschichten, 24stündigen Wechselschichten im 14tägigen Rhythmus und Wochenarbeitszeiten von 60 bis über 84 Stunden von allen Industrien den größten Anteil der Arbeiter in dieser Arbeitszeitkategorie stellte.[4] Die Ablehnung derartig langer Arbeitszeiten durch eine reformbewußte Öffentlichkeit, die in diesen „barbarischen" Arbeitsverhältnissen ebenso eine Gefahr für die Gesundheit der betroffenen Arbeiter wie für deren soziale und politische Integration sah, brachte der amerikanische Präsident Warren G. Harding im Sommer 1923 mit der öffentlichen Feststellung zum Ausdruck, daß der Zwölfstundentag ein Anachronismus im amerikanischen Leben sei.[5] Diesem Urteilsspruch, der auf einem breiten gesellschaftspolitischen Konsens beruhte, beugte sich die amerikanische eisen- und stahlerzeugende Industrie freiwillig, wenn auch widerstrebend.

Nach der Einführung des achtstündigen Dreischichtsystems 1923/24 verlor sich das öffentlich-politische Interesse schnell wieder, und da weder legislativ noch tarifvertraglich gebunden, wäre es für die eisen- und stahlerzeugende Industrie ein leichtes gewesen, die Arbeitszeiten allmählich wieder zu verlängern. Die entspannte Lage auf dem Arbeitsmarkt in der zweiten Hälfte der zwanziger Jahre und die Schwäche der amerikanischen Gewerkschaften machten eine besondere Rücksichtnahme auf die Arbeiterschaft unnötig, denn dank der erfolgreichen Ausrottungstaktiken der Arbeitgeber gegenüber jeder gewerkschaftlichen Organisation verfügten die Arbeiter über wenige Möglichkeiten der Gegenwehr.[6] Darüber hinaus hatte die eisen- und stahlerzeugende Industrie als einen der wichtigsten Gründe gegen die Einführung der

---

[4] *Monthly Labor Review*, Bd. 15 (1922), S. 319.

[5] Vgl. Robert K. Murray, *The Harding Era. Warren G. Harding and his Administration*, Minneapolis, Minn. 1969, S. 237f.

[6] Für die Schwäche der amerikanischen Gewerkschaften in den zwanziger Jahren vgl. allgemein Irving Bernstein, *The Lean Years: A History of the American Worker 1920—1933*, Boston 1960; spezifisch für die Situation in der eisen- und stahlerzeugenden Industrie David Brody, *Steelworkers in America. The Nonunion Era*, New York 1969, bes. Kap. 13, sowie David H. Kelly, *Labor Relations in the Steel Industry: Management's Ideas, Proposals, and Programs, 1920 to 1950* [Maschinenschrift], Diss., Bloomington, Indiana 1976, bes. Kap. 2.

Achtstundenschicht stets den Wunsch der betroffenen Arbeiter selbst nach langen Arbeitszeiten angeführt, wegen des damit verbundenen Mehrverdienstes, so daß eine erneute Arbeitszeitverlängerung nur folgerichtig gewesen wäre. Trotzdem hielt die Industrie im großen und ganzen am einmal eingeführten achtstündigen Dreischichtsystem fest, wenn auch bei Ausbruch der Weltwirtschaftskrise 1929 festgestellt wurde, daß immer noch oder wiederum etwa sechs Prozent der Eisen- und Stahlarbeiter regelmäßig zwölf Stunden pro Tag und gelegentlich sogar noch länger arbeiteten.[7]

Offensichtlich war das Experiment mit dem Achtstundentag auf amerikanischer Seite wesentlich positiver als auf deutscher Seite ausgefallen, wo die eisen- und stahlerzeugende Industrie nach fünfjähriger Praxis die Rückkehr zum zwölfstündigen Doppelschichtsystem erzwang. Dabei war die mentalitätsmäßige Ausgangsposition der Arbeitgeber in der Beurteilung der Arbeitszeitfrage auf deutscher und amerikanischer Seite durchaus identisch und reichte bis in die Vorkriegszeit zurück. Aufgrund der für die eisen- und stahlerzeugende Industrie typischen tätigen und beobachtenden Arbeitsleistung, die eng verzahnt war, vermochte man auf Arbeitgeberseite keine physische Überbelastung der Arbeiter durch zwölfstündige Doppelschichten zu erkennen, denn schließlich war Arbeitsbereitschaft nicht Arbeit, sondern „freie" Zeit. Ferner versprach man sich wegen der angeblichen Einflußlosigkeit der menschlichen Arbeitsleistung auf die Maschinenleistung keine Produktivitätsgewinne durch Arbeitszeitverkürzung. Deshalb gab einerseits die Furcht vor einem möglichen Verlust der internationalen Wettbewerbsfähigkeit, andererseits die Möglichkeit einer Aufwertung der für Arbeitszeitverkürzung agitierenden Gewerkschaften den entscheidenden Ausschlag für den Widerstand gegen eine Einführung des achtstündigen Dreischichtsystems. Angeblich konnte weder die deutsche noch die amerikanische eisen- und stahlerzeugende Industrie, obwohl vor Kriegsausbruch die beiden leistungsstärksten der Welt, die höheren Lohnkosten der verkürzten Arbeitszeit verkraften.[8] Noch 1922, als die amerikanische Industrie sowohl produktionstechnisch als

---

[7] Siehe E. M. Hartl/E. G. Ernst, *The Steel Mills Today. The Twelve-Hour Day and the Seven-Day Week Go On*, in: *New Republic* vom 19. 2. 1930, S. 7—9; für die Arbeitszeitdiskussion siehe I. Steinisch, *Acht Stunden sind besser als zwölf*... [wie Anm. 3], Kap. III.

[8] A.a.O., Kap. I.

auch erzeugungsmäßig eine international unbestrittene Führungsposition innehatte, hielt Elbert H. Gary, der Leiter der United States Steel Corporation, des größten Stahlkonzerns der Welt, die Einführung des achtstündigen Dreischichtsystems für einen Versuch, die Industrie zu ruinieren.[9]

Allerdings trat trotz dieser Arbeitszeitverkürzung der Ruin der amerikanischen eisen- und stahlerzeugenden Industrie nicht ein, gleichermaßen löste auch die Rückkehr zum zwölfstündigen Doppelschichtsystem die Probleme der deutschen eisen- und stahlerzeugenden Industrie nicht. Vielmehr handelte sich letztere durch die Arbeitszeitverlängerung eine beständige Unruhe in ihren Betrieben ein und sah sich gezwungen, einen unablässigen Grabenkampf gegen erneute, wenn auch schrittweise Arbeitszeitverkürzungen zu führen, die sich trotz allem nicht verhindern ließen.[10] Warum aber die deutsche eisen- und stahlerzeugende Industrie selbst im letzten Drittel der zwanziger Jahre, ungeachtet der verbesserten wirtschaftlichen Lage, ihren Widerstand gegen das achtstündige Dreischichtsystem nicht aufgab, obwohl das zwölfstündige Doppelschichtsystem mittlerweile international zu einem Anachronismus geworden war, lag nicht unwesentlich in den Rahmenbedingungen von Revolution und Inflation begründet, die nach Kriegsende die Umstellung auf den Achtstundentag begleitet hatten.

I

Die Einführung des Achtstundentages unter den Bedingungen von Revolution und Inflation

Der politische Umsturz durch den Ausbruch der sozialen Revolution am 8./9. November 1918 diktierte im Deutschen Reich mit einem Schlag die allgemeine Einführung des Achtstundentages in Industrie und Wirtschaft. Den veränderten machtpolitischen Verhältnissen sowie der revolutionären Ausrufung des Achtstundentages als gültiger Normalarbeitszeit trug das am 15. November 1918 zwischen den Interessenverbänden der Arbeitgeber und den Gewerkschaften abgeschlossene Zentralarbeitsgemeinschaftsabkommen Rechnung, an dessen Zu-

---

[9] Siehe *Iron Age* vom 28. 12. 1922, S. 1719.
[10] Siehe dazu ausführlich Bernd Weisbrod, *Schwerindustrie in der Weimarer Republik. Interessenpolitik zwischen Stabilisierung und Krise,* Wuppertal 1978, Kap. IV, 1 u. 2.

standekommen der bekannteste Vertreter der rheinisch-westfälischen Schwerindustrie, Hugo Stinnes, maßgeblich beteiligt war, der 1922 seine Autorität ebenso effektiv für einen Appell zu Mehrarbeit und Abschaffung des Achtstundentages einzusetzen wußte.[11] Mit der zunächst geheimgehaltenen Einschränkung der Internationalisierung legte das Abkommen die Einführung des Achtstundentages ohne Lohnkürzung fest. Damit waren die bis dahin noch in der eisen- und stahlerzeugenden Industrie bestehenden Hoffnungen, durch die sofortige Einwilligung in die Gewerkschaftsforderungen aus der Vorkriegs- und Kriegszeit, wie Verkürzung der Samstagschichten auf acht Stunden und Umstellung der Hochofenwerke auf das Dreischichtsystem, die Abschaffung der zwölfstündigen Doppelschichten in den Stahl- und Walzwerken zumindest zu verzögern, zunichte gemacht.[12] Kaum eine Woche später konkretisierte zudem die sozialistische Revolutionsregierung die neue Arbeitszeitregelung durch den Erlaß einer Demobilmachungsverordnung, die am 23. November 1918 in Kraft trat.[13]

Infolge der revolutionären Entwicklung war die möglichst schnelle Durchführung des Achtstundentages nicht mehr eine wirtschaftliche, sondern eine politische Überlebensfrage, und unter diesem Druck vollzog sich der Übergang vom zwölfstündigen Zweischichtsystem zum achtstündigen Dreischichtsystem in erstaunlich kurzer Zeit. Obwohl gelegentlicher Mangel an qualifizierten Arbeitskräften vor allem in den Thomas- und Walzwerken Ausnahmeregelungen nötig machten, war Anfang 1919 die achtstündige Schicht in den Betrieben der eisen- und stahlerzeugenden Industrie weitgehend etabliert.[14] Vor dem Hinter-

---

[11] Vgl. Gerald D. Feldman, *German Business Between War and Revolution: The Origins of the Stinnes-Legien Agreement*, in Gerhard A. Ritter (Hrsg.), *Entstehung und Wandel der modernen Gesellschaft. Festschrift für Hans Rosenberg*, Berlin 1970, S. 312—341; ferner *Mark-Stabilisierung und Arbeitsleistung. Rede von Hugo Stinnes gehalten am 9. November 1922 im Reichswirtschaftsrat* (Broschüre), Berlin 1922.

[12] Siehe die Arbeitszeitverhandlungen in Gerald D. Feldman, *The Origins of the Stinnes-Legien Agreement: A Documentation*. Unter Mithilfe von Irmgard Steinisch, in: *Internationale wissenschaftliche Korrespondenz zur Geschichte der deutschen Arbeiterbewegung*, H. 19/20 (Dez. 1973), bes. S. 61 f., 70 ff., 85; ferner Rundschreiben des Arbeitgeberverbandes für den Nordwestlichen Bezirk des Vereins Deutscher Eisen- und Stahlindustrieller (Arbeitnordwest) vom 12. 11. 1918, Historisches Archiv der Gutehoffnungshütte (HA/GHH), Nr. 300140/8.

[13] *Reichsgesetzblatt*, Jg. 1918, S. 1334—1336.

[14] Vgl. *Vereinbarung für die Übergangszeit*, Rundschreiben des Arbeitnordwest vom 21. 11. 1918, Bundesarchiv Koblenz, R 13 I/189.

grund der zügigen wirtschaftlichen und militärischen Demobilmachung, der damit verbundenen Furcht vor einer drohenden Massenarbeitslosigkeit und weiterer politischen Radikalisierung stellte die Einführung des Achtstundentags trotz der Notwendigkeit, einen vollen Lohnausgleich gewähren zu müssen, was angesichts der langen Arbeitszeiten in der eisen- und stahlerzeugenden Industrie nicht unerheblich war, noch ein verhältnismäßig kleines Übel dar, dessen Kosten sich wegen des Rohstoff- und Auftragsmangels, der häufigen Produktionseinstellungen und Verrichtung unproduktiver Arbeiten sowie der politischen Lohnerhöhungen kaum kalkulieren ließen.[15] Demgegenüber kamen die positiven Auswirkungen der Arbeitszeitverkürzung deutlich zum Tragen. Durch gesetzliche Verordnung, aber auch aus politischer Vorsicht ohnehin nicht in der Lage, den teilweise aufgeblähten Belegschaftsumfang den Erfordernissen der Friedenswirtschaft umgehend anpassen zu können, ließ sich die Einrichtung einer dritten Schicht zunächst als Arbeitsstreckung durchaus begrüßen und die Arbeitszeitverkürzung selbst als wichtige Maßnahme der Arbeiterbeschwichtigung und Arbeitererholung betrachten.[16] Angesichts der katastrophalen Ernährungs- und Versorgungslage gab es für die von Unterernährung und körperlicher Überanstrengung gezeichnete Arbeiterschaft kaum eine andere Möglichkeit, als durch Leistungsverringerung Gesundheit und Körperkräfte zu schonen. Die Arbeitszeitverkürzung kam diesem Bedürfnis entgegen, das sich auch in dem Insistieren der Arbeiterschaft auf Abschaffung der Akkord- und Prämienentlohnung artikulierte.[17]

Unter den Rahmenbedingungen des politischen und wirtschaftlichen Bankrotts war das logische Resultat dieser betriebsorganisatorischen Neuerungen eine weitere Verschärfung des drastischen Produktionsabfalls, der für die eisen- und stahlerzeugende Industrie wegen des Verlustes von Elsaß-Lothringen und den dortigen Werksanlagen sowie der Unterbrechung des Verbundsystems zwischen den links- und rechts-

---

[15] Für die katastrophale Rohstoff- und Verkehrslage siehe die Wirtschaftsberichte des Reichswirtschaftsministers an den Reichspräsidenten, die monatlich abgefaßt wurden. Bundesarchiv Koblenz, R 43 I/1147; ferner sehr informativ: *Jahresberichte der Gewerbeaufsichtsbeamten und Bergbehörden für das Jahr 1919. Amtliche Ausgabe,* Bd. 1, Berlin 1920, bes. S. 269 ff., 497 ff., 596 ff. u. 699 ff.

[16] Vgl. z. B. *Beispiel für einen Anschlag!,* Rundschreiben des Arbeitnordwest vom 16. 11. 1918, HA/GHH, Nr. 300140/8.

[17] Siehe *Jahresberichte der Gewerbeaufsichtsbeamten für 1919*... [wie Anm. 15].

rheinischen Unternehmen doppelt schwer wog.[18] Gegenüber 1913 sank die Zahl der betriebenen Hochöfen im deutschen Reich 1919 um mehr als die Hälfte (313 : 152), die Produktion von Roheisen (16 764 000 t : 6 284 000 t) und Walzstahlfertigerzeugnissen (13 119 000 t : 5 230 000 t) um fast zwei Drittel und die Rohstahlerzeugung um mehr als die Hälfte (17 812 000 t : 7 932 000 t).[19] Langfristig mußten die Produktionseinbußen den Übergang vom wirtschaftlichen Substanzverlust durch Kriegsauszehrung und Kriegsniederlage zum völligen Wirtschaftsruin bedeuten, der durch die politisch bedingte Unmöglichkeit, die Arbeiterschaft in vollem Umfang an der Krise teilhaben zu lassen, nur noch beschleunigt werden konnte. Aus dieser Zwangssituation schuf der Währungsverfall einen Ausweg. Der sinkende Wert der Reichsmark erlaubte im Inland eine großzügigere Lohnpolitik, stellte auf dem Auslandsmarkt preismäßig einen kaum zu überbietenden Wettbewerbsvorteil dar, erleichterte dadurch die Rückeroberung der Auslandsmärkte, was die notwendigen Devisen für die Rohstoffbeschaffung einbrachte. Deshalb begann die eisen- und stahlerzeugende Industrie zunehmend den Auslandsmarkt zu bevorzugen, und unter dieser Konstellation fiel die Höhe des Lohnkostenanteils vergleichsweise weniger ins Gewicht, als die Notwendigkeit, die Produktion zu steigern.[20]

Seit Mitte 1919 vermehrten sich die Vorstöße in der eisen- und stahlerzeugenden Industrie, durch die Rückkehr zu einem leistungsorientierten Lohnsystem die Produktivität zu steigern.[21] Nach den Berichten der Gewerbeaufsichtsbeamten war das Resultat der Wiedereinführung von Akkordarbeit und Prämienzahlung im August 1919 in manchen Fällen, so in einem großen gemischten Werk Rheinland-Westfalens, eine Verdoppelung der Arbeitsleistung.[22] Tatsächlich zeigte die Produktion in der zweiten Hälfte des Jahres steigende Tendenz, doch wurde erst 1921/22 ein deutlich verbessertes Produktionsvolumen erreicht, das aber immer noch hinter der Vorkriegsleistung zurückblieb.[23] Zu dieser Zeit stand die Produktionsbehinderung durch

---

[18] Vgl. Gustav Hempel, *Die deutsche Montanindustrie*, Essen 1969, S. 109—112.
[19] *Stahl und Eisen*, Sonderheft: *100 Jahre Stahlwirtschaftliche Organisationen*, 94. Jg., Nr. 21 vom 10. Oktober 1974, S. 1018—1020.
[20] Siehe Gerald D. Feldman, *Iron and Steel in the German Inflation 1916—1923*, Princeton, N.J. 1977, bes. Kap. 2 und 3.
[21] Siehe Hauptvorstandssitzung des VDESI vom 3. 2. 1920, Bundesarchiv Koblenz, R 13 I/157; ferner *Jahresberichte der Gewerbeaufsichtsbeamten für 1919*... [wie Anm. 15].
[22] A.a.O., S. 606.
[23] *Stahl und Eisen*, Sonderheft... [wie Anm. 19], S. 1018—1020.

die „schematische" Festlegung der täglichen Arbeitszeit auf acht Stunden schon im Mittelpunkt der öffentlichen Kritik, die von der eisen- und stahlerzeugenden Industrie angeführt wurde. Ersten Auftrieb hatte diese Arbeitszeitkampagne durch die deutlichen Anzeichen einer Markstabilisierung im Sommer 1920 bekommen, denn nicht nur die eisen- und stahlerzeugende Industrie hielt mit dem möglichen Wegfall der Inflationsvorteile auf dem Weltmarkt eine Arbeitszeitverlängerung sowohl zur Produktionssteigerung als auch zur Produktionskostensenkung für unumgänglich. Obwohl die Valutastabilisierung eine temporäre Erscheinung blieb, erhielt die Kampagne gegen den Achtstundentag weitere Nahrung durch die Versuche der Reichsregierung, das Provisorium der Demobilmachungsverordnung über die Arbeitszeit durch ein ordentliches Gesetz abzulösen, über das jedoch zwischen Arbeitgebern und Gewerkschaften keine Einigung zu erzielen war.[24]

Schließlich ging es der eisen- und stahlerzeugenden Industrie nicht allein um die Beseitigung des allgemein in Industrie und Wirtschaft vielbeklagten „Schematismus" des gesetzlichen Achtstundentags, sondern um die Rückkehr zum zwölfstündigen Doppelschichtsystem. Für die Arbeiterschaft und die Gewerkschaften war dieses Ansinnen indiskutabel, denn schon vor dem Krieg hatte man gemeinsam mit Vertretern der Sozialreform auf staatliche Abhilfe für die überlangen Arbeitszeiten in der eisen- und stahlerzeugenden Industrie gedrungen und deren wirtschaftliche sowie soziale Verschwendung angeprangert.[25] In der Auffassung der Industrie hatte die praktische Erfahrung mit dem Achtstundentag jedoch die größere Effizienz des Zehnstundentages und des zwölfstündigen Doppelschichtsystems klar unter Beweis gestellt.[26] Diesen Befund stützten einschlägige Werksstatistiken, allerdings hatte die Gutehoffnungshütte in Oberhausen „wegen der Un-

---

[24] Vgl. R. R. Kuczynski, *Postwar Labor Conditions in Germany* (= *Bulletin of the U.S. Bureau of Labor Statistics*), Washington, D.C. 1925, S. 104—107; ferner Gerald D. Feldman/Irmgard Steinisch, *Die Weimarer Republik zwischen Sozial- und Wirtschaftsstaat: Die Entscheidung gegen den Achtstundentag*, in: *Archiv für Sozialgeschichte*, Bd. 18 (1978), S. 353—439.

[25] Für die Arbeitszeitdiskussion vor dem Ersten Weltkrieg vgl. I. Steinisch, *Acht Stunden sind besser als zwölf...* [wie Anm. 3], Kap. I.

[26] Schon Mitte 1920 sprach man in der eisen- und stahlerzeugenden Industrie offen von dem Achtstundentag als einem „nationalen Unglück". Siehe Hauptvorstandssitzung des VDESI vom 22. 6. 1920, Bundesarchiv Koblenz, R 13 I/158; vgl. ferner *Die Arbeitszeitfrage in Deutschland: Eine Denkschrift verfaßt von der Vereinigung der deutschen Arbeitgeberverbände* (= Schriften der VDA, H. 8), Berlin (1924).

Inflationäre Wirtschaftsentwicklung und Arbeitszeitproblem 403

möglichkeit der Erfassung der statistischen Daten" von vornherein darauf verzichtet, die Hüttenwerke in ihre Arbeitsleistungsstatistiken miteinzubeziehen, und sich auf die Walzwerke einschließlich deren Fertigerzeugnisse beschränkt, wo der Faktor Arbeitskraft besser meßbar war.[27] Andere Unternehmen waren weniger zurückhaltend, wie die Arbeitszeituntersuchung von Karl Knackfuß zeigt, die von den Hochofenwerken bis zu der Weiterverarbeitung alle Betriebsabteilungen erfaßte und auf den statistischen Erhebungen verschiedener rheinisch-westfälischer Werke beruhte.[28] Daß seine Untersuchungsergebnisse, die seines Erachtens die produktionsschädigenden Auswirkungen des Achtstundentags beweisen, nur mit großen Vorbehalten zu benutzen sind, macht das Beispiel der Gutehoffnungshütte deutlich. Zum einen sollten nach den Aussagen der Werksdirektion selbst diese Arbeitszeitstatistiken den „Nachweis führen ... daß in der Achtstundenschicht weniger geleistet wird als vor dem Kriege in der Zehnstundenschicht". Zum anderen war man sich durchaus klar darüber, daß eine „Reihe von Zufälligkeiten" nicht auszuschließen war.[29] Welcher Art diese „Zufälligkeiten" unter anderem sein konnten, läßt die nachfolgende Produktionsstatistik einer Walzstraße zumindest teilweise erkennen.

---

[27] Siehe GHH, Hauptverwaltung, Statistik über einen Vergleich der Leistungen in der Achtstundenschicht und Zehnstundenschicht, 1918—1921, HA/GHH, Nr. 300140/12.
[28] Karl Knackfuß, *Die Arbeitszeit-Frage in der rheinisch-westfälischen Eisen- und Stahlindustrie. Ihre Entwicklung und produktionstechnische Bedeutung*, Diss. Köln 1927, bes. S. 15.
[29] Siehe Niederschrift über die am 5. 12. 1922 in der Hauptverwaltung abgehaltene Besprechung über „Vereinfachung der Lohnverrechnung", HA/GHH, Nr. 300140/12.

TABELLE

*Produktionsleistung bei 8stündiger und 10stündiger Schicht
1919—1921*

Vergleichsbasis: 1. Halbjahr 1914 mit einer monatlichen Durchschnittsleistung von 3,160 t pro Schicht und Arbeiter.
GHH, Walzwerk Oberhausen, Träger- und Grobstrasse.

Monat	Jahr	Gesamt-Erzeugung in t	Schichten à 8 Std.	Arbeiter-zahl	Leistung pro Arbeiter u. Schicht in t	in % von 1914
Januar	1919	1838	725	29	2,530	80,07
	1920	3680	1592	68	2,31	73,1
	1921	3517	1561	68	2,252	71,27
Februar	1919	456,4	215	30	1,123	67,18
	1920	3465	1483	68	2,336	73,92
	1921	3010	1443	68	2,085	65,98 [a]
März	1919	487,3	188,56	32	2,584	81,77
	1920	3370,7	1513	68	2,227	70,47
	1921	3172	1476	68	2,142	67,78 [b]
April	1919	1214,9	479,375	33	2,534	80,19
	1920	3221	1401	68	2,3	72,78
	1921	3759	1651	68	2,276	72,03 [c]
Mai	1919	1658,4	684,5	31	2,423	76,68
	1920	3388	1454	68	2,3	73,73
	1921	2943	1360	68	2,164	68,48 [d]
Juni	1919	1703	731	30	2,329	73,7
	1920	3713	1676	68	2,214	70,06
	1921	3615	1586	68	2,278	72,09
Juli	1919	2041	849	29	2,402	76,01
	1920	3867	1751	68	2,208	69,88
	1921	3536	1596	68	2,214	70,06
August	1919	1792,5	673	31	2,663	84,27
	1920	3915	1632	68	2,398	75,89
	1921	3475	1599	68	2,173	68,08 [e]
Sept.	1919	2367	1141	29*/50**	2,074	65,63
	1920	3498	1698	68	2,059	65,16
	1921	3332	1598	68	2,085	65,98 [f]

Monat	Jahr	Gesamt-Erzeugung in t	Schichten à 8 Std.	Arbeiter-zahl	Leistung pro Arbeiter u. Schicht in t	in % von 1914
Oktober	1919	4043	1731	68	2,336	73,92
	1920	3919	1673	68	2,342	74,11
	1921	4037	1588	68	2,541	80,41 [g]
Nov.	1919	3382	1482	68	2,282	72,22
	1920	3388	1421	68	2,383	75,41
	1921	3704	1498	68	2,471	78,20
Dezember	1919	3233	1430	68	2,26	71,52
	1920	3518	1640	68	2,145	67,88
	1921	3863	1404	68	2,750	87,03 [h]

* Bis 15.
** Ab 15.

[a] Verminderung durch leichtere Profile.
[b] Verminderung durch schlechte Spezialfabrikation, viel Walzenwechsel.
[c] Wenig Störungen, daher bessere Schichtleistung.
[d] Verminderung: Auf der einen Schicht keine eingearbeitete Ofenbelegschaft, infolge fristlosen Austritts verschiedener Arbeiter.
[e] Verminderung durch schlechte Profile.
[f] Verminderung durch leichtere Profile und Betriebsstörungen.
[g] Vermehrung: Anreiz durch neuen günstigeren Akkord.
[h] Verminderung durch häufigen Walzenwechsel.

Aus: HA/GHH, Nr. 300140/12.

Nicht anzuzweifeln und mit einigen wenigen Ausnahmen allgemein typisch war die gegenüber 1914 deutlich gesunkene Produktion pro Schicht und Arbeiter. Ob damit gleichzeitig die geringere Arbeitsleistung im Achtstundentag und Dreischichtsystem gegenüber dem Zehnstundentag und Zweischichtsystem bewiesen ist, bleibt jedoch fraglich. Hinter einer derartigen Schlußfolgerung steht nämlich implizit die Annahme, daß alle anderen produktionsbeeinflussenden Faktoren weitgehend konstant geblieben seien, was allein wegen der Kriegseinwirkungen schlichtweg nicht zutreffen kann. In welchem Umfang aber gerade andere Faktoren neben dem Faktor Arbeitskraft, wie Auftragsspezifikationen, Materialbeschaffenheit, Energieversorgung, Zahl und Qualifikation der Belegschaftsmitglieder usw., die Produktionshöhe beeinflußten, demonstriert in Ausschnitten obige Statistik. Diese muß zudem hinsichtlich der Fluktuationen im Produktionsvolumen trotz konstanter Arbeiterzahl zu denken geben. Offensichtlich war der Grund für vermehrte oder verminderte Arbeitsleistung häufig nicht präzise zu bestimmen, vor allem aber schlagen sich selbst so wichtige politische Geschehnisse, wie zum Beispiel der Generalstreik während des Kapp-Putsches im März 1920, nicht unmittelbar im Produktionsergebnis nieder. Darüber hinaus fällt die vergleichsweise hohe Pro-Kopf-Produktion Anfang 1919 auf, als man durch die plötzliche Umstellung auf das Dreischichtsystem gezwungen war, mit wesentlich kleineren Belegschaften pro Schicht auszukommen. Damit stellt sich aber unter anderem auch die Frage nach der ausschlaggebenden Bedeutung und Verantwortlichkeit der Werksdirektionen, für eine produktivere Ausnutzung der Arbeitskraft bei verkürzter Arbeitszeit Sorge zu tragen. Grundsätzlich läßt sich daher anhand obiger Statistik lediglich der Tatbestand der gesunkenen Produktionsleistung pro Arbeiter und Schicht als gesicherte Erkenntnis ablesen, während über die Ursachen des Produktionsabfalls spekuliert werden muß.

Dieser Vorbehalt gilt in noch stärkerem Maße für die von Knackfuß zusammengestellten Statistiken, in denen er Belegschaftszahlen und Produktionshöhe im Monatsdurchschnitt für die Jahre 1913, 1922 und 1924 vergleicht, aber nur in Extremfällen knappe Hinweise auf die spezifischen Produktionsbedingungen der einzelnen Werke gibt. Da Knackfuß auch auf die erheblichen Differenzen in der Belegschaftssteigerung und der Pro-Kopf-Erzeugung nicht näher eingeht, kommt er zu Durchschnittswerten, die im großen und ganzen den Standpunkt der Arbeitgeber stützen, die den Rückgang der Produktion pro Arbeiter mit durchschnittlich 40 Prozent veranschlagten und dafür den Achtstundentag wegen der ungünstigeren Arbeitsweise und den höheren Belegschaftsziffern verantwortlich machten.[30] Diese einseitige Schuldzuweisung kann angesichts der Rolle der eisen- und stahlerzeugenden Industrie als Bremsblock im Arbeitszeitfortschritt der Vorkriegszeit kaum überraschen, und die Demobilmachungsverordnung über die Arbeitszeit vom 23. November 1918 war nicht dazu angetan, einen Prozeß des Umlernens einzuleiten.

Die gesetzliche Erlaubnis, daß die Arbeiter in kontinuierlichen Industriezweigen jede dritte Woche eine 16stündige Wechselschicht verfahren durften, war so ziemlich das einzige in der Demobilmachungsverordnung enthaltene Zugeständnis an den Produktionscharakter der eisen- und stahlerzeugenden Industrie.[31] Statt auf 48 Wochenstunden verkürzte sich dadurch für gut die Hälfte der Hochofenarbeiter und etwa zehn Prozent der Arbeiter in den Stahl- und Walzwerken, die produktionstechnisch bedingt ohne Rücksicht auf die Sonntagsruhe sieben Tage in der Woche arbeiten mußten, die Arbeitszeit nur auf 56 Wochenstunden.[32] Mit einer regulären Arbeitszeit von 84 Wochenstunden bis Kriegsende verkürzte sich die Wochenarbeitszeit für diese Arbeiterkategorien durch die Umstellung auf das achtstündige Dreischichtsystem also um insgesamt 28 Stunden oder 33 1/3 Prozent. Die gleiche prozentuale Arbeitszeitverkürzung galt für die übrigen Arbeiter in den kontinuierlichen Betrieben, denn hier sank die reguläre Wochenarbeitszeit von 72 auf 48 Stunden. Auch in den Werkstätten und Tagesbetrieben, wo der Zehnstundentag und die 60 Stundenwoche ausschließlich der Pausen die reguläre Arbeitszeit gebildet hatten, fiel die Arbeitszeitverkürzung mit zwei Stunden täglich und zwölf Stun-

---

[30] *Wirtschaftliche Auswirkung der Achtstundenschicht in Hüttenwerken*, in: *Stahl und Eisen*, 44. Jg. (1924), Nr. 37, S. 1102—1105; K. Knackfuß, *Die Arbeitszeit-Frage...* [wie Anm. 28], S. 19ff. Demgegenüber zeigt Hans Schönfeld, *Kritische Studien zum wirtschaftlichen Problem des Zwei- und Dreischichtsystems in Hochofenbetrieben* (= Schriften der Gesellschaft für soziale Reform, H. 79), Jena 1926, am Beispiel empirischer Betriebsanalysen, daß nicht in erster Linie die Arbeitszeitverkürzung für die Belegschaftsexpansion und Produktionsminderung verantwortlich gemacht werden könne, vielmehr u. a. die Folgen des Krieges ungleich schwerwiegender seien. Ferner verweist er auf den relativ geringen Anteil der Löhne an den gesamten Produktionskosten.
[31] Vgl. *Reichsgesetzblatt*, Jg. 1918, Art. 7, S. 1335.
[32] Die Angaben über die Anzahl der betroffenen Arbeiter beruhen auf den statistischen Daten der Vorkriegszeit. Siehe *Jahresberichte der Königlich Preußischen Regierungs- und Gewerberäte und Bergbehörden für das Jahr 1911. Amtliche Ausgabe*, Berlin 1912, S. 516 und *...für 1912*, Berlin 1913, S. 236.

den pro Woche, das heißt 20 Prozent, beachtlich aus.[33] Hinzu kam die rigorose gesetzliche Beschränkung der Überstunden, die nur in Notfällen erlaubt waren und von der behördlichen Genehmigung ebenso abhingen wie von der Einwilligung der Belegschaft. Damit war die Dispositionsfreiheit der Werksdirektionen drastisch beschnitten, denn Überstunden waren gewohnheitsmäßig das Schmieröl für einen reibungslosen Produktionsverlauf, mit dem der für die eisen- und stahlerzeugende Industrie typische Stoßbetrieb und die nicht eben selten auftretenden Betriebsstörungen bewältigt wurden.

Plötzlicher Auftragsdruck, unregelmäßige Wagengestellung durch die Eisenbahn, anfallende Reparaturen, Unfälle, Erkrankungen oder Bummelei der Arbeiter ließen sich mit Überstunden ausgleichen, von denen vor dem Krieg im Schnitt über die Hälfte der Eisen- und Stahlarbeiter mit umgerechnet einer 30 bis 40minütigen Verlängerung pro Schicht betroffen waren.[34] Die Klagen nicht nur der eisen- und stahlerzeugenden Industrie über den „Schematismus" der gesetzlichen Arbeitszeitregelung waren daher verständlich, denn für letztere entfernte die Demobilmachungsverordnung über die Arbeitszeit einen der wichtigsten Stützpfeiler in ihrer Betriebsorganisation. Zwar gelang es der eisen- und stahlerzeugenden Industrie schon im Mai 1919, eine erste Sonderregelung, der weitere folgten, von den Demobilmachungsbehörden zu erwirken, damit zumindest die notwendigen Wartungs- und Aufräumarbeiten wie in der Vorkriegszeit vor Beginn der Schicht und insbesondere am Sonntag bei teilweisem Betriebsstillstand durchgeführt werden konnten,[35] doch erübrigte sich damit nicht die Anpassung

---

[33] Die Pausenverordnung für die Großeisenindustrie vom 19. Dezember 1908 brachte theoretisch eine Arbeitszeitverkürzung auf 10 Stunden pro Schicht, da in den kontinuierlichen Betrieben eine zweistündige Pause obligatorisch wurde. Da jedoch ein Teil der Arbeitsbereitschaft auf die Pausenzeit angerechnet werden konnte und sich zudem die Arbeiter häufig nicht von ihrem Arbeitsplatz entfernen durften, um bei Bedarf einspringen zu können, muß die effektive Arbeitszeitverkürzung erheblich geringer veranschlagt werden. Anders lag der Fall in den nichtkontinuierlichen Betrieben, wo eine zweistündige Pausenzeit während der zwölfstündigen Schicht die Regel war. Dazu ausführlich I. Steinisch, *Acht Stunden sind besser als zwölf...* [wie Anm. 3], Kap. I.

[34] Das Überstundenunwesen in der eisen- und stahlerzeugenden Industrie hatte maßgeblich zu der Pausenverordnung von 1908 geführt, die u. a. auch die Werke zur Einführung von Überarbeitsverzeichnissen verpflichtet hatte. Deren Auswertung erfolgte durch die Gewerbeaufsichtsbeamten. Vgl. die zusammenfassenden Ergebnisberichte in den *Jahrbüchern für Nationalökonomie und Statistik*, III. Folge, Bde 40, 42, 44, 46, Berlin 1910—1914.

[35] Siehe *Jahresberichte der Gewerbeaufsichtsbeamten für 1919...*, S. 271, 501, 603, 701;

an die neuen Arbeitszeitverhältnisse. Anscheinend aber kam es mit Ausnahme der unumgänglichen Einführung einer dritten Schicht zu keiner weitergehenden Anpassung, zumindest deutet die starke Belegschaftsexpansion darauf hin. Gegenüber 1913 hatten sich nach den Angaben von Knackfuß die Belegschaftszahlen 1922 durchweg um mehr als 50 Prozent, zum Teil sogar um über 100 Prozent erhöht.[36] Offensichtlich hielt man statt organisatorischer Straffung des Betriebsganges und entsprechender Reduzierung der Belegschaften an dem überkommenen System einer überhöhten Belegschaftszahl pro Schicht fest, um so weitgehend gegen alle Störungen abgesichert zu sein. Das war bei der größeren physischen Beanspruchung der Arbeiterschaft im zwölfstündigen Zweischichtsystem notwendig und finanziell tragbar, machte bei einem achtstündigen Dreischichtsystem jedoch die Standardargumente der Kostengünstigkeit durch größere Produktivität und — für die eisen- und stahlerzeugende Industrie fast noch wichtiger — größere Zuverlässigkeit der Arbeiter weitgehend zunichte.[37]

Ohne Zweifel trug einerseits die Inflexibilität der Arbeitszeitregelung durch die strikte Überstundenbeschränkung zu diesem möglichen Verharren im überkommenen betriebsorganisatorischen Muster bei, andererseits schlugen sich hier die Einflüsse der Kriegserschöpfung, Revolution und Inflation deutlich nachteilig nieder. Erstens machte der abgenutzte Zustand der Betriebsanlagen ausgedehnte Reparaturarbeiten unumgänglich, was zumindest eine Teilursache für das überproportional starke Ansteigen der Belegschaftsziffern sein dürfte. Zweitens ließ zudem die unzureichende Material- und Energieversorgung einen regelmäßigen, durchorganisierten, da vorplanbaren Betriebsgang und Produktionsverlauf kaum aufkommen.[38] Drittens erhöhten der Ausbruch der Revolution und die politischen Unruhen die Konfliktbereitschaft der Belegschaften und verstärkten dadurch deren Unzuverlässigkeit und verminderte Leistungsfähigkeit, die ein Resultat der

---

siehe auch Gerhard Erdmann, *Die deutschen Arbeitgeberverbände im sozialgeschichtlichen Wandel der Zeit*, Berlin 1966, S. 136.
[36] K. Knackfuß, *Die Arbeitszeit-Frage...* [wie Anm. 28], S. 22—25.
[37] Vgl. Franz Wieber, *Die Arbeitszeit in ununterbrochenen Betrieben der Grosseisenindustrie. Bericht an die Internationale Vereinigung für gesetzlichen Arbeitsschutz*, Berlin 1912.
[38] Siehe H. Schönfeld, *Kritische Studien...* [wie Anm. 30], bes. S. 28 ff. u. 44 ff.; vgl. ferner Anm. 15.

physischen Erschöpfung durch die Kriegsentbehrungen war.³⁹ Die für eine größere Produktivität des Achtstundentags erforderliche bessere Arbeitsdisziplin und Leistungsbereitschaft konnte unter diesen Umständen kaum aufkommen, und nicht zuletzt die fortschreitende Inflation sorgte maßgeblich dafür, daß auch nach dem Abklingen der Revolutions- und Demobilmachungswirren keine überzeugende Besserung eintrat.

In den Worten der Arbeitgeber hatte der „verhüllende Nebel der Inflation" die Kosten des Achtstundentages verdeckt, denn die Geldentwertung machte eine präzise Kostenkalkulation unmöglich, reduzierte zudem die Bedeutung eines ausgewogenen Verhältnisses zwischen Produktionshöhe und aufgewandten Lohnkosten.⁴⁰ Auf der Arbeiterseite wiederum verloren die Lohnanreize für eine gesteigerte Arbeitsleistung immer mehr an Gewicht, selbst die traditionellen Unterschiede der finanziellen Honorierung von leichter und schwerer, qualifizierter und wenig qualifizierter Arbeit verflüchtigten sich mit zunehmendem Kaufkraftverlust.⁴¹ Neben dieser lohnmäßigen Leistungsdemoralisierung ergab sich zusätzlich durch den Funktionsverlust des Geldes die Notwendigkeit, Güterbedarfsdeckung für das tägliche Leben zu betreiben, was mindestens ebenso wichtig wurde wie der Bezug eines Geldlohnes aus geregelter Arbeit. Die zunehmende Schwarzarbeit und das mangelnde Arbeitsinteresse müssen vor diesem Hintergrund gesehen werden und waren kaum, wie die Klagen der Arbeitgeber zu interpretieren versuchten, eine ursächliche Folge des Achtstundentags.⁴²

Mit dem am 13./14. Dezember 1923 den Gewerkschaften mit Hilfe der staatlichen Schlichtung abgerungenen Mehrarbeitszeitabkommen, das mit Ausnahme der 24stündigen Wechselschichten und einem freien Samstagnachmittag für die Arbeiter in den nichtkontinuierlichen Betrieben die Vorkriegsarbeitszeit der allgemeinen Zwölfstundenschicht

---

³⁹ Zur Kriegsverelendung vgl. Jürgen Kocka, *Klassengesellschaft im Krieg 1914—1918* (= Kritische Studien zur Geschichtswissenschaft 8), Göttingen 1973, bes. S. 12 ff.

⁴⁰ So ein Direktor der GHH in Oberhausen, E. Hofmann, *Wirtschaftliche Auswirkungen der Achtstundenschicht in Hüttenwerken*, in: Stahl und Eisen, 44. Jg. (1924), Nr. 37, S. 1101.

⁴¹ Vgl. *25 Jahre Arbeitnordwest 1904—1929*, hrsg. vom Arbeitgeberverband für den Bezirk der nordwestlichen Gruppe des VDESI, Berlin 1929, S. 153 f.; R. R. Kuczynski, *Postwar Labor Conditions...* [wie Anm. 24], S. 142 ff.

⁴² *Jahresberichte der Gewerbeaufsichtsbeamten für 1920...*, S. 264 u. 638 f.

einschließlich einer zweistündigen Pause wiederherstellte,[43] begann die eisen- und stahlerzeugende Industrie die Wende einzuleiten. Dabei kam ihr der Wegfall der behindernden Demobilmachungsverordnungen ebenso zugute wie der durch die Kündigung des Tarifvertrages zum 1. Oktober 1923 durch die Gewerkschaften entstandene tariflose Zustand.[44] Neben dem Belegschaftsabbau, der in manchen Werken gegenüber 1922 bis zu 50 Prozent und mehr betrug, setzte man erneut eine deutliche Lohndifferenzierung durch, so daß die Lohnspanne zwischen einem Hilfsarbeiter und einem Facharbeiter im Schnitt 25 Prozent betrug.[45] Im Gegensatz zur Inflationskonjunktur kam es in der Absatzkrise nach der Währungsstabilisierung nicht mehr auf eine möglichst hohe Produktion an, die 1924 teilweise unter den Stand von 1921 zurückfiel,[46] sondern auf eine Senkung der Selbstkosten.[47] Diesem Ziel fiel der Achtstundentag zum Opfer, da die Arbeitszeitverlängerung einerseits den Lohnabbau für den einzelnen Arbeiter, falls er nicht arbeitslos wurde, milderte, andererseits den Unternehmern erhebliche Einsparungen bei den Lohnkosten ermöglichte. Entscheidend für die Arbeitszeitfrage war dabei jedoch, daß die Rückkehr zum zwölfstündigen Doppelschichtsystem als integraler Teil der wirtschaftlichen Reinigungskrise 1923/24 betrachtet wurde, die die wirtschaftliche Erholung in der zweiten Hälfte der zwanziger Jahre einleitete. Daß damit aber die These der höheren Produktivität kürzerer Arbeitszeiten für das achtstündige Dreischichtsystem in der eisen- und stahlerzeugenden Industrie noch keineswegs widerlegt ist, zeigt das amerikanische Beispiel, das zugleich die Voraussetzungen für eine erfolgreiche Arbeitszeitverkürzung spezifiziert.

[43] Siehe Abkommen und Verhandlungsberichte in Gerald D. Feldman/Heidrun Homburg, *Industrie und Inflation. Studien und Dokumente zur Politik der deutschen Unternehmer 1916—1923*, Hamburg 1977, S. 362—374.
[44] Vgl. G. D. Feldman/I. Steinisch, *Die Weimarer Republik zwischen Sozial- und Wirtschaftsstaat...*, in: *Archiv für Sozialgeschichte* [wie Anm. 24], S. 387 ff., bes. S. 404.
[45] K. Knackfuß, *Die Arbeitszeit-Frage...* [wie Anm. 28], S. 64—67; *Wirtschaftliche Auswirkungen der Achtstundenschicht in Hüttenwerken*, in: *Stahl und Eisen*, 44. Jg. (1924), Nr. 37, S. 1103.
[46] *Stahl und Eisen*, Sonderheft... [wie Anm. 19], S. 1018—1020.
[47] Vgl. *Geschäftsbericht des Arbeitnordwest für 1924*, Archiv der Mannesmann AG (Phoenix-Rheinrohr-Archiv), P 8/25/23/2; ferner *Wirtschaftliche Auswirkungen der Achtstundenschicht in Hüttenwerken*, in: *Stahl und Eisen*, 44. Jg. (1924), Nr. 37, S. 1104; für die Gesamtproblematik vgl. G. D. Feldman, *Iron and Steel in the German Inflation...* [wie Anm. 20], Kap. 6.

II

Der Übergang zum achtstündigen Dreischichtsystem unter den Bedingungen wirtschaftlicher und machtpolitischer Stabilität

Zeitpunkt und Modalitäten der Einführung des achtstündigen Dreischichtsystems in der zweiten Jahreshälfte 1923 waren für die amerikanische eisen- und stahlerzeugende Industrie überaus günstig, denn unterdessen war es unter anderem gelungen, die Auswirkungen der Kriegswirtschaft und Demobilmachung erfolgreich in den Griff zu bekommen und in eine neue „Normalität" zu überführen, die sich deutlich an den Zuständen der Vorkriegszeit orientierte. Gerade für die eisen- und stahlerzeugende Industrie war dieser Umstellungsprozeß schwierig, da der Krieg der Industrie einerseits eine einmalige wirtschaftliche Blüte beschert, andererseits aber die wirtschafts- und sozialpolitischen Arrangements aus der Vorkriegszeit zerstört hatte.[48]

Die Politik informeller Preiskartellbildung zwecks Marktstabilisierung war mit der Kriegshausse für Stahl und Eisen 1915/16 in die Brüche gegangen, durch staatliche Festpreise 1917 wieder hergestellt worden und ging mit dem schnellen Rückzug des Staates aus der Wirtschaft nach Kriegsende erneut verloren. Das bedeutete konkret, daß das gegenüber dem letzten guten Geschäftsjahr 1913 bei Kriegsende um rund 100 Prozent gestiegene Preisniveau sich während der Nachkriegskonjunktur 1919/20 noch einmal um bis zu 60 Prozent erhöhte, um in der zweiten Jahreshälfte 1920 abrupt in eine Talfahrt der Preise und Produktionshöhen überzugehen.[49] Sinkende Nachfrage bei gleichzeitig beträchtlich erweiterten Produktionskapazitäten — allein die United States Steel Corporation hatte ihre Produktionskapazitäten für Rohstahl während des Krieges um das Äquivalent von zwei Drittel der Rohstahlkapazität des deutschen Reiches vor Kriegsausbruch erhöht — führten zu einem Preiskrieg und Konjunkturtief, in dem nur die starken Unternehmen überlebten.[50] Selbst der Konjunktureinbruch

---

[48] Vgl. dazu ausführlich I. Steinisch, *Acht Stunden sind besser als zwölf...* [wie Anm. 3], Kap. II.

[49] Siehe *Iron Age* vom 10. 4. 1919, S. 969, und a.a.O. vom 4. 1. 1923, S. 1—3.

[50] *Annual Statistical Report of the American Iron and Steel Institute for 1913—1922*, New York 1914 ff., jeweils S. 1; für die verstärkte Konzentrationsbewegung nach Kriegsende vgl. Gertrude G. Schroeder, *The Growth of Major Steel Companies, 1900—1950* (= The John Hopkins University Studies in Historical and Political Science, Series LXX, No. 2), Baltimore, Md. 1952.

während der Finanzpanik 1907/8 war nicht so drastisch ausgefallen wie die Rezession 1921.[51] Mitte des Jahres war lediglich ein Viertel der Produktionskapazitäten ausgelastet, die Jahresproduktion insgesamt nicht höher als 1908. Allerdings setzte nach diesem absoluten Tiefstand eine Trendwende ein, 1922 erreichte die Produktionshöhe schon wieder den Vorkriegsstand und 1923 hatte die Industrie zu einer halbwegs stabilen Konjunktur zurückgefunden mit einem Preisniveau, das in etwa dem Stand des letzten Kriegsjahres entsprach.[52]

Was für die Industrie eine temporäre Reinigungskrise im Prozeß der Umstellung auf den freien Markt der Friedenswirtschaft war, stellte sich für die Eisen- und Stahlarbeiter mehr als eine Eliminierung ihrer Kriegsgewinne dar. Dank der staatlichen Sozialpolitik während des Krieges, die die Einhaltung gewerkschaftlicher Lohn- und Arbeitszeitstandards zur verbindlichen Richtlinie machte und zum ersten Mal das Koalitionsrecht der Arbeiter schützte,[53] hatten die Eisen- und Stahlarbeiter ebenfalls beträchtlich vom Krieg profitieren können. Ohne direkt von der sozialpolitischen Intervention betroffen zu sein, sah sich die eisen- und stahlerzeugende Industrie aufgrund des verengten Arbeitskräftemarkts zu einer schnellen Anpassung an die neuen Verhältnisse gezwungen. Um mögliche Arbeiterunruhen vorzubeugen und gewerkschaftliche Organisationsversuche ebenso wie Arbeitszeitzugeständnisse abzuwehren, schlug sie den Weg lohnpolitischer Großzügigkeit ein.[54]

Unter der Führung der United States Steel Corporation verdoppelte sich in der eisen- und stahlerzeugenden Industrie bis 1919 der nominale Durchschnittswochenlohn.[55] Allein die Einführung des Achtstunden-

---

[51] *Iron Age* vom 15. 6. 1922, S. 1679f.

[52] *Iron Age* vom 28. 7. 1922, S. 209, und a.a.O., vom 4. 1. 1923, S. 3.

[53] Siehe Gordon S. Watkins, *Labor Problems and Labor Administration in the United States During the World War* (= University of Illinois Studies in the Social Sciences, Bd. 8, Nr. 3), Urbana, Ill. 1919; für die arbeiterfreundliche Politik Präsident Woodrow Wilsons vgl. John S. Smith, *Organized Labor and Government in the Wilson Era, 1913—1921: Some Conclusions*, in: Labor History, Bd. 3 (1962), S. 265—286.

[54] Für die Arbeitspolitik der eisen- und stahlerzeugenden Industrie vgl. D. Brody, *Steelworkers in America*... [wie Anm. 6], S. 180—213, sowie Melvin I. Urofsky, *Big Steel and the Wilson Administration. A Study in Business-Government Relations*, Columbus, Ohio 1969, S. 248—278.

[55] Paul H. Douglas, *Real Wages in the United States, 1890—1926*, New York 1930, unveränd. Nachdruck 1966, S. 126; ferner Charles A. Gulick, *Labor Policy of the United States Steel Corporation*, New York 1924, S. 56—68.

tages als Lohngrundlage Anfang Oktober 1918 brachte den Eisen- und Stahlarbeitern einen Lohnzuschlag von zehn Prozent bei zehnstündiger und sechzehn Prozent bei zwölfstündiger Schichtdauer ein. Zum ersten Mal stiegen die Löhne schneller als die Lebenshaltungskosten, und der Reallohnvorsprung blieb auch während der Nachkriegskonjunktur 1919/20 erhalten, da die steigenden Lebenshaltungskosten durch eine weitere Lohnerhöhung von zehn Prozent im Februar 1920 aufgefangen wurden.[56] Erst die Krise Ende 1920 brachte die Umkehr. Drastische Lohnkürzungen bei gleichzeitiger Abschaffung des Achtstundentages als Lohngrundlage halbierten fast die Nominallöhne der Eisen- und Stahlarbeiter in weniger als einem halben Jahr und eliminierten temporär den Reallohngewinn, da die Lebenshaltungskosten weniger rapide sanken.[57]

Allerdings vermittelt der steile Lohnsturz 1921 noch kein adäquates Bild von den tatsächlichen materiellen Einbußen der Arbeiterschaft, denn mit den Lohnkürzungen gingen Massenentlassungen parallel. Bei Kriegsende und im Konjunkturhoch Anfang 1920 beschäftigte die eisen- und stahlerzeugende Industrie über eine halbe Million Arbeiter, von denen Mitte 1921 knapp die Hälfte übriggeblieben war, so daß die Belegschaftszahlen geringfügig unter dem Stand von Anfang 1915, dem Beginn der Kriegshausse lagen.[58]

Daß die eisen- und stahlerzeugende Industrie im Gegensatz zum Beispiel zum Kohlenbergbau oder der Metallverarbeitung in der Lage war, derart radikal Belegschaftsumfang und Lohnkosten den veränderten wirtschaftlichen Bedingungen anzupassen, ohne auf Widerstand zu stoßen,[58a] verdankte sie ihrer erfolgreichen Liquidation der gewerkschaftlichen Organisation in ihren Betrieben. 1918/19 war es der American Federation of Labor, dem Dachverband der amerikanischen Gewerkschaften, durch einen umfassenden Organisationsfeldzug gelungen, einen Gutteil der Eisen- und Stahlarbeiter zu organisieren. Trotzdem lehnte die United States Steel Corporation als anerkanntes Sprachrohr der Industrie prinzipiell alle Verhandlungen mit den Gewerkschaften ab. Um sowohl die Anerkennung ihrer gewerkschaftlichen Organi-

---

[56] *Iron Age* vom 5. 2. 1920, S. 418.
[57] *Iron Age* vom 12. 4. 1923, S. 1053.
[58] *Ebda.*
[58a] Man war sich durchaus klar darüber, daß in keiner anderen Industrie die Lohnkürzungen in derart scharfem Ausmaß erfolgt waren, verband mit dieser Erkenntnis jedoch die Forderung gleichzuziehen. Siehe *Iron Age* vom 27. 10. 1921, S. 1087.

sationen als auch die Einführung des Achtstundentages zu erzwingen, traten Ende September 1919 rund eine Viertelmillion Eisen- und Stahlarbeiter in den Streik, der Anfang 1920 erfolglos abgebrochen werden mußte. Zum Teil unter der Auflage eines schriftlichen Verzichts auf jede weitere gewerkschaftliche Organisation kehrten die Arbeiter im Einzelarbeitsvertrag an ihre Arbeitsplätze zurück. Die Niederlage war so vollkommen, daß erst unter dem besonderen staatlichen Schutz des Koalitionsrechtes während der Wirtschaftskrise in den dreißiger Jahren ein neuer gewerkschaftlicher Organisationsvorstoß erfolgte, dem endlich Erfolg beschieden war.[59]

Als Anfang 1922 eine Beschleunigung der konjunkturellen Aufwärtsbewegung einsetzte und langsam einer stabilen Konjunktur Platz machte, konnte die eisen- und stahlerzeugende Industrie daher befriedigt feststellen, daß sie weitgehend zu den Verhältnissen der Vorkriegszeit zurückgefunden hatte. In kaum einem anderen Industriezweig war die Anpassung an die Normalität der Friedenswirtschaft so drastisch verlaufen, und mit der Konjunkturverbesserung geriet die eisen- und stahlerzeugende Industrie von zwei Seiten unter Zugzwang.

Höhere Löhne in anderen Industriezweigen machten im August 1922 eine 20prozentige Lohnerhöhung nötig, um dem sich abzeichnenden Arbeitermangel zu begegnen. Weitere Lohnerhöhungen 1923 brachten den Eisen- und Stahlarbeitern erneut einen Reallohngewinn.[60] Allerdings drohte diese Entwicklung die einzige positive Auswirkung der Wirtschaftskrise zunichte zu machen. Im Unterschied zur Vorkriegspraxis hatte die eisen- und stahlerzeugende Industrie im Konjunkturtief 1921 nicht wie gewohnt zwecks weiterer Lohnkostenersparnis zu Arbeitszeitverlängerungen gegriffen, sondern zu Kurzarbeit und Reduzierung der zwölfstündigen Schichtzeiten.

Im Oktober 1920 arbeiteten schätzungsweise 18 Prozent der Hochofenarbeiter, 22 Prozent der Arbeiter in den Bessemer Stahlwerken, 30 Prozent der Arbeiter in den Siemens-Martin-Stahlwerken und 25 Prozent der Arbeiter in den Grobwalzwerken im Achtstundentag, und diese Zahlen erhöhten sich im folgenden Jahr.[61] Zum Beispiel hatte sich angeblich die Zahl der Arbeiter mit einer regelmäßigen zwölfstündigen

---

[59] Dazu ausführlich: David Brody, *Labor in Crisis: The Steel Strike of 1919*, Philadelphia-New York 1965.
[60] *Iron Age* vom 12. 4. 1923, S. 1053, und a.a.O., vom 24. 8. 1922, S. 508.
[61] *Iron Age* vom 1. 6. 1922, S. 1515.

Arbeitszeit in der United States Steel Corporation zwischen Oktober 1920 und März 1922 von 32 Prozent auf 14 Prozent reduziert.[62] Trotz des Drucks von seiten der Öffentlichkeit hatte die Massenarbeitslosigkeit 1921 jedoch keine grundsätzliche Abschaffung des Doppelschichtsystems in Gang gebracht, und in der Befürchtung, daß mit der besseren Konjunktur und möglichem Arbeitermangel sich der Zwölfstundentag im Vorkriegsausmaß erneut in der eisen- und stahlerzeugenden Industrie etablieren könne, begann unter maßgeblicher Beteiligung des Handelsministers Herbert Hoover, dem bekannten „Self-Made Millionaire" mit sozialem Engagement, ein organisierter öffentlich-politischer Feldzug für die Abschaffung zwölfstündiger Arbeitszeiten.[63]

Studien von seiten der Ingenieursverbände über die ökonomische Verschwendung überlanger Arbeitszeiten, die wirtschaftliche Tragbarkeit und technische Durchführung des achtstündigen Dreischichtsystems in der eisen- und stahlerzeugenden Industrie komplementierten Artikelserien über die soziale Verschwendung überlanger Arbeitszeiten in den einschlägigen Presseorganen, und am 18. Mai 1922 sahen sich die führenden Eisen- und Stahlindustriellen ins Weiße Haus in Washington D. C. geladen, um mit dem amerikanischen Präsidenten Warren G. Harding persönlich die Abschaffung der zwölfstündigen Doppelschichten zu diskutieren.[64]

Danach begannen die großen Unternehmen aktive Vorbereitungen für die Umstellung auf das achtstündige Dreischichtsystem zu treffen, das mittlerweile schon in verschiedenen kleineren Unternehmen Einzug gehalten hatte.[65] Wegen des hinhaltenden Widerstandes der United States Steel Corporation verzögerte sich die Arbeitszeitverkür-

---

[62] United States Steel Corporation, *Minutes of Annual Meeting of Stockholders, 17. 4. 1922*, in: *Addresses and Statements* by Elbert H. Gary, comp. by the Business History Society, Bd. 6, 1927.

[63] Vgl. Charles Hill, *Fighting the Twelve-Hour Day in the American Steel Industry*, in: Labor History, Bd. 15 (1974), Nr. 1, S. 19—35; ferner I. Steinisch, *Acht Stunden sind besser als zwölf...* [wie Anm. 3], Kap. III.

[64] *Ebda.;* ferner *Survey* vom 5. 3. 1921. Das ganze Heft war den Arbeitsverhältnissen in der eisen- und stahlerzeugenden Industrie gewidmet. Die bekannteste Studie von seiten der Ingenieure, die von Handelsminister Herbert Hoover gefördert und von Präsident Harding mit einem Vorwort versehen worden war, kam von den Federated American Engineering Societies, Committee on Work-Periods in Continuous-Industry, *The Twelve-Hour Shift in Industry*, New York 1922.

[65] *Iron Age* vom 9. 8. 1923, S. 325—328.

Inflationäre Wirtschaftsentwicklung und Arbeitszeitproblem

zung bis Mitte 1923, verlief dann aber aufgrund einer schwachen und nur temporären Konjunkturabflachung um so reibungsloser. Anfang 1924 war die Einführung des achtstündigen Dreischichtsystems weitgehend abgeschlossen, und statt des Ruins stellte sich eine neue Prosperität ein, die zudem von weiteren Produktivitätsgewinnen begleitet war.[66]

Sorgfältige organisatorische Vorbereitungen und allmählicher Übergang zum achtstündigen Dreischichtsystem, begleitet von einer Straffung der Betriebsorganisation, Verkleinerung der Belegschaften pro Schicht, paritätischer Aufteilung des Lohnkostenausgleichs zwischen Arbeitgeber und Arbeiter, was für letztere einen Lohnverzicht von rund 16 Prozent pro Schicht bedeutete, und Anpassung des Akkord- und Prämiensystems an die verkürzte Schichtzeit waren einerseits die Gründe, die auch im Kreis der Arbeitgeber für einen gewissen Enthusiasmus über die gelungene Umstellung auf das Dreischichtsystem sorgten. Andererseits hielt sich durch die strikte Beschränkung des Achtstundentags auf die Doppelschichtler in den kontinuierlichen Betrieben die Arbeitszeitverkürzung in Grenzen. Für rund die Hälfte der Eisen- und Stahlarbeiter, die in den Werkstätten als Tagesarbeiter oder Reparaturhandwerker arbeiteten, blieb der Zehnstundentag weiterhin bestehen. Je nachdem, ob sich ein Unternehmen auch zur Eliminierung der Sonntagsarbeit bereitfand, variierte daher die regelmäßige wöchentliche Arbeitszeit, die 48, 56 und für die Tagesarbeiter sogar 60 Stunden betragen konnte.[67] Die durchschnittliche Wochenarbeitszeit lag in der zweiten Hälfte der zwanziger Jahre zwischen 54 und 55 Stunden,[68] was deutlich macht, daß sich die eisen- und stahlerzeugende Industrie mit der Einführung des achtstündigen Dreischichtsystems noch lange nicht dem gültigen Arbeitszeitstandard einer 48-Stundenwoche verschrieben hatte.

---

[66] Am 25. Mai 1923 hatte Elbert H. Gary als Vorsitzender des Arbeitszeitausschusses und Präsident des American Iron and Steel Institutes dessen Ergebnisbericht bekanntgegeben. Letzterer enthielt ein klares, wenn auch kein endgültiges Votum gegen die Abschaffung des Zwölfstundentages. Die Reaktion war ein öffentlicher Aufschrei, und nach erneuter Intervention Präsident Hardings gab Gary endlich nach. Vgl. I. Steinisch, *Acht Stunden sind besser als zwölf...* [wie Anm. 3], Kap. III; siehe den Produktivitätsindex in *Historical Statistics of the United States, Colonial Times to 1957*, Washington, D.C. 1960, Series W24—38, S. 601.

[67] Siehe United States Bureau of Labor Statistics, *Bulletin*, No. 567, S. 3f.

[68] *Ebda.*

Darüber hinaus stellte die Arbeitszeitverkürzung für die Betriebsorganisation allgemein keine einschneidende Maßnahme dar, denn der für diese Industrie typische unregelmäßige Betriebsgang durch plötzlich auftretende produktionstechnische Störungen oder unerwarteten Stoßbetrieb konnte nach wie vor mit Hilfe ausgedehnter Überstunden bewältigt werden, die, angeblich um einer zurückhaltenden Arbeitsleistung von seiten der Arbeiterschaft vorzubeugen, zudem nicht höher entlohnt wurden.[69] Unter diesen Bedingungen wird verständlich, warum auch auf seiten der Industrie die Vorteile des achtstündigen Dreischichtsystems anerkannt wurden, dessen lohnkostensteigernde Wirkung man auf unter fünf Prozent veranschlagte.[70] Diese positiven Begleiterscheinungen der Achtstundenschicht wurden schlagwortartig wie folgt umrissen:[71]

1. Steigerung der Produktivität und Produktion durch größere Effizienz;
2. Größere Zufriedenheit der Arbeiter;
3. Beseitigung der Drückebergerei;
4. Niedrigere Arbeiterfluktuation;
5. Kein Bummeln und Blaumachen.

III
Vergleichende Schlußbetrachtung

Warum die deutsche eisen- und stahlerzeugende Industrie in ihrer fünfjährigen Praxis mit dem Achtstundentag angeblich keine positiven Erfahrungen hatte machen können, lag nicht zuletzt darin begründet, daß sie teilweise bewußt dazu tendierte, die Folgen des Krieges und der Inflation mit den Auswirkungen der Arbeitszeitverkürzung zu verwechseln, die sich, und das war entscheidend, allerdings auch nicht oder nur schlecht wechselseitig isolieren ließen. Ob der Produktivitäts- und Produktionsverlust ein Resultat der schlechten Material- und Energieversorgung, der abgewirtschafteten Betriebsanlagen und mangelnden Betriebsorganisation einerseits, oder der sozialen Spannungen, Verelendung und der mangelnden Arbeitsbereitschaft der Belegschaften

---

[69] *Interview with Elbert H. Gary, Chairman, in response to Inquiries by Representatives of 26 different newspapers, July 6, 1923*, in: *Addresses and Statements* by Elbert H. Gary, Bd. 6.
[70] Siehe *Survey-Graphic* vom 1. 1. 1927, S. 465.
[71] *Survey-Graphic* vom 1. 2. 1924, S. 492; ferner *Iron Age* vom 15. 11. 1923, S. 1321 f.

andererseits, oder die direkte Folge der Arbeitszeitverkürzung war, ließ sich innerbetrieblich vielleicht noch grobrastrig klären, kaum aber in jedem einzelnen Fall und gewiß nicht in der Kumulation der Ursachen. Von betriebsfremder Seite war die Einschätzung der Situation noch unübersichtlicher, so daß die Position der Unternehmen, niedrigere Produktionsziffern mit dem Achtstundentag kausal zu verbinden, zugleich logisch einleuchtete und nur schwer konkret zu widerlegen war. Jedoch waren die verschiedenen Gründe, mit denen die Industrie generell die geringere Produktivität der Achtstundenschicht zu erklären versuchte, überaus fadenscheinig. Argumente von der Art, daß der Maschinenpark im Dreischichtsystem stärker als im Doppelschichtsystem in Mitleidenschaft gezogen würde, da drei statt zwei Arbeiter Bedienung und Wartung vornähmen, waren schließlich kaum mehr als Bauernfängerei, ferner waren Zweifel an der Aussagekraft der eigenen Statistiken ebenfalls durchaus vorhanden.[72] Kaum weniger kläglich waren zudem die Versuche, den alten Einwand aus der Vorkriegszeit, daß die Arbeitsbelastung im zwölfstündigen Doppelschichtsystem gegenüber dem achtstündigen Dreischichtsystem geringer sei, wiederzubeleben, was weder die deutsche noch die amerikanische eisen- und stahlerzeugende Industrie überzeugend nachzuweisen vermochte. Wenn man auf der weitgehenden Einflußlosigkeit des Faktors Arbeitskraft auf die Produktionshöhe vor allem in den Hochofen- und Stahlwerken bestand und dabei das hohe Ausmaß der Arbeitsbereitschaft betonte, war schließlich kaum einzusehen, warum die Arbeiter im achtstündigen Dreischichtsystem weniger in den Genuß dieser Arbeitsbereitschaft kommen sollten und dadurch den Wegfall geregelter Pausenzeiten kompensieren konnten, beziehungsweise, falls sich die Arbeitsbereitschaft im Achtstundentag verkürzen ließ, letzteres sich nicht produktivitätssteigernd zu Buche schlug.[73]

Trotz dieser Widersprüche erklärt dieses Argument jedoch die Renitenz beider Industrien gegenüber dem Achtstundentag, die in erster

---

[72] *Wirtschaftliche Auswirkung der Achtstundenschicht in Hüttenwerken*, in: Stahl und Eisen, 44. Jg., (1924), Nr. 37, S. 1103.

[73] Das Problem der Arbeitsbereitschaft zieht sich wie ein roter Faden durch die gesamte Arbeitszeitdiskussion, wurde aber in den USA nach Kriegsende durch die Ingenieursstudien stärker unter dem Vorzeichen ineffizienter Betriebsorganisation debattiert. Für das Aufwärmen alter Argumente auf deutscher Seite vgl. M. Schellewald, *Zur Frage der Arbeitszeit für die Feuerarbeiter der Hüttenwerke*, in: Stahl und Eisen, 44. Jg. (1924), Nr. 46, S. 1446—1455.

Linie in der Furcht vor höheren Lohnkosten begründet lag. Dieses Problem konnte die amerikanische eisen- und stahlerzeugende Industrie eindeutig zu ihren Gunsten lösen, denn die Einführung des achtstündigen Dreischichtsystems stellte nicht mehr als eine mäßige und in den Augen der breiten Öffentlichkeit längst überfällige Reform dar, deren Kosten durch Lohnkürzungen und Arbeitsintensivierung zudem überwiegend zu Lasten der betroffenen Belegschaften gingen. Demgegenüber mußte die deutsche eisen- und stahlerzeugende Industrie nicht nur einen vollen Lohnausgleich und Überstundenzuschläge gewähren, sondern die kurzfristige Einführung des allgemeinen Achtstundentages, seine stringente Fassung durch die Demobilmachungsverordnung vom 23. November 1918 und die rigorose Beschränkung der Überstunden revolutionierten gewissermaßen ihre Betriebsorganisation von außen. Ferner gaben weder die sozialen und politischen Rahmenbedingungen noch die schwierige wirtschaftliche Situation positive Anstöße für eine durchgreifende betriebliche Reorganisation, wie sie auf amerikanischer Seite stattfand. Vielmehr verdeckte die Inflation, die die internationale Wettbewerbsfähigkeit der deutschen eisen- und stahlerzeugenden Industrie sicherstellte, diese Notwendigkeit temporär, da das Problem der Lohnkostensteigerung zunächst zurückgestellt werden konnte. War es aus dieser Perspektive schon das Einfachste und Naheliegendste, unter den schwierigen wirtschaftlichen Bedingungen der Stabilisierungskrise Ende 1923 auf der Ineffizienz des Achtstundentages zu bestehen, da die notwendige Lohnsummenersparnis über den Weg der Gleichzeitigkeit von Arbeitszeitverlängerung, Belegschaftsabbau und Lohnkürzung ohne große Anforderungen an das betriebstechnische Organisationsvermögen der Werksdirektionen bewerkstelligt werden konnte, so drängten auch noch andere Auswirkungen des allgemeinen Achtstundentags in die gleiche Richtung.

In der Sicht der deutschen Schwerindustrie hatte die allgemeine Gültigkeit des Achtstundentages zusammen mit der Inflation die traditionelle Hierarchie in der Lohnstruktur und der Arbeitszeitlänge der Arbeiterschaft zerstört. Die Folge dieser produktionsschädigenden Lohnnivellierung und Gleichmacherei in der Arbeitszeitregelung sah man in der Abwanderung der Arbeiterschaft in die Industriezweige, in denen die Arbeit leichter war. Schon 1919 hatte die eisen- und stahlerzeugende Industrie Schwierigkeiten, die Schwerarbeiterpositionen vor allem in den Hochofen- und Stahlwerken zu füllen, die vor dem Krieg vielfach von italienischen und polnischen Arbeitern besetzt worden waren, deren Zuzug nach dem Krieg ausblieb.[74] Damit bewegten die deutsche Seite ähnliche arbeitsmarktpolitische Sorgen wie die amerikanische eisen- und stahlerzeugende Industrie, die durch die 1916 beginnende restriktive Einwanderungsgesetzgebung nicht mehr wie vor dem Krieg mit einem Überangebot an billigen Arbeitskräften rechnen konnte und deshalb bei einer Verkürzung der Arbeitszeit um ihre lohnpolitische Wettbewerbsfähigkeit fürchtete.[75] Daß sich letztere dem arbeitsmarktbedingten Lohndruck nicht entziehen konnte, zeigen die Lohnerhöhungen in den Jahren 1922 und 1923; jedoch bestand in der amerikanischen Wirtschaft keine enge Verzahnung der Lohn- und Arbeitsbedingungen zwischen den Industrien wie auf deutscher Seite, wo die Bergarbeiter traditionell den Anspruch auf die kürzeste Arbeitszeit bei Spitzenlöhnen erhoben, während hohe Löhne aufgrund langer Arbeitszeiten die eisen- und stahlerzeugende Industrie arbeitsmarktpolitisch wettbewerbsfähig gemacht hatten. Nicht zuletzt deshalb stellte die Schwerindustrie die treibende Kraft hinter der Kampagne für die allgemeine Abschaffung des Achtstundentages dar, denn ohne eine allgemeine Rückkehr zum Zehnstundentag war die Verlängerung der Schichtzeit im Bergbau von sieben auf acht Stunden und die Wiedereinführung des zwölfstündigen Doppelschichtsystems in der eisen- und stahlerzeugenden Industrie nicht durchsetzbar.[76]

Darüber hinaus verbanden sich mit dem Übergang zu einer deflationistischen Finanz- und stabilen Währungspolitik auf deutscher Seite in der Arbeitszeitfrage wirtschaftliche Überlegungen mit politischen Absichten, die sich für die amerikanische eisen- und stahlerzeugende Industrie schon erledigt hatten. Der schnelle Rückzug der amerikanischen Regierung aus der Privatwirtschaft nach Kriegsende und die Streikniederlage der Eisen- und Stahlarbeiter hatte die volle Dispositionsfreiheit der amerikanischen eisen- und stahlerzeugenden Industrie wieder hergestellt und das durch den Krieg in Frage gestellte machtpolitische Verhältnis der Vorkriegszeit wieder vollständig restauriert.[77] An dieser

---

[74] *Jahresberichte der Gewerbeaufsichtsbeamten für 1919...*, S. 600.

[75] Siehe bes. die Berichterstattung über das Zusammentreffen der Industriellen mit Präsident Harding in *Iron Age* vom 25. 5. 1922, S. 1448 f.; die Einwanderungsgesetzgebung sollte die ‚nordischen' Länder gegenüber den osteuropäischen Ländern, aus denen die Masse der Eisen- und Stahlarbeiter sich rekrutiert hatte, begünstigen. Vgl. Maldwyn Allen Jones, *American Immigration*, 6. Aufl., Chicago-London 1969, S. 268—277.

[76] Vgl. M. Schellewald, *Zur Frage der Arbeitszeit...*, in: *Stahl und Eisen*, 44. Jg. (1924), Nr. 37, S. 1455.

[77] Vgl. M. I. Urofsky, *Big Steel...* [wie Anm. 54], S. 292—343.

Tatsache rüttelte die von einer reformbewußten Öffentlichkeit erzwungene Abschaffung des Zwölfstundentages absolut nicht. Demgegenüber erschwerte der Umstand, daß die politische Machtergreifung der Arbeiterschaft im November 1918 der deutschen Industrie und Wirtschaft den allgemeinen Achtstundentag aufgenötigt hatte, eine vorurteilsfreie Prüfung der Vor- und Nachteile des achtstündigen Dreischichtsystems beträchtlich. Sowohl auf der Arbeiter- als auch auf der Arbeitgeberseite hatte die Revolution den Achstundentag zum Symbol der veränderten machtpolitischen Verhältnisse gemacht, und der Konfrontationskurs, den die deutsche Schwerindustrie in der Arbeitszeitfrage einschlug, zielte eindeutig darauf ab, den neugewonnenen politischen Einfluß der Arbeiterschaft zurückzudrängen, die Gewerkschaften entscheidend zu schwächen und neben der Arbeitszeitverlängerung gleichzeitig auch die Lockerung der Tarifvertragsfessel durchzusetzen.[78] Diese Versuche, den durch die Schärfe der wirtschaftlichen und politischen Krisensituation im letzten Viertel des Jahres 1923 geschaffenen breiten gesellschaftspolitischen Konsens über die wirtschaftliche Notwendigkeit einer allgemeinen Arbeitszeitverlängerung, der bis in die Arbeiterschaft reichte, als eine willkommene Gelegenheit zu nutzen, nach Möglichkeit auch die machtpolitischen Verhältnisse der Vorkriegszeit wieder herzustellen, schlugen fehl. Auf Arbeitgeberseite mußte man sich mit der durch die Arbeitszeitverordnung vom 21. Dezember 1923 gesetzlich sanktionierten Rückkehr zum zwölfstündigen Doppelschichtsystem begnügen.[79] Allerdings sorgte das rigorose Vorgehen der Schwerindustrie für eine dauerhafte Vergiftung der Tarifbeziehungen, die nur durch die verbindliche staatliche Schlichtung überspielt werden konnte.[80] Der Staat wurde zum letzten

---

[78] Vgl. das Urteil von R. R. Kuczynski, *Postwar Labor Conditions*... [wie Anm. 24], S. 106; ferner G. D. Feldman/I. Steinisch, *Die Weimarer Republik zwischen Sozial- und Wirtschaftsstaat*..., in: *Archiv für Sozialgeschichte* [wie Anm. 24], S. 388 ff.

[79] Die neue Arbeitszeitregelung legte in den kontinuierlichen Betrieben eine 58 Stundenwoche bei Tagschicht und 60 Stundenwoche bei Nachtschicht ausschließlich der Pausen fest, was eine durchschnittliche Wochenarbeitszeit von 59 Stunden ergab. In den nichtkontinuierlichen Betrieben der Weiterverarbeitung wurde der Zehnstundentag wieder eingeführt, allerdings mit einer verkürzten Arbeitszeit am Sonnabend, so daß hier die Wochenarbeitszeit ausschließlich der Pausen 57 1/2 Stunden betrug. Siehe den Abdruck des Arbeitszeitabkommens in G. D. Feldman/H. Homburg, *Industrie und Inflation*..., S. 372—374.

[80] Für die Notwendigkeit, die Arbeitszeitverlängerung mit einer verbindlichen staatlichen Schlichtung eng zu verknüpfen vgl. Uwe Oltmann, *Reichsarbeitsminister Brauns*

Schiedsrichter in der Festsetzung der Arbeitsverhältnisse, da die beiden Tarifparteien zur selbständigen Kompromißfindung unfähig waren, und aus diesem Grund blieb die Arbeitszeitfrage auch in der zweiten Hälfte der zwanziger Jahre in Deutschland mehr eine politische Machtfrage als ein zu lösendes technisch-wirtschaftliches Problem.

Summary

It is generally well known that the struggle over the Eight Hour Day contributed heavily to the socio-political conflict that undermined the stability of the Weimar Republic. Equally well known is the leading role German heavy industry played in abolishing the Eight Hour Day at the end of 1923. What is not so well known, however, is the fact that at about the same time the American steel industrialists put up an equally tough fight against the introduction of the Eight Hour Day and the Three Shift System. In their defence they employed arguments very similar to those used by their German counterparts. But whereas the latter never gave up their resistance, the American steel industry — admittedly under heavy political pressure — voluntarily introduced the Three Shift System in 1923 and, even more important, on the whole maintained it although no union or law prescribed it. One convincing reason certainly was the discovery that the Eight Hour Shift System in comparison to the former Twelve Hour Shift System paid in terms of better productivity and production as well as better labor relations. Since the German steel industrialists had to live with the Eight Hour Day and Three Shift System for five years, the question naturally arises why they did not discover anything positve about the shorter worktime. The answer becomes fairly clear when the political

in der Staats- und Währungskrise 1923/24. Die Bedeutung der Sozialpolitik für die Inflation, den Ruhrkampf und die Stabilisierung, Phil. Diss., Kiel 1969, bes. S. 188—280; Zu dem daraus resultierenden Kampf der eisen- und stahlerzeugenden Industrie gegen das Schlichtungswesen vgl. Gerald D. Feldman/Irmgard Steinisch, *Notwendigkeit und Grenzen sozialstaatlicher Intervention. Eine vergleichende Fallstudie des Ruhreisenstreits in Deutschland und des Generalstreiks in England*, in: *Archiv für Sozialgeschichte*, Bd. 20 (1980), S. 57—117.

framework, socio-economic setting and the actual conditions under which the Eight Hour Shift was introduced in both industries are examined.

First, the American steel industry managed to get rid of labor unrest, unionized workers and high war-time wages during the depression of 1920/21 and only introduced the Eight Hour Shift System once social and economic stability prevailed again. Second, it never introduced the general Eight Hour Day but only the Eight Hour Shift which meant eight hours for the shift workers and ten hours for the day workers. Third, the change-over from the Twelve Hour-Two Shift System to the Eight Hour-Three Shift System was made gradually after quite a period of careful preparation and, what is more, entirely on the terms dictated by management. The reverse was true for the German experience. The revolutionary workers forced the universal Eight Hour Day, the change-over from the twelve hour to the eight hour shift was made within a very short time and under conditions of social and economic upheaval, both of which did not further high productivity and production, or amicable labor relations or economic planning and rationalization. What occured, therefore, was a fusion of the worktime problem with other social and economic issues. The Eight Hour Day became closely associated with negative experiences which were first and foremost due to revolution and inflation. Thus, the German industrialists never were able to develop a more objective stance towards the hours of work question in contrast to their by no means less anti-union and autocratic American counterparts.

VERZEICHNIS DER MITARBEITER

1. Die Mitarbeiter des Bandes *Die deutsche Inflation. Eine Zwischenbilanz / The German Inflation Reconsidered / A Preliminary Balance**

BÜSCH, Prof. Dr. Otto (geb. 1928), Professor für Neuere Geschichte und Sozial- und Wirtschaftsgeschichte, Freie Universität Berlin

CHILDERS, Thomas, Ph. D. (geb. 1946), Associate Professor of History, University of Pennsylvania, Philadelphia, Penn./USA

FELDMAN, Gerald D., Ph. D. (geb. 1937), Professor of History, University of California, Berkeley, Calif./USA

HOLTFRERICH, Prof. Dr. Carl-Ludwig (geb. 1942), Professor am Kennedy-Institut, Freie Universität Berlin

HUGHES, Michael L., Ph. D. (geb. 1949), Visiting Assistant Professor of History, State University of Iowa, Ames/USA

JAKSCH, Prof. Dr. Hans Jürgen (geb. 1930), Alfred-Weber-Institut für Sozial- und Staatswissenschaften, Universität Heidelberg

KUNZ, Andreas, Ph. D. (geb. 1948), Forschungsstipendiat, Europäisches Hochschulinstitut, Florenz

LINDENLAUB, Priv.-Doz. Dr. Dieter (geb. 1937), Wirtschaftswissenschaftliches Seminar, Universität Tübingen

MERKIN, Gerald (geb. 1922), Principal Lecturer, Portsmouth Polytechnic, Portsmouth/Großbritannien

MOELLER, Robert G., Ph. D. (geb. 1949), Assistant Professor of History, Columbia University, New York, N. Y./USA

OSMOND, Jonathan P., B. A. (geb. 1953), Lecturer in History, University of Leicester, Leicester/Großbritannien

RITTER, Prof. Dr. Gerhard A. (geb. 1929), Professor am Institut für Neuere Geschichte, Universität München

SCHRÖDER, Prof. Dr. Hans-Jürgen (geb. 1938), Professor am Historischen Institut Neuzeit I, Universität Gießen

---

* Herausgegeben von Gerald D. Feldman, Carl-Ludwig Holtfrerich, Gerhard A. Ritter, Peter-Christian Witt (= Veröffentlichungen der Historischen Kommission zu Berlin, Bd. 54. Beiträge zu Inflation und Wiederaufbau in Deutschland und Europa 1914—1924, Band 1), Berlin-New York: Walter de Gruyter 1982.

TRUMPP, Dr. Thomas (geb. 1931), Bundesarchivdirektor, Koblenz
TSCHIRBS, Dr. Rudolf (geb. 1946), Oberstudienrat, Goethe-Schule, Bochum
WITT, Prof. Dr. Peter-Christian (geb. 1943), Professor am Fachbereich Geschichte, Gesamthochschule Kassel

2. Die Mitarbeiter des vorliegenden Bandes

BLOOMFIELD, Jonathan, B. A., Ph. D. (geb. 1950), Wissenschaftlicher Mitarbeiter, University of East Anglia, Norwich/Großbritannien
BOROSS, Elizabeth A., Ph. D. (geb. 1939), Wissenschaftliche Mitarbeiterin, University of East Anglia, Norwich/Großbritannien
BOUWSMA, William J., Ph. D. (geb. 1923) Professor of History, University of California, Berkeley, Calif./USA
FELDMAN, Gerald D., Ph. D. (geb. 1937), Professor of History, University of California, Berkeley, Calif./USA
HOLTFRERICH, Prof. Dr. Carl-Ludwig (geb. 1942), Professor am Kennedy-Institut, Freie Universität Berlin
KERNBAUER, Dr. Johann (geb. 1949), arbeitet an einer Geschichte der Österreichischen Nationalbank
KINDLEBERGER, Charles P., Ph. D. (geb. 1910), Professor of History, Harvard University, Cambridge, Mass./USA
LANDAU, Prof. Dr. Zbigniew (geb. 1931), Professor an der Szkoła Główna Planowania i Statystyki w Warszawie (Hochschule für Planung und Statistik), Warschau
MAIER, Charles S., Ph. D. (geb. 1939), Professor of History, Harvard University, Cambridge, Mass./USA
PATTON, Craig (geb. 1952), Graduate Student, University of California, Berkeley, Calif./USA
RITTER, Prof. Dr. Gerhard A. (geb. 1929), Professor am Institut für Neuere Geschichte, Universität München
SARGENT, Thomas, Ph. D. (geb. 1943), Professor of Economics, University of Minnesota, Minn./USA
STEINISCH, Dr. Irmgard (geb. 1946), Wissenschaftliche Mitarbeiterin, Institut für Neuere Geschichte, Universität München
TOMASZEWSKI, Prof. Dr. Jerzy (geb. 1930), Professor an der Universität Warschau
WENDT, Prof. Dr. Berndt-Jürgen (geb. 1934), Professor am Historischen Seminar, Universität Hamburg
WEBER, Dr. Fritz (geb. 1947), Forschungsassistent, Creditanstalt-Bankverein, Wien
WITT, Prof. Dr. Peter-Christian (geb. 1943), Professor am Fachbereich Geschichte, Gesamthochschule Kassel

HISTORISCHE KOMMISSION ZU BERLIN

Vorstand

WOLFGANG TREUE (Vorsitzender)
PETER BAUMGART / OTTO BÜSCH
PETER CZADA / HELMUT ENGEL
WOLFRAM FISCHER / GERD HEINRICH
STEFI JERSCH-WENZEL / GEORG KOTOWSKI
ILJA MIECK / WOLFGANG RIBBE
HENRYK SKRZYPCZAK / WILHELM TREUE
WERNER VOGEL / KLAUS ZERNACK

Kirchweg 33 ('Mittelhof'). D-1000 Berlin 38 (Nikolassee)

VERÖFFENTLICHUNGEN DER HISTORISCHEN
KOMMISSION ZU BERLIN

Beiträge zu Inflation und Wiederaufbau
in Deutschland und Europa 1914 bis 1924, Band 1
Herausgeber: Gerald D. Feldman, Carl-Ludwig Holtfrerich,
Gerhard A. Ritter, Peter-Christian Witt

DIE DEUTSCHE INFLATION
Eine Zwischenbilanz

THE GERMAN INFLATION RECONSIDERED
A Preliminary Balance

Groß-Oktav. XXIV, 431 Seiten, 2 Tafeln. 1982. Ganzleinen DM 82,–
ISBN 3 11 008721 9 (VHKB, Band 54)

Inhalt / Contents

Erster Teil / Part One
Zur ökonomischen und statistischen Analyse
Toward an Economic and Statistical Analysis

Zweiter Teil / Part Two
Zur deutschen Wirtschaftspolitik und zu den
internationalen Wirtschaftsbeziehungen
Toward the Analysis of German Economic Policy
and of International Trade

Dritter Teil / Part Three
Zu gesellschaftlichen und politischen Auswirkungen
Toward the Study of Social and Political Consequences

Preisänderung vorbehalten

Walter de Gruyter  Berlin · New York